Commercial Mortgage Loans and CMBS: Developments in the European Market

Third Edition

Commercial Mortgage Loans and CMBS: Developments in the European Market

Third Edition

Editor
Andrew V. Petersen

SWEET & MAXWELL   **THOMSON REUTERS**

First Edition   2006   Editor: Andrew V. Petersen
Second Edition   2012   Editor: Andrew V. Petersen
Third Edition   2016   Editor: Andrew V. Petersen

Published in 2016 by Thomson Reuters (Professional) UK Limited trading as Sweet & Maxwell,
Friars House, 160 Blackfriars Road, London, SE1 8EZ
(Registered in England & Wales, Company No.1679046.
Registered Office and address for service: 2nd floor, 1 Mark Square, Leonard Street,
London, EC2A 4EG)

For further information on our products and services, visit *www.sweetandmaxwell.co.uk*

Typeset by YHT Ltd, London
Printed and bound by CPI Group (UK) Ltd, Croydon, CR0 4YY.

No natural forests were destroyed to make this product: only farmed timber was used and
replanted.

A CIP catalogue record for this book is available from the British Library.

ISBN: 978-0-414-05744-9

Thomson Reuters and the Thomson Reuters Logo are trademarks of Thomson Reuters.

Sweet & Maxwell ® is a registered trademark of Thomson Reuters (Professional) UK
Limited.

Crown copyright material is reproduced with the permission of the Controller of HMSO and
the Queen's Printer for Scotland.

Foreword

How the world has changed during the four years since the previous edition of this book. In his Foreword to the 2012 edition, Christian Janssen, the then chairman of CREFC Europe, took stock of a CRE finance market still struggling to recover from the global financial crisis, and looked forward with anticipation towards the emergence of a more diverse and resilient market.

Eventually, the barren post-GFC years did indeed give way to a strong and broad recovery across all sub-sectors and most geographical markets, with strong CRE markets and good credit availability, through to late 2015. Since then, a new period of increased uncertainty has begun, heralded by the build-up to, and entrenched by the aftermath of, the UK's vote for Brexit in the June 2016 referendum on EU membership.

At the time of writing, the CRE finance market certainly looks a great deal more sober and resilient than in 2007, where we had a largely overexposed and undercapitalised banking sector. In many markets, including the UK and Ireland, most of the pre-crisis legacy has been resolved and banks are lending again. Leverage levels are moderate, and a newly diverse array of lenders is providing a broader range of products. Despite significant challenges in some parts of Europe, this feels like a market that is functioning broadly as it should and the Chapter detailing the lending markets in France, Germany, Italy and Spain reflects that.

Yet, as ever, scratch the surface and a more complex and nuanced picture emerges. The real estate cycle does not stop turning, and neither does the regulatory one. After a storm of post-crisis interventions in financial regulation (often affecting CRE finance markets), the need for a more considered and coordinated approach is becoming ever clearer. Some countries still have a long way to go to resolve legacy loans, and neither occupational market strength nor credit availability are distributed evenly across the continent. European CMBS has so far failed to re-establish itself as a significant part of the landscape, depriving the market of the data, liquidity and diversification benefits it could provide. Intercreditor relationships continue to evolve as new and traditional providers of senior and mezzanine debt work out how to work together. Quite aside from increasing currency volatility, a strange new world of low, zero or negative interest rates is posing new challenges and opportunities for the use of derivatives. These are among the issues that preoccupy CREFC Europe and the industry, and are covered by chapters in this book.

Gratitude is due to all the contributors to this book. They have, and have shared, an enormous amount of technical, legal and commercial expertise and experience, both about matters that are of obvious interest, and about topics and products that may seem arcane or only for the specialist. Our industry should preserve and build on this knowledge and by doing so we can hope to avoid both repeating the mistakes of the past, and needlessly reinventing the wheel.

Finally, I would like to thank the editor, Andrew Petersen, for his vision, drive and persistence in marshalling all that expertise to bring this timely new edition to the bookshelves.

Madeleine McDougall

Chair, CREFC Europe

Head of Institutional, Lloyds Banking Group

November 2016

Preface

In the years leading up to 2007, the remarkable and unprecedented explosion in the use of commercial real estate (CRE) debt resulted in investors scrambling for relatively inexpensive financing off the back of rising real estate asset values. The opportunity for yield and returns, for all parties throughout the capital structure, helped propel the meteoric rise in real estate debt and CMBS transactions. The first edition of this book chartered the development of the innovative CMBS product during this time. However, the provision of capital, during this boom period, tended to be very capital intensive and in respect of the commercial mortgage loan market, of a longer-term nature, mostly funded by balance sheet banks using relatively shorter-dated funds, thus allowing them larger spreads through effectively taking maturity transformation risk. This position could not continue indefinitely and in 2008, the global financial crisis (GFC) manifested itself on a scale and with such far reaching impact as never seen before. As a result, the commercial mortgage loan and CMBS markets are currently unrecognisable to the markets that existed on the publication of the first edition of this book in 2006.

Since 2008, there has been an unprecedented level of intervention by the world's central banks and state bail-outs of the financial and capital markets as well as a new regulatory framework aimed at trying to minimise the risk of these events occurring again. This third edition will, in continuing the examination undertaken in the second edition, consider the CRE debt and CMBS markets in the context of this post-GFC world. Indeed, now following the vote of the UK to leave the European Union towards the end of June 2016, as this edition was being finalised, it will also examine the markets in the context of a post-Brexit vote. The consequences of the UK's decision to leave the EU on the CRE finance market in the UK, and indeed the rest of Europe, are imponderable. For the time being, the UK remains a member of the EU. It will always be part of Europe. As no author possesses an all seeing crystal ball, this examination will be based solely on what is known since the Brexit vote and not predict into the future, into a period where the process of leaving the EU will be uncertain and certainly volatile. Each Chapter has been written against this backdrop. It is hoped that, as with the first two editions of the book, this edition, expanded to cover the wider CRE debt markets in France, Germany, Italy and Spain, will prove a timely and useful publication, as it is the case that real estate throughout Europe remains a tremendously important asset.

After all, one of the most striking developments in the global debt and capital markets over the last decades has been the metamorphosis of real estate from an asset class that had been famously regarded by institutional investors as illiquid and cumbersome outside the US. It is fitting then, that Chapter 1 begins by going back in time, splitting such analysis up into three separate periods: up to 2007, 2007 to 2012 and post 2012, to examine the evolution of the CRE and CMBS markets in an effort to understand and to determine whether European CMBS will, going forward, once again be an important source of funding and risk diversification tool and resurge from its form that exists at the time of writing and whether the financing of CRE can continue to adapt and evolve on a journey based on financial innovation.

Chapter 2, in recognising that whilst CRE and bank lending have a sym- biotic relationship—CRE markets can be volatile and are prone to cycles - provides an understanding of how property cycles occur and, in particular, the crucial role that debt flows can, and have, played in creating significant volatility in the development and structure of Europe's CRE lending mar- kets pre and post GFC.

Chapter 3 explores the development and structure of Europe's CRE lending markets post-GFC and highlights their importance to the financial markets generally. The Chapter first looks in detail at the structure of the CRE market in Europe, focussing on bank lending, covered bonds and CMBS, exploring how Europe's markets differ to those in Asia Pacific and North America. The Chapter then considers the evolution of the markets during the GFC, before concluding by looking at predictions for the future of CRE markets in Europe.

Chapter 4 consider the loan origination process in detail—the very heart of the CRE debt markets, for without loans there would not be a CRE debt market—outlining and explaining the key stages of the CRE loan origina- tion process from the viewpoint of a senior lender. Given the broad nature of the topic, it is drafted with a focus on the UK CRE lending market, although the vast majority of the methodologies described therein are applicable across the whole of the European markets.

Chapters 5, 6 and 7—in a nod to the leveraged market that exists at the time of writing—consider the world of intercreditor agreements and the opportunities for utilising subordinated debt structures. Chapter 5 exam- ines the emergence of subordinate debt structures including the key prin- ciples and pricing of such structures; the common key principles of intercreditor terms surrounding subordinate debt structures; the economics and business case for utilising mezzanine debt and/or AB debt; and the continued use of borrower debt buy-backs. Chapter 6 then focuses in fur- ther detail on the key commercial terms and provisions of an intercreditor agreement, whilst Chapter 7 considers in detail the key legal terms and provisions.

Chapter 8 examines why development finance has become so popular during this phase of the real estate cycle, by questioning whether the search for yield, at a time when there is a surplus of savings looking for a safe home, is driving the popularity of development finance, or whether, such popularity is driven by an ageing population in the developed world looking for a safe return in their extended retirement, or from sovereigns and UHNWs in the developing world, looking for a high quality assets to preserve a portion of their wealth. Its conclusion, that perhaps lenders pull away from development (or begin development) at the wrong time is revealing. It further demonstrates that development finance can be an opportunity and a well remunerated form of lending, paying higher margins on deals with an average of less than three years compared to the lower margins on a four-five year tenor on investment loans, as will be discussed further in the final Chapter to the book.

Servicing and asset management remain key issues in 2016. Chapters 9, 10 and 11 consider how the role of a facility agent, servicer and special servicer has been transformed since the vintage 2004-2007 originations and legacy deals of 2008-2014 and how servicers have had to adapt in the post-GFC world. These chapters conclude that, in 2016 as in 2012, as liquidity in both the commercial mortgage loan and CMBS markets remains relatively stagnant, servicers face challenges to their own businesses, as legacy deals begin to run off and the attendant fee income begins to evaporate. Lessons have been learned as a result of the GFC and the naivety and shortfalls seen in pre-GFC transaction documents has begun to be addressed in post-GFC CMBS documentation (considered in detail in Chapter 11). Wider powers and increased discretion are being given to the servicer and special servicer (e.g. the power to sell a defaulted loan) and the ability for servicers / special servicers to be replaced has been widened, making it easier to hold a servicer to account for their actions and incentivise them to achieve the best results for noteholders in the most proactive way. Servicers of the future will need to be more than just servicers, reliant on CMBS portfolio instructions; those with real estate experience, experienced asset management platforms and investment teams will be best placed place to profit from the next boom, or indeed the continuing bear, as these three Chapters conclude.

In Chapter 12, we discover that derivatives, such as interest rate swaps, caps and floors, prevalent within a wide range of CRE financings in Europe remain relevant despite—and on some levels as a result of—the continuation of historically low variable interest rate indices such as LIBOR and EURIBOR since 2009. It examines how, in recent years, lenders have adapted to the prospect (and now in some cases, the reality) of negative interest rate environments. The Chapter also focuses on the trend of third-party interest rate hedge providers and their impact on the overall process of arranging CRE financings and addresses why hedging requirements exist in the first place. After several years of extraordinarily low interest rates, whilst it may be only natural to begin to perceive interest rate risk to be low, it is actually quite the opposite, for two reasons. The first is that because interest rates are so low, it reasons that there is far more room to travel in the other direction. The second is that central banks are actively seeking this result. With extremely low interest rates, an economy is closer to a deflationary spiral than in a higher interest rate environment, so it follows that central banks will effect policies guiding the market toward more "normal" levels of interest rates when the risk of deflation is high. It's a fascinating read on modern times and our interest rates being so low for so long—much lower and longer than anyone could have anticipated.

In 2012, the last edition of this book included a Chapter on the evolving role of issuers and trustees in European CMBS transactions. Such a Chapter was not considered necessary in the 2006 first edition. At such time, the European CMBS market was a robust and vibrant part of the securitisation industry and the role of the issuer and trustee was considered in quite a different light then and involvement in litigation was not a particular feature. However, the period between the publication of the first edition and the publication of the second edition was a tumultuous period for the global CMBS market and for its participants. During this period, the GFC occurred, and the market saw a decrease in value (at times, a very significant decrease in value) of the underlying CRE as well as the inability of borrowers to refinance the securitised facilities at maturity. This fundamental deterioration in real estate market conditions placed the securitisations under stresses which were not anticipated when the transactions were structured and executed. As a result of these stresses, by the time the second edition of this book was being prepared, the role of various parties in the CMBS market had evolved from those previously envisaged, and often the parties at the forefront of this evolution were those appointed to have an ongoing role in the transaction (such as the issuer, the trustee and the servicer). As such, when the second edition was prepared, it was felt that the evolving role of the trustee and issuer in CMBS transactions warranted further analysis and whilst the issues discussed in the second edition remain relevant at the time of writing, it is timely that a new edition is used, through Chapter 13, to explore in greater detail one of the themes noted in 2012: the increase in litigation. Such an increase in litigation in CMBS transactions has had a positive impact on the role of trustees and issuers in these transactions, since Courts have become more familiar with structured finance transactions and the intricacies of these deals, which in turn has potentially made court determination of construction issues more attractive and efficient to parties involved. Contractual interpretation of the grey areas in a structured finance deal may, in time, be viewed as a positive development.

The role of the rating agencies in CRE lending and the wider debt capital markets is examined in Chapter 14. Rating agencies serve an essential role in the securitisation market by providing independent opinions about the creditworthiness of bonds backed by loans. For CMBS the multi-step rating approach includes property, loan, legal and structural analysis. At the loan level, the way rating agencies analyse CRE loans is not too different from an originator's or debt investor's underwriting process examined in Chapter 4. However, in the context of CMBS, tranching and pooling add another layer of complexity to the risk assessment and for both loan-level and CMBS rating analysis, a rating agency typically has to strike a balance between transparency and accuracy, considering that employing excessively complex models risks that the rating process becomes a black-box. In a transitioning market, it is extremely important for rating agencies to maintain credit standards and provide timely opinions about the creditworthiness of rated debt. Whilst the role of the rating agency is ever evolving, as the European securitisation market adapts to new regulations and market conditions; going forward, there is no doubt that rating agencies will play an increasing role in the larger CRE market aside from only CMBS.

Chapter 15 is very contemplative as it considers the key drivers of credit performance for European CRE loans originated in the run-up to the GFC and derives what may be insightful and valuable lessons from an underwriting and structuring perspective for CRE lenders. It starts by setting out a brief overview of the legacy of CRE lending in Europe following the downturn, focusing on CRE debt maturity profiles, the manifestation of different types of CRE lenders, as well as origination trends, recognising that the European CRE lending landscape evolved substantially during the GFC, through an initially brief disruption period immediately post-GFC, followed by a growth period and culminating in what seems to be a more normalised (or new normal!) market at the time of writing. The Chapter concludes by identifying and analysing various factors that may have affected the credit performance of European CRE loans. It is a very useful Chapter to attempt to learn lessons from.

European financial markets are currently in the most extensive period of financial regulatory reform in living memory. The two central and inter-related objectives of the global reform agenda are the strengthening of the world's financial institutions and the extension of regulatory oversight. Accordingly, it is fitting that this edition devotes two Chapters, in Chapters 16 and 17, to consider the current regulatory environment for CRE finance and the numerous incentives, including the latest proposals on risk retention (rules put in place to mitigate the perceived risks of the pre-2008 "originate to distribute" model in the securitisation market and the subsequent GFC), which are, at the time of writing, under increasing consideration by regulators and governments. Chapter 16 concludes that there is a risk that the complexity of regulation, and the fact that it is often difficult to apply with certainty to common real world situations, together with the rapid pace of change across a number of areas, may itself act as a deterrent to investment. Against this background, Chapter 21 examines certain recommendations developed by a UK CRE industry group for a more coherent, considered regulatory framework for CRE finance markets, before the concluding Chapter to the book considers the opportunities based on the existing framework.

Given the importance of continental Europe to the CRE finance markets, it would be remiss of this book not to focus on certain major economies driving the debate and presenting some of the opportunities for investment in CRE and CRE debt in Europe post the GFC in Europe. The first edition did this and country specific Chapters return for this edition. As a result, Chapter 18 includes sections on the respective lending markets in France, Germany, Italy and Spain.

CRE has been an increasingly important asset class for Islamic compliant transactions and banks since the publication of the first edition of this book in 2006. Ten years later, Islamic-compliant financing is on a growth trajectory, based on demographic trends, rising investible income levels and investment in European CRE by Middle Eastern investors led by relatively stable political and legal environments. Moreover, it is estimated that 29.7% of the global population will likely be Muslim by 2050, against 23.2% in 2010. The proportion of Muslims in Europe is, at the time of writing, around 6% of the population and projected to be 8% by 2030. This creates a large market and consumer base to consider, such that the topic of the importance of Islamic finance continues in this edition and is dealt with in Chapter 19, which recognises that in the wake of Brexit, some parameters have changed in relation to Islamic-compliant investment in UK CRE: the immediate fall in the pound / US dollar exchange rate makes the UK more attractive for those investors in non-Sterling pegged economies; potential UK tax cuts and incentives have been mooted to draw investment; and there is, at the time of writing, a predicted short to mid-term decline in UK real estate values. However, the Chapter also recognises that most fundamentals of such investment have not changed: Islamic finance has never been governed by EU law in the UK or elsewhere; the UK has one of the most Islamic friendly legal environments with the most legislation of any of the EU countries to assist Islamic finance from a political and tax perspective; the English language, English law and the English courts remain attractions for overseas investors; and the need to draw overseas investment to the UK became more important than ever. Thus Brexit may be a spur to further such investment rather than an impediment.

Moreover, when discussing real estate the force of globalisation cannot be ignored. The GFC demonstrated (perhaps for the first time) the myriad ways in which financial markets and economies are inextricably linked and interdependent. Whilst investment in European CRE has long been regarded as a relative value play for many global investors, North American interest in European CRE has, in particular, proven to be an effective counterweight to the traditional interest of European investors in US CRE opportunities. There are many reasons why US investors looked to the Old Continent in the wake of the GFC in the New World. One reason is that European CRE, which had long been valued as a source of diversification, became more attractive as US mortgage markets were broadly affected by the fall in the residential sector and CRE properties were affected by the steep fall off in tenant demand in US markets. Another is the weakening trend of the US dollar in relation to major European currencies, which affects the demand of US investors for future cash flows denominated in those currencies, no more so than what occurred since the Brexit vote, when Sterling fell precipitately over 10%. While it remains to be seen how the investment story will play out in light of Brexit and the long-running efforts of the EU to avert hard devaluations by Eurozone member states, it appears that continuing uncertainty over European fiscal and monetary policy will provide additional attractive occasions for opportunistic private equity investors to obtain interests in fundamentally strong CRE at favourable prices, albeit caveated and subject to regional and political uncertainty arising from the economic climate in the Southern European jurisdictions and the fallout from Brexit. The implications behind all of this are considered in detail in Chapter 20, which touches on some of the strategic and tactical issues that potential investors should be prepared to address when investing in European CRE. These include country-specific features; differences and similarities between investments through interests in mortgages, mezzanine notes and B-pieces; CMBS in Europe and the United States; the CRE debt secondary markets; and problems associated with the economic pressures in the Eurozone. Investing against the grain, again...

The establishment of real estate as a global asset class in its own right is unlikely to be reversed and I have no doubt that real estate will re-emerge as a popular asset class. Such re-emergence will, be dictated in large part by the confidence in our financial architecture. Any developments or products we can provide to help restore market confidence as well as remove or reduce risk can only be a good thing. Thus Chapter 21 outlines the origins and relevance of, and the prospects for, two proposals for improving financial system resilience in the face of the CRE cycle discussed in Chapter 2. One of the proposals—for a comprehensive CRE loan database—seeks to improve the quality of information available to regulators and market participants. The other proposal seeks to introduce a structurally counter-cyclical element in CRE finance markets, by promoting the use of long-term value-based LTV ratios in risk assessment by lenders and regulators. The proposals were put forward by an independent industry group which was formed in 2012, during an unusually reflective and introspective period for the CRE industry. It concludes by setting out how might a sustainable, diversified and efficient CRE finance market look.

As the concluding Chapter 22 was finalised in mid-2016 and the news-flows around the world were considered, many market participants would have agreed that it remains a challenge to be optimistic, given the backdrop of macro-economic uncertainty, geo-political stress and political uncertainty present in the world in mid-2016. Against this backdrop, investors and lenders alike need to be underwriting with an exit strategy in mind and to be confident on the assets and their fundamental investment qualities over time. With the Brexit process evolving and, at the time of writing, a controversial US election campaign reaching a conclusion, that will be finished as you read this edition, there remain many challenges in allocating capital in existing financial markets, where many asset classes are trading at or close to all-time highs and it is often difficult to calculate an asset's intrinsic value. In short, the CRE lending market is experiencing an Age of Great Uncertainty, and with uncertainty comes both challenge and opportunity.

The Chapter concludes by acknowledging that innovation in adapting to the challenges faced by the sector will continue, as is already seen in the arrival of specialist debt funds and fixed rate products of short and long durations on offer. In addition to traditional sources of capital, debt market participants in Europe will need a more global perspective in seeking out capital to allocate to CRE debt. South-East Asia, the Americas, the Middle East, Russia, Japan and importantly China, will all have an increased role to play in the European CRE debt markets post 2016 and for the next decade and beyond. Those individuals and organisations that can embrace this by realising that we are in an Age of Great Uncertainty on a global scale, and be the quickest to adapt to this shifting landscape and rise and adapt to these challenges, will succeed and prosper. After all, as Chapter 22 concludes, it was the teachings of Charles Darwin that taught us: it is not the most intellectual of the species that survives; it is not the strongest that survives; but the species that survives is the one that is able best to adapt and adjust to the changing environment in which it finds itself.

When conceiving the first edition of this book in 2005, my desire was to produce a book that included a vital mix of business chapters alongside legal chapters: a new generation of textbook spanning the sometimes achingly visible gap between business people and their professional advisors. Over ten years later and two further editions along, the worthwhile act of bringing together specialist industry professionals in a true collaboration between principals and advisors, embraces this important and beneficial concept once again. Long may it continue.

Finally, on a personal note, I wish to thank my wife Sarah and my daughters, Livia and Isobel, for their infinite patience and continuing understanding in putting up with my absences at weekends and evenings whilst working on this book.

Andrew V. Petersen

November, 2016

Acknowledgement

Many people have been involved in bringing this book to fruition. It is hoped that the mentioning of the names below will go some way to thanking those listed for all the time and effort they have contributed.

First and foremost, thanks must be directed at the authors. When I began approaching potential contributors, I was amazed at the depth of expertise we still have in this industry, and indeed new expertise that has developed as a result of the factors at play in the market. Each author was enthusiastic and unwavering in producing their respective chapter. Without their self-less undertaking, this volume would have not reached publication.

Acknowledgment is further due to the assistance given in the production process by Lucy Haworth of K&L Gates. Lucy must be singled out for succeeding in the mammoth task of producing the book's glossary of terms and abbreviations. The glossary acts as a valuable stand alone tool to assist readers wishing to understand this important area. It could be published as a stand alone piece in its own right!

I also want to thank Madeleine McDougall, Chair of CREFC-Europe at the time of writing, for contributing the foreword to this volume and acknowledge the collaboration received from CREFC-Europe, in particular Peter Cosmetatos, its Chief Executive Officer and Carol Wilkie, its London Managing Director. CREFC-Europe carries out sterling work promoting the real estate industry in the midst of an incredibly important and difficult time dealing with numerous market initiatives and EC regulatory issues, the outcome of which will shape our industry for years to come. If this book can assist in some small way, alongside their work, then it is only fitting that its current Chair has the first words and Chapters written by its CEO appear at Chs 16 and 21.

The continuing enthusiasm for the project from within K&L Gates should also be mentioned, especially from the Firm's Chairman and Global Managing Partner, Peter Kalis and Tony Griffiths, London Administrative Partner, each for recognising this project as a truly collaborative effort, bringing together many lawyers from across our global law firm and for each being supportive and permitting the K&L Gates' contributors the time to undertake this work.

Finally, I would like to thank Thomson Reuters and in particular our commissioning editor Nick Bliss, for helping to make all of this possible with his foresight to commission the third edition. Also, I am grateful to

Cari Owen who took over from Nick and the editorial team who under-
took—with great success—a difficult job and ensured this volume was
published efficiently and promptly.

Andrew V. Petersen

November, 2016

Contents

4   The Loan Origination Process   65

Klaus Betz-Vais,
Lloyds Banking Group

5   Leverage and the use of Subordinate Debt   107

Andrew V. Petersen,
Partner and Practice Area Leader-Finance, K&L Gates LLP

6   The Modern Intercreditor Agreement: Commercial Terms and Issues   125

Duncan Batty,
M&G Investments

Laurence Griffiths,
US Bank Trustees Limited

Clare Tanner,
Special Counsel, Litigation, K&L Gates LLP

Elizabeth Lovett,
Assistant Vice President, Global CMBS, Structured Finance, DBRS

Christian Aufsatz,
Senior Vice President, Global CMBS, Structured Finance, DBRS

Georghios Anker Parson and Nassar Hussain,
Brookland Partners LLP

Peter Cosmetatos,
CEO CREFC Europe

Stephen Moller,
Partner, K&L Gates LLP

**22   Challenges and Opportunities for Commercial Mortgage
      Loan Markets**   549

Craig B Prosser,
Landesbank Baden-Württemberg

Abbreviations

A full glossary is provided in the Appendix.

AAOIFI	Accounting and Auditing Organisation for Islamic Financial Institutions
ABCP	Asset Backed Commercial Paper
ABS	Asset Backed Securities / Securitisation
ADR	American Depository Receipts
AFC	Available Funds Cap
AFFO	Adjusted Funds From Operations
AIF	Authorised Investment Funds
AIF	Alternative Investment Funds
AIFM	Alternative Investment Fund Manager
AIFMD	Alternative Investment Fund Managers Directive
AIM	Alternative Investment Market of the London Stock Exchange
ALA	Allocated Loan Amount
ALTA	American Land Title Association
AREA	Asian Real Estate Association
AUM	Assets under Management
AVM	Automated Valuation Models
BBA	British Bankers' Association
BCBS	Basel Committee
BCO	British Council for Offices
BIPRU	FSA's Prudential Sourcebook for Banks, Building Societies and Investment Firms
BIS	Bank for International Settlements
BOV	Broker's Opinion of Value
Bp	Basis Point
bppa	Basis Points Per Annum
BPF	British Property Federation
CAGR	Compound Annual Growth Rate
CBO	Collateralised Bond Obligation
CCR	Controlling Class Representative
CDO	Collateralised Debt Obligation
CDO2	Collateralised Debt Obligation Squared
CDS	Credit Default Swaps
CFC	Controlled Foreign Company
CEBS	Committee of European Banking Supervisors
CEE	Central and Eastern Europe
CESR	Committee of European Securities Regulators
CGT	Capital Gains Tax

CIL	Community Infrastructure Levy
CIS	Collective Investment Scheme
CLN	Credit Linked Note
CLO	Collateralised Loan Obligations
CMBS	Commercial Mortgage Backed Securitisation / Securities
CMO	Collateralised Mortgage Obligation
CMSA	Commercial Mortgage Securities Association
CMU	Capital Markets Union
CMVM	Portuguese Securities Commission
CNMV	Comisión Nacional del Mercado de Valores
COE	Cost of Equity
COMI	Centre of Main Interest
CP	Commercial Paper
CPR	Constant Prepayment Rates
CRA	Credit Rating Agency
CRD	Capital Requirements Directive
CRD 2	Capital Requirements Directive 2
CRD 3	Capital Requirements Directive 3
CRD 4	Capital Requirements Directive 4
CRE	Commercial Real Estate
CREFC	Commercial Real Estate Financial Council
CREFC IRP	Commercial Real Estate Financial Council Investor Reporting Package
CRR	Capital Requirements Regulation
CSA	Collateral Support Agreements
CSA	Credit Support Annex
CSWA	Capital Structure Weighted Average
CTL	Credit Tenant Lease Loan
CVA	Company Voluntary Arrangement
CVE	Control Valuation Event
CVL	Creditors' Voluntary Liquidation
DCF	Discounted Cash Flow
DOL	Department of Labor (US)
DPO	Discounted Pay Off / Discounted Purchase Offer
DSCR	Debt Service Coverage Ratio
DTAA	Double Taxation Avoidance Agreements
EAD	Exposure at Default
EBA	European Banking Authority
E-IRP	European Investor Reporting Package
EC	European Community
ECB	European Central Bank
ECON	Committee on Economic and Monetary Affairs
EEA	European Economic Area
EFTA	European Free Trade Association
EIOPA	European Insurance and Occupational Pensions Authority
EL	Expected Loss

EMEA	Europe, the Middle East and Africa
EMIR	European Market Infrastructure Regulations
EONIA	Euro OverNight Index Average
EPF	European Property Federation
EPRA	European Public Real Estate Association
ERISA	Employee Retirement Income Security Act 1974 (US)
ERV	Estimated Rental Value
ESF	European Securitisation Forum
ESMA	European Securities and Markets Authority
ESRB	European Systemic Risk Board
ETF	Exchange Traded Fund
EU	European Union
EUIR	European Union Insolvency Regulation
EURIBOR	Euro Inter-Bank Offered Rate
FATCA	Foreign Account Tax Compliance Act
FCA	Financial Conduct Authority
FDI	Foreign Direct Investment
FDIC	Federal Deposit Insurance Corporation (US)
FFI	Foreign Financial Institution
FFO	Funds From Operations
FHCMC	Federal Home Loan Mortgage Corporation (Freddie Mac)
FIRREA	Financial Institutions Reform, Recovery and Enforcement Act 1989 (US)
FNMA	Federal National Mortgage Association (Fannie Mae)
FRI	Fully Repairing and Insuring Leases
FSB	Financial Stability Board
FSF	Financial Stability Forum
FSMA	Financial Services and Markets Act 2000 (UK)
GAAP	Generally Accepted Accounting Principles
GACS	Garanzia sulla Cartolarizzazione delle Sofferenze
GCC	Gulf Cooperation Council
GDP	Gross Domestic Product
GFA	Garantie Financière d'Achèvement
GFC	Global Financial Crisis
GIC	Guaranteed Investment Contract
GNMA	Government National Mortgage Association (Ginnie Mae)
GOEF	German Open-Ended Funds
GSIFIs	Globally Systemically Important Financial Institutions
GSE	Government Sponsored Entities (US)
HEL	Home Equity Loans
HIRE	Hiring Incentives to Restore Employment Act 2010 (US)
HMRC	Her Majesty's Revenue & Customs (UK)

HNWI	High Net-Worth Individual
HVRE	High Volatile Real Estate
IBOR	Inter-Bank Offered Rate
ICE	ICE Benchmark Administration Limited
ICE LIBOR	The ICE Benchmark Administration Limited London Inter-Bank Offered Rate
ICR	Issuer Credit Rating
ICR	Interest Cover Ratio
IDB	Islamic Development Bank
IFRS	International Financial Reporting Standards
IFSB	Islamic Financial Services Board
IMF	International Monetary Fund
INREV	Investors in Non-Listed Real Estate Vehicles
IO	Interest-Only
IOSCO	International Organisation of Securities Commissions
IPD	Interest Payment Date / International Property Databank
IPF	Investment Property Forum
IPRE	Income Producing Real Estate
IRAP	Italian Regional Tax on Productive Activities
IRB	Internal Ratings-Based Approach
IRES	Italian Corporate Income Tax
IRP	Investor Reporting Package
IRR	Internal Rate of Return
IRS	Internal Revenue Service (US)
ISCR	Interest Service Coverage Ratio
ISDA	International Swaps and Derivatives Association
ISE	Irish Stock Exchange
IVASS	Italian insurance supervisory authority
LGD	Loss Given Default
LIBOR	London Inter-Bank Offered Rate
LLP	Loan Loss Provision
LMA	Loan Market Association
LOC	Letter of Credit
LP	Limited Partner
LPE	Limited Purpose Entity
LSE	Luxembourg Stock Exchange
LTC	Loan-To-Cost
LTV	Loan-To-Value
LTRO	Long Term Refinancing Operation
LSA	Liquidity Subordinated Amounts
M	Effective Maturity
M&A	Mergers and Acquisitions
MAD	Market Abuse Directive
MAR	Market Abuse Regulation
MBMP	Multi-Borrower Multi-Property
MBS	Mortgage Backed Securities / Securitisation

MCR	Minimum Capital Requirement
MFC	French Monetary and Financial Code
MFH	Multi-Family Housing
MGS	Malaysian Global Sukuk Inc.
MiFID	Markets in Financial Instruments Directive
MTN	Medium-Term Note
NAMA	National Asset Management Agency
NAREIT	National Association of Real Estate Investment Trusts (US)
NAV	Net Asset Value
NCREIF	National Council for Real Estate Investment Fiduciaries (US)
NICE	Non Inflationary Consistent Expansion
NIM	Net Interest Margin
NOCF	Net Operating Cash Flow
NOI	Net Operating Income
NPL	Non-Performing Loan
NPV	Net Present Value
NRSRO	Nationally Recognized Statistical Rating Organizations
NSFR	Net Stable Funding Ratio
NSMIA	National Securities Markets Improvement Act 1996 (US)
OA	Operating Advisor
OC	Offering Circular
OECD	Organisation for Economic Co-operation & Development
OEIC	Open Ended Investment Company
OER	Operating Expense Ratio
OIC	Organisation of the Islamic Conference
OSCRE	Open Standards Consortium for Real Estate
OTC	Over-The-Counter
OTD	Originate to Distribute
P2P	Peer-to-Peer Lending
PAIF	Property Authorised Investment Fund
PD	Probability of Default
PFIC	Passive Foreign Investment Company
PIA	Property Industry Alliance
PIC	Property Investment Certificate
PIC	Property Income Distribution
PIIGS	Portugal Ireland Italy Greece Spain
PIK	Payment in Kind
PLN	Property Linked Note
PUT	Property Unit Trust
PC	Practical Completion
PMA	Property Market Analysis
PMP	Professional Market Parties
PRS	Private rental sector

QEF	Qualifying Electing Fund
QFC	Qualifying Floating Charge
QIB	Qualified Institutional Buyer
QIS	Qualified Investor Scheme
QIV	Qualifying Investment Vehicle
QRS	Qualified REIT Subsidiary
RAC	Rating Agency Confirmation
RBA	Ratings Based Approach
RBC	Risk Based Capital
RCF	Revolving Credit Facility
RED-SIG	Real Estate Derivatives Special Interest Group
REIT	Real Estate Investment Trusts
REMIC	Real Estate Mortgage Investment Conduit
REO	Real Estate Owned
REOC	Real Estate Operating Company
RICS	Royal Institution of Chartered Surveyors
RIE	Recognised Investment Exchange
RIS	Regulatory Information Services
RMBS	Residential Mortgage Backed Securities
ROC	Return on Capital
ROE	Return on Equity
RTC	Resolution Trust Corporation (US)
RW	Risk Weight
RWA	Risk Weighted Assets
S&L	Savings & Loan
SAREB	Sociedad de Gestión de Activos Procedentes de la Reestructuración Bancaria
SCR	Solvency Capital Requirement
SDLT	Stamp Duty Land Tax
SEC	Securities and Exchange Commission
SF	Supervisory Formula
SIV	Structured Investment Vehicle
SLE	Specialised Lending Exposures
SME	Small and Medium Enterprises
SMMEA	Secondary Mortgage Market Enhancement Act 1984 (US)
SOCIMI	Sociedades Anónimas Cotizadas de Inversión Inmobiliaria
SONIA	Sterling Over Night Index Average
SPE	Special Purpose Entity
SPV	Special Purpose Vehicle
STS	Simple, Transparent and Standardised
SWF	Sovereign Wealth Fund
TALF	Term Asset Backed Securities Loan Facility (US)
TARP	Troubled Asset Relief Programme (US)
TIN	Taxpayer Identification Number
TMP	Taxable Mortgage Pool
TOGC	Transfer of a business as a Going Concern

TRS	Total Return Swap
TWRR	Time-Weighted Rate of Return
UBTI	Unrelated Business Taxable Income
UCC	Uniform Commercial Code (US)
UCIT	Undertakings for Collective Investment in Transferable Securities
UKAR	UK Asset Resolution Limited
UNCITRAL	United Nations Commission on International Trade Law
UL	Unexpected Loss
VAT	Value Added Tax
VATA 1994	Value Added Tax Act 1994
VPV	Vacant Possession Value
VEFA	Vente en État Futur d'Achèvement
VRE	Voting Rights Enforcement
WAC	Weighted-Average Coupon
WAFF	Weighted-Average Foreclosure Frequency
WALS	Weighted-Average Loss Severity
WAM	Weighted–Average Maturity
WAULT	Weighted-Average Unexpired Lease Term
WBS	Whole Business Securitisation

Chapter 1

The Commercial Mortgage Loans and CMBS Markets: Legacy and current positions

Andrew V. Petersen,

Partner and Practice Area Leader-Finance, K&L Gates LLP

1.1 Introduction

Commercial real estate (CRE) is a tremendously important asset, as the content of this book will discuss. However, the CRE lending and commercial mortgage-backed securities (CMBS) markets are, at the time of writing, largely unrecognisable to the markets that existed on the publication of the first edition of this book, published in 2006. Between the first edition[1] and the second edition, published in 2012,[2] such markets have witnessed seismic structural shifts. Numerous financial institutions with strong histories were consolidated or were nationalised and, through the chaos of the GFC, CRE and the CRE capital markets had a visible presence throughout, with nearly all real estate values across the globe suffering unanticipated catastrophic declines.

The provision of capital to the CRE industry, which tends by definition to be very capital intensive and of a longer-term nature was, during the boom period up to 2007, mostly funded by balance sheet banks using relatively shorter-dated funds, thus allowing them larger spreads through effectively taking maturity transformation risk. This position could not continue indefinitely. Due in a large part to the deterioration that began in the US sub-prime mortgage market in the second half of 2007, this position led through contagion, interdependence and interconnection, to a deep crisis for the global securitisation markets, across all asset classes, which developed in 2008 and in the subsequent years quickly morphed into the GFC.

With the GFC came a decrease in leveraged M&A transactions, falling share prices, a weakening of the global economy and the shutting down or freezing of the global real estate capital markets, ending the seemingly

---

[1] A.V. Petersen, *Commercial Mortgage-Backed Securitisation: Developments in the European Market*, 1st edn (London: Sweet & Maxwell, 2006).

[2] A.V. Petersen, *Commercial Mortgage-Backed Securitisation: Developments in the European Market*, 2nd edn (London: Sweet & Maxwell, 2012).

unstoppable growth of issuance in European and US CMBS markets witnessed prior to the summer of 2007. This development was not a cyclical change, as had occurred in the past, but a major structural change, giving rise to questions over the viability of the CMBS "originate-to-distribute" model, based in part on structural weaknesses revealed in the securities themselves. Such questions, dealt with throughout this book, will also need to be addressed post 2016, as many believe that the impact of this structural shift, still evident at the time of writing, may persist until 2020 and beyond.

Given this backdrop, and the backdrop of the UK's vote for Brexit in the June 2016 referendum on EU membership (the consequences of which continue at the time of writing) the markets witnessed an unprecedented level of intervention by the world's central banks and state bail-outs of the financial and capital markets, and this third edition will consider the ongoing effect of such interventions and their effects on these markets in the context of a post GFC world. In doing so, this Chapter will consider the legacy markets for CRE financing and CMBS and will examine the markets at the time of writing. In doing so, it is necessary to go back in time to examine the evolution of the CRE and CMBS markets in an effort to understand and to determine whether European CMBS will, going forward, once again be an important source of funding and risk diversification tool and resurge from the form in which it exists at the time of writing. Thus, when we consider the legacy European commercial mortgage loan and CMBS markets that exist at the time of writing, we can split such analysis up into three separate periods: up to 2007, 2007 to 2012 and post 2012.

1.2 The European CRE loan and CMBS markets prior to 2007

The first edition of this book chartered the introduction and development of the innovative CMBS product in Europe up to 2006. During this period, as a result of technological improvements and the lowering of global investment barriers that freed CMBS from the restrictions of US REMIC rules, the development of the product proved remarkable in its ability to address the needs of borrowers, loan originators and investors, in a way few would have thought possible. This transformation resulted in an explosion of issuance, as the CMBS market in Europe reached €46 billion (more than double the total for 2004), peaking at €65 billion in 2007. This issuance came off the back of a boom in CRE financing, fuelled by an overheated CRE market, fostered by the availability of plentiful and cheap funding, coupled with relatively low capital requirements that established real estate as a global asset class in its own right.

The European bank lending sector was, up to 2008, the key and biggest provider of financing to the CRE market, providing around 90% of the financing to the sector as banks with significant balance sheet capacity (but not strength, as it turned out) grew their exposure to real estate substantially during the period 1997 to 2007. This was predominantly as a result of falling interest rates which stimulated demand for real estate following the technology market crash and dotcom bust of early 2000s as investors sought solace in longer-term assets that effectively hedged interest rate risk. During the period from 1997 to 2007, given the relatively low development of other forms of financing, CRE financing was one of the fastest growing lending classes for banks, particularly in the UK, Germany, Ireland and Spain. The largest CRE lenders were made up of UK, German and Irish banks (in each case lending both domestically and internationally). Spanish banks also generated a large CRE exposure, although primarily domestic (see further the Spanish lending section contained in Chapter 18). Prior to this period, commercial and residential real estate debt was held on the balance sheets of mortgage lenders, such as banks, building societies and insurance companies. To the extent that a secondary market existed for this debt, it was largely a club syndication and participation market. Securitisation through the issuance of CMBS played a small (historically around 10–12% the total outstanding debt in the sector), but meaningful, role in funding European CRE throughout this development and it is important to understand its origins.

1.2.1 The birth of commercial mortgage-backed securitisation

Whilst the US claims to be the birthplace of CMBS, securities, in the form of European mortgage bonds, have existed in Europe for over 200 years. Nonetheless, it is true that CMBS in the modern form ultimately did not become popular in Europe until after the 1980s following the widespread acceptance in the US marketplace where many of the legal structural foundations of the modern CMBS market were put into place, paving the way for the growth of the modern CMBS industry. Such growth was based on the changing dynamics of real estate lending that had its origins in the 1970s, particularly as US government-sponsored enterprises, such as the Federal National Mortgage Association (Fannie Mae) and the Federal Home Loan Mortgage Corporation (Freddie Mac) began to facilitate increasing growth in home ownership by guaranteeing mortgage-backed securities backed by portfolios of US mortgages.

CMBS in the US received a further catalyst for growth with the advent of the savings and loan crisis of the late 1980s. The crisis led to a seminal event in the development of the modern US CMBS industry, with the passage of the Financial Institutions Reform, Recovery and Enforcement Act (FIRREA) in August, 1989. Among other things, it imposed stricter capital standards on regulated commercial lenders and created the Resolution Trust Corporation (RTC). The RTC was charged with resolving failed thrift institutions and disposing of the assets of these failed institutions. In the early 1990s, the RTC, and later the US Federal Deposit Insurance Corporation (the FDIC), began to reduce the inventory of assets that they had acquired from failed depository institutions during the savings and loan crisis. The biggest portion of the RTC's inventory consisted of a portfolio of mortgage loans, which by August 1990 was estimated to be more than US $34 billion that had been originated and held by depository institutions that the RTC controlled. It was quickly realised that selling those loans one by one was neither efficient, nor, in the final analysis, even achievable. As the market for mortgage-backed securities had developed dramatically up to this time, the RTC, in a significant step in the evolution of the mortgage capital markets, turned to the then novel concept of private-label securitisation of assets that did not conform to the Fannie Mae or Freddie Mac underwriting standards as a way to dispose of this overhang of now publicly owned private debt.[3]

The success of the RTC's CMBS programme resulted in private-label mortgage conduits bursting forth in the early 1990s as a way of funding and securitising vast pools of commercial and multi-family loans. It is during this period, through financial innovation, that the alchemy of securitisation truly prospered as the "originate-to-distribute" business model took hold where mortgages were originated with the sole intention of distributing them or selling them on in the market shortly after being written, thereby passing the risk of default to another financial institution. Such alchemy allowed risky mortgage assets to be mixed in a melting pot of potions to be turned overnight into highly-rated investment grade assets based on a wide range of investor demand and appetite. Meanwhile, the European securitisation markets, whilst lagging behind the developing market in the US, slowly metamorphosed into a European securitisation industry based on three types of securitisation methods:

- "On-balance sheet securitisation", such as covered mortgage bonds and Pfandbrief-style products;
- "Off-balance sheet pass through" securitisation, where assets are transferred to a trustee for the sole purpose of issuing asset-backed securities; and
- "Off-balance sheet pay through" securitisation. This development and growth was as a result of the diversity of the European markets in terms of the types of underlying assets, types of security and the applicable taxes, regulations and laws that permeate throughout Europe.

The introduction of the euro currency towards the end of the 1990s resulted in a reduction of the currency translation risks of cross-border transactions, translating into an increase in issuance fuelled by strong investor demand, which formed the basis for the creation of a relatively large European MBS

---

[3] See further Ch.1 of the 1st edn. The RTC's famous "Series C" transactions marked the first time that commercial mortgages were packaged and securitised in large volumes. These programmes not only helped to resolve the overhang of the savings and loan crisis, but also created standard templates for securitisable loan terms, securitisation structures, loan servicing conventions, property information reporting templates and the like, paving the way for the growth of a vibrant commercial mortgage conduit securitisation industry.

market. A UK-centric, fixed rate market in the late 1990s quickly developed. During this time, CMBS transformed the CRE market. What was initially an isolated, self-contained business funded by domestic (and often geographically local) banks and insurance companies, investing a fixed "real estate" allocation of capital into the CRE markets for portfolio purposes and holding those mortgage loans on their balance sheets to maturity, transforming itself into a business funded by the broad global capital markets.

By the late 1990s, fixed income investors invested in rated bonds throughout the capital stack, up and down the risk curve enabling the spread of risk. A growing number of boutique, high-yield real estate players further emerged to invest in the below investment grade segment of the risk curve. CMBS led to an enormous increase in the availability of finance and became a major driver of economic growth in western markets. However, the autumn of 1998 witnessed the Russian rouble debt crisis which, whilst shaking the industry to its core, also matured the industry,[4] such that (for a time) there were tightened underwriting standards throughout the early years of the 2000s, a period which also led to a high-yield market for subordinate tranches of CRE loans.[5]

In the UK, prior to 2004 listed real estate companies or corporates were the major issuers of CMBS as it was mainly used as a financial or capital raising tool; a means for such entities to borrow directly from the capital markets to finance investments more efficiently on longer terms than borrowing directly from banks. CMBS proved attractive due to capital efficiencies resultant from the CMBS product with margins offered through a CMBS financing, often lower than through conventional bank debt funding. Thus, a price arbitrage developed between bank lending and CMBS lending. Then from 2005 to 2007, following the birth of banks' conduit programmes (described below), CMBS began lending in increasing amounts, direct to highly geared CRE investors, such as private equity funds and property funds, leading to a dramatic shift in the use of CMBS from a long term financing to a shorter term funding method. The loans originated by these programmes were often set up by investment banks or commercial banks, which would then deposit the loans to capital markets issuing entities for packaging and distribution to investors.[6] These investors, broadly speaking, saw bonds backed by commercial mortgage debt, not as an isolated "alternative investment" but simply as one among many core investment opportunities, which were pursued with more or less vigour depending upon perceptions of relative value. This led to a range of assets being financed through securitisation conduit programmes, such as operating businesses made up of pubs, hotels and nursing homes through to offices, retail properties and industrial properties. With this development, the CMBS industry morphed into a major source of capital, with 75% of all

---

[4]   See further Ch.1 of the 1st edn.
[5]   See further Ch.5.
[6]   See further Ch.3 of the 1st edn and Ch.4 herein.

outstanding CMBS bonds that still exist at the time of writing, issued between 2005 to 2007, mostly all through conduit programmes. Thus through CMBS, CRE and its funding depended, in a very material way, upon direct access to the capital markets. It is worth setting out what exactly the CMBS product consists of for those readers unfamiliar with the product.

1.2.2 *Key features of CMBS*

CMBS is largely a mechanism for capital transfer established on a methodology of channelling capital into real estate debt based on cash flows generated by separate pools of commercial mortgages through the creation and issuance of securities. This methodology, based on an indirect real estate investment, is a means of providing liquidity to the markets by issuing securities whose payments are backed by illiquid real estate. In essence, illiquid assets are converted into securities that can be sold to investors, through a product, designed to spread risk, through the method of pooling and repackaging of cash-flow producing commercial mortgage loans by mortgage originators, usually in the form of off-balance sheet vehicles in the form of newly formed special purpose vehicles (SPVs). The SPVs issue securities backed by the CRE loans that are then sold to investors in the global capital markets. Instead of requiring the originator to hold all of the credit risk of a CRE loan until maturity, thereby inefficiently trapping capital of the originator, CMBS provides the originator a way of selling the CRE loan upon origination and using the funds received to originate further loans. The process produces fixed income fees for the bank through the creation, sale and underwriting/arranging of the product, and, on occasion, at the same time reducing the mortgage originators' capital requirements/ capital relief. The process and its economics, will be discussed further in Chapter 4.

The move in the late 1980s and early 1990s to securitise US mortgage debt effectively remedied one of the primary impediments to real estate becoming a global asset class, that of illiquidity, at the same time serving as a useful credit portfolio risk management tool for CMBS originators. Cash flows from whole loans can be (i) isolated from the individual whole loans and reassembled in a number of ways (based on investor demand) to pay principal and interest (in normal market conditions at a lower amount than the rates received from the borrowers, thereby providing additional income to the CMBS originators), and (ii) stratified by interest rate, risk and duration, thereby boosting the volume of lending available for CRE, via a tradeable security that provides investors with an income stream backed by real assets. Such investor demand drives the value of the sum of the securities to equal or exceed the par amount of the loans backing these securities.

A very important feature of CMBS is the dispersion of risk through the tranching of credit risk based on subordination, so that the pool of mortgage assets (together with any credit enhancement) can effectively be tranched all the way from triple-A rated securities to non-investment grade securities that bear the first loss of risk on the assets in the pool. The securities in a CMBS are rated by international credit rating agencies (CRAs),[7] such as Moody's, Standard & Poor's, Fitch Ratings and DBRS, based on a methodology which recognises the different levels of risk, return, order of payment and degree of credit support. The credit ratings proffered by the CRAs became, over time, a crucial indicator of risk as investors relied on such ratings as they themselves were often not in a position to evaluate the quality of, or risk factors associated with, the underlying assets. Indeed, often investment criteria for senior tranche investors were based on the fact that two of the three largest CRAs had provided the same rating and thus an element of reliance of CRAs undertaking the task instead of investors took hold.

By creating tranched capital structures for investments in pools of mortgage debt, CMBS transactions permit investors in senior tranches ranging from triple-A, with the first claim on payments (thus reducing risk but also providing a lower return), to obtain highly-rated exposures to diverse pools of financial assets at a yield greater than that for comparably rated corporate or sovereign debt. Whilst investors in subordinate tranches (the so-called "first loss" piece, as these notes are the first to absorb losses and consequently receive the highest rate of returns), only receive payments once the senior tranches have been paid (i.e. based on a waterfall principle), such investors can obtain leveraged exposures to diverse pools of financial assets without the risk of margin calls.

Such tranching led to the investor base for CMBS becoming highly targeted based on differential risk-return appetites. Treasury departments of banks, structured investment vehicles (SIVs), asset backed commercial paper (ABCP) conduits, insurance companies and pension funds, were the major participants in the most highly-rated tranches, due to many of these entities being required to only hold highly-rated securities, which presents the risk of a forced sale in the event of a rating downgrade of the triple-A notes. The drive for these institutions into senior CMBS tranches was based on the need for a return on a product with triple-A credit ratings. That attracted similar high ratings as compared to government bonds or treasuries, but because interest rates were at historic low levels, offered much lower yields. On the other end of the scale, real estate investors, hedge funds and other opportunistic high yield investors with a high tolerance for risk or a keen understanding of the underlying real estate assets, invested in the most subordinate tranches that provided credit support for the more senior tranches. The participation of SIVs and the ABCP conduits, as leveraged buyers of CMBS, proved controversial, as they engaged in arbitrage by funding their investments through issuing short-term debt, by way of ABCP and repurchase or "repo" agreements or arrangements at low

---

[7] See further Ch.14. for a discussion of the role of the rating agencies in commercial mortgage lending and the wider debt capital markets.

interest rates and then buying CMBS longer-term securities that paid a higher rate of interest. SIVs were thus highly-leveraged vehicles, mainly held and treated as off-balance sheet by banks subject to capital requirements in relation to their balance sheets (as the banks had no direct claim to the bonds). As banks wanted to take on more debt to make the returns that MBS offered, the banks made such investments through SIVs and ABCP conduits. As soon as the ability to raise short-term funding in the market disappeared with the advent of the liquidity crisis, the SIVs were either liquidated (to the extent they were allowed to do so) or brought onto the balance sheet of the banks to protect and preserve the bank's reputation and positions in the market, thereby rendering them unable to purchase CMBS but more importantly still keeping the risk of default within the banking system. This effectively eradicated a large section of the investor base and as buyers for the product disappeared, the CMBS market effectively closed in the second half of 2007.

1.3 The CRE market: 2007 to 2012

Between 2007 and 2012, the CRE market witnessed a severe cut back from bank lenders, due to the uncertainty of value of the assets they had lent against during the boom years. Moreover, regulatory pressures surrounding the banks' capital and its use and a general contraction in the inter-bank lending market, with bank lenders less than enthusiastic to lend to each other, further contributed to such cut back. As a result, banks continued to shrink their balance sheets and the shadow banking sector (discussed below) continued to reduce their exposure to real estate. Further, the value of the assets held on the balance sheet of banks continued to cause concern, as one important consequence of the examination of such assets in the market that developed during this period was the increasing difficulty of valuing such assets. Such difficulty also highlighted tensions with international accounting standards, particularly the "fair value" system that requires banks to mark the value of their assets to market price. Post 2007, this resulted in banks and other holders of real estate debt marking values to a virtually non-existent market. When market value is the price that a fair-minded buyer is willing to pay to a seller that does not need to sell, there is a real question raised as to how one values the assets held on balance sheet that cannot be sold at any price because the market for such assets has effectively closed down. This problem was recognised by the Basel Committee, which in 2009 issued guidelines to banks to allow flexibility in marking asset values to illiquid market valuations, particularly where one or more of the transactions (i.e. asset sales) have occurred at less than expected value due to illiquid market conditions.

Overall, the CRE sector received a limited amount of financing from CMBS markets during 2007 to 2012. Most of the CMBS bonds not able to be securitised, due to the shutting down of the CMBS markets, were retained by banks and used to obtain liquidity from the Bank of England (in the UK) and the European Central Bank (ECB) (throughout Europe). Further, the markets witnessed a contraction of lending against CRE by other credit providers such as funds, hedge funds and other institutional investors, the so-called "shadow banking" sector. It is estimated that the shadow banking system comprised in excess of 80% of the total credit provided in the US economy prior to the financial crisis of 2007–08. Once the short-term money markets and CMBS markets effectively shut down in 2007–08, the shadow banking system shrank dramatically with important consequences. In particular, the declining profitability of the funds (particularly hedge funds) caused in some cases a dramatic rise in redemption requests from investors. Faced with a large number of redemption requests, some funds were forced to liquidate large portions of their CRE debt portfolios, in many cases through forced sales at well below book value for the assets (a process akin to the one witnessed immediately post the UK's vote for Brexit in the June 2016 referendum on EU membership). This had a knock-on effect on the broader CRE and CMBS markets by contributing to a general decline in value and liquidity.

1.3.1   European CMBS market between 2008 and 2012

In the UK, between 2008 and 2012, there were eight CMBS transactions issued. This contrasted with the period from 2004–07 where there were hundreds of new issuances. These included transactions from Deutsche Bank's DECO platform in 2011 and 2012, true sale securitisations of the Chiswick Park and Merry Hill loans and Vitus German Multifamily deal.[8] The other securitisations were from two corporates that used CMBS to raise funding totalling £3 billion. Tesco Plc brought four CMBS issues to the market, totalling £2.64 billion, backed by rental payments from properties occupied by Tesco Plc. Land Securities Plc issued £360 million of CMBS backed by rental payments from a UK government body. These issuances had several common characteristics that appealed to institutional investors: (i) they were single tranches with no subordinate debt; (ii) they were backed by investment grade credits; (iii) they carried fixed coupons; and (iv) were relatively long dated, with maturity dates ranging from 2027 to 2040. As such, they resembled investment grade corporate bonds and did not represent a true re-opening of the CMBS market, as investors were primarily taking credit risk rather than property risk.

1.3.2.   Challenges to re-establishing a viable European CMBS market

Re-establishing a sustainable market in CMBS, since the markets were effectively frozen during this period, proved challenging. This was because CMBS became associated with a number of disadvantages.

Firstly, because of the insistence of CMBS loans being originated to SPVs, to minimise insolvency and other creditor risk, CMBS noteholders, following a

---

[8]   See Deco 2011-E5, Deco 2012-MHILL and FLORE 2012–1.

default, had to rely on the underlying cash flow generated by the properties, since there was no guarantee against other funds. This led to performance issues, with some commentators and regulators branding CMBS as being "toxic" assets, which contributed to the GFC. In this regard, it is important to differentiate between the US and Europe (including the UK). As discussed above, in the US, certain products, such as subprime residential mortgage bonds and Collateralised Debt Obligations (CDOs)[9] created from these bonds, performed poorly through the GFC. The delinquency rate of US subprime loans in 2010 rose above 50%. In Europe, however, these same products were not created and the assets backing most securitised products, including CMBS, performed reasonably well during this period, with statistics suggesting that the CRE loans that were securitised were of higher quality on average than the CRE loans that were not securitised in the UK. This theme will be developed further in Chapter 15.

Secondly, being off-balance sheet and existing effectively in the shadow banking market CMBS historically has not been subject to banking supervision or regulations, thus creating the possibility of moral hazard based on weakening underwriting standards. As set out above, CMBS allowed a CRE loan originator to avoid the individual credit risk of its borrowers, however, it also (it was argued) reduced the originator's incentive to ensure the borrower had the ability to repay (based on higher levels of equity) or ensuring through strong underwriting, loan terms and provisions (for example, trapping of cash; interest reserve war chests) based on the real estate providing for payment. Thus, this argument, taken to its extreme, was based on the premise that, where the originator retained no risk and was compensated merely for making CRE loans, regardless of how well those loans were underwritten and without any regard to whether or not that loan would be repaid, there was no incentive for the originator to maintain strict underwriting standards (so called "covenant light" loans), leading to a shift in focus of the originator from maintaining high credit standards to generating maximum volume of product. As was witnessed with the spread of the contagion from a US sub-prime crisis to the GFC, the ease by which large financial institutions were able to package up loans into securities and sell those securities in the global capital markets allowed the risk of mortgage defaults to spread well beyond traditional mortgage lenders to investors that may or may not have understood real estate and the risk of having an indirect investment in it.

Finally, there was during the period of 2008 and 2012, and continues (to a lesser extent) at the time of writing, a considerable amount of overhanging CRE debt in need of refinancing. This is due to the fact that CMBS securities (generally around 10 years) are not matched to the underlying loans (typically around five to seven years) raising the risk that borrowers are not able to obtain refinancing at the time of their loan's maturity dates.

---

[9] See Ch.11 of the 1st edn.

1.3.3. Refinancing risk

Given the catastrophic decline in CRE values after 2007, most LTVs on CRE loans rose in excess of 100%. This resulted in many borrowers being in negative equity. As most CMBS loans do not amortise (preferring instead a single repayment bullet at maturity), it was predicted that those high LTVs would persist for many years to come. Thus, whilst it remained the case that most UK CMBS and loans continued to out-perform balance sheet loans, it was predicted that there was in 2012 refinancing risk for CMBS of around €75 billion, owing to a gradual maturing of existing CMBS. Based on a prediction that up to 50% of all UK CRE that required refinancing might not even be suitable for CMBS origination (not being standardised enough to be trusted by investors) and with an estimated €25 billion of equity capital outflow from real estate markets due to open ended funds terminations, it was predicted in 2012 that there existed a total financing shortage for the European CRE sector of around €400–€700 billion. Of the £56 billion of UK CMBS bonds outstanding, £27 billion was due to be repaid over the next 10 years. These bonds were predominantly of the "conduit" variety, which were issued by investment bank programmes from 2005 to 2007, as described above. Given CRE loans tend to have an average duration of five to seven years, preceding the peak in CMBS bond maturities in 2014, a wave of UK CMBS loans, totalling about £19 billion, matured in 2012 to 2014. This topic will be dealt with in further detail in Chapter 3.

Debt held against UK CRE continued to fall from £228.1 billion in 2011 to £212.3 billion in 2012, a drop of 6.8%.[10] The 2012 *UK Commercial Property Lending Market Report* by De Montfort University (*De Montford Report*), found that "while the overall level of debt was falling and progress had been made in dealing with the distressed legacy debt, there was a long way to go with between £72.5 billion and £100 billion struggling to be refinanced on current market terms when the debt matures as it has a loan-to-value ratio of over 70%." The 2012 *De Montford Report* further recognised that although progress had been made in addressing the legacy situation, banks still faced a significant overhang of pre-recession CRE debt held on their balance sheets, with around £51 billion due to mature in 2012 and £153 billion—72% of outstanding debt—by year-end 2016.

Bright spots in the 2012 *De Montford Report* showed loan originations on the increase and new lenders to the market increasing their market share to circa 8%. However, this was a mere drop in the ocean compared to the level of deleveraging—in 2012 Morgan Stanley expected €1.6 to €3 trillion of total

---

[10] See *UK Commercial Property Lending Market Report* by De Montfort University, which remains the UK's largest independent property lending survey (the *De Montford Report*). In 2012, the survey of 72 lending teams from 63 banks and other lending organisations said that 2011 started with some optimism for the commercial property lending market, including the first CMBS issue since 2007, but that this changed dramatically during the second half of 2011 as the Eurozone sovereign debt crisis heralded "extremely tough times" to the economy.

loan reduction between 2012 and 2015, as banks endeavoured to increase capital, recover funding, improve profitability and generally refocus business models. Morgan Stanley derived this number from the sum of the specific CRE deleveraging plans already announced by some banks (approximately €300 billion of loans) and it estimated that up to €300 billion of exposure might not be entirely rolled over as banks retrenched and refocused their business, and thus reduced their cross-border loans or simply reduced LTVs. To put this into context, this was equivalent to five times the annual real estate transactions between 2008 and 2012 in Europe.[11]

1.4   The CRE market: 2012 to the present day

Since the second edition of this book published in 2012, there has been an upward trajectory in the CMBS market, although not necessarily in Europe. In the US, lenders issued $94 billion in new loans in 2014 and US CMBS issuance ended 2015 above $101 billion (although at the time of writing 2016 is unlikely to reach this amount). There were 16 CMBS transactions issued in the UK between 2012 and the end of 2015, twice the number in the previous period following the GFC. Notable transactions included the £450m Intu (SGS) Finance Series 1 and £350m Intu (SGS) Finance Series 3 issued as part of a £5 billion programme, the base prospectus of which was published in March 2013, the £463m Isobel Finance No. 1 Plc and the Westfield Stratford City CMBS in relation to a £750m loan secured by a charge over Westfield shopping centre in central London.

Some issuances, such as Westfield Stratford City Finance Plc had similar characteristics to those post 2008, where issues had single tranches and long maturity dates were the norm, in order to appeal to institutional investors since 2012. However, other transactions have been more complex than during 2008 to 2012. Few CMBS issued between 2012 and 2015 have had a maturity date beyond 2030; DECO 2013-CSPK Limited for example has an August 2019 maturity date. Rates payable on notes have been primarily floating, multi-tranched and with varied ratings. Magni Finance DAC, for example, has five note classes with ratings ranging from A to unrated junior notes. In addition, Mint 2015 was an example of an unusual multi-currency CMBS, which issued £251.2m and €131m notes, further to the securitisation of £75m and €30m mezzanine debt in 2014, backed by hotel properties in the UK and the Netherlands. This suggests some re-opening and recovery of the CMBS market and an increasing risk appetite of CMBS investors.

More importantly, the refinancing risk caused by the overhang of pre-recession debt, discussed above as identified by Morgan Stanley in 2012, has not been as severe as initially forecast. Moody's stated in December 2015 that "the much vaunted 'refinancing wave' in 2016 and 2017, during

---

[11] See Morgan Stanley's Blue Paper 15 March 2012 "Banks Deleveraging and Real Estate—Implications of a €400–€700 billion Financing Gap" (the *Morgan Stanley Report*) p.17.

which loans originated with 10-year terms during the 2006 and 2007 pre-crisis peak mature, caused little more than a ripple", noting that "about half of the original issuance levels have since paid off or defaulted and of the remainder about three quarters appear well positioned to refinance, even if 10-year Treasury rates rise by up to 2%." In its CMBS Surveillance Maturity Report for February 2016, Morningstar predicted that the total remaining amount of loans still to mature in 2016 and 2017 is now approximately $150 billion—it expects $56.98 billion of CMBS loans to mature in 2016 and $99.88 billion in 2017. Morningstar has reported that most CMBS loans originated before the market's peak of 2006–07 have been able to refinance, and the delinquency rate is at a seven-year low as at February 2016.[12] See further Chapter 3.

UK CRE loan origination increased from £45 billion in 2014 to £53.7 billion in 2015 according to the 2015 *De Montford Report*. There has also been a continuing growth in the market share of non-bank lenders for loan originations, which has increased to 9%, and the market share of insurance companies has steadily increased to 16% of the market in 2015. This has begun to add diversity to funding sources in the CRE market. CREFC-Europe has endorsed the growing role of institutional capital in addition to bank lending in the CRE debt market as a means of enhancing financial stability, and delivering stable long-term income. The 2015 *De Montford Report* will be further discussed in Chapter 15.

This growth in market share has been partly attributable to deleveraging by banks; by the end of 2014, the CRE loan book of the six largest UK banks had shrunk by 56% to £68 billion.[13] At the time of writing, deleveraging appears to be drawing to a close. The total amount of outstanding CRE debt in the UK at year-end 2015 was £168.4 billion, representing a 1.9% increase from £165.2 billion at year-end 2014, and the first increase recorded since 2008, whereas it had dropped by 6–10% in each of the preceding five years.[14] According to the 2015 *De Montford Report* (the latest report at the time of writing), the deleveraging process has been secured by refinancing of assets at lower LTVs and an increase in equity-only CRE investment. This has been further supported by rising CRE values. By the end of 2015 lending refinanced before the end of 2007 together with new lending before the end of 2007 dropped to 15% of the total CRE debt stock in Europe. The pace of deleveraging between 2007 and the time of writing has varied between different countries. Ireland has significantly reduced its exposure and deleveraging in Germany and Spain appears to have decelerated. Spain, for example saw a 34% reduction in closed loan sale transactions in CRE and residential loans between 2014 and 2015. In Italy on the other

---

[12] See CMBS Surveillance: Maturity Report February 2016 Remittance https://ratingagency.morningstar.com [Accessed 24 August 2016].
[13] See APL CREFC Europe INREV ZIA "Commercial Real Estate Debt in the European Economy 2016" p.28.
[14] See Ch.15 and *UK Commercial Property Lending Market Report* (De Montfort University, 2015).

hand, the country's banks were slow to adopt deleveraging plans and only began significantly deleveraging in 2014; in 2015 it posted €5.3 billion of CRE and residential loan trades, which was 8.2 greater than in 2014 and 23 times greater than in 2013.[15]

However, 71% of respondents to the CREFC Market Outlook Survey in 2016 believed that CMBS spread volatility would be "somewhat" volatile, with geopolitical events, deteriorating credit standards, and contagion from volatility in other asset classes being likely causes of spread volatility in 2016. Although 65% of respondents to the 2016 CREFC Market Outlook Survey expected a total CMBS issuance of between $100 and $125 billion in 2016, there was only €885m placed issuance between January and July 2016 in Europe compared to €4.25 billion during the same period in 2015 and in the first quarter of 2016 there was a total of $17.8 billion priced in the US, down 32% against the previous year.

Looking beyond 2016, there therefore appears to be a mixed picture. In relation to new issuances, although there are signs of CMBS market recovery, heightened volatility may impact CMBS and factors in the financial world unrelated to the underlying performance of CMBS may negatively affect the CMBS market, as will be discussed in the final chapter of this book. Moreover, in relation to maturities, Morningstar projects that the borrowers' ability to pay off CMBS loans on time will become progressively more difficult through 2017, because of lax underwriting standards and estimated net cash flow projections that were never realised.

1.5. Conclusion

As stated above, the European CRE and CMBS markets have undergone a dramatic structural shift since 2007 and the central banks that regulate them have, since the advent of the GFC, faced unprecedented challenges. Such a structural shift has highlighted (as did the Russian rouble crisis of 1998), that in disintermediated credit markets, such shifts and crises can quickly morph into a GFC, where investors flee to the relative quality of government treasury securities and where subordinate interests cannot be sold for any price. During the GFC, SIVs (a historic readily available market for CMBS) largely disappeared, and alongside the shifting investor base, originators' business models changed—perhaps forever. Given these changes, it is predicted that, at the time of writing, CMBS will remain only a marginal provider of CRE capital over the medium term due, in a large part, to the seismic shifts that have brought regulatory challenges, such as:

---

[15] See CBRE Capital Advisors "European Commercial Real Estate Finance 2016 Update" and the Italian NPL Market section in Chapter 18.

- Basel III,[16] that by increasing the amount of capital financial institutions must hold to ensure solvency during periods of financial stress, in turn makes it more costly for such institutions to hold CMBS;

- Article 122a of the CRD, which came into effect in January 2011 (replaced in January 2014 by arts 405–409 of the Capital Requirements Regulation), the so called "5% skin in the game" provisions.[17] Bank and insurance investors in all securitisations now need to ensure that the transaction originators retain 5% "skin in the game", meaning that they retain a 5% interest (first loss or vertical) in every CMBS transaction they bring to market. The retention rule has not prevented the resumption of primary issuance in funding-motivated products like prime residential mortgage-backed securities (RMBS) and consumer asset-backed securities (ABS) because originators typically retained an equity interest even before the crisis. However, the risk retention rules have materially altered the economics of CMBS issuance, which was heavily reliant on a conduit "originate to distribute" model. Investment banks were the sponsors of these conduits and retaining 5% exposure in every new transaction over its lifetime translates into a significant drain on capital;

- significant derivatives legislation, with the European Commission's proposed derivatives legislation potentially forcing European CRE companies and funds to collateralise their interest rate swaps on floating rate loans. In Europe, CRE loans are typically floating rate and swapped to fixed in order to hedge the risk of interest rates increasing. If borrowers were forced to cash collateralise these swaps, the cost of borrowing on a floating rate basis would increase. Chatham Financial estimates that €64.9 billion of working capital could be required across EU Member States to comply with the legislation. If the proposed legislation is passed, borrowers may prefer to use fixed rate loans or to hedge via out of the money caps. Fixed rate loans could be conducive for issuing fixed rate CMBS, as is the norm in the US. However,

---

[16] Basel III was introduced due to criticism of Basel II, based on risk-weighted assets, with the risk weighting given to certain assets based on ratings given by CRAs. The lower the credit rating, the greater the risk weighting given to the asset. Unfortunately, the Basel II requirements, which have been widely adopted, resulted in financial institutions across the globe seeking out similar asset classes and similar highly-rated securities that would carry lower risk weighting, as under Basel II, banks were given the opportunity to define the risk weighting of each asset on their balance sheet using their internal risk models, under three methodologies (standardised, foundation or advanced internal ratings based (IRB)), which were characterised by increasing levels of sophistication. The introduction of the Basel II discipline often resulted in banks being able to reduce the risk parameters applied to their assets and thus reduce the level of equity held against them, a move that has since been widely criticised. As a result, falls in the market value of these highly-rated securities have been felt throughout the financial markets and capital adequacy rules designed to improve the stability of individual banks, have instead increased the level of systemic instability.

[17] See further Ch.16 and the detailed discussion in Ch.17. The skin in the game provisions are attempting to combat the cyclicality and thus periodic crises of the CMBS markets by aligning the interests of the issuers and the investors. With a focus on minimising risk and strengthening underwriting standards, originators and those that securitise will be required to retain some of the risk of the loans they originate or package as part of a CMBS.

European borrowers have traditionally rejected fixed rate loans due to the prepayment penalties that are incurred if the property is sold and the loan prepaid; changes to the IFRS accounting standards; and shifting and conservative rating agency treatment[18];

- Solvency II, is an EU supervisory regime for insurers and reinsurers, introducing new capital requirements and tiering. Since 1 January 2016 Solvency II has required insurance companies to hold capital against the risk of loss in the market value of their assets. CMBS is classified as a Type 2 securitisation, excluding it from favourable treatment; even AAA rated tranches have a higher risk weighting than CRE equity. This means that CMBS has become more expensive for insurers relative to Type 1 securitisations and many other asset classes. The requirement for risk weighting can be removed through matching adjustments where longer-dated real estate debt investments are of a similar duration to long term insurance liabilities. The fact that there is prepayment and extension risk for the repayment of securitisations means that CMBS are unlikely to qualify as eligible for matching adjustment. On the other hand matching can be made possible in relation to direct CRE lending. This incentivises insurance companies to invest directly in CRE rather than securitised debt. It is unlikely therefore that the growth of alternative sources of direct lending in CRE will be replicated to the same extent in the CMBS market; and

- as a result of the Financial Conduct Authority's (FCA) guidance on "slotting", a method for assigning risk weights to lending exposures, greater scrutiny has been placed on the internal models used by banks in lending to specialised assets, including CRE. Slotting puts loans into four categories depending on their LTV and capital weightings can range from 50% to 250%. Banks have been expected to reduce their exposure to balance-sheet intensive asset financing and commercial real estate lending, which was previously one of their biggest on-balance-sheet activities. The British Bankers' Association, in a response to the European Commission noted that "the changes to the Securitisation framework and the imposition of the supervisory slotting approach for Specialised Lending (especially infrastructure lending) have lessened the attractiveness of these asset classes. We think that these rules overestimate the capital requirements leading to the adverse impact upon these asset classes."[19]

1.5.1 Challenges to the wider European commercial mortgage market

Based on the reasons highlighted throughout this chapter, it remains the case that, at the time of writing, CRE lending is less attractive for banks than it was prior to 2007. CRE lending has transformed from purely property

---

[18] See further Ch.14.
[19] See British Bankers' Association response to DG FISMA consultation paper on the possible impact of the CRR and CRD IV on bank financing of the economy and Ch.16.

focused to a relationship-driven business. Unlike in 2005–07, post GFC, the quality of the sponsor (ultimate equity owner of the property) of the non-recourse CRE loans and the prospects of ancillary business with the sponsor, have become more important than ever. As a consequence, quality prime sponsors stand the best chance of obtaining a loan secured by non-prime properties. Such transformation is based on a number of factors. In the *Morgan Stanley Report*, Morgan Stanley attributed the reduced appeal of CRE lending to five factors (that whilst published in 2012, are still relevant at the time of writing):

(i)   Financing is not easy and is expensive, especially for long-term tenures. The boom in CRE financing between 2004 and 2007 was fostered by the availability of plentiful and cheap funding for the banks, coupled with relatively low capital requirements. That is not to say that all long-term lending is dead. Issuance of Pfandbriefe covered bonds in Germany, for example, although more expensive than in the past, still provides substantial financing for the industry.[20] However, volumes are greatly reduced, and this will continue to constrain new business;

(ii) capital is getting tighter, especially as under Basel III there is no dif-ferentiation of the risk associated with low LTV loans (the regime currently gives CRE loans secured on underlying assets as a higher risk weighting than unsecured corporate bonds).[21] This may mean that banks are no longer able to make a return on CRE lending that covers the cost of equity, and indeed in some cases they may be loss making;

(iii) CRE relationships are less profitable than corporate client relation-ships. Ultimately, despite the fact that banks have over-extended their balance sheets to the real estate sector, this is still a marginal activity and one that does not relate to their core client base. Also, compared to corporate lending, it provides lower ancillary revenues;

(iv) huge cyclicality makes the business less attractive. The peak-to-trough loan loss provisioning in CRE is significantly higher than that of any corporate lending activity; and

---

[20]   See further Ch.2. and the German Lending Market section contained in Ch.18.

[21]   This is subject to review under "Basel IV"; in the first consultative document published by the Basel Committee on Banking Supervision in 2014, real estate risk weights were to be based on the LTV ratio and the debt-service coverage ratio rather than the previous 35% flat rate and under a second consultative paper published in December 2015, the Basel Com-mittee on Banking Supervision has proposed to use the loan-to-valuation (LTV) ratio as the main risk driver for risk weighting purposes, and to use a three-category classification (from less to more risky) from general treatment for exposures secured by real estate where repayment is not materially dependent on rent/sale of the property; a more conservative treatment for exposures secured by real estate where repayment is materially dependent on cash flows (i.e. rent/sale) generated by the property; and a conservative, flat risk weight for specialised lending real estate exposures defined as "land acquisition, development and construction". See Basel Committee on Banking Supervision "Second consultative docu-ment—Revisions to the Standardised Approach for credit risk" December 2015 (issued for comment by 11 March 2016).

(v)   there tends to be more pressure from governments and regulators to keep financing corporates and SMEs in sectors that are more crucial for the real economy.

Further, banks face other issues when trying to deleverage:

- lack of alternative financing is the single biggest issue banks encounter when trying to reduce their loan exposure. If borrowers cannot find alternative sources of funding, they cannot repay, unless they sell the underlying assets;
- falling property prices mean that borrowers find it hard to sell and repay, while quality of exposure declines and LTVs increase. This often makes loan extensions and other forms of restructuring of CRE loans that otherwise would be in breach of LTV covenants more likely; and
- swap transactions linked to loans may also prevent banks from selling down exposure more aggressively. As CRE companies prefer to take loans at fixed rates and banks tend to want to lend at variable rates, banks usually sell an interest rate swap contract to the company that takes the loan. These swap contracts are becoming an issue when banks try to offload the loans, as they may be forced to take losses on the swap, especially if contracts have been put together when interest rates were higher.[22]

Further challenges to the commercial mortgage loan market include a proposal put forward in April 2016 by the Basel Committee that banks, rather than using the IRB model (see fn.23), be subject to the same standard risk assessment model and recognise "slotting", already used by banks in the UK (as referred to above). The institutions that could be most affected by this latest Basel pronouncement are continental European banks that have incurred significant expenditure in implementing IRB risk assessment models to help them to maintain low costs of capital. If this regulation is implemented, it could increase the capital requirements for European banks interested in specialised income-producing loans, including CRE finance.

However, the fragility of the bank's balance sheet during the GFC has highlighted how the CRE market needs CMBS and its access to global capital markets. This means that CMBS certainly has a supporting role to play and may eventually prove to be most competitive in financing yieldly, secondary properties that are not suited for on-balance sheet lending by banks. In other words, CMBS could eventually become the equivalent of the high yield market for CRE finance with LTV potentially limited to 50–60% and required spreads in excess of 500bp.

---

[22] See the *Morgan Stanley Report*, pp.22–26 and Ch.12.

Moreover, this chapter has shown that when discussing European CRE it is clear that globalisation cannot be ignored.[23] The globalisation or internationalisation of capital has played an integral role in the financial crisis, with both benefits and disadvantages. Such globalisation can provide for access to global markets, thus reducing financing costs and allowing for business cycles to be smoothed, but it can also allow for the rapid transmission of economic shocks between economies. As discussed above, investors are able to purchase a wide variety of securities offered on various international markets (by way of example, Swedish farmers had exposure to single parent families in Illinois), which has in turn allowed the impact of the sub-prime crisis in the US to spread around the world. Further, it also allows for regulatory arbitrage as financial institutions or investors transfer their operations and investments to jurisdictions they perceive as favourable. Regulatory arbitrage results in jurisdictions with inadequate regulation creating risks for other jurisdictions due to the interconnection of economies and markets.

As regards real estate, the GFC highlighted that, whilst real estate remains an essentially local illiquid asset, its financing is not and our real estate finance markets and economies are inextricably linked and interdependent and it is very hard to dislocate the economic forces that they produce. After all, one of the most striking developments in the global debt and capital markets over the last decade has been the powerful journey and metamorphosis of CRE in creating a truly global market for CRE finance, investment and development, an asset class that had been famously regarded by institutional investors as illiquid and cumbersome. However, if the last decade will be remembered for this development, the following decade will be remembered for the creation of the post-GFC banking and financial regulatory landscape that affects real estate (and its financing, investment and development) as discussed further in Chapters 16, 17 and 21.

The establishment of real estate as a separate asset class will not be reversed and it is undeniable that real estate will continue to be viewed as a popular asset class. Given that the GFC was as much due to a crisis of confidence as to any other factors, such re-emergence will, in a large part, be dictated by the confidence in our financial architecture. Any developments or products the CRE market participants can provide to help restore market confidence, such as greater regulation and transparency, more sustainable lending, improved reporting standards, clarity over servicing standards and servicer responsibilities[24] and more standardised and clear documentation (particularly uniformity surrounding intercreditor arrangements),[25] that will hopefully reverse credit rationing and soften the impact of widespread de-

---

[23] See A.V. Petersen, *Real Estate Finance: Law Regulation & Practice*, (London: LexisNexis, 2008 1st edition and 2014 2nd edition).
[24] See further Ch.21.
[25] See Chs 5, 6 and 7.

leveraging, as well as remove or reduce risk to investing in real estate, can only be a good thing. However, the overriding aim must be to strike a balance between market reform (through all of the above) and efficient markets. It is our financial architecture. Markets are essential to human development through economic advancement and human well-being and should not be impeded or innovation suffocated such that they cannot function. Nor should markets be allowed to operate with unintended consequences which sow the seeds for future crises. After all, this Chapter has highlighted that we have been down this road before and whilst this crisis remains structural rather than cyclical, the desire to reform must be accompanied by caution. The remaining Chapters in this book will examine the markets in this light, to determine whether the funding of CRE through commercial mortgage loans and CMBS can continue to adapt and evolve on a journey based on alchemy and financial innovation.

Chapter 2

Property Cycles and their Nature

Robin Goodchild,

International Director—Global Research & Strategy, LaSalle Investment Management

2.1   Introduction

CRE and bank lending have a symbiotic relationship. The CRE market relies on the flow of debt capital, in conjunction with equity, to fuel its activity; for lenders, CRE is their main source of security for the loans they underwrite. Most of the time the inter-relationship is mutually beneficial—lenders derive good returns from their property loans and the CRE market functions effectively, meeting the demands of business for warehouses to store goods and distribute them, providing offices for a wide range of service companies, and shops and other types of space for retailers. However, CRE markets can be volatile and are prone to cycles. As a result, the quality of security provided can be compromised, which can cause lenders significant stress and possible losses.

The purpose of this Chapter is to provide an understanding of how property cycles occur and, in particular, the crucial role that debt flows can play, and have played, in creating significant volatility. The sudden fall in values impairs loan quality because it causes Loan-to-Value (LTV) ratios to increase, sometimes to the extent that the loan exceeds the value of the security. This happened across the developed world, and in some emerging markets, in 2008/09 following the Global Financial Crisis (GFC).

The evidence provided is predominantly from the UK, because that is the market with the longest time series of reliable CRE data.[1] Notwithstanding the analysis presented is generally applicable in other developed markets and, while every country's CRE market has its own idiosyncrasies, operating within its own unique institutional framework, all are prone to cycles even if their magnitude varies and can be disguised by property valuation/appraisal practices (discussed below).

---

[1]   Data is available from the 1960s. The US and Australia have the next longest CRE returns series which date from 1978 and 1985 respectively. The longest real estate time series is an index of house prices along the Herengracht, Amsterdam that commences in 1628—Eicholtz P (1997) 'A Long Run House Price Index: The Herengracht Index, 1628–1973' *Real Estate Economics* Vol 25 pp.175–192.

The Chapter commences with a description of how cyclical CRE markets have been. It then progresses to an explanation of how this cyclicality occurs starting with some economic literature before describing experiences gained while working through different cycles' phases as well as their key drivers. There is then a discussion of property valuation/appraisal practices given their crucial importance in the CRE lending process. The Chapter concludes with review of current market prospects, particularly where markets are in their cycle, and how lenders should react.

2.2 The Prevalence of Property Cycles

Since 1971, the UK has experienced three major CRE cycles. On these three occasions, property values fell by 40% or more in real terms, i.e. after allowing for inflation. This timing is apparent from Figure 1 in 1974/5, 1990/2 and 2007/9. The causes of these cycles are examined throughout this chapter. At this point in the analysis, the key point is their scale. Declines in value of 40% are clearly most disconcerting to those who make loans secured on CRE and are presuming that the asset will be a good security for that loan throughout its life (see also Table 2).

Figure 1: UK Property 1968-2015: Three Big "Boom & Bust" Cycles

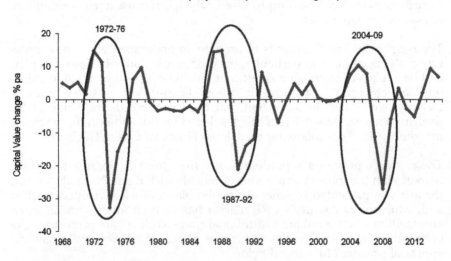

Source: LaSalle, IPD, ONS

While similar data across all commercial property types are not available back to the 1960s for other countries, there are data on the capital values for prime offices in the leading global financial centres from the mid-1970s. These are shown in Figure 2 (with the numbers again adjusted for inflation).

The series for the London City (as opposed to London West End) has been highlighted and it is immediately apparent that London City office values appear to have been relatively stable compared with the values in many other financial centres. However, in London City values still fell by 75% between 1988 and 1992 and by 50% following the GFC. The value declines in New York and Tokyo were greater in both periods, while values in Sydney declined by 80% in the early 1990s crash.

Figure 2: Capital Values for Major Global Markets, 1976–2015

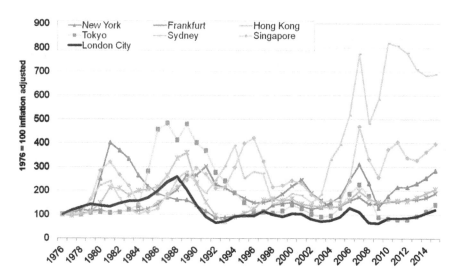

Sources: PMA, Wheaton & Barranski, Vallis, Devaney, Turvey, RICS, Bjorklund & Soderberg

Thus it is readily apparent that London and the UK are not unique in having CRE cycles. The Asian markets of Hong Kong and Singapore are especially volatile, tending to move to their own rhythm, for example, with their own cycles peaking in the mid-1990s coinciding with the Asian crisis at that time. However, since the mid-2000s, office values in all these financial centres appear to be more correlated, peaking around 2008, bottoming out in 2009/10 before recovering steadily.

Further evidence of the CRE's cyclical nature is provided by a report from the World Economic Forum. This is an important contribution to the body of knowledge about cycles based on an analysis of case studies from around the globe that span 40 years. The case studies relate to both commercial and residential property cycles, providing some insightful proposals as to how the volatility of markets may be reduced in the future.[2]

---

[2] "Emerging Horizons in Real Estate: An Industry Initiative on Asset Price Dynamics", *Executive Case Studies* (Geneva: World Economic Forum, 2015).

2.3 The Economic Literature on Cycles

The economic literature on cycles has been relatively neglected in modern times, yet it is deep and mature. Economists generally recognise four types of cycle, each with different durations. These are:

- The Inventory cycle of three to five year duration associated with Kitchin (1923);
- The Fixed Investment and Business cycle of 7–11 years duration associated with Jugler (1862);
- The Infrastructure Investment cycle of 15–25 years duration associated with Kuznets (1930); and
- Long waves driven by innovation and technological change with durations of 45–60 years and associated with Kondratieff (1925) (also known as Kondratieff Waves).[3]

The cycles of most interest to CRE practitioners are the Fixed Investment and Business Cycle (Jugler) and the Infrastructure Investment cycle (Kuznets). The Business Cycle is important because it drives occupier demand for space. The Infrastructure Cycle, also referred to as the Building Cycle, was probably first observed by Homer Hoyt.[4] More recently, Foldvary (2007) building on Hoyt's analysis, identified an 18-year real estate cycle for the US stretching back to the early 19th century. While this mixes commercial and residential cycles, the pattern shows remarkably consistent frequency (see Table 1).

Table 1: The Great US 18-Year Real Estate Cycle

Peaks in Land Value Cycle	Interval (years)	Peaks in Construction Cycle	Interval (years)	Start of Depressions[5]	Interval (years)
1818	–	–	–	1819	–
1836	18	1836	-	1837	18
1854	18	1856	20	1857	20
1872	18	1871	15	1873	16
1890	18	1892	21	1893	20
1907	17	1909	17	1918	25
1925	18	1925	16	1929	11
1973	48	1972	47	1973	44

---

[3] See A. Korotayev and S. Tsirel, "A Spectral Analysis of World GDP Dynamics: Kondratieff Waves, Kuznets Swins, Jugler and Kitchin Cycles in Global Economic Development, and the 2008-2009 Economic Crisis" (2010) *Structure and Dynamics* Vol.4, 1, pp.3–57.

[4] H. Hoyt, *One Hundred Years of Land Values in Chicago* (New York: Arno Press, 1933).

[5] Foldvary defines a 'depression' as beginning during a recession when GDP falls below its long-run trend.

1979	6	1978	6	1980	7
1989	10	1986	8	1990	10
2006	17	2006	20	December 2007	18

Source: Foldvary, F (2007). *The Depression of 2008*, The Gutenberg Press, Berkeley p.5

Foldvary identified peaks in land values and construction activity, and discerned that economic downturns followed usually within two years. He presciently predicted in 1997 that the next downturn would be in about 2008, 18 years after the 1990 downturn, assuming no major interruption such as a global war.[6]

The most significant exception to Foldvary's 18 year pattern is the period between 1929 (the Great Crash followed by the Depression of the 1930s) to 1973, when the first post-war global oil shock occurred. His explanation for this extended period is because of World War II and it is noticeable that his pattern is also affected by World War I. However, the slow economic recovery during the 1930s and the changes introduced to reduce risk-taking and prevent a recurrence, notably the Glass-Steagall Act, might have caused the cycle to be more drawn out, even without the war.

Another important analysis of US real estate cycles is by Pyhrr et al.[7] They provide a comprehensive review of the various theories of cycles and their nature, as well as their strategic implications for property investors. A further focus is why cycles matter, given the scepticism of many in finance who believe in the "efficient market hypothesis", which suggests that market prices are always a rational distillation of future expectations—a concept which surprisingly has not been completely discredited by the GFC. The work of Mueller also merits reference, as he has pioneered an approach to identifying the cyclical position of office and other sub-markets. However, his emphasis is more on rents, vacancy levels and development pipelines than on capital markets.[8]

The evidence from the UK is remarkably similar. The most comprehensive real estate analysis is by Barras which includes a review of building cycles in London since the 18th century together with a comparison of US and UK experiences. He concludes as follows:

> "There is evidence of up to four building cycles of different duration. The basic endogenously generated building cycle is a major cycle of 8–10 years [a Jugler cycle], consistent with a construction process that on average lasts for

---

[6] F. Foldvary, "The Business Cycle: A Georgist-Austrian Synthesis" (October, 1997) 56 (4) *American Journal of Economics and Sociology* pp.521–41.

[7] S. Pyhrr, S. Roulac and W. Bonn, "Real Estate Cycles and Their Strategic Implications for Investors and Portfolio Managers in the Global Economy" (1999) *Journal of Real Estate Research* 18(1) pp.7–68.

[8] See, for example, G. Mueller, "Real estate rental growth rates at different points in the physical market cycle" (1999) 18(1) *Journal of Real Estate Research* pp.131–150.

around two years. Building investment also shows some evidence of a shorter 4-5 year minor cycle [a Kitchin cycle], reflecting the demand-side influence of the business cycle, and a 40-50 year long [Kondratieff] wave, revealing the impact of intermittent technological revolutions. The most prominent cycles in building activity are the long cycles which occur every 15–20 years [a Kuznets cycle]. These are in part a result of the coalescence of the major cycle and the long wave, and in part a product of the tendency for every other major [Jugler] cycle to be subject to speculative investment pressures which create a particularly volatile boom-bust cycle."[9] (Author's additions in square brackets)

Moreover, Barras identifies that "... three long cycles—occurring in the early 1970s, the late 1980s and the mid-2000s—are apparent in different economies and for all sectors of building" (i.e. both residential and commercial). He further notes that office cycles have been converging globally with much more synchronicity between markets in the mid-2000s than in the late 1980s. Barras' analysis is a combination of economic history together with neo-classical theory. He summarises the mechanisms at work in an elegant, if complex, schematic which incorporates forces from both the Real Economy and the Capital Markets (see Figure 3).

Figure 3: How the Building Cycle works

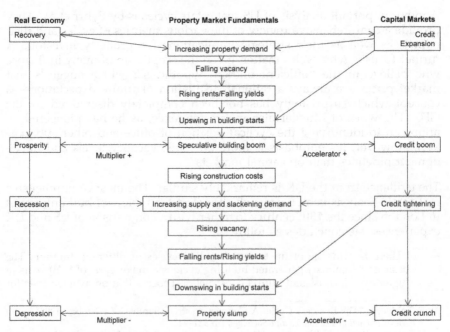

Source: Barras (2009), p.80

---

[9]   R. Barras, *Building Cycles: Growth & Instability* (West Sussex: Wiley-Blackwell, 2009), p.325.

These cycles result from the fact that new buildings take time to construct. Thus, when there is an increase in demand for CRE space, there is a lag in delivering that supply. In the interim, while new developments are under construction, the market can send misleading signals. Rent "spikes", particularly for offices, are likely because businesses compete aggressively to secure the limited space on offer. Firms perceive a profitable opportunity they want to exploit immediately, and are not prepared to wait. Moreover the cost of business space is usually a small proportion of the total project cost (typically 10–20%—the main cost component is labour) so they are prepared to pay more in rent rather than miss the opportunity.

These market signals tend to be amplified by the feedback between the Real Economy and the Capital Markets (see Figure 3). Developers need finance to construct new buildings and that capital can be equity and/or debt. During the initial stage of the cycle, lending to developers and property owners is highly profitable because CRE values are rising and this encourages further lending. The latter stages of an upswing also tend to be a time of high business confidence which reinforces the favourable climate for CRE lending.

The powerful signals created in an upswing are well illustrated by the history of skyscraper building. The desire to be the developer of the tallest building in the world, or a region, is a powerful elixir. However, they are very risky projects because their construction is both more complex and takes longer than a low rise structure, increasing the risk that market conditions will have changed in the meantime. Ever since the invention of the modern elevator, waves of skyscraper construction have tended to coincide with the peak of a boom, or later. For example, the Empire State Building, New York, was completed in 1931, having been conceived in the late 1920s and remaining 75% vacant for a decade.[10] The Burj Khalifa, (formerly the Burj Dubai), the world's tallest building today at 829.8m (2,722ft), was completed in 2010, construction having started in 2004.

Barras sums up the challenge for markets as follows:

> "The formation of expectations in real estate markets is uniquely difficult because of the uncertainties deriving from the long lead times in construction, market rigidities, infrequent transactions, heterogeneous stock, imperfect information and the long asset life over which the future investment returns must be projected. The informational inefficiencies created by these features of the property market make the formation of rational expectations all but impossible. Furthermore, the speculative nature of much development creates a tendency for confidence itself to be cyclical, reinforcing the cycle as sentiment switches between optimism on the upswing and pessimism on the downswing" (ibid, p.78).

---

[10] Unsurprisingly it was nicknamed the "Empty State Building" during this period according to L. Mumford, *The City in History: Its Origins, Its Transformations, and Its Prospects* (New York: Harcourt, Brace & World, 1961).

This speculative nature can also be explained with concepts from behavioural finance, notably, "optimism", "overreaction" and "herding", all of which can generate a "manifestation of collective madness"[11] that is also associated with financial crises, e.g. the events leading up to the Lehman's collapse in 2008. These speculative forces, more easily computed qualitatively as the balance between greed and fear, were major drivers of the market in the three UK CRE cycles since 1970. They have been well captured in a number of books because they make great stories.[12]

2.4   Phases of the Property Cycle

A CRE cycle goes through four distinct phases. These are:

- Boom
- Bust
- Recovery
- Equilibrium

The Boom and Bust are the essence of a big cycle. The Recovery phase is more surprising, but has been apparent in each of the three UK CRE cycles since 1970. The Equilibrium phase is the period between the volatile Boom/Bust/Recovery and during which values are relatively stable. Table 2 shows the data behind the decomposition of the cycle into these different phases.

Table 2: Decomposing UK Property Cycles

Cycle	Data	Boom	Bust	Recovery	Equilibrium
Early 1970s	Dates	1972–73	1974–76	1977–78	1979–86
	Capital Value Change	27.9%	−49.2%	16.4%	−17.0%
	Rental Value Change	17.4%	−26.2%	−5.5%	−6.1%
Late 1980s	Dates	q2 87 – q3 89	q3 89 – q1 93	q1 93 – q2 94	q2 94 – q4 03
	Capital Value Change	29.5%	−39.3%	12.8%	−3.9%
	Rental Value Change	−31.2%	−24.9%	−6.4%	0.4%

---

[11]   See Forbes W, *Behavioural Finance*, (West Sussex: John Wiley & Sons, 2009), p.91.

[12]   For the early 1970s, J. Plender, *That's the way the money goes: The Financial institutions and the Nation's Savings* (London: Andre Deutsche, 1982); for the late 1980s, A. R. Goobey, *Bricks and Mortals: Dreams of the 80s and the Nightmare of the 90s—the Inside Story of the Property World* (London: Random House Business Book, 1992).

Cycle	Data	Boom	Bust	Recovery	Equilibrium
Pre-GFC	Dates	q4 03 – q2 07	q2 07 – q3 09	q3 09 – q3 10	q3 10 to date
	Capital Value Change	28.1%	−46.1%	10.4%	5.5%
	Rental Value Change	−2.6%	−9.7%	−6.9%	−7.0%

NB: All value changes are cumulative, not annual changes, and adjusted for inflation

Sources: LaSalle, MSCI/IPD

The Boom phase has a variety of forms but generally reflects at least two consecutive years where capital values increase by 10% or more. During 2004–07 values increased by 28% but with negligible real rental growth. In other words, the value growth was driven solely by yield compression. This contrasts with both 1972/3 and 1987/8 where there was strong rental value growth that drove the boom in values, though yield compression played a part in the earlier cycle. In all cases the Boom phase emerges from a period of fairly stable values and goes on to generate a real capital value increase of around 30%.

The Bust phase is marked by a sharp decline in capital values which takes two to three years to find a floor. The collapse in capital values begins with yields rising sharply but with little change in rents. This decline is then reinforced by rents falling materially, as the negative effects from the Capital Markets feed back into the Real Economy (see Figure 3 above). Moreover, the scale of decline reflects value movements in the Boom phase: thus in the 1990 Bust there was significantly more rental decline than in the most recent downturn, reflecting the 1980s boom in rents (see Table 2).

Bust is followed by Recovery, the most interesting part of the cycle for investors, because it is the best time to "make money". This Recovery phase is a period of rapid but short-lived capital growth as yields compress towards their pre-bust levels, despite rents continuing to decline (see Table 2). The Recovery phase reflects that the Capital Markets have overreacted during the Bust. Values are pushed down too far, while the market is risk averse to a point where savvy, contra-cyclical investors recognise that pricing is attractive.[13] This change in sentiment is quickly picked up by other players and the market dynamic turns sharply. It is noticeable, however, that the Recovery phase has become progressively shorter (see Table 2), suggesting that the industry may have learnt from previous cycles.[14]

---

[13] See Goodchild, 'Property Cycles: Reflections by Dr Robin Goodchild' (2015), LaSalle Investment Management, *http://www.lasalle.com/documents/Global-Real-Estate-Universe-February-2015.pdf* [Accessed 7 September 2016], for how investors may exploit this opportunity.

[14] This would accord with part of George Soros's theory of "Reflexivity", see G. Soros, *The Age of Fallibility* (New York: Public Affairs, 2007).

The Recovery phase is followed by a period of relatively stable values named Equilibrium. Generally capital values move in a range of +/– 5% pa during this phase, though this is not an immutable rule. It continues until the next break out into a Boom marking the commencement of a new cycle.

2.5   Drivers of Property Cycles

There are three key drivers of property cycles. They are:

- Economic growth
- The volume of development
- Availability of credit

Economic growth as manifested through the business cycle is always a major driver of property markets. As shown in Figure 4, there is a high correlation (0.58) between the changes in UK real GDP and annual real capital value from commercial property. But the correlation is not perfect and it is noticeable that the three big Boom and Bust cycles coincide with every *second* global recession. Thus property values did not decline much during the downturns of 1981/82 and 2001/2. Moreover, the three recessions coinciding with these Booms and Busts tend to be deeper, reflecting the complex feedback loops between the economy and property markets discussed above (see Figure 3).

Figure 4: UK Property Cycles, GDP & Recessions, 1968-2015

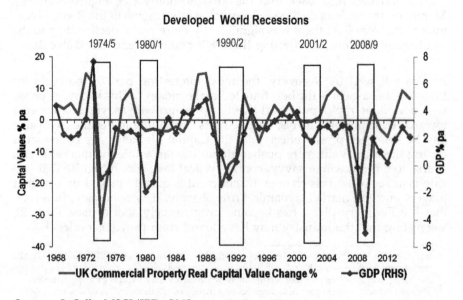

Sources: LaSalle, MSCI/IPD, ONS

The evolution of UK office development is shown in Figure 5. The peak of 1990 stands out, as does a lower peak in 2008 after which production immediately collapsed on both occasions. But there is a third peak in 2001 coinciding with the collapse of the dotcom stock market crash. While output fell in 2002/3, it stabilised at a much higher level than after either 1990 or 2008.

These data may point to the market anticipating demand better after the late 1980s Boom as a result of improved market information. This would also explain why there was little rental growth in the 2000s because there was much less of a mismatch in the market fundamentals. The evidence suggests it did not require a spike in rents to stimulate new construction as developers commenced projects ahead of the increase in demand. Thus while development was an important cause of the 1980s Boom and Bust, its impact in the last cycle was much more muted.[15]

Figure 5: UK Office development, 1980–2015

Sources: LaSalle, BCIS, ONS

In contrast, the ready availability of credit played a key role in each of the three big cycles over the last 45 years. In the UK, there was a rapid increase in lending to property companies associated with the upswing phase of each cycle, which was then followed by a collapse when a significant volume of bad loans needed to be written-off and/or worked out. This is evidenced by

---

[15] In the early 1970s there was a short lived development boom following the election of a Conservative government (in 1970) so development played a role in 1972/3 Boom (see case study in World Economic Forum (2015)).

the sharp change in the proportion of bank lending to CRE companies following each big cycle (see Figure 6). The ready availability of credit was a
key driver of the late 1980s crisis both in the US, associated with the Savings
& Loans crisis documented in the first edition of this book, and in Japan
with its banking system taking more than a decade to recover from its 1980s
property boom.[16] The role of credit in the last Boom around the world needs
little amplification, as the nickname "Credit Bubble" implies.

Figure 6: Commercial Real Estate Lending, 1969–2015

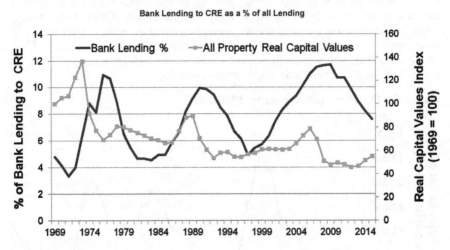

Sources: Bank of England, MSCI/IPD

With the benefit of hindsight, it is hard to understand how such rapid
increases in lending can re-occur so frequently. It is well understood that
there is a fundamental conflict in banking between expanding a loan book
through increasing market share and making prudent lending decisions.
Competitive pressures normally cause lending margins to tighten as
bankers seek to write more business, often to inexperienced players. The
result, if taken to excess, is under-pricing of risk and substantial losses
when the market turns down.

Data from the Bank of England provides guidance as to why lenders find
real estate so seductive (see Figure 7). During the upswing phase, here
2000–2006, loans to property companies showed negligible write-offs
(<0.1%), in contrast with general commercial lending where losses were
rarely below 0.5% pa. Thus, to a banker with no knowledge of property's
cyclicality, the repayment experience would encourage further property
lending and increasing market share. Once the crisis struck, losses increased

---

[16] One of the case studies in World Economic Forum (2015) is about the Japan market in the
1980s.

Figure 7: Loss Rates on Commercial Loans 1994–2013

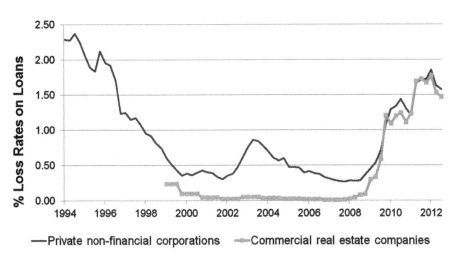

Source: Bank of England and Bank calculations

Lending by UK monetary financial institutions. The series are calculated as annualised quarterly write-offs divided by the corresponding loans outstanding at the end of the previous quarter. The data are presented as four-quarter moving averages and are non-seasonally adjusted. Lending in both sterling and foreign currency, expressed in sterling terms.

Figure 8: Evolution of Delinquency Levels for US CMBS loans 2000–15

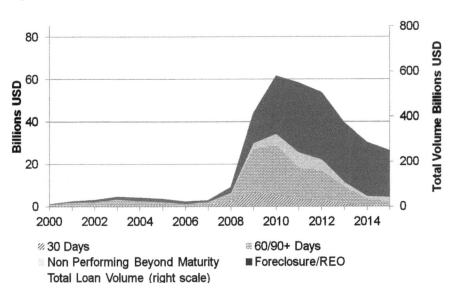

Source: Trepp LLC

sharply and are likely to be understated by this data because banks take a while to recognise the full decline in property values and their impact on borrowers.[17]

Data from the CMBS markets show a similar picture. As was discussed in the previous Chapter, the European CMBS market was embryonic in the period prior to 2008. Notwithstanding the highest rates of loss are observed on loans originated between 2005 and 2007.[18] There is much more data for US CMBS and there loss rates were also very low until immediately after the GFC when the volume of delinquent loans increased sharply (see Figure 8). The delinquency was concentrated in loans originated in a small number of vintages (2005–07) because US CRE moved in a similar pattern to the UK, though value declines occurred more in 2008/09 than 2007/08. It is also clear from Figure 8 that the volume of CMBS loans originated in the US increased significantly prior to 2008.

Thus the role of credit availability may be seen as the most important driver in all three property cycles. Despite the lessons from the past, new lenders emerge in each upswing without direct experience of previous cycles and the same mistakes are repeated. Moreover, the turnover of staff in the main commercial banks militates against the learning experience being retained, especially where there have been significant lay-offs in the downturn.[19]

2.6 Lending on Volatile Property Values

The usual approach that a lender adopts before offering a loan secured on property is to commission an independent valuation or appraisal report for the asset.[20] The purpose of this report is to advise on both the capital value of the property and its suitability as security for a loan, for example, the robustness of the income stream for an investment property.

What precisely do the estimates of valuation provided represent? Valuations undertaken by members of the Royal Institution of Chartered Surveyors (RICS) and "approved valuers", must follow the guidance set out in the RICS "Red Book".[21] This requires a valuation to represent 'open market value' which is defined as:

---

[17] One bank among the sample wrote off nearly 20% of its commercial real estate loans (J. Benford and J Burrows, "Commercial property and financial stability" (2013) *Bank of England Quarterly Bulletin Q1)* p.49.

[18] See Trepp LLC, *The Mid Year—CRE Market on the High Wire* (Doylestown, PA: Commercial Real Estate Direct, 2016).

[19] M. Wolf, *The Shifts and the Shocks: What We've Learned—and Have Still to Learn—from the Financial Crisis* (New York: Penguin Group, 2014), stresses that the credit markets are inherently unstable and need to be regulated much more tightly than in the past if future crises are to be avoided.

[20] Appraisal is the description used in the US and generally where American practice is dominant. See further Ch.4 describing the loan origination process.

[21] Its formal name is the RICS 'Valuation—Professional Standards'.

"The estimated amount for which an asset or liability should exchange on the valuation date between a willing buyer and a willing seller in an arm's length transaction, after proper marketing and where the parties had each acted knowledgeably, prudently and without compulsion."

In essence this can be summarised as the price the property would sell for, after proper marketing, at the date of valuation. It is therefore a point estimate at a single moment in time. It is not providing any assurance that the value reported will endure; that will depend on the future course of the market.

But, to the unwary, the terms "value" and "valuation" in general parlance imply at least some duration. Yet a Red Book valuation can be relied on only for as long as market conditions do not change. Furthermore, a Red Book value is not an "assessment of worth", i.e. at the valuation price, the investment can be expected to deliver returns in the future in line with market expectations for assets of that type.

Figure 9: Bank of England's Investment Valuation Approach (Q2 2015)

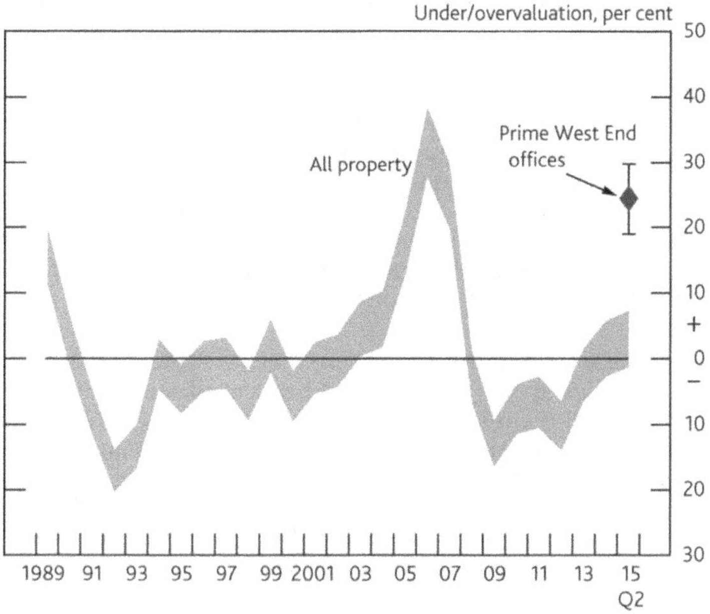

Sources: Association of Real Estate Funds (AREF), Bloomberg, Investment Property Forum, MSCI and Bank of England calculations.

Notes
Investment valuations are based on assuming property is held for five years with the cash flows from the rent and sale discounted. It is assumed that the property is sold at a rental yield (in line with long-run averages fifteen years). The sale proceeds and rental income are discounted by the ten-year gilt yield plus a risk premium. The swathe represents varying assumptions on the average through the cycle risk pre-

mium, given the inherent uncertainty in measuring it; the lower end of the range is from a survey of investors from AREF and the higher end is a risk premium derived from the long-run relationship between gilt yields and property yields. For more details see N. Crosby and C. Hughes, "The Basis of Valuations for Secured Commercial Property Lending in the UK" (2011) 4 (3)Journal of European Real Estate Research, pp.225–242.

The Investment Property Forum commissioned an expert group to investigate the challenges presented to the CRE market by the GFC and the preceding Boom. Its report was published in 2014 entitled "A Vision for Real Estate Finance in the UK". This criticised the use of spot values for property lending and proposed that a more long term assessment, or appraisal of worth, should be used instead, as this would give a much better indication of a durable "fair value" on which to lend. This idea has been taken up by the Bank of England (see Figure 9) as more fully described in Chapter 21. Currently this approach is being employed to provide guidance on overall market stability, rather than to the value of individual assets, and this may be the best approach to take. The Bank of England, and other central banks, can use the insights from this analysis to inform their advice to banks and other lenders as to their general CRE exposure.

Valuation/appraisal practice differs around the world. This is not so much because the formal rules differ significantly—most adopt the International Valuation Standards Board's definition of market value quoted above. One of the key reasons is the volume of transactions occurring in a market. Valuation practices rely principally on analysing transaction evidence from sales of properties comparable to the asset being valued; the more comparable evidence available, the higher the likelihood that the reported value accurately reflects the likely sale price for the relevant asset.

The valuer's task is more difficult where there are few market transactions or the volume dries up, as often occurs when a market is weak and/or there is general financial distress. In some countries, valuers do not adjust their valuations without clear market evidence that a change in level has occurred, i.e. transactions have completed at a new price point. In other markets, notably the UK, valuers are more prepared to adjust their estimates without hard transaction evidence, but where it is clear that, if deals were to occur, they would take place at a different level.

Thus valuation practices can disguise the degree of volatility a CRE market displays. The best evidence for this is some data provided by MSCI/IPD and shown in Figure 10. The volatility (as measured by the standard

Figure 10: Limits of Appraisal Data for Measuring Market Risk

Valuation practices around the world vary

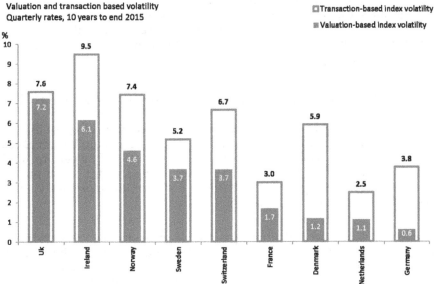

Valuation and transaction based volatility
Quarterly rates, 10 years to end 2015

☐ Transaction-based index volatility

■ Valuation-based index volatility

* Comparison of Quarterly Transactions Linked Index and Appraisal Based Index (excl. capital expenditure) volatility by market

Source: MSCI

deviation of quarterly capital values) in valuation/appraisal based property indices have long been recognised as "smoothed", i.e. their volatility is under-stated.[22]

MSCI/IPD have calculated national property indices based on the transactions reported within their national samples. These show higher, and often much higher levels of volatility than the appraisal based indices. For the UK, the transaction index is only marginally more volatile (5%) in comparison with Denmark and Germany, where the appraisal based indices understate the "true" volatility by 5 times and 6 times respectively.

---

[22] This phenomenon was first identified in the UK by G. Blundell and C. Ward, "Property portfolio allocation: a multi factor model" (1987) *Land Development Studies*, Vol. 4, pp. 145–156 and in the US by D. Geltner, "Estimating market values from appraised values without assuming an efficient market" (1993) (8) 3 *Journal of Real Estate Research*, pp.325–345. See also T. Key and G. Marcato, "Index Smoothing and the Volatility of UK Commercial Property", *Investment Property Forum Research Report* (2007).

Excluding these three outliers, the appraisal indices understate the volatility in transaction prices by 75%.

These data also show that market stability does vary between countries, though all show a minimum "true" volatility of 2.5% per quarter. CRE lenders, who operate internationally, need to be mindful that valuation practices do vary between countries and reflect those differences in their decision-making.

2.7   So how should CRE lenders deal with market volatility?

Lenders using CRE as a security must first and foremost recognise that the asset class functions within a cyclical market. During an Equilibrium phase, the market can be reasonably stable and so most CRE loans perform well. However the potential for a Boom/Bust/Recovery sequence is ever present and the longer the gap since the previous big cycle, the more likely a new big cycle is to occur.

Leaders can instruct valuers/appraisers to provide historic data about assets which are potential security. This could include the average equivalent yield, ideally over the last 20 years (to cover a full cycle) but over the last 10 years as a minimum. This can then be compared with current equivalent yields and so provide some guidance about relative long term value. Information about historic rental growth over a 10 or 20 year time frame would also be helpful. This, together with the yield data, would enable a long term estimate of fair value to be derived in line with the Bank of England's suggested approach (see Figure 9 above). Better lending decisions should result especially when the market starts to overheat during a Boom phase. Lending can then be reduced at the most dangerous point in the cycle and/or hedges put in place to mitigate a potential decline in values.

Lenders should also monitor CRE markets much more closely than was the case prior to the GFC. Commercial banks should have their own CRE research teams and all the lenders should be monitoring activity to understand, as far as possible, where the markets are in their cycle at all times. This should inform Credit Committee decisions and encourage them not to allow lending covenants to soften just at the time when the market is at its most vulnerable to a shock. Moreover, late in the cycle is the time to be especially wary of investors with little market experience in real estate. Investing in and developing CRE looks a very easy way to make money in the run up to a Boom. Often such sponsors are not using much, if any, of their own equity but raise pools of capital from high-net-worth investors. Such investors may not appreciate all of the risks in CRE investment nor the potential need for more capital if values decline or simply to keep an asset income producing.

If lenders monitor the CRE market closely they should avoid the worst effects of the market cycle. The most important pitfall is the temptation to write new business when the market is growing through offering more competitive terms given, for example through reducing the protection provided by loan covenants. Pro-cyclical behaviour should be avoided at all costs.

2.8 Future Prospects

So what does all this analysis suggest will happen in the current cycle? At the time of writing, the gateway real estate markets made a rapid recovery from the GFC after 2009 and this momentum then spread to most second tier cities. The keenest demand is for prime buildings but investors are increasingly looking at more secondary quality assets too. This demand is driven by the general search for income in an environment of low bond yields in a world that seems to be awash with low risk capital, whether from central banks' quantitative easing or from the global savings glut that emerged in the last decade—principally from the countries running trade surpluses.

Pricing for prime real estate is back to pre-crisis peak levels in many markets and even exceeding them in some cases. Given what happened in 2008/9, it is not surprising that some investors are getting nervous and concerned that another correction is imminent. Moreover, the volume of transactions stabilised during the first half of 2016 and even declined in some markets, notably in the UK at least partially because of fears following the Brexit referendum. The (much more than) $64 million question is when will the next market peak occur?

The key thesis of this Chapter is that the pattern of CRE cycles is well established, so there is a presumption that economic cycles will continue to operate as in the past. Thus the next big property cycle should peak around 2025, i.e. 15–20 years after the last peak.

But why might this presumption be wrong? There are a number of reasons for believing that the current property cycle could be shorter or longer than the norm. There was a large gap in both the US and UK sequence of cycles between the 1929 and 1973 peaks. World War II almost certainly played a large role, but how much of this stable period was due to the restrictions placed on banks' ability to increase lending during the 1930s to prevent a repeat of the 1929 Great Crash? These restrictions remained in place for 20 years of the post-war period up to the mid-1960s (see above).[23]

---

[23] Although the Glass-Seagall Act was not formally repealed until 1999, its limitations on deposit taking banks also engaging in investment banking was steadily loosened by banking regulators from the 1960s.

Banks and the capital markets in general are subject to much increased levels of regulation as a result of the GFC, whether from national bodies or from the Bank of International Settlements through the Basel II, III & IV rules. It is likely that these restrictions will make it harder for mainstream banks to expand credit availability so readily in the future. However, the markets are likely to find ways around these restrictions through, for example, new sources of debt entering the market from institutions other than banks that are subject to different regulatory regimes, or even none. As will be discussed throughout this book, this change has, at the time of writing, started to occur in Europe with insurance companies and debt funds filling the void left by the banks. The innate instability of credit markets has already been highlighted. Regulation in the future will need to be tighter, much more contra-cyclical and politically brave; but this is only possible if the lessons of the GFC are learned properly.[24]

The global economy is struggling to recover from the GFC and it is likely that average levels of growth to 2020 will be lower than during the last 20 years. The world benefitted hugely during that earlier period from a range of favourable forces, notably the extraordinary growth of China and the huge increase in global trade. It is virtually impossible for the world to receive a similar boost in the coming years; instead the slowing of globalisation from increased geo-political tensions or working off the overhang of excessive debt is more likely to constrain growth. Even if growth exceeds expectations, central bankers are likely to be quicker to slow expansion to prevent booms rather than follow the Greenspan doctrine of letting markets run their course and then supporting the recovery, i.e. they are more likely to do what central bankers have always been charged with—"removing the punch bowl before the party gets out-of-hand".

A third reason to hope that the next peak will be later than around 2025 is simply "memory". The scale of this downturn should have caused memories of its events to be seared into the minds of market players and policy makers more deeply than in the past. As a result, it would seem reasonable to expect that the same mistakes will not be made again. But sadly, history suggests that this expectation is likely to be naïve.

Can the present cycle be much shorter, particularly given the rapid recovery in some real estate markets post 2012? Barras explains the fact that a big real estate cycle generally occurs every other business cycle because the excesses of the last big cycle are absorbed in the next business upswing without generating much new construction. Development is not required because of the overhang of space from the previous boom. This explanation accords well with the markets of the 1980s. However, levels of development were not so high in the upswing ending in 2007/08, at least in Europe and North

---

[24] See World Economic Forum (2015) for some important ideas as to how the credit markets can be improved. For the UK specifically, see also Real Estate Finance Group, *A Vision for Real Estate Finance in the UK* (London: Investment Property Forum, 2014).

America, so that there is not so much vacant space to absorb now. That boom was driven by capital markets rather than the real economy; the increase in capital values came from yield compression not rental growth. Thus a construction boom could emerge more quickly in this cycle than history would suggest, and accelerate the Boom and Bust.

Currently, in the major markets globally, development activity is generally under control, and debt levels are well below 2006/07 volumes, with much less reckless terms, i.e. lower loan-to-value ratios and better income-cover ratios. Capital flows have increased though, driven by institutional and high-net-worth equity from around the globe with debt availability returning remarkably quickly too. As a result, prime yield levels have been pushed down to pre-crisis levels in many markets by the weight of money. However spreads over local 10 year sovereign bonds (the conventional benchmark) are generally at average levels or above, so relative real estate valuations can still be justified.

It is unusual for institutional investors to change their minds, radically switching from buying to selling without a special trigger. Experience from the UK in the late 1970s shows that real estate was then expensive relative to the other main asset classes based on yield levels (see Figure 11) following a period of rapidly increased investment driven by a desire for inflation-protection.[25] While yields did increase slightly over a number of years (1983–5), they did not rise sharply until after the upswing had peaked in 1988/9. However, in 2016 domestic institutions are no longer the dominant players in the UK CRE market. The funds that insurance companies are investing come predominantly from retail investors allocating their savings to real estate investment products. In 2007, some of those retail investors were quick to switch their money out of the market at the first sign of market decline; this caused the first stage of the market collapse which was then amplified after Lehman's failed in September the following year.

At the time of going to press, the UK electorate has just voted to leave the EU and inflicted a significant, negative shock to their domestic economy as well as business confidence in both Europe and the rest of the world. This shock is adversely affecting CRE markets and is likely to cause capital values to decline materially, possibly by 15–20%, particularly for the volatile Central London office markets. While this decline is less than half the scale experienced during a typical Bust phase (see Table 2 above), it would still be substantial and require careful monitoring, especially by mezzanine debt lenders. Stress in retail investor funds is the most likely, initial transmission mechanism through which a shock to general business confidence moves into the UK direct property market as those funds are forced to sell properties to meet redemptions.

---

[25] UK inflation averaged 13.8% pa during the 1970s. Real estate delivered 16.2% pa in the decade outperforming stocks at 14.2% pa and government bonds at 10.2% pa.

Figure 11: UK Asset Class Yields 1975–2015

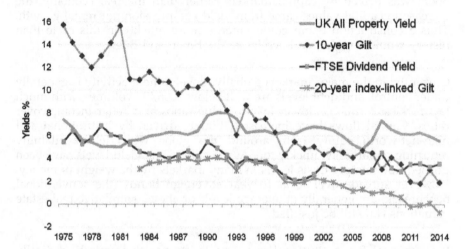

Source: Datastream, CBRE

Thus, at least in the UK, there is a very high probability of a mid-cycle correction, which will push the concept of the market remaining in an Equilibrium phase to the limit. However, the correction should not be on the same scale as a typical Bust phase, both because the up-cycle has not been sufficiently strong to constitute a Boom, and because lenders have behaved responsibly maintaining prudent credit controls; the increase in capital values during 2014/15 arose from the weight of equity capital, not from the ready availability of cheap debt.

2.9 Conclusion

CRE markets are inherently cyclical. A cycle of 15–20 years duration has been observed in both the UK and the US over a number of centuries. There have been three major cycles observed in an increasing number of markets, peaking in 1973/74, 1989/90 and 2007/8. In all cases, a sharp downturn in capital values occurred after each Boom, which had significantly negative effects for CRE lenders.

Lending on CRE can be a highly profitable activity while property values are stable or increasing. At such times, it is natural for lenders to wish to increase their exposure. However, increased lending feeds the upcycle and has played an important role in causing all the Boom-Bust cycles since 1970.

Lenders using CRE as security for a loan must recognise the market's cyclicality and should always monitor activity most carefully. They should also never forget the sage advice of the late Alistair Ross Goobey:

"Whenever the [new cycle] starts, there will be new participants, who will be less constrained by the experience of this recession than those who lived through it. They will repeat many of the mistakes of the 1980s, as many of the companies repeated the mistakes of the 1970s. The market will then be driven to levels which will prove unsustainable."[26]

Those who experienced first-hand the CRE lending markets from 2002–2007 should share their experiences with those who did not. The latter should learn as much as possible about past big cycles so they can avoid reprising the same errors.

---

[26] Ross Goobey A (1992)—sadly his advice was ignored in the period prior to the GFC.

Chapter 3

Commercial Mortgage Loans, CMBS and its role in the wider Real Estate Debt Capital Markets

Nigel Almond,
Head of Capital Markets Research, Cushman & Wakefield

Hans Vrensen,
Consultant Director, Research & Education, CREFC Europe

3.1 Introduction

This Chapter explores the development and structure of Europe's CRE lending markets over the past decade and highlights their importance to the financial markets generally. The Chapter first looks in detail at the structure of the CRE market in Europe, focusing on bank lending, covered bonds and commercial mortgage backed securities (CMBS), exploring how Europe's markets differ to those in Asia Pacific and North America. The Chapter then goes on to look at how the market has evolved during the GFC before concluding by looking at predictions for the future of CRE markets in Europe.

3.1.1 Importance of Lending to Commercial Real Estate

Lending to CRE entities has played, and continues to play, an important role in the functioning of Europe's CRE markets. Since the turn of the 21st century, debt outstanding to CRE vehicles across Europe grew nearly three-fold to €1.9 trillion (See Figure 1). This is equivalent to 60% of the total value of commercial property located in Europe held for investment purposes. Of this, close to €1.8 trillion is held by banks on their balance sheet, in the form of bank lending and covered bonds. This is equivalent to around 7% of all bank lending to non financial corporations, although in some markets, such as the UK, lending to CRE has been even higher at over 10% of all lending.

Figure 1: Growth in outstanding debt to European CRE

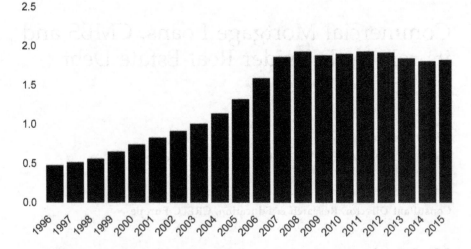

Source: Cushman & Wakefield Research

As Figure 1 illustrates, the increase in the availability of cheap debt from banks during the period 2003–2007 was especially strong. This supported the strong growth in Europe's CRE investment market. The €240 billion 2007 transaction volumes across Europe represented a near tripling in four years from the €88 billion in 2003. In the wake of the GFC, growth in outstanding debt slowed, before turning negative in 2009. The lagged response in the outstanding debt from the peak in property values in 2007 was due to the fact that lines of credit agreed towards the peak of the market, were only gradually drawn down subsequently. This lag effect is a normal response in the market. The subsequent reduction of the out-standing debt reflected the fact that redemptions and write-downs on loans were higher than new loan originations, for the first time in over a decade. The weakness in new loan originations led to a collapse in transactional investment activity which reached a decade low of €78 billion in 2009. As liquidity slowly returned to lending markets there was, from 2010, a strong recovery in transaction volumes with investment reaching a new record of over €280 billion in 2015. The growth in investment activity through this last cycle was largely driven by the injection of more equity as outstanding debt over the period actually fell through 2011 to 2014 (see Figure 2).

Figure 2: European investment activity and change in outstanding debt

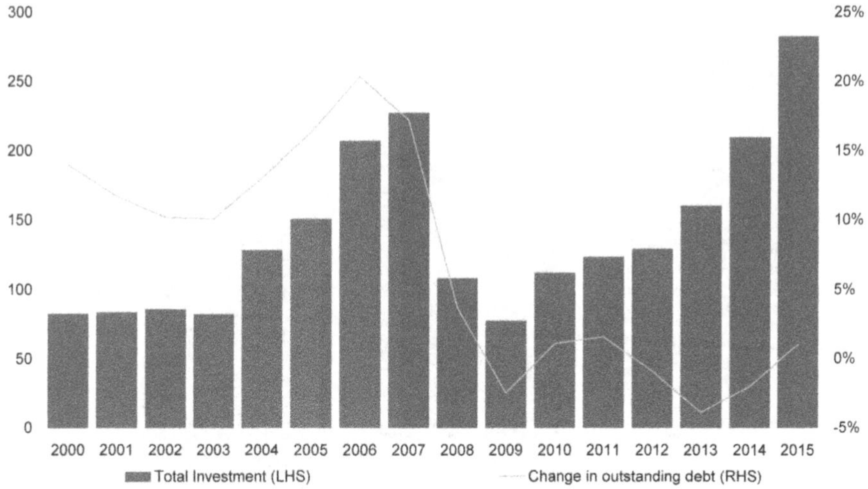

Source: Cushman & Wakefield Research

3.2 Structure of Europe's debt markets

Lending on European CRE has long been dominated by banks. Towards the peak of the market in the last cycle, 79% of debt was secured through bank lending. A further 11% was through covered bonds, which are originated through, and remain on the banks' balance sheet. The remainder was secured through CMBS (7%)[1] and Property Company bonds (2%). In this respect, Europe's market is similar to Asia Pacific in the dominance of bank lending for the CRE market. However, it does contrast with North America, where just over 50% of the outstanding amount is secured by banks, where CMBS accounts for a further 18% and institutions a further 12%, providing a more diverse funding base (see Figure 3).

The diversity of funding sources in North America is likely to be one of the main reasons why the region was better placed than Europe to weather the storm thrown up by the GFC, as will be set out in section 3.4 below.

---

[1] See Chs 1 and 4 for more detail on the CMBS market.

Figure 3: Outstanding debt by lender type, 2015

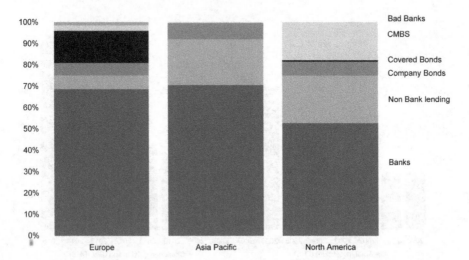

Source: Cushman & Wakefield Research, Standard & Poor's, Verband deutscher Pfandbriefbanken, Bloomberg, ECBC

Across Europe, the share of bank activity in the CRE sector has remained strong over the past decade, although its share has diminished somewhat, due to increased activity in both non-bank and covered and company bond issuance (see Figure 4). Of course, there are variations in the structure of lending sources across markets, so it is worthwhile examining in more detail the key areas of bank lending, covered bonds and CMBS.

The above data is based on outstanding amounts, and therefore still reflects to an extent the historic dominance of banks. There is a lack of transparency on data covering new lending across Europe, although the De Montfort Lending survey in the UK, does provide some indicators for trends in major markets. The latest release covering trends in 2015 showed UK banks had a 34% share of new originations in 2015, its lowest level on record. Non-banks, including institutions, maintained a strong 25% market share, with other overseas banks making up the rest.

3.2.1 Bank lending

At the beginning of the 21st century, as discussed, banks accounted for almost 90% of lending to CRE across Europe. Whilst the share of total lending has slowly reduced, bank lending still remains the most dominant source of funding, accounting for over three quarters of the total debt outstanding on CRE. Close to 60% of the outstanding debt, comprising over €740 billion, is secured against assets in France, the UK, Italy, Germany and Spain (see Figure 5). A further 20%, is secured against assets in the Nordics

Figure 4: Outstanding debt by lender type 2004–2015

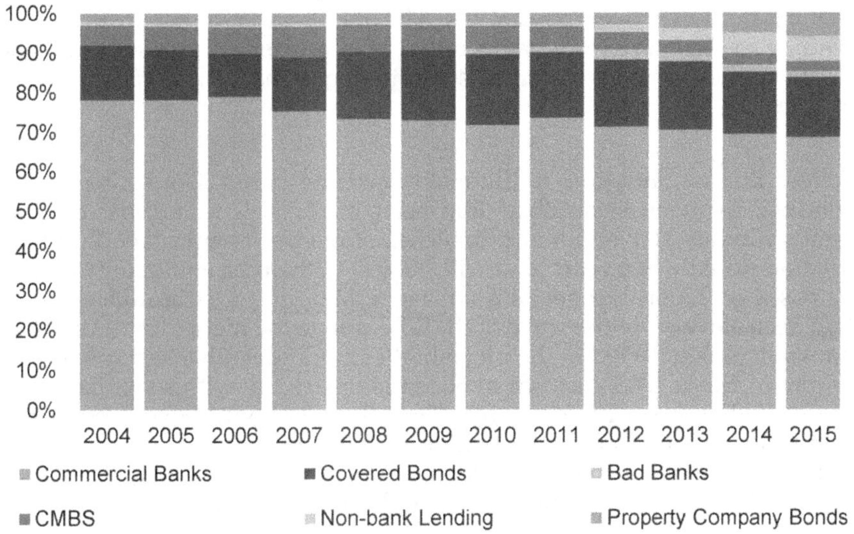

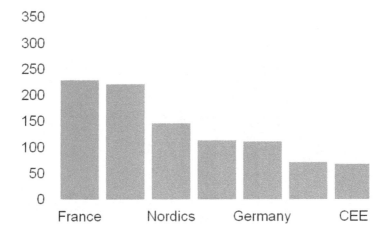

Source: Cushman & Wakefield Research, Standard and Poor's, Verband deutscher Pfandbriefbanken, ECBC

Figure 5: Banks' outstanding debt to real estate by geography, 2015

Source: Cushman & Wakefield Research

49

and Benelux totalling €240 billion. German assets represent just 9% of the outstanding amount to banks. This is around half of the value of outstanding bank debt to UK assets, even though the invested stock in Germany is just 20% lower than the UK. The main reason for the lower value of lending to Germany from banks reflects the greater reliance on the Pfandbriefe market, which is Germany's covered bond market, detailed in section 3.2.2 below.

Across Europe, investors traditionally focus on banks as a source of debt funding. In many established European markets, it is not just domestic banks who are active, but also branches of overseas banks. Lending terms are traditionally five years, and will, subject to the type and quality of asset, be based on Libor/Euribor plus a margin. Margins vary through time, and had been elevated in the wake of the GFC due to the higher funding costs of banks. This is reflected in the much higher credit default swap spreads (see Figure 6). Since 2008, these have been rising steadily with a significant gap emerging between different banks. This diversity could offer a competitive advantage to some banks should they wish to be active in the market.[2] Since 2014 this spread has narrowed significantly as banks and financial markets benefited from central bank policies and returned back to normality.

Figure 6: European Bank five year Credit Default Swaps

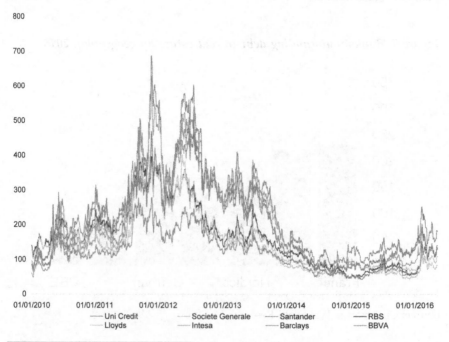

---

[2]   See further Ch.22 where the opportunities for lenders in this market are addressed.

Source: Bloomberg

Lending by institutions other than banks, in the CRE market in Europe, is limited and reliable data is not widely available. The non-bank lenders who are active have often tended to focus on more niche types of collateral, including doctors' surgeries, healthcare and student accommodation. Loans are typically longer in duration, up to 20 years, where there is limited competition with traditional banks. Some lenders have started lending on a fixed rate basis also.

3.2.2 *Covered bonds*

The European covered bond market has grown and developed over recent years, increasing its share of the CRE lending market to 18% by the end of 2009, and is now the second largest source of finance against European real estate after bank lending. However, the market itself is not new and in Germany[3] covered bonds date back to 1769. In Spain,[4] the other major market in Europe for covered bonds, legislation dates more recently to the 1980s. Both these countries now have well established covered bond markets.

Although the funding is effectively provided by banks, covered bonds are secured by a cover pool of mortgage loans to which bond investors have a preferential claim in the event of default. Unlike other asset backed securities, such as CMBS, these bonds remain on the bank's balance sheet and assets can be replaced in the pool. In the case of the German Pfandbriefe market, there are also strict eligibility criteria for loans to be included in the cover pool. This differs from terms available from traditional bank lending. For example, property financings may be included in the cover pool only up to 60% of the prudently calculated mortgage lending value. Similar restrictions are also imposed with Spanish Cédulas, although there are some exceptions in the case of construction and residential premises where the limit is raised to 80%.[5] Consequently, covered bonds are seen as a safer source of funding than traditional bank lending, underlined by the fact that there has not been a Pfandbriefe default since 1901 and no defaults have been reported on Spanish Cédulas.

As stated above, the majority of collateral secured by European covered bonds is in Germany, representing 51% of the market. This reflects the dominance of the Pfandbrief market. Assets in Spain account for a further 21% of the European covered bonds market. Overseas lending is permitted in both the German and Spanish regulations, with the UK at 9% and France

---

[3] In Germany, the covered bond market is the Pfandbriefe. See further the German Lending Market section contained in Ch.18.

[4] In Spain, the covered bond market is the Cédulas. See further the Spanish Lending market section contained in Ch.18.

[5] See 2015 ECBC European Covered Bond Fact Book for more detail.

at 7%, keys targets. The combination of these four countries, represent over 85% of the collateral in European covered bonds (see Figure 7).

Figure 7: Covered bond outstanding debt to real estate by geography, 2015

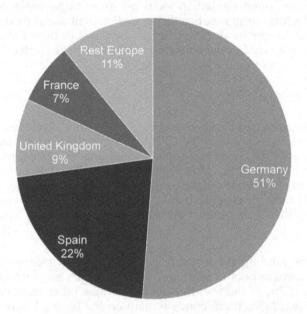

Source: Cushman & Wakefield Research, Verband deutscher Pfandbriefbanken, ECBC

The security offered by covered bonds has also been a benefit during the GFC. Whilst growth in bank lending to real estate slowed markedly in 2007 (12%) and 2008 (1%), the covered bond market remained resilient with growth rates of 47% and 29% respectively. Those banks which have provided such covered-bond funded lending, have also benefited from the European Central Bank's covered bond purchase programme. The first tranche ended in 2010 with €60 billion purchased. A second programme was launched in November 2011, with a limit of €40 billion. The programmes were superseded by the more recent long term refinancing operation (LTRO), a three year term loan facility provided by the European Central Bank. In September 2014 the ECB initiated a third programme for a scheduled period of two years. Reports have pointed towards over €300 billion of asset purchases under the various programmes.

3.2.3 CMBS

As was discussed in Chapter 1, the European CMBS market grew from virtually nothing in mid 1990s, with the amount outstanding reaching a peak of €146 billion in 2007. The European CMBS market has witnessed a severe cutback since 2007,[6] with little new issuance taking place or predicted. The amount outstanding according to data from Standard and Poor's has fallen back to €146 billion by year-end 2015 (less than one third of the peak), reflecting redemptions and write-downs. In 2016, at the time of writing, the CMBS market still represents 3% of the outstanding debt in the European CRE sector. Given the new regulatory regime and limited issuance pipeline, it would be reasonable to expect a further decline in the short term. The majority of assets underlying these bonds are located in the UK and Germany, which combined, represent over 80% of the collateral, with the remaining assets mostly located in Italy, Spain and the Netherlands (see Figure 8).

Figure 8: European CMBS Outstanding, 2015

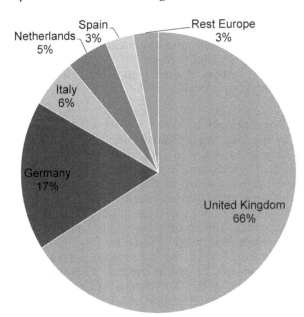

Source: Standard & Poor's

As set out in Chapter 1, unlike traditional bank lending or covered bonds, CMBS removes the loan off the bank's balance sheet. It grew in popularity in Europe during the mid-2000s enabling banks to repackage loans for sale in the capital markets, and raising fresh capital. In Europe, CMBS has traditionally involved both single high quality assets, and portfolios of loans. Since the onset of the GFC, issuance of new CMBS in Europe has been highly limited with just a handful of transactions as new regulatory requirements limit investors' ability to hold CMBS bonds.

---

[6] See Ch.1 section 1.3.

3.3 Deleveraging in the market

Despite the pressures on banks to shrink their balance sheets, the amount of debt outstanding in the European CRE market remains elevated at €1.8 trillion, just 6% off the peak in 2008. The scale of debt remaining in the market has been surprising and the pace of deleveraging has been slow. In part liquidity supports to banks enabled them to delay the deleveraging process.

During 2008 and beyond, many banks chose to roll-over loans with impending maturity dates due to refinance given the liquidity restraints. As the GFC continued, those loans that were unable to be refinanced, but were still performing, were extended, in some cases up to a period of five years. Maturity date extensions have continued, albeit at a lesser pace since 2012. There seem to be a number of reasons for banks to extend maturities, including swap breakage costs and banks' inability to absorb losses when collateral is enforced, especially when this might have triggered further reserves on a larger portion of their loan. This behaviour has inevitably delayed the deleveraging process.

The pace of deleveraging has varied by market. In a number of major markets such as the UK, Ireland, Spain and the Netherlands, banks and governments have been active in removing distressed assets off balance sheet. The total debt outstanding in these markets has shrunk by 18%, 22%, 46% and 25% respectively since the peak in the market. In these markets, bad banks have been created to remove assets from individual banks and to allow these bodies to work out assets. In 2012 close to €50 billion of assets were held by bad banks. The progressive sale of loans has seen the value of assets shrink by nearly half, to €27 billion by the end of 2015. Ireland has been ahead of the curve with the National Asset Management Agency (NAMA) seeing commercial loans in Ireland fall from near €16 billion in 2011 to €6 billion by end 2015. The Spanish bad bank SAREB was formed after NAMA and held over €19 billion of commercial loans in 2012 across Spain, which have subsequently shrunk to under €15 billion. Over the same time the Dutch bank Propertize has seen its assets nearly halve to €2 billion.

Whilst the volume of debt outstanding has slowly receded, the growth in equity across Europe has remained robust and has been rising at a faster pace. The difference between the two cycles could not be starker. In the period 2003 to 2009 the value of stock held by investors grew by over 50%, driven by a 87% increase in debt. Equity grew just 16%. Since 2009, the market has posted a rise of 22%, driven by equity of 63%. In contrast, debt shrank by 3% over this period.

Figure 9: Change in debt and equity through the cycle

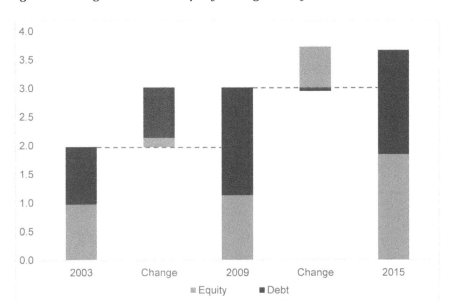

Source: Cushman & Wakefield Research

This faster growth in equity[7] has therefore helped to drive down overall leverage ratios. There are, inevitably, variations across markets. In a number of core European markets, such as France, Germany and the UK, loan to value ratios (LTVs) have been on the decline in the last couple of years (see Figure 10), in part reflecting modest declines in debt, but mostly as a consequence of rising levels of equity. Whilst this may not be good news for banks, it provides breathing space for borrowers who may have been under water. In some markets, such as Sweden, LTVs have been low and remained below the European average, reflecting more conservative lending. At the other end of the scale are more troubled markets, such as Ireland and Spain, where capital values have fallen significantly. However, a recovery in equity values and a shrinkage in the debt burden is leading to falls in aggregate leverage in the market, evident over the last couple of years. This has coincided with a growing appetite among investors to seek opportunities in these markets, especially many opportunistic funds which have the capacity to buy direct assets and loans.

---

[7]   Equity refers to the equity proportion of the commercial real estate holdings of, for example, institutions, private property companies and individuals, unlisted property vehicles and listed property companies including REITs. Debt is stripped out by applying a different gearing ratio for each investor group.

Figure 10: European LTVs

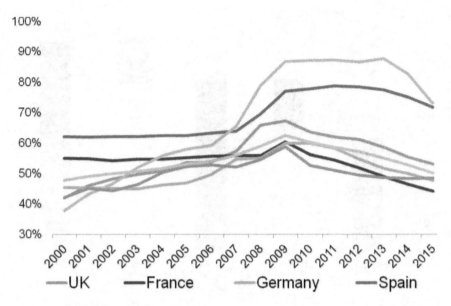

Source: Cushman & Wakefield Research

The rise of the bad banks was part of the wider response to the deleveraging process across Europe and in dealing with the wall of refinancing faced by many banks. In 2012 research by DTZ (now Cushman & Wakefield) estimated there to be close to €1 trillion of loans outstanding due to be refinanced between 2012 and 2015. This was over half the total debt outstanding at the time. As a result of falling values and a reduction in LTVs at refinance, a funding gap emerged. The gap can be defined as the difference between the existing debt balance and the debt available to replace it.

At its peak it was estimated that a gap of €140 billion existed across Europe in 2012. The gap grew in response to increased regulatory pressures from the European Central Bank (ECB) and European Banking Authority (EBA) who required banks to hold extra capital across all loans held on their balance sheet (not just real estate) in order to meet possible stresses imposed by a series of annual stress tests on the banking system. The results of these tests were in effect to force banks to scale back the volume of assets held on balance sheet with estimates suggesting banks' aggregate loan books (including real estate) should shrink by up to 7–8%.

During 2012, a number of banks—including Commerzbank, Société Generale, DG Hyp, Yorkshire Bank and Clydesdale Bank withdrew from the market or retreated to their home markets, as a means of reducing their exposure to CRE. In Europe, which is heavily reliant on banks for funding, any withdrawal proved unwelcome.[8] It also came at a time when it was estimated that over €1 trillion of debt was due for refinance over the period 2012–2015.

Analysis conducted at the time showed efforts in the market to plug the funding gap as new sources of finance, previously not available, began to emerge. Thus through time the funding gap began to shrink, supported by the growth in alternative sources of finance; including the rise of non-banks and insurers making direct loans; funds and institutions; along with the growth in bond issuance. By the last report published in May 2014 the gap had reduced to €124 billion, with the biggest gaps in France, Germany, Spain and the UK. However, the authors noted that finance from alternative sources would effectively shrink this gross gap to a net €36 billion. In some markets like France, Germany and the UK, alternative finance led to a surplus, though in Spain a net gap remained. Through time it was suggested that the surplus in some markets would shift to those with more problems, thus eroding the overall gap to zero.

Non-bank lenders are not new to the market. Back in the 1970s many institutions were active lenders. Many withdrew from the market after the early 1970s banking crisis. One of the few lenders to remain active was Aviva (Norwich Union), who by 2007 had a commercial loan book in excess of £10 billion, though mostly secured against more niche sectors, for example doctors surgeries. In the noughties, Aviva was joined by a number of US insurers who sought to gain a foothold in the market. By 2007 non-banks had loan balances in excess of €16 billion, equivalent to a market share of less than 1%. Since then there has been a steady rise of new entrants, including AXA and Allianz in Europe as well as US-based insurers such as Cornerstone (Mass Mutual). Other active institutions include AIG, Legal & General, MetLife, M&G and Canada Life. Numerous funds also emerged from traditional equity investors, including DRC, LaSalle, Longbow, Renshaw Bay (now GAM) and Savills IM to name but a few. By year end 2015 it is estimated that these non-banks held loan balances of €117 billion, reflecting a greater market share of 6%.

Additionally, as highlighted above,[9] the US has a more diverse source of finance that supports lending capacity. Of note, is the share of activity by insurers and other institutions who are traditionally more conservative lenders. Whilst institutions tended to be less active at the peak of the market, relative to commercial banks, this meant they were less exposed to the downturn in values and the market, and were thus able to lend at the bottom of the market cycle and increase their market share whilst banks

---

[8] In late June 2012 Commerzbank deemed all CRE lending as non-core. With a European CRE loan book totalling close to €70 billion based on data published in the July 2011 EBA stress tests, it was a significant lender to CRE.

[9] See Figure 3 above.

were less active (see Figure 11). Growing diversity in lending sources is seen as a benefit to the market, and whilst they may not prevent crises, they may lessen their impact.

Figure 11: US loan originations index by source

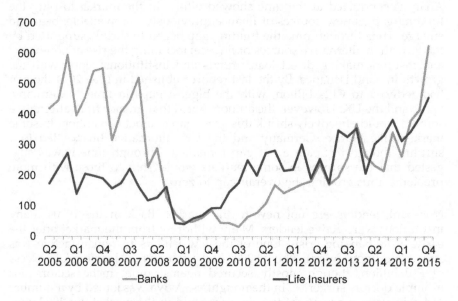

Source: Mortgage Bankers Association

Beyond the growth of alternative lenders has been the emergence of a loan sales market in Europe that was never previously there to the extent that may be witnessed in 2015–16. The market for loan sales grew from €25 billion in 2012 to over €86 billion in 2015, and followed sales of over €80 billion in 2014 (Figure 12). To date the loan sale market has been dominated by loans in the UK and Ireland, although an increasing number are evident in Spain and Italy.

Figures from Cushman & Wakefield[10] showed that Ireland's NAMA and the UK's UKAR were the biggest vendors, with RBS, Ireland's Permanent TSB and GE, some of the other major vendors. Some of these vendors might have not been distressed sellers. Still over 40% of sales were by other organisations. On the buy-side, this has been dominated by US private equity funds with Cerberus, LoneStar and Blackstone the major buyers. Oaktree, CarVal and Apollo also appear in the top 10 buyers.

---

[10] See European Loan Sales Market Q4 2015, Cushman & Wakefield.

Figure 12: European Loan Sales

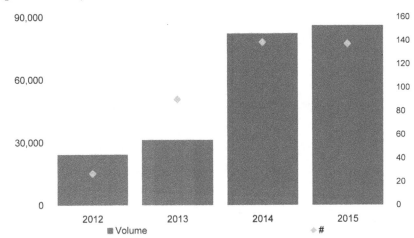

Source: Cushman & Wakefield

As the market moves forward and the cleaning of balance sheets nears a close in some markets, there may be witnessed a growing pipeline in others, with Spain, Italy and Germany prevalent, as well as the Netherlands, as its bad bank Propertize[11] ramps up its sale process. Many of these loan portfolios contain performing, partly performing and non-performing loans. The cumulative sale of over €200 billion in loan portfolios, many at significant discounts, has been an effective way to reduce bank's balance sheets exposure to CRE.

3.4   Current attitudes towards lending

The environment for lending has changed since the publication of the second edition of this book in 2012 and some of these trends are evident in a regular survey by Cushman & Wakefield. At the time of writing the most recent survey was released in February 2016. This survey showed that the majority of lenders remained focused on the three core markets of UK, France and Germany, which represent close to 50% of lending activity. The results also showed an increased appetite to lend in Spain and also across the Nordic markets. The former underscores the transformation in activity and willingness to move lending up the risk curve. In contrast the appetite to lend in Italy remained weak. Appetite to lend was stable in Benelux and CEE markets (Figure 13).

---

[11]   At the time of writing it is reported that a joint venture between JP Morgan Chase and Lone Star were leading the bidding to take control of Propertize.

Figure 13: Geographic focus of lending activity

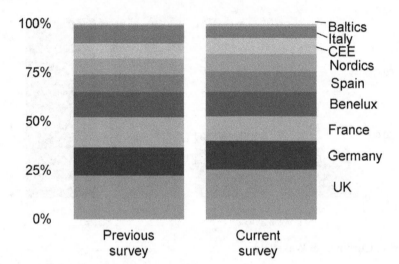

Source: Cushman & Wakefield Research

Whilst a majority of lenders (81%) stated that originations were either stable or up and equally moving forward a high proportion of lenders expecting originations to be stable or higher. However, those reporting an increase over the next six months shrunk from 56% to 41%, implying that the pace of increase could be slowing. A similar trend is also evident for refinancing, although a far higher proportion of lenders report stable levels of activity and this is set to increase further as at the time of writing.

On a positive note the outlook for overall loan books is one of expansion, with fewer expecting loan books to decline in 2016. This implies that the workout of loans and write downs is nearing an end; combined with new lending and refinancing, lenders expect some expansion in loan books. Further, lenders remain positive for 2016 overall, with over 90% expecting lending activity to increase or remain static compared with 2015 levels, with the balance evenly split (Figure 14).

Figure 14: European loan book expectations, Q4 2015

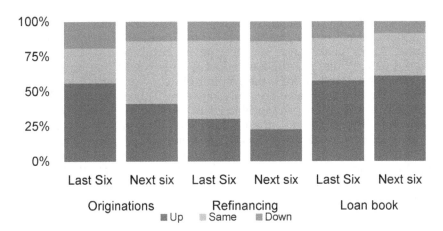

Source: Cushman & Wakefield

The majority of lenders in the survey (57%) remain engaged in senior lending, which was consistent with previous surveys. In contrast with the past, a higher proportion (20%) of lenders were engaged in whole loans. This style is now a clear second preference for lenders, ahead of mezzanine finance and stretch senior. Many lenders will offer a whole loan and then syndicate either the senior or mezzanine position later.

Attitudes towards lending by style in both Tier 1 and Tier 2 & 3 markets has changed little since 2015. In line with previous surveys there was a greater willingness to lend on non-prime standing investment in Tier 1 markets. There was also a greater propensity to lend towards pre-let development in Tier 1 markets, although the proportions have changed little.

Looking forward, the outlook remains broadly stable, with the majority of lenders seeing no change in their level of lending activity. This is a step change in attitude compared with previous surveys which reported a greater willingness to increase in all markets. This is consistent with attitudes in the previous section, where the pace of lending is expected to slow.

One clear trend to emerge was greater caution towards speculative development, with the balance of lenders (those expecting a rise less those seeing a fall) negative in both Tier 1 and Tier 2 & 3 markets. In Tier 2 & 3 markets there was marginally stronger appetite for pre-let development. This was consistent with the limited supply pipeline and willingness to develop where risks are lower. It was noted that caution towards speculative development was contrary to evidence Cushman agents were witnessing in the market where lenders appeared to be giving a warmer reception to the idea. See further Chapter 9.

3.5   Conclusion

As this Chapter has highlighted, lending to CRE across Europe has played an important role in the growth and development of Europe's investment market. At its peak, aggregate gearing in Europe's investment market reached 62%. Whilst gearing has reduced, largely reflecting an increase in the value of equity holdings, the amount of debt outstanding to European CRE has remained elevated and only between 2012 and the time of writing has it shrunk below the peak level in 2008. The slow response in the market can largely be put down to the liquidity supports put in place by central banks. These have enabled banks to extend and amend loans, in many cases up to a period of five years. This has provided banks with the required breathing space to manage their troubled loan books, without the need for enforcing collateral and releasing stock to the market at highly distressed prices.

Whilst lending markets have, at the time of writing, returned to normal with lenders across Europe able to refinance and provide new loans, the workout of legacy debt continues. At the end of 2015, Cushman & Wakefield reported that they were tracking over €70 billion of live or planned loan sale across Europe from both bad banks and other lenders. This compared to sales of over €80 billion in 2015. This underscores the remaining tasks still facing the market and the increase injection of equity into new deals has clearly facilitated investment returning to record levels.

Europe's reliance on banks as its main source of funding for CRE has also highlighted a weakness in the market when alternative sources to date have been relatively limited. At its peak, around 90% of lending to CRE in Europe came through banks. The only limited participation by other sources, mostly CMBS, but also some through insurance companies, is now changing. This is in stark contrast to North America, where traditional bank lending represents just over 50% of outstanding lending. There, other sources of finance, CMBS and lending from insurance companies and other institutions, represent a much higher proportion of activity. This, combined with longer lending terms, up to 10 years, insulates the market from short term volatility in capital values and reduced lending capacity from particular lending groups.

Changes are underway and the arrival of alternative funds and institutions into the European market has led to a shift in the balance. Whilst the pace is slow, non-bank lenders (funds and institutions) now have a 6% market share, with bond issuance providing a further alternative source at a further 6%. Banks (including covered bonds) now represent just 84% of the market, their lowest share since record began in the mid-1990s. It is expected that this trend will continue, as banks find effective ways to deal with new capital reserve requirements, like those proposed in the Basel IV revisions. Institutions are likely to remain longer term players. Funds are more uncertain, though with data showing funds that mature from 2020 onwards, and many having extensions, there are still a few more years of growth to come. One of the key questions remaining is whether CMBS will be providing a potential alternative funding channel.

Chapter 4

The Loan Origination Process

Klaus Betz-Vais,

Lloyds Banking Group

4.1 Introduction

This Chapter outlines and explains the key stages of the CRE loan origination process from the viewpoint of a senior lender. Given the broad nature of the topic, for convenience, it has been drafted with a focus on the UK CRE lending market, although the vast majority of the methodologies described herein are applicable across the whole of the European market.

The Chapter will examine the six phases of originating a CRE loan, together with a commentary on some of the key areas where theory may diverge from practice. The phases are as follows:

1. Deal sourcing
2. Preliminary underwriting, debt sizing and pricing
3. Agreement of key terms between the parties
4. Legal and commercial due diligence
5. Documentation
6. Closing

Whilst there is a clear sequential nature to the process, depending on commercial imperatives such as time available, it is possible to run any combination of steps 2–5 in parallel.

4.2 The organisation of a CRE lending business

In order to understand the CRE loan origination process, it is first necessary to understand the roles and responsibilities of some of the key actors in that process. These will change from franchise to franchise, but all CRE lending businesses will likely have some delineation between the duties of various team members. Some key ones are as follows:

Coverage: Coverage bankers are responsible for the majority of client interactions. This can include sourcing of new opportunities, negotiation of commercial terms, managing the loan creation process (by acting as a "master of ceremonies"), dealing with day-to-day client queries, monitoring post-closing covenant compliance and, in extremis, assisting with the work-out process should a loan become distressed.

Credit: The credit team is the guardian of the originating institution's balance sheet. To this end, they usually have the final discretion as to whether a loan is funded and will work closely with the coverage bankers to understand the risks of a potential financing and the structures proposed to mitigate those risks. They will usually also have views on the nature and quality of the underlying properties which will inform their decision making.

Loan administration: Loan administration is usually seen as a middle office function. The role of the loan administration team is usually to disburse funds, inform the client of what payments are due and when, ensure compliance certificates, information and monitoring reports are received on a timely basis and manage eventual repayment.

Others: Depending on the nature and size of an organisation there are a number of other teams that could be involved in loan creation. These can include the treasury team whose responsibility it is to ensure that funds are available for disbursement as required by the loan documents, a rates team whose responsibilities are to assist and implement hedging strategies for the borrower, a property underwriting team (usually ex surveyors) whose job is to understand and advise on the nature of the underlying properties that are the subject of the financing, an agency team whose job it is to administer syndicated facilities independently of the arranging bank in order to avoid conflicts of interest and also potentially a transaction execution team who run the documentation and due diligence process once outline terms have been agreed, so as to free the coverage team up for sourcing new business.

4.3   Deal sourcing

Deal sourcing is the responsibility of coverage bankers who will usually deploy a mix of strategies in order to win mandates from their clients. The broader the mix of strategies utilised and the larger the volume of deals seen by the coverage bankers, usually the better range of outcomes as it enables them to pick and choose the best opportunities.

There are a number of methods commonly used to source opportunities as follows:

1. **Personal contacts** are the most common ways of sourcing deals in the CRE lending market in Europe, despite disruptive technological innovations in virtually every other similar industry. A good coverage banker will have a roster of client relationships built up over a number of years which will form the genesis of the majority of his or her pipeline.
2. **Debt brokers** have become a much more prevalent feature of the European market since 2010. These are companies and individuals whose role is to match borrowers with funders and who can add value (especially for occasional borrowers) given their depth of knowledge of market terms and relative propensity of different debt capital providers to lend at various pricing and leverage points.
3. **Conferences and industry events** such as MIPIM and Expo can provide a forum for borrowers and lenders to interact.
4. **Advertising and franchise leverage** can generate leads via calls and queries from borrowers who have had no previous direct interaction with a particular lending platform.

4.4 Preliminary underwriting, debt sizing and pricing

Once an opportunity has been presented to a coverage banker, their next step is to assess it in the context of risk appetite and pricing aspiration at the lending organisation he or she is employed by. This process will vary from firm to firm but in all cases should be driven by a desire to **minimise probability of default** and **loss given default** at any given leverage and pricing point whilst **maximising returns**.

At this stage of the origination process, the amount of information will usually be limited but notwithstanding this, there are a number of analyses and methodologies that can be employed to assist with this task. These can be categorised as follows.

4.4.1 Property fundamentals

These are the core features of the properties that will form the security package for the loan and will usually comprise the quality (is the property new or old, is the specification suitable, what is the quality of the fit out, to what degree is investment required, can it be subdivided if large), the location (micro and macro location, supply of and tenant demand for similar properties, saleability) and the tenancy profile (what is the lease length profile, are the tenants strong covenants, what rents are payable, what is the estimated rental value on re-letting, how long will the property be void following the end of a lease, what are the void costs during this period, what are the costs of re-letting).

4.4.2 Sensitivity and break even analysis

In order to understand default risk and value break points in a variety of stress scenarios, it is advisable to run a sensitivity analysis for three of the key determinants of property value and consequently loan repayment: rent, occupancy and yield levels (ROY). A useful way of combining these is via a ROY table as shown below:

Figure 1: An example ROY (rent, occupancy and yield) table

A	B Rate gap to forward	C RY shift gap	D Break even rent	E (Disc) / Prem to ERV	F Break even occupancy GBP Per Sq. Ft.						
					13.82 (30.0 per cent)	15.79 (20.0 per cent)	17.76 (10.0 per cent)	19.74 ERV	21.71 10.0 per cent	23.68 20.0 per cent	25.66 30.0 per cent
Day 1 3.41 per cent	(0.74 per cent)	(1.93 per cent)	4.61	(76.7 per cent)	63.8 per cent	60.6 per cent	58.0 per cent	55.8 per cent	54.0 per cent	52.4 per cent	51.1 per cent
6.00 per cent	1.85 per cent	0.66 per cent	7.96	(59.7 per cent)	77.0 per cent	72.4 per cent	68.7 per cent	65.6 per cent	63.0 per cent	60.8 per cent	58.9 per cent
7.00 per cent	2.85 per cent	1.66 per cent	9.25	(53.1 per cent)	82.1 per cent	77.0 per cent	72.8 per cent	69.4 per cent	66.5 per cent	64.0 per cent	61.9 per cent
8.00 per cent	3.85 per cent	2.66 per cent	10.54	(46.6 per cent)	87.1 per cent	81.5 per cent	76.9 per cent	73.2 per cent	70.0 per cent	67.2 per cent	64.9 per cent
9.00 per cent	4.85 per cent	3.66 per cent	11.83	(40.0 per cent)	92.2 per cent	86.1 per cent	81.1 per cent	76.9 per cent	73.4 per cent	70.4 per cent	67.9 per cent
At Maturity 4.15 per cent	--	(1.19 per cent)	5.03	(74.5 per cent)	65.5 per cent	62.1 per cent	59.3 per cent	57.1 per cent	55.1 per cent	53.5 per cent	52.0 per cent
6.00 per cent	1.85 per cent	0.66 per cent	7.18	(63.6 per cent)	74.0 per cent	69.7 per cent	66.2 per cent	63.3 per cent	60.9 per cent	58.8 per cent	57.1 per cent
7.00 per cent	2.85 per cent	1.66 per cent	8.34	(57.7 per cent)	78.5 per cent	73.8 per cent	69.9 per cent	66.7 per cent	64.0 per cent	61.7 per cent	59.8 per cent
8.00 per cent	3.85 per cent	2.66 per cent	9.51	(51.8 per cent)	83.1 per cent	77.9 per cent	73.6 per cent	70.1 per cent	67.2 per cent	64.6 per cent	62.5 per cent
9.00 per cent	4.85 per cent	3.66 per cent	10.67	(45.9 per cent)	87.7 per cent	82.0 per cent	77.4 per cent	73.5 per cent	70.3 per cent	67.5 per cent	65.2 per cent

A ROY table is interpreted as follows:

- The table is set up to reflect debt levels both at the commencement of the loan ("Day 1" rows) and the anticipated debt level at maturity (bottom 5 rows);
- Column A stresses the loan for a series of interest and cap rate scenarios—these are best thought of as reflecting the debt yield (income divided by loan amount) on the loan;
- Column B compares the debt yields in column A to a range of anticipated refinancing rates at the maturity of the loan which is itself the sum of the forward rate and an anticipated margin. The greater the

68

positive gap, the more resilient the loan is to refinancing risk driven by interest rate increases;

- Column C compares the debt yields in column A to the reversionary yield (RY) of the underlying properties. Again, the greater the positive gap, the more resilient the loan is to value falls as reflected by a widening (reversionary) cap rate;
- Column D shows the break even rent, in this case on a GBP per sq ft metric, to generate each debt yield on a fully let basis. Column E compares these to the ERV of the security property. The greater the discount to ERV, the easier it should be to re-let the properties to achieve each given cap rate; and
- Section F is a corollary of columns D & E in that it shows the necessary degree of occupancy of the security property at differing rental levels (ERV, discounts and premiums to ERV) to achieve each level of debt yield.

A well-structured CRE loan should be resilient to falls in value (increases in required debt yield) with the additional constraint of falling rents. If, having stressed both of these factors, the ROY table indicates an achievable level of occupancy, the risk of loss to a lender is likely low.

4.4.3 Financial modelling[1]

Financial modelling is an essential part of the loan sizing process. The primary purpose of financial modelling is to identify cash flow and value risks which may manifest themselves during the term of a facility and enable these to be managed and mitigated via loan structuring. It is almost always advisable to model future cash flow, as purely valuation driven lending may expose the lender to a number of risks, not least of which is the ability of the borrower and/or underlying security to service the loan and comply with proposed loan covenants.

Unlike a sensitivity analysis, the financial model is there to primarily illustrate the probability of default over the loan term.

CRE debt modelling is complex and requires a disciplined approach to model creation. A good model will allow a user to take a large volume of non transparent data (tenancy and property schedules) and synthesise this into a clear, easy to understand projection. This can be used to gain an informative "at a glance" picture of the underlying property/properties and enable the loan to be structured in such a way as to manage the cash flow and value risks of the transaction.

---

[1] This section draws on the CREFC-Europe Guidelines for Due Diligence on Real Estate in the UK to which the author contributed. The Guidelines are available here: *http://www.crefc europe.org/wp-content/uploads/2015/02/CREFC-Europe-DD-Guide-Final.pdf* [Accessed 5 August 2016].

Given the "bespoke" nature of most real estate leases and transactions, a lender will usually prefer to create its own model but, if this is not practicable (and/or to check the lender's own model and analysis) an external party may be engaged to assist.

4.4.4 Model design

Any form of financial model should consist of three main elements:

Inputs	The drivers of the outputs and need to be clearly identified as such—either statements of fact (e.g. the length of an in-place lease) or assumptions about the future (e.g. the length of time it will take to re-let).
Calculations	Formulae that should not contain any hard numbers—calculations process the inputs to build up the model so that it can produce clear and useable outputs.
Outputs	Selected key calculations reproduced to give an indication as to how a transaction may perform and identify the key risks which may manifest themselves during the loan term.

Excel spreadsheets can be used in financial modelling but are extremely prone to error, as there is no built-in data integrity checking and no internal process for determining whether the formulae are logically or commercially correct. It is best practice to create separate sheets for inputs, calculations and outputs.

4.4.5 Type of model

Generally, CRE financing models fall into one of two categories

a)   **Deterministic**—the predominant type of underwriting model which employs defined and fixed inputs reflecting current reality or future assumptions and generates a discrete set of cash flows driven by these to show one particular (usually conservative) scenario;

b)   **Stochastic**—these replace certain key inputs with random variables, e.g. the "Monte Carlo" simulation, a modelling method run using multiple iterations of key inputs sampled from underlying probability distributions and a statistical analysis of the results (such as probability of default and loss given default) to provide a more holistic interpretation of the underlying risks. When designing or using such a model it is vital to determine whether the underlying probability distributions:

    i.   are correct (historically stochastic models have used distributions that take too narrow a view of the range of potential outcomes); and

ii.   have been correctly correlated or correlated at all (this has ten-
        ded to be ignored in the past resulting in too narrow a view of
        potential outcomes—i.e. lending transactions thought to be
        lower risk than they actually were).

4.4.6 Inputs required and responsibility for their provision

When underwriting a loan, the lender should list information requirements
early to give all parties the ability to satisfy them on a timely basis. Most of
this information will also be required on an ongoing basis whenever
covenants are tested (usually quarterly). Two broad categories of information are required, namely transaction level information and property level
information

Transaction level information includes information on the proposed facility
such as facility amount, cost of the financing and the debt repayment
profile:

Figure 2: Typical transaction level information

Data point	Responsibility for provision	Data point	Responsibility for provision
Loan term	Borrower & Lender	Swap / cap rate (if hedged)	Lender (use quarterly month actual / 365 rate from Bloomberg) to determine midmarket rate, credit spread by agreement between Borrower & Lender
Purchase price	Borrower		
Loan amount	Borrower & Lender		
Margin	Borrower & Lender		
Arrangement fee	Borrower & Lender	ISCR covenant	Borrower & Lender
Commitment fee	Borrower & Lender	DSCR covenant**	Borrower & Lender
Monitoring fee	Borrower & Lender	LTV covenant	Borrower & Lender
Drawdown profile	Borrower & Lender	Yield on Debt covenant**	Borrower & Lender
Amortisation profile	Borrower & Lender	Tax rate	Borrower & Lender
Allocated loan amounts*	Borrower & Lender	Release pricing multiple*	Borrower & Lender

*Portfolio transactions only **Optional

Property level information includes information on the terms of the leases, the valuation of the properties and assumptions as to re-letting:

Figure 3: Typical property level information

Data point	Responsibility for provision	Data point	Responsibility for provision
Tenant name	Borrower	Lease end date	Borrower
Tenant guarantor*	Borrower	Lease break option dates*	Borrower
Type of space (office /retail etc.)	Borrower	Lease extension dates*	Borrower
Tenant rating*	Borrower	Lease break penalty payments*	Borrower
Guarantor rating*	Borrower	Lease extension or non exercise of break option incentives*	Borrower
Lease type (fixed term or rolling)	Borrower	Anticipated void period	Borrower & valuer
Property associated with lease	Borrower	Anticipated void rate	In the UK Valuer or Lender (via the Valuation Office Agency web site www.voa.gov.uk)
Net lettable area	Borrower	Void rates transitional relief	
Parking spaces*	Borrower	Anticipated service charge and insurance expense	Borrower
Current gross rental income	Borrower	Anticipated rent free letting incentive	Borrower & valuer
ERV at reletting	Borrower & valuer	Anticipated letting fees	Borrower & valuer
Indexation provisions*	Borrower	Anticipated new lease length to first break	Borrower & valuer
Lease start date	Borrower	Anticipated re-letting capex, net of dilapidations	Borrower & valuer
Lease income start date	Borrower		

*Not always applicable

Other relevant information will include the address of the property, any payments due under ground rent or head lease agreements, information on the values of the underlying properties, quantification of corporate over-heads, asset management expenses and other non-recoverable items and details of capex programs to be implemented.

4.4.7 Creating the model

The model should be prepared in the following manner:

- calculations should be built up logically and step by step (if too many are done in a particular cell at once, these are difficult to check or later modify);
- the model should be quarterly and calculations should be, at least, quarter accurate (although day count accurate calculations are

strongly preferable, particularly where a property or portfolio is leased to a small number of tenants);

- income calculations should be done at a lease-by-lease level (a summary total of the lease by lease calculations should then be brought into a separate sheet or section where the transaction level cash flows can be calculated);
- property disposals during the term should be catered for including the anticipated excess deleveraging from release pricing as a result of such disposals;
- apart from generating a projected cash flow, the model should include a stratification of the underlying property/portfolio (the calculations for this should be done separately);
- for a lender's basic underwriting cash flow, the model should generally be run to the earlier of first break or lease end—no extensions or lease renewals should be assumed;
- a premium should be built into the swap rate to allow for adverse interest rate movements between the underwriting date and the actual funding date;
- the model should be sufficiently flexible so as to add leases if appropriate;
- the model should include basic data integrity and error checks—for example if a lease is input as ending before the model start date, this should be flagged as a potential error; and
- cash flows should be assessed using certain assumptions, for example relating to re-letting (the market convention for projected income calculations, and hence covenant testing, is to ignore these so that, if space is vacant, it is assumed not to re-let—a model should therefore only be used for covenant testing if it can assume a full run off of all leases and any other relevant provisions of projected rental income calculations).

4.4.8 Modelling conventions

There are several modelling conventions specific to the UK CRE market:

- leases are assumed to be fully repairing and insuring (FRI or in US "triple-net"), such that while a property or part of a property is let, the tenant is assumed to pay the rent and all outgoings;
- where there is a lease rent free period, it is assumed the tenant pays for all service charge, insurance, rates and other outgoings;
- generally, there is a short grace period (this may be longer for newly constructed properties) from the termination of a lease before "empty" business rates are charged, reflecting grace periods provided by legislation;
- rent payments are due on calendar quarter end dates (usually 25 March, 24 June, 29 September and 25 December); and

- interest payment dates are two to three weeks after rent payment dates, i.e. between the 15th and 25th of the month following (usually April, July, October and January).

4.4.9 Outputs

The outputs of the model need to clearly and accurately identify and summarise the key transaction risks. They should neither be too detailed, nor so high level such that risks are hidden. The following is a basic set suitable for most transactions:

- a granular annual operating cash flow identifying gross rental income, break penalties, void costs, letting fees, head lease payments and other non-recoverables to result in a net cash flow figure, less net capital expenditure (re-letting capital expenditure less anticipated dilapidations payments) and lastly, the amount of cash that is paid to the borrower (or needs to be injected) after financing costs and tax;
- a summary quarterly cash flow which starts with consolidated net rental income and deducts net capital expenditure, interest, tax and amortisation;
- key loan metrics on a quarterly basis (Interest Cover Ratio (ICR), Debt Service Cover Ratio (DSCR), yield on debt, Loan to Value (LTV) and debt per sq ft;
- a list of top 10 or top 20 tenants along with key data on their leases (term to first break, term to maturity, total rent paid, ERV, sq ft occupied, rent per sq ft);
- summary property details (income, Estimated Rental Value (ERV), area and vacancy);
- an annual breakdown of terminating leases by income for a ten or fifteen year projection period (i.e. 10% of income breaks in year 1, 5% in year 2, etc.);
- the weighted unexpired lease term and the weighted unexpired lease term to first break;
- the portfolio vacancy;
- a breakdown of the properties by income and space type (office, retail, logistics, etc.).

4.5 Sponsor financial capacity and experience

The nature of the sponsor who stands behind a borrower is key to determining whether a loan will be made and on what terms. There are in principle three key aspects of sponsor quality which need to be examined on most transactions:

4.5.1 Experience

The experience of the sponsor and its management team is essential in ensuring that the security property is kept in a good condition, occupied, the business plan is successfully implemented and, if unexpected adverse events occur (e.g. tenant defaults), these can be mitigated. Needless to say, the more transitional the properties, the more important the experience and skill of the sponsor.

4.5.2 Financial capacity

Most UK CRE loans are made on a non-recourse basis and must consequently be structured to assume that no financial support from the owner of the property will be forthcoming in the event that the loan runs into difficulties. Notwithstanding this, the financial capacity of the sponsor continues to play an important role, as a well capitalised sponsor with substantial resources will be in a better position to provide a solution in a distressed situation, be it by de-leveraging the structure, injecting additional funds to improve the underlying collateral or providing a guarantee to mitigate the risk of uncertain future events.

4.6 Business plan review

By their very nature most commercial properties are subject to a variety of risks including the need to re-let on a periodic basis, risks of upkeep and obsolescence, impact of macro-economic conditions on demand and the presence or prospect of competing stock.

All borrowers should consider these risks and address them in a business plan that will be reviewed by both the coverage bankers and the credit team. A business plan must be credible, cover a variety of downside scenarios and address and consider how each business plan initiative will be funded.

4.7 Interest rate management

As will be discussed further in Ch.12, it is important to consider interest rate management strategies at the outset of a transaction as these will have an important impact on the probability of a loan defaulting. Typically, at the time of writing, most senior lenders expect interest rate risk to be managed via a swap or a cap (for floating rate loans) or via a fixed rate loan structure. Swaps and fixed rate loans have the advantage of providing a highly predictable stream of interest payments and are therefore attractive to lenders seeking to minimise risk, but may have termination costs in the event of early prepayment of the debt facilities. Caps by contrast still provide protection, but given that these tend to be purchased "out of the money",

75

a lender will usually assume the cap rate in its underwriting, which may limit loan proceeds as this typically tends to result in an increased probability of default. Where a disposal programme is envisaged for a portfolio, or where a sponsor wishes to preserve the ability to sell properties opportunistically, a combination of swaps and caps may be utilised to provide an optimal result for both borrower and lender.

4.8 Pricing

Once the quantum of loan has been established, it is then necessary to price the facility. There are broadly two key drivers of pricing:

1. The balance sheet cost of the lending institution for any part of the debt that it chooses to retain; and
2. The price at which the part of the loan which will not be retained can be sold at, either in the loan or capital markets.

4.8.1 Pricing the retained component of a loan

Where lenders originate loans for their balance sheet they need to do so at rates of interest and fees that exceeds their cost of capital. This capital is comprised of equity and different types of debt.

Different types of lenders have different pricing models (for example, a bank will price principally on a cost plus basis whereas a fund may have an absolute target level of return), but irrespective of the institution, the pricing of a CRE loan should be a combination of that lender's basic cost of capital (debt and equity), the operational cost or making and administering the loan, a provision for loss derived from the risk profile of the financing and a profit element.

All banks use a risk weighted assets (RWA) approach to price loans. The (simplified) principles behind this are as follows:

a) The lender determines the risk profile of the loan using a combination of the above approaches and assigns the loan a rating.
b) That rating determines what proportion of the loan balance counts for RWAs by applying a percentage—for example a low risk loan will have a low RWA percentage (perhaps 30%) and a higher risk loan will have a high RWA percentage (say 150%) although the RWA percentage ultimately depends on the regulatory framework applicable to the lender, with different lenders subject to different rules and having different levels of flexibility.
c) The loan balance is multiplied by the RWA percentage to determine the total RWA.

d) The total RWA is then multiplied by the bank's capital ratio target to determine the amount of equity that is to be allocated against that loan.
e) The anticipated returns net of costs are then compared against the equity allocated in order to determine whether the return on equity over the life of the loan is of a sufficient high level.

An example is shows below:

Loan (£100.0 million)* ×RWA percentage (75%) = £75.0 million
RWA's* ×desired capital ratio (10%) = £7.5 million equity allocation

Profit after costs = £1.0 million per annum/£7.5 million equity = 13.3% return on equity

4.8.2 Pricing the component of a loan distributed to the loan market

The component of a loan that is distributed in the loan market is priced in a similar way to the retained component, with the key difference being that returns market participants are likely to require will be focused on their pricing rather than the originating lender's cost of capital.

When pricing a loan for distribution in the loan market, the originating lender will usually look to make a profit on the sale in the form of a "skim". This is a differential between the margin and fee the loan is originated at, versus at which it is sold. For example, an originating bank might advance a loan with a 1.00% up-front fee and a 300bps margin but sell it down to another bank at a fee of 0.60% and a margin of 275bps. The originating bank can therefore be said to have made a skim of 0.40% on the up-front fee and 25bps on the margin.

4.8.3 Pricing the component of a loan distributed to the capital market

As was discussed in Chapter 1, pre GFC, a large number of CRE loans distributed in the capital markets were done via a CMBS exit. At the time of writing the CMBS market is proceeding through a period of uncertainty which will be explored throughout this book, although if the CMBS market was to return to levels consistent seen prior to the GFC, it is worth highlighting the economics of the business of a CMBS originator.

These can be broken down into several component parts and are conceptually very straight-forward and simple: an originator makes loans at a certain level of pricing, packages them into securities and sells them to investors at tighter pricing levels. The pricing difference is the retained profit for the originator. The basic economics for portfolio and originate-to-distribute lenders are fundamentally similar. The main difference to portfolio lenders is that CMBS originators remove the credit risk from the balance sheet upon closing of the CMBS, and that they endeavour to monetise the excess spread by selling it to third party investors.

However, it is useful and important for the purposes of this Chapter to analyse the details of the CMBS originate-to-distribute model to understand how the economics of CMBS origination are derived and how CMBS originators might be able to do it in the future. The economics of a loan are relatively simple. The borrower will pay the lender origination fees, interest, principal and under certain circumstances prepayment fees. In a few instances and in more speculative loans there might be payment in kind (PIK) interest components, exit fees and profit share arrangements, but it would be generally accepted that these are not likely in CMBS loans. The costs associated with the origination of a loan, i.e. documentation, due diligence, valuations, etc. would generally be paid for by the borrower and therefore would not affect the economic dynamics. While traditional CMBS issuance could comprise fixed or floating rate bonds, the vast majority of "conduit" issuance is in floating rate format, which will be the focus of this Chapter as it considers the life cycle of a typical CRE loan.

As discussed in Chapter 1, CRE has traditionally been viewed as a fixed income asset class, due to the relatively fixed nature of the rental income generated by the CRE assets. While there is some empirical evidence that over longer periods of time, CRE asset values and rental income do provide a moderately effective hedge against inflation, it is, however, poorly correlated with short-term interest rate movements. Therefore, given that CMBS issuers need to originate actual or effective floating rate assets, the originator will, as discussed in Chapter 12, also generally enter into hedging arrangements to hedge the interest rate risk. This is traditionally done, as discussed above, mostly with swaps or sometimes caps. If the loan is a floating rate loan, the swap is entered directly with the borrower, and if the loan is a fixed rate loan the lender will enter into a swap with its derivatives desk and novate it to the CMBS vehicle. Whichever approach is used, hedging activities traditionally comprise a significant portion of the economics for a CMBS loan originator. Meanwhile, whilst the loan is on the originator's balance sheet, it earns interest in excess of the short-term funding costs of the bank or the CMBS desk. This is defined as "positive carry".

Once a pool of sufficient size and with the right degree of diversity and compatibility has been assembled, the structuring, rating and documentation process takes place. The costs associated with these activities are generally borne by the originator of the CMBS.

At the time of writing, whilst most loan originators try to optimise their economics by syndicating parts of loans, generally the higher leverage portions of loans, i.e. junior loans or B pieces (see Chapters 5, 6 and 7), the fundamental mathematics of the exit strategy are the same as if the whole loan is securitised. The basic reasons for syndicating the junior portion of the loan range from simple—rating agencies might assign a low rating to a highly levered loan, there might not be strong demand for such a tranche— to structurally more nuanced—the required coupon for a lowly rated tranche might cause the tranche to be either priced at a discount or be susceptible to available funds caps. Lenders follow a simple decision making process: if B pieces or junior loans can be sold at higher prices/ lower margins to loan investors than to bond investors, then loan origina- tors act rationally and sell the loans to loan investors instead of re-packa- ging them as CMBS securities.

Once a CMBS has been marketed and sold and bonds have settled, the economic tally of originating the deal can be assessed. An originator aims to sell all the bonds in a CMBS, but if it fails to do so, it will generally be required to hold any unsold bonds on its trading book at the appropriate mark-to-market (with possibly a resulting loss). For the purposes of this analysis, it is assumed that originators sell all of the bonds. Generally, the margins on the bonds are set at a level so that the bonds can be sold at par. In some circumstances, particularly for the most junior classes, either because the net interest margin of the loans is not sufficient to pay the full margin on all the bonds (either from day one or under certain prepayment scenarios), then the margin of certain bonds will be set at a level lower than the market clearing discount margin, leading to below par pricing.

In order to illustrate the economics of CMBS origination a hypothetical, but not atypical, CMBS conduit transaction is analysed below. Figure 4 portrays a £500 million securitisation structure of eight loans with the characteristics of Figure 5 below. The securitisation is comprised of five tranches, and utilises a simplified sequential pay structure with an X-class (or deferred consideration) and running transaction costs of 15bps per annum.

Figure 4: Sample CMBS Structure

	Bond Size	Bond Balance (£)	Price (%)	Price (£)	Margin	Discount Margin
			Securitisation Structure			
AAA	75%	375,000,000	100.00%	375,000,000	0.25%	0.25%
AA	10%	50,000,000	100.00%	50,000,000	0.40%	0.40%
A	7%	35,000,000	100.00%	35,000,000	0.70%	0.70%
BBB	5%	25,000,000	100.00%	25,000,000	1.00%	1.00%
BB	3%	15,000,000	95.912%	14,386,729	2.00%	2.75%
Total/W.A.	100%	500,000,000	99.88%	499,386,729	0.39%	0.41%

Figure 5: Sample Loan Collateral Pool

Loan Collateral Pool

Loan	Balance	Amortisation	Margin	Term (Years)
1	140,000,000	1% Per year	1.12%	6.00
2	106,000,000	Interest Only	1.05%	5.50
3	78,000,000	1 Year IO, 1% per year	0.90%	7.00
4	55,000,000	1.75% per Year	1.40%	6.00
5	39,000,000	Interest Only	0.70%	5.00
6	27,000,000	1.5% per year	0.78%	6.50
7	16,000,000	2 Year IO, 1% per year	0.95%	7.00
8	39,000,000	2% per year	1.25%	5.00
Total/W.A.	500,000,000		1.06%	5.95

A range of economics (low and high) has been chosen, as different types of transactions have different levels of costs and profit. As demonstrated in the above example, the transaction generates a profit for the originator of approximately 1% to 3%, i.e. £5 million to £15 million (see Figure 6). As shown below, the significant part of the economics and the vast majority of profits of the CMBS originator are determined by the value of the excess spread and its ability to be extracted in an efficient and timely manner by way of an X-class note (see Chapter 4 of the previous edition of this book and Chapter 13 for further discussion of the development of X-class notes) or deferred consideration.

Figure 6: Summary of Sample Economics for a £500 million CMBS

	Low	High	Footnotes
Loan Origination	-100.00%	-100.00%	
Origination Fees	0.35%	0.65%	
Carry	0.25%	0.60%	1)
Derivatives P&L	0.15%	0.40%	2)
Securitisation Origination Expenses	-0.35%	-0.55%	3)
Sale of Bonds	99.88%	99.88%	4)
Sub-Total (%)	**0.28%**	**0.98%**	
Sub-Total (£)	1,386,666	4,886,666	
X-Class/Deferred Consideration (%)	0.80%	2.19%	5), 6)
X-Class/Deferred Consideration (£)	4,005,708	10,950,000	
Total (%)	**1.08%**	**3.17%**	
Total (£)	**5,392,374**	**15,836,666**	

Assumptions/Footnotes

1)	Assumes 6 months hold, Loan Interest at L+80/120 (Low/High), Funding at L+0/50
2)	Assumes 3-8bps profit PV-ed
3)	Legal, Accounting, Rating
4)	Junior Bonds might be sold at
5)	High End Value assumes PV of zero prepayment
6)	Low End Value assumes PV of worst prepayment scenario in 10,000 Monte-

Figure 7: Sample Excess Spread Cashflows—Base Case

The key feature of these interest-only X-class payment streams is that they can cease if loans prepay or default. In a CMBS transaction backed by a pool of loans with an expected average life of six years, if no prepayments occur and all loans perform to maturity, the X-class would expect to receive excess spread cash flows for six years (see Figures 6 and 7).

If loans prepay before maturity this will directly lead to reduced excess spread payments, and therefore a reduction in the potential profits an originator would make.

In Figure 8, certain loans prepay during the transaction with the reduction of the cash flows seen in the reduction in the height of the bars representing the quarterly payments to the X-class.

Figure 8: Sample Excess Spread Cashflows—Prepayment Case, No Prepayment Fees

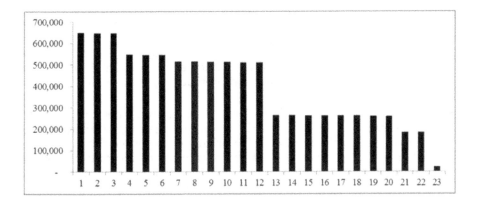

Hence, the importance in a CMBS transaction of loan level call protection (protecting against reduced excess spread due to loan defaults is a more challenging task). In Europe, call protection may be achieved by the inclusion of prepayment fees in the loans. While some longer-dated CMBS transactions may utilise prepayment lockouts, or defeasance structures, some may utilise more sophisticated yield maintenance or make-whole provisions.

Figure 9 shows the same prepayment profile as Figure 8, with the significant difference that, particularly in the early years of a loan, prepayment fees were paid when loans prepaid, increasing the cash flows at the time of the prepayment and compensating the X-class investor for the future reduction of excess spread.

Figure 9: Sample Excess Spread Cashflows—Prepayment Case, With Prepayment Fees

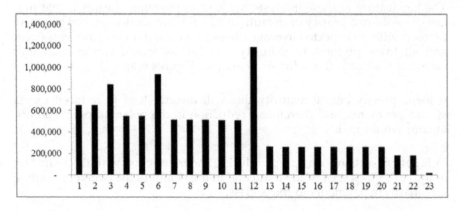

The design of prepayment fees and structuring to optimise the stability of the excess spread is an interesting, complex and controversial topic, but is beyond the remit of this Chapter.

Whilst complex, given a set of fixed inputs, it is entirely possible to determine the pricing of a loan structured for CMBS distribution and achieve a set level of profit. However, as discussed in Chapter 1, at the time of writing, the CMBS originator faces a number of additional challenges, which make executing a successful and profitable CMBS exit more difficult:

- **Extended execution period**—There is generally a three to 12 months delay between the time of origination and the time at which CMBS bonds are actually sold. A CMBS originator might require three to six months to accumulate enough reasonably compatible or homogenous collateral to put together a pool of loans. At the height of the CMBS market, some platforms issued over one €/£ billion of CMBS per year (some significantly more). Most conduit platforms issued less than that and therefore the accumulation period was reasonably long. In addition, the fact that European CMBS issuers did not combine or pool their loans, contributed to the extended periods of time to achieve reasonably sized pools of loans. Once the pool is assembled, originators required approximately three months to get the deals rated by the rating agencies, document the transaction and market the bonds.

- **Uncertain rating outcome**—The outcome of the rating process is uncertain. While a number of the CMBS issuers believe they have good approximations to rating agency models, such statements are difficult to reconcile with the reality, particularly given that the rating agencies never release detailed parameters to replicate their models. While, as will be seen in Chapter 14, rating agencies may have internal models to analyse loans, a significant component of their analysis and eventual capital structure allocation is based on subjective "non-model" overrides. The high degree of variability in rating outcomes is due to the different analytical approaches used by each rating agency, which may lead to rating agency "shopping" and arbitrage.

- **Lack of homogeneity**—Additional variability is partially due to the fact that loan documentation, loan structuring, leases, etc. vary from jurisdiction to jurisdiction, from loan to loan and from originator to originator. The lack of a homogenous European lending market (as will be seen by the discussion of the major Western European lending markets in Chapter 18) and therefore the ability to make the analysis more predictable and formulaic, make the rating outcome more volatile and unpredictable.

- **Lack of credit hedging**—The lack of instruments to hedge credit spreads exposes CMBS originators to economic risks. The vast majority of the CMBS market in Europe is a floating rate market. While loans can be originated as floating rate loans as well as fixed rate loans, all "conduit style" fixed loans are hedged with interest rate swaps or caps that effectively hedge the interest rate risk between the origination of the loan and the issuance of the (mostly) floating rate bonds. However, originators have few, if any, cost effective choices to hedge credit spread variations over such extended period, making it very difficult to ensure that the economics expected at loan origination are actually realised when the CMBS is priced.

- **CRE value volatility**—CMBS originators are exposed to CRE values changing between the time of origination and CMBS sales which could affect the credit quality of the loans. This can have a positive outcome if values improve during the hold period, or be negative if values deteriorate. For example, a 65% LTV priced at LIBOR plus 300bps could become a 70% LTV and be mispriced by the time it is securitised, or become a 60% LTV and have a successful and highly profitable CMBS execution. See further Chapter 21 for a discussion on how a focus on long-term value may address this risk.

- **Negative convexity and adverse selection**—Another somewhat uncontrollable factor is the tendency of borrowers to prepay loans, sometimes while they are still on the lender's balance sheet. Generally, the loans being prepaid are the ones which have improving credit characteristics, such as increasing CRE values, and are therefore able to get higher leverage and tighter pricing from other lenders. The ones with deteriorating credit attributes may not prepay as readily.

As discussed further in Chapters 16 and 17, regulatory requirements post GFC have changed the economics of CMBS origination from the "golden era" of 1998–2007. In particular, CMBS originators are, at the time of writing, required to retain 5% of the risk on their own balance sheets, either by holding 5% of the bonds or retaining 5% of the loan and selling the remaining 95% interest to the issuing vehicle. This has the effect of both reducing returns and also increasing capital usage, hindering a successful return of a CMBS market seen pre-GFC.

4.9   Agreement of key terms between the parties

Once preliminary underwriting, sizing and pricing are complete, the loan originator must agree key terms with the borrower in order to have a clear basis on which to proceed. This is usually done via a "heads of terms", (HoTs) which is a set of agreed principles which precede the signing of the (negotiated) loan agreement and which the parties intend to be reflected in the written contract. They set out the basis of the financing on broad terms. HoTs may also be referred to as a "memorandum of understanding", a "letter of intent" or a "term sheet".

HoTs are typically not legally binding although if this is the case it is important to clearly state this in the document. Occasionally heads of terms may be legally binding in which case they are may referred to as an "offer letter". Needless to say where HoTs are legally binding then they must be approved by the credit team prior to issuance.

HoTs may be either "short" or "long" form. Short form HoTs are usually one or two page documents which memorialise only the absolutely key parameters of a real estate financing whereas long form terms may run to many pages and can cover a variety of loan parameters which may be of concern to both the borrower and lender to clarify at an early stage.

A number of commercial areas covered in short and long form HoTs are described below.

4.9.1   Short form heads of terms

The following areas are usually covered in short form HoTs. These assume that the loan is floating rate and needs to be structured in a form which is distributable in the loan or capital markets.

Sponsor	This is usually the over-arching business or fund that is proposing to acquire the property. It is distinct from the borrower in that it is the "controlling mind" behind the transaction rather than the Borrower which is likely to be set up as subsidiary of the Sponsor so as to avoid direct recourse to it.
Shareholder	This is the direct parent of the Borrower, controlled by the Sponsor. It is generally desirable to have an intervening bankruptcy remote entity between the Sponsor and the Borrower as it avoids a situation where the entity that has granted security over the shares of the Borrower to the Security Agent may be insolvent (see further the following Chapter).
Borrower	The acquiring entity for the CRE asset (or the parent of a holding company—see further the following Chapter). It will usually be controlled by the Sponsor. Where the Borrower has not yet been incorporated, it is usual to state in the HoTs that it needs to be incorporated in due course, must be bankruptcy remote and acceptable to the Lenders.
Ultimate Owner(s)	This is the ultimate beneficial owner of the Sponsor business. It is important to understand who this is for KYC purposes and also to enable change of control language to be drafted correctly in the loan agreement or term sheet.
Ultimate Controller	This is the ultimate controller of the Borrower. It will often be the same as the Ultimate Owner, but in certain circumstances such as where a fund is the beneficial owner of an asset, the Ultimate Controller may be a general partner of the fund and a different entity. Again defining this is important for KYC and change of control purposes.
Guarantor	There may sometimes be a guarantor of a loan (for example the Shareholder or a related entity of the Sponsor). If so this should be defined.
Obligor(s)	These are usually the Borrower and the Guarantor.
Facility Agent	This is the party that administers the loan for the lenders in all respects (passing on information, calculating covenant compliance, etc.) apart from the holding of security.
Security Agent	This is the party who is responsible for holding and administering the Lender's security.
Arranger	The originating lender who is arranging the financing.

85

Lender(s)	The Arranger and any other lenders participating in the financing.
Hedge Counterparty	The provider of any hedging products.
Finance Parties	Typically the Facility Agent, the Security Agent, the Arranger, the Lenders and the Hedge Counterparty.
Property(ies)	A description of the security properties—address, size, key tenants, passing rent and ERV.
Amount	This is the basis of calculation of the amount of the loan to be advanced. At minimum, it should be the lower of four (calculated) amounts:

- The amount of the loan initially contemplated (e.g. £200 million);
- An amount that does not exceed the assumed loan to value (LTV), e.g. 65%;
- An amount that does not exceed the assumed loan to cost (LTC), e.g. 65%;
- An amount that does not result in an interest service coverage ratio (ISCR) of less than a certain level, e.g. 3.00x.

Availability	This is the period that the loan will be available for drawing. For an investment loan this is typically a number of business days after signing, for a development loan this will be the period during which the development will be ongoing.
Repayment	The date at which the loan needs to be repaid usually expressed as a number of years from the first Interest Payment Date.
Amortisation	This is any fixed repayment that will need to be made to the Lenders.
Security	Describes the security package that the lenders expect. This will typically include a first mortgage over the security properties, a fixed charge over the shares of the borrower and any intercompany debt as well as any other security that is available or desirable (e.g. a fixed charge over a number the Borrower's bank accounts).
Valuation	A description of the basis on which the security properties will be valued and how often the valuation needs to be updated.
Financial covenants	The financial covenants that the Borrower will be expected to comply with over the term of the financing. These are typically split into two categories, "hard"

and "soft". A breach of hard covenants will trigger an event of default whereas a breach of a soft covenant will usually only result in an accelerated repayment of the loan through a cash sweep or other mechanism. The financial covenants may relate to a number of parameters but in an investment loan will usually include any combination of the following:

- LTV—maximum levels which trigger soft and hard defaults
- ISCR—minimum levels which trigger soft and hard defaults
- Yield on Debt—same as ISCR
- WAULT(B)—Weighted Average Unexpired Lease Term (to Break), minimum levels which trigger soft (and occasionally hard) defaults.

Margin	The rate above the relevant reference rate (e.g. 3M LIBOR, 3M EURIBOR, EONIA etc.) which the lender charges on an ongoing basis for drawn balances. Usually quoted in basis points (bps).
Interest	The amount of interest payable on each Interest Payment Date. Usually a combination of the relevant reference rate and the Margin.
Interest Payment Dates	These are dates (usually quarterly) on which interest must be paid. These are usually set a few weeks after each rent collection date in order to give the Borrower time to chase late payments of rent.
Arrangement fee	A one off fee paid to the Lenders for arranging and structuring the financing package. This should be expressed as a fixed amount in currency. It is usually paid in one amount upfront.
Commitment fee	A fee for undrawn commitments, typical in the case of development financings. This is usually expressed as an annual fixed percentage (e.g. 1.25%) and is paid on Interest Payment Dates.
Prepayment and cancellation fees	These are one off fees (expressed as a percentage of the amount prepaid or cancelled) which are payable if the loan is repaid prior to the repayment date. These usually reduce over time to reflect the reducing opportunity cost to and foregone profits of the Lenders as a result of the early repayment. They may be structured to reduce on a quarterly or annual basis.

Monitoring / agency fees	These are fees (usually expressed as currency amounts) payable to the Facility and Security Agent for their services.
Other fees	Any other fees (e.g. coordination fees payable to the Arranger) agreed between the Borrower and the Finance Parties.
Interest rate management	A description of any interest rate management strategies to be implemented by the Borrower in conjunction with the Hedging Counterparty. This can include swaps, caps or combination thereof.
Costs	A description of how the Finance Parties' costs will be borne and any reimbursement arrangements agreed with the Borrower or Sponsor.
Confidentiality	These are confidentiality provisions relating to the HoTs and any information provided by any party to any other party until the date of signing of the Facility Agreement.
Exclusivity and break costs	Provisions relating to exclusivity periods provided by the Borrower to the Arranger and details of any break fees payable by the Borrower or Sponsor if the financing is aborted or executed with another lender.
Lapse of terms	The period after which the terms lapse.

4.9.2   Long form heads of terms

Apart from the matters covered in a short form heads of terms, a number of additional topics may be covered by a long form HoTs, some common examples of which are described below:

Subordinated creditors	Details of any subordinated creditors and proposed subordination or intercreditor arrangements.
Extension options	Details of any loan term extension options and extension criteria relating to these.
Margin flex	The mechanics by and economic terms under which the Arranger may increase the margin on the loan to assist with distribution.
Mandatory prepayment	The circumstances under which the loan must be repaid prior to the original repayment date. These can include KYC failures, change of control or beneficial ownership and illegality.

Representations and warranties	Key representations that the Obligors will be expected to make at each drawdown date and on a repeating basis on Interest Payment Dates.
Rental income collections	The mechanism by which rental income is collected by the managing agent of the property, the amounts that the managing agent may retain to pay costs and into which Borrower account (controlled by the Facility Agent) surplus funds should be deposited.
Payment waterfalls	The sequence and priority of payment from the Borrower's rent account (controlled by the Facility Agent) to the Finance Parties and ultimately the Borrower both pre and post Default.
General undertakings	General obligation that the Obligors will abide by during the term of the loan (e.g. not incurring any other indebtedness).
Property undertakings	Obligations the Borrower undertakes in respect of the security Property (e.g. restrictions on entering into, granting, amending, waiving, surrendering and forfeiting leases and consenting to assignments, subleases and rent reviews without Lender consent).
Information undertakings	Information undertakings of the obligors (e.g. provision of accounts, up-to-date tenancy schedules, ongoing KYC requirements).
Events of default	Circumstances which give rise to an Event of Default under the finance documents. These will typically include such things as non-payment of interest or principal, breach of Financial Covenants and insolvency of the Obligors, Sponsor, Ultimate Owners or Ultimate Controllers.
Conditions precedent	Any key conditions precedent to the disbursement of the loan such as corporate authorisations, satisfactory site visits, provision of a satisfactory business plan and due diligence requirements.
Insurance	Requirements relating to the insurances to be put in place in respect of the Property and the identity of the insurer. These can include the status of the Lenders (e.g. composite insured), notice periods that must be given prior to cancellation of any insurance and rating requirements for insurers.
Balance sheet management	Provisions relating to distribution of the loan including information disclosure, assistance by the Obligors and Sponsor and mechanics for re-tranching of the loan.

Publicity   How publicity around the provision of the loan will be managed.

Once heads of terms have been agreed between the originating lender and the borrower, due diligence and documentation can commence.

4.10   Legal and commercial due diligence[2]

Due diligence is the process of factual and legal investigation, research, analysis and discovery into the relevant borrower, asset, sponsor and other principal parties, typically undertaken by a prospective buyer, lender or investor prior to entering into a transaction.

The main purposes of due diligence are:

- to establish whether the relevant asset is sound for the purposes of investment or loan security;
- to verify information given, financial projections and/or assumptions as to the ownership, value and condition of the property, made in connection with the company, asset or transaction generally;
- to identify any risks inherent in the transaction or asset and mitigate these where possible;
- to comply with applicable statutory or regulatory requirements; and
- generally to assist the buyer, lender or investor in analysing the legal and, to the extent possible, factual issues associated with the relevant transaction, and deciding whether to proceed.

In a CRE lending context, the precise scope of the exercise will vary depending upon the nature and value of the transaction and/or asset, the lender's existing knowledge of the borrower, timing and cost considerations, but typically it involves an analysis of the buyer's/borrower's business plan, a review of the buyer's/borrower's, solvency, funding and tax position, enquires into the background, experience and credit record of the buyer/borrower, sponsors and/or other principal parties, a physical inspection of the property, a valuation of the property, an investigation of/report on the title to the property and/or legal restrictions affecting its use, a review of the stability of the rental income stream, the creditworthiness of the occupational tenants, the terms of the occupational leases and insurance and asset management arrangements, consideration of the principal insurances and consideration of the nature of the security to be granted and enforcement issues.

---

[2]   This section draws on the CREFC-Europe Guidelines for Due Diligence on Real Estate in the UK to which the author contributed. The Guidelines are available here: *http://www.crefc europe.org/wp-content/uploads/2015/02/CREFC-Europe-DD-Guide-Final.pdf* [Accessed 5 August 2016].

The purpose of requiring separate reports for different due diligence areas is to ensure that the best quality advice is available. Individual areas can be very specialised and necessitate particular expertise.

The two fundamental concerns of a lender are likely to be the ability of the borrower to repay the loan and the value (in both legal and monetary terms) of the security. These will shape the nature and extent of the due diligence—for example if the loan is being underwritten primarily on the basis of a sponsor guarantee, the level of property due diligence may be less than for a transaction where the asset is the only or primary collateral.

For a lender, the primary purpose of due diligence is to assist with the internal underwriting and credit review processes. In an acquisition finance context, a lender will often, to save costs and avoid duplication of reports, seek to rely on the due diligence carried out on behalf of the buyer and, whilst in many cases this will be acceptable where the respective interests coincide, consideration should be given to undertaking an independent review as that will not always be the case. It is also critical, in such a case, that the lender is able to rely on the reports provided for the borrower. The results should help to ensure that the appropriate provisions are included in the loan documents, the correct security is taken and all relevant conditions are imposed and satisfied.

Due diligence can be divided into four broad categories—transactional due diligence, property due diligence, tenant due diligence and insurance related due diligence. Consideration should also be given to the basis for instruction of due diligence reports and subsequent reliance issues.

4.10.1 *Transactional due diligence*

This category of enquires, checks and diligence relate to the commercial nature of the transaction and will usually be undertaken at an early stage by or on behalf of the lender. The principal purpose is to verify that there are no material structural flaws in the transaction structure and that the information and appraisals upon which the credit decision to lend is based are accurate and reasonable in the circumstances.

- **KYC and anti-money laundering**—These will vary from jurisdiction to jurisdiction but are principally designed to identify and check all principal persons involved with the buyer or borrower in order to facilitate a lender's duty to report any criminal or suspicious activity or circumstances. This is one of the reasons why it is important at the term sheet stage to identify the ultimate owners and controllers of the borrower and restrict these from changing without lender consent. The overall effect is to impose specific obligations upon organisations and professionals (including banks, funds, lawyers, accountants and surveyors) to check identities of individuals with whom they deal and the source of monies they receive. This due diligence is not optional—

any breach of the requirements could lead to criminal prosecution of the individual and/or organisation concerned.

- **Legal structure/ownership**—In order to facilitate the KYC exercise and assist with other components of the legal due diligence process a full understanding of the ownership structure is required, both in order to understand the financial resources of the ultimate owners (which give some comfort that in the event of distress they may be able to provide credit support whether or not there is a legally binding obligation to do so) and also to confirm that the laws of each relevant jurisdiction are compatible with taking or granting security over the jurisdiction in which the security property is located and that each entity is properly constituted with power and capacity to enter into the transaction. This comfort is usually given in the form of a legal opinion.

- **Legal opinion**—This is a document prepared by the lender's legal advisors and is intended to confirm that all the necessary formalities have been complied with, including that the borrower/security provider is duly incorporated and has the necessary capacity and authority, the borrower/security provider is not subject to any formal insolvency process, the documents and security created are validly executed and legally binding on and enforceable against all relevant parties and that the choice of law in the documents is compatible with, and judgments of the relevant courts are enforceable in the relevant jurisdiction. It should also highlight any post completion requirements (e.g. payment of taxes and/or registrations) that need to be addressed. A legal opinion should be provided by a law firm competent to practice in the relevant jurisdiction. It is rarely possible to provide a totally "clean" unqualified opinion and certain assumptions (for example that all parties other than those the subject of the opinion have full power and capacity to enter into the documents/transaction) and qualifications (e.g. as to any provisions of the relevant law which might inhibit or restrict enforcement) will therefore usually be made, but that said there should be no exclusions which effectively negate the value of the opinion itself.

- **Tax due diligence**—there may be taxes and withholding requirements which may take priority over the claims of the lenders and adversely affect the income from the security properties, particularly with the plans, at the time of writing, to restrict interest deductibility for tax purposes. The purpose of the tax due diligence is to identify these in order to enable mitigating actions to be taken.

4.10.2 *Property due diligence*

The focus of any CRE loan should be the underlying assets which form the core component of the lender's security package. In the past, mistakes have often been made by lenders where there has been overreliance on numbers in spreadsheets and valuations and consequently full property due diligence should be undertaken, bearing in mind in the process that the lender may become the owner of the asset if the borrower defaults.

- **Property inspection**—A physical inspection of the property being offered as security is very important in order to get a feel of what the property is actually like and the area in which it is located. During the visit a lender should also assess the conformity of physical outline of the property to any plan available, the occupants of the property (if it has been sub-let), the nature and status of surrounding buildings and competing stock, the area where the building is located in the context of transport, infrastructure and new development and the physical condition of the building and state of repair.

- **Development appraisal**—Most due diligence exercises focus on the existing state of the security properties at the date of origination only. Where the assets are long let and in excellent condition this may be sufficient, however where there is a business plan which is heavily reliant on re-letting or redevelopment, a development appraisal should be undertaken. This may be undertaken by an independent professional or by the valuer. The appraisal should consider the costs and valuation implications of the strategy proposed by the borrower, the impact on cash flows from the properties over the loan period and sensitivity analysis and scenario testing to determine a range of potential outcomes with a particular focus on adverse scenarios.

- **Asset and property management**—The proper and efficient management of a property is important in preserving and/or enhancing its value. It is important to draw a distinction between "property management", which is the day to day administrative management of a property including rent collection and service charge management and "asset management", which is the strategic asset planning required in order to meet the Borrower's long term objectives including letting, planning, refurbishment/repositioning and redevelopment. Asset and property managers should have appropriate professional qualifications, experience and track record of managing similar properties and systems and procedures in place for discharging their duties (especially in the context of handling monies from rental collections and service charge payments). Should the asset or property manager not perform as expected then it is important they can be replaced. If either is connected with the sponsor then it is important to put in place strict governance in relation to how monies are handled and when they may be extracted from the security pool. The asset and property manager's contractual arrangements with the borrower must be reviewed and have their duties and responsibilities both clearly defined as well as ensuring that none are omitted. Both need appropriate levels of professional indemnity and fidelity insurance and should have a separate duty of care with the lenders covering such matters as which accounts rental monies are paid into. Consideration should also be given to their fees and expenses—these should be fully disclosed, at market levels and covered in any financial appraisal and the loan documentation should specify when and how these can be paid.

- **Valuation**—Valuation reports are part of the standard package of due diligence for investment in, or lending secured on, property. A valuation underpins the investment or lending criteria and, in the context of it and other due diligence reports, crystallises the issues into an impact upon value. All lenders should therefore ensure that they can justify actions through professional valuations from firms with a coverage and skill-set appropriate to the portfolio or property in question—especially so since the advent of the valuer negligence claims seen in 2015 and 2016 and discussed further in Chapter 13. Valuations are typically instructed by lenders, although borrowers may instruct their own valuations but these will not be decisive for covenant testing purposes. A valuation is an opinion of the price that would be achieved for the sale of an asset (free of any corporate holding structure and encumbrances) at any given time assuming an adequate marketing period had elapsed. It is a snapshot as of the valuation date—it does not provide any indication of the future per-formance of the asset (although opinions on this can be expressed through report commentary or additional requested valuation bases). A valuer should provide valuations on appropriate bases to match both the asset being considered and the type of finance provided. The most common valuation bases are:

  1. Market Value—the valuer's opinion of the price that could be achieved for a sale of the property (ignoring any holding vehicle) on the valuation date assuming that a reasonable marketing period has elapsed;
  2. Market Value on the Special Assumption of Vacant Possession—often requested for commercial properties to assess the down-side risk, this is the valuer's opinion of the price that could be achieved if the property were sold on the valuation date fully vacant: a vacant possession value (VPV). A common mistake made by lenders is to assume that the VPV estimated by the valuer is the VPV at the point in the future when leases have terminated—this is not the case and the VPV at lease termination date is likely to be lower than current VPV (as building condition and therefore marketability generally declines over time);
  3. Market Rent or estimated rental value (ERV)—this is the valuer's opinion of the rent that can be achieved for the property if let on market terms (revealing whether rents under existing leases are higher or lower than prevailing rates);
  4. Reinstatement Cost Assessment—whilst not a formal valuation basis this is often requested as part of a finance valuation for checking the level of buildings insurance in place (it is usually provided on a non-reliance basis and should not be used for assessing buildings insurance cover—this should be commis-sioned from a qualified building surveyor).

- **Report or certificate on title**—This is a report usually prepared by the Borrower's legal advisors on the title, and other principal legal issues arising, with regard to the property to be provided as security. It should test, from the legal perspective, the assumptions made and information given concerning the property, and should state that the title is suitable for security purposes should the lender/mortgagee need to enforce. Ownership/title (including principal head lease terms) should be confirmed in all cases. A report on title should include an analysis of the results of searches of the local property register, local authority and any other entity where information on encumbrances and other matters affecting the property may be held, a review of the title documents, including subsisting mortgages and documents creating encumbrances to which the property is subject, a review of the relevant leases, an assessment of replies to questions commonly asked of property owners prior to sale/charging and consideration of the potential effects of any material relevant legislation or general legal provisions (for example legislation relating to tenant's security of tenure) which would qualify the specific provisions of any lease or title document. The report should include an explanation of any defects/omissions, an assessment of the implications and recommendations for remedy or mitigation and a general explanation of the potential effects of any material relevant legislation. As the lender often relies on a report prepared on behalf of the borrower, the lender's legal advisors will normally produce an overview report, which will highlight any issues which should be brought to the lender's attention in the context of financing or refinancing the purchase of a property. However, such an overview report will not amount to a further due diligence exercise and it is therefore critical to ensure that the lender can rely on the underlying certificate/report.
- **Mechanical & electrical (M&E) and structural survey**—This is a report (usually commissioned by the Borrower) that covers the physical quality of each building on a property from a technical, infrastructural, and architectural point of view and identifies potential or known technical deficiencies, compliance issues and risks. It should cover the regulatory compliance status of the buildings and surrounding sites, an evaluation of the current quality of the buildings and technical installations, a description of measures to achieve compliance and to address potential or known liabilities and repair issues from a technical, infrastructural, and architectural point of view. The report will usually also include a statutory compliance (including fire protection) review and investigations into the structure, fabric, external areas and mechanical, electrical and other systems of any building located on the property. Optional items such as flexibility in use, pre-assessment according to sustainability schemes (e.g. LEED, BREEAM, DGNB), a spot check measurement of areas, assessment of OPEX costs, completeness of handover documentation and insurance reinstatement cost can also be included.

- **Measurement survey**—The purpose of this report is to measure the security properties so as to ensure that, amongst other things, the valuation is accurate. Results should not only comprise floor plans but also highlight tenant areas and identify discrepancies in comparison to existing documents in order to facilitate assessment (by other consultants) on issues such as rental income and cash flows.
- **Environmental survey**—Environmental due diligence should always be undertaken as the presence of environmental contamination may have a material adverse effect on the value of the security properties. Generally this will be carried out in two stages—a preliminary desktop assessment to determine the potential for risk (in the UK knows as a "Phase I report") followed by further investigations to address areas or properties of high potential risk. A property can potentially be impacted by environmental issues, but the risks are greater for those that have historically been used for purposes (for example as a landfill site, mining or certain industrial processes such as rendering) that may have left a legacy of contamination, where current activities may be causing contamination, where surrounding properties currently or historically may have the potential to contaminate and/or adversely impact the security property and where deleterious materials (for example asbestos) were used in the construction of the property. Intrusive investigation is sometimes required if it is considered environmental contamination may be present in the ground. This can comprise a range of measures including installing boreholes, sampling soils and groundwater or assessing physical site characteristics such as the integrity of any underground storage tanks.
- **Planning report**—Unless there are indications of planning non-compliance, this is rarely required for existing properties where no redevelopment or change of use is contemplated. Where these aspects form a significant component of the business plan then a planning report should be commissioned. This will determine what (and to what extent) planning factors affect the development, redevelopment and/or change of use potential of the property, verify that all requisite consents have been obtained and that no changes have occurred which could affect the validity of these and/or require further approvals and check that all conditions to which any such consent is granted have been complied with.
- **Utilities report**—Where a development is being contemplated a specialist report may be advisable to check what services are available to the site, whether these have sufficient capacity (taking into account expected additional usage and demand) and what works are required to connect to the mains supply. Planning or construction matters and/or legal issues requiring an easement, licence or wayleave may also arise where the supply crosses other land.
- **Mining report**—Historical mining activity may physically affect a property, causing ground movement as the workings collapse and the ground consolidates as well as shafts forming a preferential pathway for the migration of potentially explosive gas. The presence of mine

works will typically be flagged during a standard environmental due diligence process and if this is deemed high risk a further specialist mining survey may be required.

- **Unexploded ordnance (UXO)**—Some properties may have been subject to bombing during World War 2. A basic ordnance assessment report will be undertaken as part of an environmental survey, however where development and deep excavation is contemplated in the business plan it may be appropriate to commission a UXO report.
- **Flood risk report**—A basic flood risk assessment will be carried out as part of the environmental survey but a specialist report may be appropriate to investigate further if this risk is deemed to be high.
- **Rights of light report**—In the UK a "right of light" gives a property owner (a "Dominant Owner") the legal right to receive light through defined apertures in buildings on their land. The burdened landowner (a "Servient Owner") cannot substantially interrupt this (for example by erecting a building in a way that blocks the light) without the consent of the Dominant Owner, who is prima facie entitled to an injunction to protect its right. The Dominant Owner may have express rights of light (set out in an agreement between the Dominant Owner and the Servient Owner) or, more commonly, undocumented prescriptive rights (acquired by 20 years' enjoyment of light over land owned by the Servient Owner). These are of particular concern where development or redevelopment is being contemplated and a specialist survey may be required to identify prescriptive rights. Specialist surveyors can provide advice as to whether such rights may subsist and/or whether specific designs will amount to an interference.
- **Infrastructure report**—Where a property is located close to an actual or proposed major national infrastructure development, for example a major waterway, port, power station, new road or railway a specialised report may be appropriate to identify any unusual risks to the property such as compulsory purchase.
- **Energy efficiency/performance**—Buildings in most developed jurisdictions are now subject to energy certification schemes and compulsory inspections for equipment such as of boilers and air-conditioners (new buildings will usually be required to comply with higher standards in this respect). A consequence of these is that some form of certificate must be made available to new tenants and purchasers of property. Generally, these may only be issued by competent, licensed persons and must be commissioned before marketing a property for sale is started. Where the properties to be financed do not meet current or future energy performance standards, the cost of bringing them into compliance should be assessed as this will have an impact on both the value and the borrower's business plan. In the UK, 2018 regulations will make it unlawful to let properties in England and Wales which do not meet a prescribed minimum energy performance standard (MEPS).

4.10.3 Tenant due diligence

The leases, the rental income from which forms an important part of the security underlying any CRE loan, are only as good as the ability of the tenants to meet the obligations outlined in them. It is therefore almost always appropriate to undertake due diligence into the credit quality of tenants and, if relevant, their guarantors. The amount of diligence required is driven principally by the concentration of tenants in the relevant property or portfolio—the ICR and LTV ratios for a loan which finances a property, which is single let or let to a small number of tenants (for example an office block), is far more sensitive to tenant failure than one secured on a multi-let building, such as a shopping centre.

There are a number of resources and techniques which can be used to judge tenant credit quality and quantify the risk of tenant default in the short/medium term. The most common are shown below (these are usually most effective when used together to build up a detailed picture of a company's financial health in the context of the market in which it operates).

4.10.4 Rating agencies

Tenants who issue publicly tradable debt securities (e.g. bonds) may have a rating from one or more of Standard & Poor's (S&P), Moody's, Fitch or DBRS. Each has a slightly different way of describing credit risk depending on the type of obligation issued, as will be discussed in Chapter 14.

A copy of the rating report from the rating agency, which contains commentary and analysis underlying the determined rating, can also be obtained but there is usually a cost to this. Where a borrower has several types of debt outstanding the most relevant rating is usually the "senior unsecured debt" rating which most closely approximates to the ranking of unpaid lease obligations in case of insolvency.

4.10.5 Credit checking agencies

Credit checking agencies can be a useful source of information where tenants are smaller and have not issued publicly tradable debt securities. Two of the largest credit checking agencies are Dun & Bradstreet (D&B) and Experian but, whilst reports from both of these contain useful data (especially where underlying properties are leased to large numbers of smaller tenants) it is important to remember that, given these agencies' high volume and low margin business models, there is a limit on the amount of analysis that each can perform and therefore individual ratings may present a misleading picture.

As a matter of good practice, external valuations should contain these wherever possible.

Experian

Experian have a system known as a "Delphi" score which indicates the risk of failure. The main Delphi score bands are reproduced below:

Delphi score band	Proportion of scored companies falling into band	Risk of failure
0	N / A	Serious Adverse Information or Dissolved
1 – 15	18.94%	Maximum Risk
16 – 25	9.92%	High Risk
26 – 50	23.94%	Above Average Risk
51 – 80	28.52%	Below Average Risk
81 – 90	14.08%	Low Risk
91 – 100	4.60%	Very Low Risk

Dun & Bradstreet

Dun & Bradstreet operate both a credit scoring system and a rating system. The rating system consists of a financial strength component and a credit risk indicator which is D&B's view of the likelihood of business failure within the next 12 months. The current financial strength and credit risk indicators are summarised below:

Financial strength indicators:

Based on Net Worth	Based on Capital	Net worth (GBP)
5A	5AA	> GBP 35,000,000
4A	4AA	GBP 15,000,000 – GBP 34,999,999
3A	3AA	7,000,000 – 14,999,999
2A	2AA	1,500,000 – 6,999,999
1A	1AA	700,000 – 1,499,999
A	AA	350,000 – 699,999
B	BB	200,000 – 349,999
C	CC	100,000 – 199,999
D	DD	70,000 – 99,999
E	EE	35,000 – 69,999
F	FF	20,000 – 34,999
G	GG	8,000 – 19,999
H	HH	Nil – 7,999

Credit risk indicators:

Risk indicator	Probability of failure	Guide to interpretation
1	Minimal risk	Good covenant
2	Low risk	
3	Slightly greater than average risk	Satisfactory covenant but needs monitoring
4	Significant risk	Unsatisfactory covenant – may well default – confirm quantum of rental deposit
--	Insufficient information	

4.10.6   Altman's Z-Score Model

A well known model for predicting financial distress is Altman's Z Score model. This uses variables which have been shown to be effective indicators and predictors of corporate distress and attempts to predict the probability that a firm will enter bankruptcy proceedings by applying weightings to a number of key financial ratios as follows:

	Public company	Private company
Inputs	X_1 = (Current Assets – Current Liabilities) /Total Assets X_2 = Retained Earnings/Total Assets X_3 = Earnings Before Interest and Taxes/Total Assets X_4 = Market Value of Equity/Book Value of Total Liabilities X_5 = Sales/Total Assets	X_1 = (Current Assets – Current Liabilities) /Total Assets X_2 = Retained Earnings/Total Assets X_3 = Earnings Before Interest and Taxes/Total Assets X_4 = Book Value of Equity/Book Value of Total Liabilities X_5 = Sales/Total Assets
Model	$Z = 1.2X_1 + 1.4X_2 + 3.3X_3 + 0.6X_4 + 1.0X_5$	$Z' = 0.717X_1 + 0.847X_2 + 3.107X_3 + 0.420X_4 + 0.998X_5$
Outputs	$Z > 2.99$ – low risk of failure $1.81 < Z < 2.99$ – elevated risk of failure $Z < 1.81$ – corporate distress	$Z > 2.9$ – low risk of failure $1.23 < Z < 2.9$ – elevated risk of failure $Z < 1.23$ – corporate distress

The model appears to be accurate in the short run, with an estimated 80%+ of firms with a Z score indicating corporate distress filing for bankruptcy within one financial statement period of the test being run but it is not recommended for use in analysing financial companies.

4.10.7 Credit default swap spreads

Credit default swaps (CDS) are a form of derivative, similar to insurance, entered into between a lender seeking protection from a credit risk and a counterparty who insures that risk. They are classed as swaps or contracts for differences as, when the relevant credit event occurs, the lender exchanges its loan for an agreed amount (usually the principal amount of the loan) with the counterparty. The premium charged by the counterparty is known as the CDS spread and, the higher this is, the higher the perceived market risk of a credit event occurring to the borrower.

CDS spreads can be a leading indicator of corporate distress in the public debt markets, in contrast to credit ratings which tend to be lagging indicators, but they are generally only available for very large borrowers for whose debt there is a high volume of CDS trading. They can be downloaded from Bloomberg and, whilst they are not always directly comparable between all borrowers, a good rule of thumb is that CDS spreads of less than 200 basis points (bps) are indicative of lower risk and spreads in excess of 500bps a good indicator of current or near term corporate distress.

4.10.8 Financial statement analysis

Financial statement analysis is the most effective way of judging the credit quality of smaller tenants although is also time consuming and may therefore not be suitable for large multi-let properties.

There are a number of standard analytical techniques that may be applicable to a business which, if used properly, can give a good insight into the creditworthiness of a tenant. In order to calculate these it is necessary first to extract a number of data points from the financial accounts. These include:

Net debt	The net amount of financial indebtedness that a company is carrying. It can be calculated as follows: Net Debt = Short Term Debt + Long Term Debt + Unfunded Pension Scheme Liabilities + Current Tax Due + Net MTM on Derivatives − Cash and cash equivalents
EBITDA	Earnings Before Interest, Tax, Depreciation and Amortisation. It is calculated by reversing all interest, tax, depreciation and amortisation out of net income (if the depreciation and amortisation expense is not shown on the face of the income statement then it can usually be found in the notes to the accounts).
EBTDAR	As EBITDA, but interest is not stripped out and rent payments are.
Interest	The net interest expense of the company

Leverage ratio (Net debt/EBITDA)—This shows how relatively indebted the tenant is by relating its net debt as a multiple of one year's EBITDA (the higher the ratio, the more indebted the company and hence the greater the risk of financial distress). A normal operating company that does not operate in a sector where high debt levels are normal (e.g. the property industry) with a ratio of less than 3x is generally considered to be conservatively geared. Ratios of between 3x and 6x are generally considered an indicator of a higher risk of default and ratios in excess of 6x (typical in leveraged buyout structures) are generally considered dangerous to the viability of a firm.

Interest Coverage Ratio (EBITDA/Net interest expense)—This shows how many times net interest expenses are covered by EBITDA (the lower the ratio, the greater the risk that the tenant will be unable to pay interest and may subsequently fail). A normal operating company that does not operate in a sector where high debt levels are normal would be considered conservatively geared if this ratio were in excess of 4x. Ratios of below 2x are generally a sign of over-gearing and an indicator of likely upcoming financial distress.

Rent cover ratio (EBTDAR/Rent)—This shows the headroom between the rent the tenant is paying and earnings available to meet that rent. It is typically used in sale and leaseback and OpCo/PropCo transactions, where the property is let to a single tenant, as a method of increasing the amount of debt that is available. A ratio of any less than 2x leaves the tenant vulnerable to not meeting its rental obligations as a result of a trading slowdown.

Apart from the ratio analysis outlined above, it is also worthwhile checking the following:

a) audited accounts should state that the business is a going concern and the audit opinion should be unqualified (a qualified, disclaimed or adverse audit opinion is a sign of financial irregularities which may threaten solvency); and

b) the firm should have an adequate liquidity profile—indications of this include having a reasonable amount of cash on hand, the presence of overdraft facilities and a staggered debt maturity profile (in the absence of these, even a firm with large profits and a high tangible net worth may be unable to pay its rent).

4.10.9 Insurance due diligence

The object of insurance due diligence is to determine historic exposure, examine the sufficiency of current insurance arrangements in force or proposed by the borrower and also assess whether risks currently insured will continue to be insurable in the future.

Depending on the type of transaction a lender may require a number of types of insurance to be put in place prior to advancing funds and then be maintained during the term of the loan.

Types of insurance

- **Buildings insurance** covers repair and reinstatement of the subject properties for a variety of risks;
- **Public liability insurance** protects against third party claims arising out of the ownership and management of the property—often included as a separate section in the buildings insurance policy;
- **Environmental risk insurance** covers liability arising from pollution and/or "clean-up" costs;
- **Professional indemnity insurance** should be taken out by any professional (e.g. a valuer, solicitor, or other professional or report provider) engaged in connection with a property against future claims for negligence;
- **Latent defects insurance** covers damage by unforeseen risks (e.g. rectification of a structural defect) not included in other policies and independent of the establishment of liability;
- **Warranty insurance** may be used where a sale agreement imposes warranties and indemnities upon the seller, but, if these cannot be given or there are concerns about the warrantor's ability to meet any claim, insurance may give comfort to the buyer and funder;
- **Defective title insurance** insures a defect in the legal title to the property (e.g. an old restrictive covenant prohibiting the current or proposed use);
- **Fidelity insurance** is distinct and separate from professional indemnity insurance and covers fraudulent actions by a party (for example a legal advisor stealing funds held on its client account).

A lender often has specific insurance requirements which necessitate amended or replacement cover. The lender will also want to be satisfied that the insurers are of sufficient financial status to support the credit rating of the loan and may also want a loss payee clause that provides for claims proceeds (usually above a specified amount) be paid only to it, thus avoiding the risk that a borrower might misappropriate these. There is also normally a requirement for the borrower and/or the insurers to notify the lender of any changes and non-payment of premium (allowing the lender to take appropriate steps to keep the cover in place).

The loan agreement will normally require insurance of any building against "all risks" in its reinstatement value plus loss of rent (usually for three years) if damage renders the property unlettable or triggers rent suspension clauses in leases. The loan documents may also require the lender to be an insured party in its own right (i.e. a composite insured, providing parallel cover unaffected by any act or omission of any insured parties) as anything less, for example interest noted, joint/co-insured or a general interest endorsement, may not be sufficient.

Copies of the actual policy documents with full schedules, reinstatement valuations, up-to-date endorsements and accurate and complete rent schedules should be vetted by an independent advisor (not the insured's placing broker) as documents prepared by other parties cannot be relied upon (especially where a third party is arranging the cover).

4.10.10   Other due diligence considerations

A due diligence report is only as good as:

(a)   the instruction letter which governs the appointment of the report provider;
(b)   the form of reliance on that report provided to a lender; and
(c)   the degree to which and amount of liability and professional indemnity insurance the author of the report has in place which the lender may call upon if the findings of the report are found to be erroneous resulting in an economic loss.

4.10.11   Instruction letters

The scope of engagement must be set out in a formal engagement letter written by the consultant/professional or in an instruction letter prepared by the buyer or lender. Ideally, this should be countersigned by the receiving party to confirm acceptance and is often subject to negotiation.

Such a letter should usually expressly set out and list an outline of the transaction contemplated, a description of the relevant property, confirmation of the type/purpose of report including the form and extent of reporting required, any exclusions, any particular assumptions to be made or disregarded, details of when the report is required, confirmation of any limitation or cap on the liability of the report provider plus details of their professional indemnity insurance and confirmation of fee basis and disbursements and/or other expenses agreed to be paid.

4.10.12   Reliance letters

Most due diligence reports contain restrictions on disclosure to, and reliance by, third parties. Any lender financing the purchase of real estate will, however, want to ensure it can rely on those reports because it or its advisers will have reviewed these and the decision to lend made on the assumption that the information contained in those reports is accurate. The lender will want to be able to claim compensation from the report provider for damages if the report is incorrect and, as a result, it suffers loss.

A lender will typically expect to be able freely to disclose each report to all relevant finance parties, including future finance parties and its advisers and rating agencies and other parties such as servicers.

4.11 Documentation

Once terms have been agreed, the documentation process follows, usually simultaneously with due diligence. The majority of larger CRE loans in the European market are documented on the basis of pre-prepared LMA REF facility agreement. See section 5.2.6 of Chapter 5.

4.12 Closing

Once due diligence is complete, the loan has been documented and conditions precedent are satisfied, the final stage of the origination process is closing (i.e. funding) the loan. Care must be taken by the originating lender to ensure that funds are available for disbursement following its commitment—this can be a particular issue for lenders whose own sources of funds require funding calls to be made in good time to investors. Cut off times for money transmission networks (e.g. CHAPS) should also be borne in mind.

4.13 Conclusion

In summary the CRE loan origination process is surprisingly complex, with a large number of steps needing to be undertaken between deal sourcing and closing, usually within tight timeframes. Coordination of the parties and professional advisers is key, and this is perhaps the most important function of the coverage bankers running a transaction. Whilst there will always be a temptation in the face of borrower pressure to disregard or cut corners or parts of the process, that temptation should always be balanced by remembering that CRE loans are typically advanced for longer maturities during which market conditions may radically change, and that the economics of CRE loan are in effect identical to a sold put option on the security property, and therefore the origination process must be handled with the utmost care.

Chapter 5

Leverage and the use of Subordinate Debt

Andrew V. Petersen,

Partner and Practice Area Leader–Finance, K&L Gates LLP

5.1   Introduction

As highlighted throughout this book, a significant development in the capital markets over the last two decades has been the arrival of real estate debt on the global stage as an asset class in its own right. Based on its increasing popularity, the financing and investment of CRE flourished in the market in the period up to 2007, as a result of a highly competitive CRE lending environment, yield compression and the evolution of attractive capital market exits.[1]

During this period, lenders were forced to be more innovative in structuring CRE loans to keep pace with (i) investors' vociferous appetite for CRE assets, (ii) the escalating need for leverage, and (iii) their competitors. As a result CRE quickly became seen not only as a hard asset but also a financial one. Consequently, lenders were forced to provide much higher amounts of leverage than they traditionally did, or may have been comfortable with. However, with the capital markets providing an exit, banks were able to package this additional leverage in a way that appealed to investors across the risk-tolerance spectrum and accommodated a mortgage borrower's desire, to constantly maximise leverage.

Moreover, CRE borrowers' demands for even more flexibility and leverage led to lenders undertaking a constant balancing exercise, between origination volume and their return on their product, without compromising any securitisation or syndication exit, or, in the environment that exists at the time of writing, a club deal exit.[2] This led to a marketplace where subordinate debt structures became commonplace.

In the US, where subordinate debt structures first emerged, originating lenders discovered that dividing or splitting a whole loan into multiple tranches enabled them to create a variety of debt instruments which would appeal to a broad array of investors, while meeting the demands of their mortgage borrowers for greater leverage and flexibility. For example, on a

---

[1]   See further Ch.1.
[2]   See further Ch.3.

highly-leveraged property, the related financing was typically structured so as to produce an investment grade portion of the debt that was included in a CMBS, with the remaining portion of the financing split into one or more subordinated tranches, often tailored to meet the requirements of the anticipated purchaser. Thus, for example, a certain investor's risk and return preference might cause such an investor to prefer a slice of the debt that represented 60–70% of the overall leverage of the financing; with other more opportunistic investors with more aggressive risk and return tolerances preferring more deeply subordinated, higher risk, higher-yielding tranches of the financing, at 70% plus. Methods adopted to achieve this balance or alignment of rights was achieved through the introduction of subordinated debt (junior or mezzanine) and the bifurcating of the commercial mortgage whole loan.

This development was not a new development in "traditional" (i.e. non-securitised or non-capital markets) global CRE finance transactions, with commercial mortgage loans with related bifurcated subordinate debt appearing frequently in the market. Gradually, such structures found their way into the CMBS market and 2003 witnessed one of the first European uses of an AB loan structure included in a CMBS deal, where the underlying whole loan was split into a separate participation in the underlying loan, with only the senior tranche being securitised and the junior tranches were held outside the CMBS.

Following this, between 2003 and 2007, the CMBS lending market witnessed a proliferation of highly complex modelled subordinate debt structures incorporating a concept of bifurcated or trifurcated real estate loans, comprising of A-1 or A-2, B, C or even D tranches, senior-subordinate tranches and mezzanine or junior debt. As discussed below and in the following Chapter, this practice generated highly flexible structures that built upon the emergence of CMBS as a product of innovation.[3] A product that allowed the subordinate debt to be tailored to comply with the demand in the market, the underlying borrowing group structure and the available lenders (and their legal and regulatory requirements).

Whilst the CRE financing market continues to operate at a vastly reduced level to the boom years of 2000 to 2007, at the time of writing, an improving and growing funding market is emerging. This means that, in an increasingly competitive market, senior lenders are able to pick and choose the deals and the pricing on such deals, with an increasing amount of senior debt becoming available for good secondary assets with secured income, as well as higher-priced defensive subordinated or stressed/distressed loan-on-loan financing. This is true, even of certain senior lenders that write cheques for substantial senior whole loans that internally will tranche or syndicate the loan to a mezzanine provider or fund set up or controlled by

---

[3] Andrew V. Petersen (ed.) *Commercial Mortgage-Backed Securitisation: Developments in the European Market*, 1st edn (London: Sweet & Maxwell, 2006), Ch.1. and 2nd edn (2012).

such senior lender. Thus, it has become a rare exception for real estate loans not to be structured with some form of multiple separate subordinate debt. Such structures apply to both single and multi-borrower transactions.

In this Chapter, the debt underlying such structures (mezzanine or tranched junior) will be referred to as subordinate debt and generally take one of the following two forms:

- a mezzanine loan interest which is documented pursuant to a separate loan and secured by a separate (or shared) security package ranking behind the security interests securing the senior or whole loan, or in certain cases a separate security pledge over the equity in the borrower (mezzanine debt);
- a B Loan within an AB loan structure, where the single whole loan is tranched into senior and subordinated tranches which are secured by a single security package (AB debt).

This Chapter will examine:

- the emergence of subordinate structures including the key principles and pricing of such structures;
- the common key principles of intercreditor terms surrounding subordinate structures[4];
- the economics and business case for utilising mezzanine debt and/or AB debt;
- the emergence of recent developments surrounding discounted purchase options (DPO).

5.2 The key principles of subordinate structures

It is important to understand the economics behind subordinate debt structures. Therefore the key principles that underpin such structures must be examined, while noting that there can be variations on all of these principles, as no two deals are the same and that each deal will be faced with unique characteristics based on asset type, obligor or borrower group structure (including any legal and regulatory and other restrictions regarding granting of security or historic tax liabilities).

5.2.1 Mezzanine debt

A typical mezzanine secured credit facility (the mezzanine facility) will comprise a term facility that is subordinate to, but coterminous with a senior loan facility. Often the mezzanine facility may increase by any

---

[4] Note that the key commercial terms and provisions of an intercreditor agreement will be considered in detail in the following Chapter and the key legal terms and provisions will be considered in Ch.7.

payment in kind (PIK) or other amounts accrued. Typical leverage will be an aggregate of the senior facility and mezzanine facility capped at a certain percentage (say 80%) of value of the underlying real estate portfolio. The senior facility will fund a lower percentage of the value, typically in the range of 60–70% LTV.

5.2.2 Mezzanine debt pricing

At the time of writing, there is no "typical" pricing of mezzanine debt. Pricing will be dependent on a number of factors, including the size and quality of the deal, the nature of the asset, the number and type of lenders chasing the deal, the economic power of the underlying sponsor and the jurisdiction of the underlying assets. For deals occurring at the time of writing, mezzanine pricing will be in a range from percentages in the high single digits to mid-teens per annum (all-in coupon) of which an element will often be structured to be payable in cash (cash pay interest) and an element may be PIK-ed.

Mezzanine debt may be further structured where the mezzanine lender receives a percentage of excess profits once the sponsor achieves a certain level of internal rate of return (IRR) known as a profit participation. The profit participation will be in addition to any fees and interest payable on the deal. Typically, a mezzanine lender will want to be compensated for its debt being repaid prior to the maturity date. Although, a voluntary pre-payment will be permitted at any time after the first year of the term mezzanine facility, prepayment fees will be payable to the mezzanine lender to protect a certain fixed level of return (say 1.35 times equity multiple) on the mezzanine debt. For example, if the mezzanine facility is prepaid and the mezzanine lender has not received a minimum of 1.35 times on the original principal amount of the mezzanine facility, then the mezzanine borrower will compensate the mezzanine lender for the difference between the amount actually received by the mezzanine lender and an amount equal to 1.35 times of the original principal amount. Alternatively, the mezzanine lender may agree an exit fee equal to a specific percentage of an amount repaid or prepaid.

Key terms of a senior loan facility sitting above a mezzanine facility may include: loan to value covenants, with a hard event of default triggered if LTV or ICR values raise above a certain percentage; a cash sweep triggered if LTV values are above a certain percentage, funded by equity or excess cash, and upon such sweep being activated monies being swept to repay the senior loan or placed in reserve to be retained for future cash flow shortages. A cash sweep will often continue until the LTV or ICR values reduce below a certain percentage on two consecutive interest payment dates (IPD).

5.2.3 Borrower PIK election period

Typically, on any IPD where there is a cash trap event caused by triggers in the senior facility which has the effect of stopping cash pay interest to the mezzanine facility (The PIK election does not apply to hard events of default), the borrower may make a PIK election where the total coupon is accrued or rolled and forms part of the mezzanine facility balance until the occurred amount is paid down by the borrower. Typically, the borrower will be limited to a maximum of two PIK elections during the term of the mezzanine loan and will not be able to use its PIK election if this would cause a breach of the mezzanine facility hard default covenants. Following any PIK election quarter where the borrower has no remaining PIK elections, a mezzanine facility event of default will be triggered if the mezzanine facility is not cash paid on any remaining IPD (and the cash escrow released to the mezzanine lender).

5.2.4 Typical mezzanine security package

In a senior/mezzanine funding structure, the senior loan will typically be advanced to the property owning company (the Senior Borrower) while the mezzanine loan will typically be advanced two levels, above the Senior Borrower, to the shareholder of the shareholder of the Senior Borrower (the Mezzanine Borrower). The Senior Borrower's shareholder (the Senior Parent) provides "insulation" to the senior lenders that mitigates the risk of the mezzanine lenders bringing claims against the senior lenders' own obligors.

The loan advanced to the Mezzanine Borrower will be on-lent to the Senior Parent and in turn on-lent to the Senior Borrower, in each case by way of an unsecured 'pay as you can' subordinated loan that will be contractually subordinated behind the senior loan and the mezzanine loan.

In a very simplistic case, the rental income stream from the Senior Borrower will then be utilised on a periodic basis:

- first to make payment of all fees, costs, expenses, interest and principal repayments due on the senior loan;
- secondly, provided there is no continuing default on the senior loan, up streamed to the Mezzanine Borrower to make payment of all fees, costs, expenses, interest and principal repayments due on the mezzanine loan.

For so long as the senior loan is in default, typically no payments are allowed to be made in respect of the mezzanine loan and all amounts available for distribution will be applied in repayment of the senior loan (or trapped in a senior controlled account) until it is repaid in full.

Subject to the differences in the overall structures and underlying borrower groups, security for a typical mezzanine facility will consist of the same typical security package expected for a senior facility, albeit on a sub-ordinated basis, which shall include the following:

Shared with the senior facility (on a subordinated basis) or separate second ranking, each to the extent applicable:

- legal charges over the properties;
- fixed and floating security over all the assets of the borrower(s), including without limitation all bank accounts, material contracts (such as managing agent contracts), insurance (including being co-insured), the hedging arrangements related to the mezzanine facility and all shareholder and other intra-group loan balances;
- deed of subordination between the mezzanine lenders and any shareholder loans or equity confirming neither interest nor repayment of any shareholder's loans or equity permitted until mezzanine facility fully repaid;
- a duty of care letter from the managing agents, if any; and
- any other security as required under the senior facility.

This is typically in the form of common or shared security whereby the senior security agent holds the security on trust for the benefit of the senior and the mezzanine finance parties, but sometimes by way of separate second ranking security. In both scenarios, the mezzanine finance parties will not be able to enforce such security interests until the senior finance parties have been repaid or enforced their security. In addition, the mezzanine finance parties will also take a first ranking charge over the shares in the Mezzanine Borrower and in the Senior Parent and over any intra-group loans made to the Mezzanine Borrower and to the Senior Parent. The common security is held for the benefit of all lenders, whereas the mezzanine security is granted solely for the benefit of the mezzanine finance parties. The mezzanine finance parties are typically free to enforce the first ranking mezzanine security following an event of default on the mezzanine loan for the purposes of taking control of the equity in the Mezzanine Borrower or the Senior Parent, subject to any restrictions in the intercreditor agreement.

In addition, based on potential deal structure and requirements of the mezzanine lender, a first ranking pledge of shares in the mezzanine bor-rower (or any other appropriate entity depending on the final structure of the transaction) representing control over the entirety of the properties. It is often requested that, in an acknowledgment of the credit support the mezzanine facility is providing and the first loss position it is in, such security is separate and not part of the security package for the senior facility and without any turnover obligation to the senior lenders upon exercise/enforcement or exercise of voting rights attaching to such shares.

112

Given the subordinated nature of the mezzanine loan, a senior default will always cross default and cause a default of the mezzanine loan. However, a mezzanine default should not result in a default of the senior loan.

5.2.5 Valuation

Often, the mezzanine lender shall, at the mezzanine borrower's expense, have the right once per year to call for a valuation in accordance with the RICS "red book" or at any time if it reasonably believes there may be a default or at any time if an event of default is outstanding. Typically, if the mezzanine lender uses this right (in addition to the standard annual valuation provided to the lenders at the borrower(s) expense) that the mezzanine lender will bear the costs of such additional valuation to the extent that this valuation does not result in a cash sweep or an event of default.

5.2.6 Documentation

The mezzanine facility will normally be documented by a facility agreement and related security documentation which are normally based on the Loan Market Association (LMA) documentation[5] used for the senior facility (often using the same form of senior facility after it has been negotiated with the senior borrower/sponsor), this agreement will set out (inter alia) the conditions precedent to drawing, representations and warranties, under-takings, events of default triggers, borrowing costs, pro-rata sharing, set-off, and other provisions usual for such transactions.

The mezzanine facility agreement outlines the relationship between the mezzanine borrower and mezzanine lenders, and an intercreditor agree-ment[6] outlines the relationship between lenders.

The 2012 Draft Guidelines and the LMA ICAs contemplate a transaction structure where two loans are advanced to finance CRE assets: a senior loan to the property owning entity (the propco) and a mezzanine loan to a mezzanine borrower (who is the sole shareholder of the parent of the propco). The effect of this structure is to structurally subordinate the

---

[5] On April 16, 2012, in an attempt to aid transparency and liquidity in the market, the Loan Market Association launched its recommended form of single currency term facility agreement for use in real estate multi-property investment transactions. The new document has assisted standardise the approach taken to real estate specific issues by reducing the time spent negotiating boiler-plate type clauses.

[6] On 10 June 2014 the Loan Market Association published a form structural subordination intercreditor agreement and in August 2016 the LMA produced a contractual subordination intercreditor agreement (the LMA ICAs) providing boiler plate and a structural framework. Whether an intercreditor agreement is based on the LMA ICAs or another form, commercial arrangements between lenders have been subject to on-going discussion and development and so, to supplement the 2012 Draft Guidelines, CREFC has in 2016 produced commentary on these commercial developments (the Intercreditor Agreements—commentary on recent commercial developments.

mezzanine loan to the senior loan. The intercreditor agreement, includes, amongst other provisions, the right of the mezzanine lender to freely enforce its security without triggering a change of control default or mandatory prepayment obligation under the senior facility. The right of the mezzanine lender to cure a senior event of default and the right to purchase the senior facility if accelerated may also be included. In addition to the foregoing, the senior lender will agree not to change any payment date or maturity, increase or vary any fee or interest payable, increase or vary principal or require amortisation or prepayment, or amend events of default without the prior written consent of the mezzanine lender. Often, it is required that the senior lender consult with the mezzanine lender prior to enforcing its security.

The documentation will also contain conditions precedent, undertakings and covenants, representations and warranties, customary for the financings the subject of the deal and in a form and substance satisfactory to the parties and at a minimum mirroring the conditions precedent under the senior facility. Both the commercial and legal terms of an intercreditor will be dealt with in the following two Chapters.

5.2.7 *The typical features of AB debt structures*

There are certain common features existing within AB debt structures.[7] One such feature is that, although B lenders lack the right to enforce the mortgage loan security they do typically benefit from certain rights following monetary events of default on mortgage loans, in a recognition that they are (as described above for mezzanine debt structures) in the first loss position.

Such rights are not usually available to junior first loss piece holders in a CMBS, known as the "B piece holders". The B piece holders in a CMBS hold the most junior note interest in a securitised pool of CMBS loans. They hold the "last pay" "first loss" note which do not represent individual loans and have no direct relationship with the mortgage borrower, and should not be confused with the B lenders or B loan holders.

B lenders are not obliged to exercise these rights, which vary from deal to deal and ultimately depend on the sophistication and the needs of the

---

[7] AB Structures were very popular in Europe from 2003 to 2007. See further A.V. Petersen, *Commercial Mortgage-Backed Securitisation: Developments in the European Market*, 1st edn (London: Sweet & Maxwell, 2006), Ch.8. As described herein, their popularity has lessened with the demise of the availability of financiers (and the absence of a fully functioning European CMBS market) that are prepared to arrange or originate a whole loan that will cover the whole of the required debt, although they are still used by certain senior lenders that originate a whole loan and internally tranche such loan into an AB structure and are, at the time of writing, emerging in the marketplace, in an attempt to be economically the same as a senior/mezzanine structure, necessitating the LMA launching their contractual subordination agreement in August 2016 and the CREFC-Europe launching commentary on such intercreditors in 2016.

parties. In theory, B lenders would generally only exercise their rights if the expected recoveries from the mortgage loan would thereby be enhanced. The exercise of cure and repurchase rights (which usually include the B lender's right to purchase the A loan as a means of avoiding enforcement proceedings by the A lender following a mortgage loan payment default by making whole a mortgage loan payment) has implications for the A loan and thereby the rated bonds and in such cases, the structure of the inter-creditor and servicing agreements are extremely important and require detailed analysis and consideration.

5.2.8   *The attraction of AB structures*

AB structures were very popular during the growth of the European CMBS market in the decade up to 2007. From the perspective of the most junior investor in a CMBS, as payments to the B loan can be subordinated to the A loan in an AB structure, CMBS transactions with AB loans are preferable to CMBS transactions without such a structure. This is because, depending on the transaction structure, as we have seen above, payments to the B lender may be cut off entirely following an underlying mortgage loan monetary event of default until the A loan has been redeemed in full.

Thus, by creating a B loan that is held outside the CMBS, loss severity can be viewed as having been reduced as, following a loan monetary event of default, the A lender benefits from the subordination of payments to the B loan by having the ability to take control over the whole loan and instigate enforcement proceedings before a shortfall has occurred on the A loan, and therefore the rated bonds. This allocates the risks associated with incor-porating the additional debt efficiently throughout the market and is pre-ferable to a standard CMBS, in which senior noteholders gain control only after realised losses have eroded the value of the junior CMBS notes. Fur-thermore, this results in an improvement of the subordination levels of the rated securities versus the subordination levels if the entire loan was included in the CMBS.

However, for multi-loan CMBS transactions, which may pool together various A loans, the additional credit support provided by the sub-ordinated B loans is specific to the individual A loans to which the B loan relates and is therefore not provided to the entire transaction, usually resulting in higher credit enhancement being expected for the lowest-rated level of securitised notes. If losses incurred on any one loan exceed the amount of the B loan, the excess will be allocated to the lowest-rated class of notes.

It is important to note, however, that although a higher percentage of the rated securities are considered investment grade in a pool that is made up of A loans, the investment-grade debt as a percentage of the first-mortgage debt (the first-mortgage debt equalling the combined total of all A and B loans) is not higher. In fact, in most cases the investment-grade debt as a percentage of the first-mortgage debt would be lower than if the entire loan were deposited into the CMBS. This is due to the weaker form of credit support provided by the B loans that are not cross collateralised, compared to subordinate bonds, which are cross collateralised. For instance, in a pool made up of A loans, if a loan incurs losses, upon the erosion of the B loans, losses would continue upward into the rated securities and not to the other B loans held outside of the CMBS.

At the time of publication of the 2012 Draft Guidelines it was felt that whole loan structures would not typically find market favour. However, at the time of writing it has become apparent that certain lenders and equity sponsors have a preference to utilise whole loan structures when con-structing debt finance packages. This is because whole loan structures can have certain advantages over structural subordination models—both on the borrower and on the lender sides.

From a prospective B loan purchaser's perspective there are several benefits to an AB structure. First, the B loan is secured by a preferred form of security, a first mortgage. Also, for many of the institutional B loan pur-chasers, risk-based capital reserve requirements are less onerous for B loans than that of subordinate bonds. Having to reserve less capital against B loans effectively increases their overall net yield. When contrasted with investing in subordinate bonds, the primary benefit of the B loan is the ability to isolate risk to one asset. Unlike a subordinate bond where losses can be incurred from any one asset in a pool, the loss potential of a B loan is limited to the asset(s) serving as security to the B loan. This makes it easier than in a whole loan CMBS, where the originator, when placing a pooled bottom class of risk, has to try and sell this risk to an investor willing to take the first loss risk on all of the loans in the pool. As a result, risk is effectively dealt with much more discretely and the risk assessment of potential sub-ordinate debt investors is also much more efficient since the due diligence process of evaluating one asset (the B loan) is considerably easier than evaluation of a pool of subordinate bonds. This is especially so in the European market where there is a multitude of loans and variety of asset classes within pools. Another benefit, as discussed above, is the ability to either purchase or cure upon an event of default. While this feature may not always be a viable option, it may be a potential exit strategy. Further, on the lender side there is additional flexibility offered to arrangers in being able to originate a whole loan and determine the sizing and pricing of the tranching at a later stage. Quicker execution may therefore be available if a whole loan structure is used.

5.2.9 Why utilise subordinated structures?

Given the additional complexity of subordinate structures, the natural question to ask is why incorporate this type of instrument into real estate debt transaction? It would be much simpler to just have one lender and one loan. But from a business standpoint, the use of subordinate debt is important to a number of stakeholders in a real estate transaction.

From the sponsor's point of view, mezzanine debt typically carries a return that is lower than the return required by the common equity and allows the sponsor to invest less cash in a transaction, whether it is for an acquisition, or, refinance. This additional leverage can be accretive to the deal and usually helps to enhance the deal's internal rate of return (IRR).

From the senior lender's point of view, since mezzanine debt is structurally subordinate to the first mortgage, it provides credit enhancement and a significant capital buffer against collateral value deterioration. Moreover, by incorporating subordinate, the senior lender is able to reduce the amount of risk they would otherwise have to hold on their balance sheet.

From the mezzanine lender's perspective, subordinate debt produces a higher yield than senior debt, because there is more risk involved on a relative basis, but is still collateralised.

5.3 Key principles of a senior/mezzanine intercreditor agreement

As discussed above, in a subordinate structure, the legal relationship between the lenders is delineated in an intercreditor agreement (intercreditor), which both grants and limits certain important rights (which may have an impact on the senior lender), to the subordinate lender. Whilst the next two Chapters will examine the key commercial and legal terms and provisions of an intercreditor agreement in detail, this Chapter will briefly set out certain key structural features.

The list below is not intended to be exhaustive and there can be variations on all of these principles as no two deals are the same and each deal will be faced with unique characteristics based on asset type, obligor or borrower group structure (including any legal and regulatory and other restrictions regarding granting of security or historic tax liabilities). The principles below represent the key terms and principles for an intercreditor governing the relationship between a senior loan (senior loan) made by a senior lender (the senior creditor) and a mezzanine loan (the mezzanine loan) made by a mezzanine lender (the mezzanine creditor). In such a hypothetical case, the principal terms that may be included in the intercreditor are as follows:

5.3.1 *Acceleration/enforcement*

The senior lenders will have the right, subject to any applicable cure rights the mezzanine lenders may have and subject to certain standstill periods relating to the mezzanine lenders' rights to acquire the equity in the Mezzanine Borrower and their rights to acquire the senior debt from the senior lenders, to take any enforcement action in respect of the senior loan including enforcement of its security (whether common security or stand alone first ranking security) once the senior loan is subject to a continuing event of default. In recognition of the subordinated nature of the mezzanine loan, the mezzanine lenders will have no right to enforce their interests in the common security or their standalone second ranking security until the senior loan has been repaid in full or if the senior lenders otherwise consent or, following a fairly lengthy period of time (and often subject to a raft of other conditions) after the senior lenders have failed to take enforcement action following the occurrence of a senior event of default. In the event that the mezzanine lenders do instruct the enforcement of common security this does not afford the mezzanine lenders with the right to control or direct how the security is enforced and the common security agent would still act on the instructions of the senior creditors. Any proceeds of enforcement would be applied first to discharge the senior debt in full and, once discharged, be applied in and towards the discharge of the mezzanine debt. The mezzanine creditor may require the mezzanine loan facility agent/ security trustee to exercise voting rights under the first-ranking share pledge over the mezzanine loan borrower (or if the mezzanine loan borrower is the same as the senior loan borrower, over the borrower's parent company) if an event of default (other than a material default (as defined below)) is outstanding.

The senior creditor shall not require nor instruct the senior loan facility agent/security trustee to take any enforcement action under any security unless it has first consulted with the mezzanine creditor or if the period to exercise any mezzanine lender cure rights have expired.

It is common practice in senior-mezzanine lending structures which include structural subordination, for the mezzanine lenders to have security over the shares in the Mezzanine Borrower. Upon an event of default under the mezzanine loan agreement (which would not in itself constitute an event of default under the senior loan agreement), the mezzanine lenders would be entitled to enforce the share security and acquire all (but not some) of the shares in the Mezzanine Borrower, effectively to step into the equity of the Mezzanine Borrower and, indirectly, the Senior Parent and, in turn, the Senior Borrower.

Exercising these acquisition rights is ordinarily subject to a number of conditions, including curing any remediable senior events of default that are then continuing.

5.3.2 Permitted payments

The intercreditor will contain waterfalls setting out the priority of payments prior to and following the occurrence of a material default. Prior to a material default (as defined below), interest and principal payments (including any prepayment fees) made by the borrower are to be applied in accordance with the loan agreement.

Upon the occurrence and continuance of a material senior default, cash will be distributed sequentially according to a post-default waterfall resulting in a cessation of cash to the mezzanine creditor and diversion of cashflow to the senior creditor. This will be dealt with in further detail in the following Chapter.

5.3.3 Limit on senior loan

Often any senior loan headroom concept in an intercreditor will be capped at 5–10% to deal with the provision of property protection loans. This means that any increase in the amount of senior loan above any permitted headroom will rank behind the mezzanine loan (excluding any increase in amount of mezzanine loan).

5.3.4 Cure rights

Upon the occurrence of an event of default (other than certain insolvency related events of default) which is remediable, the mezzanine creditor may remedy that default within grace periods between certain fixed periods (say 15 business days in relation to a payment default and 20 business days in relation to other defaults)—each period will be negotiated depending on the circumstances of the deal.

It will often be requested that cure periods for defaults other than payment defaults should be unlimited for so long as the mezzanine creditor is diligently pursuing a cure, again to be negotiated on a case by case basis. Further, the mezzanine creditor may request that it may take such action to remedy as it considers desirable in the circumstances. For remedy of a payment default or financial covenant default, certain actions may be expressly permitted including:

- prepaying the senior loan (excluding default interest and prepayment fees);
- paying the amount of the shortfall;
- placing a deposit on behalf of the senior loan facility agent/security trustee into a cure loan deposit account in an amount equal to the additional amount of net rental income which would have been required to have been received by the obligor to have complied with the relevant financial covenant; or
- obtaining and delivering to the senior loan facility agent/security trustee an unconditional and irrevocable standby letter of credit payable on demand and in an amount equal to the additional amount of net rental income which would have been required to have been received by the obligor to have complied with the relevant financial covenant.

The mezzanine lenders will be limited in the number of times they can exercise their cure rights. Typically, an intercreditor will provide a limit on the number of times that a payment default can be cured, so that the cure right may not be exercised more than a fixed number of times, say twice consecutively in any one 12-month period and no more than four to six times during the term of the facility. It will further be requested that there shall be no limit on the number of times a payment default may be cured where such default is continuing for a 90-day period or more and that there will be no limit on curing other defaults (to the extent the borrower's cure rights are unlimited). An intercreditor may also specify the numbers of cures are limited to one more than the Senior Borrower has under the senior facility agreement. Each time the Senior Borrower exercises a cure right it reduces the number of cures available to the mezzanine lenders and vice versa.

Often it will be provided that any repayment of cure payments made by the mezzanine creditor in respect of cure rights will rank behind the senior loan but ahead of the mezzanine loan. Further, during the exercise of cure rights (and the applicable grace periods for making cures), the senior creditor shall be prohibited from taking enforcement action in respect of any relevant event of default.

For so long as the mezzanine lenders are exercising their cure rights within the permitted timeframe the senior lenders will be prohibited from taking any enforcement action with respect to the event of default which is the subject of the cure rights. However, if another senior event of default occurs which the mezzanine lenders are either not entitled to cure or are not exercising their right to cure, then the senior lenders will be entitled to take enforcement action in respect of that event of default.

5.3.5 *Purchase/buy-out rights*

In recognition that it is best to have an incentivised mezzanine lender in the deal compared to a dis-incentivised sponsor or borrower, the intercreditor will typically provide that at any time after the occurrence of any event of default under the senior loan or any enforcement action, the mezzanine creditor may elect to acquire the senior loan at par plus accrued interest, any swap breakage costs and funding break costs incurred by the senior creditor as a result of the transfer but excluding prepayment fees and default interest or at a price as otherwise agreed between the lenders.

5.3.6 *Amendment rights*

In further recognition of the interconnection between the senior loan and the mezzanine loan, an intercreditor will often provide that certain material economic provisions of the senior loan finance documents must not be amended or waived without the prior consent of the mezzanine creditor. These are dealt with in detail in the following two Chapters.

5.3.7 Consultation

An intercreditor may provide that a senior creditor and a senior loan facility agent/security trustee will notify and consult with the mezzanine creditor (without the need for their approval save for enforcement action) before taking any formal step to exercise any remedy against the borrower or taking any enforcement action (which shall require the approval of the mezzanine creditor), save where the senior creditor reasonably determines that immediate enforcement action is necessary in order to prevent the material diminution to the value, use or operation of the security or a material adverse effect to the interests of the senior creditor under the senior loan finance documents—the so-called senior creditor override—a provision that acknowledges the position of the senior loan and its security and the position of the senior creditor in maintaining control of its security and its recovery on the senior loan.

5.3.8 Developments involving DPOs

A major effect that emerged in 2007 as lenders/investors withdrew credit was the ever-decreasing pool of investors buying CMBS. With the origination/distribution model that CMBS shops had relied on effectively closing down, many originators and holders of debt, faced with the prospect of having to sell the logjam or overhang of assets remaining on their books that were destined for a CMBS execution, turned to borrower or sponsor affiliates to buy some of their own debt. The lack of liquidity in the market drove pricing and values down, thus borrowers and sponsors saw sense for them to use available cash to purchase perfectly good debt (in their eyes).

Thus the DPO market was born and with the market evolving very rapidly and investors in short supply and senior bankers (and their new state shareholders) demanding the mortgage-laden balance sheets of the banks be cleared out before the prospect of any true market in CRE lending commencing once again.

A DPO purchase is not without its challenges. In most cases, CMBS documents do not provide for such a transfer without the involvement and agreement of the CMBS parties, being the issuer, noteholders and the B lender. Often CMBS servicing agreements[8] will state that except as contemplated by the issuer deed of charge and the intercreditor agreement, a servicer will not be permitted to dispose of any loan or any B piece. In addition, the usual forms of power of attorney granted under a CMBS deal normally expressly prohibit a servicer from selling the debt to the borrower. Further, typically an intercreditor will not provide for the sale of the debt or B piece and the issuer deed of charge often states that a sale of any of the issuer's loans is not permitted unless the note trustee is enforcing its

---

[8] See further Ch.11.

security or its sale back to the originator under the original mortgage loan sale agreement. Moreover, as far as an issuer is concerned, it is usually restricted from disposing of its assets unless it has the consent of the note trustee. The note trustee would usually not give its consent unless it gets the consent of the most senior class of noteholders.[9] Moreover, the intercreditor will often contain an absolute restriction on the B lender selling its loan to the borrower or an affiliate of a borrower. Therefore, the B lender would need the consent of the issuer and the facility agent to undertake such a sale.

Notwithstanding these challenges and any prohibitions in the intercreditor, the DPO market still, at the time of writing, remains popular and consent to a transfer of the B loan to a borrower/sponsor affiliate may be sought on the basis that the rights of any B lender (that is also a sponsor or borrower affiliate) should be turned off and should not be exercisable whilst the B lender remains a borrower or sponsor affiliate. This has the effect that, immediately following any such transfer, the B lender will not be able to exercise, have exercised on its behalf (other than by a servicer or a special servicer in accordance with the terms of the servicing agreement) or have accruing to it any cure, enforcement, consultation, approval, appointment and/or control rights (together the "Rights") otherwise available to it under the terms of the underlying credit agreement, the intercreditor and/or the servicing agreement.

Typically, following a DPO to a borrower or its affiliate, the Rights should be reinstated (1) for so long as the B lender (A) does not control or manage (in each case directly or indirectly) the management or voting rights in the mortgage borrower or an affiliate of the mortgage borrower; (B) is not controlled or managed (in each case directly or indirectly) by a mortgage borrower or an affiliate of the mortgage borrower; (C) is not party to any arrangements (the "Arrangements") with any other entity pursuant to which the mortgage borrower or any of its affiliates would have any indirect control of whatsoever nature in relation to any of the rights; and, for the avoidance of doubt, (D) is not a mortgage borrower or an affiliate of the mortgage borrower, in each case being confirmed to the reasonable satisfaction of the security agent; or (2) with respect to the whole or any part of the transferred B loans, following a subsequent transfer or assignment of such participation by the B lender, as discussed below.

Moreover, the transfer should further provide that each of the servicer and the special servicer will be required to notify the B lender (or any of its designees) with respect to material actions (as determined by the servicer and/or special servicer acting reasonably) to be taken with respect to the whole loan provided that: (A) neither the servicer or, as the case may be, the special servicer will be required to disclose any information to the B lender that, in the discretion of the servicer or the special servicer (acting reasonably), as applicable, will compromise the position of the other lenders in the

---

[9] See further Ch.13 where the role of the trustee is further discussed.

deal or reveal any strategy of the other lenders that could compromise the position of the other lenders with respect to the whole loan; (B) no such notification will be required where immediate action is required to be taken in accordance with the Servicing Standard[10]; and, for the avoidance of doubt, (C) no such rights shall oblige the servicer and/or special servicer to take into account any advice, direction or representation made by the B lender in connection with such notification.

Furthermore, the B lender should agree that, prior to any subsequent assignment or transfer of whole or any part of any transferred B loan being effective (along with the ability to exercise all or any corresponding rights), (i) the B lender either confirms or procures confirmation to a security agent that the subsequent assignee/B lender is a "qualifying lender"; and (ii) the conditions set out in each of the underlying credit agreement and the Intercreditor agreement must be otherwise complied with.

5.4   Conclusion

This Chapter has highlighted the purposes, general key features, risks, and benefits provided by typical subordinate structures. Prior to 2007, many regarded the introduction of mezzanine debt and/or AB debt as a positive development, since certain features of the structures behind such debt provided additional benefits that were unavailable to lenders in standard bilateral commercial mortgage loan financings. Such benefits may not necessarily translate into improved credit enhancement levels for loans structured as AB loans. That being said, it is generally recognised that the structural features of subordinate debt ensure that a default of the whole mortgage loan does not necessarily result in a shortfall of funds to, and therefore a default of, the senior loan. In particular, it may be seen that the cure rights of the subordinate lender, the priority of all payments to the senior loan and the enforcement rights of the senior lender reduce the probability of default of the whole loan, leading to the conclusion that subordinate structures provide benefits to rated classes of bonds in single-loan transactions.

Moreover, as is apparent in the restructuring market that has emerged since 2007, whole loan slicing and dicing ultimately creates a variety of interested parties, (whose interests are often at odds) having a variety of consent and approval rights over both "routine" mortgage borrower actions such as alterations and lease approvals as well as more complex issues such as material financial modifications. In a whole mortgage loan with multiple pari passu senior tranches, subordinate tranches and possibly mezzanine loans, it is easy to see how a once relatively easy process quickly becomes extremely complicated and convoluted, and will require more time and

---

[10]   For further detailed discussions of the servicing standard and the rights and obligations of the servicer and the special servicer, see Chs 9, 10 and 11.

effort to process, which inevitably leads to increased costs and possibly delays in restructuring the debt.

While certain deemed consent rights are much more commonplace in an effort to streamline this process, as we shall see in the following two Chapters, any insolvency proceedings are bound to be infinitely more complex, with the potential for large-scale conflict among the various stakeholders. Nowhere is this more apparent than in the market conditions witnessed since 2008. In the post GFC market that exists at the time of writing, workouts and stressed properties are more apparent than in the last decade and the role of the intercreditor in such workouts are usually not viewed as a productive outcome to the innovative structuring that has developed over the last few years, as the parties to the intercreditor attempt to agree what rights they thought they had.

In past real estate cycles,[11] a mortgage borrower may have only had to negotiate with one secured creditor, a mortgage bank or at worst a small syndicate of such banks. With the continued popularity of utilising subordinate debt in a transaction, the economic tightrope is walked by many interested parties—hedge funds, distressed debt funds or opportunistic "vulture" funds, even borrower or sponsor affiliates together with numerous lawyers representing each of the parties. In the end, only time will tell if the overall impact slicing and dicing, and the effect of intercreditor arrangements, have had a detrimental impact on mortgage borrowers, originating lenders, the restructuring of commercial mortgage and CMBS loans and commercial mortgage loan servicing in general. What is certain is subordinate debt and the intercreditors that are required to document such structures are here to stay.

---

[11] See Chs 1 and 2.

Chapter 6

The Modern Intercreditor Agreement: Commercial Terms and Issues

Duncan Batty,

M&G Investments[1]

6.1 Introduction

As highlighted in the previous Chapter, of all the legal documents entered into in real estate finance transactions, arguably the intercreditor is the document which has undergone the mostly pronounced shift from its pre GFC form. Whilst loan agreements have been bolstered with credit enhancing features like cash sweeps and security packages have been supplemented with security over intra-borrower group subordinated debt, ultimately the basic rights and obligations of the parties are consistent with the equivalent pre GFC documents. The same cannot be said of an intercreditor, where rights and obligations are now fundamentally different.

At its most basic, the intercreditor agreement sets out the rights, obligations and ranking of the claims of the senior and junior lenders, facility agent(s), security agent(s) and hedge counter parties vis a vis each other. There is of course much more detail and nuance than this and it is these more detailed commercial provisions which will be explored below, and in the following Chapter the legal provisions will be explored in further detail.

One element needs to be emphasised at the outset: this Chapter is not designed to provide a view on what is "right" or "wrong" or whether certain positions should be accepted by certain parties. These decisions will of course be negotiated on a deal by deal basis depending on the circumstances in question and the relative negotiating position of the parties. Rather this Chapter is designed to highlight some of the key commercial issues, concepts and points of negotiation.

---

[1] This material contains the opinions of the author but not necessarily those of M&G Investments and such opinions are subject to change without notice.

6.2 Structure

The first question to consider is the deal structure, as the precise format of the intercreditor will depend on this and how the junior debt is to be brought into the overall transaction. As was discussed in the previous Chapter, post GFC, the bulk of junior debt has been loaned through structurally subordinated mezzanine loans. Under this structure the senior loan is typically advanced to the property owning vehicle or vehicles and the junior loan is to a borrowing entity further up the corporate structure from the senior borrowers under its own loan agreement. In turn the junior loan is downstreamed to the senior borrower by way of intercompany loan and cash flow is transferred up the structure to the mezzanine borrower by way of interest payments on the inter company loan. In this Chapter this loan structure shall be referred to as a "structurally subordinated" loan. The popularity of this structure has meant this has received attention from industry bodies, with organisations such as the LMA and CREFC producing template documentation, term sheets and guidance notes.[2]

The alternative approach is to utilise an A/B loan structure. Under this structure both senior and junior loans are advanced to the same borrowing entity under a single loan agreement or "whole loan", with a single amount being loaned and a single coupon being paid by the borrower. This structure was very popular pre-GFC and as discussed in the previous Chapter is becoming more prominent in the market at the time of writing.

There is a third approach which is something of a hybrid, whereby a separate senior loan and mezzanine loan are advanced to the same borrowing vehicle under separate loan agreements.

The intercreditor agreement will of course need to be tailored to reflect the structure used. Many of the provisions below are relevant for both structures but nuances for each structure will be highlighted where relevant. In this Chapter the term "senior lender" is used to describe both the senior lender under a structurally subordinated loan and the A lender under an A/B loan and the term "junior lender" is used to describe both the junior lender under a structurally subordinated loan and the B lender under an A/B loan. Where specific differences depending on structure are relevant these have been highlighted.

6.3 Who should be party to the intercreditor?

This may seem a very basic question but it does warrant discussion. Clearly the various lenders in the deal will need to be party to the intercreditor in their relevant capacities, usually either as senior lender, junior lender or

---

[2] Further in August 2016 the LMA have produced a contractual subordination intercreditor agreement with CREFC-Europe also publishing guidelines in 2016.

both. In addition, anyone with an interest in the security package and cash flow should be party, most likely to be a hedge provider where deal cash flow is funding ongoing hedge payments and the security package is securing any out of the money mark to market exposure on the hedge. The facility agent and security agent (both for the senior loan and mezzanine loan where relevant) should be party, as their role in relation to payment and other administration and holding security respectively will be dictated by both the loan agreement and the intercreditor.

The main question is whether the borrower should be party. In a structurally subordinated loan there is usually no debate about this: the intercreditor will impose certain obligations on the borrower (for example in relation to intra-company loan payments to transfer cashflow up the structure to pay mezzanine loan interest) therefore the borrower needs to be party. This does however give the borrower details of certain rights of the lenders vis a vis each other and may give the borrower an advantage in a negotiation with either or both lenders at a later date, such as in a distressed scenario.

The situation is not so clear cut in an A/B loan. Here the intercreditor will set out the quantum of the senior and junior loans and the returns being paid to each alongside the various other rights of the lenders against each other. The lenders may not wish to give away this information to the borrower and this keeps intra lender rights away from borrower eyes—this may result in certain economic information being dealt with in a side letter between the lenders. The downside of this is that if the borrower is not a party then the intercreditor clearly cannot operate as a variation to the loan agreement which in turn introduces the prospect of the junior lender being affected by an available funds cap. This occurs where junior interest payments are shut off and cash for these is diverted to delever the senior loan. Should this happen then the respective senior and junior balances have moved out of line from their day one position so the single coupon paid by the borrower will not be enough to fund all senior and junior interest and the junior will have no ability to claim the shortfall from the borrower. This could be avoided by making the borrower party to the A/B intercreditor and creating an obligation on the borrower to pay both senior and junior interest even if the principal balances become misaligned in this way. The desire to resist revealing economics to the borrower may override this and it is a risk the junior lender will have to accept in this structure.

6.4 Security Interests and Enforcement

6.4.1 "Common Security"

When it comes to the security over the properties and other assets which are the subject of the financing taken by both the senior and junior lenders and regulated by the intercreditor (known as the "common security") the standard position is that the senior lenders control the timing and method of enforcement of this common security at their discretion, subject to some nuances worth noting:

1.   The senior lender will often be obliged to give the junior lenders a short notice period before taking any enforcement action to give the junior lender the chance to act themselves, for example by curing. The senior lender will usually look for an override so that this requirement can be dispensed with should they consider urgent action to be necessary.
2.   The junior lender will usually seek a contractual reassurance in the intercreditor that the senior lender will use reasonable endeavours to maximise the proceeds of recovery. This is tantamount to an extension of the duty owed by the senior lender at law to the equity holder and, provided the wording does not exceed this general duty, does not impose additional obligations on the senior lender. The senior lender should of course ensure that there is a carve out for the actions of insolvency practitioners they appoint so they are not liable for the actions of any third party practitioner they engage.
3.   In scenarios where the junior lender does not have any separate security which they can enforce independently (discussed below), they may seek an ability to force enforcement action after a specific time period of non-action by the senior lender. This seeks to give the junior lender some sort of ability to force activity rather than being stuck in a passive position ad inifitum. From the senior lender's perspective the time period involved needs to be considered carefully, in particular whether this might give long enough to conclude restructuring discussions with the borrower or whether the period can be extended if these discussions are progressing positively. Consideration should also be given to a value cover test before the senior lender is obliged to take enforcement action, so the senior lender cannot be forced to enforce when there is a chance they may not fully recover.

6.4.2 *"Junior lender only" security*

A feature of the post GFC market has been the desire of junior lenders to have their own security which they can enforce independently of the senior lender. Typically this consists of shares in an entity further up the chain of ownership from the senior borrowers and sits alongside the common security. This separate security gives the junior lender a self-help type remedy but does create a number of issues to be considered.

In a structurally subordinated loan context this security instrument can be easily created—there is a separate junior loan which this piece of security can clearly secure. In an A/B context matters are not so clear—there is only a single whole loan after all and so a separate payment obligation which could be secured by this share security does not exist. In theory this can be achieved in an A/B context by expressing this share security to secure the payment obligations under the whole loan, but to state in the intercreditor that the junior lender is the sole party able to enforce this share security. However careful analysis of the legal regimes involved is needed before concluding that this can definitively have effect.

The enforcement of any junior only share security also has consequences:

(a) this enforcement will almost certainly trigger a change of control under the senior loan so the junior lender will want a carve out from this should they enforce. The senior lenders may not automatically be prepared to agree to this unless there are restrictions on the identity of the holder of the shares post enforcement and administrative matters like KYC/AML have been taken care of;

(b) the senior lender should ensure in their initial due diligence that any enforcement by the junior lender does not create any tax consequences to the overall lending structure, for example de-grouping charges or clawbacks due to the change of ownership and measures taken or restrictions imposed if this is relevant;

(c) the senior lender should take care to ensure that junior lender enforcement does not prejudice their own enforcement ability. This could happen where the junior lender takes share security over the parent of the senior borrowers. If the junior lender enforced and put the parent into an insolvency process which triggered a moratorium, the senior lender may not be able to enforce its share security over the senior borrowers whilst the moratorium prevails. This can usually be avoided by including another intermediate company between the senior borrowers and the entity over which the junior lender has share security; and

(d) the junior lender may wish for a period post enforcement during which outstanding defaults on the senior loan can be cured (for example there may be matters which cannot be cured until they formally take control). On the contrary, the senior lender may not be prepared to waive change of control unless all issues on the senior loan have been dealt with, so a negotiation over cure rights and standstill periods whilst these are being dealt with is likely.

6.5 Cashflow and Payments Waterfalls

The cashflow arrangements under a structurally subordinated loan and an A/B loan fundamentally differ, however the general principles of payment arrangements are relatively similar. In (very brief) summary, under a structurally subordinated loan, cash flows through the various accounts and payments waterfalls under the senior loan agreement, before being transferred to a mezzanine account and then flowing through a separate account and waterfall arrangement under the mezzanine loan. This is not necessary under the A/B loan as there is a single cashflow with respect to the whole loan, which is allocated between senior lenders and junior lenders under the intercreditor agreement. Note here that it is not just rental income which needs to be considered but also the application of disposal proceeds and other potential income of the borrower such as surrender premia and insurance proceeds.

The general principle however is that, provided certain specific trigger events have not occurred, contracted payments are made to both the senior lenders and the junior lenders as set out in the senior and junior loan agreements (in a structurally subordinated loan) or under the whole loan agreement and intercreditor (in an A/B loan). Should these trigger events occur then payments to the junior lenders cease (subject to certain exceptions), with excess cashflow being taken by the senior lender and applied to amortise the senior loan. This trigger point is typically the occurrence of a "Material Senior Default".

6.5.1 Material Senior Default

One of the key concepts in the intercreditor is the Material Senior Default. This features in a number of the key provisions of the document in addition to cashflow, for example when the junior lender purchase right arises.

The circumstances for the Material Senior Default are, in essence, the point at which the senior lender has become deeply concerned about the underlying loan it has made. The usual construct therefore is for a Material Senior Default to be triggered upon a non-payment default, a senior financial covenant default, an insolvency event and enforcement action being taken. These are explored in more detail as follows:

(a) Non-payment—this seems logical, with a non-payment being one of the most serious defaults. Both non-payment of principal and interest should be covered. In a senior and mezzanine loan the non-payment is clear to see—the senior loan has its own independent payment obligations and it is clear when these have not been met. The A/B loan is a little less clear and there is sometimes a debate over whether the Material Senior Default should be triggered on non-payment of the whole loan or just the A loan. The standard position is that the trigger is non-payment under the whole loan—the borrower is under a single payment obligation and it has not been able to comply with this and so is in a heavily stressed position, even though the A loan may still be covered. The junior lender counter to this is that the A lender is in a better position than they would be a structurally subordinated arrangement where the trigger would only be non-payment of the senior loan only.

(b) Senior financial covenant breach—this is a heavily negotiated section of the intercreditor. As the title suggests, this tests the loan metrics against the senior loan only. As per non-payment, in a structurally subordinated loan, matters are a bit more straightforward as these covenants will be set out in the senior loan agreement itself and there is a clear senior loan and interest obligation to test against. In an A/B loan this is not the case and the intercreditor will usually include a regime to test against the A loan only, with the methodology following that of the whole loan covenants but looking at the A loan and interest only. It is worth noting here that this creates an additional testing obligation which will create more work for the servicer or whoever monitors this.

The main area of debate here concerns the trigger point for the senior financial covenant breach. The starting point is the whole loan (or mezzanine loan in a structurally subordinated context) level. The junior lender will usually require the senior loan covenant to be tripped some time after this—they want an element of breathing space after the whole loan or mezzanine loan covenant is breached before payments to them are shut off to try and negotiate directly with the sponsor or take their own enforcement action where they have their own share security. What the senior lender can accept is ultimately a credit matter in the circumstances of the deal looking at the senior loan position at the point of the whole loan or mezzanine loan default. It may be that the senior loan is also very stressed at this point so no headroom can be given, or it may feel some further deterioration can be absorbed before getting too concerned. Of course, a sudden shock such as a major fall in value or a significant decrease in income may override any mezzanine breathing space built in to the covenant levels.

(c) Insolvency—this trigger again seems entirely logical and bites in the times of extreme stress. Typically the insolvency triggers will mirror those in the underlying loan agreement (usually by cross reference to the relevant clauses). There is usually not a great deal of negotiation of this limb, although the junior lender should take care to ensure the drafting covers "actual" insolvency events rather than preliminary steps, for example a "meeting with creditors" could in theory include an initial discussion with lenders over restructuring terms and which would not be a "true" insolvency event.

(d) Enforcement action—this trigger is an extension of the other limbs: if matters have become so serious that enforcement action is being taken by the senior lender then it will not be prepared for payments to be made to the junior lender. There is still scope for discussion about this trigger point in relation to what should constitute "enforcement action". The senior lender will seek for this to be as wide as possible; the junior lender will try and limit this to "true" action like appointment of receivers rather than anything which could be considered a preliminary step.

Whilst the circumstances above represent the typical framework of the Material Senior Default concept, there may be other deal specific circumstances which could feature in the provision. Given the importance of the concept, these would need to be fundamental matters affecting the credit and would need to be addressed at an early stage with the junior lender.

Examples could be not signing or regearing a key lease by a certain date or not selling an asset for a certain price with a certain timeframe. Where these elements are a fundamental part of the underwriting of the deal and their failure to occur materially impacts the credit position, then there is a stronger argument that they should be included. These will usually be heavily resisted by the junior lender, especially where they are items which they cannot cure.

6.5.2   *Payment flows following a Material Senior Default*

As mentioned above, typically a Material Senior Default means all payments to the junior lender cease and all cash is applied to pay senior principal and interest. However, the junior lender will typically seek to negotiate exceptions to this cessation of payments. Often they will seek for interest they would have received to be transferred to an escrow account and held for a certain period (say six months). If the Material Senior Default has ceased (for example due to a temporary issue) or if the senior lender has not taken enforcement action at the end of this period, then this amount will be released back to the junior lender. This provides the junior lender with protection against temporary short term issues and gives the senior lender an incentive to take action to deal with the issue rather than sitting on their hands with nothing being paid to the junior lender. In the event that enforcement action is taken then this amount will be applied to pay down the senior loan. The junior lender may also seek to negotiate payments for junior loan agency fees or corporate costs of the junior borrowers in a structurally subordinated loan context to ensure that the junior loan continues to be serviced and the junior borrowers can continue to operate.

In an A/B loan context the junior lender needs to take particular care where the borrower is not party to the intercreditor. In this scenario there is a finite cashflow representing the borrower's payment obligation under the loan. Part of this cashflow is to be used to pay interest and principal on the junior loan and the borrower, not being party to the intercreditor, does not know what this is. Following the Material Senior Default (subject to the exceptions above) this junior interest and principal element of the cashflow will actually be applied to pay down the senior debt only, reducing the proportion of senior and increasing the proportion of junior debt in the overall deal. This in turn means an available funds cap is hit: there will not be enough cash to pay the interest expected by both the senior lender and the junior lender going forward and the situation will become more pronounced as time continues. The junior lenders return from the deal is therefore eroded. As the borrower is not party to the intercreditor and has no idea of these arrangements, the junior lender will not be able to make a claim for this lost return.

The same issue does not apply in a structurally subordinated loan where interest under the separate junior loan continues to accrue if not paid. The issue arguably will not arise if the borrower is a party to the intercreditor—

the junior lender will argue here that the intercreditor varies the loan agreement and creates two separate debt obligations payable by the borrower, so interest on the junior loan continues to accrue when not paid. The borrower will of course resist this, reasoning that they have met their payment obligations under the whole loan and have therefore discharged their duties.

6.6 Junior Lender Purchase Option

The right for the junior lender to purchase the senior loan is relatively common in intercreditor agreements, both for structural subordination and A/B deals. Junior lenders request this right to enable them to take ownership of the senior loan and therefore take control of the total debt stack, allowing elements like work outs and restructurings to be driven by the junior lender. The junior lender may view prospects for the underlying property or the workout strategy differently to the senior lender and want to eliminate the senior lender from the process to ensure their agenda can be pursued without interruption.

Of course, the senior loan will continue to earn the senior interest rate following the purchase and will therefore dilute the junior lender return. The junior lender will also have to come up with a proportionally large amount of capital to make the purchase given the senior loan will usually occupy the bulk of the total debt in place.

The right to purchase is typically triggered on a Material Senior Default occurring or the senior lender giving notice of their intention to take enforcement action. This seems logical as this is the point matters are stressed and the senior lender will take control of cashflow, so the junior lender exercising this right will allow them to take back control.

The purchase price for the senior loan will usually be specified in the intercreditor and will usually require a purchase at par (rather than market value) plus accrued interest and break costs at the point of purchase. Whether prepayment fees should be included is usually a matter of debate. The senior lender may argue here that they are being forced to transfer which is akin to being forced to accept a voluntary prepayment from the borrower and therefore prepayment fees should apply. To put it another way the senior lender may have been perfectly happy to continue to collect their coupon in the circumstances, particularly if they consider covenant breaches to be temporary, so would expect a prepayment fee if they were to be prepaid. This is particularly important when matching adjustment eligibility is being sought and disapplication of prepayment fees through no action of the senior lender may impact capital treatment. One potential compromise here is for the purchase price to include prepayment fees if the purchase is prior to the senior lender notifying the junior lender of its intention to take enforcement action, but to exclude prepayment fees afterwards. The rationale here is that if the senior lender has decided the situation is sufficiently serious to warrant enforcement action then they may well settle to be paid back at par without any additional prepayment fee.

Mechanically, any transfer to the junior lender will typically take place by way of transfer certificate under the transfer provision of the loan agreement. Timing surrounding any transfer will typically be a matter of negotiation—the junior lender will usually want a specific period to get the necessary approvals and assemble the capital to make the purchase and to know that the senior lender cannot enforce during that period; in return the senior lender will only be prepared to commit to not take enforcement action for specific periods. This situation is especially relevant where the junior lender needs time to assemble the capital to make the purchase, for example a debt fund which needs to call cash from its investors. One solution to this is to give a short timeframe for the junior lender to commit to make a purchase and then a longer period to assemble the capital if the commitment to purchase has been made, balancing the senior lender desire to minimise the period of uncertainty surrounding with the time requirements of the junior lender.

Finally there is the issue of hedging arrangements to consider. The senior lender may not be able to continue to provide hedging arrangements for the senior loan if they are not also the lender, so may require the transferee of the loan to also take a transfer of the senior hedging arrangements. Again this will impact the economic position being purchased by the junior lender and may not be possible under the constitutional documents of the junior lender.

For all of these reasons it is perhaps no surprise that this right is rarely exercised by the junior lender and is more of a theoretical right rather than an extremely useful practical tool.

6.7 Cure Rights

Typically the intercreditor will include the ability for the junior lender to cure certain curable breaches of the senior loan. From a practical perspective these are most likely to be non-payment events or financial covenant breaches. The junior lender wants this ability to delay problems under the senior loan, for example when they think there is a temporary issue, and ensure that their cashflow is maintained and drastic action like enforcement is not taken by the senior lender.

Typically the method of cure is aligned to that given to the underlying borrower in the loan agreement and cures will be aggregated with those given to the borrower to ensure there is a limit on these. In the structurally subordinated loan then the intercreditor sets these items out and, as the borrower is party, can include provisions whereby the borrower agrees that any cure payments operate as an additional advance under the junior loan and that the exercise by the junior lender of a cure right removes a borrower cure right under the loan agreement.

The A/B intercreditor does introduce difficulties, however, where the borrower is not party to the intercreditor. In terms of the number of cures, the borrower will not be aware that the B lender has exercised a cure right and has not agreed to the B lender cures being aggregated with their cures under the loan agreement. Therefore if borrower cures after the junior lender has exercised a cure right they can do so under the loan agreement regime. In turn the senior lender should be aware this could mean that cure rights are exercised on more occasions than initially contemplated (note that where the borrower cures first then the position is clear: that borrower cure takes one cure away from the junior lender).

Secondly, the method of cure and the impact of this needs to be considered. Typically the underlying loan will provide for a cure by paying down the loan to achieve compliance or by depositing funds which would, if applied to pay down the loan, achieve compliance. The aim of the senior lender here is to de-risk, and reducing their balance in this way does this. The matter is clear where the borrower does this: the debt balance is reduced (or will be once deposited cash is used to pay down debt) with the corresponding reduction in the obligations under the loan. Where the junior lender does this in an A/B context the position is not so clear. The junior lender knows that they will hit the available funds cap if the senior and junior debt balances become misaligned and this will become more pronounced if part of the A loan becomes permanently extinguished rather than diluting the junior lender return by paying interest at the A rate. In addition, the borrower is not aware of any principal reduction as the "repayment" is outside of their eyeshot under the intercreditor. The method to effect this junior lender cure in the A/B context is to say that the junior lender cure occurs by way of a transfer of the relevant part of the A debt to the junior lender (at par and usually with any other items the borrower would have paid by curing under the loan agreement such as break costs and prepayment fees where relevant). This ensures that the senior debt balance is reduced, meeting the senior lenders' need and preserves the debt balance so part of the junior loan now earns interest at the A rate, diluting the junior return but to a lesser extent than if the relevant part of the A debt had been permanently extinguished.

Finally, timing of the cure is a matter of negotiation. The junior lender will usually require a period after the borrower's cure ability has expired to make their cure (the junior lender will not want to cure if the borrower may also do so). As per the purchase option above, the compromise position is often a shorter time period for the junior lender to commit to the cure and then a longer period to effect this.

6.8   Voting Rights and Decision Making

The intercreditor will typically include a regime regarding lender voting which overrides the regime set out in the underlying loan agreements. This is necessary for both senior and junior lender who would find it intolerable for certain terms of the senior/junior (as appropriate) loan to be amended without their consent.

The main clauses of the senior and junior loans which cannot be amended (or waived to create the same effect) without the consent of the other lender are:

(a)   economic terms such as interest rate arrangements and fees—the junior lender cannot accept the senior loan increasing its coupon and reducing cashflow available to them; the senior lender cannot accept the additional stress put on the borrower by junior lender increasing their coupon;

(b)   repayment arrangements—the junior lender does not want senior repayment arrangements changing, whether through additional amortisation taking up cashflow, by extensions pushing back the time they can take action or by changes which might bring forward the maturity of the senior loan. Note here there is sometimes an option for the senior lender to grant a short extension of the senior loan (say six months) without junior lender consent to ensure a refinancing which has been slightly delayed is not prejudiced. The senior lender concerns are reciprocated in relation to equivalent amendments to the junior loan;

(c)   debt quantum—again the junior lender cannot accept additional senior ranking debt being introduced ahead of them into the deal and the senior is unlikely to accept the additional pressure that extra junior debt brings. Note here that sometimes the senior is allowed to introduce a small amount of senior debt into the structure (usually capped at 5% of the senior loan) for emergency matters which need to be paid and junior debt may be allowed to be brought in for matters like cures up to certain specific amounts;

(d)   financial covenant and cash sweep levels—both the senior and the junior lender will not want the other's financial covenants to be amended. Making these tighter increases the likelihood of default under senior and junior loan so will be resisted by both parties. The junior lender may also have an interest in the senior lender not relaxing their financial covenants as they may be taking some credit support from the senior covenants (in particular cash sweeps due to the implicit deleveraging of the junior loan from prepayment of the senior loan). Each party should also restrict amendments to the method of calculation as well as the covenant levels—changes to calculation methodology could make covenants more difficult to comply with;

(e)   cashflow arrangements—cashflow arrangements will be heavily reviewed by all parties at the outset to ensure they are comfortable with payment flows through the structure, so it will usually not be acceptable for these to be changed. This is particularly important in a structurally subordinated loan where cash needs to flow through senior and junior loan accounts in a prescribed way to ensure payments at the relevant levels of the structure are made; and

(f)   creation of "more onerous obligations"—a catch all provision will usually be included preventing the parties from agreeing to any changes which create "more onerous obligations" on the relevant borrower. This seems a relatively reasonable and pragmatic solution to the issue that neither senior nor junior lender wants the other to amend their loan in a way which can increase the risk of default in the other loan and saves a lengthy list of potential amendments to every clause in the underlying loan documents.

There may also be other deal-specific items to consider, for example leasing activity requirements or timing of mandatory disposals. Note also that these restrictions do not restrict matters which have been pre-agreed in the senior and junior loan documents at the outset, for example property protection loans. The lenders should therefore conduct a thorough review of each of their document packages before entering into the loans to make sure they are comfortable with them at the outset.

Whilst these restrictions do protect the lenders vis-à-vis each other, they do make the loan somewhat more cumbersome to manage and may meet resistance from a borrower wary of prolonged debates for consents and waivers.

These restrictions also do mean that a full restructure of either senior or junior loan in stressed circumstances is likely to be impossible without the consent of the other lender, introducing the scope for lenders to be difficult to extract "hold out" value. The most obvious situation for this is when the junior lender is out of the money (i.e. real estate value is below the senior loan principal) and refuses to consent to a restructuring plan to try and create some "nuisance value" from their position. One potential solution to this is a "control valuation event" type principle, whereby junior lender rights are excluded in the event that real estate value is below the senior liabilities. This protects the senior lender (and to some extent the borrower) but will be heavily resisted by the junior lender, who will argue that the value fall could be temporary so cannot tolerate amendments being made which could cut them out of the picture during this period. The junior lender will also argue that the borrower always has to be involved in any restructuring discussion and the junior lender should not be excluded from proceedings whilst the borrower remains involved. Compromises may exist in relation to the matters which can be changed without junior lender consent in this "control valuation event" situation, for example it not applying to the absolutely key items but other less important matters being

137

covered. Reference to the transferability may also be relevant—the senior lender may be able to get comfortable with the likelihood of the original junior lender not seeking to exploit this "nuisance value" but, if the junior loan is freely transferable, there is no guarantee that the original junior lender will continue to hold the loan through its term. A concept whereby the "control valuation event" applies to transferees from the original junior lender may warrant exploration.

Another element often debated in this context is the existence of a "deemed consent" provision for matters falling outside the key elements identified above. Under this mechanism, if the senior lender agrees to an item then the junior lender will be deemed to have given their approval. This scenario usually exists in the A/B loan in a roundabout way—these type of items will usually require majority lender consent rather than all lender consent, so the senior lender will usually be able to force these through by virtue of holding a majority lender position. The same is not the case in the structurally subordinated loan: here there are separate senior and mezzanine loan agreements typically on mirror terms (save for the key economic items) and borrower consent under both loan agreements are needed. Junior lenders typically resist this, arguing that their rights under their loan agreement should not be able to be overridden in this way, so this is one aspect where the A/B loan structure improves the position of the senior lender.

6.9   Transferability and Disenfranchisement

Rights to transfer are typically hotly contested both under the loan agreement and the intercreditor. Lenders' concerns mirror the borrower's concerns here: the identity of their fellow lenders is an important factor in entering into the deal in the first place. Parties may also be prepared to concede certain positions under the intercreditor to some lenders but not to others. This has to be balanced by the general desire (and for some institutions the requirement) from lenders to be able to transfer their holdings in loans without restriction. For that reason it is unusual for the intercreditor to impose more restrictions than conceded to the borrower in the underlying loan agreement.

The lenders should however consider whether specific positions are being taken due to the identity of the day one lender (whether senior or junior) and if so then consideration should be given to building mechanics into the intercreditor to switch off or switch on certain provisions should the original party transfer their holding. This will of course meet resistance due to the impact this has on liquidity.

Lenders can also potentially protect themselves with pre-emption rights, rights of first refusal or "last look" type provisions, so that they have an option to step in if the other party is looking to transfer. The decision as to whether to take on the position being sold or live with the incoming lender can then be made at the time of transfer.

As was discussed in the previous Chapter, a further consideration relating to the transferability of the loans is disenfranchisement. The usual position is, not surprisingly, that entities which hold an interest in both the senior loan and the junior loan are disenfranchised for voting purposes under both loans. It is relatively hard to negotiate this to the contrary but care should be taken to ensure that the drafting is not too wide to create some unintended consequences, for example including "Affiliates" where lenders are large organisations might include entities which technically fall within the definition but which in reality are not at all connected. Looking at this another way, where lenders are funds then disenfranchisement may need to encompass funds managed by the same manager which hold an interest in both the senior and junior loan.

6.10 Conclusion

This Chapter has aimed to give an insight into the key commercial elements for parties to consider when negotiating intercreditor agreements. At the time of writing, there is no real "market standard" position on these items: instead they are very much negotiated on a deal by deal basis according to the unique terms of the deal and the relative negotiating power of the parties. Even from a deal structuring perspective there is no evidence of clear preference for a structurally subordinated lending structure or a whole loan structure, with each having their own positive and negative features (see above and the previous Chapter for more detail about this). Structural subordination has been most popular in the post GFC environment but there has been an increasing use of whole loans, especially from institutions which seek to originate a loan to the borrower, carve this up and then sell the senior or junior piece to a third party. Without a clear preference for either structure it is important to be aware of the issues which arise for both structures and for negotiations to be framed accordingly. Where there is a bit more standardisation in the market is in respect of the legal terms, which are covered in more detail in the following Chapter.

As we have seen from the previous Chapter, subordinate debt is a valuable feature of the real estate finance market, adding flexibility into the capital structure and increasing the options available for both lenders and borrowers. As the post GFC market becomes more mature and increasingly complex lending structures arise to meet lender and borrower demand, the prevalence of subordinated debt may well increase. In turn this means that intercreditor agreements will continue to be entered into and the points of negotiation will continue to be relevant for market participants.

Chapter 7

The Modern Intercreditor Agreement: Legal Terms and Issues

Diego Shin,

Special Counsel, K&L Gates LLP

Philip Moore,

Executive Director, Highbridge Principal Strategies

7.1 Introduction

When this Chapter was published in the preceding edition to this book in 2012, the main focus of the discussion on intercreditor agreements was the A/B intercreditor as such senior/junior lender arrangement was, and for the most part continues to be, the most relevant document setting out the relationship, rights and obligations of senior and junior lenders where the senior loan is placed into a CMBS transaction. Given the lack of new CMBS transactions at that time and that any such new CMBS deals were being structured on a simpler basis (i.e. single loans, single borrowers and backed by stronger performing real estate assets) if compared with the more vibrant and active period before the GFC, the issues discovered from working out stressed CMBS transactions, the losses that many B lenders faced in the market and the simpler structure of CMBS transactions overall, legitimately resulted in a fairly obvious conclusion that A/B intercreditors were perhaps not as necessary as they had once been before.

This conclusion, that can fairly be said was shared by the marketplace overall, resulted in very little notice of the A/B intercreditor in favour of the senior/mezzanine intercreditor, the latter more relevant in the market place and accompanied by the introduction of new specialist alternative lenders in the marketplace providing that extra space of necessary capital that traditional senior lenders were no longer able or willing to finance. This point was acknowledged to such a degree in the market place that the Commercial Real Estate Finance Council (CREFC) and Loan Market Association (LMA) produced guidelines and, in the latter case, a template intercreditor agreement between the period 2012 and 2014 which relegated any discussion of the A/B intercreditor to the back of the room.[1] Rightly so, the senior/mezzanine intercreditor was the main discussion point, the most useful document to concentrate on in practice and an attempt to standardise the basic framework of such an agreement was undertaken by the LMA as referred to above.

So whilst the senior/mezzanine intercreditor remains the more relevant and commonly used transaction document out of the two, the A/B intercreditor has, as discussed in the previous two Chapters, resurfaced at the time of writing. The reason for this may well be due to the flexibility it provides—it does not require that the pricing and tranching of the loan be set out at the time of the origination of the underlying loan, it does not require the more cumbersome borrower group structure to be organised and maintained and it may well be just a lot quicker to put in place. This Chapter will look at intercreditor agreements in both their senior/mezzanine and A/B variants. For these purposes, as in the previous two Chapters, references to "senior loan" will be used interchangeably to refer to the senior or "A" interest in a whole loan, the actual whole loan itself or, in the context of a senior/mezzanine structure, the senior component of that arrangement, whilst references to a "junior loan" may refer to either a "B loan" or "B tranche" of a whole loan or a subordinated interest to such whole loan, be it a mezzanine or other interest. The use of the term "junior loan" may also be deemed to include references to more subordinated tranches in a whole loan in the context where there are more than two tranches of debt. Naturally, where the distinction is of paramount importance to differentiate a senior/mezzanine arrangement from an A/B whole loan structure, this will be highlighted. What this Chapter is not intended to discuss are intercreditor agreements in the context of subordinated loans, debt or equity provided by companies related to the underlying borrowers and which would otherwise be expected to be fully subordinated to the interests of third party lenders financing the transaction save to mention that senior/mezzanine intercreditor arrangements will typically also accomplish the purpose of setting out the subordination of such intragroup debt to third party financing.

7.2 Basic principles

When discussing intercreditor agreements in the context of CRE transactions, practitioners tend to differentiate between intercreditor agreements establishing the rights of lenders in either a senior/mezzanine lending arrangement or as lenders in a whole loan scenario. The former consists, in simple terms, of at least two distinct loans being made to two separate entities in a borrower group where the senior loan is made to the property owning vehicle, or immediate parent thereof, which obligations are secured

---

[1]   However, the LMA in August 2016 in recognising the market's move to contractual subordination published a template intercreditor agreement. Further CREFC-Europe published guidelines in 2016 on contractual subordination intercreditor agreements.

by, among other things, a mortgage over the relevant property while the mezzanine loan is made to a holding company (typically at least two steps removed from the ownership of the senior borrower vehicle) which will be secured by the same security securing the senior loan as well as by (again, among other things) "independent" security which only benefits the mezzanine lenders over the equity interests in the mezzanine borrower. The latter involves discussing the rights of lenders in respect of the same loan to which such lenders are parties, made to the same borrower or borrowers and secured by the same security package which loan is tranched, usually with no visibility of the borrower as to the arrangement, setting a contractual subordination between of a junior tranche to a senior tranche of such loan.

As to the reasons why lenders and/or borrowers will prefer using one form of deal structure over another will be due to various reasons but these will take into account the requirements of the lenders in terms of their respective security packages and enforcement rights thereupon, the complexity and cost of operating multiple layers of special purpose vehicles necessary to set up a senior/mezzanine loan structure, the availability of a mezzanine lender at the outset of the transaction to clearly define the sizing and pricing of the transaction, speed of execution and whether a CMBS exit is being contemplated for the senior portion.

Figure 1: Typical Senior/Mezzanine Structure

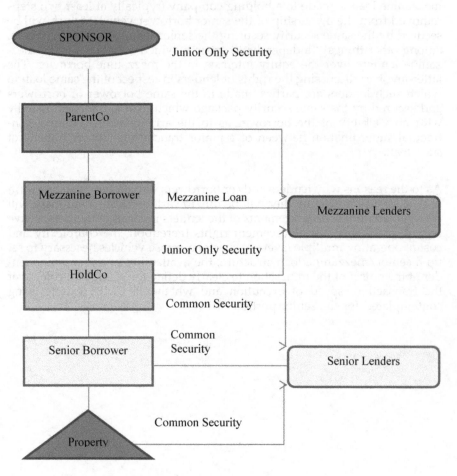

Figure 2: Typical A/B Structure

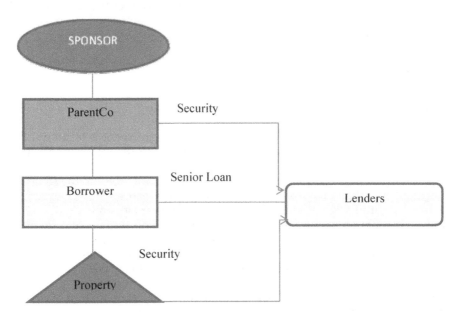

Apart from the differences resulting from the senior/mezzanine model being based on the existence of two separate debt obligations at different levels in the borrower group structure with the consequential operational considerations that such entails when compared to a whole loan A/B structure, historically one of the most distinguishing features of the senior/ mezzanine structure has been the possibility for mezzanine lenders to have the possibility to pre-empt enforcement by the senior lenders on the occurrence of a mezzanine loan event of default. This would be possible as the occurrence of an event of default under the mezzanine loan will, in certain circumstances, occur before there is an event of default under the senior loan primarily as a result of the occurrence of a financial covenant breach at the mezzanine loan level, without it being so severe as to trigger the equivalent senior loan financial covenant, or the unavailability of cash to pay amounts outstanding under the mezzanine loan after having paid regular payments under the senior loan in full.

If that mezzanine loan event of default occurs prior to the occurrence of a senior event of default, the usual position under an intercreditor agreement between the senior and mezzanine lenders will, whilst prohibiting the mezzanine lenders from exercising any enforcement rights over any security given for the benefit of the senior lenders (including the mortgage over the related property), allow the mezzanine lenders to exercise enforcement rights over security given exclusively for its benefit. Typically this will consist of share security over, and security over intragroup loans made to, the mezzanine borrower which would allow the mezzanine lenders to take control of the mezzanine borrower and, by virtue of the same, control the senior borrower effectively becoming the new owner of the borrower group structure.

7.3 Priority of payments

7.3.1 Introduction

One of the primary purposes of an intercreditor agreement is to set out the respective lender's right to cashflow generated from the underlying loan.

In a senior/mezzanine structure this will either usually refer to the separate payment waterfalls incorporated into the senior loan and the mezzanine loan taking into account that the related intercreditor agreement will set out the subordination of the mezzanine lenders' position to the senior loan or the intercreditor agreement will set out the full waterfall applicable to distributions under each of the senior and mezzanine loan. These will usually be subject to certain exceptions as there will likely be circumstances where the mezzanine lenders will be entitled to receive certain payments before the senior loan has been paid in full. This may include disposal proceeds in connection with the sale of properties under the loan, proceeds received in connection with the enforcement of the junior only security, payment of funds received from the equity intended to pay down the mezzanine loan, current interest due and payable and, to the extent the principal amount of the senior loan exceeds the principal balance of the senior loan at the time of the origination of the senior loan, it would be usual for that difference (or an amount in excess of a pre-agreed amount or percentage) to be subordinated to the mezzanine lenders' position. As each of the senior and mezzanine loans will set out what amount is due to each of the lenders and the obligors will be a party to the senior/mezzanine intercreditor agreement, the borrowers will have full visibility on what amounts are due to each of the lenders as well as when and in what circumstances they will be paid.

In an A/B intercreditor, the relevant whole loan agreement will set out a payment waterfall that should ensure that costs associated with the running of the income producing property securing the loan and the operational costs of the borrower (usually a special purpose vehicle (SPV)) are met and, if applicable, any hedging costs relating to any borrower-level swaps, are paid in priority to the distribution of any amounts to the loan finance parties. Following payment of such expenses and any fees, costs and expenses due to the relevant agents of the loan, together with amounts available to pay principal and interest due under the loan, will be paid to the lenders, although the underlying whole loan agreement will usually not set out how those amounts are to be distributed amongst the lenders. In this respect, it is therefore not necessary for the borrower to be privy to the arrangements between the lenders, and the actual rates to be paid to each of the lenders can be set out in separate fee letters agreed between such lenders.

The allocation of amounts due to be distributed under an intercreditor agreement (be it under a senior/mezzanine intercreditor, by reference to the senior and mezzanine loan, or under an A/B intercreditor agreement, where the relevant waterfall will likely be contained in the same A/B intercreditor agreement) will, in common practice, hinge on whether certain triggering events have occurred. A senior/mezzanine intercreditor agreement will usually refer to a payment stop event preventing payments flowing after discharging amounts due under the senior loan from being paid to the mezzanine lenders. On the other hand, in an A/B intercreditor, there will likely be separate waterfalls that would apply depending on whether certain material events of default are in occurrence in respect of the related loan. Usually, these payment stop events, in the case of a senior/mezzanine intercreditor agreement, or material events of default, in an A/B intercreditor agreement will encapsulate, at a minimum: (a) a default in the payment of interest, principal and other amounts due on the senior loan (in a senior/mezzanine structure) or whole loan (in an A/B structure); (b) a default under certain covenants linked to the cashflow coverage or the loan to value ratio again in respect of the senior loan or whole loan depending on the intercreditor; and (c) certain insolvency events relating to the borrower and related obligors under the senior loan or whole loan, as the case may be. Other than the preceding, additional events can be and are commonly included as well, though this will be subject to negotiation between the lenders due to the effect that such events have on the distribution of amounts and ultimately, on the scenarios in which the junior lenders will be absorbing a loss, since the junior loans in such arrangements provide credit enhancement for the more senior positions in the related loan. A junior lender will also seek to ensure that it has the right to cure, where possible, as many of the events will either constitute a payment stop event for purposes of the senior/mezzanine loan intercreditor or may trigger a waterfall switch for purposes of the A/B intercreditor as further discussed below.

The above, in the context of a senior/mezzanine structure, needs to take into account that due to the existence of two separate loans and waterfalls under the underlying loan documentation that, save for certain exceptions as discussed above, payments will be sequential. The senior loan obligations will be discharged on any given interest payment date before the mezzanine lenders are entitled to receive payment. The exceptions to this will be negotiated, but will typically include the application of disposal proceeds, for instance, where prior to a payment stop event may be distributed on a pari passu and pro rata basis. There may also be cash trap or cash sweep events in the senior loan waterfall which will usually apply to surplus funds available under the senior loan waterfall after regular amounts due under the mezzanine loan are paid. From a mezzanine lender's perspective, it may well be necessary to include a consent right over the release of such cash trapped amounts particularly if such release is made at a time where amounts due to the mezzanine lenders have not been paid in full.

Furthermore, if a payment stop event occurs in a senior/mezzanine structure, cash that would have otherwise been paid to the mezzanine lenders may either be swept to amortise the senior loan or may be diverted and escrowed for a certain period of time. A usual scenario is that such escrowed amounts will be held and trapped on successive interest payment dates for say two interest periods and if in the intervening period there is an acceleration event under the senior loan, then such cash may be applied towards repayment of the senior loan. If such a payment stop event is cured or corrected, then such escrowed amounts will be released to the mezzanine borrowers.

7.3.2 Waterfalls

7.3.2.1 Senior/mezzanine waterfalls

A senior/mezzanine intercreditor will refer to the senior and mezzanine waterfalls contained in the underlying loan agreements. It is also possible, as discussed above, that the senior/mezzanine intercreditor will incorporate a single waterfall instead as an amalgamation of what would have been included in each of the senior and mezzanine loans and this will dispense with the need of incorporating separate waterfalls in the loan documents. In either case, the form of the waterfall or waterfalls, as the case may be, will be a standard sequential waterfall (either taken alone or together) accommodating the payment buckets necessary to deal with the payments under the loans. In the event of separate waterfalls in each of the senior and mezzanine loans, the senior loan will contain a bucket allowing for payments to be made to the mezzanine lenders by transferring an amount necessary to make such payments directly to the related mezzanine loan account.

The ordinary sequential nature of the waterfalls where amounts owing to in respect of the senior loan will be paid in priority to payments due under the mezzanine loan may be subject to certain exceptions agreed between the lenders. Primarily, there may be agreement that mandatory prepayment proceeds received in connection with a disposal of properties may be distributed pro rata between the lenders. Also certain prepayment events affecting lenders individually (i.e. mandatory prepayment due to illegality and/or increased costs) may be agreed to be paid to the affected mezzanine lender outside of the usual subordination of the mezzanine lender position. There may also be circumstances where the lenders have agreed that amounts available by the related mezzanine borrower's equity may be paid to the mezzanine lenders without those funds being applied first to discharge any senior amounts due. Naturally, this is not an exhaustive list and will be subject to agreement between the lenders.

Other exceptions to the usual senior/mezzanine subordination relate to the amounts by which the senior loan balance may increase if compared to the original senior loan balance at origination. This includes property protection loans or cure loans and the concept of a senior headroom. Property protection loans or cure loans are usually included in loan agreements to allow the lenders to make certain payments that the borrower should but has not paid. These will typically include amounts due under headleases, insurance policies, hedging arrangements, taxes and other costs related to the preservation or protection of the security granted to the lenders. When advanced by a lender, these amounts will accrue interest (at the same rate as amounts advanced as principal by the lenders and, sometimes, the pre-agreed default rate) and will be expressed to be repayable by the borrower on demand. If advanced by the senior lenders, these amounts will usually be expressed to be repayable in advance of ordinary principal and interest due to the senior lenders.

Given that the advancing of such further amounts will increase amounts due under the senior loan which will be paid in priority to amounts due under the mezzanine loan, mezzanine lenders will attempt to control the advancing of those amounts to the borrower as well as limit the quantum that would rank senior to their position. Mezzanine lenders will (i) seek to ensure that the purpose for which those amounts may be advanced are clearly set out and limited; (ii) consider negotiating with the senior lenders to have a first refusal right to make those advances instead of the senior lenders; and (iii) attempt to cap the total amount of any such advances to the borrower by setting a maximum amount or percentage (usually 5–10% of the balance of the senior loan at origination) that could be advanced by the senior lenders with any excess over that maximum amount being agreed to be subordinated to the mezzanine loan position. In the event the mezzanine lenders procure a right to advance such property protection loans, those amounts could be advanced to the mezzanine borrower and funnelled down to the senior borrower by way of intragroup loans, the mezzanine lenders would pay the same to the senior lenders as a cure or the senior lenders in the first instance would make such advances which would then be acquired by the mezzanine lenders by making a payment for those advances to the senior lenders (subject to certain limitations arising from the acquisition of such senior advance).

To the extent the senior waterfall contains a cash trap or cash sweep, care would need to be taken by the mezzanine lenders to ensure that the triggers for either of the above would not result in monies not being made available to keep the mezzanine loan payments current. Ordinarily, it would be expected that such cash traps or cash sweeps would apply after the bucket in which an amount necessary to pay mezzanine loan amounts then due has been extracted from the senior loan waterfall to the mezzanine loan waterfall.

Lastly, the senior/mezzanine intercreditor will set out the triggers which stop payments being made to the mezzanine lenders. Usually these will include payment defaults, financial covenant breaches and insolvency of the senior obligors under the senior loan. When such payment stop event occurs, it is usual for the amounts that would otherwise been payable to the mezzanine lenders to be extracted from the waterfall and placed into escrow. Once in escrow, the relevant provisions will ordinarily provide that such amounts will be released to the mezzanine lenders or released through the waterfalls once the relevant payment stop event has ceased to be continuing (and, in some instances, for a certain additional period of time beyond that date to provide for a stabilisation period). In the event there is cash trapped in the related escrow account on an acceleration of the loan, such cash would be available to pay down the senior loan. It is also not uncommon to see a limit placed on the amount of time such diverted funds may be held in the escrow account or on the continuance of the payment stop event trigger if the senior lenders have not taken enforcement action within an agreed period of time. It may also be the case that amounts due in respect of the mezzanine loan which are otherwise trapped may have to be released to the mezzanine parties before the payment stop trigger ceases to be continuing, such as in the case of ordinary agency fees due under the mezzanine facility agreement.

7.3.2.2 A/B pre-default and post-default waterfalls

An A/B intercreditor agreement will usually set out a pre-default waterfall and a post-default waterfall. The pre-default waterfall will determine the allocation of payments before certain events of default have occurred. The post-default waterfall will set out the allocation of payments after such events have occurred.

There may be some variation to a typical pre-default waterfall from deal to deal (e.g. junior loans which have some element of amortisation may rank in priority to amortisation on senior loans) but a typical pre-material default waterfall is set out below:

> "For so long as no Material Event of Default is continuing, on the later of the date that amounts are distributed in accordance with the Credit Agreement or the date that payments are due with respect to any Hedging Arrangement that relates to such amounts, such amounts shall be distributed as between the Finance Parties (in replacement to the order set out in the Credit Agreement) as follows:
>
> - *first*, in or towards any payment due under any **Hedging Arrangements** (whether or not periodic payments or payment as a result of termination, provided that such termination is not due to a default of or termination resulting from the related swap counterparty);
> - *secondly*, in or towards payment of all fees, costs and expenses due and payable to the **Security Trustee** and its agents under the Finance Documents, (including all fees and expenses of the **Servicer and Special Servicer** as agents of the Finance Parties pursuant to the terms of the Servicing Agreement) and all amounts expended in connection with the preservation

of the rights of the Finance Parties under the Finance Documents, including the preservation of the Property as security for the Whole Loan;

- *thirdly*, in or towards payment of **interest due and payable** (after taking into account any Cure Payment made in respect of a Non Payment of such interest) to the **Senior Lende**r under the Credit Agreement (including the portion of Break Costs (and income earned thereon) up to the amount necessary to make a complete payment of interest on the Senior Loan at the Senior Loan Rate for the related Interest Period);

- *fourthly*, in or towards payment of **interest due and payable to the Junior Lender** under the Credit Agreement (including the portion of Break Costs (and income earned thereon) up to the amount necessary to make a complete payment of interest on the Junior Loan at the Junior Loan Rate for the related Interest Period);

- *fifthly*, in or towards **payment to the Senior Lender and the Junior Lender, pro rata,** according to the amounts due to each of them, **of principal due and payable** in respect of the Senior Loan (after taking into account any Cure Payment made in respect of a Non Payment of such principal) and the Junior Loan respectively;

- *sixthly*, in or towards payment of **Default Interest** received on the Whole Loan to the Senior Lender and the Junior Lender, pro rata, according to the outstanding principal on the Senior Debt and the Junior Debt as of the beginning of the related Interest Period;

- *seventhly*, in or towards **reimbursement** on account **of any Cure Payments** made by the Junior Lenders pursuant to this Deed;

- *eighthly*, in or towards payment to the Senior Lender and Junior Lender, pro rata, other than to the extent such amounts are paid above, of **all other costs, fees and expenses due and payable** under the Finance Documents; and

- *ninthly*, in or towards payment to the **swap counterparty** with respect to any Hedging Arrangement entered into with respect to the Whole Loan **in relation to termination payments** when the swap counterparty is the defaulting party or reason for termination.

- *Notwithstanding the above*, if there are insufficient collections to pay all amounts of principal and interest due and payable to the Senior Lender and the Junior Lender (or any of them) in accordance with this Clause, the full amount of such shortfall shall be allocated to the Junior Loan."

In contrast to the above, upon the occurrence of a relevant triggering event, a post-default waterfall typically provides that payments due to the lenders are to be distributed sequentially, in order to ensure that higher ranking lenders receive their payment in full, prior to any amounts leaking out, to pay amounts due to the more subordinated classes of lenders. The intercreditor agreement position here may be different than under the underlying loan agreement, as the occurrence of the material event of default, for these purposes, may or may not involve an acceleration of the whole loan. Therefore, the post-default waterfall trigger may cause available proceeds to be applied to pay off lenders in full, whilst such amounts may not necessarily be presently due and payable under the whole loan itself.

Alternatively, it is not uncommon to see waterfalls that provide a staggered approach whilst a material default is continuing (e.g. a payment default) but, prior to acceleration of the whole loan, amounts received from the borrower would be applied firstly to pay amounts due and payable to the A loan whilst amounts that would subsequently be due to the B loan or more subordinated classes of lenders would be placed into an escrow account. The period during which such amounts may be retained in such an escrow account will usually be limited, pending either the acceleration of the loan, or the cure of such default by the junior lenders. If the loan is accelerated, or the default is not cured, amounts in the escrow account would be applied towards payment of amounts due in respect of the A loan, with any excess flowing to the more subordinated positions. If, however, the whole loan is not accelerated within a certain period (a period which is subject to negotiation but, as an example, it may be 90 days to match an interest period), then such escrowed amounts together with any accrued interest in the escrow account would be released to be applied against the B loan, or more subordinated positions in the debt stack. Such retention periods are usually structured to motivate the A lender to assess the impact of the relevant default and to determine whether it should seek to accelerate the whole loan and enforce the related security. However, from a junior lender perspective, such may be seen as an attempt by the A lender to build up a reserve to the detriment of the junior lenders.

An example of a sequential post-default waterfall is set out below:

"For as long as a Material Event of Default is continuing, on the later of the date that amounts are distributed in accordance with the Credit Agreement or the date that payments are due with respect to any Hedging Arrangement that relates to such amounts, such amounts shall be distributed (in replacement to the order set out in the Credit Agreement) as follows:

- *firstly*, in or towards payment of any amounts due under any **Hedging Arrangements** entered into with respect to the Whole Loan (whether or not periodic payments or payments as a result of termination, provided that such termination is not due to a default of or termination resulting from the related swap counterparty);
- *secondly*, in or towards payment of all costs, fees and expenses due and payable to the **Security Trustee** under the Finance Documents (including all fees and expenses of the **Servicer and Special Servicer** as agents of the Finance Parties pursuant to the terms of the Servicing Agreement) and all amounts expended in connection with the preservation of the rights of the Finance Parties, including the preservation of the Property as security for the Whole Loan;
- *thirdly*, in or towards payment of **interest due and payable to the Senior Lender** under the Credit Agreement (including the portion of Break Costs (and income earned thereon) up to the amount necessary to make a complete payment of interest on the Senior Loan at the Senior Loan Rate for the related Interest Period);
- *fourthly*, in or towards repayment of **all principal outstanding on the Senior Loan** (whether such amount is due or not);
- *fifthly*, in or towards payment to the Senior Lender of the **Senior Lender's** pro rata portion of all other **costs, fees and expenses** due and payable under the Finance Documents;

- *sixthly,* in or towards payment of the **Senior Lender's** pro rata portion of **Default Interest** received on the Whole Loan based on the outstanding principal on the Senior Debt as compared to the Whole Loan as of the beginning of the related Interest Period;
- *seventhly,* in or towards **reimbursement** on account **of any Cure Payments** made by the Junior Lender pursuant to this Deed;
- *eighthly,* in or towards payment of **interest due and payable to the Junior Lender** under the Credit Agreement (including the portion of Break Costs (and income earned thereon) up to the amount necessary to make a complete payment of interest on the Junior Loan at the Junior Loan Rate for the related Interest Period);
- *ninthly,* in or towards repayment of all **principal outstanding on the Junior Loan** (whether such amount is due or not);
- *tenthly,* in or towards payment of the **Junior Lender's** pro rata portion of **Default Interest** received on the Whole Loan based on the outstanding principal on the Junior Debt as compared to the Whole Loan as of the beginning of the related Interest Period; and
- *eleventhly,* in or towards payment to the Junior Lender of the **Junior Lender's** pro rata portion of all other **costs, fees and expenses** due and payable under the Finance Documents; and
- *twelfthly,* in or towards payment of any amounts due under any **Hedging Arrangements** entered into with respect to the Whole Loan in relation to termination payments, when the swap counterparty is the defaulting part or reason for termination."

7.3.3 Hedging[2]

The above A/B waterfalls contemplate that lender-level hedging, benefiting all, is in place in respect of the loan. If hedging is exclusively in place at the borrower level, then the loan agreement waterfall will usually deal with its payment in priority to payment of amounts due to the lenders under the loan. If, in contrast, no lender level hedging is to be entered into for the benefit of the junior loan, then the CMBS waterfalls would have to deal with the allocation of amounts payable to the related hedge counterparty. Typically in CMBS, there will at least be a basis swap to address the mismatch between the dates on which interest and principal are due on a loan and the date on which proceeds are to be distributed to CMBS bondholders under the CMBS and the floating interest rate mismatch that may arise as a result. Accordingly, if a lender-level swap pays on any date, after which amounts are due on the underlying loan, the actual date of distribution of such amounts, for the purposes of the intercreditor agreement, should reflect that latter date as the date of distribution of amounts under the intercreditor agreement.

A hedge counterparty will expect that the main hedge payments due to it rank at the top of the waterfall. In the context of CMBS, this is important, as the CMBS bonds will require having adequate hedging arrangements in place, as a default in the payment of such amounts will not only result in the

---

[2] See further Ch.12.

probable termination of the underlying hedging arrangement and break costs due to such hedge counterparty, with the corresponding reduction in proceeds available to be distributed to bondholders, but also in the impossibility of bringing in a replacement hedge counterparty if required. However, not all payments due to a hedge counterparty will rank in priority. If break costs are due to a hedge counterparty, for reasons which are imputable to such hedge counterparty (e.g. termination event under the related hedging arrangement in respect of a hedge provider or the failure by the hedge provider to meet its obligations under the related hedging agreement following a ratings downgrade), such amounts will be expected[3] to be subordinated to amounts due to the lenders.

7.3.3.1 *Case law in the US and England*

Three cases, two in the US Bankruptcy Court in the Southern District of New York and one in the UK's Supreme Court, in each case relating to the bankruptcy of Lehman Brothers and its affiliated companies, in and around September 2008, have evidenced that US and English law disagree on the validity of such subordination clauses or "flip clauses" when triggered by the filing of insolvency proceedings of the related hedge counterparty.

The first, *Lehman Bros Special Financing v BNY Corporate Trustee Services Ltd (Re Lehman Bros Holdings, Inc)*[4] related to two series of credit-linked synthetic portfolio notes issued by an Irish SPV (Saphir) created by Lehman Brothers under the so-called Dante Program. At issue was whether Lehman Brothers Special Financing (LBSF), as credit default swap provider to the transaction, had been validly subordinated under the provisions of the transaction documents, which were expressed to be governed by English law, in respect of its entitlement to distributions in the collateral (being certain triple-A rated bonds) securing the transaction upon the filing of its voluntary case under US bankruptcy law, specifically Ch.11, in October 2008.[5] Prior to an event of default under the related hedging arrangement imputable to LBSF, LBSF would have been entitled to payment of proceeds produced by the collateral in priority to certain bondholders (in this case *Perpetual Trustee Company Ltd*), who would otherwise have been due such amounts as payment due under the related bonds. Upon the occurrence of such an event of default, the priority of payments would be "flipped" and the calculation of the amount due to LBSF as a result of the termination of the hedging arrangement would vary, each favouring *Perpetual* to the det-

---

[3] For instance, see *Swap Criteria for European Structured Finance Transactions*, DBRS, June 2011, pp.17–18.

[4] 422 B.R. 407 (Bankr. S.D.N.Y. 2010).

[5] Lehman Brothers Holdings, Inc (LBHI) bankruptcy filing in September 2008 was also an event which was capable of triggering an event of default under the credit default swap, as LBHI was the credit support provider and its bankruptcy filing was an express event of default. However, this distinction is immaterial for purposes of the above as each of LBHI's and LBSF's bankruptcy filings predate the date on which the hedging arrangements were notified to have been terminated on behalf of Saphir.

riment of LBSF. As there was no issue of triable fact, Judge Peck heard the matter as a motion of summary judgment and concluded, among other things, that the "flip" to the priority of payments as a result of the insolvency of LBSF breached US bankruptcy law[6] and any attempt to enforce such provisions would violate the automatic stay provided for under the US bankruptcy law. Interestingly, this motion for summary judgment was being heard contemporaneously with proceedings brought by *Perpetual* in the English courts and Judge Peck noted that "[i]n applying the Bankruptcy Code to these facts, this Court recognises that it is interpreting applicable law in a manner that will yield an outcome directly at odds with the judgment of the English Courts." For purposes of the US litigation, the case was subsequently settled before appeal to the US District Court and accordingly, the decision is ultimately only persuasive for the purposes of whether it is a binding precedent for future litigation.

Similarly, *Lehman Brothers Special Financing v Ballyrock*[7] related to a hedging arrangement entered into between LBSF and the issuer in a CDO transaction, Ballyrock. Under the related master agreement and indenture, LBSF would have been entitled to a priority ranking in the related waterfall if amounts were due to it as a result of the termination of the hedging arrangements, except that if such termination was due to LBSF or Lehman Brothers Holdings Inc (LBHI), as credit support provider under the hedging arrangement, among other reasons, due to either having instituted or having instituted against either of them bankruptcy proceedings. The termination payment would be subordinated to the payment of bondholders and capped in the amount of $30,000. Accordingly, upon LBHI's bankruptcy filing in September 2008, Ballyrock exercised its right under the hedging arrangement to call for an early termination date, under all transactions entered into in respect of the hedging arrangement and a termination payment due to LBSF of approximately $404 million was determined. Ballyrock subsequently liquidated its assets and after distribution of

---

[6] Specifically under each of: (1) s.355(e)(1) of the US Bankruptcy Code, which reads: "Notwithstanding a provision in an executory contract or unexpired lease, or in applicable law, an executory contract or unexpired lease of the debtor may not be terminated or modified, and any right or obligation under such contract or lease may not be terminated or modified, at any time after the commencement of the case solely because of a provision in such contract or lease that is conditioned on (A) the insolvency or financial condition of the debtor at any time before the closing of the case; (B) the commencement of a case under this title; or (C) the appointment of or taking possession by a trustee in a case under this title or a custodian before such commencement." (11 USC (2011) s.365(e)(1)); and (2) s.541(c)(1)(B) of the US Bankruptcy Code which reads in part "... an interest of the debtor in property becomes the property of the estate ... notwithstanding any provision in an agreement, transfer instrument, or applicable non-bankruptcy law ... that is conditioned on the insolvency or financial condition of the debtor, on the commencement of a case under this title, or on the appointment of or taking possession by a trustee in a case under this title or a custodian before such commencement, and that effects or gives an option to effect a forfeiture, modification, or termination of the debtor's interest in property". (11 USC (2011) s.541(c)(1)(B)).

[7] *Lehman Bros Special Financing Inc v Ballyrock ABS CDO 2007-1 Ltd and Wells Fargo Bank, N.A., Trustee (Re Lehman Brothers Holdings, Inc)*, 452 B.R. 31 (Bankr. S.D.N.Y. 2010).

amounts due to the bondholders proposed to further distribute a remaining amount of $137 million to bondholders on the next scheduled payment date. Upon the announcement of the proposed distribution of such amounts, LBSF filed a complaint against Ballyrock for a declaratory judgment to obtain, among other measures, a judgment that such proposed distribution would be in violation of applicable bankruptcy law. On a motion to dismiss such complaint, Judge Peck again found that, also citing *Lehman Bros Special Financing v BNY*, the flip clause was susceptible to being interpreted[8] as an ipso facto provision that could not be enforced to deprive LBSF of its rights on account of its bankruptcy filing. Furthermore, there was a detailed discussion of the safe harbour provisions in US bankruptcy law then set out in *Lehman Brothers Special Financing v BNY*. Such provision allowed, notwithstanding a bankruptcy filing, a swap participant to exercise any contractual right it may be entitled to under the terms of the related hedging arrangement to liquidate, terminate or accelerate a hedging arrangement upon a bankruptcy filing of the other party[9] Judge Peck, in his judgment, made it clear that such safe harbour was to be construed to permit termination and not, as in this case, to subordinate a right to payment but for the bankruptcy filing.

In *Belmont Park*,[10] the UK Supreme Court heard the final chapter in the *Perpetual* case saga. Rather than being based on carefully worded legislation, applicable English law relevant in this case hinged primarily on English common law and the "anti-deprivation rule" under English insolvency law. The Belmont group were a series of bondholders, other than *Perpetual*, who owned bonds in other series of bonds issued by Saphir. Following decisions by the High Court and Court of Appeals favouring the bondholder view that the "flip" clause was valid and worked to subordinate LBSF's expectation of payment from proceeds realised on the related collateral, Lord Collins, in his leading judgment, found that it is "desirable that, so far as possible, the courts give effect to contractual terms which parties have agreed",[11] that "there is a particularly strong case for autonomy in cases of complex financial instruments such as those involved

---

[8]   Given that the matter heard was in the context of a motion to dismiss filed by Ballyrock, a full hearing at trial on the matter would subsequently determine whether such the enforcement of such clauses would violate US bankruptcy law.

[9]   Specifically, s.560 of the US Bankruptcy Code, which reads in part: "[t]he exercise of any contractual right of any swap participant or financial participant to cause the liquidation, termination, or acceleration of one or more swap agreements because of a condition of the kind specified in section 365(e)(1) of this title or to offset or net out any termination values or payment amounts arising under or in connection with the termination, liquidation, or acceleration of one or more swap agreements shall not be stayed, avoided, or otherwise limited by operation of any provision of this title or by order of a court or administrative agency in any proceeding under this title ..." (11 USC (2011) s.560).

[10] *Belmont Part Investments PTY Ltd v BNY Corporate Trustee Services Ltd and Lehman Bros Special Financing Inc* [2011] UKSC 38.

[11] Citing Lord Neuberger in *Perpetual Trustee Co Ltd v BNY Corporate Trustee Services Ltd* [2009] EWCA Civ 1160; [2010] Ch 347 (CA) at [58].

in this appeal"[12] and specifically, the transaction (and the "flip" clause) had been entered into in good faith and there never had "been any suggestion that those provisions were deliberately intended to evade insolvency law".[13] Furthermore, Lord Collins considered that it was "possible to give a policy [the anti-deprivation rule] a common sense application which prevents its application to bona fide transactions which do not have as their predominant purpose, or one of their main purposes, the deprivation of the property of one of the parties on bankruptcy."[14]

Consequently, the practical lesson to be learnt as a result of the above cases is that, whilst the "flip" in a waterfall triggered as a result of an insolvency filing of the party otherwise entitled to payment is valid under English law, care should be taken to verify whether the jurisdiction in which main bankruptcy proceedings may be brought against that party will also recognise such clause. Given that US courts may steer towards finding such clauses in breach of US bankruptcy laws, parties may wish to minimise any adverse impact by, where possible, entering into such arrangements with counterparties subject to, for example, English law where possible.

7.3.4 Losses due to shortfalls

The primary goal of either form of intercreditor agreement is to ensure subordination of, in the case of a senior/mezzanine structure, the mezzanine debt to the senior debt or, in the case of an A/B structure, the junior tranche to the senior tranche. One area where this is important is, in the context of an A/B structure, allocation of losses. In a senior/mezzanine structure, the analysis is considerably simpler as due to the application of both a senior and mezzanine waterfall (or, in the alternative, an integrated waterfall as discussed above) the sequential application of available cash flow will result in a clear conclusion that in most payment scenarios the senior loan will be paid in priority and the mezzanine lenders will ultimately face the first risk on insufficient cash flow being available to pay both debt obligations. As the borrowers in such senior/mezzanine structure will have visibility as to what is due to each lender, the failure to pay any amount due will be a payment default of the related borrower.

In an A/B structure, the pre-material default waterfall sample included at section 7.3.2.2, the last paragraph of that clause ensures that the intended credit enhancement that the B loan represents, in favour of the A loan, is preserved in the circumstance where there is a shortfall in available proceeds, even when the pre-material default waterfall applies. This may occur, for instance, following a work-out or restructuring of the loan where the loan, after having been paying under the post-material event of default waterfall, reverts to the pre-material default position but, for instance, the

---

[12] [2010] Ch 347 (CA) at [103].
[13] [2010] Ch 347 (CA) at [109].
[14] [2010] Ch 347 (CA) at [104].

amount payable by the borrower under the loan has been reduced. This paragraph ensures that when a payment is to be made in respect of each of the A loan and B loan where the B loan would, save for the shortfall, have been entitled to any payment in priority to the A loan (as in the case of the sample pre-material default waterfall above), available proceeds are first allocated to meet amounts owing in respect of the A loan, with the B loan absorbing the loss. This may be applicable even in a situation where the borrower is current on all amounts it is obliged to pay under the whole loan which is a different conclusion that what would arise under a senior/ mezzanine structure were the payment deficiency would be imputable to a payment default by the related borrowers.

7.3.5   *Interest rate creep/payment shortfalls*

A diminution of the amount of principal outstanding on an A/B senior loan may have a negative impact on the availability of proceeds, to meet amounts due under more subordinate tranches. As noted above, lenders in the debt stack will agree to an interest rate on their participations that will be calculated based upon the overall rate payable by a borrower under the whole loan. Senior (or A) lenders, given their ranking in the waterfall and their priority in respect of recoveries from proceeds generated by the underlying collateral, will agree to a rate of interest that matches the level of risk they are agreeing to in the transaction. Correspondingly, subordinated (or B) lenders will invest and accept subordination only if they are paid a rate commensurate to their own position's level of risk.

An example of what is called "rate creep" can be explained by assuming a whole loan in the amount of £100 million is entered into at a rate of 9% per annum. The whole loan is subsequently tranched into an A loan in the amount of £70 million at a rate agreed between the lenders of 6% per annum and a B loan in the amount of £30 million at a rate of 16%. If the A loan is hyperamortised in priority to the B loan in, for example, £5 million that results in a weighted average on the combined A loan and B loan of approximately 9.07%, which means that the whole loan interest rate payable by the borrower under the loan agreement would no longer be able to sustain the B loan rate. This scenario may occur if the post-default waterfall triggers occur, which results in hyperamortisation of the A loan, in priority to the B loan and then the waterfall shifting back, as a result of a cure of the event, to the pre-default waterfall. Another example may be if part of the A loan is wiped out or forgiven. One way to address this issue is to ensure that the A loan rate is expressed to be net of the B loan rate. In the second example, the consent rights typically afforded to the B lender will require that prior to any change to the amount of any payment due under the loan, the prior written approval of the B lender be obtained.

There are no clear cut solutions to the resulting issue caused by such payment imbalances. Traditionally, such losses have been absorbed by junior lenders as described above. It is now not uncommon to see the junior interest rate being set out in the A/B intercreditor agreement as the lesser of the junior interest rate agreed between the senior and junior lender at the time the junior lender acquired its interest in the whole loan and an interest rate that would match the amount of available cashflow available to pay junior interest after application of the A/B waterfall. This yields the same result of the junior lender absorbing the loss and the junior lender potentially being paid less than the pre-agreed interest rate. One attempt to minimise the impact of the payment imbalance on the junior loan is by using default interest payable by the borrower under the whole loan to allow junior lenders to "catch-up" at least part of the amount that would be due to them, which in any event is an imperfect solution as it is unlikely that any default interest payable by the borrower would be sufficient to allow the junior lenders to recoup the full amount of pre-agreed interest. On the other hand, a clear solution would be to make the tranching of the loan and the "A note" and "B note" interest rates visible to the borrower ultimately making the borrower liable to pay the full amount of interest on the "B note" in the event of a shortfall. This may be accomplished by making the borrower a party to the A/B intercreditor agreement or by factoring the tranching of the loan into the terms of the whole loan itself, which would evidently be subject to negotiations between the parties including whether the borrower would be willing to accept that the pricing for the whole loan may not necessarily match the original all-in interest rate that it may have thought it had agreed.

7.4 Amendments, waivers and consents

7.4.1 *Entrenched rights v control valuation*

In Europe, there are two general approaches to resolving the issue relating to the amount of control given to subordinated lenders. The first, requiring that either any amendments, waivers or consents, or those relating to an enumerated list of specified actions in respect of the whole loan, cannot be taken without the consent of the subordinated lenders, which are commonly denominated "entrenched rights". Any actions outside that list would be taken by the servicer, special servicer or senior lender as relevant. Rating agencies have traditionally not favoured the existence of entrenched rights in a CMBS context.[15] The second, subjecting any subordinated lender approval rights in respect of any amendments, waivers or consents relating to an enumerated list of actions to a "value out" provision (a "control valuation event"). Under such a provision, if the underlying properties

---

[15] "It is common for the junior lender to have consent rights with respect to issues that will affect the characteristics and/or credit quality of the loan. However, Fitch expects that these consent rights to be structured such that they do not interfere with the day-to-day management of the property, servicing of the loan and, in particular, the timing of the enforcement process. Where amendments can be undertaken only in case all (senior and junior) creditors agree, the question is whether these consent rights grant too much power to the junior creditor." *Fitch Ratings*; pp.4–5.

securing the whole loan have depreciated in value to cover both the senior debt and a specified portion of the related subordinated debt, then such approval rights would be disapplied. An example of a control valuation provision is provided below:

> "A 'Control Valuation Event' will occur if at any time, the Market Value of the Property is less than the aggregate of: (i) the A Debt then outstanding to the A Lender; and (ii) twenty-five per cent of the B Debt outstanding to the B Lenders at the date of this Deed."

Hence, if the value of the property, as determined by a valuation obtained pursuant to the terms of the intercreditor agreement, securing the whole loan falls below the full amount of the A loan plus 25% of the B loan, at the time the intercreditor agreement is entered into, the B lender will cease to be able to exercise the relevant control rights. Such calculations will be based on valuations obtained at the times or upon the occurrence of certain events, as set out in the intercreditor agreement. This may or may not coincide with the timings for obtaining valuations under the underlying loan agreement. In fact, such valuations at times cannot be used for the purposes of determining whether a control valuation event is in existence. If a control valuation event is determined to exist, the affected lender will usually have the right to obtain, or instruct the servicer or special servicer to obtain, another valuation at the cost of such lender. The servicer or special servicer may then have the discretion, to be exercised in accordance with the servicing standard, as to which valuation to use for determining the existence of a control valuation event.

The position described above in connection with A/B intercreditor agreements is not vastly different to the position in senior/mezzanine intercreditors, particularly when contemplating that all or part of the senior loan in such structure is placed into a CMBS. More often that not, when a CMBS is not contemplated for the senior loan, the rights of mezzanine lenders in connection with a modification or consent of the terms of the senior loan would be entrenched. This means that the mezzanine lenders would have to affirmatively consent to a modification of the terms of the senior loan which is likely would have a material impact on the mezzanine loan be it in connection with an alteration to the amounts that rank senior to the mezzanine loan or to the operation of the borrower group or properties. In order to ensure that any amendments or consents that may be permissibly given by the senior lenders with or without the consent of the mezzanine lenders are capable of being implemented without further consequence, it would be usual for the mezzanine lenders to be dragged along with a consent or amendment permissibly given by the senior lenders under the terms of the senior loan agreement and intercreditor agreement so that such item would not cause an event of default under the terms of the mezzanine loan.

However, such purported amendments or consents given in respect of a senior loan, where it is intended that all or part of such senior loan will be placed in a CMBS, will be subject to a value threshold having the same effect as a control valuation event as described above in connection with A/B intercreditors. This will result in the mezzanine lender express consent rights over modifications or consents made by the senior lenders under the senior loan being switched off once the value of the underlying property has fallen below the amount of the senior loan and a buffer.

7.4.2 Common actions requiring consent

An intercreditor agreement may provide for a combination of both methods described above, i.e. a set of entrenched rights or rights subject to a control valuation event and a list of items in respect of which the facility agent or, if applicable, the servicer or special servicer would be required to consult the relevant subordinated lender on in any event.

Whilst the list of actions that will require the consent of the junior lenders will naturally be subject to intense negotiation and vary from deal to deal, there are a few that form a very basic list from which negotiations usually start. A sample list is provided below relating specifically to an A/B structure but which can be extrapolated for a senior/mezzanine structure:

> "The [Agent, Servicer or Special Servicer] may not amend or waive any term of any Finance Document or exercise or refrain from exercising any consent, approval, discretion or determination, contained in any Finance Document having the same commercial effect in a manner or to an extent which would or could result in:
>
> (a) any change to the date of payment of any amount to a Lender under the Finance Documents;
> (b) a reduction in the Margin or a reduction in the amount of any payment of principal, interest, fee or other amount payable to a Lender under the Finance Documents;
> (c) a change to the currency of any amount payable under the Finance Documents;
> (d) an increase in, or an extension of, a Commitment;
> (e) any change to the basis upon which a payment is calculated in accordance with the original provisions of that Finance Document;
> (f) any amendment, waiver or supplement to a Financial Covenant or an Event of Default under the Credit Agreement;
> (g) a release of an Obligor;
> (h) a release of any Security other than in accordance with the terms of the Finance Documents; or
> (i) any change to the right of a Lender to assign or transfer its rights or obligations under the Finance Documents ...''

The first four items listed above will impact the junior lender's economics in the transaction and will naturally be an area that the junior lender will wish to ensure is not amended without its consent. For the reasons provided in section 7.4.1, the junior lender will also wish to limit any amendments to the economics relating to the senior piece, or any amendment under paras (e) and (f) which can result in a change to the applicable waterfall or lead to the acceleration or enforcement of the loan, that may have an impact on the junior lender's rights to payment (including cash flow). Paragraphs (g) and (h) address the credit quality of the asset and (i) ensures that the lender may exit the transaction on the originally agreed terms, if so desired. Other items are commonly negotiated and added on to the list on a case-by-case basis (i.e. relating to the administration and quality of the underlying property or further events that may result in a change to the applicable waterfall which may result in proceeds being cut off from the junior lender). These will vary depending on the transaction and the bargaining power of the related parties. However, care should be taken to ensure that such actions that may be required for the day-to-day management of the property are not unduly restricted or subject to the delay that a formal approval or consultation process will entail, particularly in a post-default scenario where the servicer or special servicer will be required to take a more active role.

If compared with a sample list of items requiring mezzanine lenders' consent under a senior/mezzanine intercreditor, similar areas of coverage and areas of difference may be identified mainly accounting for the difference between the A/B and senior/mezzanine loan structures where, in the latter case, there are two separate loan agreements entered into with borrowers at different levels in the borrower group structure:

"(a) increase the Loan Margin or provide for additional margin to be payable (except to the extent that such increase or addition is contemplated by the Finance Documents);

(b) change the basis on which interest, fees or commission are calculated under the Facility Agreement, unless the relevant change: (i) is contemplated by the Finance Documents; (ii) is minor or administrative and not prejudicial to the Mezzanine Lenders; (iii) does not increase the overall cost to the Obligors of the Secured Liabilities; or (iv) relates to reasonable fees or charges in connection with amendment, waiver or consent requests;

(c) increase the principal amount of the Facility;

(d) increase the overall cost to the Obligors of the Secured Liabilities;

(e) change the currency of any amount payable under the Finance Documents;

(f) change the timing of payments under the Facility Agreement (including (i) any change to the definition of the term 'Interest Period' in the Facility Agreement or (ii) an extension or reduction of the term of the Loan);

(g) change the provisions relating to hedging or the definition of 'Majority Lenders' in the Facility Agreement;

(h) cause existing financial covenants, events of default or defaults contained in the Facility Agreement to be more onerous on the Obligors or introduce new financial covenants to the Facility Agreement;

(i) change, or grant to consent to an amendment to, the provisions governing the disposals that are permitted under the Finance Documents which would make such disposals more onerous for the Obligors or to amend the Release Price payable for a permitted disposal, unless a Loan Event of Default is continuing and the disposal otherwise is a Distressed Disposal permitted under the Intercreditor Agreement;

(j)   change, or grant consent to an amendment to, the provisions governing the type or proportion of insurance proceeds, expropriation proceeds and recovery proceeds which must be applied in prepayment of the Loan;

(k)   change, or grant consent to an amendment to, the negative pledge, the provisions restricting the payments of dividends or other distributions or the insurance covenant contained in the Facility Agreement;

(l)   change, or grant consent to an amendment to, the provisions of the Facility Agreement governing the ability of affiliates of the Obligors to purchase participations in the Secured Liabilities;

(m)   release any Loan Security other than expressly permitted pursuant to the terms of the Facility Agreement or the Intercreditor Agreement;

(n)   amend or waive or provide a consent in respect of the accounts or priority of payment provisions of the Facility Agreement unless it is contemplated by the Finance Documents or a minor or technical change or correction which is not prejudicial to the Mezzanine Lenders;

(o)   result in a cross default of the Secured Liabilities to any default under any Mezzanine Facility Liabilities or subordination of the Secured Liabilities to any indebtedness;

(p)   permit the Finance Parties to acquire any direct or indirect equity interest in a Mezzanine Borrower or any additional interest based on cashflow or appreciation of the Properties;

(q)   without prejudice to any permitted Distressed Disposals, release, waive or compromise any Mezzanine Borrower Liabilities;

(r)   consent to a change of control pursuant to the terms of the Facility Agreement; and

(s)   change or release the guarantee or indemnity under the Facility Agreement other than as permitted under the Intercreditor Agreement with respect to a Distressed Disposal."

As in the case of the A/B intercreditor discussion above, the list of amendments in this senior/mezzanine sample can be subdivided into items:

(i)   protecting the mezzanine lenders' economics in the deal. For example, paragraphs (a), (b), (c), (d) and (e) are conceptually the same as the items covered in the first four paragraphs of the A/B intercreditor list above. This is expanded to cover other items that would have a similar economic effect by extending the related interest period or term of the senior loan (paragraph (f)), changing the hedging requirements (paragraph (g)), changing financial covenants particularly in the case where there are cash traps or cash sweeps that could prevent amounts being available to pay mezzanine obligations (paragraph (h)), which would have an impact on the amount of any prepayments (paragraphs (i) and (j)) which amounts may be subject to distribution to the lenders other than sequentially as discussed in section 7.2.3.1 above or which would impact either the availability of funds for the mezzanine borrower to pay the mezzanine loan (paragraph (k) or the actual priority of payments (paragraph (n)));

(ii)   preventing unexpected triggers for an event of default under the senior loan which would have a detrimental effect on the mezzanine lenders having a period of time between a mezzanine event of default and a senior event of default to take steps to minimize issues at the borrower or property level (paragraph (h) and (o));

(iii) protecting the availability of the common security and the continuance of the mezzanine debt (paragraphs (m), (q) and (s)) and any interference with the availability of any mezzanine only security to the mezzanine lenders (paragraph (p)); and

(iv) changing the relationship with the borrower by either permitting a change of control (paragraph (r)) or allowing the borrower or affiliate thereof to become a lender (paragraph (l)).

In a senior/mezzanine intercreditor, a similar set of consent rights will be afforded to senior lenders in respect of proposed amendments or consents granted by the mezzanine lenders under the mezzanine loan. These will be principally aimed at restricting the mezzanine lenders from agreeing with the mezzanine borrower modifications that could have an adverse impact on the cash flow of the group by increasing the amount of the mezzanine obligations.

In each of A/B intercreditors and senior/mezzanine intercreditors, it is common for the consent requirements discussed above to be subject to a snooze/lose provision whereby if the party whose consent is required prior to the implementation of the proposed amendment or consent has failed to respond by a particular time, such lenders' deemed consent to the proposal will be considered approved. Further, if the proposed amendment/consent is given in respect of a senior loan in a senior/mezzanine loan structure, it will usually be provided that such amendment or consent is deemed also given in respect of the equivalent provision in the mezzanine loan by the mezzanine lender.

7.5 Cure rights and purchase option

7.5.1 *Cure rights*

As noted in the previous two Chapters, cure rights are an important feature for junior lenders, in order to avoid, in the case of A/B structures, a switch of the pre-material default waterfall to the sequential post-default waterfall or, in the case of senior/mezzanine structures, the occurrence of a payment stop event and, in each case, to halt the taking of enforcement action by the senior lender. In addition, such a feature will normally prevent the transfer of the whole loan or senior loan (as the case may be) to special servicing, as will be further discussed below. These rights will usually allow the junior lenders to remedy a payment default and certain other defaults that are by their nature capable of being remedied. The precise list of defaults that the senior lender will agree that the junior lenders may cure will be negotiated on a case-by-case basis, but in addition to a payment or monetary default, it is not uncommon for the junior lenders to be also permitted to cure financial covenants (i.e., loan to value or debt service covenants set out in the loan agreement). Defaults which cannot be remedied by a payment may, at times, be included, though they would in practice be very difficult to cure if at all. Regardless, insolvency defaults would be excluded and to the extent that defaults other than those that can be cured by payment are included, they will usually be events that may be corrected by the borrower, after the fact, such as a breach of representation or undertaking to perform certain actions.

The amount of the cure payment to be made on the occurrence of a payment default will include not only the amount of the shortfall but to the extent, in the context of a CMBS, the issuer, as A lender or senior lender, has obtained an advance or has made a drawing under the securitisation liquidity facility. The cure payment will also be made to include any related interest and other amounts, including any break costs, that will be payable by the issuer on such advanced or drawn amounts on the following interest payment date. It is possible that the intercreditor agreement provides for the payment of certain additional amounts, though a junior lender will naturally wish to minimise the number of costs that may be chargeable as part of the cure payment.

7.5.2 Exercise of cure rights

The procedure followed in respect of the exercise of cure rights will usually commence upon the agent, servicer or special servicer becoming aware of the curable default and the giving of a notification to the junior lender, entitled to make such cure, within a predefined period of time. To the extent that the cure is being made under an A/B intercreditor agreement, the junior lender will make the cure directly to the senior lender without the borrower necessarily being aware. If, however, the cure is made pursuant to a senior/mezzanine arrangement, the cure will either be expressed to be a direct cure payment made by the mezzanine lender to the senior lender or the amount of the cure will advanced or deemed to have been advanced by the mezzanine lender to the mezzanine borrower which in turn will make the advance down the intragroup loan arrangements in place to the senior borrower to put it in funds to make the cure. In the latter case, it will be a fresh advance under the mezzanine loan which will increase the amount of the mezzanine liabilities. In the former, such cure may ultimately require a subrogation by the mezzanine lenders making the cure to the senior loan amounts that have been paid and which will continue to be outstanding as between the senior lender and the senior borrower.

If the curable event is a payment default, the junior lender will generally be permitted to make a payment, in an amount equal to the payment shortfall due to the senior or more senior lenders, or, in the case of an A/B structure, if such payment default only results in a shortfall to that junior lender, or those other junior lenders which are subordinated to it, but there is enough cash to pay the senior amounts due in full, waive on its own behalf and on behalf of any other lenders which are subordinated to it, such shortfall as between the lenders. In the latter case, such waiver would not waive amounts due by the borrower and those amounts would continue to be due by the borrower but would, for the purposes of the intercreditor, be considered waived in order to prevent such event from constituting a material event of default leading to the consequences discussed above. If, on the other hand, such event is a financial covenant default, this may be required to be cured by making a prepayment of the loan/senior, in the case of a loan to value covenant breach, in an amount equal to such amount as would be necessary to ensure that the covenant is subsequently observed. Alternatively, if the event is a debt service or interest cover covenant, it may be provided that such default may be cured by depositing an amount that would cure such default in a controlled escrow account or obtaining an irrevocable letter of credit, payable on demand from a bank or other financial institution meeting certain ratings thresholds, which would provide additional security for the whole loan/senior loan albeit this choice is more common under A/B structures. Ultimately, if a subsequent material event of default occurs which is not, or is incapable of being cured, whether by its very nature or as a result of cure rights having been exhausted, such escrowed amounts would be available, or such letter of credit could be called, to pay down the whole loan in accordance with the post-material default waterfall. If the financial covenant is subsequently rectified, which may require that compliance with the covenant be maintained for a certain number of consecutive interest periods, any escrowed amounts would be released to the paying curing lender. In senior/mezzanine structures it is more typical for cures to be expressed as a prepayment or repayment of the senior loan.

Cures are typically required to be made within a prescribed period of time. This period will be negotiated between the lenders, but will account for the nature of the default and the impact any delay caused by the cure process would have on the senior lender. In addition, lenders who need to undertake internal processes to source the cash in the amounts required to make such cures will build in enough time to ensure that such rights can be effectively exercised. Further, any payment cures, other than any escrowed amounts as discussed above, will be reimbursed to the paying lender in accordance with the priority of payments of the applicable waterfall(s). Such reimbursement will be made after all amounts of principal, interest, expenses and other items due to the more senior lenders have been paid.

No enforcement action will be permitted to be taken during the period afforded to the junior lender to cure the related default save, if agreed, in the event that immediate action is required to preserve or protect the senior lenders' position. The intercreditor agreement would not necessarily provide a grace period or equivalent upon the occurrence of any other event of default which is not subject to junior lender cure right. In order to address any concerns with the length of time afforded to the junior lender to cure the default, the intercreditor agreement may provide that the junior lender would have a reduced period to notify the agent that it will be making a cure and then have an extended period in which to complete the cure. If the junior lender fails to respond or notifies that it will not be making a cure, the period during which no enforcement action would be permitted would be shorter than if such period was intended to provide the junior lender some time to actually effect the payment or other cure. From a ratings perspective, excessively long grace periods would be considered as detrimental to the credit quality of the senior debt.

7.5.3   Limits on number of cures

In order to avoid a scenario in which recoveries under the loan would have been greater had the loan and the related security been enforced earlier, rather than waiting whilst the loan was continuously being cured, junior lender cure rights are usually limited both in the number of consecutive cures that can be effected as well as in the total number of cures that would be permitted during the life of the transaction. Usually cures will either be permitted, in the case of an A/B structure, no more than twice in consecutive interest periods and between four and six times during the life of the deal, which will vary, among other reasons, according to the length of the term of the transaction or, in the case of a senior/mezzanine arrangement the number of times that the senior borrower has the ability under the terms of the senior loan agreement to effect a cure plus one or two additional times. The number of times a cure may be effected by a junior lender will be subject to negotiation between the lenders.

7.5.4   Purchase option

It may be considered that a purchase option granted to the junior lenders to acquire the more senior loans, upon the occurrence of a material event of default or payment stop event, is mutually beneficial to both categories of lenders, in that the senior lenders would be repaid the loan at par and the junior lender is able to preserve or gain control of the related loan in circumstances where its right to cashflow may be halted due to a shift to the applicable waterfall, the occurrence of a payment stop event or it ceases to be able to exercise consent or consultation rights as a result of the occurrence of a control valuation event or equivalent trigger. However, it is often not a practical solution for a junior lender, due to the likely problems surrounding the performance of the loan and the amount of the purchase price that would have to be committed to effect the acquisition. For these reasons, it is not an option that is commonly taken up by junior lenders.

The option is often triggered on the occurrence of the same trigger events that will cause a shift to or stop to the payments under the applicable waterfall in related intercreditor agreement. There may be circumstances where the junior lender may be able to have included, within the purchase option trigger events, additional items that may result in a decrease in available cash flow to the junior lenders (e.g. increased costs resulting from

167

the transfer of servicing from a primary servicer to a special servicer) or its loss of consent or consultation rights.

The purchase price will usually be determined by the agent, servicer or special servicer and will normally include:

- the outstanding principal amount of the loan being acquired;
- all accrued and unpaid interest, fees, costs and expenses and other amounts owed to the selling lender;
- any funding break costs of the selling lender;
- any amount, including fees, costs and expenses and VAT chargeable thereon due to the servicer and/or special servicer in respect of the loan;
- any interest or other finance charges (including, break costs) payable or which would be due on the next interest payment date by the senior lender with respect to any advance or drawing made by a liquidity facility provider or otherwise in connection with the loan; and
- the reasonable costs and expenses incurred by the selling lender as a result of the acquisition.

Whether default interest and prepayment fees are included in the above will be negotiated on a case-by-case basis, but it is fairly common for such items not to be included. Further, if there is lender level hedging arrangements in place, in respect of the senior loan being sold, relevant hedging termination costs would be included in the above list if such hedging arrangements are not being transferred across to the purchasing junior lender.

7.6   Enforcement

As noted in the previous Chapter, the rights of a junior lender to instruct enforcement action are set out in the intercreditor agreement. Any enforcement rights also depend on the security the junior lender holds in respect of the loan. For example, if the junior lender is a B lender under the whole loan, it would be expected that the junior lender and the senior lender would share an interest in the security whilst, if the junior lender's position is that of a mezzanine-type lender, it may have its own separate subordinated security package ranking behind the senior security.

Ordinarily, intercreditor agreements as used in European CRE financing transactions, will either provide the junior lender with no right to cause an enforcement, or a limited right of enforcement. In the former case, the rights granted to the junior lender to cure a specified list of defaults, or to acquire the senior loan upon a material event of default (for which see above) would be argued by a senior lender as representing sufficient protection for a junior lender, faced with a probable enforcement scenario. In the latter case, the junior lender could be prevented from taking any such action through a control valuation type of event. Such tests would ensure that the value of the underlying property is sufficient to cover a full recovery of the senior loan plus an addition buffer, normally determined to be 125% of the senior loan. Further, a junior lender would be prohibited from taking any steps to accelerate the relevant junior loan or enforcement action until the expiry of a standstill period provided that the senior creditor has not itself accelerated the senior loan or commenced any enforcement action.

The length of any standstill period, applicable to the junior lender, would vary depending on the nature of the default in question, such as a payment, financial covenant or other default. These periods are typically heavily negotiated between the parties but it is usual, particularly pre-2007, to see periods oscillating between 90 and 150 days from loan default. On expiry of the standstill period, if the relevant default remained outstanding or, the security trustee or special servicer had not taken any enforcement action and provided always that a control valuation event had not occurred in respect of the relevant junior loan, the junior lender would be entitled to take or instruct the relevant agent or special servicer to take enforcement action.

Absent any right of the junior lender to instruct enforcement action, the senior lender would commonly be able to direct enforcement action. Any such instructions from the senior lender would remain subject to any cure or purchase option rights and timetables, in respect thereof, to which the junior lender would be entitled. During such periods, the senior lender would not be entitled to take enforcement action as discussed above. Usually, when exercising such rights, the senior lender would not be obliged to take into account the interests of the junior lenders, when instructing the relevant party to take enforcement action. In some transactions, the junior lender may be able to have an indirect influence on the enforcement process, by being able to terminate and propose the appointment of its preferred special servicer. Certain conditions will be attached on the identity of any such proposed special servicer will be discussed in Chapters 9, 10 and 11, though this right ensures, that for so long as the junior lender has enough equity in the deal, it will be able to have some degree of influence on the management of a specially serviced loan. This power to terminate and appoint a special servicer, will typically be provided in situations where the whole loan is being serviced on behalf of both the senior and junior lenders. However, the inclusion of such a right and additional consent and consultation, as discussed above, may be afforded to the junior lenders in circumstances where the junior loans are not being serviced.

Although the above scope of junior lender enforcement rights is commonly seen in Europe, there may be some variations to the above depending on the transaction in question. For example, certain transactions may provide the junior lender with the power to require the disposal of properties at any time, once enforcement of the whole loan has commenced, if any such disposal proceeds would be sufficient to repay the senior loans. The principle behind these types of variants is to afford the junior lender with a greater voice in the process, where there is enough value in the transaction to repay the senior loans and any additional costs in full.

One of the distinguishing features of the senior/mezzanine intercreditor arrangement has been the ability of the mezzanine lender to be able to enforce its own separate security to gain control over the mezzanine borrower and, by virtue of the same, the senior borrower and obligors. As in a senior/mezzanine structure there are two distinct loans made at two different levels in the borrower group structure, the mezzanine lender would obtain security interests over its borrower and share in the security granted by the senior borrower to the senior lender. This sharing of security would either take place by way of having the same security interests securing both the senior and mezzanine loan obligations (where the intercreditor would specify the priority of recovery of the senior loan over the mezzanine loan) or by way of separate security where the senior lenders would benefit from a first priority security interest and the mezzanine lenders from a second priority interest. However, the mezzanine only security over the mezzanine borrower would only benefit the mezzanine lenders.

As, in the case of financial covenants, there are instances where the mezzanine loan could potentially be in default prior to the occurrence of an event of default under the senior loan (for example and in addition to the occurrence of a financial covenant default, the occurrence of a payment default under the mezzanine loan whilst enough cash had been available to ensure that outstanding amounts owing the senior loan on a given payment date had been paid in full). This earlier trigger, if compared with the timing of the occurrence of a senior event of default, allows the mezzanine lender to be able to enforce the mezzanine only security and gain control over the mezzanine borrower. The senior/mezzanine intercreditor agreement would specify the circumstances in which such mezzanine only security enforcement could take place, what steps would have to be taken by the mezzanine lender following it gaining control of the mezzanine borrower and the consequences that would flow as a result to the rights of the mezzanine lenders under the intercreditor agreement.

The senior/mezzanine intercreditor agreement would typically provide that the right of the mezzanine lenders to exercise the enforcement over the mezzanine only security could take place following a mezzanine event of default and may be subject to a pre-agreed consultation period between lenders. The effect of the acquisition of the mezzanine borrower shares will require that the mezzanine lender or any agreed transferee, within a prescribed period, complies with any senior lender "know your customer" diligence requirements as well as cures any outstanding senior loan events of default outstanding and it would be agreed that the resulting change of control of the borrower group would not in itself result in a breach of the terms of the senior loan. Given that the mezzanine lender following such acquisition will be both in control of the borrower group and the mezzanine lender for purposes of the senior/mezzanine arrangements, it would be expected that the senior lenders would require that certain rights granted to the mezzanine lenders under the intercreditor agreement be disapplied (such as any consent rights in respect of any proposed amendments or waivers of the terms of the senior loan documents, cure rights exercisable by the mezzanine lenders to cure any senior loan curable defaults and any rights to instruct the enforcement of the common security).

Whilst traditionally this mezzanine only security enforcement feature has been associated with senior/mezzanine loan structures it is, at the time of writing, being more frequently proposed in A/B structures which raises issues as to how this can be implemented into a whole loan structure where the security afforded by the borrower would, in principal, secure the entirety of the whole loan debt. As in contrast to a senior/mezzanine arrangement, the A/B structure relates to a whole loan there are structural issues as to how a separate component of the security package (a share security) can be enforced by a B lender without triggering the enforcement of the entirety to the whole loan debt. If this feature is proposed in connection with a A/B structure, care would need to be taken by the lenders to ensure that it works within the way the loan has been originated and, from a B lender's perspective, whether in fact it could in practice be exercisable without triggering unanticipated consequences.

7.7   Transfer restrictions

During the GFC it became increasingly common that borrowers or affiliates of borrowers, in an attempt to maximise opportunities raised by financial institutions, needed to address relevant regulatory capital requirements, raise liquidity and dispose of loan assets. Such parties sought to purchase and/or pay off positions in related loans at a discount (so-called DPO),[16] in order to reduce leverage and influence loan administration processes, including prospects of enforcement. Such a trend has also been seen in secondary market trading of whole loan CMBS, where positions have been acquired to exert control over the appointment of special servicers and the consequent influence such would have over the administration and enforcement process of a non-performing loan.

Historically, limitations on the parties to whom a junior lender or senior lender have been able to transfer part or the entirety of the position in a loan have been typical and would be included as a restriction on transfer in an intercreditor agreement. These have typically followed Loan Market Association (LMA) standards, where the transferee is expressed to be a financial institution, or by way of the inclusion of either a general but narrower description of the type of entities to which such interests could be

---

[16]   See Ch.5.

transferred and/or the inclusion of a "black list" of lenders to which transfers would be prohibited. Such restrictions have been aimed at addressing the potential misalignment of objectives between lenders, whose motivations are influenced by other interests, than ordinary lenders ultimately concerned in achieving a full recovery of proceeds due to it under the loan.

In order to address concerns of undue influence of sponsors, borrowers and their affiliates in the day-to-day administration of a loan, post-GFC transactions have sought to restrict the rights which such parties may be entitled to exercise upon an acquisition of the loan. This is dealt with under the related documentation by providing for the:

- disapplication of voting rights in approving any consent, waiver, amendment or any other matter;
- removal of any right to attend any meetings between the other lenders when dealing with matters pertaining to the loan;
- removal of any right to receive any communications or notices prepared for the benefit of the other lenders;
- exclusion of any benefit in the security package securing such loan;
- cessation of any entitlement to receive certain payments (e.g. tax gross-up payments or increased costs); and
- excluding the amount held by such lender from any computations used to determine the identity of the requisite proportion of lenders constituting a majority position.

upon such party acquiring an interest in the loan. This is also relevant for purposes of the enforcement of mezzanine only security where the mezzanine lender acquires control over the borrower group as described in section 7.6 above. Furthermore, upon the securitisation of the loan any such acquisition by a related party would be prohibited. Similarly, post GFC whole loan CMBS deals have also gone a step further by treating any bonds held by the sponsor, borrower and their affiliates as if they were not outstanding and, accordingly, carrying no rights for the purposes of any quorum required to pass a resolution of bondholders, computing the necessary majorities required to approve a written resolution and giving instructions to the relevant note trustee.

7.8 Negotiating intercreditors from an investor's perspective

Having discussed the technical aspects of intercreditor agreements above and how, in particular, junior lenders might approach the negotiation of these documents and what such parties try to achieve through these discussions, will now be discussed. What follows is not meant to give an exhaustive view on how to negotiate the finer details of the above, but more to give a framework to the practitioner.

Typically, the vast majority of what is documented in an intercreditor agreement will only come into play when a transaction starts going wrong and there are issues relating to the borrower's performance of its obligations. When the deal is performing, a lender will usually only be concerned about when and in what amount it will get paid and accordingly there is no great need to look beyond what is expressed in the payment waterfall. However, the vast majority of what is contained in a typical intercreditor agreement will deal with theoretical outcomes, once things start to go wrong. It is therefore paramount to have a clear idea of what parties are trying to achieve in terms of rights at the outset of the negotiation. This will depend on the asset type, the leverage and also on the other parties involved in the negotiation and the way parties anticipate they might react in a default situation.

Taking the sections above in order, the following is a non-exhaustive list of commercial issues worth consideration for each category.

7.8.1   Waterfall

In an intercreditor, the key thing to consider, aside from the initial ordering of payment, are the events that can cause this ordering to change. Typically these are linked to events of default, but the precise parameters are often up for discussion. For instance, as a mezzanine lender, one should always push to restrict the events that can cut off such lender's cashflow to certain limited events of default. In practice, from a mezzanine lender's perspective, a mezzanine lender's position is best protected if it is subject to any payment stops only upon the occurrence of a Material Event of Default (Payment Default, Financial Covenant Default or Insolvency Event). It is also common for the mezzanine lender to push for the mezzanine coupon to still be paid when a cash trap event is triggered as opposed to the occurrence of an Event of Default. On the other hand, if a senior lender, the converse applies. Other points to note are where the hedging payments rank. This will depend on the relative negotiating power of the hedge provider. The particular payments to consider are hedging breakage costs, as these are the most volatile as exemplified by the period 2008 to 2012.

7.8.2   Hedging

The main argument is typically whether the swap should rank senior or pari passu with the senior lender. It is widely accepted that the swap would rank senior, but one would expect this might change given the issues caused by long dated super senior swaps in the structures being worked out at the time of writing.[17] The other points of discussion are usually where

---

[17]   See further Ch.12.

termination payments rank and when the swap counterparty itself defaults. From a junior lender perspective, there is usually no real position to take here, unless it is to use it as a giveaway point for something else.

7.8.3 Servicing

This is very much transaction specific and the main discussions are typically around the level of fees. If the CMBS market is ever properly resurrected to pre-2007 levels, one would anticipate a lot of discussion around the powers of servicers, as discussed in Chapters 9, 10 and 11. There has been a lot of difficulty caused by the lack of clear guidelines for servicers, in particular, at how servicers look after the interests of different lenders with different priority rankings. At the time of writing, the agency role contemplated in most modern intercreditors provide for as little discretion as possible, as this usually completely controlled by the majority (senior) lenders.

7.8.4 Entrenched rights

The basic principle is that all classes of lender are going into a transaction on a set of pre-agreed terms and these terms should not be varied on an ongoing basis, given that this changes the credit profile for the other parties to the transaction. Senior lenders have attempted to modify these clauses, in order to have the discretion to vary the term of their senior loan. From a junior lender perspective, the only power a typical junior lender can accept to give to a senior lender, in these situations, is limited to extensions and or certain waivers, e.g. senior lenders may be permitted to be more lenient if they so decide without junior lender consent. A junior lender should not accept any rights for a senior lender to make their loan more onerous for the borrower, without junior lender consent as that takes the parties closer to a senior default with the usual anticipated consequences. Another mechanic that has been resurrected is the concept of control valuation events that can switch off a junior lender's rights. This should be restricted due to the potential volatility of third party appraisals and should not be necessary if the remainder of the entrenched rights clause is structured well.

As a junior lender one should expect that the overall structure and profile of the senior position should not change throughout the life of the deal in a way to make the deal more risky for the junior lender. This is achieved by restricting the senior lender's ability to increase economics, tighten covenants, change the amortisation profile or charge increased fees on a bilateral basis with the borrower. Other restrictions should be added to prevent the modification of the security and release pricing arrangements over the underlying collateral.

174

7.8.5   Cure rights/purchase options

These are key rights in the context of a default as they allow the junior lender to keep the loan alive and avoid being "cut off/out" by the senior lender if they believe that there is value left in the asset for the junior loan. The key is to ensure that there are sufficient cure rights available and to distinguish between junior lender cure rights from those afforded to the borrower under the underlying loan documents, if at all possible. This will allow junior lenders more time to fix a problem. If these cure rights are deficient, it may become necessary for junior lenders to buy out the senior loan. This is usually done by auctioning a purchase option. This option is usually linked to a default. In this regard, from a junior lender perspective, the key point is to make sure any prepayment or exit fees are waived in the case of the purchase option being exercised.

From a practical standpoint it is important to make sure that any arrange-ment agreed above can be made to work within the constraints applicable to the junior lender in approving and drawing capital as the sums needed to cure can be material. This is dealt with by agreeing the time periods that the junior lender has to both signify their intent to exercise an option to cure or to buy out but also the time period they have to complete on the payment/acquisition. It is also important to secure additional cure rights above and beyond the borrower's for a junior lender. This allows a realistic prospect of being able to control and step in to a distressed situation if a borrower runs out of cure options.

7.8.6   Security package and enforcement

This is the most important part of the intercreditor agreement, as this will govern how recoveries are made and who can control that process. In the market that exists at the time of writing, it appears to be widely accepted that the senior lender has unfettered rights to enforce on their security package, which principally in senior/mezzanine loan structures, will usually include a first ranking mortgage and first ranking share pledge on the asset holding company. The key from a junior lender perspective is therefore to seek, at the time of the structuring of the transaction, a senior share pledge at a company higher up in the structure, with the ability to enforce on that share pledge, without needing the consent of the senior lender and without triggering a change of control event for the senior loan. The ability to enforce can be achieved by setting covenants on the junior loan to be more sensitive than the senior loan covenants, such that a junior loan default is triggered before a senior loan default. It is also key to make sure that the senior loan does not cross default with the junior loan for this mechanic to work properly. The last things to avoid are senior lender attempts to tie obligations to cure senior events of default to the enforce-ment of this separate share pledge.

If all the above points are achieved, a junior lender should have structured a position where they can step into the equity with minimal disturbance to the senior financing in place, which is a precious commodity in today's senior debt-constrained marketplace as it goes to the heart of the ability for, particularly, a mezzanine lender to be able to step in and control a distressed situation and ultimately attempt to control the outcome.

These mechanics are tricky to set up and are usually the subject of intense negotiation. The key flashpoints for a mezzanine lender (in particular, but exportable to an A/B arrangement where the step-in right is provided for in the structure, as discussed above) are usually:

- Events that trigger the right for the mezzanine lender to step in:
    i) Mezzanine only events of default: tighter covenants or milestones for example.

    ii) Common events of default where the mezzanine cures the senior Event of Default.

- Any hoops the mezzanine lender has to jump through before they can step in
    i) Senior "know your customer" requirements.

    ii) No adverse tax effects on the structure.

    iii) Requirement to cure senior Events of Default either pre or post step in.

- Ability to assign the step in right to third parties:
    i) Affiliates of the original junior lender.

    ii) Pre-agreed whitelist expressly authorising the transfer to certain pre-identified potential transferees.

    iii) Qualifying Institution concept (i.e. financial institutions typically both experienced in the CRE sector as well as holding a certain amount of investment in similar positions on their books).

- Time periods to signify the intention to step in and to execute the step in.

Setting up the mechanics above in a way that is executable in practice is challenging as there are multiple scenarios and outcomes that need to be catered for. The assignability of the right to step in is always a hotly contested point as senior lenders need to accept the possibility that anybody that benefits from this right may end up being a sponsor of the transaction.

7.9 Conclusion

The key to successfully negotiating intercreditor agreements rests in the ability to understand, manage and ultimately accommodate the requirements and concerns of the different classes of participating lenders.

Senior lenders typically require control over the collateral and an ability to control outcomes once certain levels of distress have been crossed. The junior lender's best outcome is thus to be able to control situations effectively before they reach that stage and give themselves the time to be able to effect a turnaround. This is usually achieved by structuring the junior covenant package, cure/buyout rights and, particularly in a senior/mezzanine structure, step in rights to work as a system giving multiple "bites at the apple" whilst keeping the senior lenders comfortable.

Knowing what is a practical solution versus a theoretical right is also key. Negotiations often reach a crossroads on the most hypothetical of points, whilst more important practical points often get much less focus. Rights to buy out senior loans are great for a junior lender on paper but need large amounts of capital to effect and therefore are not as practical as they may first seem. The inclusion or exclusion of default interest/prepayment fees and how they are allocated between the lenders, whilst seemingly important, would probably fade into the background at the time that these options are ever contemplated to be exercised. A very effective step in right is, from a junior lender's perspective, much more valuable. As a junior lender one of the greatest bugbears are control valuation type mechanics as they introduce mark-to-market type volatility to situations that require time and a cool head.

In summary, when approaching these negotiations it pays to have a roadmap in mind of the path that a lender would want to use in practice and to structure the negotiations to achieve this. This allows the prioritisation of negotiation points and a successful negotiation and concession strategy in order to secure the key points that any lender may require to be achieved at the outcome of any negotiation process.

Chapter 8

The Role of Development Finance

Jonathan Monnickendam,
Lloyds Bank

8.1   Introduction

This Chapter examines why development finance has become so popular during the phase of the real estate cycle evident at the time of writing. It will question whether the search for yield, at a time when there is a surplus of savings looking for a safe home, is driving the popularity of development finance, or whether such popularity is driven by an ageing population in the developed world looking for a safe return in their extended retirement, or from sovereigns and UHNWs (Ultra High Net Worth) in the developing world, looking for high quality assets to preserve a portion of their wealth. Ultimately, whatever the answer, there is no doubt that the demand for low risk assets has increased and so has the definition of what is acceptable to the extent that prime real estate is now included. Even though real estate (even the finest real estate) can be both volatile and illiquid, yet only a small increase in the allocation to real estate by global fund managers can have a significant increase in the demand for real estate markets, markets which are far smaller and heterogeneous than mainstream assets classes, and often parochial. Thus investors are looking at established prime assets, considering that the yield—the income element of anticipated return on real estate—is more attractive compared to the more mainstream investments such as gilts. Historically, such investors are correct, but it is yet to be seen if the risk premium for real estate, seen at the time of writing, is a sufficient reward for the volatility in capital values and uncertainty over rental growth in a slower growing world.

8.2   Why the appeal of development?

There is also a question to be asked about the appeal of development in 2016, in comparison to the previous cycle (see further Chapter 2 for a detailed discussion of the property cycles and their nature). The last property cycle resulted in investors looking to secondary or even tertiary office buildings and shopping centres around the UK, typically found in the lesser cities and lesser towns. A problem with such assets however, was that whilst they may have the same kinds of tenants found in the largest and most prime shopping centres that would be found in or near to the biggest cities, the difference was of the absence of a deep investor base for the shopping centres in smaller towns. The tenants may have been the same, but the investor base simply was not there outside the big cities and major locations, once the cycle turned. In a similar way, in the previous cycle, investors looked at OpCo/PropCo structures that separated the operating business from the property business and put the property business into a separate vehicle. The idea was, that by placing the operating and property businesses into separate entities, with a long lease between linking the two whole businesses, this would able the borrower to borrow more, and by placing the properties with eager investors, create a demand for a new property class. This was certainly the case in the leisure sector, in gyms and sports clubs and racquet clubs. However, as was seen during the GFC, there was no depth to the investor market when tested.

In addition, in the last cycle there were lenders willing to provide close to 100% of the finance required on standing stock, allowing investors to make significant returns whilst risking only limited equity. This raised the question of why take the risk of a development when you make an even greater return on a standing asset through high leverage? In mid-2016, the route of high leverage does not really exist, as mainstream banks are now constrained by what the degree of leverage that they can offer. As discussed in the opening Chapters of this book, there are any number of debt funds that will provide significantly more leverage than the banks, but in the cycle seen post GFC, price is more congruent to the risk. It is more expensive and there is less of it.

In 2015–2016, institutional investors and others have begun to look at development finance in the belief that by creating an asset, by creating a new office building or a new logistics hub, they will be creating value and they will be able to keep the developer's profit. At the point of completion of the development, they can decide whether to hold the asset or sell it to an institutional investor looking for a modern configured building with good tenants. For much of the cycle post GFC, the focus has been on London, office and residential, and more recently logistics as the internet displaces and compliments established forms of retailing.

At the time of writing, there is a feeling that London has peaked (albeit the UK's vote to leave the European Union and the fall in sterling that immediately followed it has given prime City a reinvigorated boost, but it is too soon to tell whether this will last) and the focus is on the Big 6 Cities, where there is a shortage of modern configured stock across all classes. For example, if an occupier is looking for an office building in Manchester, the chances of finding something of scale and modern other than in one or two schemes is slim. This is because not very much has been built since 2006–2007 and the stock that was built then was probably put into planning some years before that. Of course there are other opportunities in the market in addition to development finance.

Finally, the demand for development finance is also aimed at new segments of real estate. At the ULI conference in May 2016, there was concentrated discussion of interest from institutional investors in operational assets. By operational, it is meant assets where there is no occupational lease that gives a guaranteed flow of rental income, upwards only and with the obligations falling on the tenant, which is the traditional lease in the UK. Instead investors have to take the risk of the operating business, with the rent paid as a result of the performance and management of the asset. Unsurprisingly, the interest through 2015–2016, has been strongest in sectors with strong defensive characteristics, ones that will perform well throughout the cycle. Examples of this would be student accommodation and more recently, PRS ("private rental sector"). That is to say every year students will turn up, they will stay for approximately 51 weeks of the year and given the growth characteristics of the UK university education system and the high regard within which the UK is viewed by overseas students and their parents, there will be another flow of students coming through next year paying market rent.

In providing an answer to why development finance is proving so popular in 2015–2016, this Chapter will consider:

(i)   the definition and introduction of development finance;
(ii)   a framework for assessment in three parts, business risk and financial risk protection;
(iii)   a review of each element of the framework;
(iv)   comment on the segments of the development market as seen in mid-2016; and
(v)   the conclusion.

It should be noted, as pointed out in the preface to this book that this Chapter has been written in mid-2016, following the UK's vote to leave the EU in June 2016 referendum, in a market where demand for development finance remains strong, even as the demand for investment finance appears to be slowing.

8.2.1   *The definition and introduction of development finance*

The definition of development finance that will be used throughout this Chapter has three elements which when added together create a situation whereby the asset has very little value, no income producing ability until practical completion (PC) and the recovery value on the land will be highly correlated to the performance of the asset. If the asset is completed as expected, value is created and the loan is repaid.

The key aspects are:

1.   asset specific finance;
2.   that leads to the creation and completion of a performing asset;
3.   which is capable of sale or refinance at PC or stabilisation.

Taking each of those three phrases: asset specific means that the asset is the sole source of repayment. This is important because this sets the transaction apart from the rest of the business. By contrast, many property companies in the UK, the REITs and the like, will undertake developments but will build them using a general corporate funding structure. That is to say they have a revolving credit facility (RCF) which they use to fund the development costs and that RCF is serviced by the income earned from the standing assets. They have no requirement for asset specific finance.

Secondly, the creation and completion of the performing asset is important, as a development creates an asset and once this process has commenced it does not make commercial or economic sense to stop this creative process, as a lender or a borrower. Thus getting it through to PC is very important. If a development is stopped half way through the process, the equity has no value and more than likely the debt will have limited value as well. A half complete shopping centre is worth much less than a half let shopping centre.

Thirdly, the asset has to be capable of sale or refinance at PC or stabilisation. A very important aspect of development finance is a clear understanding of what the exit is, and this should be in place at first drawdown.

For example, for an office building, a lender would want to be sure that at first drawdown the borrower has sufficient agreements for a lease to be in place, to demonstrate that the expected rent in the business plan is realistic and that the tenants are of the right quality. These are the lettings that make the lender comfortable and thereafter other lettings are for equity which will have views on how to maximise the rent on the remaining space. These initial lettings should be sufficient to allow the lender to see the development continue through to PC without interruption, since as discussed above, it makes no economic or commercial sense to stop a development whilst in progress. The combination of initial and subsequent lettings should see the asset largely let by PC, which should make it as attractive for an investment loan with a higher amount of debt. In effect, the asset will be considered to be self-sustaining and attractive, creating a rental income which is capable of supporting refinance. The importance of this third point is absolutely fundamental. As stated above, if a lender is undertaking development finance, it should always understand what its exit is and ensure that the exit is simple and clear, right from the point of first drawdown. If a lender does not have that in place from the start, then the lender is taking unnecessary risk and may well have mispriced the transaction.

8.2.2 *Development finance and other forms of lending to real estate*

Development finance is one of the three types of lending common to the real estate financing industry in the UK provided by mainstream lenders. The other two are investment finance and general corporate funding, usually though RCFs.

Investment finance is secured upon existing stock that is performing assets with a rent roll where the issue is not how to get the thing built, but how to manage the asset once it is built, so as to nurture the right kind of income and see it grow. The lender has certainty, as it is lending to an identifiable pool of assets and tenants and any significant change to that pool requires lender approval. It may be an office building with a limited number of tenants, which appears quite straightforward but obviously carries event risk due to the lack of diversity and the maturity profile of the leases. Should one of those tenants fall away, a significant part of the rental income will be lost. By contrast, in a retail environment, a lender should feel comfortable with the demand for the vacant space because of the draw created by strong anchor tenants on long leases, whilst recognising that lesser retailers will come and go, giving a multi-tenanted shopping centre characteristic, similar to an operational asset.

The third variety of property finance is RCF. This is a structure typically used by publicly quoted borrowers, in particular whereby given their strength and visibility and sometimes a rating by credit rating agencies (see further Chapter 14). The class of borrowers will be able to borrow on a largely unstructured basis, that is to say, their reputation allows them to acquire and dispose of assets at will and with little involvement from lenders who are perhaps more concerned about winning the next bond mandate. The lender has less certainty over the pool of assets and must have complete trust in the borrower; hence it is typically available to those publicly quoted. The certainty gained by the structure is replaced by lower leverage and the exposure of the business to the public eye; from auditors, disclosures to the stock exchange and ultimately public censure for failure.

8.2.2.1 *Compared to project finance*

Some regard development finance as similar to project finance, such as schools, roads, bridges and hospitals, but development finance is very different, hence the different structures used. For instance, if analysing the provision of a school, a lender would look at the two big questions: performance risk and payment risk. Performance risk would entail questions around whether they can build it and operate it, and whether the operator is of sufficient quality to ensure the asset is created to the right standard within the allowed costs. The payment risk would focus on the ability of the off-taker to pay for the use of the asset. However, such analysis is not sophisticated enough, because in project finance there is typically a single off-taker of a (quasi-)sovereign quality on a very long contract from the outset, such that there should be no doubt over the payment risk. The main risk arises from the concept of availability, that the asset is fit for purpose, for an agreed percentage of the time, and is of a standard that the operator has to achieve to receive full payment. By contrast in real estate, the focus is typically on the multiple off-takers of lesser quality (tenants on shorter leases, finding their replacements when leases expire). The concept of availability does not really exist in real estate as most obligations relating to the availability of the asset fall on the off-taker under the FRI lease.

8.3   Framework for Assessment

One way to look at a development finance transaction is to divide the framework assessment into three areas—

1.   business risk;
2.   financial risk; and
3.   protection.

Business risk looks at the asset side of the balance sheet and combines the land, the intellectual capital that comes with it (both the planning permission and relationships with planning authorities), and finally the equity which may come from an unrelated source, but needs to be fully invested before debt is drawn.

Financial risk looks at the liability side of the balance sheet. The usual focus is on the debt structure which in some corporates can be complicated, but in a development deal there is a single source of debt which may involve more than one lender but always within a single structure. Once the loan has been signed it is straightforward, with drawings under this structure to take place each month against an agreed drawdown profile, with work done certified by a lender's project monitor. There is of course hedging to be agreed too. The real focus in a development deal is on the position at exit, at PC or shortly after; engineering a situation at first drawdown that allows for a clear exit. This will involve demonstrating that the asking rent is reasonable, by achieving sufficient lettings to give comfort that the client's strategy is viable and that the break-even rent for the lender on the remaining space is a modest relative to the current market rate.

There is one other critical factor, unrelated to the above, to consider and that is stock selection; choosing the deals that are most likely to happen, within the agreed term sheet and commenced by the expected date. Development finance differs from investment finance in that a borrower does not have a ready standard debt structure. Instead the structure of the lend is bespoke, agreed over a period of time as the deal evolves. In addition, there are a number of reasons, even when the financial structure is agreed, that the deal does not proceed as quickly as expected. This can happen before work on site starts, e.g., an objection to the planning permission just before expiry of a judicial review period, that is sustained. Moreover, it can happen after work on site has begun with the unexpected discovery of important archaeological remains, which will delay the start of the construction and push back the expected date of PC.

Clearly some of this cannot be foreseen, but one skill for an originator looking to hit his/her income target for the year is stock selection. It can be argued that this is another element of the intellectual capital of the borrower, but for a lender the conclusion is clear: make sure there is a large enough pipeline of development deals to allow for unexpected delays.

8.3.1 Business risk—who is the sponsor?

For deals using development finance it is more important to know the sponsor behind the scheme. There are three elements to the sponsor: the intellectual sponsor, the financial sponsor and the wider professional team.

First is the intellectual capital behind the deal. Often the intellectual sponsors are small outfits, as few as 5–20 people, who have an excellent record in finding sites, buying them, owning them outright or having access to them under an option to buy. Such teams can be proficient in buying sites without planning permission, working up the business plan, engaging with the community and getting the local authority on side and then obtaining planning permission. At this stage they introduce a financial sponsor as they themselves do not have the equity to make the development bankable.

Identifying the track record of the individuals behind the intellectual sponsor is not always as easy as might be expected, as property is a highly highly fragmented business, making it difficult to know what the team and the individuals therein have done in the past and especially how they behaved in the difficult times of 1990 and 2008; did they stay to work out troubled assets even though their equity had no value at the time, or did they simply hand the keys to the lender and walk away? There are many property professionals who operate below or away from the trade press, so a lender may have to do significant research.

Identifying the financial sponsor is easier because they are larger organisations, often financial institutions with a recognised regulator. Due diligence for this sponsor should be far easier. Once they have made that financial contribution in the form of the equity that goes in ahead of the debt, a lender should further be sure that the financial sponsor has the additional equity, the deep pockets, to resolve unexpected situations when one aspect of the development goes awry. In addition, the financial sponsor will often bring its own intellectual capital, akin to best practice, created by working on a number of different schemes with a range of intellectual sponsors.

8.3.2 Business risk—the professional team and understanding the development

In most development deals the sponsors will engage a number of highly specialised professional teams. A lender can regard this as an extension of the intellectual capital of the sponsor because developers will want a settled and experienced team of professionals around them that have worked together before, giving confidence that the development will be delivered, complete with variations along the way. In addition, the small teams of the intellectual sponsor do not have the time or resource to search for the ideal specialist for each development, preferring to have a team of reliable professionals who can work together and on whom they can call.

The supporting cast of professionals for a development may be long, but the roles are self-evident, so there is no need to go into detail. Fortunately a lender does not have to deal with the wider team as it will appoint its own professionals to look after its interest, consisting of a limited number, whose role is understand and precis the key elements of the deal. Such professionals would typically comprise the following:

- Archaeologist
- Architect
- Development Manager
- Engineers
- Environmental expert
- Interior designer
- Leasing and sales appropriate to each sector so it could be a combination of office, retail, leisure and residential
- Main contractor
- Mechanical and Engineering experts
- Planning experts
- Project monitor
- Quantity surveyor
- Structural civil transport engineer

It is comforting to the lender to understand which professionals make up the sponsor's team. In considering the size of the team the question to be asked is: has the team built something of this size before in this location and with this mix of uses? In considering complexity, whilst architects may enjoy challenging construction techniques, a lender will want to understand what technical challenges the development contains. Moreover, does the development contain any unique source of supply—is there any part of the development for which there is a single supplier? This needs to be considered in depth when looking at developments using modular construction. As regards cash flows and contingencies the usual questions of the cash flow models—has the lender understood the key drivers stress tested them? And contingencies—what contingency has been built into costings by the developer? Finally as regards the business plan, including the letting strategy for the life of the development—is there a clear and common understanding between lender and borrower as to what will happen and what assumptions are made about growth in rent or sales values?

Review of all of the above by the lender's own professional team, most obviously the project monitor, is paramount.

Any development lender should always visit the site, to see what the proposed development looks like and how well it fits with the surrounding area. A lender should always question whether its perception fits with what is really there, as the area may have changed significantly since the last visit. In this situation, a lender should listen to advice of their own professionals and also bear in mind the research and comments from the developer's team as these provide invaluable information, integral to the decision on whether to lend. However they are professionals who are paid a fee but take no direct risk in the transaction, thus their advice should always be critically analysed, because as a lender, it is the lender's money, so a lender must be satisfied that the deal makes sense, including whether the development is congruent with the area where it is to be built.

Consequently, it is only by visiting the site that a lender can understand why a development may work. Where the location is relative to transport hubs, how it compares to competing stock, what type of tenants are in the competing stock and how much space do they take, compared to the scheme the lender is being requested to back and ultimately how attractive the scheme is to potential tenants.

After all, a lender does not have to like a proposal, a lender does not have to share the architect's taste; what is of key importance is that a lender has explored all concerns and risks, and understands and ultimately accepts, why a proposal works. This may involve challenging some of the lender's preconceptions of an area as sometimes a lender may find that an area has significantly changed in a short period of time and that what would not have worked a few years ago is now eminently practical. The development of Spitalfields was proposed many times over many years, but did not happen until there were enough positives with the site and the area, is but one example.

8.3.3 Analysing business risk—Section 106 agreements

This should not be a major issue in a development for the lender, but the relationship and agreement with the local authority granting permission is integral to a viable development. Such permissions come in the form of s.106 of the Town and Country Planning Act 1990 ("the 1990 Act") that provides a mechanism which makes a development proposal acceptable in planning terms, that would not otherwise be acceptable and the seal is a community infrastructure levy. A s.106 agreement is a legal agreement, made pursuant to s.106 of the 1990 Act, entered into between a local planning authority and persons interested in land, which imposes planning obligations. Planning obligations are typically used by local planning authorities to mitigate the negative impacts of a development and make it acceptable in planning terms. Examples of planning obligations include the payment of financial contributions, works requirements and restrictions on the use of the development. In the past, s.106 agreements have played an important role as the traditional method by which local planning authorities have funded infrastructure requirements within their areas. This role is now being challenged by a wave of reforms to the planning system introduced by the Government, such as the Community Infrastructure Levy (CIL) and reforms proposed under the Growth and Infrastructure Bill 2012–2013.

For a lender, the s.106 obligations become interesting when lending to a phased scheme. In this situation the lender will want to make sure that the s.106 agreement for that phase can be achieved during the life of the transaction into which the lender is funding. If it hasn't been achieved already, and it isn't achieved through the construction of what a lender is looking to fund, then a lender could be in a very difficult position, because there may still be obligations outstanding, perhaps on an adjacent site which means that completion is not a clean one and the local authority may still have rights over the scheme that has been built.

Often the focus of s.106 agreement is on affordable housing and the council is often assuaged with simple cash, the provision of affordable housing on a different site, or the provision of affordable on the same site as the development, at which point a lender needs to consider how the affordable housing is integrated into the whole scheme via the same entrance or a separate scheme.

8.3.4 *Analysing business risk—Cost certainty and cost overruns*

Cost inflation is an issue that all developers have to be aware of. There are a number of methods of dealing with the risk. One way of dealing with the risk is to insist on having a fixed price design and build contract with a single contractor. This passes the risk down to the contractor who fronts the whole construction contract to the developer and charges appropriately for this, providing certainty of costings but reducing the profitability of the developer. However, changes to the agreed build programme by the developer may allow the contractor to revisit costings. This requires the developer to adhere to the original plan, which sounds reasonable, until a lender remembers that tastes changes over time and what was current when the design was started may now look out of date. The developer therefore loses the flexibility to update the final finishes which are often the last part of the development to be built and make most impact. Whilst this may not be in the developer's interest, it is attractive to lenders as the construction risk has been mitigated.

Clearly the lender has to be satisfied with the strength of the contractor and this may be difficult to establish as the operating margin of a contractor is often fine. Moreover, in times of stress contractors will sometimes take on contracts at a below expected price, in the desire to maintain business and its team through the cycle, but not fix the price of the packages, only to discover that over the two or three years that the development takes place, the cost of packages has increased, but the contractor has no ability to pass them on.

The contractor may be able to absorb the additional cost or, if not, may go bust. It is important then to make sure that any business plan and budgeted costs are stress tolerant to allow for any deviation (1) for the contractor and (2) for an alternative contractor who may step in. A situation like this may see work on site come to a stop for a period whilst a replacement contractor is found and negotiations start with sub-contractors to find out who has and has not been paid. This is when the cost overruns and interest shortfall from a strong financial sponsor becomes important, as there will be cost overruns as contracts have to be revisited and interest shortfall used as the scheme will most likely be completed after the expected PC date.

There may well also be cost overruns that arise in the ordinary course of construction and without any contractor event, for no obvious reason car parks in city centre shopping schemes caused problems at a number of developments in the early noughties. If there are cost overruns, a lender would expect equity to go in first to cure it to ensure that the loan to cost ratio remains within anticipated bounds and the spend remains as expected.

8.3.5 Financial Risk—introduction

In real estate lending, financial risk focuses on the liability and the obligations that the borrower has to meet and the dates when these fall due. In a development most of these obligations will be debt which is used to pay creditors as the scheme progresses. The developer is unlikely to have many, if any, employees with the related obligations of tax and pensions. Financial risk in development finance is all about knowing that your scheme is fully funded and setting up the exit, both at first drawdown, to create the situation that when a development is approaching PC, or the point of stabilisation, that the borrower will be in a position to receive sufficient cash proceeds to pay the debt.

Once these two aspects are resolved the focus shifts to process and to ensuring the smooth running of the monthly drawdowns and payments released against certification of works, reviewed by the lender's project monitor, who has makes frequent site visits.

There can be overages, which are payments based on the profitability of the scheme to be made to a previous owner if a scheme is highly successful, but this should be a commercial transaction that sits outside the lender's security, only be paid at completion of the scheme, long after the bank has been repaid, and subordinated.

189

8.3.6 Financial risk—fully funded

A further question a lender should ask itself in terms of analysing the financial risk is whether or not the transaction is fully funded at the initial drawdown.

It is important to be able to say that on first drawdown the equity that has been invested, plus the money that a lender has committed to fund the costs through to PC, or, if it is a building for let where some lettings have been achieved but there are rent free periods (periods to which has contracted but no cash paid rent), then the development can proceed to a point where cash income starts to be paid and can be used to service ISCR (see further Chapter 4).

In simple language equity plus debt must equal or exceed the costs of the project. If not, the deal is not fully funded and a lender should not lend until it is. Regrettably situations where the answer (if asked) would have been answered in the negative, occurred in the previous cycle in lending by mainstream banks and this assisted in tarnishing development finance as being high risk. Consequently, a lender must be firm that the need to be fully funded at first drawdown is not negotiable. This point should be clarified in initial discussions with the borrower and confirmed at the time in sources and applications table to ensure that both sides have the same understanding and expectation.

For the development to work, it should be able to get a lender to a point at which the asset is completed and is income-producing as discussed above. The importance of all of this is, as discussed above, that once a development is started it makes no sense to stop. This is because in a development deal no one has a performing asset, *yet*. Looking at recovery values for a development if a lender has to stop work on site during the development period the recovery for debt will be modest at best, may be 10–20%, close or even less than to zero. Furthermore a lender will not want to cause a situation where the site is abandoned, the construction stops or the contractor goes bust. All those are very difficult to resolve. Once contractors are off site, the site will start to deteriorate, e.g. a half-built building with a concrete frame which is exposed to the elements for a long period of time. If a replacement main contractor has to be found then they will have to review the work done to date and will make the case that the more work that has been done the more difficult it is to assess the quality of that work. It will not be an attractive option for another contractor and probably not to potential purchasers of the assets when completed.

8.3.7 Financial risk—setting up the exit

Typically an exit means that at first drawdown a development should have secured sufficient presales or pre-lets to get a lender comfortable that the price point has been well tested to show that it is sufficient and realistic; and in the case of pre-lets, sufficient probably to make sure a lender has an agreed level of interest cover on the fully drawn debt.

With pre-lets, a lender will have its own view on what is sufficient. One approach is to look at the level of pre-let required to provide 1x–1.5x interest cover on the fully drawn debt and have this as a condition precedent for first drawdown. This may well require a pre-let of 30–40% of the space. A lender can then assess the break even rental level for the remaining space relative to the current demand in the occupational market. A lender may be willing to accept a lower level of pre-let if it believes that a pre-let is the anchor tenant, the one that sets the tone for the building. The term anchor tenant is used most frequently for retail but it can apply to a multi-tenanted office development as well.

Other approaches include the borrower starting with a lower level of pre-lets with the financial sponsor providing a principal guarantee if lettings have not reached a certain level at an agreed date, say PC, typically reducing debt to a serviceable level. Another option is to start with a lower level of pre-lets and limit the availability of the senior debt to an agreed covenanted level. Further drawdowns of senior debt require further lettings. This raises the question; how is the deal fully funded? This may mean bringing in a third party, such as a mezzanine lender to provide the debt to make the deal fully funded, with the result that as lettings increase, more of the senior facility becomes available and the mezzanine is reduced, all the while ensuring that the combination of equity, mezzanine debt and senior debt ensure that the deal is fully funded at all times. This route is more expensive for the borrower because mezzanine is expensive (see further Chapter 5), there are the additional fees incurred by the mezzanine lender's professional team in executing the deal, and finally the mezzanine and senior lenders will have to agree the intercreditor agreement.

8.3.8 The real estate lending cycle

Any business lending to real estate and especially developments should also take a conscious view on where the markets are in the cycle. If the typical development is expected to take three years to complete, where is the market expected to be in three years' time? This answer can be altered because within the real estate lending market many developers arrive at the same conclusion at the same time because they are working off the same model. This means that the market is rarely in balance, rather that there is an excess or a shortage. This is, of course fundamental to a lender understanding its exit. In addition to thinking about the position in the cycle, a lender needs a good understanding of competing schemes and how that development fits with developments that are taking place within a certain area. Clearly the preference is to have a development that completes first and one that has strong defensive characteristics, including limited competition.

191

8.3.9 Lender protection

There are three elements to lender protection: (i) security, (ii) enhancements and (iii) financial covenants. Business risk and financial risk have been discussed above, so now the protection that the lender has over and above the commercial transaction to give confidence to the deal will proceed as planned and the ability to intervene in certain circumstances, will be considered.

8.3.9.1 Security

The security package will typically include a fixed charge over the land, the most important part of the security, either freehold or long leasehold, as well as over the shares in the vehicle owning the land. If the collateral is leasehold, it is important to understand what rights the freeholder has over the leasehold interest and what obligations the leaseholder has to the freeholder. In some situations, involving local authorities or statutory authorities, the lender is asked to lend under a development agreement under which there is no security available at first drawdown. Instead it is only granted at or around PC when specific conditions have been met, which then allows the creation of a long leasehold interest, at which point there is security which can be charged. It is important to have a very clear understanding of all of the obligations that must be met for that lease to be granted; clearly the most transparent and commercial the obligations are the better. In such a situation, a lender is unsecured through to the point at which the lease is created. Being unsecured at the riskiest part of a development is not obviously attractive, but should not be rejected. Of course, relative to a fixed charge over the land, this is not as preferred a security, but it should be borne in mind that until the development is completed, the debt outstanding on a part completed development will have limited value and the recovery value will be modest. In summary, the fixed charge is good to have but it is not as powerful as it is in the world of investment lending.

8.3.9.2 Enhancements

These are benefits or obligations received from outside the transaction and their value lies in the fact that they are independent of performance of the project. The usual enhancement is a guarantee from an entity of substance, perhaps a financial sponsor or an entity related to that financial sponsor to cover cost overruns and interest shortfalls. It is not usually cash collateralised so that any lender should undertake its own assessment of the standing of that financial sponsor and their ability to pay under the guarantee through the life of the transaction. Typically the call under a guarantee is greater the further you are into the development.

This answers the request often made by borrowers: can the cost overrun or interest guarantee taper over time because the closer the PC, the lower the risk of a problem. This should be resisted as the work undertaken early in a development is quite simple and inexpensive, such as demolition, site clearance and piling. As a development moves closer to completion, the cost of items increases such that a lender typically will fund M&E, finishes, cladding and flooring. If something goes wrong it is expensive too, because the developer will have to remove whatever is there already, replace it with an alternative and still make it look as good as it should have been the first time. There are other enhancements; not common in the UK but in the US developers offer performance guarantees.

The cost overrun and interest shortfall guarantees are important part of lender protection because they bring fresh cash which ranks behind the senior debt to resolve issues that may otherwise have no easy resolution.

8.3.9.3   Financial Covenants

There are two important measurements which ensure that a development remains attractive to lenders. They are the loan to cost ratio (LTC) and the loan to gross development value (GDV). For mainstream UK lenders, the LTC is typically 60–65% and there may be an argument for going higher in certain situations, e.g. a building with long leases to high quality tenants. In the other direction it may be difficult to justify even a 60% LTC on assets where there is significant operating risk such as hotels, student accommodation or private rented sector (PRS), congruent with the greater volatility of income. Based on the constraint of the LTC, the loan to GDV (that is the ratio of total commitments (not the drawn loan balance)) to the expected value of the development, is typically 50–60%. If the loan to GDV is any higher then a lender should question the viability and profitability of the deal and whether the sponsor overpaid for the land. These two measures are key for keeping the deal in check. The loan to GDV is tested at the first drawdown, to ensure a viable deal but then the focus shifts to the LTC ratio, tested at each drawdown to ensure that the development is performing as expected.

There are other financial ratios worth bearing in mind, most obviously in the conditions precedent at first drawing, such as the levels of pre-sales relative to the debt and/or the level of pre-let income relative to the interest charged on the fully drawn facility. As discussed, a lender has to make sure it has sufficiently tested the market through sufficient pre-lets or presales.

8.4   Development finance: Case study of specific markets

8.4.1   Logistics market

Historically, logistics has been a higher yielding asset than most forms of real estate because the rental growth has been lower. This has the result that on day one a lender may receive an attractive coupon but would not underwrite significant rental growth. This has changed post 2011, due to an increased demand for logistics and an expanded demand for different forms of logistics. The cause is the continued rise of the internet, with new retail arrivals such as Amazon and established retailers offering home delivery, often with the option for delivery within 24 hours of placing the order. This requires a combination of logistics buildings, ranging from a limited number of the very large sheds located in a strategic locations to small local sites at the fringes of cities where those deliveries can be held, pending final delivery, the so-called "last mile", or whatever the real distance. With strong tenant demand for new units, whether large or small, rental growth in logistics is occurring, at the time of writing, for the first time in many years. The tenant quality should be strong and in some cases new to the sector, a welcome addition and bringing diversification to the investor universe so often trading at a premium to established occupiers. In addition, the lease lengths can often be long to allow for the depreciation of the fixtures and fittings, making them attractive to investors looking for that bond substitute. However, this should not distract from the credit quality of the tenant, because for all large sheds the fit out especially and the location to a lesser extent will be specific to the tenant. If that tenant fails, then a lender may have a long wait before the owner finds a new occupier. If funding the development of a large shed for a single occupier it is worth considering the ease of dividing it for use by multiple tenants.

The other side of the growth of logistics is the pain that the retail sector feels on the high street and in secondary and tertiary shopping centres, as discussed below.

8.4.1.1 Office

The office sector has been divided between London and the rest of the UK. London has seen good rental growth since the GFC, particularly in the West End. Historically, City of London rents were higher than the West End but that changed after the relaxation of the planning regime in the City, as it responded to the loss of tenants to Canary Wharf, starting in the 1990s. In 2016, the West End has had higher rents than the City of London, and growth continues there, as evidenced by a 2016 letting of £150 per sq ft in St James' Square of an upper floor to a hedge fund whereas the City has yet to exceed the £75 per sq ft peak achieved in the late 1980s. The West End benefits from the restrictions on development and height and remains a popular destination to the hedge fund sector and high end retail.

In contrast to the West End, the City of London is more open to development which means that the pressure of shortage of stock is unlikely to happen because there is in effect no planning barrier to entry. This meant that growth in rent was volatile and not sustainable because of the reliance on one sector, the financial sector and related services, occupying space in the City (questionable following the UK's vote to leave the EU following the June 2016 referendum). However, new sectors are coming into the City, forced out by the rents and space constraint in the West End. This is best illustrated by the tenant mix in the Walbrook building that, at the time of writing, is dominated by sectors taking City space. The increased diversity of tenants by sector and should make the City of London a more resilient market.

However, even in London there are new markets being established. Mid-town London is the area between the City of London and the West End where rents have traditionally been significantly lower than the two established markets. However, at the time of writing, this is no longer the case. Midtown is now regarded as being fashionable and rents there are often as high as the City if not even higher. Indeed one valuation firm specialising in Midtown presents its market as a North-South story, running from King's Cross all the way down through Farringdon through to Southbank, challenging the established perception of London as an East to West city. Some of the rental growth is due to anticipating the benefit of the Crossrail station at Farringdon. There are other examples, such as the expansion of a new business district next to Paddington station by a British Land building, the work done by Chelsfield, at Canary Wharf which continues to grow and at Kings Cross by Argent, and finally Stratford where the FCA and Transport for London are to move, which should trigger growth there.

Outside London and in the Big 6 Cities (Glasgow, Edinburgh, Leeds, Manchester, Birmingham and Bristol) rents have stabilised in the high £20s since the GFC, with Manchester breaking through into the low £30s. In many of these cities, there has simply been very little new office stock built whilst occupier demand has not been that strong and at the same time development finance remained scarce. However, there are signs of rental growth and development activity, initially in Manchester but starting to spread to the other five. This is clearly welcomed by local authorities keen to have some modern configured office stock to support the attractiveness of their cities to employers, existing and prospective. However, there is a concern that the June 2016 referendum vote will stymie this development, meaning that most of the Big 6 Cities will have very little new office stock to show for this cycle.

There hasn't been much development activity in retail since the GFC and this should not be a surprise, not just because of the impact of the GFC on availability of stock, but more importantly the way that retailer's operations had changed significantly before the GFC. The two themes in retail, the first being the reduction on demand for retail space in most locations, which leaves landlords looking for alternative uses for the surplus and often obsolete stock on the high streets and in the older shopping centres. The second is the demand for the very large shopping centres, 1m sq ft or more in areas with strong catchment areas. One current example is the revival and redevelopment of the Whitgift Centre in Croydon by Hammerson and Westfield which coincides with the rediscovery of Croydon as a dormitory suburb for London. This coincides with the expansion of the shopping centre into an experience, through the provision of quality food and beverage and of leisure which allows families to make a day out of a visit. If all of that is combined with a hotel, some open space and a major sporting and entertainment venue then you have what Quintain is creating at Wembley.

Another popular asset class in 2015–2016 is PRS. This is either a long established market from the early 20th century that is making a comeback, having been destroyed by inflation and government regulation in the 1970s, or a completely new sector which is residential by nature but with a focus on community, amenity and experience which makes the experience as important as the physical one of occupying. PRS differs from the existing buy to let market because the landlords operate at scale from purpose built buildings and appoint a professional management to provide high levels of service. PRS appeals to institutional investors searching for an income return that tracks or exceeds inflation and is reset every year so there is no waiting or appointing of professionals as happens in the five year rent review under mainstream CRE. The background to all of this is the shortage of modern housing in major UK cities. The risks to a landlord are income risk as the rental is re-set each year and will reflect market conditions at that time, both the wider economy (growth and employment) and local conditions (competing stock), and operational risk which institutional investors prefer stock to avoid. However, falling yields elsewhere has made PRS attractive. The risk to lenders is similar, but with the additional risk of the lack of pre-lets at first drawdown and the limited number of operators in the UK with experience of running PRS. However, this is a sector that should prove attractive as it is fast growing and fragmented. With significant completions due in 2016 and 2017, PRS operators have the opportunity to demonstrate their mettle in 201 and beyond.

The importance of scale and quality of service makes PRS attractive to a standardised approach to contain operating costs by using modular or volumetric construction. The means standardised flats, not just bathrooms and kitchen pods. There are other benefits to the developer through a quicker build time as units are assembled offsite, independent of events on site, and the quality of build should be more consistent as the working conditions are better. The owner then has a building which is generating income more quickly thus improving returns. The risk is the reliance on a single supplier for a very large element of the build contract which is not obviously appealing to lenders unless the supplier is part of a well-capitalised group. This may explain L&G's desire to use modular construction and own the supplier. It is early days for both PRS and modular construction but the combination should be successful.

8.4.1.2   Student Accommodation

This is a similar to PRS, being an operating business targeted at short dated lets: one year, to students, UK and overseas. There is no doubt that it is more established than PRS, being one cycle ahead, but it clearly has a narrower appeal, a smaller target market, and higher event risk, a single short letting period over the summer months through to September. At the time of writing, it appears to be a homogeneous market, yet clearly there are students of varying wealth and expectations raising the question whether there is space in the market for an expensive upmarket service orientated offering, similar to the lifestyle that the students have at home. In addition and post the June 2016 referendum, the government's views are awaited on the strong demand from overseas students: "Bad" views are that overseas students add to immigration numbers; "Good" are that they bring significant spend and a lasting admiration for all things British, useful when we have a huge current account deficit.

8.5 Conclusion

Development finance has a reputation for being high risk due to the complexity of construction, the possibility of cost overruns, letting and sales risk and to some extent poor underwriting standards. All this can make lending against standing stock as in an investment facility very appealing and less stressful than a full-on development. However, this Chapter has demonstrated that development finance can be an opportunity, as will be discussed further in the final Chapter to this book, and it can be a well remunerated form of lending, paying higher margins on deals with an average of less than three years, compared to the lower margins on a four–five year tenor on investment loans. As discussed above, the success factors for development finance are stock selection, an experienced team using reasonable leverage in a deal, which is fully funded, and has an exit which has been adequately tested prior to first drawdown, but still leaves enough room for equity to make its return.

The quantitative elements are important, most obviously that the deal is fully funded at first drawdown by known and certain sources, being equity and the various forms of debt. In the quantitative element, it is important to remember that is that there is less flexibility on the key ratios, such as LTC and loan to GDV, which also means less room for negotiation with developers. If the typical peak to trough change in property values is 40% then why would a lender lend more than 50% of the GDV on an asset which has yet to be built, has limited pre-letting and will not generate income for another three years? In other words an imprudent development lender cannot outrun the cycle and if 2015–2016 was the peak of the current cycle then stock selection and holding to those lending ratios will be central to all current lending decisions. Development finance is just the start but with the principles learned in this Chapter it certainly should be here to stay.

Chapter 9

Servicing and Asset Managing CRE Loans and CMBS Loans

James Buncle,

Director and Head of Legal, Mount Street Loan Solutions LLP

9.1 Introduction

There are many issues surrounding the asset management of CRE loans and loans held within a CMBS structure. This Chapter will tackle how the role of a facility agent, servicer and special servicer has been transformed since the vintage 2004–2007 originations, through the GFC, and go on to consider how they have had to adapt, and must continue to adapt to different market conditions and pressures. In highlighting these improvements in service levels, this Chapter will focus on the issues that the facility agent, servicer and special servicer have had to overcome in a very turbulent market.

At the time of the previous edition of this publication, the CRE market (and in particular CMBS) was barely showing signs of recovery following the GFC, due to several limiting factors, including availability of capital and poor market perception. Since then, as discussed in the opening Chapters of this book, we have seen an improvement and upturn in the CRE market, with refinancing of legacy deals, an influx of new sources of capital, and a willingness and appetite from both lenders and sponsors to forge ahead and do deals in the CRE market. The role of the facility agent, servicer and special servicer have had to adapt to this new market, by becoming much more involved and proactive in CRE financing structures than pre-GFC, in order to prove a transaction "value-add" and give confidence to all transaction parties. Whilst the markets may not witness the heady heights of 2004–2007 for some time (if ever), and the CMBS market continues to struggle at the time of writing, the green shoots of recovery have begun to take root since this publication was last visited in 2012. The question that remains to be answered is whether CMBS can overcome these regulatory (and, in many cases, reputational) difficulties in order to recover its position as a viable exit strategy for lenders seeking to reduce their balance sheet exposure, or if the securitisation market must play second fiddle to the increasing popularity of simpler methods of secondary trading (i.e. direct syndication).

This Chapter will look at the sources of capital available in the CRE and CMBS market and then deal with several other key topics such as: the

Market Abuse Regulation, servicing standards, the ability to contact respective parties within a transaction and examine the role of the special servicer and the options available to a special servicer in problematic transactions. This Chapter will not attempt to cover every eventuality on a transaction but will highlight the key fundamental issues faced by the facility agent, servicer or special servicer.

9.2   Availability of finance

As was the case in 2012, the majority of finance available in the CRE finance market continues to be focused on very good quality prime assets in prime locations. The decrease in valuation experienced by these assets is not as significant as those seen for secondary and tertiary assets. The realisation of the actual risks associated with real estate lending has partly been responsible for banks reducing their exposure to the sector. Furthermore, the continued regulations, as will be discussed in Chapters 16 and 17, being placed upon banks to ensure that they improve their capital adequacy positions has impacted upon banks' willingness to engage in CRE lending.

The shortfall in bank lending to the CRE sector created a large shortfall in funds available to refinance maturing loans, as well as to originate new transactions. This created a funding gap to the CRE market, which, in turn, created opportunities for alternative sources of financing to enter the market. As was discussed in Chapter 3, this gap was filled by an influx of lending by alternative providers of finance, including private equity, CRE debt funds, foreign banks, pension funds and insurance companies. The influx of new providers of new providers of capital has gone some way to increasing the liquidity of the CRE market, although falling margins are once again threatening to "gum-up" some of this new financing, and it has become apparent that although these new entrants can bring fresh capital, they cannot wholly replace the role played by banks in the CRE and CMBS markets.

Whilst the majority of financing still tends to be focused on the prime end of the market, the opportunities presented by an influx of capital has led to a slight upturn in trading of secondary and tertiary assets, with some specialist investors looking to focus on these asset classes and locations in order to seek higher returns, with logistics assets and business parks and shopping centres proving popular. However, there does continue to be a lack of trading of these secondary and tertiary assets when compared with the pre-GFC appetite and on the whole this end of the market remains rather illiquid, especially when the parties able to sell will not discount transactions sufficiently to entice purchasers. Until this gap is bridged, the markets are some way off from these sub-prime assets readily trading, as in previous cycles.

New types of financing have also been restricted by new regulation, as will be discussed in Chapters 16 and 17. Solvency II, for example, has incentivised insurers to allocate more capital towards directly sourced debt products. The reason for this change in allocation is due to the exceptionally high capital charge for holding securitised products, which includes CMBS, meaning that such providers of finance see a considerable advantage in relation to their returns for direct lending over any form of "collective investment products". The downside of this regulation is that it disincentivises market participants from reigniting the CMBS market and entice insurers and pension funds to buy into CMBS transactions as well as the continued origination of new debt. Both can co-exist together in the market and will only assist in plugging the funding gap.

9.3 The facility agent and the servicer

9.3.1 Role of the facility agent

It is useful to differentiate the roles performed by a servicer of a CMBS and a loan facility agent as there are very clear fundamental differences, which should not be confused when discussing types of lending products and asset management. The loan facility agent is an agent on bilateral and syndicated loans and is also an agent on loans prior to them being syndicated. The role of the facility agent has traditionally been fairly limited as they take instructions from the majority lenders and cannot use discretion unless this was negotiated into the finance documents at origination, which discretion will likely be resisted by the facility agent. The loan facility agent will be responsible for collecting rental income from borrowers and distributing these funds to the lenders on the transaction. They will also collect period reports, including property reports (if produced) along with borrower/sponsor financial information. These are then distributed directly to the lenders. The loan facility agent is then the "middle man" per se between the borrowers and lenders.

Historically the facility agent role was largely retained by the arranging or originating bank, providing a continuity of service and relationship between the arranger/originator and the borrower/sponsor. Further, this would mean that the facility agent would likely have access to all information that was available to the arranger/originator at origination and so would arguably have a fuller picture of the loan and the underlying structure and assets than other parties. At the time of writing, the rise of the third-party facility agent has been witnessed, and lenders are increasingly favouring having the facility agent role performed by an independent third party. This increased popularity of the third party facility agent has come about for a number of reasons; lenders may see such functions as a "non-core" part of their business and spin their agency teams out or close them down, alternative "non-traditional" lenders (i.e. CRE debt funds, pension funds, insurance companies, etc.) often do not have such a function in-house, and the increasing popularity of syndication, as a means to reduce a lender's balance sheet exposure, has led to participants in a lending club preferring an independent facility agent being appointed to look after the whole deal rather than having the arranging/originating bank retain oversight and potentially push the interests of their own institution.

Whilst the facility agent has historically been a mechanical and administrative function, where the role is outsourced to an independent third party it is increasingly expected that the facility agent will be able to offer more than just a "post box" service. This has given rise to a third party facility agent market, whose participants specialise in CRE financing. This knowledge means that facility agents can spot issues and work much more closely with both lenders and borrowers in order to ensure that effective asset management of the underlying CRE is undertaken, in order to preserve value in the assets and therefore protect the lenders investment.

9.3.2 *Difference between the role performed by a facility agent and a CMBS servicer*

Whereas the loan facility agent traditionally has little to no discretion in relation to a loan, the primary servicer of a CMBS, however, has certain limited discretions over and above that which has just been described for the loan facility agent. These will, depending on the particular deal, include decisions relating to the exercising of all of the respective rights, powers and discretions of each of the lenders, the loan facility agent and the loan security agent in relation to the relevant whole loan and its related security in accordance with the servicing standard. The services provided by the CMBS servicer in this regard shall usually include (without limitation) the following (all in accordance with the provisions of the relevant facility agreement and related documentation):

(a) Taking any necessary action to maintain the security in relation to any relevant whole loan and property;
(b) Monitoring each whole loan at all times;
(c) Procuring and supervising the services of third parties (excluding any sub-contracted third party) which may be necessary or appropriate in connection with the servicing of the whole loans;
(d) Collecting all payments due from the borrower in respect of any whole loan and distributing to the cash manager in accordance with the respective waterfall (see (f));
(e) Monitoring any casualty losses and administering any proceeds related thereto;
(f) Keeping records with respect to amounts paid under each whole loan and determining amounts representing principal, interest, prepayments, prepayment fees, collections on guarantees or insurance or related security, break costs, administrative charges and payments, insurance proceeds and all other amounts;
(g) Maintaining appropriate ledgers in connection with the amounts referred to in (f) above, and ensuring that correct transfers are made to the appropriate accounts;

(h) Reconciling and validating all accounts and ledgers on a quarterly basis;

(i) Conducting communications and dealings with the borrower in relation to all matters concerning each whole loan and its related security;

(j) If required by the senior lender, taking the actions referred to in the servicing agreement in relation to any amendment, modification or waiver;

(k) Giving instructions to the loan security agent in respect of the whole loan and its related security;

(l) Taking the specified actions upon the occurrence of a servicing transfer event and upon the occurrence of a specially serviced loan becoming a corrected loan;

(m) Notifying the loan security agent, the junior lender representative and the special servicer on the occurrence of a servicing transfer event, and notifying the lenders and the loan security agent upon a whole loan becoming a corrected loan;

(n) In the case of the special servicer, consulting with the junior lender representative prior to taking the specified actions;

(o) Calculating the valuation reduction amount upon the occurrence of an appraisal reduction event, obtaining an updated valuation in the specified circumstances and adjusting the valuation reduction amount to take into account such valuation;

(p) Preventing the forfeiture or irritancy of a head lease or obtaining relief on the court in respect of such forfeiture or irritancy;

(q) Taking all reasonable steps to recover and enforce all sums due to the lenders from the borrower;

(r) In the event a receiver or administrator is appointed, in the case of the special servicer, agreeing with the receiver or administrator a strategy for best preserving the loan security agent's and the lenders' rights and securing any available money from a property and agreeing the terms of and executing a receiver's or administrators' indemnity in connection with the appointment of the receiver or administrator subject to certain conditions;

(s) Establishing and maintaining procedures to monitor compliance with the terms of the finance documents regarding the insurance of the property or properties, procuring the payment of premiums under an insurance policy and, in the event any insurance policy has already lapsed or the property is otherwise not insured, informing the lenders and arranging such insurance;

(t) Negotiating, agreeing and accepting any compromise, abandonment or settlement of any claim for compensation by the loan security agent or the lenders or any claim by the loan security agent or the lenders under any insurance policy and directing amounts paid under an insurance policy to the order of the loan security agent (or in the case of loss of rent cover, paid directly into the account specified for the receipt of rental income under the relevant facility agreement);

(u) Providing additional reports, documents and information set out in the relevant servicing agreement (generally in the CREFC E-IRP format);

(v) Providing to the lenders and the loan security agent any information concerning any whole loan and its related security in order to inter alia, enable the lenders to prepare a profit and loss account, balance sheet and directors' report etc. and providing further information and reports which the lender and/or the loan security agent may reasonably require; and

(w) Providing to the lenders, in relation to each whole loan, a monthly activity report detailing any activity or action taken, if any, in relation to the relevant whole loan in the preceding month (including but not limited to lease requests, modifications, lets, etc.).

The impact of the discretions determines how the asset management of a loan or portfolio of loans is undertaken on a CMBS or balance sheet loan. When a loan is originated it will generally be executed with a cashflow that has been scrutinised, not only by an internal underwriting section of the financial institution, but also the internal credit department. Certain stresses are placed upon the loan in relation to the underlying CRE to ensure that specific market decisions will not distress the portfolio enough to provide insufficient cash to service the debt.

Many transactions have asset managers that are related to the borrower/ sponsor. When some of the first European transactions were documented the requirement in situations of sponsor and asset management relationships was that a quarter of the annual rental income was placed on deposit under the control of the servicer, in case the asset manager had to be replaced or even removed with funds from the transaction. This reserve ensured that the loan could continue to pay its debt service for at least a further quarter, whilst the servicer identified a replacement. This requirement was relaxed over the ensuing years due to borrower pressure and the quantum of transactions an actual borrower would originate with their lending bank. The rating agencies also adapted to it, as this did not affect the ratings of transactions, as the presumption was that in a conduit programme: how often would this event actually happen and were there sufficient funds from the remaining loans to cover note coupon?

Given the wider discretion given to a CMBS servicer versus a loan facility agent, and the number of (potentially unknown) holders of the notes in a CMBS, the servicer in a CMBS structure must undertake a more hands-on approach to asset management. Whereas a loan facility agent will discuss any requests or developments in relation to the management of the underlying real estate in a CRE loan before passing the same on to the lenders for a determination, in a CMBS structure this is not practical and, in many cases, may even be impossible. Therefore the servicer must use its discretion to ensure that it is fully appraised of, and involved in, any asset management strategies of a borrower (e.g. to enable the servicer to approve any works (i.e. capex) or lease requests), working alongside the borrower in terms of managing the underlying assets in order to preserve the value of the relevant assets and therefore maximise recoveries for the noteholders.

9.3.3 Whole loan versus senior loan servicing

As discussed above, servicing of a loan consists of two work streams which will depend on the status of the loan as performing or non-performing. The first denominated primary servicing is mostly administrative in nature, relating to the collection of payments due under the loan and their subsequent distribution, monitoring compliance with the loan terms and acting as liaison of the lenders with the borrower, for the purposes of any notices and requests received in connection with the loan and the collateral securing the loan. The servicer may also be appointed by the facility agent and security trustee to exercise their rights under the related loan documentation and intercreditor agreement. Upon the occurrence of a special servicing transfer event, upon a default, or it becoming apparent that the loan is imminently in danger of defaulting, the role of actively managing the loan and security can be undertaken by a special servicer who will represent the senior or all of the lenders, the facility agent and the security trustee in connection with negotiations with the borrower in order to ensure that the loan performs or reverts to a performing status as soon as possible or, alternatively, seeking to work-out or liquidate the loan in order to maximise recoveries for the lenders.

With the advent of the GFC, servicers have found that the distinction between primary servicing and special servicing has become blurred and primary servicers have been called upon to perform certain functions that in the past were carried out by special servicers. However, a loan that is past the stage of a foreseeably immediate correction will require transfer to special servicing, as the costs associated with the administration of such loan, and the expertise required in seeking a satisfactory resolution of the loan, will typically be beyond the scope of services rendered by a primary servicer.

The documentation providing for the servicing of the loan will depend on whether the whole loan will be serviced by the same servicer. If so, there are variations as to how this arrangement will be set out. In European-style intercreditor agreements (see further Chapters 5, 6 and 7), it is fairly usual for there to be an acknowledgment by the lenders that the whole loan will be serviced by one servicer for the benefit of all the lenders. It is not uncommon for the junior lenders to then become a party to the actual servicing agreement with the senior lender, servicer and special servicer. In a CMBS, this process can be quite cumbersome, as the documentation is usually agreed simultaneously, with the negotiation and finalisation of the remaining securitisation transaction documents and the involvement of additional third party lenders to the securitisation may prolong the process. Alternatively, US-style intercreditor agreements will provide a basic framework of key terms of the servicing agreement which would include, among other items, the servicing standard, the method of calculation as to when a lender becomes a controlling party for the purposes of consent, amendment and waiver rights, the criteria for transfer of the loan from primary to special servicing, the fees payable to the servicer and special servicer and the right of the controlling party to terminate and propose the appointment of a special servicer. These basic terms form the backbone of the servicing agreement and the subordinated lenders' agreement to its principal terms. Subsequently, the senior lender (being the issuer in the case of a CMBS) would, in turn, enter into the actual servicing agreement without involvement from the subordinated lenders.

When the whole loan is serviced by the same servicer, the junior lenders typically have the right to terminate and propose the appointment of a special servicer who would, in accordance with the servicing standard and the requirements of the loan documentation and intercreditor agreement (for instance, the consent and consultation of rights of the junior lenders as discussed above), be entitled to direct the enforcement strategy and make all decisions regarding the senior and subordinated loans. Similarly to junior lender consent and consultation rights, the right of the junior lender to terminate and have the right to propose the appointment of a special servicer of its choice, would be dependent on the related junior lender remaining in a "control" position in the loan, meaning that it is not affected by a control valuation event.

If the junior loans are not to be serviced by the same servicer, the inter-creditor will provide a general acknowledgement that the senior lender may cause the senior loan to be separately serviced. As discussed above, servicing fees would, in such circumstances, usually be payable by the senior lender alone. The subordinated lenders would have no further involvement in the negotiation and finalisation of the relevant documentation and would either service the related junior loan themselves, or, delegate the same to a third party. In those circumstances, given that the senior loan will be serviced and the cash management aspects of such servicing would be under the control of the senior lender's servicer, the role of any third party junior lender servicer would be limited to monitoring and receiving distributions paid to the junior lender and interfacing with the senior loan servicer, as to any consultation or consent rights that the junior lender has under the intercreditor agreement.

However, from a securitisation and rating agency standpoint, it is preferable that the whole loan be serviced by the same servicer, particularly following a default in order to minimise any disruption caused by potential conflicts between lenders and delays which may arise as a result when implementing key management actions that are required in a post-default scenario. In addition, from a practical perspective, having one servicer with the power to conduct the whole process independently will facilitate the management of the loan, again particularly in a post-default scenario.

In the context of a senior/mezzanine arrangement, common servicing of both the senior and mezzanine loan would not be as commonplace given that there is less of an operational advantage in having both loans serviced from both a senior and mezzanine lenders' perspective. Further, the mezzanine lender would ultimately wish to ensure that the servicing of its loan not be subject to the discretion of a third party, which would be obliged to take into account the interest of the senior lenders in the first instance, so it would be preferable for a mezzanine lender to retain control over the administration of its loan interests.

In a whole loan servicing scenario, whether both lenders will be responsible for payment of the servicing fee and related costs and expenses incurred by the servicer or special servicer (where there is an intercreditor dealing with the relationship between a senior and junior loan) is subject to negotiation between the parties. However, from a practical standpoint, it is in the interests of the securitisation that any potential disputes in relation to the administration of the loan are minimised and, accordingly, the servicing of the whole loan is preferable, which would be particularly relevant in the context of an enforcement or workout of the whole loan. It is also possible that the loan will include an indemnity from the borrower, making it responsible for some or part of any servicing fees incurred, particularly following the occurrence of an event of default. If so, such fees may be caught by that indemnity and would not necessarily result in a reduction in amounts available to pay the A loan and B loan. In the case of a senior/ mezzanine structure this will ordinarily not be the case, as even in circumstances where the senior loan is serviced (including the servicing of the common security) with a view of it being placed into a CMBS, the mezzanine loan will not.

If servicing fees are payable by the transaction as a whole, such fees may be taken from the top of the waterfalls. If, however, the A lender (or issuer) is solely responsible, payment may be achieved by either deducting such amounts from the amounts due to the A lender (by, for instance, reducing the amount of interest payable to the A lender) under the intercreditor agreement, or, by accounting for those amounts in the relevant securitisation waterfalls (if within the context of a CMBS deal) from proceeds already distributed to the issuer under the intercreditor agreement.

Servicing fees are broken down into firstly the primary servicing fees payable to a servicer prior to the loan(s) transferring upon the occurrence of certain events to special servicing. As discussed above, such tasks have traditionally been more of an administrative exercise, payment monitoring and borrower interface nature. As a result of the GFC and the increased levels of defaults occurring in CRE financing transactions, due to the reduced availability of capital and the general deterioration of CRE values, it has become increasingly apparent that servicers have been required to take a more active role which may include undertaking a more frequent monitoring and reporting commitment and/or some of the roles that are usually performed by special servicers. From a primary servicer's standpoint, such additional or extended obligations will usually result in an increase in the overall primary servicer's costs which were not always contemplated at the outset of the transaction when the fees were agreed. This can be addressed structurally in new transactions, for instance, transactions from 2011 have now ordinarily incorporated the possibility for the primary servicer to charge a modification fee payable by the borrower as a condition to a work-out of the loan, which is intended to prevent a premature transfer of the loan to special servicing.

Special servicing fees are the second component that may be paid at the top of an A/B intercreditor waterfall. These can include basic special servicing fees, liquidation fees and work-out fees (see further Chapter 7). Such fees are payable on top of the primary servicing fee. CMBS transactions closed since the GFC have modified these arrangements to account for the complexity and size of the loans which are aimed at ensuring that special servicers are appropriately compensated but, in respect of larger loans, are not generating excessive profits.

9.3.4   Servicing standard

As will be discussed in the following two Chapters, the servicing standard will provide the framework in which the servicer and special servicer will service the related loan. It will prioritise the factors that must be taken into account by the servicer and special servicer and will rank those factors in an order of priority which must be followed to the extent that there are any conflicts between them. Firstly, the servicer must act in accordance with applicable law. This factor serves to ensure that no liability is incurred by the servicer in conducting its administration of the loan, particularly to the extent it receives instructions from any of the lenders to take any actions that would constitute a breach of applicable law. Secondly, the servicer will have to account for the provisions of the loan agreement and other finance documents which will be the framework on which the intercreditor agreement is to operate. This is particularly relevant where the borrower is not a party to the intercreditor agreement, as any right, or, other course of action permitted under the intercreditor agreement will need to fit within the rights of the lenders and agents under the loan agreement, as the latter will represent the deal that has been struck with the borrower (see further Chapter 7). The terms of the intercreditor agreement will rank after the finance documents on the above basis. Similarly, the terms of the servicing agreement will need to conform to the rights agreed between the lenders under the intercreditor agreement, again particularly if the other lenders are not a party to the servicing agreement. The standard will subsequently set out the degree of care and standard of skill to be exercised by the servicer and special servicer. Finally, the objective of the servicer and special servicer will be to service the loan with a view towards, pre-default, the "timely collection of scheduled payments" and, post-default, the "maximisation of recoveries" for the lenders taking into account the relevant subordination agreed to between the lenders.

The servicing standard will frequently need to be considered by servicers and special servicer when considering strategies in order to deal with, particularly, non-performing loans. When assessing compliance with the servicing standard and, consequently, the servicer or special servicer's own liability to the lenders, servicers or special servicers will need to bear in mind that the objective is ultimately to ensure that recovery on the loan is enhanced "on a present value basis". Therefore, for example, strategies that seek to enhance value prior to a disposal will need to pass the test of whether the ultimate recovery will in fact be increased by taking into account, among other things, the investment involved, the period that will need to lapse before the property is disposed and the quantum of projected disposal proceeds which will be received. It is common that in making such determinations, the special servicer will wish to hedge their exposure to the lenders by engaging third party professional advisors to provide their written advice supporting the ultimate course of action adopted.

9.3.5 Special servicing transfer events

Whether specified in the intercreditor agreement or in the servicing agreement, the servicing transfer events will provide a list of events that, upon their occurrence, will result in a transfer of the loan or whole loan (as the case may be, as discussed above) from primary to special servicing. From a lender's perspective, the administration of the loan will become more active upon such transfer, as the special servicer considers and implements strategies, in accordance with the servicing standard, to recoup and maximise recoveries for the benefit of the lenders taking into account the relevant subordination between senior and junior lenders. Given that such transfer will result in the lenders, if the whole loan is being serviced, or the senior lender, if only the senior loan is being serviced and the junior lenders are not responsible for payment of servicing fees, incurring additional expense as a result of the fees chargeable by the special servicer, lenders will not wish for the servicing transfer to occur too quickly. This has resulted in primary servicers having been asked to take on a more active role than originally contemplated. However, if performance of the loan is seriously jeopardised or hindered, the lenders may have few alternatives than to accept its transfer to special servicing.

Typically, the list of events that will result in a transfer of the loan to special servicing will, at the minimum, include a payment default either at maturity or, during the term of the loan, which is continuing for a specified period of time. Furthermore, any insolvency events affecting the borrower or an obligor under the loan will also result in a transfer. The list may go on to include certain additional events which are deemed by the lenders to be material defaults, which may include a financial covenant default and/or other items as may be agreed by the relevant lenders and servicers. Given the considerations noted above, with respect to lender reluctance to incur additional fees that would be taken from funds available to be distributed to them and possibly accelerating losses upon the commencement of a disposal process, lenders will wish to avoid including hairline triggers that may cause a transfer of servicing, or will prefer to have a say in deciding whether such event should result in a transfer. Regardless, any servicing transfer will not occur during the duration of any junior lender cure period.

9.3.6 Immediate action and servicing override

The servicer and special servicer will typically be authorised to take immediate action, if it considers that such action is necessary and consistent with the servicing standard. The authority to take such immediate action will mean that the servicer and special servicer will either be able to proceed with a course of action, without having to wait for the relevant lender to provide a required consent, or, will be able to reduce any periods in which such lender is to respond. Should the servicer or special servicer take such immediate action, the servicer or special servicer will, following the taking of the required action, be required to notify the relevant lender of the action, and provide it with all reasonably requested information and must take due account of any advice or representations made by such lender.

In addition, in transactions where the whole loan is being serviced by a sole servicer and special servicer, the relevant servicer will be instructed to disregard any instructions received from a lender that conflicts with the servicing standard, irrespective of whether such lender is a controlling party under the loan. There is a lesser likelihood that such a provision is included in transactions, where the subordinated loans are not being serviced by the same servicer. However, from a CMBS rating agency perspective, there is an expectation that even in situations where the relevant junior lender is a controlling party, the relevant servicer will have sufficient authority to act in the best interests of both creditors.

9.3.7 Focusing on the real estate

One of the characteristics of the post 2007 boom decline in CRE values across Europe was the realisation that many property owners, whose assets sat within CMBS structures, lacked a fundamental understanding of how to manage complex, multi-tenanted, mixed use assets and portfolios. An abundance of cheap money and the seemingly endless increase in capital values in the run up to 2007/08 created a wave of CRE investors whose primary focus was in leveraging assets as highly as creditors would allow, extracting cash and then looking to exit as quickly as possible. In a rising market with low interest rates and aggressive lending, it's an irresistible model and the importance of understanding the assets and their true performance took a back seat to the financial engineering considerations.

When the GFC took hold and CRE values started to fall, asset trading slowed, and it rapidly became apparent that many CRE owners lacked the knowledge, personnel and financial resources necessary to react to the changing climate for CRE. Couple this with the fact that their motivation evaporated as quickly as did their equity, and the loans and their servicing and asset management were left in a perilous situation.

The post 2008 Lehman's world, where tenants want lower rents, shorter leases, longer rent-frees and more frequent breaks has left many of the newer and heavily geared landlords reeling. They have quickly found themselves out of their depth and just as quickly, it has become apparent that they often lack any detailed knowledge of their assets, have no meaningful relationship with their tenants and have little idea of how to manage active portfolios. These factors mean that when loans default, the special servicer often finds themselves faced with a plethora of problems, ranging from higher vacancy rates than were previously reported by borrowers, through to gaping holes in capex budgets and the rapid decline in values, resulting from the general assumption that every tenant intended to break their lease, or, vacate at the first available opportunity.

Throughout the early 2000s, the strategy to amass large portfolios spread over wide geographical areas, differing asset classes and even different countries, now looks totally flawed. Post GFC, the special servicer finds itself in a position of having to untangle administrative and legal headaches, whilst trying to design appropriate strategies to exit the troubled assets within the portfolios in a manner which extracts greater recoveries for the lenders. In many cases, the best recovery is likely to be achieved by an immediate sale of the underlying asset, especially where the lease and income profiles are stronger at the advent of a sale, than they would be if the asset were held in the medium term. However, as the market for secondary assets has, at the time of writing, remained challenging, the period post GFC has led to more importance being placed on developing robust asset management strategies for assets that need repositioning prior to sale.

Whilst it is important to stress that the special servicer is not a long-term asset manager, and indeed is often constrained by the lack of time brought about by the rigidity of CMBS structures, note maturities and tail periods, it is equally important to make clear that the special servicer does not want to conduct "fire sales" in circumstances where value recovery can be enhanced by applying better asset management strategies, and it is worth focusing on how asset management can deliver enhanced recoveries for creditors.

Asset management is not a new concept. Experienced, long-term real estate investors, property companies and CRE professionals have long understood the importance of sweating assets to improve their performance. As discussed above, many investors, new to the sector in the mid-2000s, did not have these skill sets to fall back on. Developing an asset management strategy for any asset involves the creation and implementation of a sound business plan at a real estate level. To do this requires an owner, or by default, the special servicer to develop a sound understanding of the underlying bricks and mortar. An appreciation of the property's micro

211

location, the occupier market it serves, and the wider economic factors affecting its performance and exit value, is vital.

The majority of assets that find their way into special servicing tend to be more difficult to sell in the market that exists at the time of writing, as they typically suffer from short lease profiles, non-investment grade covenants and a lack of investment in terms of capex and tenant improvements by the borrower. As a result, one of the first steps of a loan servicer is to analyse whether the borrower is part of the problem or the solution. If the borrower does not understand how to maximise the value of their assets and is either unwilling or unable to invest new equity or capex, they often have little of any value to contribute. The option to enforce, remove the borrower and start afresh with a new approach, delivering focused asset management is often a better way forward. In instances where borrowers do know what they are doing and have a sensible strategy, it is more likely that the special servicer will look to work with the borrower. Developing a business plan for the asset(s) requires thorough research, building knowledge and creating a strong team of multi-disciplinary professionals that can look at delivering enhanced performance.

As stated above, the starting point is to understand the real estate and what can be done with it. In order to do this, a loan servicer would typically commission a new independent valuation, often known as a "Red Book" valuation. In parallel with this process, the servicer should consider the wider- and longer-term potential to reposition the assets before disposal. This typically involves developing a strategy that might involve a combination of the following:

- re-gearing or prolonging tenant leases, by trading potentially over-rented income for longer lease commitments;
- the appointment of new agents to freshen up the marketing of vacant space;
- enhancing marketability by means of targeted capex programmes to enhance marketability;
- assessing the potential for changes of use, or re-profiling uses within buildings;
- reviewing local planning policies to assess redevelopment angles;
- pursuing dilapidations claims, either to maximise revenue to reinstate space when tenants vacate or strategically to encourage tenants to renew their leases;
- reducing a tenant's cost via better management of service charge expenditure; and
- engaging with existing tenants to see what can be done to improve the building's performance, by better tailoring the way the property operates, to suit the tenant's occupational requirements.

The potential value that can be added, via the implementation of any given asset management strategy, then needs to be considered on a net present value (NPV) basis, to help decide whether a better recovery can be obtained by selling immediately, versus implementing the medium-term business plan to optimise value. Even if the decision from the NPV analysis is to sell the assets immediately, asset management can still add short-term value, through the appointment of the most appropriate interim asset manager and/or sale agents. This enables the marketing effort to be maximised, so that the maximum number of potential purchasers are approached and then, when sales are agreed, data rooms and contracts are drafted and ready for issue as soon as heads of terms are agreed. Delays in the conveyancing and due diligence process have unwound many a good deal, so it is important that what is actually being marketed reflects the reality of what is happening on the ground. Whilst this may sound like common sense, it is easy to lose value by choosing the wrong agent or allowing a disengaged borrower to run an uncoordinated sales process.

9.4 Servicer's response time

Response times of a CMBS servicer can be key in both shortening the length of time required to achieve a resolution on a loan and controlling the leakage of funds out of a CMBS structure required to pay ongoing fees, costs and expenses (e.g. asset management costs, legal fees, valuations, etc.). There can often be significant delays in the time it takes for servicers to engage with sponsors and noteholders to examine an impending loan maturity. However, the lack of a single decision maker and appointment of advisors at all levels, (i.e. note, servicer and sponsor levels) and conflicting requirements of different creditors have also hindered the timeliness of solutions. If the servicer acts more prudently and interacts a lot earlier in the life cycle of the loan, then the length to resolution could be reduced and consequently the costs would be diluted over time.

The example of the Fox loan, securitised as the Fordgate Commercial Securitisation No.1 CMBS, which is detailed below as a case study, was one whereby the resolution was better than expected, in a difficult market (both in terms of location and assets) and did not involve a plethora of external advisors or conflict between creditors and is a strong example of proactive and timely engagement by the servicer and special servicer in order to achieve an optimum recovery for noteholders, including the junior debt which was considered "under water". The special servicer, Mount Street, was able to utilise its own in-house skills to enable its team to act in accordance with the servicing standard and ensure that recoveries were maximised. This was without the need to appoint a financial adviser or restructuring/workout expert.

Some of the key characteristics of the workout process on the Fox loan were:

- loan maturity default and transfer to special servicing in October 2013;
- £407.5m whole loan with £254m of securitised debt;

- portfolio valuation in November 2013 at £248m; and
- secured against 21 properties with five in Scotland and the remaining 16 in secondary locations across England.

A variety of workout and restructuring strategies were assessed by Mount Street, as special servicer, in order to achieve optimum recovery for noteholders, including a consensual restructure, enforcement, receivership and administration. Ultimately the following exit strategy was implemented:

- from March 2014, the sale of the junior loan was facilitated, which was ultimately purchased by an investor in May 2014;
- in April 2014, enforcement proceedings were initiated and a fixed charged receiver appointed over the English properties and calling up notices were issued in respect of the Scottish assets;
- following enforcement, the existing asset manager was retained and a new property manager appointed (and land agent appointed on behalf of the loan level security trustee of the Scottish assets) in each case to undertake marketing campaigns;
- contracts exchanged with an investor in June 2014 for £296m, resulting in a full recovery for noteholders and a considerable recovery for a junior lender that had previously been assumed as being "out of the money"; and
- the process was resolved within six weeks following enforcement of the loan and four weeks following the initial acquisition by an investor of the junior loan positions.

This case study is an excellent example of proactive servicing and effective management of a wide spectrum of interests, including a defaulted borrower, junior lenders in a seemingly out of the money position and significant interest and anticipation from investors and the market.

9.5   Noteholders' meetings

Noteholders' meetings in a CMBS deal are convened by the note trustee sending out a notice to the relevant stock exchange requesting a meeting on a certain date. The notice for this is usually three weeks at a minimum. It is sometimes very time-consuming obtaining a quorum at a noteholders' meeting. The original noteholders in a CMBS may have sold their positions many times over and people who used to deal with the bonds in-house within an institution might no longer be employed on these trading desks. As the UK does not have a bond register for loan trading, akin to those in the US, it can be difficult to discover the identity of parties. These factors all contribute to the difficulty of obtaining a quorum at a noteholders' meeting. The conclusion, dependant on the clarity of presented information, can then take weeks if not months thereafter if additional information is needed for the final decision.

9.5.1 Discovery of the identity of noteholders

It is often impossible to inject fresh equity into a CMBS structure without subordinate noteholders agreeing to being further subordinated below where the new injection of funding is placed within the structure. A fresh equity provider would clearly want there to be an advantage following its cash injection and as a minimum, they would usually expect to inject their capital which would subordinate the "out of the money" creditor classes. The fresh equity would then take a share, prior to or pari passu with, the creditors/noteholders.

As discussed above, one of the most difficult issues that a servicer faces is trying to track down the holders of each class of noteholder. This is paramount when decisions need to be made on transactions and votes need to be cast by noteholders due to quorums that are set within the securitisation documents. It has been suggested by several commentators that this would be a much easier and timely process if noteholders had to register their positions to a registrar, who would be the contact point when noteholders' meetings were to be convened. This is a practice used in the US for the loan sale market, whereby a register is kept for all holders of loans, whether traded at issuance or in the secondary market. This would clearly speed up the decision making process and reduce the usual three week notice needed to convene a meeting. However, the downside to this is the ability for a noteholder to remain anonymous if required as a private entity or fund.

9.5.2 Consequences of delayed access to noteholders and replacement of servicers

One of the consequences of delayed access to noteholders is that any delays have reflected on the servicer and the trustee, resulting in a negative view amongst noteholders of these types of institutions and the roles that they perform. The belief of noteholders can be that both these parties are not performing well and hence need replacing in the CMBS, in order to bring in a servicer or trustee that can achieve results that the noteholders want. Such replacement has proven to be difficult in certain deals, particularly in legacy CMBS deals. Historically the replacement of a primary servicer has been virtually impossible, unless it has been negligent under a transaction. However, since 2013 there have been several instances of a primary servicer on a transaction being replaced in order to bring in a servicer who it was felt, would be able to achieve a more beneficial outcome for noteholder (e.g. in the case of the Windermere XIV CMBS). The replacement of a special servicer has been more commonplace, although it is still not as easy as it perhaps should be, particularly where the requirements for replacement cannot be met (i.e. requirement for a confirmation from the ratings agencies that, as a result of the change, the ratings of the notes will not be downgraded or withdrawn).

When CMBS deals were put together in the years preceding the GFC, the primary servicer's role was akin to that of a loan facility agent with limited discretions. It was never envisaged that they would be performing tasks that they perform at the time of writing (albeit documented but not expected to undertake) and hence their replacement was never in question at the outset. Furthermore, the role of a special servicer was ultimately never expected to be needed in the European CMBS market. This view may be, in hindsight, described as naïve, but with a booming CRE lending market and economy there was never any concept of a faltering market and property prices reducing instead of increasing. Some issuing banks had chosen third party special servicers instead of setting up their own teams exactly due to the reason that they would never be needed and therefore did not need the expense of setting up a team that may never be used. Following the GFC, noteholders began to take an increased interest in their investments as many pre-GFC CMBS deals suffered severely in the crash. As a result the replacement rights of noteholders began to be tested and, in some cases, successfully exercised. When CMBS deals were transferred into special servicing, the special servicer was often in danger of being replaced, particularly if the holder of the most junior class of the notes did not agree with the then appointed special servicer's workout strategies or were concerned that their continued appointment would lead to a deterioration in their junior position. Since this book was last published there have been a large number of deals that have been transferred into special servicing and either worked out successfully or crystallised losses on the notes.

The lack of foresight in CMBS deals packaged prior to the GFC can be seen in the way that documents (servicing agreements) were drafted where they either fettered the options open to special servicers following a servicing transfer or made it difficult for noteholders to take an active role in a transaction and replace a special servicer. By way of example, as will be discussed further in Chapter 11, many legacy CMBS deals specifically prohibit the sale of a loan which is held in the CMBS. It makes sense that a primary servicer should not be able to sell a loan within a CMBS. So long as a loan within a CMBS is performing and paying its interest/amortisation then the debt on the notes will continue to be serviced, with the noteholders receiving their coupon. In the majority of legacy CMBS deals, however, the special servicer is often unable to sell a defaulted loan, as the power of attorney granted by the issuer to the special servicer expressly prohibits the special servicer from exercising this option. This means that one of the cleanest and often most cost-effective way of maximising the recoveries available is taken off the table, and the special servicer must either seek an alternative recovery strategy or else attempt to have the relevant documentation amended or overridden to allow it.

In relation to replacement of a servicer/special servicer, many legacy servicing agreements provided that certain conditions had to be met before a replacement servicer or special servicer could be appointed. One such condition often included a requirement that such a replacement could only take effect if the ratings agencies confirmed that the replacement would not lead to the ratings of the notes being downgraded are withdrawn. At the time of writing (and indeed, in the couple of years leading up to 2016), certain of the ratings agencies have been unwilling to provide any such confirmation (regardless of their opinion on the transaction or servicers in question), meaning that this condition could never be satisfied. Given that this was one of a series of conditions designed to protect noteholders, it seems counterintuitive that even with the instigation of a noteholder (i.e. replacement of a special servicer by controlling class) that a replacement can be blocked by failing to meet a redundant criteria.

It is also useful to consider the role of the note trustee. Note trustees are, at the time of writing, coming under increasing pressure from noteholders as it may be perceived that they are very reluctant to do anything due to a concern that they may incur liability as a result of doing so and/or become embroiled in litigation, although Chapter 13 will dispel this myth as trustees have played a large role on the litigation seen in 2015–2016. As a consequence, note trustees will often require an all noteholder vote to take any action that affects noteholders. This, again, increases time to resolution and adds additional costs onto the fees that go through the waterfall which eventually impacts the junior lenders or controlling class of noteholder.

9.6 Concerns of creditors and noteholders

Post 2008, many concerns exist when speaking to creditors/noteholders in relation to their holdings in CMBS. The majority of issues tend to arise as loans move towards maturity. As discussed above, creditors/noteholders often view servicers as not proactive enough in dealing with impending maturities too late in the loan cycle. Further, both servicers and trustees have also come under fire for incurring too many costs which are then run through a deal waterfall, reducing funds available for distribution to the notes.

A further concern for creditors/noteholders is the different way in which servicers report to the market. This is done through different end user repositories such as Bloomberg, CTS link, the servicer's website or the trustee's own portal. The possible lack of transparency (e.g. information being posted on websites that are password protected) may result in loan or portfolio information being inaccessible to all parties. This potentially makes the notes more illiquid, as potential buyers or deal followers are unable to assess an investment opportunity, although most servicers now provide their reports are made available to the market as a whole and are increasingly providing bespoke reporting packages, over and above the CREFC E-IRP reporting to give noteholders and potential investors greater insight into the loans and collateral. The form of reporting from individual servicers varies significantly. Most servicers provide CREFC Europe-type reporting, which has been evolving over numerous years into the current version of the European-Investor Reporting Package (E-IRP). This has increasingly become the norm in the CMBS market. However, servicers are able to provide additional reporting over and above the CREFC E-IRP reporting package which leads to an increase in useful information being made available to both noteholders and the markets as a whole.

9.6.1 Standstill—"Extend and amend"

Certain aspects of deals are currently preventing foreclosure, meaning "standstill" or "forbearance" has been more common. These include hedging that is heavily "out of the money" for the transaction and long dated swaps, which are even further out of the money due to current swap curves (see further Chapter 12). As swap counterparties often rank super senior (i.e. ranking at the top of the payment waterfall), they are less likely to agree to any amendments to finance documents or participate in anything, which would be for the benefit of the sponsor/obligor, even if such an amendment would be in the interests of the whole loan. Swap counterparties generally want their money back and to reduce their internal costs for carrying these out of the money positions. Often there is considerable conflict experienced between other finance parties such as the junior lenders and swap counterparts. This can make resolutions even more challenging due to the lack of consensus and conflicting priorities. For example, if in a particular transaction the special servicer wanted to waive certain requirements under the finance documents, where such actions required the consent of all finance parties, (which included the swap counterparty as well as the junior lender), this creates an issue, because as mentioned above, the current environment encourages the swap counterparty to refuse any type of amendment to the finance documents due to the fact that they simply want to be paid out of their swap positions. In addition, unless the junior lender receives any upside (bearing in mind that its current position is more than likely to be valueless or "under water" due to the fact that in a sale or enforcement scenario, there will be insufficient funds to fully repay the junior lender) they are not incentivised to allow the special servicer to make any changes, when the junior lender can continue to receive its current interest, so-called "clipping its coupon". Ironically, the result of such conflicts is often simply inertia and further deterioration of the collateral which does not benefit any party, and it is a unique challenge of a servicer/special servicer to liaise with all transaction parties in a timely manner in order to navigate a way through any obstacles.

The "extend and amend" restructure, or "extend and pretend" as it is also sometimes termed, represents an extension to the loan maturity date usually in exchange for an uplift in margin or a more punitive amortisation profile. It is usually only possible (by way of either documentary restriction or good practice) to extend the loans to a point occurring a specified time before the maturity of the notes, the so called "tail" of the CMBS. This tail period commonly begins at a point two years before the maturity of the notes, but can be anywhere between one and three years prior to note maturity, depending on what has been agreed on securitisation. Both of these terms developed following the GFC, whereby the "extend and pretend" term resulted in deals being extended for a period of time, often in the hope that the market would improve based on a perception that the parties who were extending were "pretending" that there was not a problem, and perhaps over time it would resolve itself and the loan would get back on track. After all a "rolling loan gathers no loss". The "extend and amend" mentality briefly improved the position somewhat, as some issues were addressed and hence the underlying deal was amended to encourage improvement and in some circumstances persuaded the equity to inject funds back in to the transaction. This mechanism provided a "hopeful" window of opportunity to "do something with" the underlying collateral. The "extend and amend" remains as a useful tool in the armoury of a special servicer, as it allows the special servicer to implement a workout strategy (i.e. additional capex works, re-gearing of leases, enhanced asset management) without completely disengaging or dis-incentivising the sponsor (i.e. by deferring enforcement action).

However, if secondary and tertiary loans are continually extended, and equity providers remain reluctant to inject further capital into a transaction, there will be a further deterioration in asset value, which would be purely as a result of reducing lease length. For example, if you have an asset which is about to mature and there is no ability to fund any capex to enhance the asset as at today you have a possible lease tail of potentially three years. If you then just extend the loan for a further year and again, there is no investment in that year to improve the asset's position in the market, then all that has happened in that one-year extension is the lease tail has diminished from three years to two years with a clear effect on the value of the asset. This raises a question, as to whether a servicer, acting as a "prudent lender", should actually just extend a loan, without a proper action plan in place to improve the asset's saleability at the end of the extension period. This is one of the skills of the special servicer; to determine the most effective way of managing a given asset in order to maximise returns for the noteholders.

9.6.2 Standstill—a case study

The example of the GSI loan securitised as part of the Windermere XIV CMBS, which is detailed below as a case study, was one whereby the resolution was better than expected, in a difficult market (both in terms of location and assets) and did not involve a plethora of external advisors or conflict between creditors. It is a strong example of proactive and timely engagement by the servicer and special servicer, using an "extend and amend" standstill to achieve an excellent result for noteholders. This initially involved the replacement of the original special servicer on the transaction with Mount Street appointed as incoming special servicer. The incoming special servicer was able to utilise its own in-house skills to enable its team to act in accordance with the servicing standard and ensure that recoveries were maximised. Again, this was without the need to appoint a financial adviser or restructuring/workout expert.

Some of the key characteristics of the workout process on the GSI loan were:

- debt secured by bespoke asset in Halle, Germany (i.e. asset was designed specifically for the tenant); and
- loan transferred to special servicing in Q1 2014 following an acknowledgement by the borrower that it would fail to repay at loan maturity (April 2014).

Within three months of appointment, Mount Street as special servicer had managed to implement the following exit strategy:

- declined a DPO offer from the borrower, which had been provisionally accepted by the previous special servicer;
- orchestrated a change of interest rate on the loan from fixed to floating, plus the deferral of default interest from Q3 2014 IPD, thereby reducing interest obligations of the borrower under the loan. This additional cash-flow had the effect of allowing the loan to be amortised to a manageable level;
- after extensive face-to-face negotiations, the borrower agreed to a restructure (via standstill) incorporating the following key terms:
    - full repayment of the loan by Q1 2016;
    - deferral of default interest (a breach of the standstill agreement would result in a reinstatement of default interest, including all accruals);
    - a new/extended lease during the standstill period would necessitate an immediate and full repayment of the loan, (including accrued default interest);
    - borrower was prohibited from refinancing/selling the asset without prior permission from the special servicer;
- standstill agreement executed by all parties in November 2014.

Following implementation of the above strategy the special servicer managed to achieve a full 100% recovery for the noteholders in Q1 2016.

9.7 Transparency

9.7.1 Market Abuse Regulation

Transparency, from an investor's point of view, must include everything associated with a loan transaction that is of value when assessing the pricing of the position held. The Market Abuse Directive (MAD) was introduced into UK legislation in 2005 and has gone some way to improve the dissemination of information flow to the market. The MAD has since been superseded/taken forward by the implementation of the Market Abuse Regulation (MAR), which came into effect on 3 July 2016. The MAR, which bears similarities to the MAD, has direct effect in EU member states and takes forward the principles of the MAD.

The framework of MAR attempts to ensure that the levels of information disclosure to the market are correct and insider dealing and market manipulation are identified and dealt with appropriately. When MAD came into force, there were a number of institutions that were unsure as to the level of disclosure required to ensure compliance. Many were also unsure of information to be published in the market place and whether such information would be market sensitive or not. This resulted in an inordinate amount of data in the capital markets that did not help an investor assess what was material and what was not, potentially delaying their due diligence prior to selling or investing into a particular issuance. This initial period was followed by a requirement to improve the quality of information disclosure and its distribution. This dissemination process has gradually improved over time with only more pertinent information being published, although, at the time of writing, there is still room for improvement, but the education of servicers and special servicers, through specific forums, has definitely assisted. With the implementation of MAR, it is not expected that institutions will display such uncertainty as they did with the implementation of MAD as, although the scope of MAR is widened when compared with MAD, the framework remains the same.

Improvement centres on the way in which this information is distributed to the market. Effective distribution of pertinent information is paramount to the success of MAR. Such distribution should be made available on a cash manager, note trustee or other related third party website enabling full access to market investors. These portals should enable easy access to information which is not password protected so that, as per the requirements of MAR, there is no restriction on accessing this information. For servicers, it is likely that a decision will be taken (as was the case under MAD) that more information, rather than less, is best and therefore they are fully covered as they have covered all bases.

An area which was not disclosed was any newly instructed valuation under a particular loan transaction. Servicers were prevented by valuers and issuing banks from releasing full valuations that were supplemental to the original valuation that was undertaken at origination. Some servicers would simply disclose the new valuation figure whereby others would release the new figure with details of the assumptions used. The assumptions are key, as sometimes they may change from day one, due to market conditions and hence a rebalance of a creditor's position may be required to include these new assumptions. If the assumptions are not known then the investor is not making a fair comparison, or in other words, using two sets of differing assumptions which inadvertently will give different values and hence cannot be compared. If the market has, however, moved and the initial assumptions are no longer valid, i.e. a long-term hold with a single tenant versus the same asset with varying lease profiles with different covenants, then it is very difficult to use the new valuation as a comparison. The issue of valuer instructions is often heavily negotiated by valuers keen to limit their exposure, as they do not want the information provided to be available and relied upon by anyone in the market. This is an understandable consideration, but the view of most servicers is that this information should be disclosed and be public, as it is pertinent to the potential value of the bonds. Therefore particular care should be taken when appointing valuers and instructing valuations in respect of assets underlying a CMBS.

9.7.2   Impact of new regulation

As the CRE financing regulatory landscape continues to change following the implementation of new regulation introduced since the GFC (i.e. Basel III and Solvency II—see further Chapters 16 and 17), and given reduced lending by banks, it has been, and will continue to be, important for the servicer/agent to be able to cope with the expected higher demands put on them by the new alternative financing sources. The servicer/agent will have to adapt to the diversification of the requirements of the varying funders including insurance companies, senior debt funds, mezzanine lenders, each having their own reporting requirements to their own investors.

Systems for a servicer/loan facility agent may well therefore become the driver behind any kind of success, as this will provide automation and ability to stress portfolios directly and give comfort to their clients. This can provide immediate benefits to servicers, but it is likely to be an expensive investment. Any system will need to cover a wide range of possibilities and provide scenario analysis to allow the addition or removal of assets and tenants to assess the effect on covenants and future debt service coverage. It must allow for upload ability of periodic reports and prior to acceptance into the system, the generation of an exceptions report. Therefore, as a minimum, a system must be able to create investor reports to the creditors, along with the simple invoicing to borrowers of their monthly or quarterly loan interest and amortisation. It should also be able to track automatically borrower obligations, such as financials, quarterly monitoring reports, etc. Servicers must continue to invest in their existing platforms in order to not only keep up with the market, but to ensure that they can perform their roles to the satisfaction of lenders/noteholders.

9.8   Levels of property data and loan information given to loan facility agents and CMBS loan servicers

It is common across all CRE financing for the borrower to be required to provide periodic reporting in respect of the assets underlying their loan to the loan facility agent. The role of the facility agent will be to take the information provided by the borrower and either pass it on to the lenders or, in the case of the more diligent loan facility agents, to review, query and test that information against the borrowers' required levels of reporting and financial (or other) covenants. In a CMBS structure, the loan facility agent will continue to collect the borrower periodic reporting and will provide the same to the servicer for distillation and inclusion in the servicer's reporting package. As the servicer's reporting is clearly an off shoot of the borrower reporting, supplied periodically by the sponsor/obligor, the servicer needs to understand exactly what is being reported by the borrower in order to relay this out to the market and the noteholder audience.

One thing that was very clear in pre-GFC deals was the differing level of property data and loan information that was given, via a loan facility agent, to a servicer of CMBS loans. This was more of an issue with third party servicers rather than in-house servicers. In-house servicers were fortunate that they had access to all information that their origination team had at hand, which included all cashflows, legal opinions of specific jurisdictions and copies of the credit papers. The detail of a credit paper would be paramount to a servicer, or even a loan facility agent, so as to see how the underwriting team and credit department have stressed the loan. This would give an insight to the servicer/loan facility agent of potential changes to watch out for as market and property fundamentals change. It must be remembered that the pre-GFC European CMBS market was a volume driven business, whereby some investors invested due to high level "credit metrics" rather than the knowledge of the underlying collateral. This applies also to the servicers/loan facility agent whereby the role of a primary servicer was initially believed to be solely that of a payment/ collection agent and hence not an employee with an ability to understand property. Since the GFC, primary servicers have sought to address this through recruiting individuals who understand property and providing learning and development packages for existing staff, in effect becoming a CRE servicing specialist.

9.9   Conclusion

As this Chapter has shown, the servicer, facility agent or asset manager has, since the peak of the market in 2007, had to review and improve their service levels to clients, but most of all attain a better understanding of the market and underlying collateral in order to deal with problematic trans-actions. There are a lot of theoretical approaches to dealing with specific examples of defaulting loans but very few practical examples. Now, almost 10 years on from the 2007 peak, and following the massive impacts of the GFC, the number of practical examples has continued to increase, with servicers gaining ever increasing knowledge of the optimum strategies required to workout maturing and defaulting loans.

However, as the market continues to falter (particularly with the advent of Brexit) and loans continue to fail to repay at maturity, due to the lack of financing available to specific assets, the intellect of the servicer, special servicer and asset manager, will undoubtedly change with each new experience of restructuring, workout or enforcement. To this end, the expectation should be that the ensuing defaulting loans will be resolved in a timelier manner, whereby the special servicer has already produced a workout strategy prior to the actual default. This means working more closely with the primary servicer of the performing CMBS, which is something that still needs to occur more often.

Since the previous edition of this book, as discussed in the opening Chapter, the CMBS market has continued to suffer, with few new CMBS issuances and even fewer being successfully placed in the market. The increasing popularity of syndication as method for deleveraging balance sheets has seen the role of the facility agent become more closely scrutinised, with many lenders expecting "servicer-lite" or "facility agent plus" services from their facility agent. With the trend towards outsourcing to third party facility agents there has been an emergence of a class of CRE-specialist facility agents that are able to handle more complex loan and deal structures. This has been boosted by the re-deployment of traditional servicing assets and personnel to cater for this increasing market. However, the challenges still remain for servicers and special servicers with respect to legacy CMBS issuance, as more loans reach maturity and default, the wits of the servicer and special servicer will continue to be tested.

Lessons have been learned as a result of the GFC and the naïvety and shortfalls seen in pre-GFC transaction documents has begun to be addressed in post-GFC CMBS documentation. Wider powers and increased discretion are being given to the servicer and special servicer (e.g. the power to sell a defaulted loan) and the ability for servicers/special servicers to be replaced has been widened, making it easier to hold a servicer to account for their actions and incentivise them to achieve the best results for noteholders in the most proactive way. More still needs to be done in order to make the servicing industry as transparent as possible, thereby increasing the confidence of investors in the CRE asset class as a whole, but positive foundations have certainly been laid. The question remains to be answered as to whether CMBS can overcome these regulatory (and, in many cases, reputational) difficulties it has suffered from in recent years, in order to recover its position as a viable exit strategy for lenders seeking to reduce their balance sheet exposure, or if the securitisation market must, in the near future at least, play second fiddle to other methods of secondary trading. The answer to that question is one which can only be answered over time, and will therefore need to be visited in a future edition.

Chapter 10

Legacy CRE Loans and CMBS Loans: Recoveries Strategies and the Deleveraging Market

Paul Lewis,
Head of Loan Advisory, CBRE Capital Advisors

Michael Haddock,
Senior Director, Global Research, CBRE Ltd

Isra Erpaiboon,
Senior Analyst, CBRE Capital Advisors

10.1   Introduction

At the time of writing, it has been nearly 10 years since the peak of the last real estate cycle in Europe and around seven years since the generally accepted trough of mid-2009. Numerous market commentators are contemplating whether the subdued conditions that exist at the beginning of Q3 2016 (a couple of weeks following the UK Referendum vote confirming the desire of the majority of the UK voting population to leave the EU—the so-called Brexit vote) may be the beginning of another correction or simply a mid-cycle pause. Despite all this, the European bank deleveraging market still remains largely active.

Central bank support and rock bottom cost of funds, combined with the sheer volume of legacy real estate loans from Europe's biggest banking crisis in living memory, have created a vastly protracted deleveraging cycle. This has spawned a new industry in its own right as private equity funds raise capital to take control of much of Europe's real estate loans before deploying strategies to gain control of and manage the underlying real estate. The loan sales market in Europe is not a new phenomenon. We have previously seen active loan sale markets in various jurisdictions to deal with localised banking crises. However, the level of European bank loan sales being undertaken post GFC is unprecedented, and may still have many years to run, and even once banks stop selling loan books, the opportunistic private equity funds that acquired them have years of undertaking difficult workout strategies to realise their investments.

This Chapter examines this deleveraging market from the perspective of both the selling banks and the private equity acquirers, considering both the macro-economic environment and specific strategies that can be adopted on a non performing real estate loan. We also consider the objectives of a special servicer on a CMBS or balance sheet CRE loan. There are considerable similarities here with the toolbox available to private equity investors, but there are subtle differences in the objectives and client base that may lead to differing results.

10.2   The European CRE Finance Landscape

After several years of revolution in the European debt market, 2015 felt more like a year of evolution. Conditions in the underlying CRE investment market continued to improve and the use of debt in those transactions continued to increase. But, in both cases, this was the continuation of an existing trend rather than the start of a new one. The same is true in the European CRE loan sales market, where after the explosion in activity in 2014 there was steady growth in 2015.

The total (nominal) value of European CRE investment debt increased very slightly over the course of 2015, from €1.08 trillion to €1.12 trillion.[1] The retirement of existing debt, either as a result of property sales or active management, offsets an increase in new lending. In fact this has been a common theme over the last few years. Although the rate at which old debt has been retired has accelerated over the last few years as market conditions have become more favourable, so too has the rate at which new CRE debt

Figure 1: Debt-Equity Split in CRE Transactions

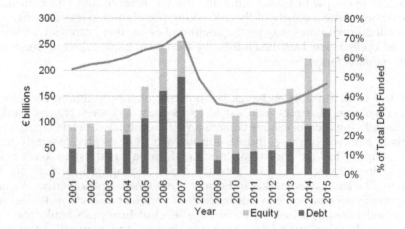

has been issued as the level of transactions has increased and average LTVs have increased.

The amount of new CRE debt issued has gone up rapidly since 2014, which is a function of the higher turnover of the investment market and the greater use of CRE debt (on average) per transaction. It is estimated that there was €62 billion of new debt issued in 2013, based on 38% out of €164 billion of CRE investment, and that this increased to €127 billion in 2015, based on 47% out of a record €273 billion of CRE investment. This increase looks steep, but viewed in the context of the pre-crisis years, it is less new debt than in either 2006 or 2007, despite a bigger underlying market.

There is still a substantial legacy of historic real estate debt on European bank balance sheets. The capital value growth in the last few years will have improved the quality of some of this legacy debt, but it remains the case that recent capital value growth has been disproportionately in the prime segments of the market, and in many cases will have been offset by lack of capital investment or active management. The fact that in most of Europe the development cycle has not yet restarted suggests that loans against development land will still, in most cases, be out of the money. These loans lie outside the scope of this Chapter, but were substantial in 2006/07. It is likely that the amount of legacy debt will continue to diminish in the next few years. Already a substantial amount has transferred into the ownership of non-bank vehicles in some jurisdictions. The combination of a strong investment market and increasingly active management of the debt stock should erode the legacy rapidly going forward.

Figure 2: CRE Debt Maturity in Europe (At end of 2015)

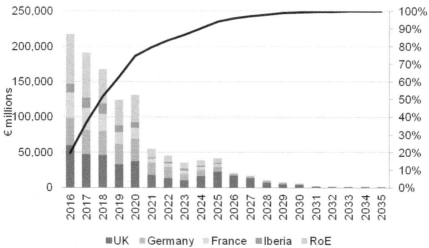

As the influence of legacy debt diminishes, the duration profile of the European debt stock is also normalising. It is estimated that about half (52%) of European CRE debt is due to mature in the period 2016 to 2019. This would be consistent with other estimates of the average duration of new loans being issued. The *De Montford Report*, for example, found that the average length of new loans granted in the UK in 2014 was 5.3 years.

The very weak transactions market in 2009/11 means that there is relatively little debt issued then, maturing now. The vast majority of CRE debt due to mature in 2016/17 is therefore legacy debt that has been either rolled over or refinanced from earlier years.

10.3   The European loan sale market

Robust activity continued in the European NPL market in 2015. CBRE Capital Advisors recorded approximately €85.8 billion of CRE and residential loan sale transactions during 2015 (excluding REOs), which shows significant 17% growth from 2014's €73.3 billion.

One trend last year was the tremendous pick-up in activity from a slow start in the first quarter, and several very large UK residential portfolios were sold in the second half of 2015. The overall €85 billion split was €47 billion of CRE and €38 billion in residential loan sales. Although residential accounted for 44% of total volume in 2015, it is anticipated that CRE loans will account for a larger portion in 2016.

Figure 3: Annual Transaction Volume (2012–2015)

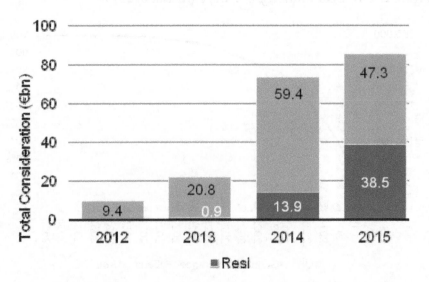

The average transaction size swelled by 25% to €924 million in 2015 up from €740 million in 2014, signifying the accelerating pace at which lenders and asset management agencies are addressing legacy loans, and the high level of liquidity in the market for absorbing large loan trades. US private equity funds continue to dominate distressed debt purchases. Private equity funds were involved in 81% of all loan trades in 2015, even more than the 78% they bought in 2014. In addition, we also see lenders in expansion phase becoming more active, acquiring 13% of 2015 transactions.

Interestingly, sales of residential loans are also increasing. Pure residential loan sales grew from €1 billion in 2013 to €14 billion in 2014, and to €38 billion in 2015. Of this €38 billion, 85% was UK assets and 9% was Irish assets.

In addition to loan portfolio sales, acquisitions of the entire lending, servicing, or real estate platforms have continued, indicative of the investors' planned activities in the specific jurisdictions. Recent examples include private equity acquisitions of businesses in Spain, the Netherlands, Italy and UK.

In terms of loan buyer liquidity, there is still an abundant supply of capital to deploy in the loan sales market. CBRE is currently tracking almost €76 billion of dry powder amongst loan purchasers across the globe, with a focus on European Investments.

As one would expect, 91% of this capital is held by US-based investment managers, while 7% are UK-based and the remaining 2% consists of fund managers domiciled in Spain, Canada, France, Italy, Japan, and Cyprus. European loan purchasers across the globe, who are currently seeking capital, have fundraising targets totalling a further €7 billion. US-based fund managers are most actively fundraising (52%), followed by UK (45%) and German (3%) firms.

10.4 The objectives of loan workout for non-performing loan purchasers

One of the striking differences we see in the deleveraging market is the difference in approach to borrower relationships and workout objectives between originating bank sellers and private equity loan buyers. This is driven by a different set of priorities and motivations. Banks' judgements and the resulting actions may be clouded by client relationships, negative publicity issues, level of book provisioning and concerns over legacy litigation. New private equity owners can often take a more objective fresh

---

[1] The euro value of the debt stock can be affected significantly by the euro-sterling exchange rate. In order to allow a like-for-like comparison the value of the 2014 debt stock is calculated on the basis of the end-2015 exchange rate.

look at loan strategies. They generally have higher return thresholds and often finite medium term (three to five year) recovery aspirations. Further, they are often operate "below the radar" and often do not consider the impact of negative publicity. Importantly, unlike for residential owner occupied loans, the workout of commercial loans is generally unregulated allowing for a much a more flexible approach. Private equity funds often undertake the loan workout in-house but may also have a subsidiary loan servicing unit or sub-contract the workout to a third party servicer. Often these servicers may also act on CMBS deals also.

10.5   The role of the special servicer in CMBS

As discussed in the previous chapter, on CMBS deals, the identity of the special servicer and the terms their appointment are generally set out when the deal is originated. The terms of such appointment are usually dealt with in length in a servicing agreement and these will be examined in further detail in the following Chapter. The special servicer is usually, but not always, the same party as the primary or master servicer. As discussed in the previous Chapter, special servicer replacements are generally under-taken by either the junior lender on a loan, the controlling class, or the controlling party in the notes. The controlling class is sometimes the junior tranche of notes in the CMBS structure, though on more recent "post crisis" deals, the control more typically moves dependent on the value of the underlying real estate assets. As the CMBS markets evolved, more repla-cements have occurred as junior lenders are more aggressively exercising their rights. Typically the Controlling Party will have certain embedded consent or consultation rights with respect to certain workout options.

Whilst the special servicer's appointment is often controlled by one class of noteholder, they will generally owe a duty of care to all classes of notes in the CMBS and often junior lenders as well.

10.5.1   *Courses of action available for successful loan workout*

Set out below is a short guide to the various options that are typically open to a special servicer of a distressed CMBS or balance sheet loan. This list is not exhaustive and a typical workout may encompass a number of different strategies. Each of the options below requires careful consideration and as a minimum will require further legal and restructuring/insolvency advice before implementation. Typically, the route that a special servicer takes will be very dependent on the specific factors relative to the deal and the requirements of the servicing standard. It is also very dependent on jur-isdictional risk, for example non-consensual solutions are currently more favoured in lender-friendly jurisdictions.

10.5.2 Consensual restructuring solutions

Consensual workouts typically consist of either a restructure of the creditor structure, terms or the debt. They almost always consist of the continued standstill or forbearance by the special servicer from taking enforcement action whilst the borrower implements an asset management strategy.

10.5.3 Extensions/amendments

Loan extensions provide the borrower with further time to either improve the value of the assets or allow for market conditions to improve. For the special servicer, these strategies have some key attractions. They are cheap and quick to implement, often require very little approval, and can be implemented without any formal consent from bondholders or other finance parties. Often loans are extended before they default thereby avoiding special servicing altogether. They may also be attractive to more junior creditors as they ensure continued payment of interest coupons and may provide enhanced "option value" by allowing sufficient time for asset value recovery and principal enhancement. Typically the servicer or special servicer will seek improved terms as part of the agreement, for example, higher margins, partial paydowns or cash sweeps. They may also make certain demands of the borrower such as new asset management resource or disposal targets.

However, as witnessed in the previous chapter, loan extensions may also have certain negative implications which need to be considered. These are:

- The potential for further asset value declines either through deterioration of market conditions or increased obsolescence of the property and consequent reduced recovery to lenders;
- They do not necessarily incentivise sponsors to improve recovery prospects;
- They do not generally allow for the introduction of new capital to maintain and improve the assets;
- They may simply be deferring a problem which in itself is not a solution; and
- They may require additional hedging arrangements.

10.5.4 Re-capitalisations

Recapitalising the equity and debt tranches of a capital stack can have significant advantages. The goal is usually to provide a more stable platform for the continued asset management of the collateral in the interests of all stakeholders. It avoids the need for a potentially damaging insolvency/liquidation process. It can often provide an incentive for the equity holders to enhance value whilst allowing the lenders to participate in any potential future value enhancement. It also allows for new capital to be introduced into the structure, allowing for further investment and value enhancement.

231

They tend to be a particularly useful tool for loans with assets that are not suitable for a liquidation strategy such as large operating businesses. Recapitalisation could typically involve one or more of the following:

1. A write-down of one or more loan tranches possibly in exchange for a new equity (a debt for equity swap) in the vehicle or a new subordinated debt piece;
2. The introduction of new capital either as new equity and debt, potentially at a more senior level to existing debt holders;
3. The amendment of debt terms or interest payable to specific loan classes or bondholders. This could also involve the deferment or "payment in kind" (PIK) or subordination of some interest payable; and
4. Using solvent restructuring techniques such as "schemes of arrangements" to implement restructures, though given the complexity of most legacy CMBS structures, this has proved relatively rare.

Whilst often attractive, recapitalisations are often not straight forward to implement and their cost and complexity may make them difficult to structure effectively. Indeed, they tend to be far less common in CMBS and CRE loans generally, than they are in corporate lending. The reasons for this are numerous but include:

- In CMBS, there is typically no mechanism for the special servicer to undertake recapitalisations unilaterally. They will often need consents from all finance parties and may be further complicated where there are also multiple tranches of bonds. Typically all classes will have to vote in favour and this may be difficult to achieve where there are conflicting economics (e.g. "in" or "out of the money"). This may be further complicated where there are other creditors with differing priorities, e.g. swap providers. To be successful, recapitalisations need careful structuring. If this is not achieved, the result may be long-term deadlock between the bondholders/finance parties which can result in further value deterioration or stagnation;
- Recapitalisations have proven very difficult to achieve on loans that represent a smaller proportion of a larger "conduit" securitisation. Often these deals do not obtain the same level of attention as the effect of the recapitalisation is diluted by the other loans in the securitisation. The exposure to other loans may also make the various consent requirements more difficult to implement; and
- The costs of these types of restructure can amount to significant levels as different lenders and bondholder classes often need their own financial and legal advisers. This can make recapitalisations a relatively expensive option when compared to other more cost-effective solutions such as enforcement and liquidation, particularly for liquid saleable assets.
- Property is generally considered to be more suitable for enforcement situations (in some jurisdictions) as there is generally less negative

"fallout" on the ultimate occupiers or underlying trading of tenants than there is in corporate lending. The one exception to this is assets that function like operating businesses. This can include healthcare, leisure or shopping centre assets.

10.5.5 Discounted pay-off (DPOs)/tender offers

As was discussed in section 5.3.8 of Chapter 5, typically discounted pay-offs will involve either a sale of the loan to a borrower, related party or the servicer undertaking to release the security on a loan in exchange for a final discounted pay off of the loan. A release of security in this way can be attractive as it can be relatively straightforward for the special servicer to implement unilaterally and cost-effectively. It avoids the negative market perception and costs of enforcement and it may enhance recoveries as the borrower may be considered a "special purchaser" and pay more than the market might. This approach may be complicated where the special servicer has no power to release a junior debt. In such circumstances the junior debt may require some enhanced level of compensation to obtain or "buy" their consent. It is a commonly used approach by private equity lenders in particular. Often, it is less commonly used in securitisation structures as the lack of an open marketing process may not be consistent with the requirement of a special servicer to maximise recoveries on behalf of all lenders.

A derivation of this approach is the tender offer, which is seen in securitisation structures where this is generally conducted at the bond level rather than the loan level. In such circumstances the borrower, sponsor or a third party may offer to buy out all the bonds in each class of a securitisation. If successful, the borrower or third party can then effectively control the senior debt. Tender offers have tended to be successful when the level of distress felt is not too high and all bondholders/lenders can receive a reasonable market price for their bonds. In circumstances where some noteholders are significantly "out of the money" it may be problematic to distribute value across bond classes in a way that all holders feel is appropriate. By their nature, tender offers are generally not handled directly by the special servicer, who only has a role to act at loan level.

10.5.6 Continued forbearance (or standstill agreements)

This is where the special servicer simply undertakes not to take any enforcement action for a pre-defined (usually short) period of time. Such a "standstill agreement" is usually put in place to buy time to undertake certain asset management initiatives or undertake a consensual sale of the property. Providing the borrower cooperates with the special servicer, this can have the effect of achieving an orderly workout or sale of the property without the negative impacts of an insolvency. It may also allow time for the borrower structure to be sold rather than the asset which has an immediate tax saving benefit. This approach does not, however, enable the special servicer to take full control of the assets and careful consideration needs to be given so as not to be at risk of becoming a "shadow director" or "mortgagee in possession". However the special servicer can usually build in certain requirements that can be imposed upon the borrower as a condition of their continued forbearance. It tends to be used as a short-term solution to achieve a specific goal, but it can also be useful as a tool to prevent the borrower from filing for an unwelcome or premature insolvency process in some jurisdictions.

10.5.7 Non-consensual solutions

10.5.7.1 *Enforcement and liquidation*

This is perhaps the most widely expected route for a special servicer to follow. Loan documents are typically well structured for such an eventuality and the special servicer can usually take enforcement action without any consent from the various bondholder classes or finance parties.

The type of insolvency procedure depends largely on the jurisdiction of the loan and the property but the special servicer would typically enforce in such a way as to retain control of the sales process, and not surrender this to a court appointed body, for example. It is also essential that the special servicer seeks to undertake the sale in an orderly well-structured fashion. Unlike non-distressed sales, the seller is usually unable to provide any representations or warranties to the buyer. Without careful pre-sale due diligence, this can provide buyers with additional risks that may have a pricing impact. In the UK, enforcement is usually undertaken by way of a fixed charge receivership process, which is usually quick and simple to implement. In some circumstances it may be possible to undertake a sale of the borrower structure, either through appointment of administrators over certain borrower entities or exercising share pledges, assuming this is within the security structure. A sale of the borrower structure may have additional tax advantages, though in reality few examples of this have been executed in practice to date.

10.5.7.2 *Enforcement and asset management*

Depending on the level of security inherent in the loan documentation and the jurisdiction of the borrower/asset, it may be possible to enforce and pursue a longer-term workout. This is usually straightforward to implement through a UK fixed charge receivership process but can more be problematic through administration or exercising of the share pledges. Often this approach will be needed where there is limited market demand for the assets or where the assets need further asset management to make them saleable. It is also useful where a change of asset manager is required, as this can often not be undertaken outside of enforcement. Often a new asset manager cannot be effective without the introduction of additional capital and the special servicer will need to consider whether there is any mechanism for the introduction of capital.

This approach has the advantage of allowing the lender to take control of the assets, without having to sell immediately and crystallise losses. A long-term enforcement process can, however, be costly and negatively impact the workout strategies, for example, by presenting a negative perception to potential occupiers or buyers. If such an approach is considered, the special servicer may also need to consider whether it is appropriate to introduce new interest rate hedging arrangements if the existing arrangements have terminated.

10.5.7.3 Sale of the loan

This approach is undertaken independently of the borrower and can therefore be consensual or non-consensual. Since 2011, loan sales have become an increasingly popular method of realising capital from distressed loans by balance sheet lenders. They have remained relatively difficult to implement in European CMBS structures originated before 2011 as servicing agreements do not typically convey the power of loan sales onto the special servicer. Some more recent deals have sought to rectify this. A sale of the loan is often perceived as a convenient way of realising proceeds without the cost and risk of a lengthy enforcement process. There is often more liquidity in the loan sales market than there is in the asset market which could further enhance recovery value. In a CMBS structure, where the special servicer has no power to implement a loan sale, the note trustee will typically require a majority of vote of all classes. As with the previously considered tender offer option, this will involve providing consent payments to more junior bond classes which often makes it uneconomic for the more senior "in the money" classes.

10.6 Definition of Servicing Standard in CMBS transactions

The definition of servicing standard has been discussed for years since the market peaked in 2007 as this has been one of the major issues impacting some servicers/loan facility agents. Some participants prefer a highly pre-scriptive "tick box" process, which dictates what can and cannot be done when using discretion. However, for others, the servicing standard is sufficient to be able to take a view on particular issues by utilising common sense and commerciality. The "tick box" process would be very constraining and would clearly reduce the ability and increase timeliness of decision making. The definition below really emphasises that the decision that a servicer has to make should be determined as if it were the owner of the loan and that it has applied the same rationale as it would do on similar commercial mortgage loans for other portfolios.

As discussed in the previous chapter, "servicing standard" typically means the requirement that the servicer services, administers, enforces and realises the debt and manages any foreclosed real property pursuant to the servicing agreement in the best interests of and for the benefit of the lenders (including any holders of notes). Often this is specified in the following or similar language:

(a) the same manner in which, and with the same care, skill and diligence with which it services and administers similar commercial mortgage loans for other third-party portfolios; and
(b) the same care, skill and diligence which it would use if it were the owner of the loans.

The result is that this is a very subjective standard with few benchmarks and broadly allows the Servicer to act as they wish with little consultation of consent from other parties. The market has sought to regulate this solely through the rating assessment of loan servicers. The CREFC guidelines released in 2012 sought to provide more structure to this servicing standard and these have been adapted to a greater degree in some "CMBS 2.0" transactions. Areas that were noted for improvement/enhancement were:

1. Greater consistency in the principles adopted by which to judge workout options;
2. Exclusion of the interests of Class X, Deferred Consideration holders or liquidity facility providers in consideration of the strategy;
3. Greater ability for noteholders of all classes to make representations to the servicer.

10.7 Conclusion

What has become clear since the advent of the GFC, is that pro-active early engagement in workouts has generally provided the best results to lenders. The lenders who have acted pro-actively to reduce their NPL books have been the first to recommence lending and return to profitability. This was well evidenced in the UK where the market as a whole benefited from workout activity in the return to a well-functioning property market which benefits the wider economy. In CMBS, pro-active activity by servicers and noteholders has tended to benefit recovery outcomes, with the 'extend and pretend' model now largely discredited in all but the very worse markets.

What has been very apparent is that since the GFC, some level of liquidity in Europe's property markets has quickly returned in some form to most sectors. In some cases this is in the form of buyers of bulk NPL portfolios, but nevertheless lenders usually have options. Too often real estate is misunderstood as an asset class. Left alone, without care and attention, tenants can leave and value can be lost. The key to protecting value is often to develop capital structure solutions that allow for the underlying real estate to be managed in the best possible way.

Going forward, post Q4 2016, there are still huge challenges to address in Europe's banking system and the deleveraging process still has a number of years to run. Even once the problem of Europe's problem loan's has shifted from the banks to the NPL buyers, creative solutions will continually need to be developed and implemented to resolve the debt overhang. This is what a good asset manager/loan servicer can do.

Chapter 11

CRE Loan Servicing in CMBS 2.0: the Legal Issues

James A. Spencer,

Partner, K&L Gates LLP

11.1   Introduction

In the last edition of this title, in 2012, a view point was taken that loan servicers were front and centre of European CRE loan workouts and restructurings in the post GFC era and their role would become increasingly more challenging, as a significant proportion of existing European CRE debt was expected to go into default as borrowers faced the consequences of being over-leveraged.

A lot has happened in the intervening period and the purpose of this Chapter is not to recount those various events. However, a number of themes do warrant mention. Since 2012, liquidity has, generally speaking, returned to the real estate lending market and underlying real estate values have seen a marked increase. The consequences have been twofold. On the one hand, a large number of legacy CMBS loans have been refinanced by the existing sponsors taking advantage of the availability of attractive debt pricing. On the other hand, special servicers (or indeed borrowers working consensually with the loan servicers) have been able, without the pressure of a fire sale type scenario, to dispose of underlying real estate and, whilst a number of deals have seen write-offs on an individual loan basis, those write-offs have generally been smaller than they would have been in 2012, due to the general rise in asset values. In short, performing loans in legacy CMBS deals have largely been refinanced whilst non-performing loans have either seen write-offs following workouts, enforcement or distressed sales or continue to be worked-out. By way of illustration, in the two year period ending June 2016, the number of loans remaining in legacy European CMBS transactions nearly halved.[1] This Chapter in the prior edition of this book looked at,[2] given where we were in the cycle at that time, the various

---

[1]   As at June 2016, the number of loans remaining in CMBS was 159, compared to 279 in July 2014—Information taken from Debtwire's "Debtwire Report: European CMBS Monthly Activity" reports dated July 2016 and September 2015.

[2]   See further Petersen, A.V., *Commercial Mortgage Loans and CMBS: Developments in the European Market*, 2nd edn (London: Sweet & Maxwell, 2012), Ch.7.

enforcement methods of servicers and those can be revisited in that edition without further discussion in this Chapter.

As discussed in Chapters 1 and 4, despite early promise, CMBS 2.0 issuance has proved modest, with German multi-family, Italian multi-loans, and English single loan deals leading the way. The role of the servicer in new CMBS 2.0 has changed but not in any dramatic way, with the introduction of greater reporting obligations, increased interaction with noteholders, the ability to dispose of the underlying loans as a tool to maximise recoveries, and a clearer framework for dealing with property protection advances, to name a few.

This Chapter will explore the role of loan servicers, their duties, obligations and rights and the key provisions of their appointment in the current vintage of CMBS 2.0 deals and will highlight some of the key differences to legacy CMBS deals.

11.2 Loan servicing and the role of loan servicers

11.2.1 What is loan servicing?

As described in the previous two Chapters, loan servicing is the process of administering, managing, collecting on and realising CRE loans and is divided into two functions: primary servicing and special servicing. Primary servicing refers to the process of collecting payments from the underlying borrower and applying those payments to the relevant creditors; put simply, cash collection and cash payment. In addition, primary servicers are responsible for the general administration of the loan, dealing with communications received from the borrower, monitoring compliance and reporting on loan performance to the finance parties and (in the securitised deals) certain of the securitisation parties.

Special servicing refers to the more "intensive care" aspects of loan servicing. Once a loan is transferred from primary servicing to special servicing, the special servicer will be responsible for dealing with non-payment and other material breaches of the underlying finance documents and for determining, and then implementing, the chosen strategy to workout or enforce the loan and its related security. Whilst a loan is being specially serviced, the primary servicer continues to carry out its role of cash management, but its duties to communicate with the borrower will vest in the special servicer.

11.2.2 Appointment of CMBS servicers

Servicers are appointed at the time a CMBS transaction is closed to service all the CRE loans securitised within that transaction on behalf of the CMBS issuer (as owner of, and lender under, those CRE loans) and the CMBS issuer security trustee (as holder of all security granted by the issuer over the loans and its other assets for the benefit of the CMBS noteholders). To carry out this role, the issuer will appoint the servicer as its agent and lawful attorney to exercise all the rights and remedies the issuer has as lender under the finance documents and, in the case of A/B loans (discussed further in Chapters 5, 6 and 7), as senior lender under the intercreditor arrangements.

CRE loans are, as discussed in Chapter 4, typically structured as syndicated loan facilities, with a facility agent being the link between the borrower and the syndicate of lenders and with a security trustee holding the security granted by the borrower on trust for the syndicate. In legacy CMBS deals, the servicer was also appointed by the facility agent and security trustee as their agent and lawful attorney to carry out and perform their duties and exercise all rights available to them under the finance documents and any relevant intercreditor arrangements. In CMBS 2.0, some deals have adopted the same approach, whereas others deals have kept the role of the facility agent and the security trustee outside the scope of the servicer/special servicer. The rationale for this is mainly because the role of the facility agent and security trustee are self-contained and, given that the identity of the facility agent and security trustee on loans marked for CMBS are typically the same entity as that which will act as servicer and special servicer on the CMBS,[3] there is no real need for that entity to appoint itself to perform that role. Where the servicer and special servicer are not appointed by the facility agent and security trustee, the facility agent and security trustee will typically still enter into the servicing agreement in order to agree to provide certain information to the securitisation parties (such as the agent providing its determination of LIBOR for the loan where LIBOR on the notes is to be pegged to the same rate (thus avoiding any basis rate risk), providing debt service calculations to the servicer and acting on the servicer's instructions with regard to making payments to the issuer).

Whilst the issuer delegates absolutely all its rights and duties to the servicer, it does not follow that the servicer is entitled to exercise such rights and duties within its absolute discretion, nor, without boundaries or limitations. The issuer (together with the facility agent, the security trustee and the issuer security trustee) will enter into a servicing agreement with the servicer and special servicer that sets out in detail what the servicer and special servicer can and cannot do in respect of the loans. The next few sections of this Chapter will discuss this in greater detail.

Servicers are granted powers of attorney from the issuer (and, where relevant, the facility agent and security trustee) and these powers of attorney are an integral part of the servicing documentation. The power of attorney typically appoints the servicer to act as the appointer's attorney in con-

---

[3] In legacy CMBS deals, the underlying facility agent and security agent was often the originating bank.

nection with all loans owned within the particular CMBS, but this power of attorney typically does not list or otherwise identify on its face which specific loans the power of attorney applies to. Whilst this approach avoids the power of attorney being cumbersome in a multi-loan CMBS transaction, it can also have the unwanted outcome of borrowers and other third parties querying or being reluctant to accept that a particularly power of attorney gives the servicer authority in respect of a specific loan. Moreover, these powers of attorney may not be sufficient or effective to enable servicers to execute all acts they may need to carry out in the discharge of their duties. This is particularly relevant for special servicers who may be taking local law enforcement action under a servicing agreement power of attorney which is often English law governed. For example, executing land charge enforcement documentation in Germany will require the special servicer to be armed with a German language and German law vollmacht (power of attorney) which on its face clearly relates to the relevant loan.

11.2.3 *Servicing standard*

As set out in the previous two Chapters, a standard feature in all servicing agreements is the obligation on the servicer to act in accordance with the servicing standard at all times. The servicing standard is one of the key principles of loan servicing, providing a benchmark against which a servicer's performance can be judged. Whilst the definition of servicing standard differs from deal to deal, CMBS 2.0 servicing agreements generally place an obligation on the servicer to service the CRE loans (i) first and foremost in accordance with all applicable laws, (ii) in accordance with the terms of the loan finance documents, (iii) in accordance with the terms of the servicing agreement and other securitisation documents to which it is a party, (iv) in the best interests of the issuer, (v) acting to a standard of care and skill which is the higher of that which it would service its own portfolio of CRE loans and that which it applies to third party CRE loans, but in each case taking into account the customary and usual standards of practice of a prudent lender of CRE loans, and with a view to the timely receipt of payments due in respect of the loans and, if a loan event of default is continuing, the maximisation of recoveries to the creditors on or before the final note maturity date.

If there is any conflict between any of these requirements, then they will apply to the servicer in the order of priority in which they are stated. Thus, for example, the servicer can't be required by the terms of the servicing agreement to do anything which would cause a breach of law, nor would the servicer be in breach of the servicing standard if it refused to take a particular course of action which a third party servicer would take if taking that action would not be in accordance with the terms of the finance documents. It is sometimes debated if an obligation on the servicer to act in the best interests of the issuer infers any greater duty than acting to the standard of care stated in (v) above, and thus a servicer may want that best interests requirement to itself be subject to the reasonable judgment of the servicer or to rank below the standard of care requirement.

Where a loan is tranched, the servicer will be required to maximise recoveries to the issuer and the junior lender as a collective whole, but taking into account the subordination of the junior lender. Whilst the servicing standard will typically rank the intercreditor agreement in priority to the servicing agreement, it is sometimes the case that the intercreditor agreement will state that, in the case of conflict with the servicing agreement, the servicing agreement will prevail (effectively overriding the conflict priority set out in the servicing standard).

As mentioned in the prior edition of this Chapter, some market participants were of the view that servicers should act in the best interests of, and maximise recoveries for, the noteholders. The market has not, however, adopted this approach. Nevertheless, as will be touched on in greater detail later in this Chapter, servicers do now have greater rights and responsibilities under CMBS 2.0, particularly in relation to the maturity of CMBS notes, to communicate with the noteholders and take their opinions into account. This may be considered as the right balance of informing the servicer of the views and thoughts of the noteholders (as a whole) at a time when their notes are due to mature, without unnecessarily hindering the servicer from performing its primary obligations of servicing the underlying loan portfolio by requiring it to evaluate (through the complex securitisation waterfalls) how decisions made at the loan level will impact each of the varying classes of noteholders.

If the servicer is instructed by the issuer, the issuer security trustee or, where relevant, the noteholders in accordance with the terms of the servicing agreement, to take a particular course of action, then the servicer is obliged to take that action regardless of whether or not it is consistent with the servicing standard (and as such the servicer can not be liable to any party for taking such action). However, servicers should seek a carve-out from that obligation such that they are not obliged to act if doing so would be illegal or likely to result in the servicer being subject to any claim or proceeding from another party.

A second important feature of the servicing standard is that it lays down the parameters for how the servicer must act in connection with any conflicts that may arise between its own interests and those of the issuer and other parties it represents. The servicing standard makes it clear that in the discharge of its duties, the servicer cannot have regard to any fees or other compensation to which it may be entitled, nor any relationship it or any related entity has with any other party to the CMBS or underlying loan, nor any ownership interest it or any related entity has in any underlying loan or in the CMBS notes. In essence, the servicer should, at all times, place the interests of the creditors above its own interests and the interests of its related entities. Whilst in practice it is often difficult for servicers to totally separate and disregard their own interests when making decisions, what should never be allowed to happen is servicers acting solely in their own best interests. By way of illustration, entities affiliated to the servicer on any particular deal may hold either junior classes of notes in that CMBS or hold (outside the CMBS) junior tranches of the underlying loans and so this element of the servicing standard is of paramount importance to protect the CMBS noteholders as a collective whole.

11.2.4 Cash collection, insurance and property protection

As mentioned above, the primary servicer will typically remain responsible throughout the life of a loan for collecting payments from the underlying borrower and then distributing those payments to the finance parties. Where the loan is tranched, this will typically involve paying the collections into a tranching account and then applying those collections in accordance with the priority of payments agreed between the senior lenders and junior lenders. In the case of a securitised loan, the servicer will pay amounts due to the CMBS issuer into the issuer's collection account. At this point, the responsibility for dealing with cash passes to the CMBS cash manager, who will distribute all amounts paid to the issuer to the noteholders and other securitisation parties in accordance with the securitisation priority of payments. As such, it should not be the responsibility of the servicer to concern itself with how loan level collections will be distributed at the CMBS level.

Servicers are also bound by fairly specific obligations relating to property insurance and property protection. Servicers must have procedures in place to monitor a borrower's compliance with its insurance obligations under the finance documents and must, to the extent of the finance parties' rights under the finance documents, cause the borrowers to comply with such insurance obligations. If a borrower is in breach of any of its insurance obligations, if the property or rental income is not insured or any policy is likely to lapse, then the servicer is obliged to use commercially reasonable efforts, subject to the servicing standard, to procure those obligations are complied with. In practical terms, assuming the borrower is not working with the servicer to remedy the situation, a servicer is most likely to first look to utilise funds standing to the credit of any of the borrower's bank accounts over which the security trustee has signing rights to pay any premiums to put such insurance in place (and is given the right to do so in the servicing agreement) and secondly it may look to make a property protection advance (discussed in more detail below) in order to do so.

As discussed above, servicers are given the right to pay amounts owed by the borrower to third parties in relation to the property, such as insurance premiums, headlease amounts, and any other amounts which in the servicer's opinion are required to protect the rights of the finance parties, from amounts standing to the credit of the blocked bank accounts of the borrower. If those accounts have insufficient funds to make the relevant payment (sometimes referred to as a property protection shortfall) and the servicer is of the opinion that it would be better in the interests of the issuer to make the payment than for it not to be paid, then the servicer is permitted to make a property protection advance by utilising one of four sources of funds—it may utilise its own funds (but there is no obligation on it to do so), it may request the cash manager releases funds from the issuer's collection account, it may request the cash manager requests a property protection drawing (from the liquidity facility provider) or it may raise funds from third parties.

Most third party European servicers do not have significant balance sheets nor lending platforms from which to fund a property protection advance themselves. If they did, then any such advance should be repaid in full on the next note payment date in the same position in the waterfall as the servicer's fees get paid, together with interest thereon (typically at the class A note interest rate). Whilst the servicer is given full authority to raise monies from third parties (and to cause such monies to be paid senior to amounts owing to the noteholders) if it considers doing so would be in accordance with the servicing standard, it is generally considered that a servicer would be reluctant to cause the issuer to be indebted to third parties and, given the immediateness in which a servicer would want to remedy such a shortfall, it would be unlikely that any third party loan could be documented and implemented that quickly in any event.[4] Thus a servicer would most likely look to the issuer's own bank accounts or to a property protection drawing to fund the property protection shortfall. If a servicer makes a property protection advance it is obliged to take reasonable steps to recover those from the borrower.

11.2.5 Reporting and provision of information

One of the primary servicer's main functions is reporting and the servicing agreement will impose a large number of obligations on the primary servicer (and, in some cases, the special servicer) to provide various parties with significant amounts of information. This section summaries these various reporting and other provision of information obligations.

In CMBS transactions, the servicer is obliged to periodically report to the note trustee, issuer and other key parties, in a standardised form, how the loan is performing (which in Europe typically follows the Commercial Real Estate Finance Council's European-Investor Reporting Package (E-IRP)). When a loan transfers to special servicing, the special servicer is required, in addition to the primary servicer's periodic reporting obligations, to provide an asset status report with respect to the securitised loan and underlying property within a specified period (usually 60 days) following the transfer of the loan into special servicing. The servicing agreement will prescribe the

---

[4]   It is worth noting that any third party funding arrangement would be unsecured and must be made on a limited recourse and non-petition basis and thus there will be a smaller world of third party lenders willing to lend on such basis.

contents of such report, which will be negotiated on a deal-by-deal basis, but, together with information on the status of the loan and underlying property it will include a summary of the special servicer's recommended strategy and course of action that it has determined will maximise recoveries. The special servicer can update this report from time to time and must modify the report if any changes are required to its strategy by the servicing standard. Together these reports are of fundamental importance to the noteholders as their primary source of information on the underlying portfolio's performance.

In the context of CMBS deals the primary servicer is also responsible for preparing, on the CMBS issuer's behalf, notices to be issued to the market which disclose non-public information which is likely to have a material impact on the value of the underlying loans.

In September 2014 the EU Commission adopted Regulation (EC) No 1060/2009 which, together with its implementing measures (in particular Regulation (EU) No 2015/3), will impose from 1 January 2017 additional disclosure requirements for structured finance transactions. Pursuant to these regulations, the issuers of structured finance transactions are obliged to publically disclose to a website set up by the European Securities and Market Association (ESMA) all transaction documents, investor reports, loan level information and other key information in relation to the transaction. The consequence for servicers is that in new CMBS transactions the servicer is the entity most likely to be contractually appointed by the issuer as the designated reporting entity with regard to all loan-level information. Article 3 of Regulation (EU) No 2015/3 sets out the generality of the information to be reported and from a servicer's perspective it will want to ensure it is only responsible for the loan-level information (through the standardised disclosure templates annexed to Regulation (EU) No 2015/3), or, if it is also responsible for providing other relevant deal information, that its contractual obligation in relation thereto is limited to the extent it is provided with the required information from other transaction parties (who should be contractually obliged to provide that information to servicers). For deals that have closed since the implementation of these regulations but before 1 January 2017, it is likely that the servicing agreements for those deals will oblige the servicer to serve notice on ESMA that it is the designated reporting entity.

ESMA was required to issue technical instructions by 1 July 2016 detailing how the reporting will take place. However, at the time of writing, the latest announcement on the matter from ESMA is that due to certain issues with setting up the website, including lack of legal basis for funding, it is unlikely that the website will be available by 1 July 2017 and, accordingly, the technical instructions were not available on 1 July 2016.

The servicer will also be obliged to ensure that the loan facility agent exercises its rights to obtain, at the borrower's cost, an annual valuation of the underlying property and, in some cases, upon a disposal of any part of the property or its compulsory purchase. The valuation will be used to determine if the real estate would be insufficient to pay all amounts owing under the loan finance documents (if it is insufficient, this is known as an appraisal reduction) and such appraisal reduction would typically result in a reduction in the commitment of the liquidity facility.

It is also now common place in CMBS 2.0 transactions, for the servicer or, if the loan has transferred to special servicing, the special servicer, to inspect the property if it becomes aware that the property has been materially damaged, left vacant, abandoned or if environmental waste has been committed. It may also carry out more frequent inspections if it is concerned as to the borrower's ability to meet its financial obligations under the loan finance documents.

11.2.6 Modifications, waivers and consent under the loan finance documents

Whilst servicers are empowered to agree to modifications, waivers and consents in connection with the loan finance documents on behalf of the lenders, they may do so only in accordance with the parameters laid down in the servicing agreement and, where applicable, the intercreditor arrangements. If the terms of the loan finance documents contemplate a particular consent or waiver, then servicers are empowered to agree to that consent or waiver provided that the servicer is satisfied (in accordance with the servicing standard) that any conditions laid down in the loan finance documents which need to be satisfied prior to such a consent or waiver being given have been met.

Servicers may also agree to consents, waivers, amendments or modifications which are not contemplated by the loan finance documents. In that regard, the servicer must be satisfied that agreeing to such matters is in accordance with the servicing standard and it must discharge its obligations to obtain the consent from or to consult with the controlling party (discussed in greater detail below). Furthermore, it is common for servicers to be prohibited from extending the maturity of a loan or changing the amount of principal, the rate of interest or prepayment fees payable on a loan, in each case without the consent of each class of noteholders. In some transactions, the servicer may be given some flexibility to extend the loan for a short period of time but never into the tail period of the CMBS (the two or three year period immediately prior to the final note maturity date) or to grant standstills for a limited period of time.

The reason for prohibiting an extension of the loan, particularly into the CMBS tail period is that the tail period allows the issuer a period of time in which to realise the loan portfolio and conclude any loan-level enforcement action (based on the projected typical timeframe for enforcement processes in any particular jurisdiction) before the notes fall due for repayment, so that the issuer can avoid defaulting on its payment obligations which would create a note event of default. As seen in the workout of legacy CMBS, obtaining noteholder consent to such loan extensions is a time-consuming and difficult process but one that the deal parties are prepared to carry out if it is the best option to maximise recoveries on the loan.

11.2.7 Enforcement

Special servicers are responsible for dealing with the enforcement and workout of specially serviced loans. Whilst a consensual workout with the borrower is preferable this frequently is not possible and so special servicers must determine how best to utilise the various rights and remedies available to the finance parties in the loan finance documentation, particularly the security, in order to maximise recoveries to the issuer. It is within the special servicer's discretion to determine in accordance with the servicing standard the best strategy to achieve this, but often the special servicer is required to notify the various parties it represents before commencing with any enforcement action and provide such parties with periodic progress updates.

Despite special servicers being granted powers of attorney to enable them to carry out enforcement action in the name of the security holders, local law requirements and practices may not recognise such powers of attorney and so special servicers may need to obtain local law compliant powers of attorney or, in some cases require the security holder itself to execute documentation in order to facilitate an enforcement procedure. When it comes to the manner of enforcement, special servicers will generally want to avoid enforcing the mortgage over the real estate to exercise the power of sale contained therein. In some jurisdictions, such as Germany, this is by far the most expensive, time-consuming route available and can take control of the process away from the special servicer. Thus, taking enforcement action of this kind is often the last resort where all other options are not viable.

It is worth noting that some enforcement procedures require the loan debt to have been demanded before the procedure can commence. The obvious risk of demanding payment from the borrower is that the directors or managers of the borrower may then be duty bound to file the borrower for insolvency. This is, almost without exception, considered unhelpful for secured creditors—not only does it add an additional level of complexity, but it will inevitably increase costs, reduce recoveries and cause significant delays, as well as risking the loss of the finance parties control over the general workout strategy of the borrower. Many legacy CMBS deals also prohibited servicers (and issuers) from granting indemnities. This created an issue on enforcement as its fairly common practice for insolvency practitioners to require indemnities from the secured creditor as part of their appointment. CMBS 2.0 deals are, as a result, often documented to permit such indemnities to be given.

One significant restriction to the workout of loans in legacy CMBS deals is that the servicing agreements typically prohibited special servicers from selling the underlying loans. Servicers frequently received offers from third parties, as well as from the underlying borrower's affiliates, to purchase the securitised loan at a discount (commonly referred to as a discounted pay off or DPO[5]) but servicers were not able to proceed even though the DPO would have been the best outcome for the issuer. Accordingly, one of the main changes in CMBS 2.0 loan servicing is the introduction of an express right for special servicers to sell defaulted loans, instead of enforcing their security, if they determine that a sale is the most appropriate course of action consistent with the servicing standard. The special servicer's right is likely to be subject to other conditions, such as the sale price must be the best price achievable in the market at the time and the sale price must be unconditionally paid in full at the time of sale (thus there can be no deferred consideration component to the sale price). Further, special servicers are often restricted to only selling the loan to third party purchasers and thus can not sell to the underlying borrower's affiliates or sponsors.

Another criticism of legacy CMBS deals is that there was a disconnect between servicers' obligations to maximise recoveries and the obligation of the issuer to repay the notes at the final note maturity date. Legacy CMBS documentation did not permit or contemplate that noteholders would want an open dialogue with special servicers to input on the approach to realise the loan portfolio before the legal maturity of the notes. In addition, when legacy CMBS deals were originally documented they were done so on the general assumption that the issuer security trustee would enforce its security package over the issuer and effectively direct the servicer to liquidate the issuer's asset. However, in practice this has not happened and ultimately such course of action is viewed as not being the best course of action to maximise recoveries.

Accordingly, CMBS 2.0 deals have introduced the concept of a note maturity plan, the consequence of which ultimately is to put the note-holders in the driving seat to determine the course of action the special servicer should take if the underlying loans remain outstanding in the run up to the legal maturity of the notes. Under CMBS 2.0, if any part of a loan remains outstanding six months prior to the final note maturity date and the special servicer is of the opinion that it is unlikely all recoveries on the loans (whether through enforcement or otherwise) will be realised before the final note maturity date, then the special servicer is required to deliver a note maturity plan to the issuer and, ultimately, to the noteholders setting out the special servicer's proposals for realising those loans. The issuer is required to then convene a noteholder meeting so that the note maturity plan can be discussed between the issuer, the noteholders (of all classes) and the special servicer. The special servicer is then obliged after that meeting to revise the note maturity plan to address the views of the note-

---

holders and to deliver that final note maturity plan to the issuer and, ultimately, the noteholders. The issuer is then required to convene a further
noteholder meeting, but of the most senior class of noteholders only, at
which the most senior class of noteholders will select their preferred proposal and after that meeting the special servicer is required, notwithstanding any requirements of the servicing standard, to implement that
proposal. If no proposal is approved by the most senior class of noteholders
then the issuer security trustee shall be deemed authorised to appoint a
receiver over all the assets secured in its favour.

As a further tool to facilitate dialogue between the servicer/special servicer
and noteholders, the servicer/special servicer's ability to convene noteholder meetings in CMBS 2.0 deals is not limited to meetings relating to the
note maturity plan. The servicer/special servicer now has the general
power to require the issuer to call noteholder meetings for such purposes as
it sees fit to put matters to the noteholders or a certain class thereof for their
consideration.

11.2.8   *Controlling party consent and consultation rights*

Despite the broad discretion of servicers under the servicing agreement, key
amendments to the terms of the underlying loans and enforcing the security
are often subject to consent rights in favour of the controlling party.

Where the whole loan is held in a CMBS, the controlling party will be the
controlling class, which is usually defined as the most junior class of notes
which, based on the aggregate outstanding principal amount of the issuer's
loan portfolio, would see more than 25% of the principal balance of that
class of notes repaid. If the loan is tranched, then the controlling party will
be the most junior lender in respect of which a CVE is not continuing
(typically defined by reference to expected recoveries, based on the most
recent valuation of the underlying real estate, being low enough that the
junior lender would expect to recover less than 25% of its principal loan
commitment), before passing to the next most junior lender, or, if there is no
other junior lender, then the senior lender. Where the senior lender is a
CMBS issuer, then the controlling party will be the controlling class.

The documentation surrounding consent and consultation rights is often
complicated and requires servicers to fully analyse the terms of the servicing agreement and, where the loan is tranched, the intercreditor agreement, to understand what matters require the servicer to seek controlling
party involvement, and whether that involvement is consent or
consultation.[6]

At the securitisation level, the controlling class will need to appoint an
operating adviser in order for its consent and consultation rights to apply. If

---

[6]   See further Chs 5, 6 and 7.

a controlling class has appointed an operating adviser it must notify the servicer, special servicer, note trustee and issuer security trustee. Most servicing agreements typically state that if the controlling class fail to do this the servicer/special servicer may proceed on the basis that no operating adviser has been appointed. Some servicing agreements (particularly in legacy CMBS) are silent on this point. In those instances, a prudent servicer may wish to contact the market, requesting any operating advisor identifies itself to the servicer.

Since the operating adviser (OA) is a single entity, it enables the servicer to communicate and discharge its consent/consultation duties more efficiently than if it had to deal with numerous noteholders within the controlling class. Whilst all deals differ to varying degrees, the consent of the OA will often be required prior to consenting to a loan extension (unless such extension is contemplated by the original terms of the facility agreement), varying the timing or amount of payments of interest or principal, deferring payments of interest for a significant period of time, varying other material provisions of the finance documents, taking enforcement action, releasing a borrower from its obligations and releasing security where it is not contemplated by the loan finance documents (e.g. where the loan is not repaid in full at maturity or where an asset sale doesn't meet the specified allocated loan amount (ALA) requirements).

Servicing agreements set out in detail the process for obtaining OA consent and often require the servicer to give 5 to 10 business days prior notification of its intended course of action and the OA is entitled to raise objection and propose an alternative course of action within that timeframe. If the OA does not respond within the specified timeframe then it is deemed to have given its consent and the servicer may proceed with its intended course of action. If the OA does respond within such period, then there is typically a period of continuing dialogue between the servicer and the OA, usually in the region of 15 to 30 days. After which, if no agreement is reached between the servicer and the OA, the servicer can proceed with whatever course of action it determined in accordance with the servicing standard.

Notwithstanding the OA consent procedure set out above, the servicer will also benefit from what is known as the servicing standard override—this entitles the servicer to take immediate action or to liaise with the OA for a shorter period of time that the servicing agreement otherwise requires, if to do otherwise would be contrary to the servicing standard. Furthermore, it also entitles the servicer to refuse to take any action if to take that action would violate the servicing standard. The servicer standard override can, therefore, be an important tool for servicers to ensure it discharges its primary duty of servicing the underlying loan and, moreover, it protects it against directions from an OA which may, by the very nature of the OA acting solely in the interests of only the controlling class, not be in the best interests of all noteholders.

251

In the case of A/B loans, the junior lender's consent rights whilst it is the controlling party are typically the same as those of the controlling class, although in some deals they can be more encompassing and, in some instances in legacy CMBS deals, the junior lender also has certain entrenched rights which it retained even after a CVE. In addition, the junior lender often had in legacy deals consultation rights with respect to any matter which the servicer considers to be a "significant action" with respect to a loan or its security.[7]

Some noteholders, however, view appointing an OA as a double-edged sword—opening oneself up for challenge from other noteholders within the controlling class for which that OA represents. As such, an OA is more likely to be appointed where one particular organisation owns the entire controlling class. Furthermore, if a noteholder appoints itself as OA, then this can limit the noteholder from trading its notes. This is because the OA, when exercising its consent and consultation rights, will become privy to price-sensitive information which may affect the price of its notes. The MAD (and the rules of the various European jurisdictions implemented MAD into national legislature) create an offense for those trading securities based on price-sensitive information, known as insider dealing.[8] Accordingly, noteholders may not wish to appoint themselves as an OA because they will not want to have their general ability to trade their notes fettered, even at the cost of losing a degree of control over the proposed actions of the servicer.

11.2.9 Special serviced loans and corrected loans

CRE loans will be serviced by the primary servicer unless and until any one of a number of events occurs with respect to the loan (known as servicing transfer events). Once a servicing transfer event occurs, the special servicer will take over responsibility for servicing that loan and addressing the particular matter which caused the loan to switch to special servicing.

The list of servicing transfer events varies from deal to deal, but typically CMBS 2.0 servicing transfer events include: (i) failure to repay the loan on its maturity; (ii) any other payment default which is more than 30 days past due; (iii) any borrower being subject to an insolvency or insolvency proceeding based loan event of default; (iv) any cross default or creditor process loan event of default; or (v) any other loan event of default occurs or, in the reasonable opinion of the servicer, is imminent, which in either case is not likely to be cured within 21 days but is likely to have a material adverse effect on the interests of the lender.

In the case of tranched loans, the intercreditor agreement will often state that a servicing transfer event will not occur for so long as the junior lender

---

7 Junior lender consent and consultation rights are discussed in more detail in Ch.7.
8 See Ch.13 of the 1st edn.

is exercising (or is within the period to exercise) its cure rights in respect of the default which has caused a servicing transfer event. However, it will not be possible to stop a servicing transfer event arising following a maturity breach or an insolvency based breach.

Despite the transfer to special servicing, as stated above, the primary servicer will remain responsible for collecting and monitoring debt service, monitoring insurance compliance as well as continuing to perform its various CMBS reporting obligations. The primary servicer will continue to receive its fee for performing these duties. However, primary servicers, have in the context of legacy CMBS deals, often found themselves in a position where the loan has not yet switched to special servicing (because although there is a loan event of default a servicing transfer event has not yet arisen) but they are nonetheless carrying out a greater level of service than was originally contemplated. As discussed below, the fee provisions in CMBS 2.0 servicing agreements goes some way to address this by permitting the primary servicer to charge additional fees in certain circumstances (although these are only recoverable from the borrower).

It is possible under the servicing agreement for a loan in special servicing to "flip" back to primary servicing if it has become a corrected loan. Typically, a loan will become a corrected loan if, in the case of payment or other monetary default, the default has discontinued for two consecutive interest periods and for any other servicing transfer event, the event which caused the transfer to special servicing event has ceased to exist.

11.2.10   Fees

Servicing fees in CMBS 2.0 are split into five components—the primary servicing fee; the servicer modification fee (which was not a feature of legacy CMBS); the special servicing fee; the workout fee; and the liquidation fee. In addition, servicers are entitled to recover out-of-pocket cost and expenses reasonably incurred in the performance of their duties.

Primary servicers are entitled to receive the primary servicing fee, which is a low basis point per annum fee calculated against the outstanding balance of all loans and payable on each note payment date. The fee rate is designed to reflect the fairly straightforward cash management and administrative nature of their role.

As indicated above and in the previous two Chapters, in practice primary servicers have often found themselves in circumstances where loans are in, or heading towards, a distressed position but have not yet been transferred to special servicing, and are carrying out special servicing functions without being appropriatly remunerated for such services. In particular, the work involved in deciding whether or not to agree to consents, waivers and modifications is often time-consuming and will often involve the preparation of internal credit papers, credit committee approval, detailed analysis of cashflows and projections. Such matters have, in legacy deals, often been dealt with in primary servicing with a view to restructuring a loan before it goes into default. Given the relatively low basis point fee which primary servicers are entitled, primary servicers will want to charge the borrower a fee for agreeing to the borrower's request. Accordingly, CMBS servicing agreements permit primary servicers (but not special servicers) charging such a fee (referred to as the servicer modification fee), provided the fee is consistent with the servicing standard and it can be recovered from the borrowers without resulting in any shortfall in current interest or any other amounts due under the finance documents. The servicer modification fee can be structured as an ongoing or periodic fee but the rate per annum can not exceed the special servicing fee rate.

Special servicers are entitled to a special servicing fee, which is a higher basis point per annum fee than the primary servicing fee and also calculated against the outstanding balance of all specially serviced loans and payable on each note payment date. This higher fee is designed to reflect the additional work and expertise required to properly service loans in special servicing. Special servicers are also entitled to two performance based fees: the workout fee and the liquidation fee. The workout fee arises where a specially serviced loan becomes a corrected loan and for so long as it remains a corrected loan. The workout fee rate is typically higher than the special servicing fee rate and calculated against all principal and interest received on a corrected loan and is intended to reward the special servicer for converting a non-performing loan into a performing loan. The liquidation fee incentivises the special servicer to maximise recoveries in the event of liquidation of a specially serviced loan or its underlying property. The quantum of the liquidation fees is, like the workout fee, typically higher than the special servicing fee but is calculated against the net liquidation proceeds received and is typically paid to the special servicer on the note payment date following receipt of such proceeds. In legacy CMBS, the liquidation fee was often stated as only being based on a liquidation of the underlying real estate following the enforcement of the security. The concern from the special servicer's perspective therefore is that if they carried out any form of consensual workout of the loan which still resulted in liquidation proceeds they would not receive a liquidation fee despite their hard work in conducting that consensual workout. Accordingly, CMBS 2.0 deals make it clear that the liquidation fee is due if the liquidation proceeds arise following the enforcement of security, the sale of a loan to a third party (but not a resale back to any originator) or through a consensual or other workout of the loan.

The securitisation level documentation architecture is usually structured such that the payment of the liquidation fee to the special servicer reduces principal recoveries to the creditors/noteholders due to the fee being paid out of funds that would otherwise be available for distribution to the creditors/noteholders. Notwithstanding how the securitisation documentation contemplates the liquidation fee being paid, there have been a number of examples of the special servicer, on behalf of the issuer, charging the liquidation fee to the borrower under the fees/costs indemnity and expenses provisions in the underlying finance documents. This can avoid a shortfall being incurred by the creditors/noteholders, but only when the net liquidation proceeds are sufficient to discharge in full all loan liabilities and cover the liquidation fee. If such proceeds are not sufficient then charging the liquidation fee to the borrower may, so far as the creditors/noteholders are concerned, have the same net effect as paying the liquidation fee at the securitisation level. Further complexity can arise if the underlying loan is tranched—in such circumstances careful consideration should be given to the terms of the intercreditor documentation as to how servicer fees are expected to be recovered from the issuer and/or the junior lender, and if charging the liquidation fee to the borrower would contradict such terms.

In legacy CMBS, the fee rates for each of the fees discussed above was fairly standardised across all deals. However, this has changed in CMBS 2.0 with fees varying quite considerably to account for the size and complexity of the deal. This change in approach reflects some market concerns under legacy deals that, because the fee percentages were effectively the same for all deals, it meant that on deals that were larger but less complex these fees represented somewhat of a windfall payment to servicers doing little work whilst on smaller more complex deals the servicer/special servicer was not being appropriately remunerated even though it may be engaged in a significant amount of work.

11.2.11   Liability, termination and replacement of servicers

The liability that loan servicers owe to their appointers is typically limited to losses and liabilities incurred as a result of the servicer's negligence, fraud or wilful misconduct. Of fundamental importance to servicers, the servicing agreement should also state that servicers are not responsible or liable for the loan portfolios performance or any shortfall in ultimate recoveries, nor the payment obligations of the issuer under the notes. Moreover, servicers are also indemnified for any losses or claims they may incur in the discharge of their duties.

Servicers who diligently discharge their obligations should remain appointed as servicer for the life of the loans, with their appointment automatically terminating when the last of the recoveries on the last loan in the CMBS portfolio has been received. However, a fundamental control right for the issuer security trustee is the right to terminate the servicer if certain material events occur with respect to the servicer. Whilst varying from deal to deal, the right to terminate the servicer will usually arise where: (i) the servicer has failed to remit funds to the issuer when due; (ii) the servicer has breached any of its other material obligations; (iii) the servicer is insolvent or any insolvency or similar proceedings have been taken or commenced; (iv) the servicer ceases to carry on its business or is unable to discharge its duties; and (v) the servicer pays all or any part of its remuneration to a noteholder. Whilst a matter of negotiation, the servicer will usually benefit from grace periods for certain of these events allowing it time to remedy the breach and avoid the issuer security trustee being able to terminate its appointment. As mentioned earlier in this Chapter, in CMBS 2.0 the servicer is often the same entity as the loan facility agent and loan security trustee and thus if the servicer terminates its appointment as loan facility agent or loan security trustee that is also usually a termination event in the servicing agreement. Conversely, if the servicer is terminated in its role as servicer, it is usually required to resign as loan facility agent and loan security trustee.

Whilst neither the issuer nor the issuer security trustee have a right to terminate the servicer without cause, the controlling class (through its OA) typically has the discretionary right to terminate the special servicer at any time and appoint a replacement special servicer of its choosing, provided that the replacement special servicer satisfies certain conditions contained within the servicing agreement. The use of this right in legacy CMBS has been a hotly discussed topic. Initially included to provide the controlling class with a degree of control in the event that the special servicer was underperforming, there have been a number of instances where the controlling class has terminated existing special servicers and replaced them with special servicers affiliated or otherwise associated with the controlling class. This has raised concerns in the market, particularly from the more senior classes of noteholders, that the newly appointed special servicer will workout specially serviced loans or otherwise carry out its duties in a manner favourable to the interests of the controlling class, disregarding the servicing standard which it should comply with at all times. CMBS 2.0 deals sometimes also give the noteholders (as a collective whole, but the controlling class excepted) the right to terminate the servicer or the special servicer.

Another problematic feature of legacy CMBS deals was that the change in servicer often required each of the rating agencies appointed on the deal to confirm that the change in servicer did not result in a downgrade of the ratings. Some of the agencies, Moody's in particular, adopted a policy of refusing to grant such confirmations and, as a result, this meant the requirements to change the servicer could not be confirmed. This legal issue has been the subject of much debate and, in some cases, the legal position has been before the English courts.[9] To address this, whilst CMBS 2.0 will still require rating agency confirmations, the securitisation documentation will make it clear that if a rating agency doesn't respond to a request for confirmation within a time period or does respond to the effect that they are unwilling to review the change in servicer, then the requirement for such a confirmation will cease to apply.

---

[9] *Deutsche Trustee Company Ltd v Cheyne Capital (Management) UK (LLP)* [2015] EWHC 2282 (Ch); *US Bank Trustees Ltd v Titan Europe 2007-1 (NHP) Ltd* [2014] EWHC 1189 (Ch).

11.3 Conclusion

Loan servicing is an integral function within CRE financings and, as this Chapter and the previous two Chapters have outlined, servicers are generally given broad powers and discretion in the performance of their roles, with CMBS 2.0 documentation addressing many of the loan servicing concerns that arose in legacy CMBS deals. The role of servicers is much clearer and better defined in CMBS 2.0, arming servicers with additional contractual rights and tools to help facilitate loan workouts and restructurings and, at the same time, enabling greater interaction between servicers and noteholders when necessary.

The future of loan servicing, however, remains a challenging market. Legacy CMBS deals will continue to run-off and, with it, so do the servicers running fees. With CMBS 2.0 issuance remaining patchy, unaided by general market conditions and the UK's decision to leave the EU, it is likely to remain fairly stagnant in the short to medium term. Accordingly, whilst liquidation fees and workout fees on legacy CMBS deals may, in part, supplement a drop in running fee income for the servicing community, servicers have to (and will need to continue to) expand their business offering more widely, so they are not reliant on an active CMBS market. Those with real estate experience, experienced asset management platforms and investment teams will be best placed to succeed in an ever challenging market place.

11.3. Conclusion

Chapter 12

Interest Rates and Hedging: How Derivatives Impact CRE Finance Strategy for Lenders and Borrowers

Mark Battistoni, Jamie Macdonald, Phong Dinh,
Chatham Financial

12.1 Introduction

Derivatives such as interest rate swaps, caps and floors are prevalent within a wide range of CRE financings in Europe, ensuring that a borrower's ability to satisfy interest cover and debt service covenants is unaffected solely by movements in interest rate markets.[1] This function is so relevant to CRE lenders' underwriting processes that it manifests as a hedging requirement in most variable-rate loans and is by definition the basis for fixed-rate financing structures. This Chapter will consider what can still appear to be a shadowy and arcane corner of CRE finance. Derivatives' relevance persists despite—and on some levels as a result of—the continuation of historically low variable interest rate indices such as LIBOR and EURIBOR since 2009. As the title suggests, it will examine how both lenders and borrowers are contemplating interest rate derivatives in conjunction with their transactions.

In recent years, as lenders have adapted to the prospect (and now in some cases, the reality) of negative interest rate environments, the lines between debt, derivatives and interest rate hedges have blurred somewhat. The first section of this Chapter unravels the conceptual knots arising when both lender and borrower employ derivatives in the same financing structure. As discussed in Chapter 4, lenders have increasingly sought to include a derivative instrument, an interest rate floor, in the financing itself to prevent erosion to their margin if the variable interest rate fell below zero. Resulting negotiations can take many different paths depending on the lender type

---

[1] Although some CRE transactions involve currency and inflation risks requiring foreign currency and inflation derivatives, these are relatively rare. This Chapter focuses on interest rate hedging, although many of the concepts will be relevant to other types of hedging. Property derivatives are not covered in this Chapter.

and certain borrower-specific negotiating dynamics.[2] Irrespective of the outcome, a new complexity arises in the transaction relative to those of positive interest rate environments.

The second section of this Chapter focuses on the trend of third-party interest rate hedge providers and its impact on the overall process of arranging CRE financings. When a borrower needs to, or prefers to, seek a hedge from a third party, the obvious repercussions can be accompanied by a host of less obvious economic and legal consequences worth noting. Market participants and stakeholders at all levels, bank and non-bank lenders, CMBS arrangers, ratings agencies, borrowers and legal advisers to name a few, can be affected in a variety of ways.

A final section addresses why hedging requirements exist in the first place. After several years of extraordinarily low interest rates, it is only natural to begin to perceive interest rate risk to be low. It is actually quite the opposite, for two reasons. The first is that because interest rates are so low, it reasons that there is far more room to travel in the other direction. The second is that central banks are actively seeking this result. With extremely low interest rates, an economy is closer to a deflationary spiral than in a higher interest rate environment, so it follows that central banks will effect policies guiding the market toward more "normal" levels of interest rates when the risk of deflation is high.

12.2 Negative interest rates, floors in loans and their effects on interest rate hedging strategies

This first section will consider the costs associated with derivatives used for hedging in CRE financings. As noted in the introduction, this will necessarily include any floor embedded in the financing as well as the hedges employed by the borrower. To be clear up-front, the floor referred to throughout this Chapter is effectively a negotiated limit to the variable index appearing in the financing documents. Sometimes it is referred to as a "minimum IBOR[3] provision". It is not a separately negotiated or documented contract like the derivatives the borrower would typically enter into

---

[2] See Briefing Note of Clifford Chance for February 2015, Negative LIBOR—implications under syndicated lending documentation: "If a Lender's imperative is to prevent potential erosion of its margin as a result of a negative LIBOR then inclusion of a Zero Floor is likely to be a high priority. However, other factors may militate against the inclusion of a Zero Floor (for example, if the transaction involves a corresponding hedging product the inclusion of a Zero Floor could result in mismatches with rates payable under the derivative). Such factors may outweigh the benefits of margin protection in some cases. Of course the borrower's perspective in any negotiation will also be critical." The Briefing Note is written with respect to syndicated loans, but is applicable more broadly to CRE financing.

[3] IBOR is "Inter-Bank Offered Rate" used generically as the variable-rate index in a CRE financing. The specific rate will have a prefix such as with USD LIBOR, GBP LIBOR, EURIBOR, and others representing the variable rates most commonly used in any given currency. Note that some currencies have multiple IBORs.

to hedge the interest rate risk under the financing. From a documentation perspective, a loan with a floor is akin to a fixed-rate loan that is only fixed in certain circumstances. To make the concepts more tangible, examples in both Sterling (GBP) and euros (EUR) will be provided to give perspectives from positive and negative interest rate environments, respectively, prevailing in mid-2016.

Note that the derivatives and their explanations below rely heavily on the concept of a forward variable rate. This rate—often referred to generically as "the LIBOR forward rate" or simply a "forward" and, in aggregate, the "forward curve"—is merely the placeholder for what the variable index will be at the beginning of each of the future interest periods being considered. No one can predict exactly what any future variable rate setting such as GBP LIBOR or EURIBOR will be, but a forward curve is the closest approximation of the market expectation to the "path" of that particular index over time. There is not a defined market for buying and selling individual forwards, but they are critical to interest rate derivatives markets. As such, forward curves need to be constructed from certain, quite detailed, market data available via inter-dealer brokers. Importantly in practice, the data arrives on a live, streaming basis as the inputs' values change continuously. Special pricing engines use these market forward rates and certain other inputs to calculate the at-market prices for derivatives, which also fluctuate continuously throughout the trading day. Again in practice, note that a derivative's price can be "stale" after only a few seconds; after a few minutes it is definitely unreliable.

Forward LIBOR and EURIBOR rates are important because they drive the pricing of derivatives such as swaps, caps and floors. In the CRE sector and many others, the most well-known derivative among these is the interest rate swap, which effectively converts a variable-rate loan into a fixed-rate loan from the borrower's perspective. A CRE borrower is concerned with the fixed rate payable under the swap and this is called the swap rate. It is helpful to think of a swap rate as the average of the forward rates during the loan term. A bit more technically, a swap rate is a balancing act in which the expected costs to one party (which pays floating each period) equal the expected costs to the other party (which pays a fixed rate.) Graphically, the chart in Figure 1 shows that the area between the forward curve and the "swap rate" line for each currency looks roughly equal on either side of the lines' intersection. It is important to note that a swap has no up-front costs. The "cost" to a borrower is the sum of the fixed payments made over the term of the swap. In undiscounted cash terms, it is roughly the fixed rate multiplied by the hedged amount multiplied by the five years of assumed hedge term. Or, it can be expressed more simply as a rate. Either way, comparison with other hedge strategies with up-front costs can be fairly straightforward as long as the approach is consistent. For this reason, the costs of other derivatives depicted below show their up-front cost (or premium payable) as well as the same amount expressed as a rate as if the premium were paid over the full term of the loan.

Figure 1: Chart with forward curves for GBP and EUR over five year period, listing five year swap rates

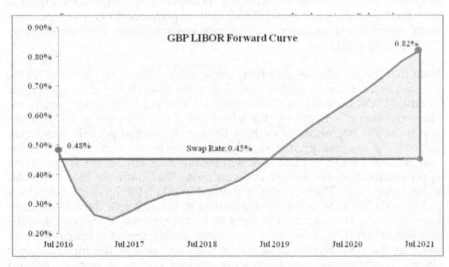

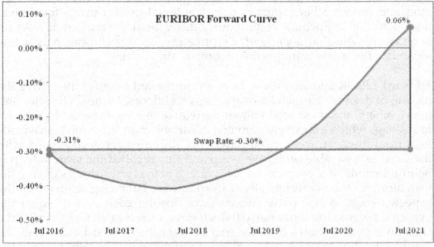

It is evident from the EUR swap example in Figure 1 that a variable-rate index and a series of forward rates comprising a forward curve can be negative, and that this leads to a negative swap rate. In derivatives markets, there is no distinction between a negative variable rate and a positive one. A negative payment means a receipt of a cash flow. There is no benefit or detriment involved, due to the balancing act described above; at inception the swap rate is merely the place at which the value of one counterparty's future cash flows equals the expected value that of the other's. If the for-ward curve is negative, the swap is expected to exchange one negative rate

262

for another. It functions just as if rates were positive, in a way. If a variable-rate loan is also indifferent to whether a variable interest rate is negative or positive, that loan hedged with an interest rate swap will also function just as if rates were positive—a variable-rate financing has a fixed rate from the borrower's perspective. If not, there is a mismatch and this is where the cost of floors becomes relevant.

Figure 2: Table with five year 0% floor costs and sample of 5yr cap costs in GBP and EUR

EUR Floor at 0%	0.45%
GBP Floor at 0%	0.17%

		Cap Strike Rates				
		1.00%	**1.50%**	**2.00%**	**2.50%**	**3.00%**
EUR	**Quarterly Premium Cost**	0.11%	0.08%	0.06%	0.04%	0.03%
	Worst-case Rate	1.11%	1.58%	2.06%	2.54%	3.03%
GBP	**Quarterly Premium Cost**	0.46%	0.32%	0.22%	0.16%	0.11%
	Worst-case Rate	1.46%	1.82%	2.22%	2.66%	3.11%

<u>*Assumptions:*</u>

5 years term, quarterly payments and resets;

For GBP Caps: 3mo. GBP Libor, Act/365 Fixed, London Business Days;

For EUR Caps: 3mo. EURIBOR, Act/360, TARGET Business Days;

Caps and floors are option contracts in which the purchaser, in exchange for an up-front premium, receives the difference between the variable-rate index and a chosen rate for a defined term. The chosen rate is called the *strike rate*. The only difference between caps and floors is in the order of the calculation of what the purchaser receives over time: for a cap it is the index minus the strike rate, and for a floor it is the strike rate minus the index. A cap protects the purchaser from rising interest rates, but enables it to "float" to the extent that interest rates fall or do not rise. A floor does exactly the opposite. Many CRE investors will be familiar with caps, as they are a popular hedge strategy choice for satisfying a financing's requirement to hedge or protect against rising interest rates. Some may also be familiar with floors, but probably in the context of an interest rate collar, which is the combination of a *purchased* cap and a *sold* floor. The latter offsets the cost of the cap and creates a band of possible outcomes for a loan's interest rate, typically with no up-front cost—thus its attractiveness.[4]

---

[4]   Note that in a collar, the fact that the floor is sold means that the bank is the purchaser so the effect is not beneficial to the borrower if rates fall.

Figure 3: Interest Rate Cap Example (GBP)

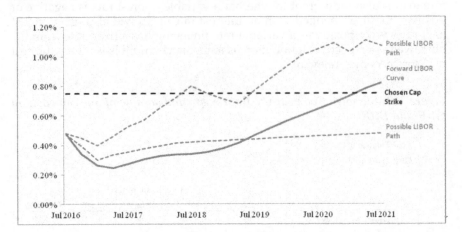

The biggest difference between swaps and options like caps and floors is the up-front cost. Again, a swap has no up-front cost whereas options only have an up-front cost for the purchaser such as a borrower. Another key difference is that there is a single at-market swap rate for a given debt profile but an unlimited number of possible strike rates an option purchaser can select. By increasing the strike rate for a cap, its premium decreases. The risk of higher all-in costs (if the variable index rises over time) increases commensurately, complicating any decision. To compare the costs of any particular cap strategy alongside a swap strategy, it is useful to spread the premium over the life of the cap to give a spread or rate, then add this to the cap strike rate. The result is a "worst-case" rate assuming the index rises to, or above, the chosen strike rate (see right-most column in Figure 2.) Although a borrower would hope that variable rates fell or stayed far below the chosen strike rate, stress-testing its interest rate assumption in this manner would be prudent. The higher potential interest costs could make the choice of a high cap strike rate less appealing than that of a lower strike rate, or indeed a swap.

Though a floor in a loan could be at any rate and its value would flex in a similar (but opposite) fashion to caps as described above, the level most often included in loan terms by lenders is 0%, so for simplicity this is the only strike rate listed in Figure 2. It is easy to underestimate the value of a floor in a loan, for two primary reasons. The forward curve, as in the EURIBOR forward curve illustrated in Figure 1, can be well below 0% and the pricing of derivatives like 0% floors factor in 100% of the extent to which the forward curve is beneath the strike rate. This reflects the expected payments by the floor seller, and is referred to as a floor's *intrinsic value*. The pricing also factors in the possibility that forward rates could actually fall further, making the payments by the floor seller larger. This is calculated as a function of interest rate volatility and time, and is referred to as a floor's *time value.*[5]

The GBP 0% floor cost is fully time value as at the time of writing, since the entire forward curve is above zero. Incidentally this comes just after the Brexit decision in the UK's EU referendum caused a sharp downward shift in GBP LIBOR expectations, underscoring this point. The implication is that if a borrower is faced with a financing with a 0% floor and wants to avoid a mismatch (why avoiding a mismatch is desirable is described in detail below), its costs could be substantial, sometimes surprisingly so. Again, for ease of comparing hedging decisions it is useful to express the premium as a rate payable over the loan term.

The subject of floors in loans is an increasingly visible and contentious one as at the time of writing. This is because negative interest rates are a relatively new phenomenon and their impact on loans and any associated derivatives is, for the most part, not intuitive to market participants. There are certain justifiable reasons why a lender (any lender, not just those in CRE) may require a floor, just as there are certain justifiable reasons why any borrower would resist its inclusion. One of the goals of this Chapter is to illustrate the objective, practical details of the impact of a floor on a borrower's interest expense—via its hedging decision—so that any discussion on the subject is more informed. To be clear, there is no "right" or "wrong" answer but there are certainly costs and additional uncertainties to lenders and to borrowers when navigating a negative interest rate environment. The costs to lenders vary by funding source and numerous other factors, leading this aspect falling well outside the scope of this Chapter. The borrower's costs are more obvious and discernible, though.

The key concept is that a floor in a loan creates at least one mismatch that manifests only to the extent that the variable index falls below the floor strike rate. The first mismatch—irrespective of the presence or type of hedging strategy—is straightforward: compared to a loan without a floor, a borrower's interest rate will be higher if the index rate is beneath the floor rate in any given interest period. The degree depends simply on how far below the floor rate the index has fallen, and a borrower might think of this mismatch leading to an "opportunity cost" of accepting the floor.

The second mismatch is more pernicious, but only occurs if the borrower has hedged with an interest rate swap.[6] Or, more accurately, it only occurs if a swap is not also accompanied by a purchased interest rate floor on the same terms at the strike rate of the floor on the loan. Unless the borrower

---

[5] Conversely, if the borrower purchases an in-the-money cap where the cap strike was lower than the then current IBOR (forward) rate, then it has *intrinsic value* and its *time value* arises from the possibility that forward rates could rise further.
[6] This mismatch would apply to any hedging strategy involving future payments such as a collar, but for simplicity the focus will only be on swaps.

has taken this extra step, the effect is *twice* the difference described in the previous paragraph. This is because on the loan the borrower is not paying a negative variable rate but on the swap, the borrower is receiving a negative variable rate. Mathematically on the swap this means it is paying the positive value of the variable rate. This would be fine if the loan acted in concert by lowering the loan interest, but the floor precludes this. The result, which is not at all intuitive, is that for any interest period in which the variable rate is negative, its interest expense will be its agreed swap rate plus the absolute value of the variable rate plus loan margin. A swap ordinarily gives a borrower a fixed rate, so it can be disheartening for a borrower to discover that not only is the swap rate not truly "fixed" but that the situation gets worse if rates fall further below zero. It is exposed to a different version of interest rate risk, but exposed nonetheless!

To correct the mismatch within the swap strategy, the borrower would have to take the extra step of purchasing the floor in the derivatives market. From Figure 2 the costs expressed as a rate paid over five years would be 0.17% for a GBP example and 0.45% for a EUR example. Adding this rate to the swap rate, which is in practical terms how the floor purchase would ordinarily be funded, gives a truly fixed swap rate in that the borrower is no longer exposed to interest rate risk due to the mismatch between loan and swap. It is also called a "floored swap". For borrowers inclined to hedge with swaps, an easy way to quantify the cost of a floor in the loan is difference between these two swap rates. This comparison for a EUR loan and swap scenario is illustrated in Figure 4 with a further table in Figure 5 detailing the ramifications on all-in interest expense as the variable index rises or falls.

Figure 4: EUR swap rates with and without the "repurchase" of a 0% floor

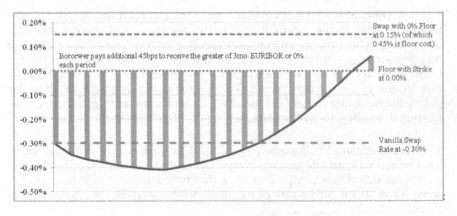

Figure 5: Effects of negative interest rates all-in costs at various EURIBOR fixing levels

Without floor "repurchase" (mismatch)					With "repurchased" floor (no mismatch)			
Vanilla 5-year Swap at -0.30%					5-year Swap At 0.15% (-0.30% + 0.45% floor cost)			
Euribor fixing		-0.80%	-0.40%	0.50%	Euribor fixing	-0.80%	-0.40%	0.50%
Loan	Borrower pays (excl. margin)	0.00%	0.00%	0.50%	Loan	Borrower pays (excl. margin)	0.00%	0.00%	0.50%
Swap	Borrower pays	-0.30%	-0.30%	-0.30%	Swap	Borrower pays	0.15%	0.15%	0.15%
	Borrower receives	-0.80%	-0.40%	0.50%		Borrower receives	0.00%	0.00%	0.50%
	All-in cost	0.50%	0.10%	-0.30%		All-in cost	0.15%	0.15%	0.15%

To merely address (as opposed to correcting) the mismatch, the borrower could also avoid the swap as a hedging strategy in favour of a cap. The borrower does not benefit from negative rates on the loan interest rate, but it will not suffer any additional running costs if rates are negative as with a swap without the repurchased floor. The costs are packaged differently as well, since the typical payment timing of a cap premium is up-front, although it is possible in some cases to pay on a periodic basis. So even if for ease of strategy comparison the cost of a cap is averaged over the loan term, in reality it may be an extra outlay at closing for a borrower to consider, especially if it is accustomed to hedging with swaps.

As a reminder, the risk of negative rates causing a mismatch for loans with floors at 0% still exists for loans in currencies in which the forward curve is well above zero. Recall from Figure 2 the difference between EUR and GBP 0% floor costs. In GBP the cost to insulate a swap against the risk of a future mismatch is lower, but still material enough to make any decision to repurchase a 0% floor a serious one.

A last note within this section is reserved for perspective. The extra interest expense for borrowers due to the 0% floor mismatch may be surprising and unwelcome, and for borrowers who typically crave certainty it may be quite discomfiting to be exposed to negative interest rate risk. Nevertheless, it is not likely to be a deal killer unless interest rates fall several percentage points below zero. Among currencies with negative variable rates, none was below –0.75% as of mid-2016. Although economists can clearly miss the mark, the general consensus is that although there is no theoretical limit to the lower bound of short-term interest rates, a practical limit exists some-where in the –1% region. Put into context of a typical CRE loan, this magnitude of interest rate risk is routinely taken when a borrower adopts a hedging strategy incorporating a cap with a strike rate 1% above the pre-vailing swap rate. This is a likely reason why the vast majority of CRE lenders have not, at the time of writing, mandated a correction of the mismatch in a borrower's required hedging by forcing the borrower to purchase the floor when choosing to swap their interest exposure. Further, there is no trend, in the authors' experience, of CRE borrowers repurchasing floors.[7]

12.3 Hedge counterparty selection and the impact of third-party hedge providers on CRE financings

Globally, since the advent of over-the-counter derivatives in the 1980s, lenders have found it more than just a matter of convenience to be able to provide derivative transactions to their clients alongside debt transactions such as CRE financings. There are certainly financial motivations in that the financial institution—often, but not exclusively, a bank—can charge a separate margin to that of the loan. Keeping the linked transactions amongst affiliates can also help to streamline the loan documentation or provide greater comfort to credit committees. In Europe, borrowers have grown accustomed to lenders also providing any required interest rate hedges since the 1990s, especially among the larger commercial and investment banks which tended to be serving the market on larger deals and eventually arranging CMBS transactions. Gradually, smaller credit institutions such as local and regional banks obtained this capability. By the middle 2000s it was exceptional for a lender on a CRE financing not to also offer a hedging transaction, and in certain cases lenders required that the hedging transaction would be executed with their derivatives trading entity.

The trend has reversed post GFC. The increasing involvement of third-party hedge provider banks comes with various repercussions for market participants. On balance the over-arching effect has been fairly positive given the evolution of the financial markets generally and, in particular, the regulatory changes precipitated by the GFC. But certain changes have been easier than others for borrowers and lenders to navigate. This section explains why the prevalence of third-party hedge providers has increased of late. Then, it examines the repercussions in some detail.

12.3.1 Non-bank lenders

The largest factor underlying the trend reversal has been the increasing participation of non-bank lenders (firms that lend but do not take deposits) in the senior loan market, arising from a funding gap due to tighter banking regulations and regulatory capital requirements as was discussed in

---

[7] In other sectors of the economy, borrowers reporting under International Financial Reporting Standards (IFRS) are more sensitive to certain accounting treatment for financial instruments such as debt and derivatives and it is more of a common practice than in Commercial Real Estate to account for an embedded derivative in a loan and to repurchase a floor in the derivatives market to correct a mismatch between the two.

Chapter 3 and with further discussion of the changing regulatory environment in Chapters 16 and 17. These non-bank lenders also typically have greater risk appetites than banks such that they often lend where banks will not, thus contributing to their proliferation and demand. This group comprises certain financial institutions, notably insurers, which can in some cases offer derivative products to customers. Debt funds and other specialist CRE lending vehicles, which almost never have the capability of offering derivatives directly to their borrowers, comprise the remainder.[8] It should be noted that some of these lenders prefer to offer fixed-rate products, which obviate the need to contemplate an accompanying hedge. For reasons including borrowers' familiarity with the hitherto dominant bank lending model, though, demand for variable-rate senior debt has been resilient. As a result, non-bank lenders in Europe have tended to offer variable-rate loans even if their preference might be for fixed-rate issuance.[9] One might also suspect that an inability to provide a hedge might make non-bank lenders less likely to impose interest rate hedging requirements on borrowers, but this has generally not been the case. Quite the opposite, many of the principals within non-bank lending firms come with experience as bank lenders or indeed CRE borrowers. As detailed in section 12.4, they are also well aware of the potential risks to their capital of not imposing a hedging requirement.

12.3.2   Credit ratings provisions

The continued presence of CMBS is another factor in the trend away from lenders delivering interest rate hedges alongside the debt as a package. This may appear to be inconsistent with the previous paragraph, as the arrangers of CMBS are almost exclusively large investment banks with extensive derivatives capabilities. The reason actually stems from the ratings of the notes. It is fairly intuitive that in order to achieve a good rating on the notes, an issuer would need to implement a conservative interest rate hedge so that noteholders are protected from the risk of interest rates rising dramatically.

This is just the beginning; ratings agencies prudently also conduct numerous stress tests as discussed further in Chapter 14. One is to consider the scenario of a dramatic decrease in the creditworthiness of the hedge counterparty bank, coupled with an interest rate environment in which that bank is in a liability position. In such an event, non-performance on the hedge would be followed by higher—potentially much higher—interest costs, which could ultimately lead to some degree of non-performance on the notes. This scenario is averted by defining certain trigger events, such as

---

[8] For a comprehensive study of the commercial lending market in the UK, see *UK Commercial Property Lending Market Report* (De Montfort University, 2015) and further Chs 3 and 15.

[9] Derivatives are far less sensitive as a topic for mezzanine debt, which is often issued on a fixed-rate basis. Or, if variable-rate, a mezzanine loan would rarely carry a hedging requirement.

certain credit ratings by selected ratings agencies falling below certain thresholds, after which a set of defined corrective measures would follow. Typically, the hedging bank would need to post cash collateral as a first measure, followed ultimately by a requirement to replace itself—at its own cost—with a more creditworthy institution unless its situation improved. Stress tests and ratings downgrade provisions were prevalent prior to the collapse of Lehman Brothers in 2008, but it was still common practice for arranging banks to provide the derivatives for the CMBS transactions they arranged. Subsequently, two changes have combined to make CMBS arrangers less likely to provide hedges on their own deals.

The first change is that the ratings agencies made the trigger events and corrective measures more robust. Few would have argued that the lessons of Lehman's collapse should be ignored, but the changes were not universally popular. This is because these more rigorous protections could lead to additional costs to a prospective hedging bank at exactly the time such costs would be most unwelcome. As such, the cost of a hedge subject to CMBS ratings provisions could be higher than the same hedge in a non-CMBS debt transaction. Importantly, the same cost increase could arise if the lender expects or reserves the right to securitise the debt at a later date. Prospective hedging banks would understandably pass this additional cost onto borrowers in the hedging rates or levels. Equally understandably, the borrower would wish to avoid these costs and be aggravated to learn of the extra costs only well after the lender selection process was concluded. This is especially true if the competitive lender selection process included other banks for which CMBS exits would not have been likely, leading to an "apples to oranges" comparison of overall financing costs.

The second change is the key in making CMBS arrangers less likely to provide hedges: banks' credit ratings have generally fallen in recent years. Unless the arranger has been one of the few banks not to see its ratings fall, it will be closer to the trigger events that would require actions and likely costs. Additionally, because banks' credit ratings have been volatile—with uninspiring outlooks on regulatory, political and macroeconomic fronts—the risk of a downgrade event appears to be high even for banks with reasonably high ratings. This combination exacerbates the cost issue described in the previous paragraph. In some instances, the direct result has been borrowers grudgingly agreeing to pay the extra (again, sometimes unanticipated) costs of hedging with the bank arranging the CMBS. In many others, though, the result is an active search to implement the hedging with third party banks able to meet the stringent ratings criteria at much lower cost. In still other cases the arranger has been unwilling to contemplate providing a hedge, for reasons such as the bank's credit rating being below the trigger event on day one of the loan.

12.3.3 Impact of third-party hedge providers on documentation process

As alluded to in this section's opening paragraph, documentation complexity tends to increase in line with the number of parties involved. Regardless of whether the entity is legally distinct, when the hedging counterparty is an affiliate of the lender or arranger, a borrower will typically see the two as the same party. In the simplest example situation a borrower goes to a "one stop shop" from which the loan is supplied by the lending desk, the hedge provided by the hedging desk, agency services provided by agency desk, and so on. In more complex situations, documentation complexity levels escalate and timelines extend as multiple parties—each perhaps with different legal representatives with slightly different viewpoints—seek to provide clarity to potential future scenarios in which trust has broken down between parties. There is a long list of items related to hedging that could be cited, but the point in this section is conceptual. Trust is less likely to break down between parties affiliated with each other, and each can likely use the same in-house legal team throughout the documentation process. It follows that if all else is equal, one can expect a less complex documentation package and shorter timeline if the hedging bank is the lender's affiliate.

It should be noted that if there is no sharing of security with the hedging bank(s) the documentation complexity could be minimal and only marginally higher with a third-party hedge counterparty. If the borrower elects

Figure 6: Indicative costs associated with Cap Counterparty Required Ratings

	Impact of Required Ratings on Cap Cost				
Required Rating Level:	None	BBB-/Baa3	BBB+/Baa1	A-/A3	AAA Bond Securitisation Compliant*
Cap Premium:	€ 260,000	€ 270,000	€ 282,000	€ 299,000	€ 350,000

<u>Assumptions:</u>
5 years cap, strike at 2.00%, 3mo. EURIBOR, TARGET Business Days, quarterly payments
The hedging bank is required to maintain the indicated Required Rating Levels from Standard & Poor's, Moody's and Fitch Ratings throughout the life of the hedge. In case it ceases to meet them, it's obliged to find a replacement bank (meeting the Required Rating Levels) at its sole cost within 30 days.
Indications provided by AA-/Aa2 rated bank, if the hedging bank has lower ratings this will result in higher cap premia as a result of their increased cost due to ratings levels.
*See S&P's "Counterparty Risk Framework Methodology And Assumptions" and equivalent from the other rating agencies for details.

to pay an up-front premium for an interest rate cap, the fact that the borrower will have no further payment obligations to the hedge counterparty means the hedge counterparty will never be a creditor. This obviates the need for the lender(s) to contemplate how security will be shared with a non-lender institution.[10] For this reason, if any lender precludes sharing security with any party hedge provider (third-party or otherwise), the documentation is likely to be fairly straightforward and predictable. The exception to this rule is if credit ratings downgrade triggers are featured; in these instances the documentation process can be quite challenging as these provisions will require future actions or potential future costs which may not align with typical bank risk management practices.

A last note in this sub-section is that even if a lender is perfectly willing to share security with a third-party hedging bank and the additional documentation burden is deemed by all parties to be acceptable, the prospective hedging bank would need to perform its own internal credit underwriting process. It would be unrealistic to expect success if the third party bank is unfamiliar with the asset or does not have a particularly well-developed lending business in the CRE asset class in a particular geography, or if the overall transaction size were not large enough to warrant the credit work entailed. In the authors' experience, the most competitive third-party hedging banks in terms of pricing and documentation are not competitive in credit underwriting for CRE assets in Europe. For this reason they are unwilling to contemplate transactions without an up-front payment of the cap premium. In short, the vast majority of cases in which a third-party bank provides a hedge entail a hedge strategy with up-front premium such as a cap.

12.3.4   Impact of third-party hedge providers on hedging strategy decisions

Whether or not security can be shared under a hedge with potential future payment obligations by the borrower can be an issue that drives borrowers' hedge strategy decisions. The cap example in the previous paragraph is a "credit-free" hedge, unless the borrower arranges to pay the cap seller the cap premium at a future date as opposed to the market standard of up-front cash.[11] Conversely, a "credit hedge" such as an interest rate swap or collar will almost never require an additional equity outlay at closing, but would likely preclude a third-party hedge provider's involvement. To summarise, unless a lender will be providing a hedge through an affiliate of the bank or

---

[10] The lenders may still include certain provisions which might not be as relevant if the hedging bank were a lender's affiliate. For one example, a collateral assignment provision would give lenders comfort that the benefit (to the lenders) of a potentially valuable hedge asset with an otherwise unrelated party to the transaction remains intact throughout the loan term.

[11] As a credit hedge, though, the cap seller would need to underwrite the credit risk and thus make this an unlikely scenario. If, however, the lender funded the cap premium with an additional loan amount, a similar effect could be achieved without the additional equity outlay by the sponsor.

insurer, certain very popular hedging strategies such as interest rate swaps may be unfeasible.

This paradigm results in the front-loading of a decision—which specific derivative transaction will be employed to best meet a hedging requirement—that in the past could well have been left until late in the closing process. A borrower's preference or tolerance for contributing the extra equity required for a credit-free hedge needs to be established fairly early on in its lender selection process. Similar to the reference to unanticipated extra costs in section 12.3.2, a borrower historically inclined to favour swaps may be surprised to learn, only after selecting a lender, that it will need to contribute extra equity to fund the up-front premium payable under a cap strategy.

A borrower may then observe that the only means to reduce the extra equity contribution to tolerable levels is to accept a relatively high degree of interest rate risk by choosing a cap with a high strike rate. This runs counter to the intent of the hedging requirement and exposes the vast difference in certainty of all-in interest expense under different hedging strategies with no or low up-front payments. As a reminder of the points covered earlier in this section, this lender could be a bank intending on a capital markets exit or a non-bank lender that is unable to provide a hedge directly to its borrower.

12.4 Hedging requirements and interest rate risk

In most cases the income from a property asset is a relatively fixed quantity. This income is not linked to the interest rate environment applicable to variable rate loans, at least in the near-to-medium term. If interest rates were to rise during the loan term, the borrower may be in a position where its income is not sufficient to cover the interest payments under a variable rate loan.[12] The ratio of net operating income (NOI) to interest expense in a given period (the interest cover ratio, or ICR) is one of the fundamental tests in CRE finance. By how much would variable rates on any given CRE loan have to rise, such that the ICR falls from fairly healthy levels (well above 1.50) to the point at which income fails to meet interest payments? Absent a hedge, for many loans this result could occur if variable rates were to rise by as little as 100 to 200 basis points. Given that variable rates can shift by these sums in a matter of months (upward as well as downward), the interest rate risk to a variable-rate loan is real.

For a simplified example, let us assume that a property produces £6 million per annum (6% NOI) and is being sold for £100 million to an investor. A lender is evaluating interest cover ratios (ICRs) for three different loan-to-value (LTV) ratios for potential loans assuming a margin over LIBOR held

---

[12] This is measured through the Interest Cover Ratio (ICR) and managed by making hedging, in some form, a condition of such loans.

constant at 250 basis points (bps). LIBOR in July 2016 is 0.52% and the table below shows the ICR test results at different upward shifts to the LIBOR assumption. The ICR Covenant is 1.50 and the ICR calculations are underlined when they are in breach.

Table 1 demonstrates the potential deterioration of ICRs if the LIBOR component of interest increases. For a loan with an LTV of 70%, a 1.50 requirement would be breached when LIBOR is shocked by 300bps in this unhedged example (c. 3.52%, a relatively average historical LIBOR rate). To the extent that the lender sees the ICR as a key lending metric and attaches strict covenants to it, a borrower would need to commit to funding additional equity as and when the ICR fell below the required level. As it is exceedingly difficult for both borrowers and lenders to accommodate such a "cash call", a more pre-emptive solution is to require that the borrower emplaces an acceptable interest rate hedge. By satisfying this requirement, a borrower will limit the extent to which LIBOR variation will erode the cash

Table 1: Unhedged ICR tests at various interest rate assumptions

Libor Assumption	3m Libor Test Rate	ICR with LTV of:		
		50%	60%	70%
Current Libor	0.52%	3.97	3.31	2.84
Libor + 100bps	1.52%	2.99	2.49	2.13
Libor + 200bps	2.52%	2.39	1.99	1.71
Libor + 300bps	3.52%	1.99	1.66	1.42
Libor + 400bps	4.52%	1.71	1.42	1.22

available for the ICR test.

The leverage effect is observable on the loan's sensitivity to movements in LIBOR. At lower LTV levels such as 50%, the margin for error is quite wide. The right-hand side of Table 1 illustrates the narrow margin for error in higher LTV scenarios. This is probably intuitive given income is held constant in the three loan examples. It is no surprise that hedging requirements can be somewhat loose (in terms of how much of the overall debt needs to be hedged) for low-leverage transactions, but when LTVs are above 50% it is typical for fairly strict hedging requirements to apply. The authors observe that requirements to hedge 100% of the debt amount for the full loan term have persisted in being quite standard for European CRE financings with LTVs at or above 60%.

Table 2 shows the same ICR calculation scenarios overlaid with the protection provided by an example interest rate hedge, a cap at 2%. The cap sets an upper limit on the LIBOR component of interest expense at 2%, which effectively sets a lower limit on the ICR test calculation under a constant NOI assumption. The cap starts to provide protection between the assumed +100bps and +200bps shift scenarios shown under the "Libor Assumption" column. For this reason, the result is the same for any scenario higher than +100bps. Note also that if a swap (not a cap as shown) on 100% of the debt were to be chosen as a hedging strategy, interest expense would be constant irrespective of the LIBOR Assumption.[13]

Table 2: Hedged ICR tests with a cap at 2.00% on 100% of the debt (80% of debt shown in brackets)

Libor Assumption	3m Libor Test Rate	ICR with LTV of:		
		50%	60%	70%
Current Libor	0.52%	3.97	3.31	2.84
Libor + 100bps	1.52%	2.99	2.49	2.13
Libor + 200bps	2.52%	2.67 (2.61)	2.22 (2.17)	1.90 (1.86)
Libor + 300bps	3.52%	2.67 (2.50)	2.22 (2.08)	1.90 (1.78)
Libor + 400bps	4.52%	2.67 (2.40)	2.22 (2.00)	1.90 (1.71)

At the risk of over-complicating the table, it also shows an interest rate cap at the same strike rate of 2% but with a slightly lower hedge ratio of 80%. For a variety of reasons, including a desire not to be "overhedged" in the event of unscheduled partial prepayments, borrowers and lenders may agree to apply the hedging requirement to a portion of the debt. This accommodation is generally on a small scale, if applicable, such as the 20% reduction illustrated in the table. The effect will be to substantially dampen, but not fully eliminate, the interest rate risk within the transaction.

Overall, Tables 1 and 2 should give a sense for the protection offered by a hedge. The ICR remains above 1.50 in all scenarios. If the lender was assessing the loan for an LTV of 70% and the maximum credit exposure they were looking at was a shock to Libor of 400bps, then a hedging requirement of 80% with a maximum strike of 2.00% should provide the lender sufficient comfort from an ICR viewpoint. As you can see in this example, calculating a lender-mandated hedge requirement can be an iterative process between LTV, maximum acceptable cap strike rate, percentage hedged and maximum exposure the lender considers in its model.

There are many other factors that may be considered when a lender sets a hedging requirement for a particular transaction, or indeed when both parties are coming to an agreement about what hedging strategy will actually be implemented. One is that the protection level can change over time. Referring to the cost-conscious investor example in section 12.3.4,

---

[13] Assuming no mismatch between loan and swap as described in section 8.2 and illustrated in Figure 5.

275

consider a borrower with substantial NOI growth projections for the later years of a facility. A lender might allow a higher cap strike rate for the latter years when the interest coverage is forecast to be greater, keeping the early year requirements tighter when income is lower. This could suit the borrower because the up-front premium of the cap with a rising strike rate for the latter years would be lower than a cap with a constant strike rate. A practical solution such as this could arise if both parties are willing to accept the higher risk profile on the grounds that the NOI growth projections are likely or realistic.

Another factor is overall suitability. Again, since each financing situation is unique it may be that a requirement has some flexibility. During this current period of persistently low and negative interest rates, some CRE lenders have permitted borrowers to postpone hedging until conditions change. The borrowers in these exceptions may elect to "float" until a certain trigger such as a benchmark swap rate rises above a certain predefined level. This exception is more prevalent on shorter-dated loans given the lower perceived likelihood of a dramatic upward shift in variable rates in the coming two to three year period. In such cases prudence would imply that both parties understand clearly at what level hedging should be triggered in order to protect against an ICR covenant. They should also think ahead to certain other considerations like timing. In a scenario of rapidly rising interest rate expectations (a pre-condition for swap rate increases that would trigger a required hedge), unfortunately there is no perfect means to ensure the hedge can be executed efficiently at or under the maximum required strike rate of the negotiated condition.

In summary, the impetus for hedging variable-rate loans is clearly for parties to a loan to gain as much certainty as they can about the cost of debt during the loan term. After all, the financing is a system in which rental income is not expected be correlated at all with the movements of short-term variable interest rates. With certainty comes lower risk to the borrower, and ultimately to the lender. The obvious uncertainty is whether variable rates will rise detrimentally over time, relative to NOI. Future interest rates are unpredictable, as are the speed of any potential changes to variable interest rates if economic conditions change. Although the protection offered by an interest rate hedge is most clearly observable in the ICR test under different LIBOR shift scenarios, there may be other means to arrive at the same conclusions.

12.5 Conclusion

Interest expense is a big line item in CRE investments, and managing it effectively over the life of an investment is in the interest (so to speak) of all parties. Market participants rightly focus a great deal of attention on the margin component of interest, but the other component (the base rate or LIBOR, depending on the type of loan) is also important, albeit for different reasons. Derivatives used to shape the non-margin component of interest expense have played an increasingly visible role in the past decade. Much recent attention to derivatives, namely specific derivatives such as 0% interest rate floors, has been well-deserved, given the impact on interest expense. Although the role continues to evolve for a variety of reasons highlighted in this Chapter, it is likely that derivatives will continue to play an important role within CRE financing packages in 2016 and beyond.

Due to the tension between margin protection, inter alia, for lenders and cost management for borrowers in a negative interest rate environment, designing and implementing the best means to mitigate interest rate risk in European CRE financings has been a balancing act for lenders and borrowers alike. Witness the proliferation of white papers, industry panels and even Google searches for "negative interest rate", and it comes of little surprise that this topic has gained importance among advisers, law firms, borrowers and their lenders alike in their commercial discussions around any CRE financing. It has been a learning process for many and in some cases it has been a painful experience for all concerned. Increased awareness of the sensitivity of a loan and any associated floor to the accompanying derivatives transactions is, in the authors' experience, a welcome side-effect of these tribulations.

This awareness will be useful as the CRE lending paradigm continues to change with the increasing relevance of non-bank lenders in a highly regulated banking environment as discussed throughout this book. Whereas bank funding has been a mainstay in Europe, there is a continuing shift to debt capital provided by private or sovereign debt funds, insurance companies, CMBS, private placements arranged by smaller specialist intermediaries, or other entities with the means to plug the "funding gap" so readily cited in the media. The role of derivatives within these other types of CRE financings cannot be assumed away. Additionally, credit rating requirements for CMBS transactions or CMBS-friendly loans directly affect the cost of such derivatives and indirectly guide the types of instruments selected to hedge the interest rate risk. In turn, both the non-bank lender sector and credit ratings requirements within CMBS transactions have contributed to the rise in third party hedge providers, whose growing role in CRE financing cannot be underestimated. Encouragingly, many stakeholders within CRE finance have launched a variety of efforts based from past experience to better equip themselves to grapple with certain subtle changes to debt capital markets for the European CRE sector.

Some of these involve derivatives: lenders and borrowers are more fully vetting at the term sheet stage the implications of a 0% floor in a loan and the potential mismatch in the hedge and the resultant cost to the borrower; lenders and borrowers increasing the specificity of acceptable hedge strategies at the term sheet stage given any floor in the loan; the allowance of third party hedge providers for non-credit intensive hedges in both on-CMBS and CMBS transactions, but especially the latter given credit ratings requirements; and all parties are paying much closer attention to the maximum liability that is possible under the hedging strategy. These are positive signs. It is clear that a focus on managing interest expense, especially in a negative interest rate environment, will evolve and continue to play an important supporting role in this market. It is not clear which of the many changes underway will be lasting and which will be fleeting. One certainty is that this balancing act is more complicated for both new lenders and the old guard with respect to the ways derivatives are selected and managed over the life of a CRE financing. Changes, a mix of both bold and subtle, are welcome.

Chapter 13

The evolving role of issuers and trustees in CMBS transactions—the epoch of litigation

Sean Crosky,

Partner, Finance, K&L Gates LLP

Laurence Griffiths,

US Bank Trustees Limited

Clare Tanner,

Special Counsel, Litigation, K&L Gates LLP[1]

13.1 Introduction

In 2012, the last edition of this book included a Chapter on the evolving role of issuers and trustees in European CMBS transactions. Such a Chapter would probably not have been considered necessary in the 2006 first edition. At such time, the European CMBS market was a robust and vibrant part of the securitisation industry, with annual issuance volumes continually increasing, both through banks using conduit programmes to securitise the loans they originated and property companies using CMBS structures to refinance their borrowings. The role of the issuer and trustee was considered in quite a different light then and involvement in litigation was not a particular feature.

However, the period between the publication of the first edition and the publication of the second edition was a tumultuous period for the global CMBS market and for its participants. During this period, the GFC occurred, and the market saw a decrease in value (at times, a very significant decrease in value) of the underlying CRE as well as the inability of borrowers to refinance the securitised facilities at maturity. This resulted in the restructuring and/or enforcement of many of the loans underlying CMBS transactions, a subject which was discussed at length in the previous edition of this book.

---

[1] The authors would also like to thank Matthew Gibbon, trainee, Finance, K&L Gates LLP for his assistance in preparing the case studies for this Chapter.

This fundamental deterioration in real estate market conditions placed the securitisations under stresses which were not anticipated when the transactions were structured and executed. As a result of these stresses, by the time the second edition of this book was being prepared, the role of various parties in the CMBS market had evolved from those previously envisaged, and often the parties at the forefront of this evolution were those appointed to have an ongoing role in the transaction (such as the issuer, the trustee and the servicer). As such, when the second edition was prepared, it was felt that the evolving role of the trustee and issuer in CMBS transactions warranted further analysis.

The Chapter dealing with the emerging role of issuers and trustees in CMBS transactions considered the position of a trustee and issuer in the pre GFC CMBS transaction as envisaged at closing. It considered a number of issues which had arisen in the years prior to 2012 in the stressed environment of the CMBS market, issues which had direct implications on the role of trustees and issuers in these transactions.

Despite the fact that it has been four years since the last edition of this book, the themes considered in Chapter 10 of the last edition largely remain current, being issues which still arise in legacy CMBS transactions. As such, with a few amendments and updates to the Chapter from the second edition, a new Chapter could have been included in the new edition of this book. However, whilst the issues discussed in the second edition remain relevant at the time of writing, it is considered that a new edition could be used to explore in greater detail one of the themes noted in 2012: the increase in litigation.

Given that CMBS issuers typically issue 10 years paper, the final stages of the life-cycle of CMBS deals (although it is difficult to predict when the life-cycle will be completed for these deals) is in 2016 apparent. A position which for many deals is accompanied by limited and reduced cashflows in the deal. In these types of circumstances, parties start to consider the documentation and their rights under the documents, and as a result, inter-creditor issues and third party claims are, as the second half of 2016 is entered, increasingly becoming common in the CMBS deals which are the subject of this Chapter. Indeed such claims have been gaining momentum since 2014.

Whilst certain of these issues can be dealt with between the parties in a consensual manner, at times this is not possible, and in these circumstances, a party or parties together may seek the adjudication of the court to resolve the issues. As such, for the current edition it has been decided to focus on the involvement of the courts in adjudicating disputes in CMBS transactions—a process with which the trustees and issuers have been necessarily involved.

Of course, seeking the involvement of the courts is generally not the first choice for parties when an issue arises—parties generally will try and consider whether there are consensual ways to resolve the issue. Often this is successful. However, in some cases, the issues in dispute relate to fundamental matters which cannot be addressed without the involvement of the court, or, the positions of various parties are so different that there is no alternative means to resolve the issue.

Experience to date indicates that the involvement of the courts in dealing with the issues that arise in CMBS transactions can rather unscientifically be split into two categories:

(i)   Disputes relating to the interpretation of the transaction documents and rights relating to various creditors. For English law transactions, these questions of interpretation are generally dealt with by way of a Part 8 proceeding (which will be considered in further detail below). These proceedings may be brought by the issuer, the trustee or another transaction party (such as a noteholder or liquidity facility provider), and often are brought with agreement by the various parties to the transaction.
(ii) Disputes relating to the action of certain parties which are purely adverse in nature. Examples include professional negligence claims against valuers in CMBS transactions, as well as litigation brought by borrowers against parties to the loans.

Section 13.3 of this Chapter will consider these in further detail through analysis of recent cases. The majority of the discussion will relate to matters considered by the English courts. There will, however, also be some discussion of matters before other courts relating to borrower litigation. It should be noted that references to CMBS transactions in this Chapter are references to CMBS transactions executed pre GFC, and as such should be read as excluding any CMBS transactions issued since 2011.

Before we consider the epoch of litigation in legacy CMBS transactions, we should make sense to remind ourselves of the role of a trustee or an issuer in these deals.

13.2   The role of the issuer and trustee in a CMBS transaction

As discussed in the Chapter to the previous edition, neither the issuer nor the trustee is involved in the arranging or structuring of a CMBS transaction, as their role only comes into effect on the closing of the transaction. Prior to that time, neither party has any formal connection with the underlying loans or the originator. Following execution of the transaction, the issuer and trustee (along with the servicer and other agents of the issuer) are the parties whose role continues throughout the life of the transaction and the parties who are required to deal with any issues which arise.

13.2.1 *The Issuer*

In CMBS transactions (as with most other securitisations), the arranger or originator will appoint a corporate services provider to establish the issuing vehicle (the issuer). Often the corporate services provider is not appointed until the terms of the transaction have been structured and negotiated and the drafting of disclosure documents and legal documents has begun. The issuer will not be involved in negotiating the commercial terms of the transaction (such as representations relating to the assets or the terms of the swaps) nor will it be involved in carrying out due diligence on the portfolio of assets or commissioning reports such as those relating to the valuation of the underlying properties. Rather, it will rely upon the arranger and reports and opinions of the advisers to the arranger (such as legal counsel and accountants).

The corporate services provider will provide directors for the issuer and will also provide company administration and accounting services. The corporate services provider is generally an organisation which provides these services to a number of issuing vehicles and specialises in the structured finance market.

The issuer will be set up as an orphan company. In many common law jurisdictions this means that the shares of the issuer will be held either directly on trust for charitable purposes or by a holding company whose shares will be held on trust for charitable purposes. In other jurisdictions, the orphan structure may be established through the shares being held by a trust or foundation structure (such as the stichting structure in the Netherlands). By this structure, the issuer is not related to the originator or any other party to the transaction. This structure is driven by rating agency requirements which require the issuer to be independent to the originator, established as an orphan vehicle and be bankruptcy remote.

On closing the issuer will issue notes into the capital markets and, with the proceeds of the issuance, the issuer will (i) where the securitisation is refinancing a portfolio of loans originated by a bank, purchase the loans from the originating bank (often the deals are called CMBS conduit deals) or (ii) where the securitisation is refinancing debt of a property company, provide a loan to the property company which will be secured over the underlying assets and may be used by the property company to refinance its existing debt or purchase new assets. A conduit deal may consist of one or a number of loans. As described elsewhere in this book, in conduit deals, the underlying loan will often be tranched, with only the senior tranche (often referred to as the "A loan") being sold to the issuer and securitised.

CMBS transactions were structured on the assumption that throughout the life of the deal the issuer would use the payments it receives on the underlying loans to repay the noteholders (and other creditors) until such time as those parties have been repaid in full. This would either be achieved through the underlying loan repaying principal throughout its life or, more often, being refinanced by the borrower at maturity, with the proceeds of such refinancing being used to repay the loan and redeem the notes accordingly. After repayment in full of its secured liabilities, the issuer would be wound up, and the securitisation would come to an end. At least this was the theory behind these structures. However, as discussed at length in the last edition of this book, events and their effect on the CRE markets have meant that things have not run in quite the way it was assumed they would in 2005–2007.

Sometimes the issuer is seen as merely a conduit to financing or a "post-box", with no real position in the transaction other than to act as the issuing entity for the financing. This ignores the legal reality of the issuer—it is a company with directors, who have duties and obligations, as well as liabilities under the company law of the entity's jurisdiction of incorporation. Sometimes an issuer may be seen as solely owing duties to the note-holders. However, this does not accord with the position under English law. Under English company law, as a general principle, the directors owe their obligations to their shareholders rather than their creditors, until such time as the entity is nearing insolvency, at which point their obligations become owed to their creditors. The obligations of the directors under company law can at times place stress on a structure. For example, the directors may have agreed to non-petition language in the documents (which essentially is a provision under which all parties to the transaction agree with the trustee not to petition for the winding-up of the issuer). However, under general company law, there may be a time in the transaction when the directors have a duty to start to wind-up the issuer, irrespective of the position under the documents. It is generally considered that such obligations take precedence to the documents, albeit they are likely to be exercised only on a very limited basis.

13.2.2 The Trustee

The appointment process of a trustee in a securitisation is similar to the process described for the corporate services provider. The trustee may be the corporate trust entity of a financial institution or it may be a stand-alone corporate trust company. In either case, the trustee will generally be an independent legal entity, separate from other parties to the transaction.

In a CMBS transaction with English law trust documents, as with other securitisations, two trusts are established under the documents. The same corporate trustee will usually act as trustee of both trusts, and the roles may be merged into one trustee position (although in the CMBS world this is not always the case). However it is important to note that in all cases, the trusts are very separate legal structures.

In a securitisation, the issuer will grant security over all of its assets to secure its obligations to its creditors (who will then be referred to as secured creditors). This security is granted to the security trustee, who is appointed to hold such security on behalf of all secured creditors of the issuer. The beneficiaries of the security trust will include the noteholders, as well as the other creditors of the issuer, such as the swap counterparty, liquidity provider, corporate service provider, third party agents and the trustee itself. This trust is referred to as the Security Trust.

The Security Trust will usually be effected through a deed of charge or security trust deed, under which the Security Trust will be established and the issuer will grant security. This document will also enunciate certain matters relating to the security trustee including powers, indemnities and liabilities, as well as the position regarding conflicts between beneficiaries. The document will also set out matters relating the acceleration of notes on a default and enforcement of security subject to the trust.

The security trustee generally will only have an active role in the event of a default at the note level, in which case, it may need to accelerate the debt due under the notes, enforce the security and liquidate the assets of the issuer (which in a CMBS transaction will be the rights of the issuer under the loan agreements underlying the structure). It should be stressed that enforcement of the security at the securitisation level is distinct from enforcement of security at the loan level. Enforcement at the loan level will be pursuant to the security arrangements at the level of the underlying loan—the security trustee is not able to enforce security over the underlying properties in a CMBS transaction, it can only enforce the security granted by the issuer. It should also be noted that an enforcement of security at either the loan level or the note level does not automatically result in an enforcement at the other level, although it may have effects (such as cessation of regular payments under the loan where the loan level security is enforced) which result in enforcement at the other level in the structure.

The second trust established at closing in a securitisation is the note trust. Under this trust, the issuer will grant to the note trustee to hold on behalf of all noteholders the covenant to pay. The only beneficiaries of the note trust will be the noteholders. The note trustee effectively acts as the conduit between the noteholders and the issuer and is the entity through which any decision making powers of the noteholders are effected.

The note trust will generally be established and the note trustee appointed pursuant to a trust deed, under which the powers, indemnities and liabilities of the trustee are enunciated. Where more than one class of notes are issued, the trust deed will also contain provisions relating to conflicts between classes and in whose interest the note trustee should act. As a general rule, the note trustee will be required to act in the interests of the most senior class of notes then outstanding.

The role of the note trustee is less limited than the role of the security trustee. The note trustee may be required to act throughout the life of the transaction, with regard to any amendments, modifications or waivers required by the issuer to the securitisation documents. The note trustee may be required to convene meetings of noteholders to discuss such issues, or it may (in conjunction with the security trustee) decide that the requested matter falls within the discretion of the note trustee. Where a default occurs at the securitisation level, the note trustee may also liaise with noteholders regarding potential acceleration and enforcement.

Throughout this Chapter, despite the separate nature of the trusts, we shall refer to the trustee in the singular, without specific reference to the different roles of a security trustee or note trustee. This is partially for ease, but also on the basis that the same entity will usually perform both roles and in the market it is not uncommon to refer to the two trustees in this manner.

13.3   The epoch of litigation

Some readers may be familiar with AP Herbert, who in addition to sitting as the independent Member of Parliament for the University of Oxford (in the days when certain universities had their own representative in Westminster), was famous for his satirical articles in Punch. These articles were written in the form of judgments of the court, and through satire highlighted aspects of the law which AP Herbert believed needed reform. Some of these satirical judgments became so famous (such as the case known as "The Negotiable Cow") that they developed a life of their own, with some people uncertain as to whether they were real or not, and some judges (fully aware of their providence) making reference to them in their own real judgments.

The interesting point is that whilst some of AP Herbert's cases are so absurd as to be impossible, others could possibly be matters which the courts could consider. It is suggested that at least one of AP Herbert's cases be read before any reader of this Chapter independently decides to look at the cases relating to CMBS transactions! It will set an interesting perspective for any reader. Whilst the cases discussed in this Chapter may not always be as amusing as those by AP Herbert, they certainly address a number of important issues and consider points which perhaps had often taken for granted. At least one judge has referred to a CMBS as a structure of Byzantine construct, perhaps a phrase which some of AP Herbert's judges may also have used had he penned a satire about them.

As noted in the last edition and above, the challenging circumstances that many of the remaining pre GFC CMBS transactions have faced, has meant that the roles of certain parties, including the trustee and the issuer, have continued to evolve in ways not anticipated when the transactions were structured and executed. In particular, as transactions near maturity, it is likely that the remaining underlying loans will be those with a more questionable credit quality, often with limited cash-flows available for distribution to investors. Frequently the loans underlying the CMBS will have defaulted and be subject to restructuring, enforcement or some other form of recovery maximisation. In these circumstances, the risk that creditors to the CMBS (being the noteholders and other secured creditors) may suffer a loss increases dramatically. As such, it is not surprising that at this time parties may consider their position closely and consider whether there are intercreditor questions (see Chapter 7) which may arise alter their entitlements or their "position" in the transaction.

As such, since 2012 issuers and trustees have regularly been involved in considering issues between various creditors in a CMBS transaction. As noted above, some of these issues may be settled in a consensual manner, through the parties coming to any agreement as to how to deal with the issue (through noteholder consent or agreement between parties) or finding a way to resolve the issue otherwise within the parameters of the transaction documents.

However, where consensual resolution is not available or possible, parties have increasingly seen the courts as an alternative means to settle the issue and provide a determination binding on all parties. Recourse to the courts is nothing new, and securitisations have periodically ended up in front of the courts. However, since 2014, the courts increasingly have been involved in considering issues facing trustees, issuers, servicers and other parties in interpreting the provisions of transaction documents across a range of structured products, including a number of CMBS transactions.

Unscientifically, this involvement of the courts can be generally divided into two areas with regards to CMBS transactions:

(i)   questions of interpretation of contractual provisions; and
(ii) disputes between parties to the transaction which results in adverse litigation.

The use of the courts to resolve issues in interpretation, as well as the potential for litigation to be an asset to issuers in securitisations (as well as a liability of course—see Chapter 10 of the last edition of this book for a discussion of litigation as an asset) has had an impact on the role of the trustees and issuers in CMBS transactions. As central parties to the transactions, trustees and issuers have more regularly been involved in seeking the assistance of the court (or being parties to matters before the court) although the vast majority relates to questions of interpretation, which as discussed further below is less adversarial in nature than traditional disputes between parties.

286

13.3.1 Questions of interpretation—what did parties to the transaction mean?

"Unlike substantive law—for instance the law of tort, or the law of property—interpretation is ultimately intuitive. There are no rules.

The reason why it is an art, not a science, is because we are ultimately trying to work out what the parties wanted to achieve from what they have said and done."

Richard Calnan[2]

"The set up and structure of the various transactions [Theatre Hospitals CMBS] seems to a simple minded property lawyer to be Byzantine in the extreme."

Mr Justice Peter Smith, (the Theatre Hospitals Case) *Citicorp Trustee Company Ltd v Barclays Bank Plc*[3]

"A highbrow is the kind of person who looks at a sausage and thinks of Picasso."

AP Herbert, An Uncommon Law, "Is 'Highbrow' Libellous?"

As CMBS practitioners will be aware, whilst the rationale and logic of a CMBS is not overly complicated, CMBS transactions, by their very nature, are highly structured deals with a number of layers. The underlying layer is the loan facility, which may, as discussed in Chapter 5, have been tranched through an intercreditor agreement under which certain aspects of the underlying facility may have been modified or amended (such as water-falls). The senior loan may then have been securitised, and further amendments and modifications may have been made to the underlying structure (or the cash flows which derive from the senior loan). This complexity, when combined with the speed at which CMBS transactions were executed in the heydays of 2006 and 2007 meant that not every issue was addressed or dealt with in the tomes of documentation produced for each transaction.

One of the main issues arising in the documentation is the fact that CMBS transactions were often considered to be "cookie cutter" deals at the securitisation level; like RMBS transactions minimal amendments were required between "repeat" deals. However, this was not necessarily always appropriate. As a general rule, CMBS transactions are not homogenous structures with identical loans. Rather, due to the nature of the financing, there will most likely have been active negotiation of each underlying facility. This means that consideration needs to be given to the structure, both legal and economic, for each loan. For example, in a CMBS there may

---

[2] Richard Calnan, *Principles of Contractual Interpretation* (Oxford: Oxford University Press, 2013).
[3] [2013] EWHC 2608 (Ch).

be a selection of loans, some of which are partially amortising, others which are bullet repayments. There may be other deals which only have one or the other type of loan in them. These differences may have a significant impact on aspects of the securitisation.

When a transaction continues to perform, the documents are generally not subject to detailed analysis post-closing. However, as noted above, when a transaction is under stress, issues often arise which require detailed consideration of the position under the documentation. It is at these times that it becomes evident that either the documents do not entirely work together or do not address certain issues.

Documentation issues are arising most frequently when the transaction is nearing default and enforcement of the underlying loans have occurred or will occur. When drafted, detailed consideration and analysis was generally not given to the position of the transaction during default and enforcement of the underlying loans, nor as to how various components of the trans-action would operate together. Issues arise, which are not specifically dealt with in the documentation. In such a situation, the servicing entity and/or the issuer and trustee (depending on what the specific issue relates to) are required to consider the parameters of their powers and any discretion which the documents may permit them. As a general statement, the parties to these deals have been proactive in addressing these issues and ensuring that a transaction is not caught in a stalemate. This has meant that the servicers, trustees and issuers have had to be engaged with a variety of highly complex issues and consider the ramifications of various positions and proposals.

For some of these issues, consideration can be given to the discretionary powers given to the trustee at the note level (or the servicer at the loan level, discussed further in Chapters 9, 10 and 11) to agree to amendments, waivers and modifications to the transaction documents. Under certain circumstances the trustee may be minded to exercise its discretion and agree to amendments etc., and as such, resolve issues relating to the doc-umentation. However, it should be stressed that such action by a trustee is discretionary in nature (i.e. the trustee has no obligation to agree to exercise the powers granted to it) and will be subject to the trustee receiving comfort on various matters, including analysis of the documents, as well as possibly being indemnified, prefunded or secured to its satisfaction. In addition, it is standard in all Eurobond transactions for these powers to be limited, such that they cannot be exercised where such action would be (or could be considered to be) materially prejudicial to the interests of the noteholders or would have an effect so fundamental that it is deemed a modification of the basic terms.

Where the issue being considered may be prejudicial to the interests of the noteholders (which, when the question relates to intercreditor rights, tends to be the case), the trustee will generally be precluded from exercising its discretion. In these circumstances, noteholder consent by way of extra-ordinary resolution may be possible. However, where different classes of noteholders have different interpretations of the issue, it is likely that such a resolution is unavailable. It is in these circumstances that issues as to con-struction and interpretation of contracts may need the assistance of the court in order to be resolved. As discussed above, since 2014, trustees, issuers and other transaction parties have sought the assistance of the court in matters relating to the interpretation of provisions within the transaction documents.

13.3.1.1 Part 8 Proceedings

For English law questions of interpretation, there is a tried and tested route for seeking the court's determination on the interpretation and construction of the provision (or provisions) in question—a Part 8 proceeding. Part 8 proceedings are used for the determination of claims that do not have a substantial dispute of fact and are capable of being resolved without some of the procedural stages, such as lengthy pleadings, disclosure and oral evidence required in standard proceedings before the English courts. Part 8 claims are typically used when seeking a declaration on the construction, meaning or interpretation of the contract, and it is in this context that they have periodically been used by parties to CMBS transactions (as well as in other structured products such as CLOs and SIVs).

As noted above, seeking the involvement of the court is often not the first route taken by parties when considering an issue in the documents. Gen-erally the parties will consider whether the issue can be resolved in an alternate manner. It should be stressed that both the trustee and the issuer have limited control over this process. Whilst they can assist the parties in considering the relevant provisions, ultimately a consensual agreement can only be reached if the parties with an economic interest in the transaction agree to such an approach within the terms of the documents. As discussed above, neither the issuer nor the trustee have such an economic interest in the transaction, and the trustee has a general obligation to act in the interests of all classes of noteholders, which would preclude it from agreeing to an approach which is prejudicial to some but not all classes of noteholders. As such, Part 8 proceedings are generally commenced after consideration and discussion of the issue between various parties to the documentation, and it becoming evident that either (i) the documents do not provide a solution to the issue or (ii) a consensual agreement as to how the provisions should be interpreted or construed cannot be reached.

Part 8 proceedings may be initiated by any party to the transaction docu-ments, and there have been instances where Part 8 proceedings relating to CMBS transactions have been initiated by trustees and issuers, as well as other parties to the documentation, such as noteholders and liquidity facility providers. Even where the Part 8 proceedings are initiated by parties other than the trustee or issuer, the issuer and trustee will generally be involved in discussions relating to the parameters of the proceedings, prior to the proceedings being initiated. For example, in Part 8 proceedings it is common that the questions for the consideration of the court are agreed by the parties prior to the hearing. In some cases, the trustee or the issuer may take a lead in formulating the questions for the court. However, even when not actively involved in formulating questions for the court, the issuer and trustee will still be involved in discussions relating to the parameters of the questions for consideration.

One of the benefits of Part 8 proceedings is the ability to ensure that the decision of the court binds all the parties to the transaction. In order to achieve this, where a certain party (or class of party) is not joined to the initial proceedings, the court may join such party or a representative of such party to the proceedings. For example, where no noteholder is a party to the proceedings (or a particular class of noteholder which may have a view on the issue being considered by the court) the court may deem it necessary to join a representative of noteholders (or the relevant class of noteholders) to such proceedings. The mechanics may vary. In the Theatre Hospitals Case, Mr Justice Peter Smith first directed that the servicer be joined as a party and identify, on a confidential basis to the other parties' lawyers only, the identity of one junior noteholder. That junior noteholder was designated as "Defendant XY" in the proceedings and the Trustee was ordered to serve all of the documents in the action upon XY who was made a representative defendant so that all the junior noteholders would be bound by the judgment. By ensuring that all relevant parties are bound to the judgment, it means that a party who does not participate in the proceedings is not able, at a later stage, to dispute a judgment unfavourable to it.

In addition, whilst the parties in a Part 8 proceedings, due to the nature of the proceedings (i.e. parties arguing alternative interpretations of the documents) may take adverse positions to each other, the process would not normally involve cross-examination of witnesses of fact or expert witnesses and thus is rather less adversarial in nature than most claims before the courts. This is due to the fact that the parties are not disputing the facts but rather solely disputing the interpretation and construction of certain provisions. As such, Part 8 proceedings are often considered an efficient way to bring an issue before the court which allows parties to present arguments as to their own interpretation without necessarily being truly adversarial in character, and being constructed in such a way as to bind all parties to the transaction. The less adversarial nature of the proceedings means that the usual "loser pays" costs rule will not necessarily apply and the parties may bear their own costs subject to the ability of the trustee and issuer to rely on their right to indemnity or other contractual entitlement. However, even in Part 8 proceedings adverse costs orders are sometimes made.

A final point on Part 8 proceedings relates to the nature of the judgments. Part 8 proceedings are often referred to as being a useful way to address an issue in the documents which may arise across a number of transactions (and even across a number of conduit issuers). As such, Part 8 proceedings may be brought on one transaction, as a "test case", with the hope that the court will give a judgment that can equally be applied to other transactions without there being any risk that parties to the other transaction will challenge the application of the relevant determination of the court. Whilst in theory this sounds commendable, it is not always an easy thing to achieve. By their very nature, most transactions will be slightly different (even across the same conduit programme), with different investors and third parties, and different sets of underlying facts. Often judgments are given which, whilst containing certain statements which may have a more general application across transactions, do not necessarily address the main point, the "test case" point in such a generic manner (or address it by way of obiter dicta, which has been criticised by certain commentators). Rather the determination is tied to the specifics of the relevant transaction. This is hardly surprising given the role of the courts (and the precedential value of a judgment of a lower court), however, it can at times be frustrating for participants in the market. It is often asked why an issue in one transaction cannot be addressed in the same manner as another transaction where the issue was subject to Court direction. Unfortunately, owing to the nature of judgments (being fact specific and only binding the parties in that transaction), unless there is a clear and unambiguous declaration as to interpretation given by the court, where the issue has significant impacts upon the rights of different creditors, it will be quite difficult to adopt the same interpretation on another transaction.

13.3.1.2 The Sompo principle

As noted above, trustees will generally be a party to Part 8 proceedings relating to a CMBS transaction. Often Part 8 proceedings will be initiated by another party to the transaction. However there are times when owing to the nature of the issue or the facts relating to the transaction (such as the transaction having been accelerated or the issue relating to the exercise of a discretion by the trustee) that the trustee is the most appropriate party to start Part 8 proceedings. Even when the trustee initiates the Part 8 proceedings itself, it may take a neutral stance and not actively argue a position. In this situation it will give parties with an economic interest in the issue the opportunity to present their positions to the court, in order for the court to give directions as to how the provision or provisions should be interpreted.

However, the trustee will always make itself available to assist the court in reaching a determination on the issue being considered. There may be times when it is recognised that there is a dispute as to the interpretation of a provision, however, for various reasons, one party to the dispute is not represented in the court proceedings. This has been seen in cases where noteholders have been reticent about taking a role in the proceedings, even though the proceedings could prejudice their rights.

This was the situation in *State Street Bank and Trust Company v Sompo Japan Insurance Inc*[4] (the Sompo case), which involved an intercreditor dispute in a synthetic CLO. In the Sompo case, despite a noteholder being joined to the proceedings, no representative of the noteholders was represented before the court. The Chancellor noted that in these circumstances, the trustee, notwithstanding its neutrality in the dispute as between various classes of creditors, had an obligation "to assist the court by bringing to the court's attention any relevant legal proposition or argument affecting the position of unrepresented beneficiaries or parties". The Chancellor further noted that a trustee in this position has been likened to a watchdog for unrepresented interests.

We have seen the Sompo principle applied in Part 8 proceedings relating to CMBS transactions. As noted above, in the Theatre Hospitals case, a representative of noteholders was joined by an order of the court as "Defendant XY". In addition, the court asked the trustee to present arguments which would have been available to the junior noteholders (who were not represented in court, despite a representative being joined). Similarly in the DECO cases (as defined below), the trustee argued a positon in accordance with the Sompo principle. When acting in accordance with the principle, the trustee is presenting such arguments in order to assist the court, and does not impact its neutrality with regard to the issues being considered. Nor does it impose on the trustee an obligation to present every argument which the unrepresented party may have available to it. Rather the trustee is only required to draw to the courts attention possible arguments.

However, the application of this principle does explain why we sometimes see the trustee presenting arguments before the court which one would usually expect to see argued by a party with an economic interest in the transaction.

13.3.1.3 Part 8 proceedings—tell us more

> "For practically every statement about how to interpret contracts, you will find a contradictory one. There is authority for just about every approach to interpretation"

Richard Calnan, Principles of Contractual Interpretation

In order to highlight the variety of issues considered by the courts in Part 8 proceedings, it is worthwhile considering a number of recent cases. Four sets of cases will be considered below, the first two involve similar questions of construction which have arisen across more than one transaction (and more than one conduit issuer) whilst the second two may have more limited application, although are still quite interesting for CMBS practitioners.

---

[4] [2010] EWHC 1461 (Ch).

It should be noted that in most of the cases a number of issues were considered by the court. The case studies have however been limited to certain questions before the court and as such, do not address all the points raised in the various judgments.

13.3.1.3.1   Special servicer transfer cases

One issue which has vexed European CMBS deals is the issue of transferring the role of special servicer. In the US, transfers of special servicers are regular events in CMBS transactions, regularly tied to the change in ownership of the B piece in a CMBS transaction.

As discussed in Chapters 9 and 11, in Europe, the possibility of transfers also exists in CMBS transactions. It is not uncommon for the controlling party to be given a similar right to terminate the appointment of the special servicer without cause (and have the right to appoint the new special servicer). However, such terminations have been very limited in the European market. This is due to a number of reasons, including the requirement to satisfy certain pre-conditions before a new special servicer is appointed. One of these conditions is the receipt of rating confirmation from the rating agencies that such transfer will not result in the downgrade of the notes. Yet, a problem has arisen in Europe due to the policy of Fitch not to provide such confirmations.

The trustees in two transactions sought the determination of the court on the rating agency confirmation point (in addition to certain other points relating to the issue of termination and appointment of a new special servicer, to which we refer the reader to the relevant cases). These cases are *US Bank Trustees Limited v Titan Europe 2007-1 (NHP) Ltd*[5] (the Titan 2007-1 case) which related to the Titan Europe 2007-1 CMBS transaction and *Deutsche Trustee Company Ltd v Cheyne Capital (Management) UK (LLP)*[6] (the DECO cases) which related to the Deco 15–Pan Europe 6 Limited CMBS transaction. In addition, as noted above, in the DECO cases, in accordance with the Sompo principles, the trustee advanced an alternative interpretation to that advanced by the representative of the controlling class.

In each case the court was asked to construe the rating agency confirmation requirement for the replacement of a special servicer in light of the fact that Fitch would not issue rating agency confirmations.

In the Titan 2007-1 case, the court's determination on this point focused closely on a provision in the documentation which at its time was quite unusual. The servicing agreement for the Titan 2007-1 transaction included a provision which stated that if a rating agency declined to issue a rating agency confirmation, then a provision requiring such confirmation would

---

[5]   [2014] EWHC 1189 (Ch).
[6]   [2015] EWHC 2282 (Ch).

be construed as though such confirmation was not required. It should be noted that such a provision is standard in CMBS 2.0 transactions in Europe. The court ruled that, on the basis of this provision, it was clear that the commercial agreement was that the failure of a rating agency to provide a rating agency confirmation should not in and of itself stop the transfer from taking place.

The decision of the High Court in the DECO case was somewhat different. Commentators have argued (and this was also recognised by the High Court) that the difference between the approaches of the court in the Titan 2007-1 case and the DECO case was due to the fact that the transaction documents Deco 15–Pan Europe 6 Limited CMBS transaction did not include the wording contained in the Titan Europe 2007-1 CMBS transaction. In addition, the documents in the Deco 15–Pan Europe 6 Limited CMBS transaction included the ability for noteholders by way of extraordinary resolution to "override" the rating agency confirmation condition (which, owing to the way the extraordinary resolutions were structured, effectively meant only the most senior class of noteholders needed to approve the transfer if the conditions were not all satisfied). The High Court held that on this basis, there was no ability to transfer the special servicing role without a rating agency confirmation from Fitch unless an extraordinary resolution of noteholders approved such transfer. In May 2016, the Court of Appeal refused an application for permission to appeal against the first instance decision in the DECO case.

Conceptually, this would seem to indicate that, solely on the point of the rating agency confirmation condition, where the documents in a CMBS transaction are drafted along the lines of the documents in the Deco 15–Pan Europe 6 Limited CMBS transaction, it may be that a servicer transfer can only occur with the consent of noteholders acting by way of extraordinary resolution. However, where they include the language from the Titan 2007-1 CMBS transaction, or language with greater flexibility on this point, such transfers may be possible notwithstanding Fitch's policy on rating agency confirmations.

13.3.1.3.2   Class X interest cases

Another issue which has arisen across a number of transactions relates to the calculation of the rate of interest on class X notes. This issue (amongst others) was considered by the court in two sets of Part 8 proceedings, one relating to one of Lehman Brothers' Windermere CMBS transactions (the *Hayfin Opal Luxco 3 S.A.R.L. v Windermere VII CMBS Plc*[7] (the Windermere case)) and the second relating to four deals from Credit Suisse's Titan CMBS transactions (*Credit Suisse Asset Management LLC v Titan Europe 2006-1 Plc*[8] (the Titan cases)). It should be noted that the decisions in both cases are

---

[7]   [2016] EWHC 782 (Ch).
[8]   [2016] EWHC 969 (Ch).

subject to part appeal, and that these appeals are due to be heard in the latter half of 2016.

Both cases related to the calculation of the rate of interest on class X notes, discussed in detail in the last edition to this book. The issue before the court related to whether or not the calculation of class X interest should take into account amounts which accrue on an underlying loan following its default (often referred to as "default interest") or whether such amounts were excluded from the calculation of class X interest. In addition, the court was asked to, amongst other issues, consider what rate of interest would apply to any unpaid amounts on the class X notes (as, owing to the nature of the payments under the class X notes, the actual rate of interest on the class X principal amount could be significant multiples of the principal (e.g. in the Windermere CMBS up to 6,001% per quarter), which certain parties contended was essentially a penalty, and as such, unenforceable).

In both judgments the court found that "default interest" on an underlying loan should not be taken into account when calculating the rate of interest on the class X notes. As both cases found that class X interest had correctly been calculated, there was no unpaid class X interest, and as such, the question of what rate of interest applied on unpaid amounts did not need to be addressed. In the Titan cases, the Chancellor specifically noted this. However, in the Windermere case, Mr Justice Snowden gave an obiter view on this issue and noted that if one used the true rate of interest on the class X notes, the rate on unpaid amounts would be exorbitant (if not extortionate) and as such fell foul of the penalty doctrine. Such statement does however rather raise another interesting question; if class X interest amounts ever were unpaid, at what rate would interest accrue on such unpaid amounts?

In any event, as noted above, both the Windermere case and the Titan cases are subject to appeal, and as such, the position may change (or be further clarified).

An interesting point about both cases is that the second edition of this book was included in oral arguments by various parties. Further, in the Windermere case, Mr Justice Snowden in his judgment quoted the last edition of this book when explaining some of the issues which have arisen with regard to class X notes, an indication of the market-leading nature of this book.

13.3.1.3.3   Theatre Hospitals case

The Theatre Hospitals case has been mentioned above, however, it is probably worth giving some more detail on this Part 8 proceeding.

The Theatre Hospitals cases related to the term "outstanding" and how to interpret the provisions disenfranchising certain classes of noteholders. It is not unusual in Eurobond transactions for noteholders related to the issuer or originator to be disenfranchised from certain matters including meetings of noteholders, the power to instruct, calculation of amounts of notes outstanding or certain determinations by the trustee. The issue arose when the underlying loans were nearing default and needed to be restructured, yet it was unclear who could provide the appropriate instructions to the trustee and others. The definition of "outstanding" disenfranchised each seller (across the two deals, there were four sellers of loans), yet one of the sellers of the loans (to whom we shall refer as "B") held notes, both directly as noteholder (the B Notes) and potentially also had an interest in certain notes which B had transferred to R under a financing arrangement, but which B continued to contractually control certain matters such as voting on amendments (the R Notes).

The court had to determine whether (i) the B Notes were disenfranchised on the basis that "seller" in the disenfranchisement clause identified B in whatever capacity; (ii) the R Notes were disenfranchised on the basis that they were beneficially held on behalf of a seller, B, since although B had no proprietary interest in the notes, it had an interest in them in an economic sense.

In addition to describing CMBS structures as Byzantine, Mr Justice Peter Smith held that (i) the purpose of the provisions was to prevent B, in its capacity as seller, from exercising its votes attached to its notes in its own interest. The preferred approach would be that the word "seller" was intended to have the effect that, when it was holding the notes as a seller, the holder was disenfranchised. B was no longer holding any notes in its capacity as seller, therefore it was not disenfranchised. Further, Mr Justice Smith also held that (ii) B held the B Notes legally and beneficially, and R held the R Notes legally and beneficially. There was no suggestion that B had acquired any interest in the R Notes; this was separate from the fact that B contractually controlled the voting of the R Notes due to other arrangements. Neither the R Notes nor the B Notes were disenfranchised.

13.3.1.3.4 Gemini liquidity facility case

The final case which is deserving of mention as it relates to Part 8 proceedings, was brought by a liquidity facility provider. It is also considered a very strong statement that the court in such interpretation matters would adopt an interpretation of a disputed term that is most consistent with business common sense.

In *Gemini (Eclipse 2006-3) Plc v Danske Bank A/S*,[9] "D" provided the liquidity facility (the LF) to the CMBS. Owing to downgrades, the LF was fully drawn as a standby facility. Following to the introduction of Basel II in Denmark, D was entitled to charge for "increased costs" (and it should be

---

[9] [2012] EWHC 3103 (Comm).

noted that this entitlement was not disputed) under the LF, however the LF also included a threshold for payments due under it, pursuant to which amounts payable over a certain threshold were treated as liquidity subordinated amounts (LSA). As such, the vast majority of the "increased costs" exceeded the threshold, and as such, could only be paid as LSA (which ranked junior to amounts due on to noteholders).

The LF permitted expenses drawings, which could be used by the issuer to meet amounts due to certain secured creditors. Importantly the LF prohibited expenses drawings being used to pay amounts due to noteholders.

The court was asked to consider whether an expenses drawing could be used to pay the LSA (and related to this issue, when the LSA would become due and payable). In his judgment, Mr Justice Cooke agreed with the arguments put forward by the issuer, essentially confirming that an expenses drawing could only be made when an amount was due and payable by the issuer and that the LSA was not due and payable until such time as all senior amounts had been paid. Mr Justice Cooke also reaffirmed that this interpretation was most consistent with business common sense.

13.3.1.3.5   The Financial List

The complex and market specific issues which arise in the type of Part 8 cases described above are such that there may be benefit in those cases being heard by a specialist judge. The Financial List became operational in the Chancery Division and Commercial Court on 1 October 2015. The Financial List helps ensure that cases which would benefit from being managed and heard by a judge with particular expertise and experience in the law relating to the financial markets, or which raise issues of general importance to the financial markets, are dealt with by judges with suitable expertise and experience. For inclusion in the Financial List a claim should: (i) relate to banking or financial matters and be for more than £50 million; or (ii) require particular expertise in the financial markets or (iii) raise issues of general importance to the financial markets.

The Windermere case was heard in the Financial List and the Titan cases were heard by the Chancellor of the High Court, a Financial List Judge, and transferred to the Financial List prior to appeal. It remains to be seen whether the further development of specialist knowledge on the part of the nominated judges of the Financial List makes Part 8 proceedings a more attractive route for transaction parties.

13.3.2   *Litigation to add value or defend value in the CMBS*

Part 8 proceedings are not the only type of litigation involving CMBS transactions. In recent years, litigation has been brought by various parties to these transactions which does not relate to questions of interpretation.

Rather this litigation is seeking damages against one or more parties to the transaction, broken down into two sets of examples:

(i) valuer negligence litigation;
(ii) borrower litigation.

13.3.2.1 Valuer negligence litigation

In the last edition of this book, a section entitled *"litigation can be an asset"* was included in the discussion of the evolving role of trustees and issuers in CMBS transactions. It considered rights attaching to the underlying loans which are transferred by the originator as part of the sale process (both contractual rights and security rights—these together are often referred to as "Ancillary Rights" or "Related Collateral") as well as the contractual rights which the issuer has directly against third parties to the transaction. The section also noted that whilst a transaction continues to perform, the assets of the issuer other than those relating to the underlying receivable originating assets and security are less likely to be actively considered (or to have any real value). However, once a transaction is in trouble and the "traditional assets" of the structure no longer have sufficient value to cover the debt owed to the noteholders, the issuer (or its agents, in particular the servicing entity) may need to consider whether there are any other assets of the structure which could increase the receipts available to the issuer to satisfy its debts as and when they fall due.

This may involve considering whether the issuer has any contractual or other claim against any third party (either directly through contractual relationships between the issuer and a third party, or as part of the assigned "Ancillary Rights" or "Related Collateral"). These may include considering whether any representations were incorrect at the time they were given (such as representations given as to the assets on the date of transfer) or whether any specialist adviser (such as a lawyer, valuer or auditor) gave advice which was negligent. In the former case, the third party may have an obligation to remedy such breach (with regards to assets, generally by repurchasing the assets in question) and in the latter, the issuer may have a claim either in contract or tort.

At the time of the writing of the last edition of this book, valuation claims were still being considered in the abstract, as there had not been any litigation relating to such matters. In the intervening years, whilst there has been considerable discussion in the CRE market regarding negligence claims against valuers, there has been limited litigation regarding this issue. This may be due to a number of the issues raised in our section on *"litigation can be an asset"* or to various other developments in the market.

However, it is worth considering the main case on this topic as part of this Chapter's analysis of litigation in CMBS transactions.

13.3.2.1.1   Titan Europe 2006-3 v Colliers

This discussion is actually an analysis of the High Court decision (*Titan Europe 2006-3 Plc v Colliers International UK Plc (in liquidation)*)[10] and the related decision of the Court of Appeal (*Titan Europe 2006-3 Plc v Colliers International UK Plc (in liquidation)*.[11]

The issuer ("T") brought a professional negligence claim against the defendant valuation company ("C") in respect of its valuation of a commercial property in Germany which had been built for the in situ tenant. When the owner of the property sought a loan, C valued the property at €135 million for the bank, partly based on the assumption that the existing tenant would continue to occupy the property and pay a significant rent. The loan was later securitised in the Titan Europe 2006-3 CMBS. The tenant later became insolvent, with its administrator quitting the lease which in turn caused the borrower to default on the loan and became insolvent. As a result the property was to be sold for only €22.5 million.

Owing to this decrease in value, T sued C for negligence. The key issues before the High Court were (i) whether T or only the noteholders could claim against C, and (ii) whether C's valuation had been negligent.

The High Court found in favour of T. It held that (i) rights arising from a debt instrument such as T's notes attached to the notes for the benefit of the holder for the time being, but the securitisation had not been structured so that the noteholders were the parties with the right to sue in respect of allegedly negligent valuations. Economically, the investors in the notes had suffered the loss. However, it did not follow that T had not suffered loss in respect of which it could claim. T was able to show that it was contractually obliged to distribute any sums received in the action to noteholders. On the premise that T could show reliance and causation, it had suffered a loss the moment it purchased the loan because it had acquired a chose in action worth less than the price paid. More generally, the courts were reluctant to accept "no loss" arguments in cases involving complex structured financial transactions as the distribution of loss could be difficult to pin down. The important points were that where the contractual structure allocated the bringing of a type of claim to a particular party, that party brought the claim, complying with any conditions for doing so, and that the proceeds were dealt with according to the contractual requirements. Applying those principles, T was entitled to bring the claim. It also held that (ii) C's valuation had been negligent. A reasonably competent valuation would have considered the fact that there was a real risk that the tenant could leave and the problems that the empty building could pose. C had failed to give sufficient weight to the fact that the property was likely to attract poor

---

[10]   [2014] EWHC 3106 (Comm).
[11]   [2015] EWCA Civ 1083.

demand because it was large, old and built to the needs of the tenant's particular business.

C appealed both decisions to the Court of Appeal, which allowed the appeal. With regard to the negligence claim, the first instance judge's finding as to the proper valuation of the property was too low; the valuation that the Court of Appeal found to be correct just fell within the 15% bracket for margin of error from C's valuation. Regarding the issue as to whether T could claim against C, as C was found not to have been negligent, the Court of Appeal did not make a finding on this issue. However Lord Justice Longmore believed that this issue was an important issue for the securitisation industry, and felt it was important for the Court of Appeal to express a view on it. In an *obiter* statement he noted that had the Court of Appeal upheld the decision of the High Court regarding the negligence of C, the Court of Appeal would have also upheld the decision of the High Court to the effect that T could sue C. The issuer's relationship with the noteholders was found to be analogous to that of a company with its shareholders.

As such, the Court of Appeal's decision gave some clarity to whether an issuer could suffer a loss and sue for such loss. However, both the High Court decision and the Court of Appeal decision also highlighted the difficulties in proving professional negligence, in particular in a case where the factual pattern was complicated.

13.3.2.2 Borrower litigation

The final type of litigation we have seen over the last few years is litigation at the loan level. As this Chapter is considering issues at the CMBS level, it may not directly fit within the parameters of discussion. However, it is deserving of discussion in this Chapter.

Since 2013, as loans go into default and are enforced, some borrowers and other creditors at the loan level have used litigation as a tool to protect their position. Owing to the nature of the claims, often the issuer and trustee are not directly involved, as the servicer or special servicer will be taking the lead on this litigation on behalf of the issuer. Market comments indicate that the claims can relate to a variety of points ranging from the origination of the loan to enforcement strategies being implemented to liquidate the defaulted loan. However, such litigation may involve the issuer, as the lender of record. As such, it is undoubtedly part of the evolving world of trustees and issuers in CMBS transactions.

13.4 Conclusion

This Chapter has considered the rise of litigation in CMBS transactions and in particular the increased use of the courts to determine questions of interpretation and construction. This increase is not surprising given where the market are in the life-cycle of CMBS transactions. As transaction cash-flows become stressed, parties may consider their position closely and consider whether there are intercreditor questions which may arise and which may alter their entitlements or their "position" in the transaction. As such parties raise conflicting interpretations of provisions and documents, and owing to the nature of the issues and its impact on various creditors, transaction parties have been increasingly seeking the courts' determination in these disputes. Of course, some might argue that these issues may have been avoided with drafting hindsight, but as always, hindsight can be a dangerous tool.

Part of the attraction in seeking the determination of the courts on matters of interpretation has been an understanding that the courts are likely to construe the documentation in a commercially sensible manner. This has not always been the case, but rather derives from a large number of cases dealing with interpretation of contracts over the last 20 years, and in particular the principles on interpretation set out by Lord Hoffmann in *Investors Compensation Scheme Ltd v West Bromwich Building Society*.[12] In this case Lord Hoffmann enunciated five principles of contractual interpretation, principles which have been generally applied by courts in subsequent cases, including cases relating to structured finance and structured products. This has given parties comfort that the court will try and achieve an interpretation which is commercially sensible where alternate views are possible.

A number of cases relating to structured finance transactions have quoted the Supreme Court's decision in *Rainy Sky v Kookmin Bank*,[13] which stated that where the language of the parties could be construed in two different ways, the aim was to adopt "the construction which was most consistent with business common sense, by an iterative process involving the checking of each of the rival meanings with the other provisions of the document and investigating the consequences. The aim is to ascertain what the reasonable person would have understood the parties to have meant by the words that they used, with such reasonable person having all the background knowledge which would reasonably have been available to the parties in the situation in which they were at the time of the contract". The courts have generally tried to adhere to this approach when considering Part 8 proceedings relating to CMBS transactions.

Of course this is not an easy task for any person, and when one adds to the equation the complexity (or Byzantine nature) of a CMBS transaction, one tends to sympathise with the judges who need to consider the issues raised in CMBS litigation.

---

[12] [1997] UKHL 28.
[13] [2011] UKSC 50.

Whilst it is not certain when the next Part 8 proceeding relating to a CMBS transaction will find its way in front of a court, it is highly likely that the courts will continue to see such cases being brought before them, and will continue to analyse complicated questions as to interpretation of provisions which necessitate analysing and addressing a number of questions. As such, it is highly likely that trustees and issuers will continue to be involved in court proceedings, and continue to see their role in these transactions evolve.

In addition, issuers and possibly trustees may be brought into litigation at the loan level. For the reasons discussed above, this could be viewed as a rather worrying situation. The assumption on closing of the transaction was that risks to the investors were largely known, or at least disclosed. However, if the issuer becomes involved in claims by a borrower, it could expose the issuer to potential liability and as such, potentially impact the possible already limited cash-flows available to noteholders.

Finally, it will be interesting to see whether further professional negligence claims are brought against valuers in CMBS transactions. Whilst the Court of Appeal decision in the Titan 2007-1 case overturned the High Court's finding of negligence, the obiter statements did indicate that an issuer could bring a claim against a valuer. Of course there are a large number of hurdles to any such claim, including the issue of limitation periods, as well as the fact that valuations are often highly complicated (as seen in the Titan 2007-1 case where various professionals gave widely varying valuations to the assets) and the usual application of the "loser pays" costs rule in the English courts. It is also noted that the professional negligence claim against Colliers by White Tower 2006-3 Plc (an issuer in a CMBS transaction) was withdrawn prior to judgment—perhaps an indication of the difficulties faced by issuers in these types of claims or of the appropriateness of settling?

In any event, the increase in litigation in CMBS transactions has had an impact on the role of trustees and issuers in these transactions. Courts have become more familiar with structured finance transactions and the intricacies of these deals, which in turn has potentially made court determination of construction issues more attractive and efficient to parties involved.

And to conclude with the involvement of the great AP Herbert in this Chapter, a final quote:

> "Justice should be cheap but judges expensive."

Chapter 14

The role of the Rating Agencies in Commercial Mortgage Lending and the wider Debt Capital Markets

Elizabeth Lovett,

Assistant Vice President, Global CMBS, Structured Finance, DBRS

Christian Aufsatz,

Senior Vice President, Global CMBS, Structured Finance, DBRS

14.1 Introduction

One of the ways to refinance CRE debt in the capital markets is CMBS. As was discussed in Chapter 1, in a typical CMBS, a loan originator sells one or more CRE loans to a special-purpose vehicle (SPV), which funds the loan purchase by issuing CMBS notes in the capital market (principal or true sale CMBS). An alternative structure is that the SPV directly lends to a CRE owner, typically arranged by an investment bank or advisor. In such agency CMBS or secured loan CMBS, the step of an originator selling the loan to the SPV falls away. Other sub-forms of CMBS include credit-tenant-lease transactions (CTL) and hybrid corporate real estate transactions, which are typically issued in the agency format.

In typical principal and agency CMBS, the notes issued by the SPV often have different seniority in relation to principal repayment (tranching); hence, they carry different degrees of credit risk. Typically, the aim of commercial mortgage securitisations is to issue some bonds that have lower credit risk than the underlying loans. This is achieved by the aforementioned tranching in combination with structural elements, including liquidity facilities, interest and/or currency hedging and appropriately rated transaction counterparties (e.g., hedge providers, account banks and liquidity providers).

Figure 1: Typical European CMBS Structure

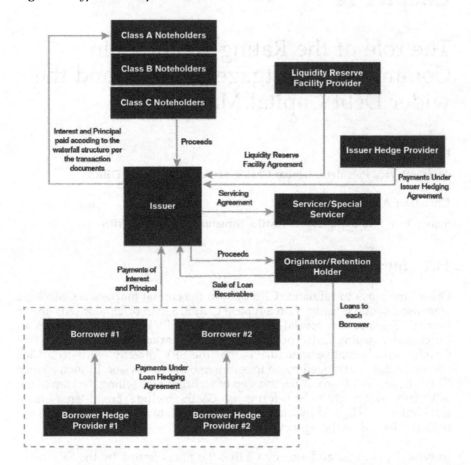

14.2   European CMBS

The first European CMBS was issued in the mid-1990s; the market experienced seven years of growth between 2001 and 2007 with annual issuance of €15 billion to €20 billion until 2004 and three years of significantly higher annual issuance before the onset of the GFC. Issuance after the GFC (European CMBS 2.0) has been sporadic, at best, for a number of reasons, including a lack of investor confidence following years of adverse loan performance and regulatory changes that significantly promote direct CRE lending for investors who would otherwise buy CMBS. More risk-adverse investors and regulatory changes have resulted in a significant deterioration of competitiveness for European CMBS lenders compared with sources of CRE debt, which hinders new issuance.

Figure 2: European CMBS issuance in EURbn

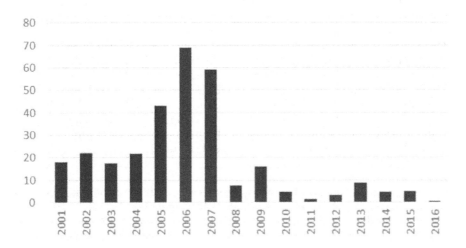

Source: DBRS Research.

Europe introduced risk retention requirements for new securitisations in 2011. Currently, most European investors are only allowed to purchase securitisation bonds if the originator or sponsor retains 5% of the exposure. While this likely had a moderately negative impact on total issuance, European CMBS 2.0 transactions, which typically securitise one to three loans, illustrate that risk retention requirements can be dealt with in CRE debt securitisations. In principal CMBS, the originator either retains a 5% vertical stake in each loan (i.e., sells 95% of the loan to the SPV) or a 5% vertical slice in each CMBS tranche. In agency CMBS, which do not have an originator, the real estate sponsor has typically retained at least 5% of the most junior debt exposure if relevant. In June 2016 the European Parliament's Committee on Economic and Monetary Affairs (ECON) published a draft report on simple, transparent and standardised (STS) securitisations. In this draft report it is proposed to increase the risk retention requirement to 20%. While it remains to be seen whether risk retention will ultimately be increased to such level, it would make CMBS issuance more expensive; a further disadvantage for securitisation compared with other sources of CRE funding. See further Chapter 17.

14.3 What is a credit rating

A credit rating is an independent opinion about the creditworthiness of, for example, corporate entities, financial institutions, sovereigns or asset-backed securities (securitisations). Credit ratings can be assigned at the issuer level (as is typical in corporate finance) or at the debt-instrument level. Credit ratings for securitisations, including CMBS, are usually assigned to the debt instruments of different seniority (tranching). Importantly, credit ratings are independent opinions about credit risk and should not be seen as investment advice or an indication of market liquidity.

The rating definitions differ by rating agency; DBRS credit ratings address the likelihood of timely payment of interest and ultimate payment of principal to the noteholders by the final rated maturity date of the notes. For CMBS, it is important to note that DBRS ratings are based on ultimate principal repayment by the final rated maturity date of the CMBS notes and not on the expected or scheduled maturity date(s) of the securitised loan or loans. If a loan is extended at maturity, the ratings may not be affected until DBRS is of the opinion that repayment is unlikely by the final rated maturity date of the CMBS.

Credit ratings are issued by rating agencies, which are independent companies. There are four major global rating agencies: Moody's Investors Service, Standard & Poor's, Fitch Rating Agency and DBRS, with several other smaller, regional rating agencies that are active in certain jurisdictions. Rating agencies aim to create greater transparency in the market by providing investors with independent credit opinions.

This Chapter will explain the rating agency process when assigning credit ratings to debt secured by CRE. Currently, this rating process is most commonly applicable to European CMBS; however, CRE loan ratings are becoming increasingly common at the request of certain investors and follow a similar process.

14.4   The rating process

In forming its opinion, a rating agency applies its rating methodology for the respective sector. For European CMBS, because of the characteristics of CRE debt, rating methodologies combine quantitative models with qualitative analysis. Typically, a credit rating agency analyst takes the lead in evaluating the loans and the CMBS bonds. Any rating decision is subject to a rating committee which reviews, discusses and votes on the analysis. Outstanding ratings and the rating methodologies themselves are subject to an annual review process.

Generally, the way rating agencies analyse CRE loans is not too different from an originator's or debt investor's underwriting process. The key factors and metrics of the analysis are the same: expected net rental cash flow of the properties, interest/debt service coverage levels, loan covenants, property valuation, market outlook, refinancing risk and loan-to-value (LTV) ratio. Likewise, the analysis of the structure of the loan and the borrower's legal structure should be similar and, in a way, a rating agency's loan rating is the same concept as an originator's or investor's internal rating for the respective exposure.

306

In the context of CMBS, a single loan is often refinanced by the issuance of debt classes with different seniorities (tranching) or the issued debt with different seniorities is backed by a portfolio of loans. Tranching and pooling add another layer of complexity to the risk assessment. As for the underlying loans, the credit risk assessment of CMBS bonds is the result of quantitative and qualitative analysis. For both loan-level and CMBS rating analysis, a rating agency typically has to strike a balance between transparency (investors and other interested parties should be able to understand the rating rationale) and accuracy, considering that employing excessively complex models risks that the rating process becomes a black-box. Ultimately, rating agencies aim to provide a credit risk grading while ensuring comparability of credit risk assessment between transactions and sectors.

14.5   DBRS European CMBS rating analysis

DBRS's European CMBS and loan rating process primarily encompasses a two-step approach consisting of the credit review and the legal review. Both reviews are done in tandem and are of equal importance. The credit review typically includes a property site visit, property and lending market analysis as well as cash flow analysis at a property and tenant level. The legal review encompasses the analysis of the contractual agreements underlying the CRE loan and the CMBS, including the loan and transaction waterfall structure; loan sale agreements; counterparties; hedging agreement; security arrangements and the corresponding legal opinions. Each rating agency has their own approach in analysing these components, which can result in different credit ratings for each class of CMBS notes.

Pool size (in terms of numbers of CRE loans) in CMBS transactions can range from single digits to several hundreds. Historically, European CMBS has been characterised by portfolios of typically fewer than 10 loans whereas most US CMBS are significantly more granular. Another difference is that most US CMBS are fixed-rate whereas European CMBS are typically floating-rate bonds.

Before the GFC there was a trend in European CMBS of securitised portfolios becoming more granular; however, at the time of writing, European CMBS 2.0 has consisted of three loans or fewer securitised loans. As a result of being a heterogeneous asset class, the European CMBS rating process is labour intensive compared with the statistical analysis of pools of relatively homogenous assets that are common in other structured finance asset classes; the analysis focuses on evaluating the credit risk of each of the underlying loans by assessing loan-property and tenant-level data.

Important participants in the rating process are the loan originator (if any) and the arranger of the CMBS issuance. In European CMBS, for principal transactions, the originator and arranger are often the same entity. During the rating process, rating agencies typically communicate with the arranger (e.g., in relation to additional data requests or in case of questions about the loan, its collateral and/or the legal structure).

In terms of timing, the rating process can be split into several phases, starting with the analysis of the loans and the property collateral. Over time, the analysis becomes more detailed and increasingly focuses on the legal aspects of the loans and the CMBS. At the end of this stage, the rating agency will typically opine on either the credit quality of the loan (in the case of a loan rating) or on a CMBS capital structure provided by the arranger. In the case of a CMBS, the rating agency typically issues its provisional ratings, which includes the publication of a press release and a presale report. The presale report details the rating agency's opinion of the transaction and is for the benefit of potential investors, who also have access to the rating analysts in case of questions.

A few days or weeks after announcement of the CMBS transaction, the legal documents are signed and funds flow (closing of the CMBS). At that point in time, rating agencies issue their final ratings and publish their final rating reports. The time between issuing provisional ratings and final ratings depends on the arranger's transaction closing schedule. During this time period, the rating agency reviews any changes to the collateral and legal documents, which are typically immaterial. That said, a material change to the transaction could result in final ratings differing from provisional ratings.

Following the closing of a transaction, rating agencies will monitor the performance of a deal on a quarterly basis until the earlier of the final rated maturity date and full repayment of the notes. The quarterly surveillance reviews include monitoring the property-related cashflows, rental performance, surveying the portfolio for delinquencies, prepayments, loan trigger events and corresponding debt service coverage ratio (DSCR)/interest coverage ratio (ICR) volatility.

The data relied on during the rating process is generally provided by the originator or arranger. The arranger generally coordinates a third-party audit of the data for accuracy. Additionally, rating agencies generally have their own internal checks and balances to validate the data accuracy. The availability of loan performance data and information relating to CMBS assets can vary widely across jurisdictions, from a very transparent public market in the US to a highly privileged and protected market in several European countries. The length of performance history varies widely across markets, even within regions, and even if data is available for a longer time period, it is not always in the format required by rating agencies and investors. If DBRS does not have sufficient data and/or information on a market and transparency of loan or property performance, it may not be able to rate the transaction or it may need to make conservative assumptions.

14.6   DBRS European CMBS rating methodology

European CRE loans are generally provided to a property owning SPV (borrower SPV) with no recourse to the ultimate equity owner (loan sponsor). As such, the borrower SPV can pay its period debt service obligations only if, on a consistent basis, cash flow exceeds its cash obligations. European CRE loans generally have shorter loan terms with minimal to no amortisation. At loan maturity, the repayment of the remaining loan balance depends on successful refinancing or the sale of the property. As a result, DBRS analyses the potential loss to a loan by considering both the term and refinance risk. DBRS defines the potential loss amount as the probability of default (PD) multiplied by the loss given default (LGD). PD is measured by the DSCR during the loan term and exit debt yield at loan maturity. LGD is measured by the LTV ratio. The DBRS rating process encompasses several steps, which are described in more detail in the following sections, to derive the potential loss amount.

Figure 3: DBRS Rating Process for CMBS Transactions

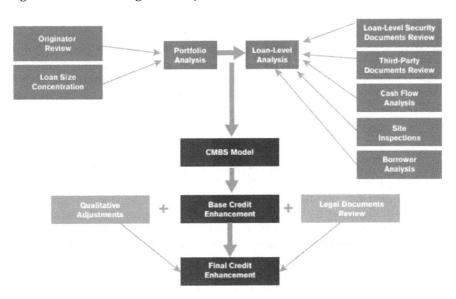

14.6.1   Property level analysis

When analysing European CRE loans and/or European CMBS transactions, DBRS begins its analysis at the property level. During the preliminary stages of the analysis, the loan and transaction legal documents may still be in the negotiation stage, but the documents required to complete the property level credit analysis are generally available since the originator or arranger has completed its underwriting process. The crux of DBRS's property analysis is an evaluation of the cash flow dynamics of each asset arising from the lease obligations in place and the projected income subsequent to lease rollover, net of projected operating expenses.

Given the concentration of most European CMBS transactions, the cashflow analysis is generally done on a property level. For more granular portfolios, the in-depth cashflow analysis may be completed for a sample of the properties and then the insights gained through this process are applied to the portfolio as a whole. The property-level analysis, which aims to determine sustainable net cashflow (NCF) at loan level and DBRS's property value assessment, includes both qualitative and quantitative analysis:

- Site visit and management meeting,
- Market overview,
- Review of the tenancy schedule,
- Cashflow analysis, and
- Review of third-party reports, including valuation.

14.6.2 *Property visit*

DBRS begins its property level analysis with a site visit and management meeting with a member of the asset management and/or local property management team. DBRS uses the site visit to determine qualitative adjustments for its property assessment and to gain local market insights. DBRS observes and discusses the property's position within the market, determines property quality and compares competitive properties. This includes a comparison of the property in terms of quality and a comparison of the tenants to other tenants within the sub-market.

For each unit of each property, DBRS completes a quantitative comparison of the in-place rent to the valuer's estimated rental value (ERV); since even within a property, the ERV for different units can differ depending on their location in the property and their usage. Leases that are signed at the peak of a market are often signed at unsustainable rental rates, so DBRS uses third-party sources (market research reports, valuations and discussions with local market participants) to identify sustainable rent and trends. In its underwriting, DBRS generally adjusts any above-market leases down to market rates with the assumption that, when the tenant has to renew, it will renegotiate its lease to a rate that is competitive within the market (see below).

It is common in European CMBS 2.0 transactions for the sponsor to have a detailed business plan to improve a property's performance. Site visits allow rating analysts to discuss the business plan with the local asset manager to fully understand the business plan and determine the feasibility of implementation. DBRS generally does not give credit to rental uplifts predicted by business plans, but may give qualitative credit on a case-by-case basis. Site visits also provide a good opportunity to measure the local market expertise of the asset manager and/or property manager.

In addition to the market knowledge gained at site visits, DBRS performs its own market research. This includes researching market trends for rental rates, vacancy levels, sales data, cap rates, construction statistics and demographics. There are several third-party data providers that provide market reports; however, finding detailed information is sometimes difficult given the lack of transparent data in most European countries. When information is not available, DBRS makes conservative estimates.

14.6.3 *Property and loan level cashflow analysis*

Ultimately, cashflow is the most important input in the DBRS model since a typical CRE borrower can only pay its periodic debt service obligations if, on a consistent basis, its NCF exceeds its cash obligations. Likewise, available NCF at loan maturity affects the exit debt yield and, therefore, the loan's refinancing prospects. Lastly, a property's cashflow generation affects the price a buyer is willing to pay.

The goal of DBRS's cashflow analysis is to determine a sustainable DBRS NCF for each property securing a loan. The starting point for the analysis is the tenancy schedule, which is provided by the arranger, generally audited by a third party for accuracy and reflected in the third-party property valuation. DBRS relies on the tenancy schedule to determine in-place rent and ERV. Credit is generally given for tenants that are in occupancy, subject to downward adjustments for tenants paying above-market rental rates as concluded in the valuer's ERV. Exceptions to this general rule of downward adjustment for over-rented units are very long-term leases to investment-grade tenants, for which DBRS typically underwrites the in-place rent. In case of under-rented properties (i.e., in-place rent is below the ERV), DBRS typically underwrites the in-place rent. DBRS also analyses the vacancy factor applied with regard to, but not limited to, historical vacancy, in-place vacancy, anticipated rollover and market vacancy. DBRS has benchmark vacancy thresholds based on property type and market that may be published in its European CMBS rating methodology.

Many leases in Europe require the tenant to pay most operating expenses, including real estate taxes, insurance, maintenance, etc. These leases are most commonly referred to as triple net or fully repairing and insuring, depending on the jurisdiction. In Germany, *Dach und Fach* leases are common and require the tenant to pay all expenses, with the exception of expenses associated with the roof and structure of the building. As a result, the DBRS cashflow analysis often includes minimal expenses. DBRS underwrites the expenses associated with vacant space that are borne by the landlord/borrower. Additionally, DBRS generally underwrites a management fee and may underwrite an additional expense plug based on historical expense. The result of sustainable rental income less operating expenses is the sustainable net operating income.

Below-the-line-item deductions include capital expenditures (capex) and leasing incentives. Capex consists of average annual expenses that should be invested into the property by a prudent property owner to maintain the property's condition and to retain its tenants or attract new tenants. DBRS finds it important to deduct these expenses regardless of a property owner's actual or budgeted capex as properties may sell for a discount if there is deferred maintenance. DBRS relies on the technical report for a cost estimate, subject to minimum expenses per property type based on historical data and market studies. Perhaps the most underestimated expense often comes from leasing incentives as new tenants are often offered a rent-free period and/or build-out expenses. Theoretically, the valuer's ERV should be net of such expenses but, in DBRS's experience, that is often not the case; hence, DBRS relies on the site visit, discussions with the property manager and the valuation to determine an appropriate estimate for leasing incentives. Based on data collected by DBRS, leasing incentives vary by point in the property cycle, property type and jurisdiction. On average, DBRS estimates leasing incentives to range from 10–15% of gross rent for new tenants and 2.5% of gross rent for rent renewals. These assumptions include the costs contributed by the property owner to build out the space and/or for rent-free periods. An additional expense for leasing broker costs is also included.

The resulting DBRS NCF is considered a stabilised figure that is sustainable over the loan term and is used throughout DBRS's quantitative analysis to determine Term and Refinancing DSCR, exit debt yield and the DBRS property value.

14.6.4 *DBRS value*

As mentioned above, the DBRS NCF is used to determine the DBRS value, which represents a stabilised value for the property collateral—a sustainable value over the loan term and refinance period. The DBRS value is determined by the rating agency's selection of a capitalisation rate or net initial yield, which primarily consider long-term historical averages based on market data. Additionally, the rating agency considers the quality and location of the real estate in the cap rate and yield selection process. The DBRS value typically represents a significant discount to the valuer's concluded market value. The discount is typically higher, (1) the more optimistic the valuer is in relation to current and future rental levels; (2) the lower the valuer's cost and capex assumptions; and (3) the more the valuer's cap rates or yields differ from historical averages. In European CMBS 2.0 transactions, the DBRS value has an average discount of approximately 20% to the valuer's market value; compared with the market's re-emergence in 2011, discounts have increased in recent years, reflecting the upward trend in certain European CRE markets.

14.6.5 Review of third-party reports

DBRS generally reviews all third-party due diligence reports that relate to the loan security which, at a minimum, includes a valuation, environmental report and technical report for each property. These reports are used to identify any possible significant contingencies such as environmental contamination, structural faults or deferred maintenance capex. If a Phase II environmental report is recommended, DBRS reviews the results. DBRS may increase the property cap rate or net initial yield it applies to DBRS NCF or make other adjustments if contamination is present and not appropriately mitigated. In certain instances, generally where loans are secured by highly diversified portfolios, only a sampling of the technical and environmental reports may be produced and provided. In some circumstances, DBRS may apply a penalty if the scope or the sample size are deemed to be insufficient.

The third-party reports typically also include valuations for all properties securing the loan(s). The valuations identify macro- and micro-market dynamics, the competitive position of the properties within these markets, trends in historical operating performance, valuer forecasts for future revenues and expenses as well as key valuation metrics. Producers of third-party reports are typically large, well-known firms and, while commissioned as part of the loan origination process, DBRS expects these reports to be conducted by a third party, independently from the CMBS issuer, loan seller (originator) or arranger. DBRS reviews the valuation instruction letter and the scope of the valuation to identify whether the valuer was asked to make any special assumptions.

14.7 DBRS large loan sizing model

Following the property-level, loan-level, legal (see below) and qualitative analysis, all of the various inputs are combined in the DBRS large loan sizing model. This model is most frequently used in European CMBS transactions as it sizes each loan separately and gives limited credit for pooling multiple loans, given the limited diversity of European transactions. As mentioned above, in the European CMBS 2.0 market, the largest deal has included three loans to date. For more granular pools, DBRS would use a different model.

The large loan sizing model used by DBRS determines the debt capacity deemed to be appropriate at each rating category through a direct sizing approach. The large loan sizing model is typically used at loan level and at CMBS level by aggregating the loan-level results. The capacity of debt allowed at each rating category is determined by hurdles derived from three metrics:

• DBRS LTV

- DBRS DSCR
- DBRS Refinancing DSCR

The DSCR is generally defined as the annual NCF of a property divided by the loan's annual debt service obligation (after interest-rate hedging). The Refinancing DSCR is defined as the annual NCF divided by the refinancing constant. The refinancing constant predicts the cost of capital at the time of refinance and incorporates a DBRS stressed interest rate, an appropriate credit spread and annual amortisation. The DSCR and Refinancing DSCR are, in DBRS's view, the best measures of the default risk of a loan as they incorporate the current as well as potential stressed future operating performance of the property (NCF) and the capacity of the NCF to service the related debt (i.e. how much debt the cash flow can support). LTV, generally defined as the amount of debt divided by the asset's value, is also considered and is, in DBRS's view, one of the best measures of severity of loss.

For each property type and based on historical data, DBRS has defined minimum DSCR and maximum LTV levels for each rating category—the DSCR and LTV hurdles. The varying DSCR and LTV hurdles for each rating category can differ based on property type and sponsor strength. They represent levels of property value and cashflow stress that the loan and CMBS should be able to sustain in each respective rating category. Importantly, each hurdle is based on the DBRS DSCR and DBRS LTV and not on the respective metrics of the originator or another third party. Properties that are deemed to be riskier, given historical performance, result in a lower capacity of debt allowed at each rating category and vice versa for more stable property types. Each rating category in the direct sizing approach implies a different level of confidence or margin of safety.

Of the DBRS Term DSCR, DBRS Refinancing DSCR and DBRS LTV, the most constraining parameter determines the direct sizing of the loan. The stresses are used to determine the ratings of the loan(s), the ratings of different loan tranches and/or the ratings of each class of CMBS debt in the transaction. The cumulative proceeds at each rating category create base subordination levels that are used to compare and assign ratings to the proposed structure. The ratings and hypothetical tranching for each loan allow DBRS to compare loan quality across portfolios and enable the rating agency, the originator/arranger and investors to see how much each loan contributes to each class of the CMBS transaction.

During the modelling process, DBRS also considers the debt yield and exit debt yield as important indicators of leverage. DBRS considers a loan's debt yield to be the DBRS NCF divided by the loan amount. Similarly, the exit debt yield is defined as the DBRS NCF divided by the loan amount at maturity. The DBRS exit debt yield is typically reviewed as a check and balance to assess that the broader DSCR and LTV measures are reflective of appropriate debt loads, given an asset's stabilised NCF. DBRS uses exit debt yield benchmarks that are reversionary, stabilised and long term. Generally, the exit debt yield benchmarks are a good sign of a loan's ability to refinance at maturity, but are heavily dependent upon the property type, jurisdiction as well as collateral quality and competitiveness. The concept of exit debt yield is similar to the Refinancing DSCR: both differ by the incorporation of the refinancing constant into the latter.

14.7.1 DBRS large loan sizing example

The following example walks through the DBRS model for a hypothetical office property with a total loan amount of €50 million. The example does not take into account any qualitative adjustments, including the property's location and the loan structure.

Step 1: Cash Flow Analysis

	Valuer	DBRS
Gross Rental Income	€7,500,000	€7,500,000
DBRS Markdown	n/a	–€500,000
Net Rental Income	€7,500,000	€7,000,000
Net Operating Income	€6,500,000	€6,000,000
Net Cash Flow	€5,250,000	€4,750,000
DBRS Haircut		–10%

Step 2: Capitalisation Rate Selection

— Valuer Capitalisation Rate: 6.0%.
— Long-Term Historical Average Capitalisation Rate according to market data: 6.5%.
— DBRS Capitalisation Rate: 6.5%.

Step 3: DBRS Value Determination

— Valuer Market Value: €87.5 million.
— DBRS Market Value: €73.1 million.
— DBRS Value Haircut: –16.5%.
— Originator LTV: 57%.
— DBRS LTV: 68%.

Step 4: DBRS Metrics Analysis

Assuming a 5% interest rate, interest-only, five-year loan term and 6.4% DBRS refinance constant results in the following DBRS metrics.

DBRS Term DSCR: 1.87x.
DBRS Refinancing DSCR: 1.48x.
DBRS Exit Debt Yield: 9.5%.
DBRS LTV: 68%.
DBRS Exit LTV: 68%.

Step 4: Loan Sizing

Based on the published *DBRS European CMBS Methodology*, DBRS would use the more conservative of the resulting proceeds from the DSCR and LTV hurdles shown in the table below. In relation to DSCR, the rating agency considers the more conservative of loan-level DBRS Term DSCR and DBRS Refinancing DSCR.

Rating Category	DSCR Hurdle	LTV Hurdle
AAA	2.35	40.0%
AA (high)	2.20	42.5%
AA	2.05	45.0%
AA (low)	1.95	46.7%
A (high)	1.85	48.3%
A	1.75	50.0%
A (low)	1.72	52.5%
BBB (high)	1.68	55.0%
BBB	1.65	57.5%
BBB (low)	1.58	60.0%
BB (high)	1.48	64.2%
BB	1.45	67.5%
BB (low)	1.42	70.8%
B (high)	1.38	74.2%
B	1.35	77.5%
B (low)	1.32	80.8%

Step 5: Compare cumulative proceeds to the transaction capital stack

The following cumulative proceeds are derived from the LTV hurdles as these result in more conservative proceeds at every rating category compared with the DSCR hurdles. These proceeds are compared with the CMBS capital structure provided by the arranger to determine the ratings for each class of CMBS notes.

Rating Category	Cumulative Proceeds
AAA	€29,230,769
AA (high)	€31,057,692
AA	€32,884,615
AA (low)	€34,102,564
A (high)	€35,320,513
A	€36,538,462
A (low)	€38,365,385
BBB (high)	€40,192,308
BBB	€42,019,231
BBB (low)	€43,846,154
BB (high)	€46,891,026
BB	€49,326,923
BB (low)	€50,000,000

In this example, the cumulative proceeds are capped at the loan amount at the BB (low) rating category. As such, this loan itself would be rated BB (low) in an untranched transaction (excluding further quantitative, qualitative and legal adjustments that may be made). For example, and as discussed in more detail below, strong loan sponsorship, property diversity or some loan amortisation over the term could generally result in an investment-grade rating for this particular loan. Such adjustments would also positively affect the potential rating on the different CMBS tranches. Strong sponsorship generally affects junior tranches' ratings more positively than senior tranches; property diversity is relatively more beneficial for the rating of more senior tranches. On the contrary, negative loan characteristics, like sovereign stress and structural deficiencies, could result in the example loan and the different loan tranches being rated a number of notches lower.

14.7.2 DBRS large loan sizing example—Adjustments

The direct sizing parameters can be adjusted for quantitative and qualitative factors, if necessary. An overview of the most frequently applied adjustments is included below:

14.7.2.1 Single tenant

DBRS recognises the risk associated with properties that are leased by a single tenant as it relates to the financial strength or credit of the tenant, or lack thereof, and the length of the lease inclusive of any breaks. Often, such risks can be mitigated by a loan's structural features (e.g. reserves, letters of

317

credit, guaranteed leases that extend well beyond the loan maturity, etc.); however, in addition to potentially affecting the DBRS property value negatively, such concentrations and binary risk in a property's cash flow may warrant an adjustment to a loan's PD and, therefore, an adjustment of the direct sizing parameters.

14.7.2.2 Recourse

Loans that have enforceable recourse to a financially capable guarantor are expected to have lower PDs. As such, if the lender/issuer benefits from a full-recourse covenant from an investment-grade-rated entity, it is generally floored at the entity's rating.

14.7.2.3 Sponsor

DBRS defines a strong sponsor as one that has access to sufficient liquid financial resources to do what is economically advisable to keep the loan current in periods of economic stress. In addition, the sponsor and loan are expected to be structured in a way that does not preclude or diminish the likelihood of injections of additional equity capital in the event of economic stress. Although financial capability does not suggest that a sponsor will cover debt service payment shortfalls, unless there is significant equity to protect (neither will they cover refinancing shortfalls in an over-levered asset), DBRS generally recognises that strong sponsors are less likely to default because of a short-term cash flow shortfall and are less likely to exacerbate the losses in the event that their equity has eroded. Furthermore, to the extent that the sponsor has real, significant equity contributed in the deal, the PD is expected to be reduced and the parameters may be adjusted to reflect it.

14.7.2.4 Concentration risk and diversity benefit

The DBRS sizing parameters are designed to consider the concentration inherent in single-loan portfolios, with no benefit given to multi-loan or property pools. The parameters can be adjusted at the loan and transaction levels to account for varying degrees of diversification, such as multiple loans secured by multiple properties across multiple jurisdictions or a combination thereof. For multi-loan portfolios in CMBS, relatively more diversity benefit is given to senior tranches of the transaction.

14.7.2.5 Amortisation

To the extent that a loan amortises, the loan's DSCR reduces, but DBRS considers a positive adjustment of its LTV sizing parameters based on both the strength and the stability of the DBRS Term DSCR; however, the DSCR reduction caused by scheduled amortisation could result in DSCR becoming the constraining factor when DBRS assesses the rating of the loan or the CMBS tranches, thereby making the positive adjustment to the LTV hurdles redundant. This effect in DBRS's rating methodology illustrates that, in non-recourse CRE financing, there is a fine line between the borrower's capability to make periodic amortisation payments out of NCF and the remaining refinancing exposure. Sometimes, CRE loan agreements feature cash trap mechanisms or soft amortisation. DBRS may give credit to such loan features on a case-by-case basis, depending on the level of DBRS Term DSCR and the quality (lease expiry profile and tenant credit strength) of the NCF.

14.7.2.6 *Property release*

Loans that are secured by portfolios of properties often have provisions that allow the borrower to release the properties, subject to an arms-length sales transaction. The release provisions are defined in the loan agreement and vary by portfolio, but generally include a defined release price. In some instances, the release price is set at a predetermined factor above the allocated loan amount and, in other instances, the release price incorporates the sale price (subject to a certain minimum price). As properties are released and the loan is repaid, the allocated loan amounts of the remaining properties may decrease proportionally to the loan balance or may remain static. To the extent that the allocated loan amounts decrease proportionally, the deleveraging process as a result of property disposals is slower compared with static allocated loan amount provisions. There is a concern about adverse selection in portfolios that allows for the property releases during the loan term. The sponsor may sell the best properties, which could result in a worse collateral composition. In certain transactions, this is somewhat mitigated by different release prices for different groups of properties. DBRS may adjust the model accordingly depending on the release pricing and the expectation of adverse selection for each portfolio.

14.7.2.7 *Loan and transaction cashflow waterfall*

At borrower level, in case of additional debt, DBRS's standard assumption in its large loan sizing model is that, before and after default, the analysed loan ranks senior in relation to principal redemption. DBRS would adjust its sizing parameters in case the borrower and/or loan structure deviates from this standard assumption or in case the borrower is subject to additional indebtedness (e.g. in the form of contingent tax liabilities, etc.).

The cashflow waterfall in a CMBS transaction determines the contractual priority of payments between the parties to a transaction, both before and, separately, after any default by the issuer SPV (Issuer). Each waterfall is agreed according to the requirements of the commercial parties and, accordingly, varies by transaction. DBRS considers the cashflow waterfall of each transaction separately. DBRS typically expects the principal redemption basis to be either pro rata pay, sequential pay or modified pro rata pay. In its large loan sizing model, DBRS's standard assumption is that a CMBS transaction pays principal on a pro rata or modified pro rata basis. To the extent that a CMBS transaction pays principal in a sequential manner, DBRS may positively adjust its LTV hurdles for more senior tranches, subject to considerations related to the remaining portfolio credit quality after potential loan prepayments and/or property sales.

14.7.2.8   Prepayment scenarios

Initial portfolio diversity can be eroded because of property disposals and/ or loan prepayments. For heterogeneous pools, disposals and/or loan prepayments can also result in diminishing portfolio quality. In its analysis, DBRS considers that prepayment analysis and adverse prepayment scenarios may result in negative adjustments of the direct sizing parameters. The extent of adjustment also depends on the CMBS principal waterfall structure (see above).

14.7.2.9   Other adjustments

For typical CRE loans, additional qualitative adjustments may include but are not limited to: property quality, property market outlook, owner occupancy, specialty-use build-out, loan size, senior-ranking claims, freehold and leasehold interests, equity investment in the transaction and cashflow stability. DBRS analyses atypical loan or borrower feature (e.g. non-clean borrower SPV structure or contingent tax liabilities) on a case-by-case basis. In case of non-quantifiable risks, DBRS might not be able to rate the loan or proposed CMBS structure with its *European CMBS Rating Methodology*.

14.8   Legal Analysis

DBRS considers the integrity of the legal framework and an appropriate review and assessment of the risks associated with structural features to be critical to the overall strength of the credit ratings assigned; therefore, when analysing European CRE loans and CMBS, DBRS performs a thorough review of both the loan-level and transaction-level legal documents. With respect to transaction-level governance, European CMBS structures are similar to other European securitisation asset classes; hence, DBRS recognises common legal criteria that can apply across different asset types in each European jurisdiction and has a separate published methodology for consistency.

Amid the relatively more heterogeneous nature of European CMBS transactions, the legal analysis of CRE debt and its securitisation is very detailed at the loan and property levels. To the extent that the CRE loans or CMBS transaction is exposed to non-credit-related risks, DBRS expects such risks to be mitigated in a manner that is commensurate with the target rating level.

14.8.1 Loan Level Analysis

DBRS is asked to rate European CRE loans and loans securitised in European CMBS that are typically large. These loans are often complex and, given that loan repayment depends heavily on the property collateral, DBRS conducts an extensive review at the borrower, loan and property security levels. These reviews include but are not limited to:

- Loan agreement;
- Analysis of the effectiveness of the security given over the property or properties;
- Review of borrower-level hedging agreements and hedge counterparties, if applicable;
- Review of the borrower account structure and account banks;
- An analysis of additional loan security (e.g., pledges of shares, rental income and accounts);
- Structural setup of the borrower/property holding company;
- The ownership and control of the borrower/property holding company;
- Effectiveness of the loan security in case of insolvency of the borrower/property holding company;
- Analysis of the tax position of the borrower/property holding company and the property;
- Analysis of the key contracts at the borrower/property holding-company level, including property management agreements and material lease agreements.

14.8.1.1 Additional debt

If the loan is structured with additional debt, DBRS will also review the co-lender agreement and/or intercreditor agreement to determine the relationship between the lenders before and after loan default. If the additional debt is not structurally subordinated, DBRS will model the whole senior loan amount to account for all senior obligations and may decrease the DSCR and LTV hurdles in the large loan sizing model if the leverage is deemed to be unsustainable.

14.8.2 CMBS Level Analysis

Key legal aspects in CMBS transactions generally include but are not limited to:

- Review of the overall structure of the transaction;
- Characteristics of the SPV used to hold the CRE loans;
- Analysis of the separation of loan credit risk from seller credit risk by means of a true sale or synthetic risk transfer;

- Review of the loan servicing agreement, namely the servicing standard and the capability of the primary and special servicers to act in the best interest of noteholders;
- Review of the representations and warranties made by the seller in relation to the mortgages and properties;
- Analysis of CMBS-level hedging agreements and hedge counterparties;
- Review of CMBS-level account structure, including account banks;
- Terms and conditions of the CMBS notes, including cashflow waterfalls, triggers, tail period, etc.

It is important to note that the role of a rating agency is not to structure loans or CMBS transactions, but to opine on the presented transaction structure. As such, rating agencies generally review the documents and communicate with the arranger and arranger's counsel through a question-and-answer format. To the extent that there are non-credit-related risks that are not properly mitigated in DBRS's opinion, a model adjustment may be made to account for the additional risk.

14.8.3 *Transaction Structure*

At the CMBS level, DBRS considers a wide range of structural features, including but not limited to the cashflow waterfall, final rated maturity, transaction counterparties, liquidity facility and true sale (assuming that the mortgage loans are transferred to the SPV by way of a true sale).

14.8.3.1 *Final rated maturity*

The legal maturity date of CMBS notes is typically a number of years after the maturity date of the longest loan (tail period). The reason for this is to give transaction parties (special servicer in particular) enough time to work out defaulted loans. The tail period is considered per jurisdiction and, for currently outstanding European CMBS, typically varies from two to seven years across Europe as a result of individual countries' laws and the structure of securities. Typically, tail periods have been longer in European CMBS 2.0 compared with pre-crisis transactions; to DBRS's knowledge, the shortest tail period in European CMBS 2.0 is four years. The difference in tail periods by jurisdiction is primarily a result of different legal regimes in relation to loan workouts. For example, the UK has a very efficient enforcement process as opposed to the Italian enforcement process, which is one of the longest. Other factors that usually affect the length of the tail period include the borrower and security structure or the property type. In other words, the longer a loan workout is expected to take, the longer the tail period of the CMBS is. While keeping in mind the jurisdictional differences, as part of its rating analysis, DBRS evaluates the contemplated tail period of a transaction as at closing to assess whether the special servicer would have sufficient time to realise on the collateral in order to satisfy obligations of an issuer in accordance with the servicing standard. In DBRS's opinion, insufficient tail periods increase the risk of a fire sale and could, therefore, negatively affect recovery expectations in case of a loan default. This could, in turn, negatively affect the rating.

14.8.3.2 Transaction counterparties

There are several counterparties that each play a different role in a CMBS transaction (e.g. account banks, hedge providers and liquidity facility providers). Given the importance of each counterparty, DBRS evaluates the counterparties' credit ratings to ensure that they are commensurate with the target rating level.

14.8.3.3 Liquidity facility

Typically, the more senior notes of European CMBS are very highly rated. In contrast, the credit quality of the securitised loans' cashflow streams (interest and principal payments) is not high enough to support such high ratings on the CMBS notes; therefore, to bridge this quality gap and to ensure timely payment of interest on highly rated CMBS notes in case of adverse loan performance, transactions often include a liquidity facility provided by an appropriately rated counterparty. This facility is specifically available to provide liquidity for the structure so that the issuer can continue to meet its payment obligations in respect of interest, expenses and property protection advances, as applicable, despite cashflow shortfalls arising from delinquent and defaulted loans or unexpected/increased senior expenses that could affect scheduled interest payments on the rated notes, loan protection advances and hedging costs, as applicable. The size and presence of a liquidity facility is imperative in the rating analysis, depending on the target rating level (e.g. CMBS notes with very high ratings are typically expected to benefit from liquidity arrangements). DBRS analyses the presented liquidity facility size based on the expected pricing of the notes, the projected base rate of the notes and the expected senior expenses to determine the number of months of coverage provided by the facility, assuming that none of the borrowers pays its interest due.

14.8.3.4 True sale

In European CMBS, there are generally two ways to transfer the mortgages to the issuer in the context of a securitisation: the transfer of ownership by the originator of a portfolio of commercial mortgage loans by way of sale to an SPV (true-sale CMBS) or a property-owning company using the debt capital markets for financing through the issuance of notes. The main distinction between a true-sale CMBS and an agency/secured loan CMBS is that, in the secured loan CMBS, there is no transfer of ownership of the underlying mortgage loans to the SPV (agency CMBS). In true-sale CMBS, DBRS analyses whether the structure is sufficiently insulated from credit risk of the loan seller/originator.

A third way to transfer the CRE loan credit risk from the originator to the CMBS issuer is to use credit derivatives like credit default swaps, total rate of return swaps or guarantees (synthetic transactions). While there have been some synthetic European CMBS before the GFC, they have not reappeared in public format since that time. For synthetic CMBS, the loan-level analysis is typically equivalent to that of true-sale or agency CMBS. The transaction analysis differs, however, when accounting for the differences between the methods of credit risk transfer. See further Chapter 12 and the use of derivatives in CRE financings.

14.8.3.5 *Servicing agreement*

As discussed in Chapters 9, 10 and 11, depending on the jurisdiction, there are generally two servicing roles in a CMBS transaction: servicing and special servicing (although more than one role may be assumed by one servicer). The servicer, during the ordinary course of business of the assets, is responsible for managing payments prior to any default and for the day-to-day administration of the loan. The special servicer takes over certain functions of the servicing role when the mortgage ceases to perform within expectations, which is an important role. As such, DBRS performs on-site operational reviews with the servicers and reviews the servicing agreement.

14.9 Surveillance

Following the initial rating, DBRS monitors the ratings on a quarterly basis by surveying the performance of the collateral portfolio based on occupancy shifts, leasing activity, expense management, cashflow volatility and a review of overall market dynamics. DBRS publishes performance update reports summarising any credit issues that may have an impact on the ratings of each transaction on an annual basis at a minimum. Quarterly performance analytic reports are also published. To the extent that a property's performance changes and a change to the given ratings is warranted, there are two types of rating actions that may be taken on each class: upgrade or downgrade. If no rating change is warranted, then the ratings are confirmed. Additionally, ratings may be placed under review if there are developments that need to be monitored for a short period of time or if additional information is needed to make a ratings decision. Under review ratings are generally only kept with this designation for a short period of time until additional information is available. On occasion, there are classes of CMBS with interest payments in arrears, but the cumulative or ongoing interest shortfall is expected to be ultimately recoverable. When the interest shortfall is a question of timing and not of ultimate payments, DBRS notes this with the Interest in Arrears designations for the class(es) affected.

14.10   Conclusion

Rating agencies serve an essential role in the securitisation market by providing independent opinions about the creditworthiness of bonds backed by loans. For CMBS the multi-step rating approach includes property, loan, legal and structural analysis. At loan level, the way rating agencies analyse CRE loans is not too different from an originator's or debt investor's underwriting process. Likewise, the analysis of the structure of the loan and the borrower's legal structure should be similar and, in a way, a rating agency's loan rating is the same concept as an originator's or investor's internal rating for the respective exposure. In the context of CMBS, tranching and pooling add another layer of complexity to the risk assessment. For both loan-level and CMBS rating analysis, a rating agency typically has to strike a balance between transparency and accuracy, considering that employing excessively complex models risks that the rating process becomes a black-box. Ultimately, rating agencies aim to provide a credit risk grading while ensuring comparability of credit risk assessment between transactions and sectors.

In a transitioning market, it is extremely important for rating agencies to maintain credit standards and provide timely opinions about the creditworthiness of rated debt. The role of the rating agency is ever evolving as the European securitisation market adapts to new regulations and market conditions; going forward, DBRS expects rating agencies to play an increasing role in the larger CRE market aside from only CMBS. This could include loan ratings for syndicated CRE loans mandated by investors and more CRE exposure in other structured finance asset classes (RMBS, NPL, Covered Bonds, etc.). Regardless of the product offering, the rating agency approach will need to remain transparent and consistent with the applicable methodology.

Chapter 15

European CRE Loans: Learning from the Drivers of Historical Credit Performance

Georghios Anker Parson and Nassar Hussain,
Brookland Partners LLP

15.1 Introduction

This Chapter considers the key drivers of credit performance for European CRE loans originated in the run-up to the GFC and aims to use these to derive what may be insightful and valuable lessons from an underwriting and structuring perspective for CRE lenders. It starts by setting out a brief overview of the legacy of CRE lending in Europe following the downturn, focusing on CRE debt maturity profiles, the manifestation of different types of CRE lenders, as well as origination trends. The European CRE lending landscape evolved substantially after the GFC, through an initially brief disruption period immediately post GFC, followed by a growth period and culminating in what seems to be a more normalised (or new normal) market at the time of writing.

The Chapter then goes on to identify and analyse various factors that may have affected the credit performance of European CRE loans. These factors are collectively referred to here as the *"drivers"* of credit performance for such loans. The analysis uses charts contained in a BofA Merrill Lynch Research Report prepared by Mark Nichol[1] and employs available loan-level data (sourced from Trepp) to observe credit performance via a number of variables (such as loss amount crystallised). The dataset comprises loans securitised in European CMBS transactions in the period 2000–2013. It is believed that such data is informative, as the typical five- to seven-year term for CRE loans in the European market means that the majority of such loans originated just prior to the downturn that followed the GFC have already matured, and a large number have had time to be restructured or worked out, with final determinations as to losses/recoveries made. The availability of data is, however, also limited in some aspects, particularly in the number of variables contained in the dataset (due to the limitations of the CMBS market) and hence observed and included in the analysis set out herein. The analysis is further supplemented by drawing upon the experience in

---

[1] Historical drivers of CRE loan performance (European Structured Finance–CMBS, 19 March 2015).

restructuring or working out distressed CRE loans across a number of European jurisdictions in the context of other drivers that may also impact credit performance.

References to performance in this Chapter always relate to credit performance unless otherwise indicated.

15.2   Legacy of European CRE lending: overview

In the immediate aftermath of the GFC, following a peak in the European CRE lending markets in terms of volume of origination, there was severe disruption and relative inactivity in the market between 2009 and 2011, with debt availability limited to very few lenders and at very conservative terms. This is reflected in the chart below, which shows the volume of CRE loan originations in the UK market since 1999, by banks and non-bank lenders:

Figure 1: Volume of UK CRE loan originations across all lenders

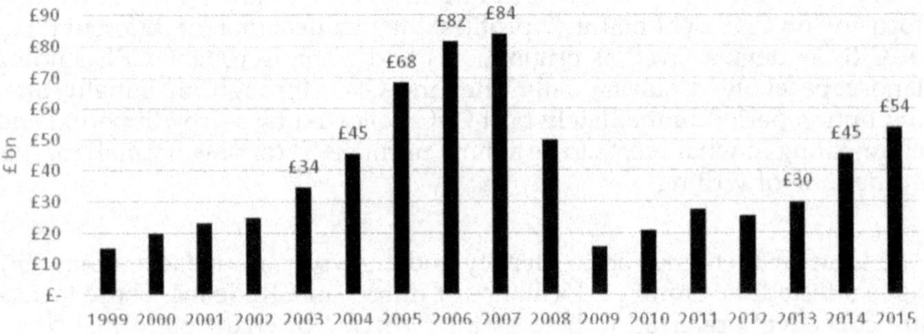

Source: *UK Commercial Property Lending Market Report (De Montfort University, 2015).*

The chart illustrates that in 2009 there is a noticeable drop in the volume of origination and even though levels have, at the time of writing, recovered to those reached in 2004/2005, they are still quite far off from the peak of the market in 2006/2007.

The European CRE lending markets started to pick up in 2011, reaching a more stable or normalised level in 2015. This stabilisation or normalisation is evident in senior debt margins[2] across Europe's largest CRE lending markets up to and including Q1 2016, as indicated in the chart below:

---

[2]   Margins over Libor/Euribor.

Figure 2: Margins for senior European CRE loans

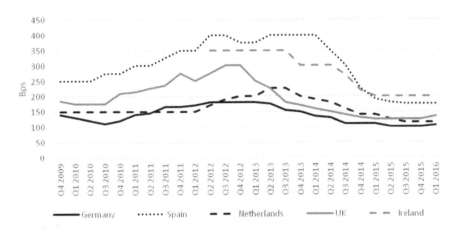

Source: CBRE Research: European Commercial Real Estate Finance-2016 Update.

Since 2008, banks have been forced to start a process of deleveraging their existing loan books, in some cases facilitated by transfers of entire loan books to government agencies/bad banks, charged with their gradual disposal, whilst some banks have proceeded to sell loan books to the market directly. This substantial deleveraging exercise has seen a select number of private equity groups, predominantly US-based, purchase European CRE loan books in bulk.

Banks have further been hit by the political and economic challenges since 2014, as well as a wave of new regulation, manifested through Basel III, CRD IV and (in the UK) slotting which has had the effect of increasing regulatory capital and liquidity requirements for banks, further deteriorating their ability to maintain their traditionally high share in the CRE lending markets, as discussed further in Chapters 16 and 17. This is expected to lead to a further withdrawal of banks from the European CRE finance market.

As a result of their gradual withdrawal from the CRE lending market, banks have been losing ground to alternative lenders, whose share of the market has been steadily increasing and who were responsible for a quarter of UK CRE loan originations in 2015.

15.2.1 Debt maturity profiles

Whilst there remains a meaningful stock of legacy European CRE debt on banks' balance sheets, they have been through a substantial deleveraging exercise since 2010. In the UK, according to the *De Montford Report*,[3] distressed legacy loans, originated just prior to the GFC, have mostly been removed from lenders' balance sheets.

The chart below indicates the breakdown of European CRE debt stock as at the end of 2014 and 2015:

Figure 3: Composition of European CRE debt stock as at the end of 2014 (RHS) and 2015 (LHS)

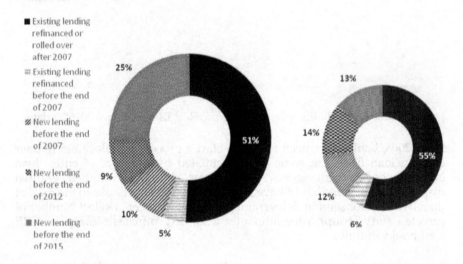

Source: CBRE Research

In 2015, the proportion of CRE debt stock comprising legacy lending refinanced or rolled over after 2007 was 51%, down from 55% in 2014. Combined with the legacy lending refinanced prior to 2007, the total legacy lending totalled 56% of the European CRE debt stock in 2015, down from 61% in 2014. The remaining 44% in 2015 comprised new lending, up from 39% in 2014.

Whilst the UK, Ireland and Spain have been the jurisdictions most successful in bringing legacy loan books to the market, Italy has been less successful in doing so despite the very large volume of legacy CRE loans on its banks' balance sheets. At the time writing, the outcome of the recent Brexit referendum held in the UK, has created further issues for Italian banks following concerns over a Eurozone slowdown and a continued period of very low interest rates by the European Central Bank (aimed at reversing a slowdown) which hurts their profitability. Share prices of Italian

---

[3] *UK Commercial Property Lending Market Report* (De Montfort University, 2015).

banks have fallen considerably since, reflecting investors' concerns. See further the discussion of the Italian NPL Market contained in Chapter 18.

The maturity profile of European CRE debt, as at the end of 2015, is illustrated in the chart below:

Figure 4: Maturity profile of European CRE debt stock as at the end of 2015

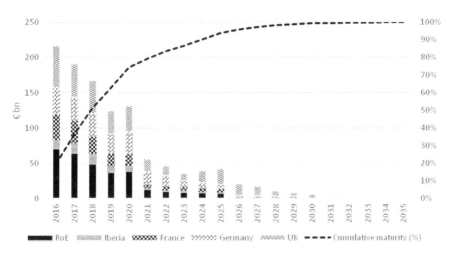

Source: CBRE Research

15.2.2 The manifestation of different types of CRE lenders

As was discussed in the opening Chapters to this book, banks have traditionally held the largest share in the European CRE finance markets. Prior to the GFC, they dwarfed any other type of lender, particularly in the period 2000 to 2007, when they significantly increased their exposure to CRE lending, with only CMBS coming someway near at the peak of the market in 2007. Up to 2014, alternative lenders such as insurance companies, pension funds and debt funds had provided very little CRE debt in the European market unlike the US market.

Since 2014, this has changed, as banks have been forced to retreat from the CRE lending market, prompting significant reductions in their CRE loan books as a result of heavy losses sustained following the GFC and increased capital requirements. The European CMBS market never fully recovered since the aftermath of the GFC and still struggles in terms of issuance as discussed in Chapter 1. The resultant debt funding gap has provided an opportunity for alternative lenders to substantially increase their CRE lending relative to prior to the GFC.

Whilst data on European CRE lending is limited, some data is available on the UK market from the *De Montford Report*, illustrated in the chart below which shows the allocation of outstanding debt in the UK going back to 1999 held on balance sheets (excluding outstanding CMBS):

Figure 5: Outstanding UK CRE loan books on balance sheets (excluding outstanding CMBS)

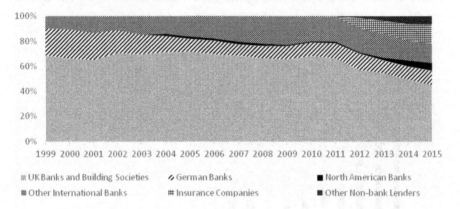

Source: *UK Commercial Property Lending Market Report* (De Montfort University, 2015).

This indicates that the share of insurance companies and other non-bank lenders has been steadily increasing since 2011, whilst the share of banks (for balance sheet lending), especially UK ones, has fallen quite significantly. The same trend is exhibited more emphatically by the volume of loan originations in the UK, as illustrated in Figure 6:

Figure 6: Volume of UK CRE loan originations

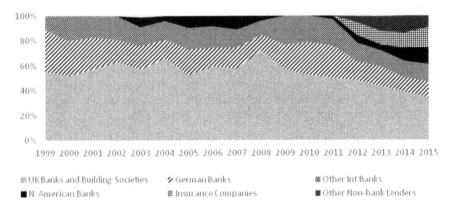

Source: *UK Commercial Property Lending Market Report* (De Montfort University, 2015).

It is notable that in 2006 and 2007, at the peak of the market in terms of volume of originations of CRE loans in the UK, the vast majority of originations were done by banks (for balance sheet and securitisation purposes), whilst this has now fallen substantially to 75% in 2014 and 2015, as a quarter of CRE loans in the UK were originated by alternative lenders (insurance companies and other non-bank lenders).

15.2.3 Origination Trends

During the period 2009–2011, the disruption in the European CRE finance markets meant that very limited CRE debt was available, from a select number of lenders who hadn't completely retrenched from the market. These lenders were subject to a large number of restrictions in terms of the type of product they could successfully deliver and therefore debt was only available for a limited subset of the CRE market (predominantly prime properties), on quite conservative terms (relatively high pricing and low LTV) and with a strong focus on existing borrower relationships.

From 2011 onwards, the gradual pick-up in the European CRE lending markets facilitated a step towards normalisation. This saw banks re-engage in new origination, albeit at more moderate levels relative to the past (and despite their simultaneous ongoing reduction in legacy CRE loan exposures), with quite conservative LTV levels, not very competitive pricing and a focus on larger ticket sizes.

Whilst there was a minor surge in European CMBS in 2013 (concentrated around the German multifamily market), this dropped materially in the two following years and the CMBS market is still, at the time of writing, somewhat disappointingly failing to show any signs of revival. The entrance of alternative lenders, with many of them focusing on mezzanine debt generating higher returns, meant that in 2013 there was a rather fragmented market in terms of a limited supply of senior debt but an excessive supply of mezzanine debt.

This has changed since 2014, with an increasing number of lenders (both, bank- and non-bank) offering increased senior debt capacity. There has also been an increasing number of lenders interested in smaller ticket sizes, which had been a gap in the market until 2014–2015.

Whilst the European CRE lending markets at the time of writing comprise a very large number of different lenders with a high level of competition, it seems that, in contrast with the pre GFC era, lenders are less willing to compete on credit/risk and structure, but will show some flexibility on economics.

At 2015 year-end, senior LTV levels, whilst on an increasing trend since 2012, are still far more conservative on average relative to the pre GFC peak. This is seen in the chart below, which shows average LTV levels offered on new loans for UK CRE investment sectors. Whilst senior lenders seek to limit the maximum LTV ratio they are prepared to underwrite post GFC, borrowers can access higher leverage through specialist mezzanine debt fund lenders whose investor base has preference for the higher returns/ higher risk associated with mezzanine loans. See further Chapters 5, 6 and 7.

Figure 7: Average LTV levels offered for new UK CRE loan originations

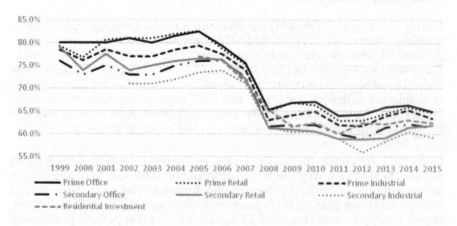

Source: *UK Commercial Property Lending Market Report* (De Montfort University, 2015).

In a similar fashion, interest cover ratio covenants for new loans are at levels which are substantially higher relative to the pre GFC era. Figure 8 shows the average interest cover for UK CRE investment sectors.

There appears to be a reluctance by banks to accept higher LTV levels or lower interest cover ratios relative to the pre GFC peak, which may be viewed as a positive development from the point of view of underwriting standards. Borrowers would ultimately like to see a more aggressive approach by lenders, but as this Chapter outlines in section 15.3.4.2 below, factors such as day-1 leverage (as measured by, inter alia, LTV and ICR levels) were very relevant to historical European CRE loan credit performance.

Figure 8: Interest coverage ratio (ICR) covenants for senior and whole UK CRE loans

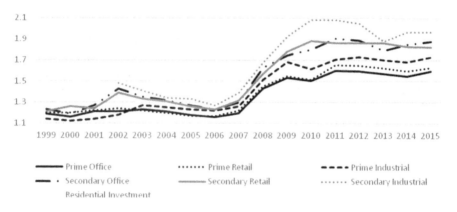

Source: *UK Commercial Property Lending Market Report* (De Montfort University, 2015).

Post GFC, lenders have been a lot more willing to compete on economics, with pricing for UK CRE lending at levels moving materially downwards from 2011 but not reaching those at the peak of the market just prior to the GFC. Figure 9 below illustrates average interest margins offered by banks and insurance companies for senior and whole loans to UK CRE investment sectors:

Figure 9: *Average interest margins offered by banks and insurance companies for senior and whole UK CRE loans*

Source: *UK Commercial Property Lending Market Report* (De Montfort University, 2015).

Surprisingly enough, the competition in relation to loan margins has not had as extensive an impact on arrangement fees, at least in the UK, as these have not moved downwards as materially, as shown in Figure 10 below, which shows average arrangement fees offered by banks and insurance companies for senior and whole loans to UK CRE investment sectors:

Figure 10: *Average arrangement fees offered by banks and insurance companies for senior and whole UK CRE loans*

Source: *UK Commercial Property Lending Market Report* (De Montfort University, 2015).

15.3 Historical drivers of European CRE loan credit performance

In this section, potential historical drivers of credit performance for European CRE loans are identified and analysed.

Based on loan performance data analysis in the BofA Merrill Lynch Research Report prepared by Mark Nichol[4] and restructuring experience relating to loans originated pre GFC, the underwriting considerations (including financial credit metrics such as LTV, ICR and debt yield determined during the underwriting process) as well as the structural features in a CRE loan financing have a material contribution in the ultimate determination of the credit performance of a CRE loan.

Such underwriting considerations and structural components of a CRE loan represent the relevant lender's response to the identification of potential risks, which may be informed by either commercial or legal considerations.

15.3.1 Availability of data

The reference period relates to loans that were securitised between 2000 and 2013, the majority of which have matured, as such loans typically had a term of five to seven years. As discussed in the opening Chapter to this book, the European CRE lending market reached a historical peak in terms of volume during the period 2006/2007 which was followed by a relatively protracted period of deteriorating credit performance. This combination of high origination volume and subsequent relatively poor credit performance provides a very informative set of circumstances for the purpose of conducting such analysis, as the identification of potential drivers is easier and the consideration of their significance in credit performance is ultimately more robust under such circumstances.

Notwithstanding the fact that the reference period is favourable from an analytical perspective, the general lack of availability of data across the European CRE lending markets, both at an aggregated level as well as a granular (loan-by-loan) level, has long been a common theme, particularly more so with the development of the notion of "big data" and the relevant ease of manipulation of such "big data" where available.

This deficiency in the European CRE lending markets partly relates to the fact that CRE lending is still predominantly a private market in Europe, making it difficult to observe transactions and related information on a systematic basis, as asymmetry of information between market participants drives a motivation for reluctance of disclosure of information on the part of

---

4   Historical drivers of CRE loan performance (European Structured Finance–CMBS; 19 March 2015).

those participants with more information relative to those with less. See further the discussion of this fact in Chapter 9. Even during the 2007 peak of the CRE lending market in Europe, only a relatively small proportion of the market was public, facilitated by the securitisation of a large volume of CRE loans in public CMBS transactions and the corresponding public disclosure of information that typically accompanies the issuance of CMBS. The only loan-level data available on CRE loans in Europe therefore, emanates from information publically disclosed in the context of CRE loans securitised in CMBS transactions.

However, this deficiency in terms of availability of data in the European CRE lending markets also relates, to a certain extent, to the heterogeneous nature of CRE loans in the European market, which ultimately makes the collection of information on a standardised basis difficult.

Thus, notwithstanding the fact that useful loan-level data are disclosed in the process of the securitisation of CRE loans in public CMBS transactions, the aforementioned heterogeneity present in the structure of CRE loans allows data to be collated in such a way that only a limited number of common variables across CMBS transactions can be observed and recorded, resulting in a relatively constrained dataset for quantitative analysis.

The lack of available data on CRE lending in Europe and the potential development of a CRE loan database, are considered in further detail in Chapter 21.

15.3.2   *Approach and analysis*

The analysis used herein employs a two-faceted approach:

(i)   **Quantitative Analysis**: employing available loan-level data (sourced from Trepp) from public European CMBS transactions, which allow inferences to be drawn in connection with drivers of credit performance. The data set analysed comprises in excess of 1,000 loans totalling c. €157.2 billion that were securitised in 184 European CMBS transactions in the period 2000–2013.[5]

(ii)   **Qualitative Analysis**: drawing upon the experience of restructuring and working out European CRE loans to draw further inferences in connection with drivers of credit performance.

The CRE loans included in the dataset are secured against underlying properties across 20 different European jurisdictions, with the main ones illustrated in Figure 11 below, by volume of origination:

---

[5]   Note that the dataset does not contain any loans that were originated in 2001, 2008, 2009 or 2010.

Figure 11: Distribution by jurisdiction

Source: Trepp, BofA Merrill Lynch Research

The CRE loans included in the data set are secured against different types of property, with office, mixed-use, retail and multifamily properties comprising the predominant majority by volume of origination as illustrated in Figure 12 below:

Figure 12: Distribution by property type

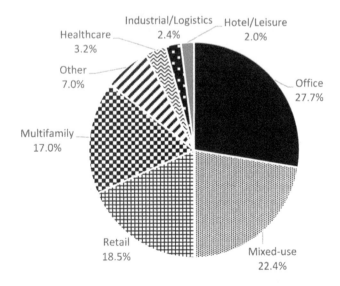

Source: Trepp, BofA Merrill Lynch Research

15.3.3 Level of losses and loss severity

Of all loans in the dataset, a loss has been determined for 150 of these, representing a c. 14.1% loss frequency by number of loans. In terms of volume, c. €157.2 billion of loans were originated in the reference period, with loans totalling c. €16.7 billion having suffered a loss and total losses amounting to c. €3.5 billion, representing a loss of c. 2.2% across all loans and a loss severity of c. 20.6% across loans that have suffered a loss. It is important to note that a 2.2% loss rate across loans in European CMBS is relatively small, when compared with the negative comments associated with CMBS transactions by the media and regulators. This is illustrated in Figure 13 below:

Figure 13: Volume of European CRE loan origination and losses

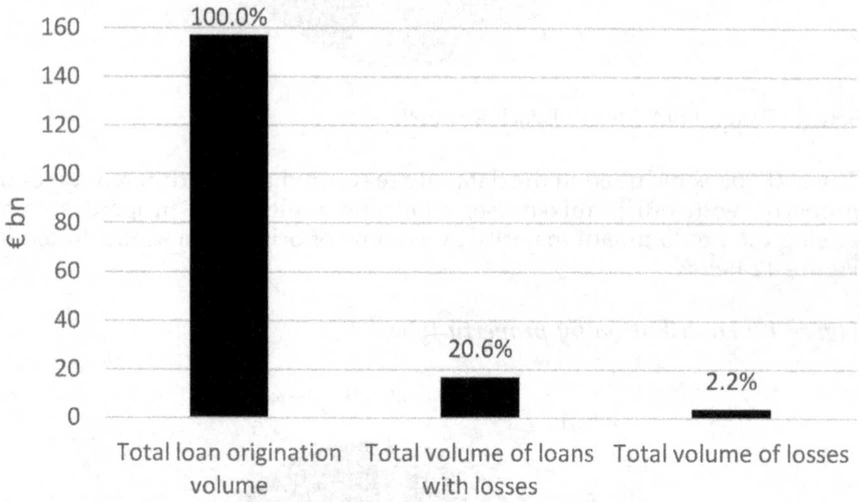

Source: Trepp BofA Merrill Lynch Research

15.3.4 Underwriting considerations and structuring drivers of credit performance

Underwriting considerations (including financial credit metrics) and structuring drivers aimed at mitigating credit risk, which are believed to be material to CRE loan performance, will now be identified and considered in turn.

15.3.4.1 Vintage

The date of origination of a loan relative to the timing of the real estate cycle was a crucial factor. As indicated below using evidence from the dataset, vintage i.e. the year in which CRE loans were originated, is a key driver of credit performance.

In the run up to the peak of the real estate cycle, lenders tend to be more aggressive in their underwriting and generate higher volumes of loans thus exacerbating the problems when the booming phase of the real estate cycle comes to an abrupt end. This is partly due to the business model and incentivisation schemes of lenders, making it difficult for them to turn off the tap, as discussed in further detail in Chapter 2.

Starting with loss frequency, in Figure 14 below, it may be seen that there is a clear trend from 2005 onwards, with loss frequency increasing steadily up to the peak of the market in 2006 and 2007.

Figure 14: Frequency of European CMBS losses by vintage

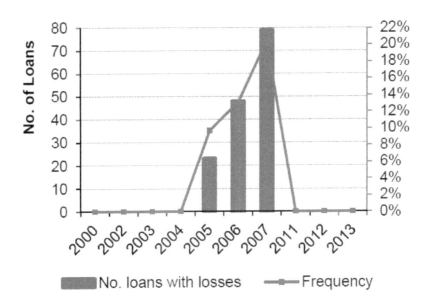

Source: Trepp, BofA Merrill Lynch Research

The trend is less pronounced when considering loss severity. Whilst there is a steady increase during the same period 2005–2007, loss severity as proportionate loss (relative to issuance volume) is not much higher in 2007 than in 2005.

Loss severity by amount of loss is quite different, with a pronounced pickup in losses from 2005 and peaking in 2007. See Figure 15 below.

Figure 15: Loan loss severity by vintage of European CMBS

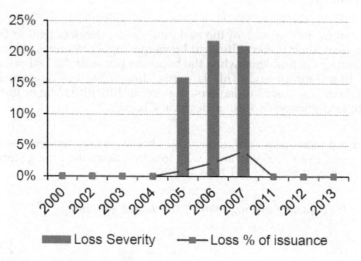

Source: Trepp, BofA Merrill Lynch Research

The corresponding booming phase of the real estate cycle (at least in the UK), is visible in Figure 16 below, which shows the evolution of UK CRE values during and subsequent to the GFC.

Figure 16: UK CRE values

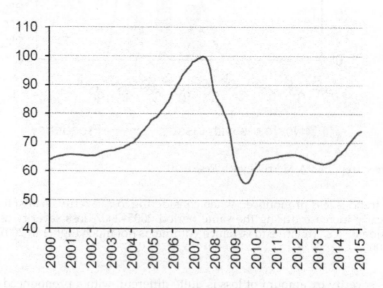

Source: IPD–Capital Growth All Property Index, BofA Merrill Lynch Research

15.3.4.2 Day-1 leverage

Day-1 leverage refers to the amount or proportion of debt that a lender will advance towards funding a particular CRE loan at the start of its term and is the single factor most reflective of the risk a CRE lender is exposed to. It will typically be driven by a number of factors, including the value of the underlying property, the expected quality and sustainability of cashflows both during the life of a loan and post maturity, location, property type, jurisdiction and the strength and incentivisation of the sponsor. The expected cashflows going forward (based on the assumptions made by the lender in deriving these) will predominantly determine the expected exit leverage, i.e. the amount or proportion of debt outstanding and due to the lender at the end of the CRE loan's term (maturity), and it is the exit leverage achievable on the basis of expected cashflows which typically drives a CRE lender's appetite for day-1 leverage, as the two are directly and inextricably linked.

Whilst, as discussed further in Chapter 4, the assumptions a lender will typically make in its underwriting and structuring processes are aimed at mitigating several risks, a big risk to mitigate is the refinancing/repayment risk present in a CRE loan. However, a number of risks are difficult to eliminate and not always easy to predict. This could be due to a change in market circumstances in the intervening period between the start of a CRE loan's term and its maturity, both in the property markets (cap rates, occupational lease demand, etc.) as well as the lending/finance markets (availability of debt, cost of capital, interest rates). It could also be due to property-specific factors, such as one of the key tenants entering insolvency and defaulting on its rental obligations under the lease or property obsolescence. The consequent implication of this is that the value of the property and therefore the amount or proportion of debt that can be refinanced or repaid at maturity is likely to be lower than that expected by the lender in their initial underwriting. Other things being equal, this lowers the ultimate amount recovered by either a refinancing of the CRE loan or a sale of the underlying property and implies that the higher the amount or proportion of debt at the specific point in time (which is directly correlated to the level of day-1 leverage), the higher the likelihood and therefore the higher the risk that the lender will suffer a loss. Lenders will factor in tenant quality, the strength of the location, current and future tenant demand and their perception of the status of the current real estate cycle, however, in a competitive market they will also be pushed hard by borrowers to be more aggressive and competitive.

To analyse the effect of day-1 leverage on credit performance, leverage from four different angles is considered: the loan-to-value (LTV) ratio, the interest coverage ratio (ICR), the debt service coverage ratio (DSCR) and the debt yield.

(i) Loan-to-value ratio

The LTV ratio provides an indication of leverage relative to the value of the underlying property and is calculated as the ratio of the outstanding balance of the CRE loan to the market value of the underlying property.

The deterioration in underwriting standards in the run-up to the GFC, as a result of the booming CRE markets in Europe and the competitive tension between CRE lenders at the time, is well publicised.

From the CMBS dataset this suggests that LTVs were relatively high in the European CRE lending markets even in the years prior to 2005. This is likely to be a feature of certain CMBS transactions as opposed to the wider lending market. The volume of CMBS transactions during this period was relatively low and with the ability to undertake credit-linked deals which appealed to CMBS investors, it was possible to achieve higher leverage in the CMBS markets in comparison to the bank market. See Figure 17 below.

Figure 17: Original LTV of securitised loans, as a percentage

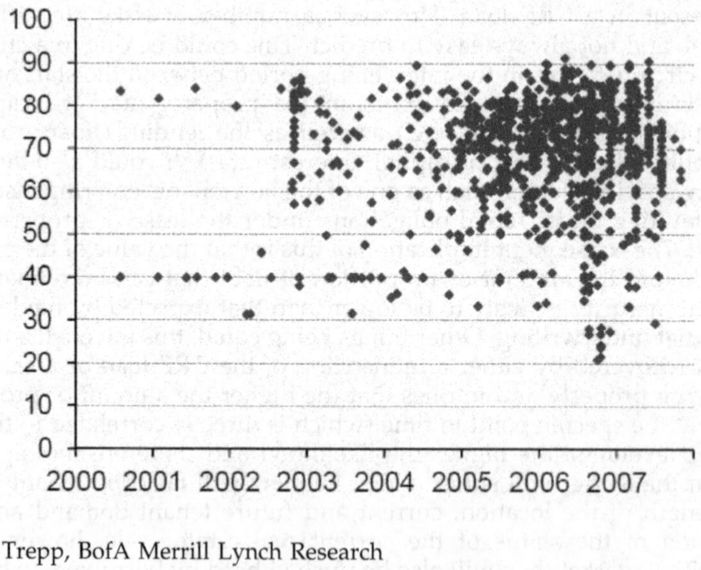

Source: Trepp, BofA Merrill Lynch Research

To facilitate the analysis of the day-1 LTV ratio as a driver of credit performance, in Figure 18 below, LTV brackets to aggregate all data points, starting at 20% and moving by increments of 10 percentage points have been created.

The frequency of losses (or loss rate) are considered, both in terms of the number of loans that have suffered losses, as well as the proportion of loans that have suffered losses, in each LTV bracket. The results are illustrated in Figure 18 below.

Figure 18: Frequency of losses by original LTV

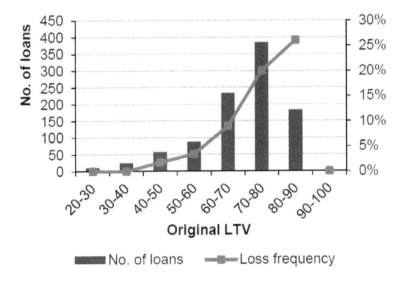

Source: Trepp, BofA Merrill Lynch Research

There is a very clear trend indicating that an increase in day-1 leverage, as measured by the LTV ratio, is correlated with an increased loss frequency. The loss frequency in terms of number of loans does not factor in the total number of loans originated in any particular LTV bracket, whilst the loss frequency as measured by the proportion of loans does, and therefore the latter could be considered a better measure of the loss frequency.

Further consideration is made in Figure 19 below to the loss severity by LTV. Whilst loss severity increases with LTV, the trend is weak due to a wide distribution of the data points (i.e. low correlation), which suggests that whilst a high LTV may result in a higher incidence of defaults, other factors may contribute to the level of loss in a more material way other than LTV.

Figure 19: Loss Severity by original LTV

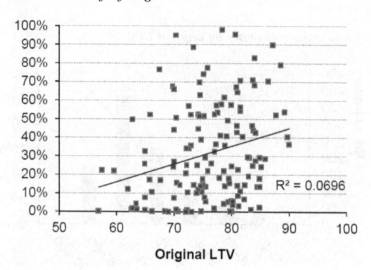

Source: Trepp, BofA Merrill Lynch Research

(ii) Interest coverage ratio (ICR)

The ICR provides an indication of leverage relative to the cashflows generated by the underlying property and is calculated as the ratio of total annual cashflows generated by the property (and available for debt servicing) to the annual interest payable on the CRE loan. A lower day-1 leverage leads to a higher ICR, suggesting a higher level of cashflow is available to meet interest payments on the loan throughout its term and a greater cushion to absorb any reductions in the cashflow generated by the underlying property whilst still meeting interest payments. As day-1 leverage increases, the ICR is reduced and a smaller reduction/stress is required in cashflows in order to create issues in interest payments on a CRE loan.

To facilitate the analysis of the day-1 ICR as a driver of credit performance, ICR brackets to aggregate all data points, starting at 1.0[6] have been created in Figure 20 below, utilising increments of 20 percentage points up to 2.5, along with an aggregate of all data points greater than 2.5 in one bracket, labelled "2.5+".

The frequency of losses (or loss rate), in terms of the number of loans that have suffered losses, are considered in each ICR bracket. The results are illustrated in Figure 20 below:

---

[6] There are no loans with an ICR lower than 1.00x in the dataset.

Figure 20: Distribution of losses by initial ICR

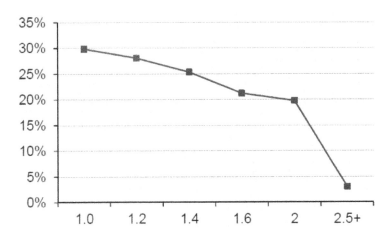

Source: Trepp, BofA Merrill Lynch Research

The results exhibit a relatively clear trend and supplement the position of many lenders today to be more cashflow-focused: an improvement in the day-1 ICR results in a lower frequency of losses. A cut-off point is visible: based on the underlying data, a day-1 ICR of 2.5 or greater seems to be the point beyond which CRE lenders are protected from negative credit performance.

The loss severity by ICR bracket is then considered, which in the same way as the LTV ratio, exhibits a weak trend due to a wide distribution. The results are illustrated in Figure 21 below.

The data again demonstrates that rather than showing that high ICR loans incur lower losses, it shows that high ICR loans are less likely to default during the term of a loan. Once a default occurs then other factors tend to apply to determine the level of loss.

Figure 21: Loss severity by original ICR

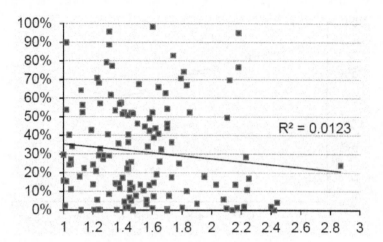

Source: Trepp, BofA Merrill Lynch Research

(iii) Debt service coverage ratio (DSCR)

Similar to the ICR, the DSCR provides an indication of leverage relative to the cashflows generated by the underlying property, however, the DSCR also takes into account the amortisation scheduled for payment during the term of a CRE Loan. The DSCR is calculated as the ratio of total annual cashflows generated by the property (and available for debt servicing) to the annual interest and amortisation (debt service) payable. For bullet CRE Loans with no amortisation during the term of the loan, the ICR and DSCR would be identical, whilst they will start deviating as amortisations starts being incorporated during the term of the CRE Loan.

A lower day-1 leverage leads to a higher DSCR, suggesting a higher level of cashflow is available to meet interest and amortisation payments on the loan throughout its term and a greater cushion to absorb any reductions in the cashflow generated by the underlying property whilst still meeting interest and amortisation payments. As day-1 leverage increases, the DSCR is reduced and a smaller reduction/stress is required in cashflows in order to create issues in meeting debt service on a CRE loan.

The dataset unfortunately does not measure DSCR levels for a sufficient number of loans to allow a quantitative analysis to be conducted in a similar fashion to that for the interest coverage ratio (ICR). However, during the relevant period under consideration, the majority of CRE loans originated in Europe were typically bullet loans or had low amortisation levels and on that basis it could reasonably be expected that the DSCR would mirror the results exhibited by the ICR (or be very similar). Therefore, in line with the

ICR, the DSCR would be expected to be a significant driver in the credit performance of CRE loans.

(iv) Debt yield

The debt yield is a financial metric that has more recently gained favour with lenders and now forms one of the key metrics to be considered in the underwriting process of a CRE loan as discussed in Chapter 4.

The debt yield is calculated as the ratio of total annual cashflows generated by the property (and available for debt servicing) to the principal balance of the CRE loan. The debt yield is a very useful metric in underwriting and structuring CRE loans, as it indicates two key parameters:

- The break-even interest rate that the underlying property can sustain for the amount of debt in question. The debt yield indicates how much scope there is for a potential rise in interest rates before a refinancing of the CRE loan (at current rental income levels) becomes restricted due to a rise in interest rates. This becomes particularly pertinent in the macroeconomic environment of extremely low interest rates (close to zero) that exists at the time of writing, whereby an increase in interest rates may be expected and lenders should factor this into their underwriting process.
- The break-even yield/cap rate that the underlying property can be sold at (at current rental income levels), in order to allow a full repayment of the CRE loan.[7] A comparison of the current property yield with the debt yield indicates the flexibility in yield-widening that may occur in the investment market, prior to the value of the under-lying property moving to a level which is below the balance of the CRE loan.

Higher debt yields for a given CRE loan therefore imply that there is less credit risk and this can be expected to be a material driver of the credit performance of European CRE loans. Amortisation or an improvement in rental levels would result in increasing debt yields over the life of a loan. It is a welcome development in European CRE lending that there is now a greater focus on debt yields both, day-1 and at loan maturity.

15.3.4.3 Amortisation

As discussed above, European CRE loans will typically have no or limited amortisation. The level of amortisation that is achievable will depend on the amount and quality of rental cashflows and whether the sponsor requires a cash yield on their investment.

---

[7] This assumes no sales costs or any other transaction costs. In practice, one must allow for *some* sales/transaction costs.

In situations where the borrower wishes a higher day-1 leverage, they are willing to forego a lower cash-on-cash return as a lender would require a commensurate increase in the rate (and therefore amount) of amortisation to reflect the higher credit risk.

Amortisation may have a considerable effect in the ultimate determination of credit performance of a CRE loan but much depends on the nature of the underlying properties. Loans secured on higher-yielding properties in secondary locations will typically necessitate higher levels of amortisation depending on day-1 leverage. Loans on higher quality properties may have higher LTVs but the amortisation may be limited due to the level of sustainable cashflow and an underwriting opinion that there is less repayment/refinancing risk.

At the 2007 peak of the market, a large volume of loans did not feature any amortisation. The subsequent drop in market values of European CRE provided the classic example of an increasing refinancing/repayment risk as such CRE loans approached maturity.

15.3.4.4 Loan Term

Many lenders pre-GFC had a typical loan term of five to seven years rather than geared to the specificity of the underlying real estate, the valuation of the properties on a longer-term basis or the business plan of the sponsor.

The peak of originations in 2006–2007 also resulted in many loans maturing at a time when debt capacity in the UK was very limited (2011–2014) resulting in a much higher default rate. In the US, most loans had a 10-year term (fixed rate market) resulting in many loans maturing in 2016–2017 when the debt markets are better positioned to provide the debt capacity necessary to refinance a large volume of loans.

The term remaining under the leases of the underlying property is an important factor in the underwriting process of a CRE loan. As discussed in Chapter 4, the weighted average unexpired lease term (WAULT) is the remaining term of the various leases, weighted by the rental income generated under each lease and is therefore a representative measure of the average remaining lease term for the entire underlying property. As well as WAULT, the granularity and diversity of leases, the credit quality of the larger tenants, and the location of a property will all be factors that determine how a lender will underwrite the sustainability of cashflows.

Most lenders focus on valuations at the outset of the loan and aim to de-leverage the loan based on this valuation as opposed to the potential valuation on maturity of the loan. Whilst difficult to do, lenders should focus more on the long term sustainable value of the underlying property factoring in where appropriate the business plan initiatives of the sponsor, with appropriate assumptions. See further Chapter 4.

In addition, the business plan of the sponsor should play an important function in determining the loan term especially if the properties need to be repositioned, improved, re-let or sold as part of a business plan. In practice, very few loan terms were based around the business plan of the borrower with a de facto five to seven year term being utilised in the vast majority of loans. A term driven more by the specifics of the underlying real estate may incentivise borrowers to meet their business plans more pro-actively. Equally, looking at longer terms on a lower leverage basis and on a long term sustainable valuation basis may smooth out some of the stresses caused by real estate lenders.

15.3.4.5 Financial covenants

A financial covenant will be used in the underwriting and structuring phases of a CRE loan to define maximum or minimum criteria in relation to certain parameters/metrics—these will typically comprise the LTV ratio and ICR. Sometimes they will also encompass other parameters/financial metrics such as the DSCR or debt yield. A breach of a financial covenant would typically be defined to constitute an event of default under the relevant loan documentation.

Alternatively, (additional) financial covenants could also be set to trigger a feature or event which is different from an event of default. The use of financial covenants, as a trigger of an event of default allows the lender to detect and mitigate the potential deterioration in the performance of a CRE loan.

Covenant-light loans (i.e. loans with limited financial covenants, in particular LTV covenants) became more common in the European CRE finance markets in 2005–2007 especially in CMBS lending, as rating agencies gave limited credit for LTV covenants. The subsequent deterioration in the performance and market values of European CRE during the downturn immediately following this period, often resulted in sponsors of the equity interests in properties owning positions which were effectively out of the money but with no ability for the lender to take enforcement action or to incentivise the borrower to pay down part of the loan.

15.3.4.6 Lender-instructed Valuations

Valuations are an essential tool in assessing the credit risk on a loan, both at the outset and on an ongoing basis. They provide important information in relation to the level of leverage and implied equity in a deal, and the quality, marketability, performance and suitability of the underlying real estate collateral as well as important market data on comparables.

The LTV ratio calculated for the purposes of testing the relevant financial covenant, will typically be done so with reference to the most recent valuation that exists, in relation to the underlying property.

Valuations are, however, not always an exact science and there will always be a certain degree of variation between different valuers. Lenders have sometimes historically accepted the practice by borrowers of "valuation shopping" where borrowers select and present their choice of valuer at the outset who they know will give the highest potential valuation. The borrower may also have the ability to select and instruct the valuer of their choice on future valuations. This may have had a role to play in the valuation negligence cases seen in the market in 2015–2016 and discussed further in Chapter 13.

Lenders should therefore provide in the relevant loan documentation that an independent valuation of the lender's choice can be instructed on an annual basis by the lender at the cost of the borrower—this allows at least annual valuations to be produced at no cost to the lender and the relevant LTV ratio calculation to be fairly reflective of the true leverage in any CRE loan.

Lenders should also differentiate between real cash equity and soft equity as a result of increased valuations of the underlying real estate. By the time refinancings were being completed from 2005 onwards, sponsors had very little or no cash equity left in deals, thus impacting incentivisation when loans defaulted at a later date.

15.3.4.7 *Portfolios: release pricing*

Whenever a lender finances a CRE portfolio, the sponsor of the equity interest in the underlying properties often likes to retain the flexibility to dispose of individual properties. To facilitate this, during the underwriting and structuring phases of a CRE loan, the lender will allocate the total CRE loan amount for the relevant portfolio across the individual properties, typically on a uniform basis using the market value of each property (giving rise to the allocated loan amount or ALA, for each property). The lender will assign release pricing to each property (as a proportion of each particular property's ALA) which will define that proportion/amount of the total CRE loan amount that the sponsor would need to repay in order for the lender to release the security related to that property only and allow its disposal.

Of course the lender would be wise not to release the relevant security for an individual property unless the corresponding amount of debt, i.e. the ALA, at a minimum, was repaid. The release pricing should therefore always be a function which is 100% or greater of the ALA for the particular property.

The credit risk here relates to the quality of the underlying properties in a relative context, i.e. compared to the other underlying properties in the portfolio. To the extent that the quality of the underlying properties differs across the portfolio, to avoid "cherry-picking" by the borrower whereby they sell the better properties first, lenders will have higher release pricing for better quality properties.

352

The level at which release pricing is set for individual property disposals, is quite material in the credit performance of European CRE loans financing portfolios—release pricing should be set at appropriately high levels for higher-quality properties.

15.3.4.8 Property Type

The main property types that senior lenders will typically finance, often referred to as the "core" property types, are office, industrial/warehouse and retail properties. These have been the traditional, mainstream property types classed under investment properties. There are also other types of property, classed as operating properties, where the cashflow is not generated through the traditional tenant-lease structure but through the revenue of the underlying business being operated in the property (although these could take the form of an OpCo/PropCo structure whereby a lease would be created). Operating properties would predominantly include hotels, healthcare properties (e.g. hospitals, nursing homes) student accommodation and multifamily properties. Senior lenders would typically have restrictions in place in relation to operating properties and would only be willing to finance certain sub-categories (e.g. hotel or where there is a lease in place to the operator). There are other lenders who specialise in operating properties and would look at all or some sub-categories.

To analyse the property type as a potential driver of credit performance, the frequency of losses (or loss rate), both in terms of the number of loans that have suffered losses, as well as the proportion of loans that have suffered losses, for each property type are considered in Figure 22 below:

Figure 22: Frequency of European CMBS loan losses by property type

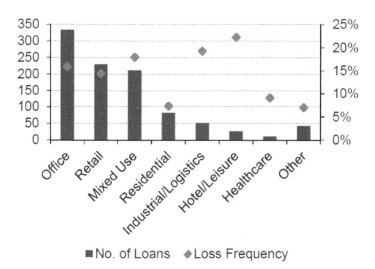

No. of Loans ◆ Loss Frequency

Source: Trepp, BofA Merrill Lynch Research

A consideration of the frequency of losses reveals some differences across different property types, when measured using the proportion of loans that have suffered a loss in any particular category. The hotel/leisure category stands out with the highest proportion of loans that have suffered a loss (just over 20%). Industrial/Logistics properties, mixed-use, office and retail properties follow within a 5% loss frequency band, between 15% and 20%. Healthcare, multifamily and other properties seem to perform better than the rest, with a loss frequency of under 10%.

When measured using the number of loans that have suffered losses in any particular category, the results for loss frequency are inconsistent, with a much higher number of loans suffering losses for office, retail and mixed-use properties. This is likely due to the much larger number of loans originated in these categories relative to the rest and this cannot therefore be treated as evidence to contradict the loss frequency by proportion of loans that have suffered a loss.

The loss severity by property type is then considered, both in terms of the actual amount of loss crystallised as well as the proportion of losses crystallised relative to the total volume of loans originated, in each category. The results are illustrated in Figure 23 below:

Figure 23: European CMBS loan loss severity by property type

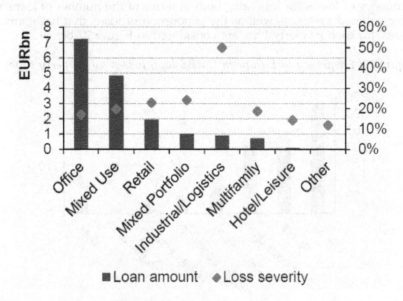

■Loan amount ◆Loss severity

Source: Trepp, BofA Merrill Lynch Research

The loss severity, when measured by the proportion of losses suffered in a particular property category relative to the total volume of loans originated, indicates that industrial/logistics properties exhibit the worst credit performance with a loss severity of c. 50%. The remaining property types follow at a distance, within a c. 15% band. Loss severity by absolute amount of loss suffered is not as accurate, predominantly due to the very large differences in total origination volumes across the various property types as illustrated in Figure 12 above.

15.3.4.9   Jurisdiction of underlying properties

It is perfectly rational to expect that the credit performance of loans is, other things being equal, best in the most creditor-friendly jurisdictions, such as the UK and the Netherlands, and deteriorates across the spectrum to less creditor-friendly jurisdictions such as Spain and Italy. At least, this would be expected to be the case when considering losses or recoveries as a measure of credit performance.

The frequency of losses (or loss rate), both in terms of the number of loans that have suffered losses, as well as the proportion of loans that have suffered losses, in each jurisdiction are considered in Figure 24 below:

Figure 24: Frequency of European CMBS loan losses by jurisdiction

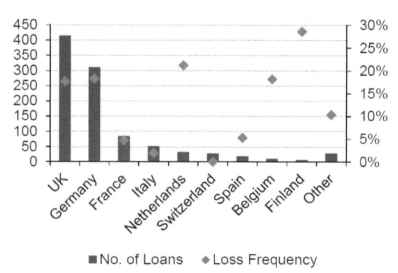

Source: Trepp, BofA Merrill Lynch Research

The results are unexpected and quite unintuitive, with the Netherlands and the UK, two of the most creditor-friendly jurisdictions in Europe showing a higher frequency of losses than most of the other European jurisdictions, including Spain and Italy. The spike in frequency of losses for the UK when measured by the actual number of loans that have suffered a loss is very likely due to the much larger number of observations in the dataset for loans originated in this jurisdiction relative to the rest. The very different number and volume of loans originated across different jurisdictions leads to a dataset which is less reliable, than if there had been a higher minimum number or volume of origination across all jurisdictions, as outliers currently skew the results substantially for jurisdictions with a very small number of loans (and volume).

The loss severity both in terms of the actual amount of loss crystallised as well as the proportion of losses crystallised relative to the total volume of loans originated, in each jurisdiction is considered in Figure 25 below:

Figure 25: European CMBS loan loss severity by country

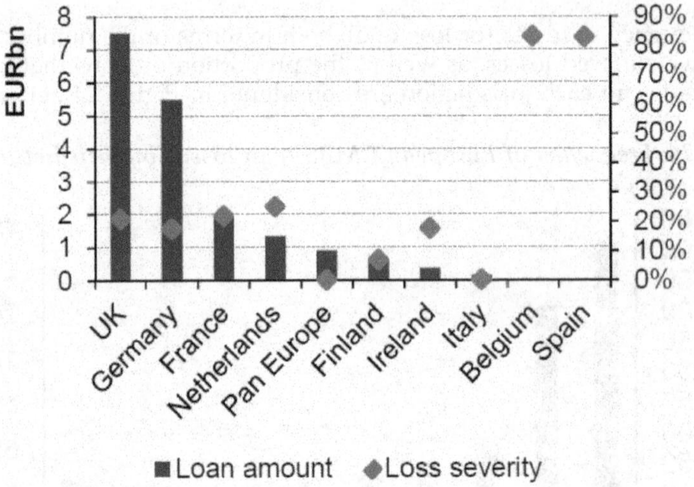

Source: Trepp, BofA Merrill Lynch Research

When considering loss severity across jurisdictions the results are slightly more intuitive. Disregarding Belgium, due to the small number of observations, Spain is the jurisdiction with the highest loss severity (measured by proportion of losses relative to total volume of loans originated per jurisdiction), consistent with the respective protracted regime in relation to enforcement. Again, the relatively high loss severity in the UK and the Netherlands are unexpected, in the context of other less creditor-friendly jurisdictions. However, results may still be distorted due to the very large differences in total origination volumes across the various jurisdictions as illustrated in Figure 11 above.

15.4 Conclusion

As alluded to a number of times in this Chapter, the dataset available to conduct meaningful quantitative analysis is quite limited, due to the private nature and information asymmetry of the European CRE finance markets. The dataset is therefore limited only to CRE loans that were securitised in public CMBS transactions, with the consequent implications that this has on the number of variables observed, but also the relevant period for which data is available.

The analysis allows the following conclusions to be drawn:

- Vintage, as an indicator of the stage of the real estate cycle, is a key driver of credit performance—the predominant majority of losses in the dataset occurred across loans that were securitised in the 2005–2007 vintage.
- The ICR, as a measure of day-1 leverage, is a key indicator of the likelihood of a CRE loan having a default throughout the term—CRE loans with an ICR greater than 2.5 seem to be cushioned sufficiently against a default during the term of a loan. However, other factors are more likely to determine the level of loss once a default has occurred.
- The LTV ratio, another measure of day-1 leverage, whilst also being a key indicator of the likelihood of a default on a CRE loan, also does not seem to play a material role in the amount or proportion of losses, which again suggests that other factors specific to each loan influence the amount or proportion of losses.
- Loans secured against hotel/leisure properties experienced the highest incidence of defaults, closely followed by industrial/logistics properties. In terms of actual loss crystallised upon occurrence of a default, loans secured against industrial/logistics properties suffered the worst losses by far, at c. 50% of the balance of such loans originated.
- Surprisingly, contrary to common expectation, the dataset indicates that the jurisdiction of the underlying properties is not a key factor in the determination of credit performance, but this is likely to be linked to limitations of the underlying CMBS dataset.

The dataset employed in preparing this Chapter predominantly relates to CRE loans that were securitised in public CMBS transactions and does not allow a direct comparison to be made in terms of credit performance between those CRE loans that ended up being securitised and those that ended up being syndicated and/or remained on banks' balance sheets. In that respect, there may ultimately be a bias in the analysis set out in this Chapter, however, it is believed that this would not change the conclusions reached regarding the key drivers of credit performance for CRE loans materially.

Chapter 16

The Current Regulatory Environment for CRE Finance

Peter Cosmetatos,

CEO CREFC Europe

Stephen Moller,

Partner, K&L Gates LLP

16.1 Introduction

In the aftermath of the GFC, there was a near universal realisation amongst regulators, market participants and the general public that "excessive and imprudent risk-taking in the banking sector"[1] had to be curbed in order to protect the solvency of individual financial institutions and reduce systemic risk. That realisation led to a sustained wave of new regulation which, at the time of writing, continues across a range of areas relevant to CRE finance, including the capital treatment of CRE loan exposures, the regulatory treatment of CMBS and other forms of securitisation, risk mitigation and clearing in relation to derivatives and the regulation of alternative investment funds.

However, the reduction of systemic risk is not the only policy objective of financial supervision. Bank lending has an important role to play in strengthening the economy and stimulating investment, an objective which is now the European Commission's top priority according to the Capital Markets Union Action Plan published last year. Regulators face a challenge in reconciling these two potentially conflicting objectives. The industry itself is only gradually beginning to assess and articulate the positive contribution of CRE finance to the economy and as an investable asset class.[2]

---

[1] The opening recital of Directive 2010/76/EU of the European Parliament and of the Council of 24 November 2010 (CRD III): "Excessive and imprudent risk-taking in the banking sector has led to the failure of individual financial institutions and systemic problems in Member States and globally."

[2] See for example *Commercial Real Estate Debt and the European Economy,* a 2016 report jointly commissioned by the Association of Property Lenders, CREFC Europe, INREV and ZIA, the German Property Federation (*http://www.crefceurope.org/wp-content/uploads/2016/07/CRE-Debt-in-the-European-Economy-2016.pdf* [Accessed 11 August 2016]).

A brief word on Brexit: the consequences of the UK's decision to leave the EU on the CRE finance market in the UK, and indeed the rest of Europe, are imponderable. For the time being, the UK remains a member of the EU and EU regulation remains applicable in the UK at least until the date of the UK's departure. This Chapter therefore considers the regulatory framework as it stands at the time of writing, as it cannot, as noted in the preface to this book, predict the future.

16.2   The commercial context

In order to understand how the post GFC regulatory agenda has affected the CRE finance market, it is necessary to go back to the years before the GFC. As discussed in the opening Chapters of this book, real estate debt played an important part in the boom leading up to the peak of the market in mid-2007 as values were driven ever higher by plentiful, cheap and often indiscriminate credit. The GFC precipitated a traumatic market collapse. Spring 2009 is widely regarded as the trough, following value falls of around 45% across UK CRE in less than two years—but anecdotal evidence and some data sources suggest that secondary property continued to fall until 2013, with the initial recovery largely limited in the UK to prime property in central London and a few other major centres.

A defining feature of the European CRE debt landscape before the crisis was a lack of diversity in financing sources. According to the *De Montford Report*, the share of UK banks and building societies in new UK origination averaged almost 58% between 1999 and 2007, with the balance shared between German, North American and other international banks. So few non-banks were active in the market before 2012 that they were not even identified as a separate category. While no comparable data source exists for the rest of Europe, it seems clear that CRE lending risk was similarly concentrated within the banking system. See the previous Chapter where the *De Montford Report* is discussed further.

The early stages of the property recovery that began in mid-2009 were largely driven by equity buyers who did not need debt. However, from around 2012, changes in the composition and structure of the CRE lending market began to emerge, as retreating banks created space for non-bank lenders. As discussed in Chapters 1 and 15, the latest De Montfort University research at the time of writing, suggests that around a quarter of new lending is now accounted for by non-banks, while the share of UK banks and building societies has fallen to around a third of the total.

Increased regulation has not been the only reason for the decline in the banks' share of the CRE finance market. Quantitative easing and a pro-tracted low interest rate environment (see Chapter 12) have also played a part by making real estate debt, with its illiquidity premium and broad risk spectrum, more attractive to fixed income investors and funds. However, it is clear that regulation (and capital requirements in particular) have played a part in reducing the capacity of the banks to lend.[3] Furthermore, as the following sections of this Chapter will attempt to show, bank regulatory capital rules discourage banks from making CRE loans or investing in CMBS transactions and the solvency capital framework for insurers under Solvency II has tended to push insurance companies and pension funds away from CMBS transactions and into direct CRE lending.

16.3   Bank regulatory capital

The global framework for bank capital adequacy is based on rules promulgated by the Basel Committee for Banking Supervision (the Basel Committee or BCBS). At the heart of the Basel Committee's rules is the concept of the capital ratio: the ratio between a bank's capital base and the aggregate amount of its risk weighted assets and off balance sheet exposures. This ratio must be at least 8%, although national regulators will often specify a higher percentage.

The 8% minimum requirement has remained constant since 1988 when the first version of the Basel Accord was introduced. However, the way in which the capital ratio is calculated has developed over time, most notably with the publication of Basel II in 2004. Basel II introduced a much more nuanced methodology for assessing the risk weights associated with assets, particularly for banks deemed sophisticated enough to rely upon their own credit models in assessing risk for regulatory purposes (i.e. banks which used the "internal risk-based approach" or IRB as opposed to the "Standardised Approach" used by other banks). Basel II went a long way to correct the perverse incentive created by Basel I for banks to invest in risky assets (under Basel I a high yielding corporate exposure had the same risk weight as an investment grade corporate exposure). However, Basel II's more sophisticated approach to risk weighting had the unfortunate side-effect of allowing banks to dramatically increase their exposure to assets with a low-risk weighting (which was not always an accurate indicator of economic risk), becoming highly leveraged in the process and often dependent upon short-term debt to finance illiquid assets. This phenomenon was central to the demise of a number of institutions including Lehman Brothers and Northern Rock as referred to in the second edition of this book.

Following the GFC, Basel II (which is now implemented in Europe by the CRR[4] and CRD IV[5]) tightened up the regulatory capital regime in two

---

[3]   In 2015, the EU Commission conducted a public consultation on the impact of bank capital requirements. All respondents from the banking industry argued that capital requirements had tended to reduce their ability to lend.

[4]   The Capital Requirements Regulation: Regulation (EU) No 5152013.

[5]   The Capital Requirements Directive IV Directive 2013/36/EU.

principal ways. Firstly, the rules on how to measure capital have become more stringent and the capital ratio has been supplemented by additional rules relating to leverage and liquidity; secondly, the risk weighting attached to certain asset classes has increased (in a way which disincentives CRE exposures). Both of these aspects are considered in more detail below.

16.4   Increased bank capital requirements, leverage and liquidity

Basel III tightens the requirements for balance sheet items to be recognised as regulatory capital and increases the amount of capital which banks are required to hold. While the minimum capital ratio remains at 8%, the capital must be of a higher quality: the minimum requirement for common equity rises from 2% to 4.5% and the minimum requirement for Tier 1 capital as a whole rises from 4% to 6%. Globally systemically important financial institutions (G-SIFIs) will be required to maintain additional amounts of common equity of between 1 and 3.5%. Basel III also introduces a new "capital conservation buffer" which restricts the ability of banks to pay dividends if their common equity ratio is less than 7% and a new "countercyclical capital buffer" which is designed to ensure that banks retain profit in good times to cover potential losses in a downturn.

Basel III also introduces a leverage ratio and two new liquidity tests to supplement the capital ratio. The liquidity coverage ratio requires banks to hold sufficient liquid assets which are unencumbered and are of sufficiently high credit quality to meet net cash outgoings during a 30 day stress scenario. The net stable funding ratio measures the amount of funding which is deemed to be dependable over a one year period against the required amount of funding which is calculated to take account of the liquidity and residual maturity of the bank's assets.

The overall capacity of banks to lend and to make other investments is therefore reduced compared with the position pre-GFC.

16.5   Bank regulatory capital treatment of CRE loans

The Basel II framework recognised that certain exposure categories presented data and modelling challenges that may make the IRB approach difficult or impossible to apply. These exposure categories are referred to as specialised lending exposures (SLEs) and include secured real estate lending (income-producing real estate or IPRE exposures). In relation to SLEs, Basel II provided a compromise solution, commonly referred to as "slotting", that introduced a modest degree of risk sensitivity for cases where the regulator of an IRB bank is not able to approve an IRB model for SLEs.

By around 2012, the UK regulator had concluded that no UK bank had data and a model of sufficient quality to gain approval for an IRB approach for its IPRE lending. All UK regulated IRB banks would therefore have to use slotting to risk weight their UK IPRE exposures. Anecdotally, it seems that little attention was initially devoted to examining how slotting might work in practice because most banks expected to use it fleetingly if at all, on their way to the more sophisticated world of internal risk models. Importantly, overseas banks operating through a UK branch are subject to supervision by their home regulator in relation to capital adequacy—and many other national regulators proved willing to approve the use of internal models for IPRE exposures by their banks (including, no doubt in circumstances that may not have passed muster in the UK).

The slotting approach requires banks to assess a loan against a number of different criteria to determine its risk weight. Both under the CRR and specifically in the UK, the criteria for assigning risk weights to IPRE exposures are organised under five "factors": financial strength, cashflow predictability, asset characteristics, strength of sponsor/developer and the security package. Each factor is broken down further into a number of 'sub-factors' (for example, for asset characteristics, the relevant sub-factors are: location, design and condition and property is under construction).[6] For each sub-factor, the bank must assign a grade from "strong" to "weak" according to specified assessment criteria (for example, in relation to location, the statement "Property is located in highly desirable location that is convenient to services that tenants desire" must be true in order to rate the asset as "strong").

The risk weighting and loss expectancy for each asset are determined on the basis of tables which take account of the overall categorisation of the asset as "strong", "good", "satisfactory", "weak" or defaulted and, for "strong" and "good" exposures, whether or not its remaining maturity is less than 2.5 years. For example, an asset which is rated as "good" and which has a remaining maturity of less than 2.5 years will be risk weighted at 50% and an asset which is "weak" will be risk weighted at 250%.

The risk weight attached to a CRE loan can be significantly higher under the slotting approach than under the IRB approach. That is particularly so for loans with strong credit characteristics, because the UK guidance indicates that "strong" "broadly corresponds" to the range of external credit

---

[6] Under the CRR, this factor is identified as "transaction/asset characteristics" and includes (under final draft regulatory technical standards published by the European Banking Authority in 2016) an additional sub-factor on financial structure which is not included in the corresponding UK framework. There are other variations at the sub-factor level. The EBA RTS can be found at *https://www.eba.europa.eu/documents* and the relevant UK provisions can be found in BIPRU 4 Annex 1 Table 2, at *https://www.handbook.fca.org.uk/handbook/BIPRU/4/Annex1.html#D2268* [Accessed 11 August 2016].

assessments of BBB- or better, which covers a very broad range of risks.[7] For example, a low LTV loan with a maturity of seven years which is rated "strong" would be risk weighted at 70% under the slotting approach, but could be risk weighted at as little at 15% using the A-IRB approach (i.e. the advanced variant of the IRB approach).

The use of slotting by UK banks gives a competitive edge to non-UK banks using the IRB approach and indeed non-banks seeking debt exposure to UK CRE. It also incentivises UK banks to finance other classes of asset which are eligible for the IRB approach or which have otherwise preferential risk weights in place of CRE assets.

16.6   Bank regulatory capital treatment of CMBS exposures

As discussed further in the following Chapter, CMBS transactions fall within the definition of "securitisation" for the purpose of the CRR and are treated accordingly from a regulatory capital perspective. In determining capital requirements for CMBS transactions and other securitisations, the CRR draws a distinction between the bank which acts as the originator and banks which are simply third party investors. In broad terms, a bank which is the originator in a true sale securitisation can treat securitised exposures as having been transferred to third parties if it achieves a transfer of "significant credit risk". For third party investor banks using the Standardised Approach, investment in CMBS is either the same or worse from a capital requirement perspective as investing in equivalently rated corporate debt of the same maturity. For example, at credit quality step 4 (which equates to a long term rating of BB+ to BB by S&P) corporate debt is risk weighted at 100%. A CMBS transaction (or another type of securitisation) with a credit quality step of 4 will be risk weighted at 350%. Re-securitisations, such as CDOs containing CMBS assets, suffer significantly tougher treatment at all levels of credit quality, with a re-securitisation transaction rated at credit quality step 4 attracting a risk weight of 650%. In contrast, covered bonds enjoy better risk weights than equivalently rated corporate debt: at credit quality step 4 covered bonds are risk weighted at 50%.

Banks investing as third parties in CMBS transactions and other securitisation transactions must ensure that such transactions comply with the "skin in the game" 5% risk retention required by art.405 of the CRR and the due diligence provisions of art.406 which require them to have a comprehensive and thorough understanding of each of their individual securitisation positions and to have formal procedures for analysing and recording various due diligence issues. The provisions of art.405 and the potential difficulties encountered in applying those provisions to structured CRE transactions are examined in detail in the following Chapter.

---

[7]   See BIPRU 4.5.11 (*https://www.handbook.fca.org.uk/handbook/BIPRU/4/5.html* [Accessed 11 August 2016]).

In general, the regulators' attitude to securitisation has softened in the years following the GFC.[8] By late 2015, the drive to rehabilitate "simple, transparent and standardised" (STS) securitisation had become one of the main planks of the European Commission's Capital Markets Union (CMU) initiative.[9] However, CMBS has not benefited from this trend in the way that other asset classes have.

Of particular importance in this context is the draft regulation published by the European Commission in September 2015 to create a European framework for STS securitisation (the "Securitisation Regulation"). Assuming it comes into law, the Securitisation Regulation will (among other things) establish the criteria for recognising securitisation transactions as STS securitisations which will be subject to more favourable bank regulatory capital treatment than other securitisations. The criteria effectively prevent any CMBS transaction from qualifying as an STS securitisation, because, amongst other reasons, CMBS transactions are subject to re-financing risk (they are not self-amortising) and in practice will not meet the concentration condition (i.e. that no one exposure represents more than 1% of the securitised pool).[10] This is a further disincentive for banks considering investing in third party CMBS transactions.

As of July 2016, the Securitisation Regulation remains in draft and is subject to further change. It is worth noting that a number of significant changes to the draft Securitisation Regulation have been proposed in the European Parliament, but if anything those changes will make securitisation transactions (including CMBS) even more difficult to accomplish going forward. It is also likely that the UK's decision to leave the EU will significantly weaken the political determination and technical capability for successful implementation of this component of CMU.

16.7 Future Developments: The Basel Committee's proposals in relation to CRE debt

In two separate sets of proposals (published sequentially rather than at the same time), the BCBS has outlined dramatic changes for (among other things) the treatment of CRE debt on bank balance sheets. The first set of

---

[8] One of the early signs that securitisation may have a positive role to play in the financial system came in September 2012, when a European Commission letter asked EIOPA, the insurance and pensions regulator, to reconsider the Solvency II calibrations for securitisation in some contexts: *http://ec.europa.eu/finance/insurance/docs/solvency/20120926-letter-faull_en.pdf* [Accessed 11 August 2016].

[9] See *http://europa.eu/rapid/press-release_IP-15-5731_en.htm?locale=en* [Accessed 11 August 2016].

[10] More information on why the evolving STS criteria cater poorly for CRE debt securitisation is available here: *http://www.crefceurope.org/wp-content/uploads/2016/05/CREFC-Europe-key-policy-points-on-qualifying-securitisation-and-CMBS-April-2016.pdf.* [Accessed 11 August 2016].

proposals is for revisions to the Standardised Approach; the second signals a sharp turn away from the use of internal models.[11] There is much to be said for these proposals, but they also contain significant weaknesses.

In relation to CRE lending, the Standardised Approach, at the time of writing, lacks risk sensitivity and so fails to ensure that higher-risk loans are backed by a suitable amount of regulatory capital. The BCBS has proposed revisions to the Standardised Approach that, among other things, would introduce a limited amount of risk sensitivity, moving from (broadly speaking) a single risk weighting of 100% for CRE lending to three different risk weightings:

- 80% for loans with an LTV of no more than 60%;
- 100% for loans with an LTV of more than 60% but no more than 80%; and
- 130% for loans with an LTV of more than 80%.

Some risk sensitivity is certainly better than no risk sensitivity. But these proposals are not unproblematic.

- The above risk weights apply specifically to CRE exposures where repayment is materially dependent on cashflows generated by the property. Generally lower risk weights apply to residential real estate, to CRE exposures where repayment is not materially dependent on the cash flows generated by the property, and to unsecured corporate exposures. It is not at all clear how strong the evidence base for this approach is. The performance of loans secured on investment CRE assets is highly correlated to the CRE cycle, but while that can mean poor performance after a CRE market crash, it is important to recognise the strong performance during the rest of the cycle, and the breadth of the CRE lending risk spectrum.
- Reliance on market value-based LTV alone is dangerously pro-cyclical, even if the property is required to be "appraised independently using prudently conservative valuation criteria", as proposed. It seems especially crude to contemplate no lower risk bracket than for LTVs of up to 60%; and a risk weighting of 130% arguably seems low for loans at LTVs higher than 80%. Chapter 21 discusses a UK industry recommendation for how this concern might be addressed.
- The proposals contemplate a single 150% risk weighting (with no risk sensitivity) for land acquisition, development and construction loans. It is true that such lending is generally riskier (and therefore more specialised) than lending against income-producing CRE. But, as with income-producing CRE, it is possible to limit risk very significantly, or to accept very high levels of risk. A single risk weighting removes any regulatory incentive to mitigate risk. By failing to ensure adequate

---

[11] See *http://www.bis.org/bcbs/publ/d347.htm* [Accessed 11 August 2016] and *http://www.bis.org/bcbs/publ/d362.htm* [Accessed 11 August 2016] respectively.

capital supports the riskiest loans, it may instead lead to adverse selection, as banks can achieve better returns on regulatory capital at the riskier end of the spectrum.

Shortly after its consultation on revisions to the Standardised Approach closed in March 2016, the BCBS published a new consultation on reducing variation in credit risk weighted assets. In important respects, this consultation marks a change from the course set by Basel II[12] which had encouraged banks to improve the sophistication with which they model risk (and the quality of the data their models rely on), allowing improved alignment of regulatory capital requirements with modelled economic risk. Now the BCBS proposes to constrain the use of internal model approaches. Specifically in relation to loans secured on income-producing CRE, models would no longer be allowed to be used, so IRB banks would have to use slotting.

This move would clearly go a long way to levelling an uneven playing field. In the UK market, for example, all banks would use either the revised Standardised Approach or slotting, removing the significant advantage enjoyed (especially for low-risk lending) at the time of writing, by overseas IRB banks with approval for an internal model for their IPRE exposures. But that step forward lays bare both the main weakness the two approaches share, and the odd inconsistencies between them:

- Neither approach caters for (or rewards) very low-risk lending. That may not be an insurmountable problem for large, prime assets where client relationships or prestige might justify bank lending, other sources of capital (debt and equity) are likely to be available, and loans are relatively easy to distribute (chiefly, in the post-crisis environment, through the syndication market). It may be far more problematic for smaller ticket and regional loans where banks may be a critical source of capital and distribution would require a functioning conduit securitisation market or similar.
- Neither approach encourages banks to focus on CRE cycle risk, even though the evidence suggests that is the best indicator of portfolio-level and macro-prudential risk. The move away from models could undermine efforts to collect better CRE loan performance data, a setback for anyone seeking a better understanding of CRE lending risk, including micro and macro prudential regulators. It will be an unfortunate irony if the regulatory response to inadequate data and inconsistent and unreliable risk models is to remove the clearest incentive to address those problems. Chapter 21 explores a UK industry recommendation for tackling the persistent informational deficit in CRE debt markets.

---

[12] The change of course is so striking that these proposals are often referred to as "Basel IV", notwithstanding that the BCBS rejects that branding.

- The different risk weighting methodologies under the two approaches could create arbitrage risk, with Standardised Approach banks motivated solely by LTV and IRB banks using a long list of defined criteria to assign risk weights. The problem could be compounded by the fact that the highest risk weights are so different, at 130% for Standardised Approach banks and 250% for IRB banks.

A few months before the BCBS published its proposals for mandating the use of slotting for all SLEs of IRB banks, the European Banking Authority launched a consultation on the slotting regime.[13] Until now, slotting has been a minority interest (other than in the UK, which accounts for 58% of all slotted exposures in the EU,[14] mainly because all UK IPRE exposures are subject to slotting—see section 3.2 above). The timing of this consultation was therefore unfortunate. No less disappointing was the fact that the EBA's goal was to reduce perceived national differences across the EU in how banks slot SLEs.

A more valuable exercise might have been to identify and address weaknesses in the slotting regime itself. For example, it would have been useful to explore whether national regulators apply the same criteria in deciding whether or not to approve an internal model for SLEs. It would also have been interesting to make slotting less procyclical, by looking at what factors might tend to skew judgments towards optimism (and risk weights down) in booming markets, and towards pessimism (and higher risk weights) after a bust.

16.8 Alternatives to bank finance

16.8.1 *Insurance companies and Solvency II*

Solvency II, which came into force on 1 January 2016, establishes a new EU wide regulatory capital regime for insurance companies and some pension funds. In important respects, it is similar to the regime already in place in the UK, so adapting to the new framework is generally understood to have presented greater challenges for continental European firms than for UK firms.

Solvency II[15] requires insurance companies to hold capital against the risk of loss in the market value of their assets in extreme circumstances. The risk is defined as the loss of value that the asset might be expected to suffer in a one year period no more frequently than once every 200 years. Just as Basel

---

[13] The European Banking Authority's 2015 consultation on how banks operate the slotting approach is available here: *https://www.eba.europa.eu/-/eba-consults-on-technical-standards-on-specialised-lending-exposures*. The EBA published its final draft regulatory technical standards in 2016: *https://www.eba.europa.eu/documents* [Accessed 11 August 2016].

[14] See section 5 of the EBA consultation referenced in the previous footnote.

[15] European Union Directive 2009/138/EC.

III permits sophisticated banks to calculate their capital requirements using the IRB approach, Solvency II envisages that sophisticated insurance companies will use internal models approved by their regulators to assess capital requirements. Other insurance companies will be required to use the "standard model" mandated by Solvency II in calculating value at risk. In general, the use of an internal model as opposed to the standard model is expected to result in a more favourable capital treatment of value at risk. That said, regulators will almost certainly have regard to the value at risk specified by the standard model in deciding whether or not to approve an internal model proposed by a sophisticated insurer; in that sense, the standard model will serve as a "base case" even for insurers which aspire to use internal models.

Solvency II distinguishes between "Type 1 Securitisations" (broadly a senior investment grade tranche of a securitisation of prime residential mortgages (or certain other types of asset) which satisfies qualifying criteria) and "Type 2 Securitisations" (i.e. any other securitisation) and "Re-securitisations" (i.e. securitisations of assets comprising or including other securitisation transactions).

The existing references in Solvency II to Type 1 Securitisations will be replaced in due course with references to STS Securitisations (as defined in the Securitisation Regulation). This is a good thing as it increases consistency between the capital adequacy rules for banks and those for insurance companies—there will be a common set of rules for determining whether a securitisation merits favourable capital treatment. However, as far as CMBS is concerned, the change has no practical effect, as CMBS is excluded from favourable treatment both under the existing definition of Type 1 Securitisation and under the definition of STS Securitisation.

The deemed risk weights are markedly greater for Type 2 Securitisations than for Type 1/STS Securitisations. For example, a "AAA" Type 1 Securitisation tranche carries a capital charge of 2.1% per year of duration under the existing rules whereas a Type 2 Securitisation tranche of equivalent credit quality attracts a capital charge of 12.5% per year of duration. For a covered bond with the same rating, the capital charge is 0.7%. This means that CMBS is expensive for insurers relative to Type 1/STS securitisations and many other asset classes.

A further issue for CMBS is that there is a linear relationship between the expected maturity of a securitisation exposure and its capital cost. CMBS transactions typically have a longer maturity than other ABS transactions and therefore will tend to suffer higher overall capital charges. In fact, investment in CMBS transactions will often carry a capital cost higher than ownership of the underlying real estate, an outcome which is impossible to justify as CMBS represents an exposure to the underlying real estate, but with the additional benefit of credit enhancement provided by equity and/or subordinated tranches of debt (not to mention liquidity and potential diversification advantages over physical real estate). By contrast, direct lending or investment in non-securitised CRE loans by insurance companies carries a relatively low capital charge.

It can be no coincidence that European insurers have moved dynamically into (non-securitised) CRE debt in recent years. De Montfort University has charted the emergence of insurance companies as a major source of new originations. In 2015 insurers were second only to UK banks and building societies, and ahead of German banks, North American banks and other international banks.

16.8.2   *Funds and shadow banking*

The term "shadow bank" is used to describe participants in the financial sector which carry on bank-like activities (and in particular the extension or maturity transformation of credit) but which are not regulated as banks. The term captures a number of diverse market players including asset backed commercial paper conduits, other securitisation vehicles and debt funds.

At the G20 Summit in Cannes in 2011, it was agreed that policies should be developed at a global level to address perceived threats to the stability of the financial system posed by the shadow banking sector, including the reliance of certain participants in the sector (for example, asset backed commercial paper conduits) on short term funding, the lack of "skin in the game" of those involved in "originate to distribute" securitisations leading to a weakening of lending standards and a general lack of transparency. Following the Summit, the Financial Stability Board has published a number of reports on the shadow banking sector, the most recent being in November 2015. The report identifies a number of potential risks in relation to the shadow banking market, including the risk that maturity mismatch arising from the short term funding of long term assets could lead to a run on shadow banks.

In September 2013, the European Commission published a communication which summarised EU policy and initiatives in relation to the shadow banking sector to date. The Commission emphasised the importance of tightening prudential rules applying to banks dealing with participants in the shadow banking sector to avoid the potential for contagion and also the need to consider extensions to the regulatory system to avoid arbitrage between the banking sector and the shadow banking sector (in other words, the risk that lighter regulation of participants in the shadow banking sector could create an incentive for activities traditionally performed by banks to move to the shadow banking sector and so avoid the scope of regulation).

European CRE lending funds are subject to the Alternative Investment Fund Managers Directive (AIFMD).[16] The AIFMD entered into force on 21 July 2013 and established a common framework across the EU for Alternative Investment Funds (AIFs). An AIF is a collective investment undertaking which raises capital from a number of investors in accordance with a defined investment policy for the benefit of those investors and which is not a UCITS fund. Anyone whose regular business is managing one or more AIFs is termed an "AIFM" (an alternative investment fund manager).

The detailed requirements imposed on investment managers by the AIFMD are beyond the scope of this book, but include the requirement for authorisation by the regulator in the appropriate member state, the requirement to appoint a custodian/depositary, (non-risk based) capital requirements, liquidity management, disclosure requirements in relation to leverage, rules in relation to risk management systems and controls, reporting and valuation requirements. These provisions generally comprise a significant barrier to entry, and specifically add to the cost of establishing a fund for the purpose of taking direct exposure to CRE loans or indirect CRE exposure through investment in CMBS securities.

The classification of an investment manager as an AIFM also has consequences under the European Markets Infrastructure Regulation (for which see section 16.9 below). AIFs managed by an investment manager which is registered or authorised in the EU will be "Financial Counterparties" which will result in additional obligations in relation to the clearing, reporting and collateral management of their derivative positions. Under art.17 of the AIFMD and the related delegated regulations, AIFs are only able to invest in a securitisation exposure if the originator, sponsor or original lender retains a net economic interest of at least 5% and if the AIFM has ensured that the sponsor and originator have sound credit granting standards and a comprehensive and thorough understanding of the securitisation positions together with appropriate procedures to monitor the securitisation. These provisions are therefore similar in scope to the requirements under art.405 of the CRR for banks investing in securitisation transactions. When the Securitisation Regulation comes into force, it will cover both credit institutions and AIFMs and so the requirements will be identical.

In summary, although funds and other entities described as "shadow banks" have increased their share of the CRE lending market at the expense of the banks (see further the previous Chapter), they too have been subject to increased regulation since the GFC and there is also a clear possibility of further regulation to deal with perceived systemic risks arising from the shadow banking sector.

---

[16] 2011/61/EU.

16.9 The European Markets and Infrastructure Regulation (EMIR)

The European Regulation on OTC derivatives, central counterparties and trade repositories (EMIR) governs clearing, reporting and margining requirements in relation to OTC derivatives. EMIR categorises parties to derivative transactions as "Financial Counterparties", "NFC+ Counterparties" and "NFC–Counterparties" and their non-EU equivalents. Entities established in the EU that are not Financial Counterparties will fall in either the NFC+ or NFC- categories, depending on the volume and purpose of the derivatives business which they and their affiliates undertake. In most circumstances, SPVs established for the purpose of real estate finance transactions will be NFC–Counterparties, although this will need to be considered on a case by case basis, particularly where the SPV is consolidated with the originator group.

SPVs established in the EU are subject to the reporting obligation under EMIR which requires them to report their derivative trades to an authorised trade repository, and are also subject to rules in relation to timely confirmation of derivative trades, portfolio reconciliation and dispute resolution. Assuming that an SPV is indeed an NFC- Counterparty, it will not be subject to the mandatory clearing obligation.

While the margining requirements which apply to uncleared derivative transactions under EMIR do not apply directly to NFC- Counterparties, they will apply to banks which are the counterparties to derivatives entered into by SPVs. Up until now, market practice in both real estate loan and CMBS transactions has been for the swap counterparty to be secured by its agreed position in the post enforcement waterfall of payments rather than by any bilateral margining provisions between it and the SPV. The requirement for collateral margining therefore has the potential to change market practice in relation to CRE finance, although as at the time of writing, the regulatory technical standards which will govern margining are yet to be finalised.

The difficulty in applying the margining requirements to securitisation transactions is recognised by the Securitisation Regulation—it permits regulators to adopt technical standards to establish whether an STS securitisation transaction adequately mitigates risk for the purpose of EMIR (the implication being that a separate margining mechanism would not be necessary). Unfortunately, this is of no practical benefit for CMBS transactions because, as previously mentioned, they cannot qualify as STS securitisations.

In addition to the margining requirements, EMIR provides for increased regulatory capital charges to apply to uncleared derivatives. This will increase the cost to banks of providing interest rate swaps and other derivatives to real estate finance transactions. Inevitably, the cost of complying with the additional capital requirements and the other provisions of EMIR will need to be taken into account in banks' pricing of the interest rate swaps used in CMBS and other CRE finance transactions.

16.10   Conclusion

Post-GFC regulation has gone a long way to addressing some of the issues which gave rise to the GFC. Tighter capital requirements and increased stress testing have made banks more resistant to economic shock. The temptation for banks to over-leverage themselves has been constrained by new leverage and liquidity ratios. There is also a more critical and cautious attitude to structured finance; the "skin in the game" risk retention rules and due diligence requirements contained in the CRR acting as a brake on the "originate to distribute" model of securitisation as will be discussed in the following Chapter. At the same time, there is a risk that the existing European regulatory framework may impede the efficient functioning of the CRE finance market in a number of ways. The first, and most obvious, is the bank regulatory capital treatment of CRE lending and CMBS transactions which incentivises banks to look at other asset classes instead of CRE exposures, with implications for the availability and cost of credit for an important, enabling part of the real economy. The regulatory framework for banks also gives rise to anomalies in capital cost depending on whether the bank uses the standardised or IRB approach (and whether, if it uses the IRB approach, it uses slotting). The same is true for insurance companies using either the standard model or an internal model under Solvency II. In particular, it is problematic that the existing rules effectively discourage efficient low risk CRE lending.

The treatment of CMBS transactions for insurance companies also illustrates the potential for regulatory rules to artificially push investors into particular structures and transaction types. There is no intrinsic reason why a CMBS position should be riskier or less liquid than a direct CRE lending exposure to the same asset. Indeed, for many potential investors who may lack the experience or resources to service CRE loans, a senior position in a CMBS structure is arguably a more suitable way of investing. By attaching heavier risk weights to CMBS positions, Solvency II encourages direct lending over CMBS exposure. The diversification potential, standardised data and secondary market liquidity that CMBS can provide are lost as a result.

There is also a risk that the complexity of regulation, and the fact that it is often difficult to apply with certainty to common real world situations, together with the rapid pace of change across a number of areas, will itself act as a deterrent to investment.

Against this background, Chapter 21 examines certain recommendations developed by a UK CRE industry group for a more coherent, considered regulatory framework for the CRE finance market before the concluding Chapter of the book considers the opportunities based on the existing framework.

Chapter 17

European CRE Finance and CMBS Markets: The Impact of Risk Retention Rules

Richard Pugh,

Director and Assistant General Counsel, Bank of America Merrill Lynch

17.1   Introduction

The European Risk Retention rules came into force on 1 January 2011 in the guise of art.122a of the EU Capital Requirements Directive. From 1 January 2014, art.122a was subsequently replaced by arts 405–409 of the Capital Requirements Regulation (Regulation (EU) No 575/2103) (the CRR)).

The rules were put in place to mitigate the perceived risks of the pre-2008 "originate to distribute" model in the securitisation market and the subsequent global financial crisis that followed. Some institutions were criticised for originating poorly underwritten receivables and then offloading the entire risk into the capital markets through securitisations. Institutions that originate or purchase receivables (e.g. loans) and subsequently securitise them are now required to retain "skin in the game" in such securitisations. The premise is that if such an institution has direct economic exposure to such securitisations, it will be incentivised to only securitise high quality receivables. The hope is that by aligning the interests between the securitising institution and its investors, the quality of the assets in EU securitisations will improve.

On the whole the CRE finance and CMBS markets have adapted well to this regime. Investment banks have continued to attempt to use CMBS as a syndication strategy for their originated CRE loans notwithstanding the skin in the game requirement. Equally, investors in CMBS have taken additional comfort from securitising banks having skin in the game.

However, as discussed in the previous Chapter, there remains a considerable amount of uncertainty as to how the rules impact certain CRE financing structures beyond vanilla CMBS structures. The rules potentially extend to certain capital market and loan financings which the proverbial "Investor on the Clapham Omnibus" might not, on first glance, think of as a "securitisation".

17.2   Overview of the rules

17.2.1   *The basics*

Article 405(1) of the CRR states that:

> "An institution ... shall be exposed to the credit risk of a *securitisation* position ... only if the *originator*, sponsor or original lender has explicitly disclosed to the institution that it will retain, on an ongoing basis, a material net economic interest which ... shall not be less than 5%." [emphasis added]

Article 405(1) goes on to state that there are only five options available to retain such material net economic interest. The two options typically used for CMBS are:

> "(a)   retention of no less than 5%. of the nominal value of each of the tranches sold or transferred to the investors", and
> "(d)   retention of the first loss tranche ... so that the retention equals in total no less than 5%. of the nominal value of the securitised exposures".

Option (a) is known as the "vertical slice option" (i.e. a slice of 5% down the entire capital stack of the securitised notes) and option (d) the "horizontal slice option" (i.e. a slice of the most subordinated part of the capital stack representing 5% of the nominal value of the securitised exposures).

The CMBS can only use one retention option (or, in other words, there is no ability to combine, for example, vertical and horizontal slices to have an "L-shaped" retention) and selection of the retention option takes place when the securitisation is issued.

This 5% risk retention holding must be held for the life of the CMBS. It cannot "be subject to any credit risk mitigation or any short positions or any other hedge and shall not be sold".

The net economic interest will be determined by the notional (i.e. principal) value of the securitised CRE loans. It is not determined by the acquisition price of the assets (although typically CRE loans are sold into a CMBS at par value in any case).

17.2.2   *So far, so simple?*

As stated above, the risk retention rules apply to securitisations. However, the definition of a securitisation is not so straightforward given the wide definition European legislators have favoured.

"Securitisation" is defined as

"a transaction or scheme, whereby the credit risk associated with an exposure or pool of exposures is *tranched*, having both of the following characteristics:

(a) payments in the transaction or scheme are dependent upon the performance of the exposure or pool of exposures;

(b) the subordination of tranches determines the distribution of losses during the ongoing life of the transaction or scheme". [emphasis added]

"Tranche" means a

"contractually established segment of the credit risk associated with … exposures, where a position in the segment entails a risk of credit loss greater than or less than a position of the same amount in each other such segment …".

Therefore, instead of simply defining a securitisation as a capital market issuance of debt securities backed by underlying receivables (such as a CMBS), the definition intends to capture a much broader range of transactions. However, by being drafted so broadly, the definition also gives rise to a large amount of uncertainty. For example, it is unclear whether or not a senior and mezzanine CRE financing would be classed as a *"tranched exposure"*. Several common types of commercial real estate financing transactions are discussed in light of the definition of "securitisation" below.

17.2.3 Who has to retain?

Either the originator, sponsor or original lender has to retain the 5%. The definition of "originator" or "original lender" is of primary concern for the purposes of CMBS and CRE Finance transactions. *"Sponsor"* has a more technical meaning more suited to asset backed commercial paper conduits.

"Originator" means

"an entity which:

(a) itself or through related entities, directly or indirectly, was involved in the original agreement which created the obligations or potential obligations of the debtor or potential debtor giving rise to the exposure being securitised; or

(b) purchases a third party's exposures for its own account and then securitises them".

"Original lender" is not defined, but as a matter of plain English it is the lender that originally made the loan.

Accordingly, for the purposes of the CRE market, it is the entity that either originated the CRE loan or purchased the CRE loan after its origination that is of relevance.

377

17.2.4   Who is responsible for compliance with the risk retention rules?

Those unfamiliar with the rules may be surprised that the obligation to comply, and the penalty for non-compliance, falls on the securitisation investor (for example, a purchaser of CMBS notes) and not on the originator/securitiser putting together the securitisation.

The rules impose a compliance obligation on the following European regulated institutions: credit institutions (e.g. a bank) or investment firms[1]; alternative investment funds (AIFs)[2]; and insurance companies.[3] Such investors must ensure that a securitisation is compliant with the risk retention rules before investing in it.

Pension companies are notably absent from the rules (for now). Investors regulated outside of Europe are also outside the rules, although in practice they may find that there will be limited liquidity for any non-compliant European securitisation which they invest in.

If such a European regulated investor invests in a securitisation which is non-compliant then its regulator may impose certain penalties. For credit institutions and insurance companies this may be an increased regulatory capital charge for the holding of the non-compliant securitisation exposure. The position is different for an AIF which does not have regulatory capital requirements. The requirement for an AIF instead is to take "corrective action", which is not defined, although it is thought that this would not extend to requiring a disposal of the non-compliant position if such disposal was prejudicial to the interests of the AIF investors.

Such penalties may be imposed even if the securitisation becomes non-compliant at a later stage, through no fault of the investor.

17.2.5   Due diligence and sound and well-defined origination criteria

The rules also impose a requirement on such European investors to carry out thorough due diligence before they invest in a securitisation position. Merely relying on the originator's statement in a securitisation that it complies with the risk retention rules is not sufficient.

The rules vary depending on the type of investor. There is a general requirement for an investor to

> "demonstrate to the competent authorities for each of their individual securitisation positions, that they have a comprehensive and thorough

---

[1]   Article 4.1(3) of CRR.
[2]   Article 51(1)(d) of the AIFMD Level 2 Regulation.
[3]   Article 254(2)(d) of the Commission Delegated Regulation (EU) 2015/35 of 10 October 2014 supplementing Directive 2009/138/EC of the European Parliament and of the Council on the taking-up and pursuit of the business of Insurance and Reinsurance (Solvency II).

understanding of and have implemented formal policies and procedures appropriate to their trading book and non-trading book and commensurate with the risk profile of their investments in securitised positions".[4]

AIFs and insurance companies have additional qualitative requirements such as ensuring that the originator grants credit based on sound and well-defined criteria.[5]

However, some concession is given to investors. The CRR requires that institutions acting as an originator or original lender disclose to investors the level of their commitment to maintain a net economic interest in the securitisation. They are further required to ensure that

> "prospective investors have readily available access to all materially relevant data on the credit quality and performance of the individual underlying exposures, cash flows and collateral supporting a securitisation exposure as well as such information that is necessary to conduct comprehensive and well informed stress tests on the cash flows and collateral values supporting the underlying exposures".[6]

In addition, the originator in a securitisation is required to apply the same sound and well-defined criteria for credit-granting to exposures to be securitised as it applies to exposures to be held in its own non-trading book.[7] If this requirement is not met, then the originator may not be permitted to exclude the securitised CRE loans from its regulatory capital.

17.2.6 *Investing in non-EU deals*

Provided that a non-EU securitisation complies with the European risk retention rules, an EU regulated investor can invest in such securitisations. However, if a non-EU securitisation is not specifically drafted with EU investors in mind, there is a risk that it may not technically comply with the European risk retention rules and therefore an EU regulated investor will not be able to invest.

---

[4] See e.g. art.406 CRR.
[5] Articles 52 and 53 of the AIFMD Level 2 Regulation; art.256 of Solvency II.
[6] See e.g. art.409 CRR.
[7] See e.g. art.408 CRR.

17.3 Impact of the rules on CRE and CMBS transactions— where are the boundaries?

17.3.1 *Capital market transactions*

17.3.1.1 *Lender own-loan CMBS (tranched)*

In a classical CMBS structure, an orphan SPV issues rated notes to fund the purchase of CRE loans from the original lender. The notes will typically be listed on a recognised stock exchange and cleared through the clearing systems. They will consist of multiple tranches, where each tranche represents a specific segment of credit risk of underlying CRE loans originated by a single lender. The top tranches of issuance rank in priority to the bottom tranches in the event of an interest or principal shortfall.

Figure 1: Lender own-loan CMBS (tranched)

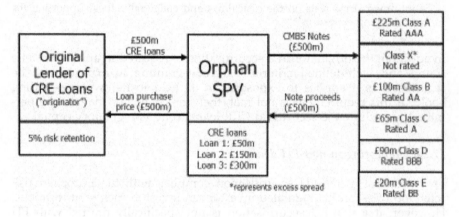

This CMBS structure clearly fits into the definition of a "securitisation" under the rules. The lender, as originator/original lender, will retain the risk either through the vertical slice option or the horizontal slice option. The amount retained will be at least 5% of the notional amount of the CRE loans being sold into the CMBS and will need to be retained for the life of the CMBS.

The lender may also comply with the vertical slice option by retaining a pari passu interest in each securitised loan.[8] So the lender can sell 95% of the CRE loan to the CMBS and retain 5% of the CRE loan. Originating banks may prefer this option as it may be cheaper from a regulatory capital per-

---

[8]   Article 5(1)(a) of the risk retention regulatory technical standards—Commission Delegation Regulation (EU) of 13 March 2014 supplementing Regulation (EU) No 575/2013.

spective for the bank to retain 5% participation in a senior loan rather than in the CMBS notes.

The technical requirement of the rules is for the originator to expressly disclose the nature of the risk retention to the investor. This is typically done through an express statement of risk retention compliance in the offering document (e.g. the prospectus).

17.3.1.1.1 Horizontal slice option

The originator would retain the first loss tranche of the CMBS notes so that the retention equals in total no less than 5% of the nominal value of the securitised exposures. In the example illustrated in Figure 1, the nominal value of the securitised exposures is £500 million. Therefore the originator would retain the first loss tranche of at least £25 million (which is 5% of £500 million) of CMBS notes.

From the capital structure in our example, that would mean the originator retaining all of the Class E Notes (£20 million) and £5 million in the Class D Notes (the next most subordinated tranche after the Class E Notes).

17.3.1.1.2 Vertical slice option

The originator would retain 5% of the nominal value of each of the tranches. Therefore the originator would retain £11.25 million of the Class A Notes; £5 million of the Class B Notes; £3.25 million of the Class C Notes; £4.5 million of the Class D Notes; and £1 million of the Class E Notes.

17.3.1.1.3 Holding a pari passu interest in each securitised loan

The originator would retain at least 5% of the loan participation in each of the securitised senior loans, being £2.5 million in CRE Loan 1, £7.5 million in CRE Loan 2 and £15 million in CRE Loan 3.

17.3.1.1.4 Other retention options

Although the options above are the most common in CMBS transaction, the rules do permit other techniques. For example, a whole loan could be split into two loans, a senior A Loan and a junior B Loan, with the senior A Loan securitised and the junior B Loan retained under option (e) of art.405(1) as a holding of a "first loss exposure of not less than 5%. of every securitised exposure in the securitisation". A/B Loans are discussed in more detail below.

It is worth noting that the X class note typically issued in a CMBS, which represents the quarterly excess spread of the CMBS (i.e. interest payments received by the SPV from the underlying CRE loans less note interest and other senior expenses) is not a valid method of risk retention. The X class note is an interest-only instrument and does not represent a "principal" exposure. See further Chapter 4 and the discussion of X class notes in Chapter 13.

It should also be noted that although the originator's credit exposure to the risk retention piece cannot be hedged, this will not prohibit the CMBS from entering into interest rate or currency hedging (see further Chapter 12).

17.3.1.2   Single tranche "CMBS"

The majority of public CMBS transactions are tranched. However, there may be situations where an SPV (typically an orphan) will issue a single tranche of notes secured over CRE loans, either in a publically listed or a private transaction. An example would be a bespoke repackaging where an investor does not want to hold participations in loans (e.g. because it is a fund that is only able to invest in securities) and therefore requests that the CRE loan receivables are repackaged into a single tranche of note securities (which may or may not be rated (and may or may not be listed)). If rated they will typically have the "*sf*" (structured finance) suffix on their rating.

Figure 2: Single tranche "CMBS"

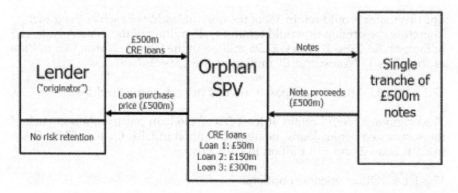

At first glance this structure looks similar to the classic form of CMBS, discussed in Chapter 1, where capital market instruments are being issued and which are secured by an underlying pool of real estate loans. The prospectus or other offering document may look very similar to the classic CMBS prospectus. As with a classic CMBS, the notes may be listed on a recognised stock exchange and rated.

However, the key issue is whether such a transaction can be said to be tranched. The prevailing market view appears to be that such a transaction is not tranched, as there is only a single tranche of notes, and therefore this transaction would not be a securitisation and therefore risk retention is not required. Ideally the offering document (e.g. the prospectus) will contain the equivalent negative statement so that the position is clear for investors. In addition, such a transaction should refrain from using the term CMBS or securitisation in the offering documents or the name of the SPV issuer in order to avoid confusing investors.

17.3.1.3 Agency CMBS (tranched)

An Agency CMBS is where a real estate investor borrows from the capital markets (rather than from a lender or lender syndicate). Figure 3 below sets out a typical structure.

The Orphan SPV issues tranched notes to capital market investors. The Orphan SPV uses the proceeds of such notes to advance a senior CRE loan to the Borrower SPV with the CRE loan secured on the underlying CRE owned by the Borrower SPV. The Borrower SPV is wholly owned by a holding company and indirectly by the ultimate Equity Holder. Interest and principal payments made by the Borrower SPV to the Orphan SPV under the CRE loan will in turn be used to pay note interest and principal.

Figure 3: Agency CMBS (tranched)

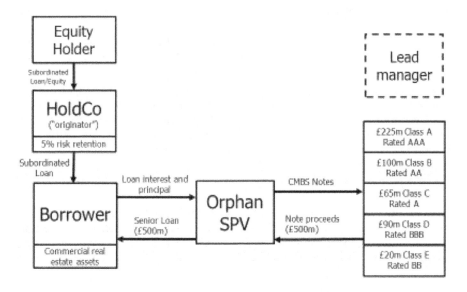

A real estate investor might want to use an Agency CMBS where, for example, the all-in costs of borrowing from the capital markets (including set-up and ongoing costs) are cheaper than borrowing from a traditional lender or lender syndicate. Another reason might be diversification of funding sources from the more traditional lenders such as banks, insurance companies or funds, amongst others.

It has been a subject of debate in the market as to whether or not a Tranched Agency CMBS would actually be classified as a securitisation[9]. The debate centres around the nature of a Tranched Agency CMBS which is akin to a real estate investor looking to borrow from the capital markets directly through a bond issue. Therefore, it is arguably closer to a corporate bond issuance than a securitisation.

However, the issuing of multiple tranches of notes by the Orphan SPV would indicate a tranched exposure to underlying credit risk (i.e. the CRE loan from the Orphan SPV issuer to the Borrower SPV) and therefore a securitisation.

17.3.1.3.1 Who is the "originator"? Square peg round hole?

If the view that a Tranched Agency CMBS is a securitisation is taken, further difficulties under the rules are encountered. It is not immediately obvious which entity should be the originator or original lender and retain the 5% risk retention in the securitisation. However the rules require someone to be nominated. Figure 3 above indicates that four parties may be considered for the nomination:

17.3.1.3.1.1 *Orphan SPV*

This entity may technically fit within the definition of originator as it has created or originated the exposure being securitised (i.e. the CRE loan made from the Orphan SPV to the Borrower SPV).

However, generally it is not legally possible for a borrower to own its own debt without such debt being legally extinguished. Therefore the Orphan SPV cannot be nominated because it cannot legally retain any of its own issued notes without them being legally extinguished.

17.3.1.3.1.2 *Borrower SPV*

As with the Orphan SPV, this entity may technically fit within the definition of originator on the basis that it is *an entity which was involved* (as the borrower) *in the original agreement which created the obligations of the debtor giving rise to the exposure being securitised.*

But this is an odd conclusion as a matter of logic. The Borrower SPV is already the debtor in relation to the securitised exposure (the CRE Loan). Accordingly, it would make no sense for the Borrower SPV to retain the credit risk in the exposure to its own debt.

---

[9] See for example CREFC Europe response to EBEA risk retention questionnaire dated 17 April 2014.

17.3.1.3.1.3   Lead Manager

It is sometimes suggested that the lead managers underwriting and marketing the notes could be construed as "sponsors" and therefore be eligible to retain the risk retention piece.

However the definition of "sponsor" is primarily intended to be applied to structures or programmes set up by a sponsor institution for the benefit of such institution, such as an asset backed commercial paper conduit.

Therefore it may not be appropriate to try to stretch this definition to the lead managers who are merely third party service providers engaged by the ultimate Equity Holder to underwrite and market the securitisation in return for a fee.

17.3.1.3.1.4   HoldCo

It may be argued that HoldCo fits under limb (a) of the definition of "originator" as an entity which itself or *through related entities* (i.e. through the Borrower SPV, its wholly owned subsidiary), directly or *indirectly* (i.e. through the Borrower SPV, its wholly owned subsidiary), was involved in the original agreement which created the obligations giving rise to the exposure being securitised.

However, this interpretation does not comfortably satisfy the regulations in relation to retention holding on a consolidated basis (art.405(2)) which are limited to EU regulated credit institutions or financial holding companies and refers only to regulatory supervision on a consolidated basis and not accounting consolidation (i.e. through HoldCo's 100% ownership of the Borrower SPV) which was expressly rejected by the European Banking Authority (EBA).[10]

In addition, this analysis has been put under further strain by a number of developments. First, the EBA has stated that the "originator" (being HoldCo in this case) must itself be of "real substance and hold actual economic capital on its assets for a minimum period of time".[11] It is not clear what is meant by this and it may cause problems where HoldCo is itself a shell entity with no other assets other than the risk retention holding. Legal counsel may need to carry out a detailed analysis of the activities of HoldCo before any conclusion can be reached. Second, it is anticipated that the STS Regulation (the Simple, Transparent and Standardised Securitisations regulations which are still to be implemented) will prohibit an entity from being be an originator where it is established or operates for the "sole"

---

[10] See pp.7 and 21–22 of the European Banking Authority Report on Risk Retention dated 22 December 2014.
[11] See pp.24–25 of the European Banking Authority Report on Risk Retention dated 22 December 2014.

purpose of securitising exposures. Again a detailed legal analysis may be necessary to determine this. Further, as discussed in section 17.7 below, there have been recent proposals that an entity should be an EU regulated entity in order to qualify as an originator. If these proposals are implemented, many HoldCos would no longer be able to qualify as an originator as they would not be EU regulated.

Notwithstanding the above, the view has been taken to date that the HoldCo being the originator is the only logical possibility for the Tranched Agency CMBS structure.

17.3.1.3.2 How to retain? Round peg square hole?

If HoldCo is taken to be the originator, consideration must be given to how it can retain a 5%. net economic interest in the securitisation. It would be contrary to the commercial purposes of the Agency CMBS if the HoldCo was to retain a net economic interest in the Senior Loan (or the issued notes funding the Senior Loan) as the purpose of the structure is for HoldCo, via the Borrower SPV, to access senior CRE funding from the capital markets, and not for HoldCo to provide part of this senior funding itself. Therefore HoldCo will need to consider other ways of holding the material net economic interest.

As 100% owner of the Borrower SPV, HoldCo already has a credit exposure to the Borrower SPV (and therefore indirectly to the securitised Senior Loan). Accordingly it could be argued that this equity exposure is an eligible form of retention under option (e) of art.405(1) as a holding of a "first loss exposure of not less than 5%. of every securitised exposure in the securitisation".

Alternatively, the balance of the Borrower SPV's real estate financing will often be from a subordinated loan from HoldCo (the injection of equity financing through a subordinated loan rather than an equity interest is usually more tax efficient as interest payments on debt are tax deductible). Given that the loan-to-value of the senior loan acceptable to the Agency CMBS noteholders will typically be significantly less than 95%, this subordinated loan will therefore represent more than 5% of the total debt funding of the Borrower. Therefore this subordinated loan may constitute, albeit indirectly, a material net economic interest under the retention rules. The relevant risk retention option here would be art.405(1)(d), with the holding of the subordinated loan being a retention of what is effectively the first loss tranche.

For the same reasons as those in relation to HoldCo above, it may also be possible to designate the Equity Holder (or intermediate companies in the ownership structure) as the originator through its equity exposure to the Borrower.

From a documentation perspective, the relevant offering document should contain a positive statement that the transaction is a securitisation which will be complied with through HoldCo's credit exposure, therefore expressly disclosing compliance to investors as required by the rules, allowing them to invest. In addition, the lead manager(s) may also want contractual comfort that the transaction will comply with the securitisation rules, for example appropriate representations and warranties from HoldCo in the note underwriting agreement.

Although compliance with the rules through the HoldCo option may be the right result for a Tranched Agency CMBS (which some would argue should not be a securitisation in the first place), this is a good example of where the application of the rules beyond the classic CMBS quickly becomes complex and uncertain. It is not helpful that in order to comply with the rules one is forced to form a view on what is the intended spirit of the rules rather than the black letter.

17.3.1.4 Single tranche Agency "CMBS"

Some Agency deals are issued by way of a single tranche.

Figure 4: Single tranche Agency "CMBS"

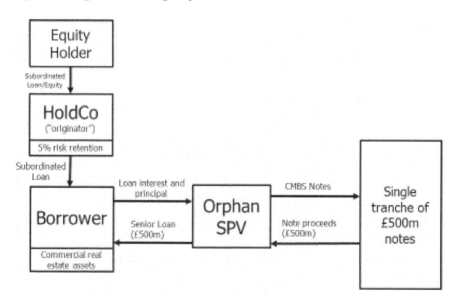

As with a single tranche CMBS, this structure may at first glance look similar to the classic CMBS structure described above and in Chapter 1. However, the key is whether such a transaction can be said to be tranched. Again, the prevailing market view appears to be that such a transaction is not tranched, as there is only a single tranche of notes, and therefore this transaction would not be a securitisation and therefore risk retention is not required. Accordingly, these types of deals will sometimes not even be described as CMBS in order to avoid investor confusion.[12]

As with the single tranche CMBS, the relevant offering document will ideally contain an equivalent negative statement and the lead manager(s) may look for additional contractual comfort.

17.4   Loan transactions

17.4.1   *Senior loan secured over CRE (with or without mezzanine finance)*

A vanilla senior CRE loan is not considered to be a securitisation. This is the case even where there is also mezzanine finance in the structure.

Figure 5: Senior loan secured over CRE

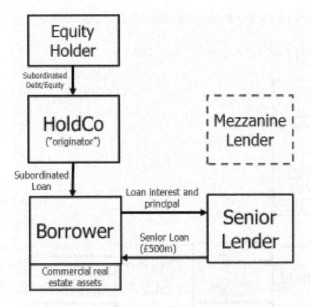

There are two arguments typically raised in this regard. Firstly, Recital 50 of CRR states that

> "an exposure that creates a direct payment obligation for a transaction or scheme used to finance or operate physical assets should not be considered an

---

12   See e.g. Westford Stratford City Finance Plc £750,000,000 Commercial Real Estate Loan Backed Floating Rate Notes due 2024 (issued on or about 16 October 2014).

exposure to a securitisation, even if the transaction or scheme has payment obligations of different seniority".

Although Recital 50 may have been drafted with project finance transactions in mind, a typical CRE finance transaction will involve the financing of physical assets (the underlying real estate). Secondly, that CRE is a physical asset, and therefore cannot be said to fall under the definition of an "exposure". "Exposure" really means a "receivable" such as a loan.

17.4.2   A/B Loan structure

An A/B Loan structure is where the Senior Loan is itself tranched into a senior "A Loan" and a junior "B Loan" (sometimes also called a "B Piece").

Figure 6: A/B Loan structure

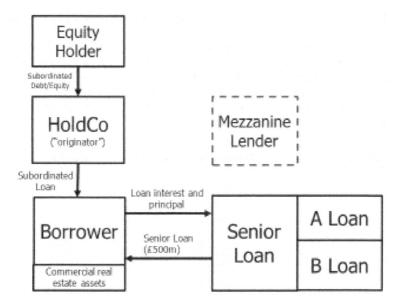

As was discussed in Chapters 5, 6 and 7, these structures were common pre-2008 when A Loans were often securitised into a CMBS with the higher margin B Loan separately sold to real estate debt investors. However A/B Loans are not as popular in the market at the time of writing (although they are having somewhat of a renaissance, as evidenced by the publication by the LMA in August 2016 of a contractual intercreditor agreement and the CREFC-Europe 2016 guidelines) and accordingly there has been limited consideration and analysis of the application of the risk retention rules to them.

Arguably, such structures have the same overall credit exposure as our vanilla Senior CRE Loan described in the section above and therefore, for the same reasons, should not be considered securitisations.

However, it has been suggested that the position is less clear where a Senior Loan is tranched into A and B Loans but the A Loan is not immediately securitised into a CMBS.

17.4.3 Senior loan secured over CRE loans (a "loan on CRE loan")

The "loan on CRE loan" has been a common theme of the market in recent years, particularly in connection with the disposals of large pools of non-performing CRE loans.

In this structure, a Senior Lender will provide senior (and sometimes mezzanine) finance to the Borrower (a newly created acquisition vehicle). The Borrower will use such senior funding, together with subordinated funding from the Equity Holder (via HoldCo) to purchase a pool of CRE loans. The underlying loans themselves will typically have the benefit of a mortgage secured over CRE and other security common to a CRE loan. However the Borrower (which will be the lender of record under the underlying loans) will have the direct benefit of this underlying security, and not the Senior Lender. Instead the Borrower will grant security over its interests in such loans to the Senior Lender.

Figure 7: Senior loan secured over CRE loans ("loan on loan")

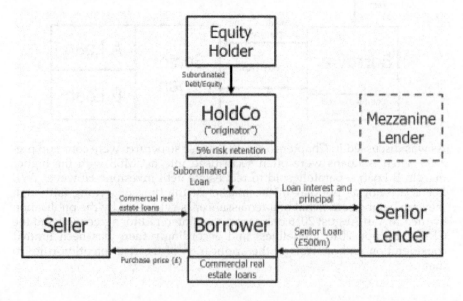

17.4.3.1   A securitisation? You cannot be serious!

This structure has caused a large amount of discussion and disagreement in the context of the risk retention rules.

The Senior Loan is a form of credit risk which is associated with an exposure or pool of exposures (i.e. the underlying CRE loans). The Senior Loan payments may be dependent upon the performance of such exposures (especially if the underlying pool of CRE loans are performing). The Borrower will typically finance its purchase of the CRE loans though a mixture of senior debt (from the Senior Lender) and junior debt (from the Equity Holder, via HoldCo). Therefore the exposure to the credit risk of the underlying CRE loan pool might be said to be tranched and to fall within the technical definition of securitisation.

If the funding provided to the Borrower by the Equity Holder (via HoldCo) is instead by way of debt-like equity instruments such as profit participating notes (rather than subordinated debt) then this may still constitute tranching. Conversely, if such funding is provided by way of simple common equity, then this may not constitute tranching (and therefore no securitisation), although the tax benefits of subordinated debt or debt-like instruments will often mean that simple common equity is not a tax efficient option.

Despite requests from the market for clarification,[13] the regulators have refrained from opining on whether or not the term securitisation applies to this sort of private loan transaction. However given the wide definition of securitisation, it can arguably apply to private transactions.

Recital 50 of CRR (as discussed in more detail above) does not provide much guidance here, as the focus here is on the financing of underlying receivables (CRE loans) and not physical assets.

Indeed, most law firms with CMBS expertise have taken the view that this transaction may be a securitisation. Accordingly, a Senior Lender in its capacity as "investor" in such securitisations may insist on a number of contractual enhancements to the loan agreement to ensure that it will be compliant with the risk retention rules (given it will bear the risk of "investing" in (or lending to) a non-compliant deal). Such contractual enhancements may include a representation and warranty from the originator that it will continue to hold at least a 5% exposure to the underlying CRE loans in accordance with the European risk retention rules, together with a covenant not to hedge or otherwise dispose of this exposure. This may give the Senior Lender comfort that if its local regulator takes the view that such loan exposures are securitisations then the Senior Lender can

---

[13] See for example CREFC Europe response to EBEA risk retention questionnaire dated 17 April 2014.

demonstrate it is investing in a compliant transaction and has undertaken the required investor due diligence.

The Senior Lender may have reason to be even more conservative in this analysis if it is looking to syndicate or securitise the Senior Loan. In the case of syndication, from a reputational perspective the Senior Lender may not want to run the risk of syndicating a loan to its buy-side clients if there is a risk of the loan later being labelled as a non-compliant securitisation. The buy-side client may also experience impaired liquidity if it wants to on-sell the loan and some of its buyers take the view that the loan may be non-compliant. In the case of a CMBS exit, if the loan is itself a securitisation, then a CMBS exit would be a "re-securitisation" with the adverse capital treatment that such a designation brings on an investor in such CMBS.

The suggestion that a loan on CRE loan is a securitisation can be something of a shock to a CRE borrower that is used to simple vanilla CRE loans and sometimes even to its legal counsel as well (who are more likely to be banking lawyers rather than securitisation lawyers). Accordingly, they may resist this analysis, arguing that the rules were never intended by the regulators to cover private loan transactions.

By way of comparison, it is also worth noting the approach of the European asset backed securitisation loan finance market. In these transactions, typically there is a senior loan financing the acquisition or holding of a pool of underlying receivables (e.g. residential mortgages, auto loans, unsecured consumer loans) together with junior debt from the equity holder. These types of financings are typically classified as securitisations by the senior lenders for the purposes of risk retention and regulatory capital and the loan agreements and lender contractual protections are structured accordingly. However, the only difference between a loan on CRE loan and these types of financings is that the receivable is a CRE loan rather than, for example, a residential real estate loan. The risk retention analysis conducted thus far has argued that they are the structurally the same and therefore should be subject to the same conclusions that they may be classified as securitisations.

17.4.3.2 Who is the originator? Square peg round hole revisited

Assuming that such transactions are classified as securitisations, it is not clear which entity would then be classed as the originator (as with the Tranched Agency CMBS example above):

17.4.3.2.1 the Seller:

The Seller may fall under the definition of original lender. However a third party Seller will simply want to sell all of its interests in the CRE loans to the Borrower as part of a planned disposal of its asset portfolio. It is unlikely to want to retain a 5% interest in the sold CRE loans for the life of the Senior Loan.

17.4.3.2.2   the Borrower:

The Borrower is the purchaser of the loans therefore technically it would fit under limb (b) of the definition of originator (i.e. "[an entity which] purchases a third party's exposures for its own account and then securitises them"). However the Borrower cannot legally retain a debt exposure to itself.

17.4.3.2.3   the Senior Lender:

The Senior Lender is making the loan as an investor and will not fall under the definition of originator. In addition, as discussed in the Tranched Agency CMBS example it does not seem appropriate to try to stretch the definition of sponsor to include a Senior Lender.

17.4.3.2.4   HoldCo:

As with the Tranched Agency CMBS analysis, the better approach may be to rely on the concept of an indirect or related entity in the limb (a) definition of originator to classify HoldCo as the originator (i.e. "[an entity which] itself or through related entities, directly or indirectly, was involved in the original agreement which created the obligations or potential obligations of the debtor or potential debtor giving rise to the exposure being securitised").

Following the same approach, consideration must also be given to the subordinated loan from HoldCo (as the originator) as representing at least 5% exposure in the transaction (the loan-to-value in a loan on CRE loan will almost always being much less than 95%). The relevant risk retention option here could be art.405(1)(d), with the holding of the subordinated loan being a retention of the first loss tranche.

As with the Tranched Agency CMBS analysis, this conclusion is difficult to argue and maintain under the strict definitions and the legal analysis is complex. In the comparable asset backed securitisation loan financing transactions referred to above, legal counsel will often go into an extremely detailed analysis as to whether HoldCo is of "real substance". The conclusion is very much on a case by case basis and may be complicated where HoldCo is itself a shell entity with no other assets other than the subordinated loan to the Borrower. In addition the recent proposals (discussed further in section 17.7 below) that an entity should be EU regulated in order to qualify as an originator would mean that, if such proposals are adopted, many HoldCos will no longer qualify as they are not EU regulated.

Notwithstanding, market participants have felt this conclusion to be within the spirit of the rules as things currently stand.

Adopting this approach means that in most cases, the loan on CRE loan structure should be implicitly capable of complying with the risk retention rules. All that remains is to satisfy the technical requirements of *the originator ... explicitly disclosing to the institution that it will retain, on an ongoing basis, a material net economic interest,* and for the originator to agree not to hedge or sell the retained interest. This can be met through appropriate HoldCo representations, warranties and covenants in the senior loan agreement or a side letter.

For the same reasons as HoldCo above it may also be possible to designate the Equity Holder (or intermediate companies in the ownership structure) as the originator through its equity exposure to the Borrower.

17.5 Amending a pre-2011 securitisation

Care should be taken if amending a pre-2011 legacy securitisation in any way, particularly if such amendment results in changes to the securitised assets (e.g. a CRE loan in the securitised pool is replaced by another loan). This could result in the (previously exempt) pre-2011 securitisation being brought within the scope of the risk retention rules.

17.6 The US risk retention rules

Any European CMBS entered into from 24 December 2016 will also be subject to the Dodd Frank US risk retention rules unless it falls within one of the exemptions, such as the foreign transactions safe harbour.

It is beyond the scope of this Chapter to go into the detail of these rules, which are at least as complex as the European rules, although Chapter 20 considers these rules in further detail. However if a European CMBS is looking to include US investors in primary issuance (for example in reliance on the exemption from the registration requirements of the US Securities Act of 1933 provided by Rule 144A), or if the originating bank or assets have a connection with the US, then the foreign transactions safe harbour may not be available and the CMBS may have to comply with the US risk retention rules as well as the European risk retention rules. This may cause material complexities in the structuring of the risk retention. It should also be noted that the Dodd Frank rules put the obligation to comply on the originating/securitising institution (rather than on the investor).

17.7 Conclusion

As discussed in the previous Chapter, the European Commission's proposals on Simple, Transparent and Standardised Securitisations contain material changes to the risk retention rules[14]:

- First, the definition of originator will be narrowed so that "an entity shall not be considered to be an originator where the entity has been established or operates for the sole purpose of securitising exposures". In order to be an originator an entity will need to demonstrate a "broad business purpose" beyond just retaining the retention piece. This may create additional challenges, for example in the nomination of HoldCo as originator in transactions such as a Tranched Agency CMBS or a loan on CRE loan.

- Second, the proposals impose a direct obligation to comply with the risk retention rules on the originator and the original lender. This may put added pressure on any borrower and lender institutions (and their legal advisers) who to date have taken the view that a loan on CRE loan is not a securitisation. If a regulator was to disagree and consider such structures a securitisation then the borrower (as originator) may have a direct liability for breach of the regulations if it cannot demonstrate that such transaction has complied with the rules. There remains some uncertainty under the proposals as to whether such a breach would result in criminal as well as civil liability.

At the time of writing, it is not certain when these rules will come into effect but mid to late 2017 is thought to be the earliest likely date.

Further, on 6 June 2016, Rapporteur Paul Tang MEP (who is in charge of steering the proposals through the EU Parliament) published a report on "Common rules on securitisation and creating a European framework for simple, transparent and standardised securitisation". The report proposed additional material changes to the risk retention rules beyond the current EC proposals described above. In particular, the report proposed (i) increasing the required risk retention from 5% to 20%; and (ii) requiring that an entity must be an EU regulated entity in order to qualify as an originator. This report is not binding, but may influence how the new rules are ultimately drafted. However if these proposals are implemented it is clear that they will have a material impact on CMBS and those CRE Finance transactions caught by the definition of securitisation.

---

[14] Article 4 of European Commission's proposal for a Regulation of the European Parliament and of the Council laying down common rules on securitisation and creating a European frame work for simple, transparent and standardised securitisation (dated 30 September 2015).

Chapter 18

European Lending Markets

18.1 Introduction to French Commercial Real Estate lending

Antoine Corpet,
Owner, Polyreal Limited

Jean-Pierre Cherbit,
Head of France Real Estate Structured Finance, Société Générale

18.1.1 Introduction

This Chapter is based on a CREFC training presentation on the French lending market and is more an overview and introduction targeted to non-French market players, rather than a Chapter dedicated to French CRE lending specialists.

On paper, France is an attractive market for commercial real estate (CRE) lenders. The market is comparatively larger than many other European countries, with Paris being the largest office market in Europe. France was also, for a number of decades the largest shopping centres market (17.66 million sq m GLA) in Europe and has been overtaken only by Russia (17.7 million sq m GLA) in 2014, but is still ahead of the UK (17.1 million sq m GLA).

France also benefits from a highly transparent CRE market, ranking 5th in the world and 3rd in Europe in the 2016 JLL's Global Real Estate Transparency Index.

However, whether rightly or not, France is not seen as attractive as the UK or Germany (see the German Lending Market Chapter contained in this Chapter 18) by some foreign CRE Lenders. This is mostly due to some market characteristics, particularly:

- France is perceived as less creditor friendly than the UK or Germany;
- The short lease structure (comprising three, six and nine years) has an impact on lending terms;
- There is a certain lack of legal predictability on enforcement procedures, particularly after the Coeur Défense default in 2008; and

- French banking monopoly rules create a certain barrier to entry, mostly for alternative lenders.

To put things in perspective, this Chapter will first present an overview of the French CRE lending market size in comparison with other major European CRE lending markets. A second section will cover market segmentation and a third part, loan structures and pricing. A final section will cover some French CRE lending market characteristics, with a special attention to structures available to mitigate insolvency risk.

18.1.2 Overview of the French lending market

There is multiple data available on the French CRE lending market but data is not always consistent and this Chapter uses what was perceived as the most accurate information available.

18.1.2.1 The French CRE Investment market

Before describing the French lending market, it is interesting to have a brief overview of the size the French CRE market and CRE Investment market, as it is a good proxy to estimate the size of the lending market.

Figure 1 below gives interesting information on the CRE stock in various European countries.

Figure 1: Estimated size of total CRE market (€ bn)—September 2014

	AT	BE	CZ	DK	FI	FR	DE	HU	IE	IT	NL	PL	PT	ES	SE	UK	EU	EA
Estimated size of total CRE Market (€ bns)	27	44	12	41	45	275	317	7	20	99	11	26	22	55	131	432	1,664	1,816

Source: MSCI

The above information needs to be analysed on a relative basis: according to MSCI data, France, with a total CRE stock of €275 billion, is the third largest market in value, after the UK (€432 billon) and Germany (€317 billon); the fourth market is Sweden with €131 billion. On an absolute basis, these numbers still have to be taken with a pinch of salt, as they are not always consistent with other information available in the market. MSCI data may not cover the entire market or the definition of CRE market might be more restrictive than other data sources. For instance, the Cushman Wakefield outstanding debt data, used later in this Chapter, indicates a volume of French CRE backed private and public debt of £287 billion in 2014 and an average LTV ratio of 48%, which would indicate a total market size of nearly £600 billion. However, the hierarchy between the major EU countries remains unchanged.

In terms of CRE investments, the ranking is also similar, with France being the third largest investment market behind the UK and Germany, but in front of Sweden.

2015 was a record year in terms of volume of CRE investment in Europe: over €245 billion was invested—a year-on-year increase of 22% and a 6% increase on the 2007 investment peak. With €26 billion of investments, France was again the third largest CRE investment country in Europe, but far behind the UK (€92.5 billion) and Germany (€55 billion).

Figure 2: 2015 full-year investment volume and yoy growth

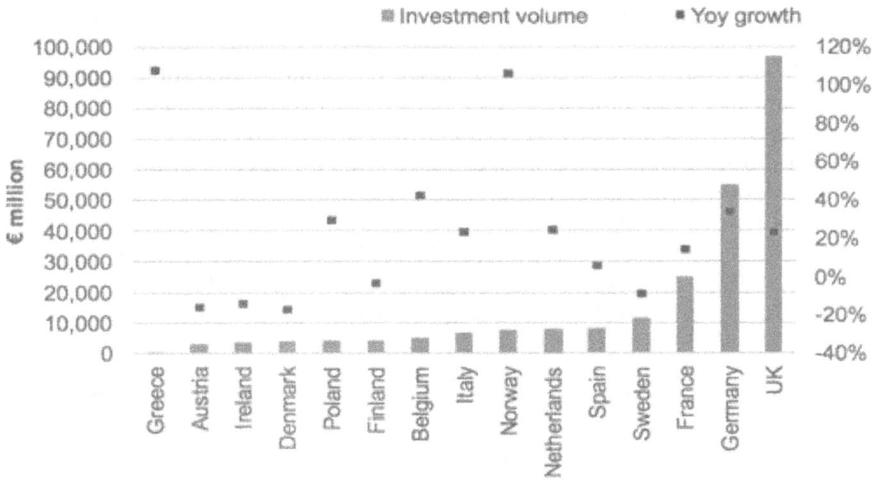

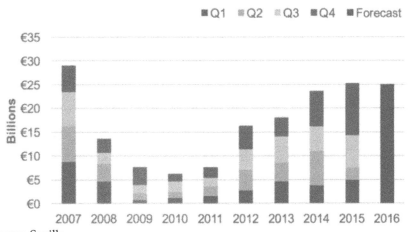

Graph source: Savills

As shown in figure 3, French investment volumes were above their 2014 levels in 2015, but slightly below their record volumes of 2007.

Figure 3: France Investment Volume 2007–2016

Source: Savills

18.1.2.2 French outstanding CRE loans v the UK and Germany

France is the second largest European CRE lending market after the UK, almost at par with Germany. Figure 4 shows that the outstanding volumes of CRE loans have been steadily growing since 2000, while the UK and Germany have decreased post GFC, the former most significantly than the later. There are several explanations to this phenomenon:

— There has been less volatility in CRE values in France compared to the UK or Germany. French values have remained relatively stable through the GFC, which explains the relative stability of the outstanding debt amounts with new loan production being based on steadier valuations. Figure 5 below gives an overview of CRE yield volatility in various countries and France appears to be the county which had experienced the lowest amount of property yield volatility.
— French banks have done fewer enforcement procedures than their British and German counterparts and there has been potentially more "extend and pretend" management of French loan books. French enforcement procedures are generally lengthy and lenders tend to negotiate loan extensions or restructure loans in partnership with their borrowers.
— The above figures also could confirm the good balance sheet and credit management by French banks, which were less aggressive pre-crisis than British or German banks in terms of LTVs and loan covenants. This is the result of operating in a less creditor friendly environment, but also the result of the lessons learned by French lenders during the 1990s CRE crisis in France.

Figure 4: Outstanding CRE loans volumes in major EU markets

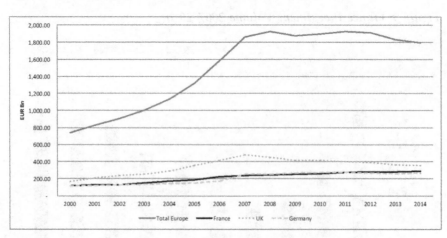

Source: Cushman Wakefield

400

Figure 5: Low volatility of French CRE Yields

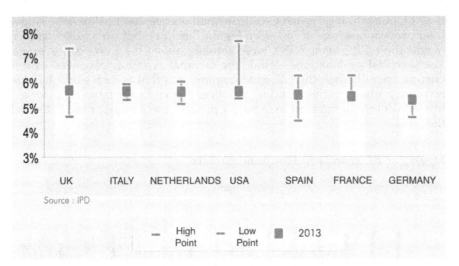

Source: IPD

In 2014, France represented approximately 16% of the outstanding CRE debt in Europe, slightly ahead of Germany but far behind the UK. With such a market share, France is definitely an attractive market for lenders, as only the UK or Germany would present similar or higher market depth.

Figure 6: Major EU countries' shares of the CRE lending market

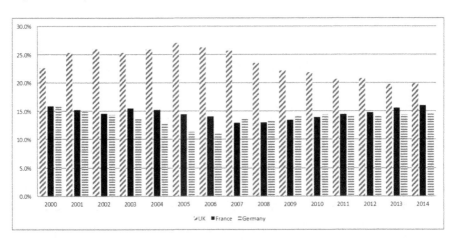

Source: Cushman Wakefield

18.1.2.3   French CRE gearing v other European markets

In 2014, outstanding French CRE loans had an average LTV of 48%, below the European average of 53% (see Figure 7 below); but up to 2006, French outstanding CRE loans LTVs were actually above the European average. The potential explanations include the fact that France is perceived as less creditor friendly than the UK and Germany and that French banks have to be more cautious in their lending practice. French Banks have also worked towards deleveraging their loan books, probably as a result of the 1990s and the GFC.

Figure 7: CRE gearing in European markets

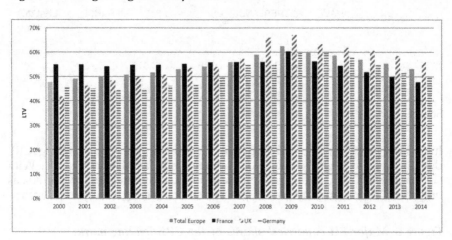

Source: Cushman Wakefield

Lower average gearing is another attractive feature of the French market, which also denotes that competition between lenders is not as high as in the UK or Germany.

18.1.2.4   French CRE loan maturities v other European markets

French loan maturities are on average shorter than in the UK and Germany. As shown in Figure 8, most French CRE loans in 2014 were maturing within five years. This is mainly due to the way leases are structured in France, where leases tend to have shorter maturities than in the rest of Europe (generally nine year maturities, with break options at the end of year three and year six). Another important explanation is the large proportion of CRE loans in the French market which have short-term maturities (usually three years) provided to French developers or estate agents ("marchlands de biens").

Figure 8: Maturity Profile of European Debt Stock (as at end 2014)

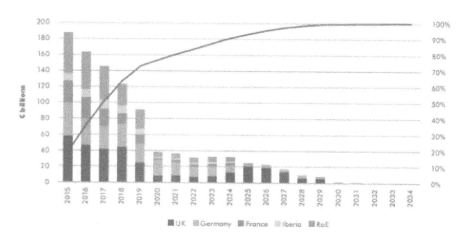

Source: CBRE Research

18.1.2.5 *Market Segmentation by borrower and property types (French banks only)*

As obtaining detailed market data is always a challenge, the following information on market segmentation by borrower and projects types is based on the Banque de France reports that only cover French banks.

French banks are still very active in the development market as shown in Figure 9, below.

The large size of the property developers market may explain why average loan maturities are short, as loans to developers usually have shorter maturities.

As shown in Figure 10, French Banks' loan production are approximately 50% backed by residential properties and 50% by CRE. Traditionally, a large portion of the CRE loan production was backed by office properties. However, during the GFC, French banks favoured retail and logistic properties, which were perceived as more stable than offices. Data after 2012 is not available, but it can be expected that the share of office backed loans has probably increased to it pre-crisis levels.

18.1.2.6 *Market segmentation by lender type*

This section is an attempt to map the CRE lending market by lender type and is based on market experience, which is therefore slightly subjective. As shown in Figure 11, it is possible to map the market by loan size, making a distinction between prime and Paris properties, versus non-prime properties that are usually located in the French regions.

403

Figure 9: Production breakdown by borrower type

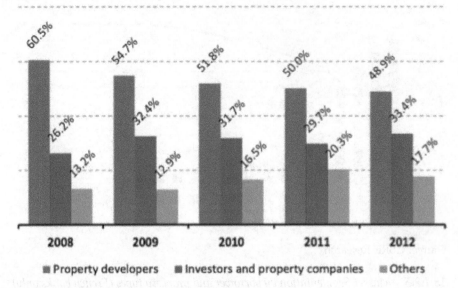

■ Property developers   ■ Investors and property companies   ▨ Others

Source: SGACPR's annual inquiry

Figure 10: Production breakdown by property type

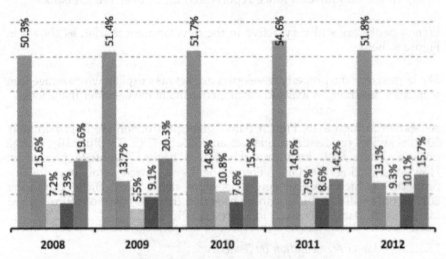

▨ Residential ▨ Offices ▨ Industrial, Warehouses, Cafés/Hotels/Restaurants, Parking lots ■ Retail ▨ Others

Source: SGACPR's annual inquiry

Figure 11: Market segmentation by lender type

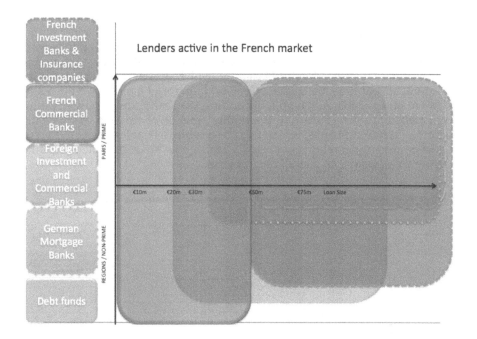

Large French Banks cover the entire market: their investment banking arms tend to finance the larger properties or portfolios, while their commercial bank arms tend to focus on the smaller loans in regional markets. The typical cut-off in terms of loan size for an investment bank is between €30 and €40 million.

German mortgage banks have a positioning somewhat similar to French banks' investment banking arms, but with a narrower approach: they tend to focus mostly on prime Paris properties and are fairly less active in the regions. Their cut-off loan size is usually around €30 million for the smaller banks and €50 million for the larger players.

Foreign investment and commercial banks used to be more active in the French market before the GFC. They now tend to operate in the large loans space and are mostly relationship driven, following their international clients in France but not actively looking for local opportunities.

Debt funds still represent a relatively small portion in the market and are either focused on small mezzanine loans or above €20 million senior loans. The funds active in the market are yield-driven and therefore are not necessarily financing prime properties, which attract low margins.

18.1.2.7   Lenders' market shares in the French market

As shown in Figure 11, French commercial banks clearly dominate the French CRE lending market, followed by German mortgage banks, with a pick up after 2007. Between 2007 and 2008, German Pfandbrief banks were probably the only lenders active in the market, mostly due to sourcing funds via the German Pfandbrief market, which was the only cheap source of capital at that time. Since then, German Pfandbrief banks have been able to maintain their market share, but funding via Pfandbrief is now at par or even potentially less attractive than other sources of funding. As a result, German Pfandbrief banks, which used to be able to beat French commercial banks on pricing on relatively low LTV loans, now have difficulties offering pricing as attractive as some French banks.

Figure 12: CRE Lenders' market shares in the French market

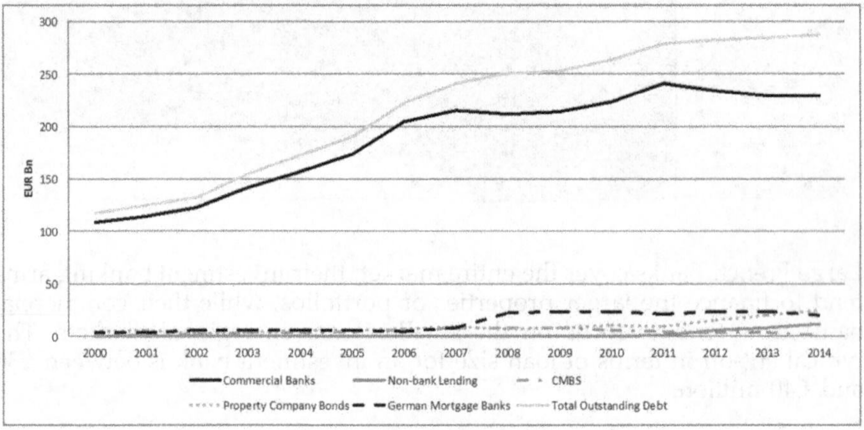

Source: Cushman Wakefield

In recent years, the volume of property company bonds in the market has increased significantly. Bonds are popular as there are many large listed real estate companies in France that can issue bonds at very attractive pricing. The decrease in bank lending after the GFC has also opened the bond market as an alternative source of financing for large and well capitalised, often listed, CRE investors. The bond market is also an alternative to the banking monopoly rules, as debt funds can buy bonds even if they are not legally entitled to lend.

Non-Bank lenders represent a small proportion of the market, mostly due to the French banking monopoly as debt funds needs to joint venture with a band to be in a position to lend or can alternatively buy bonds issues by real estate companies.

Finally, CMBS had never really taken off in France, even before the GFC. This is mostly due to French regulations, which was perceived as less creditor-friendly than the UK or Germany. The default of the Coeur Défense CMBS transaction does not help this perception, even if the European CMBS market starts to pick up again, which is, however, unlikely in the environment that exists at the time of writing.

Figures 13, 14 and 15 show interesting lenders' segmentation discrepancies between France, the UK and Germany.

Figure 13: CRE lenders' segmentation in France

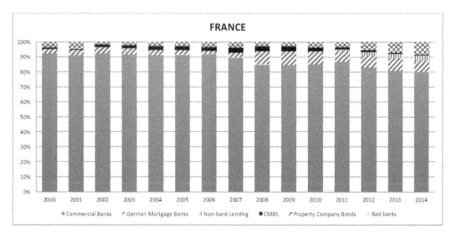

Source: Cushman Wakefield

Figure 14: CRE lenders' segmentation in the UK

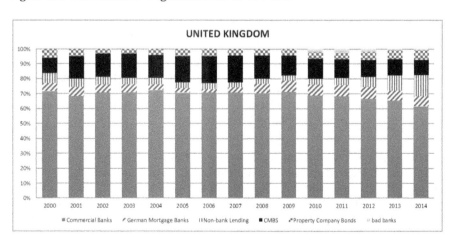

Source: Cushman Wakefield

Figure 15: CRE lenders' segmentation in Germany

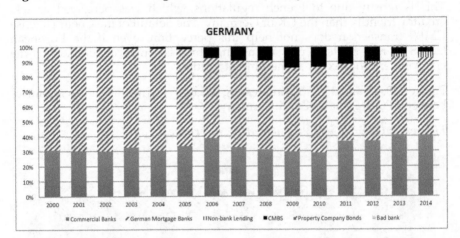

Source: Cushman Wakefield

18.1.2.8   Typical lending terms

French lending terms tend to be very different across the various segments of the market. Large prime transactions tend to attract large pan-European lenders offering terms and lending structures in line with the terms and structures seen in the UK or Germany. On the non-prime/regional markets, lending terms and loan structures varies more than the above.

18.1.2.8.1   Prime Lending terms: How France compares to other European countries?

CRE loans backed by prime properties are mostly found in the wider Paris region and are mostly office and retail, but also luxury hotels. The market is dominated by French banks, but with intense competition from European and international lenders. Prime lending terms and debt structures are therefore fairly similar to other large prime European markets such as the UK and Germany. Figure 16 gives an idea of margins in this segment of the market across major European CRE markets.

Prime CRE loans tend to have maturities of five to seven years, with similar loan structuring features as in other European Prime markets. LTVs tend to be lower in France than the UK and Germany, with 65% LTV still a ceiling for many senior lenders. However, mezzanine is widely available. Margins are usually higher than in the UK of Germany, but low leveraged loans (<50% LTV) backed by super prime properties can attract margins below 100bps.

Figure 16: Prime lending terms in France

FRANCE

	Q1 2015	Q1 2014	Q1 2013
LTV	50% - 70%	50% - 70%	55% - 65%
MARGINS	1.25%-2.25%	1.40%-2.50%	1.90%-3.00%
RATING	5	4	4
MEZZ	Strong	Strong	Strong

UK

	Q1 2015	Q1 2014	Q1 2013
LTV	65%-70%	60% - 65%	55% - 65%
MARGINS	1.20%-2.00%	1.75%-2.50%	2.50%-3.00%
RATING	5	5	4.5
MEZZ	Strong	Strong	Strong

GERMANY

	Q1 2015	Q1 2014	Q1 2013
LTV	55%-75%	55% - 75%	55% - 75%
MARGINS	0.60%-1.75%	0.80%-1.75%	1.20%-2.00%
RATING	5	5	4.5
MEZZ	Strong	Strong	Strong

SPAIN

	Q1 2015	Q1 2014	Q1 2013
LTV	55%-65%	50%-60%	40%-50%
MARGINS	2.25%-3.75%	3.00%-5.00%	5.00%-6.50%
RATING	4	3	2.5
MEZZ	Limited	Limited	None

LTV	Senior Prime LTV
MARGINS	Prime Margins
RATING	Market Liquidity (1-5)
MEZZ	Availability of Mezz
	(None, Limited, Good, Strong)

Source: Cushman Wakefield

In terms of loan covenants and credit structures, French loans are structured with tighter covenants and more structuring features, like reserve funds, to take into account the short French leases and the more challenging enforcement environment.

18.1.2.8.2 Non-Prime/Regional lending terms in the French Market

The French non-prime lending market tends to be mostly in the regions, except for retail properties. Typically, loans are below €20 million and French banks dominate this market segment, with little competition from foreign lenders. Some German and foreign private banks are however active in this market segment.

This segment of the market has a lot of variations in terms of loan structures:

Long term fully amortising investors' loans: a relatively large proportion of the market includes 15 to 20-year fully amortising loans. They are fixed-rate loans, not floating rate loans with a swap. Starting LTV can be higher than market average and margins quite competitive. Limitations are the lack of tailor-made structures and the high prepayment penalties.

Short-term developers or estate agents *"marchlands de biens"* loans: This segment in the market is constituted either by loans to developers or loans to estate agents/*"marchlands de biens"*. They are usually interest-only loans with high LTVs and maturities shorter than three years. They also often benefit from a sponsor guarantee.

409

Prime loan copycats: These loans benefit from similar structuring to the prime loans described above. They are usually larger than average loans made by domestic investment banks or foreign lenders and they utilise LMA type documentation.

Figure 17: Non-prime types of loan structures and pricing

	Short term developers or estate agents' loan	Long term fully amortising investors' loan	The "prime loan copycat"
Maturity	1 to 3 years	10 to 20 years	5 to 7 years
Typical LTV	65% to 80% LTV	55% to 70% LTV	50% to 60% LTV
Amortisation	No amortisation	Fully amortising	I/O or contractual AM
Margins	2.00% to 4.00%	1.50% to 3.00%	1.5% to 3.0%
Hedging	Floating rate loans (sometimes with a cap)	Fixed rate loans	Capped or Swapped

18.1.2.9 Specificities of the French lending market

18.1.2.9.1 Development/VEFA loans

Vente en État Futur d'Achèvement (VEFA) or "sale in future state of completion" contracts are regulated development contracts, which were initially designed to protect residential buyers of off-plan properties against the default of their home builders. The same principle applies to CRE, and VEFA loans represent the largest portion of the CRE development financing market.

In a VEFA contract, the buyer and the developer sign a reservation contract ("*contrat de reservation*"). This contract includes items such as the guaranteed price of the property when built, payment stages which coincide with the different phases of the property's completion and technical specifications. The buyer usually pays a 5% deposit when signing the reservation contract, which is then deducted from the total purchase price.

In a VEFA loan, the bank usually finances the buyer, but you can also have specific arrangements where the bank finances the developer and the buyer commits to buy at completion, like in a traditional forward sale agreement. In both cases, the advantage of the French VEFA against other EU development financing structures is the fact that the bank provides a completion guaranty or construction bond (GFA or "*Garantie Financière d'Achèvement*"). While construction bonds are not standard in other EU markets and not available for all projects, the French completion guaranty is completely standardised and available for most projects. This gives a lot of confidence to the parties and clearly protects the buyer against adverse events that could occur during the construction project such as the bankruptcy of the developer.

18.1.2.9.2   The Property Leasing market or "Crédit-Bail Immobilier"

The property leasing market is quite large in France, with approximately 12% of the outstanding CRE debt (see Figure 18 below). This is different from the UK, where, at the time of writing, leasing is virtually non-existent, but similar to Germany where leasing also represents a fairly large portion of the CRE "lending" market.

Leasing is used by many SMEs in non-prime markets where the investment market is slim. Property leasing is used as an alternative way of financing CRE properties, as lessees can get higher implied LTVs than a traditional mortgage loan (potentially 100% financing). There are also interesting tax benefits for lessees as the lease payments are entirely tax deductible, while only the interests (not the amortisation) are deductible in a traditional mortgage loan. Property leasing has a significant advantage for the lessor, compared to tradition loans, as there are no enforcement issues should the lessee stop paying its lease payments. This is an interesting feature in the French market where enforcement procedures are long. This allows weaker sponsors to have access to funding and eventually acquire the property at the end of the lease, which generally has a purchase option.

The major limitations of the credit bail structure are the expensive contractual and tax breakage costs. The tax arbitrage described above is only available for a minimum contract length (usually 12 or 15 years). If the lessee breaks its lease to purchase the property, previous tax deductions are suddenly clawed back and due to the tax administration.

Figure 18: The French CRE leasing market

French property leasing market (EUR million)	2011	2012	2013	2014	2015
Industrial buildings (factories, light industrial, warehouses, etc)	1,927	1,542	1,406	1,150	1360
Commercial buildings (retail, supermarkets, hotels, restaurants, etc)	2,014	1,622	1,373	1,566	1167
Office buildings	803	937	891	1,259	1411
Other buildings (Clinics, Hospitals, cinemas,etc)	932	966	588	558	691
Total production	5,676	5,067	4,258	4,533	4,629
Total Outstanding Amounts	34,075	34,967	35,395	35,367	35,568
% ot total CRE Debt outstanding	12.2%	12.4%	12.4%	12.3%	n/a

Source: ASF

18.1.2.9.3   Factors that impact French CRE lending and how loans are
             structured

As already mentioned above, there are a number of local factors that impact
the way French CRE loans are structured.

The first major factor is that French leases are typically shorter than in other
European countries. French leases are typically nine years with break every
three years (3–6–9). It is possible to find 12-year leases, but leases beyond 12
years are virtually non-existent, as they attract additional taxes. To mitigate
the lease break risk, lenders tend to have lower LTV loans and usually
structure cash reserve to mitigate the lease rollover risk.

The second major local factor that impacts the way French loans are
structured is that France is a less creditor friendly country than the UK or
Germany. As a result, lenders structure loans with lower LTVs and tighter
covenants. It is not uncommon to have debt service coverage ratios a 1.20x
to 1.30x while DSCR levels would be much lower in the UK.

Other structuring tools to be considered to protect lenders in France are the
double Lux Co structure, the *Fiducie Sûreté*, and the golden share, which are
described in detail below.

18.1.2.10   France: Banking Monopoly Rules and alternative sources of lending

One of the particularities of the French lending market are the French
banking monopoly rules, where lenders must be licensed or otherwise
entitled to carry out banking business in France. Pursuant to the French
Monetary and Financial Code, only an institution that is licensed as a credit
institution in France or recognised as such in France, through the EU's rules
on mutual recognition, can conduct banking transactions in France on a
regular basis.

There are a number of exceptions to the French banking monopoly:

—   Insurance and reinsurance companies governed by the French *Code des
    assurances;*
—   Securitisation vehicles;
—   Intra-group treasury transactions with companies having direct or
    indirect share capital links between them, provided that one of the
    contracting companies has effective controlling rights over the others;
    and
—   Securities (such as bonds).

One particular feature of the French market is that, due to the "banking
monopoly" restrictions, private debt funds cannot make loans available to
borrowers incorporated in France (or French branches of foreign companies), nor can they commit to make a loan available (regardless of whether

or not that loan is eventually funded). Consequently, mezzanine debt, unitranche debt and more generally any debt to be underwritten or made available by such private debt funds must take the form of a bond instrument rather than that of a loan.

18.1.3 Creditor friendliness, enforcement procedures, structuring solutions and best practices seen in the market

18.1.3.1 Creditor friendliness and the Cœur Défense enforcement

The current perception of French creditor friendliness is linked to the Cœur Défense enforcement procedure that received a lot of press coverage and worried a lot of foreign lenders who are now more cautious when lending in France.

18.1.3.1.1 What happened with Cœur Défense?

The Cœur Défense saga started soon after the collapse of Lehman Brothers in September 2008. Cœur Défense is the largest single office complex in Europe with 180,000 sqm in Paris' La Défense business quarter.

The asset formed the collateral of a CMBS, Windermere XII, structured by Lehman Brothers, who were also the hedging counterparty. The hedging documentation included the obligation to substitute the hedge counterparty in case its credit rating fell below a minimum level. This caused a default under the loan agreement, which prompted the French borrower to file for protection under the safeguard procedure with the Paris commercial court.

The court opened a safeguard proceeding for the French borrower but also for the Luxembourg holding entity. The opening of the safeguard proceeding immediately triggered a mandatory stay of proceedings: As a result, creditors could neither enforce their mortgage in France, nor their share pledge in Luxembourg.

The borrower also obtained an order from the Paris Commercial Court to the effect that the lessees should pay amounts due under the leases to the judicial administrator in escrow, preventing the creditors from exercising their rights under the *Dailly* security assignment. The order also provided that the judicial administrator could debit from the amounts held in escrow the amounts necessary for the maintenance of the Cœur Défense complex.

Five years after the start of the proceedings, a definitive safeguard plan was finally adopted by the Versailles Court of Appeal in February 2013. The safeguard procedure ended in July 2014. The Versailles Court of Appeal confirmed the enforceability of the security assignments of lease receivables (*"cession Dailly"*) even upon insolvency of the lessor.

This major case law in France confirmed the enforceability of rental assignments under the so-called *"Dailly"* assignment mechanism, meaning that the cash flows originating from the lease of the property will not be caught by the insolvency of the landlord.

The exit from insolvency was made possible with the acquisition by Lone Star of the PropCo as well as ultimate holding company together with buying out in the secondary market all the junior classes of notes issued by Windermere.

Following such acquisition, backed by its new sponsor, the PropCo was then able to borrow €935 million from Bank of America Merrill Lynch and pay off the securitised loans, which finally allowed for the full repayment of the outstanding senior classes of notes.

18.1.3.1.2   Update on French insolvency law

The *"Sauvegarde"* or safeguard procedure was introduced in French law in 2006. This is a form of insolvency proceeding inspired from the US Chapter 11 proceedings. Safeguard is open to any company that faces difficulties that it is unable to overcome. The opening of such a proceeding immediately triggers a mandatory stay of proceedings until the completion of the safeguard process. The company's management remains in full control of its day-to-day operations, subject to supervision by a court officer. The safeguard proceeding was introduced to protect French employees and was not meant to be applied for CRE SPVs.

The 2014 "creditor-friendly" reform of French insolvency law is a partial response to the *Cœur Défense* story. It introduced a conciliation mechanism with the reinforcement of the "new money" priority ranking. The safeguard procedure was slightly amended by introducing the possibility for creditors to propose an alternative restructuring plan and the potential conversion of the safeguard into a receivership without the debtor's consent. Another reform is expected in the near future to strengthen the rights of the lenders, particularly the ability to oust shareholders who refuse to agree with a recovery plan which would result in the dilution of their shareholdings.

French insolvency law is still not perfect and, as mentioned above, many lenders are still reluctant to lend in France for that reason. Several structures are available to mitigate the risk associated with the *sauvegarde* procedure.

18.1.4   Structuring solutions used by international lenders

18.1.4.1   The double Luxco

The aim of the double Luxco structure is to take control of the safeguard procedure, not to prevent the opening of safeguard. There is more flexibility of enforcement under Luxembourg law, which is perceived as a "creditor friendly" jurisdiction.

There are already many available articles discussing why and how to set up a double Luxco structure. As a result, the objective of this Chapter is to describe the concepts behind this structure.

Figure 19: Double Luxco structure

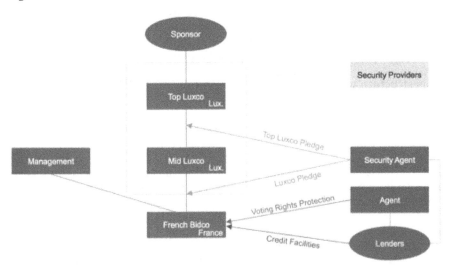

At a very basic level and as described in Figure 19, the double Luxco structure allows the security agent to enforce its share pledge on the Top Luxco. In the case of Cœur Défense, the security agent was unable to exercise its share pledge on the Luxembourg holding company because of the European Insolvency Regulation, which includes a concept of Centre of Main Interest (COMI). In the case of Cœur Défense, the borrower was able to claim that the Luxembourg holding company had its Centre of Main Interest in France and therefore was protected by the *Sauvegarde* and therefore prevented the lenders from enforcing their share pledge in Luxembourg. By introducing a top Luxco, whose centre of main interest cannot be in France, as it only holds the shares of another Luxembourg company, it is possible for a Lender to enforce its share pledge in Luxembourg and take control of the transaction.

However, the "double Luxco" structure, which had until a few years ago been put in place almost systematically, especially for large transactions, has been declining in popularity. This trend may be explained by the complexity of the structure and the significant related costs that it generates. As a result, the double Luxco is mostly applicable to larger transactions *and* foreign lenders. It would make little sense for a French borrower to create a

415

Luxembourg holding company to get financed. The same logic applies to French lenders. Double Luxco structures are therefore mostly used by foreign lenders that finance foreign CRE investors who would have invested through Luxembourg anyway. Current competition in the French lending market also reduces the appetite for such structures, as lenders proposing a double Luxco structure might appear as less competitive.

18.1.4.2 Taking control of the borrower through the granting of a "golden share"

Another potential structure is the "golden share" structure: If a safeguard is initiated, the Agent is entitled to dismiss managers of the French entity and to appoint new managers of its choice (without having to enforce its security interest over the shares of the French or Luxembourg entity).

This structure was used in the refinancing of Cœur Défense (together with the double Luxco structure), as an additional protection for the Lenders.

18.1.4.3 Isolating the collateral by placing it in a "security trust" or French "Fiducie"

In the French *Fiducie* structure, the ownership of certain assets (shares, cash, receivables, and the like) is transferred to a trustee to secure the payment of a loan. In the event of a default, the assets may be sold by the trustee to pay the loan.

The *Fiducie-sûreté* is much more efficient that a traditional pledge and has already been used in some significant restructurings and in real estate transactions with real estate SPVs, where the tax issues can already be avoided. The *Fiducie-sûreté* is certainly a good alternative to the double Luxco, even if it is still expensive to put in place.

18.1.5 Conclusion

Despite some relative bad press after the Cœur Défense default, France remains an attractive market for CRE lending: the French market is, depending on data sources, the second or third largest in Europe and competition between lenders is not as fierce as in the UK or Germany. French insolvency law has recently evolved in a positive direction and new structures give more protection to lenders.

The *Coeur Défense* case has probably attracted too much attention and as a result, many market players can't see the forest for the trees: lending volumes have remained relatively stable in France during the GFC while they dropped dramatically in other markets. There has been fewer enforcement procedures than in the UK or Germany and French banks remained strong during the GFC with no French CRE loan books being sold or transferred to an official "bad bank", although there has been some deleveraging or partial sale of loan portfolios occurring at some French banks. This shows that the fundamentals of the market were sound and that French lenders have been good at managing their loan books. Some may say that there has been a lot of "extend and pretend" among local lenders, which may be partially true, but it is probably not the worst strategy to manage CRE loan books, which are backed by cyclical assets by definition.

18.2 German Lending Market

Markus Hesse and Ahmed Elfeky,

IRE I BS

18.2.1 Introduction

In this Chapter, the International Real Estate Business School (IRE I BS)–University of Regensburg will provide a summary of the German Debt Project, where the authors have provided a detailed view on the market structure of German CRE lending (with a focus on institutional investment properties including residential).

The 2015 report (covering the years 2010 to 2014 plus a future outlook) is based on 24 face-to-face interviews with German CRE lenders all over Germany. Furthermore, the authors analysed a data pool of some €122 billion via a detailed data questionnaire. Based on this portfolio the authors will forecast the overall market structure of the German CRE lending market.

This Chapter will commence with an overview of the German lending market, including an illustration of the competitive status of the market, the overall performance of new business and loan books (i.e. the overall market portfolio), CRE loan maturities and a commentary on the long-term trends of the Pfandbrief market up to the year 2015. The Chapter will then discuss in detail how the German market is structured with respect to location, property type, lot sizes as well as market shares by type of lenders. In terms of lending conditions in Germany, this Chapter provides an overview of margins as well as LTVs trends and discussed NPLs. The Chapter concludes with a brief overview on the German CMBS market (based on data provided by Fitch for the GDP report).

18.2.2 Overview of the German lending market

18.2.2.1 The level of competition in the German lending market

From a highly elevated level there has been a further rise in competitive pressure in the year 2015 which continues into the year 2016. There is some consolidation in terms of the number of players, while at the same time there are new market entrants. Figure 1 illustrates the change in competitive dynamics observed by the financial institutions compared to six months before. The flattening of the bars, shown in Figure 1, is due to the marked rise in levels alone, i.e. the competitive pressure keeps rising, albeit not as sharply as a consequence of the levels. This trend continues to be triggered less by the competitive pressure generated by alternative suppliers, such as debt funds and insurance companies (they are particularly active in sub-markets, in particular), but rather by the very high "homemade" competitive pressure created by the German banks. In contrast to the UK, the market share of international lenders active in the German market is very low. Thus "homemade" can be taken literally. This very high level of competition is very important to bear in mind when analysing the overall market condition in this Chapter.

Figure 1: Perceived change in the competitive situation
(Comparison between the current and previous 6-month periods)

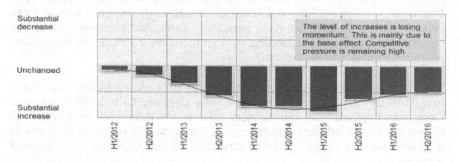

Source: IRE I BS

18.2.2.2   German outstanding CRE loans and new business

18.2.2.2.1   New business

The growth of new business in the German CRE lending market since 2014 has been impressive. Growth in new business also remained high in 2014 at 9%. The growth is not in double digits, as it had been in previous years; however, measured in terms of absolute figures, the increase still represents a dynamic expansion in new business (in particular when it is compared to the GDP growth of the economy). Extrapolated to the market as a whole, the business expansion amounted in 2014 to around €10.6 billion (compared to 2013 of €15.6 billion). The growth in new business to finance investment properties is supported on two fronts: CRE financing rose by 6.3%, and there was a double-digit rise of 16.9% in new business in the area of institutionally-held housing.

Figure 2: Growth in new business *(Changes compared to the previous year)*

Figure 3: Portfolio growth *(Changes compared to the previous year)*

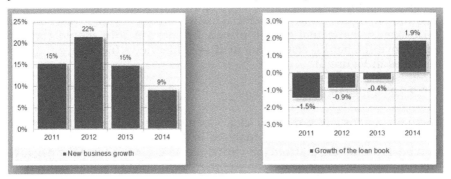

Source: IRE I BS   Source: IRE I BS

Despite the sustained strong growth in new business (Figure 2), there was only a modest rise in the volume of the total loan book (Figure 3). While loan book figures had remained virtually stable or had been in slight decline in previous years (Figure 3) despite the strong growth in new business, a rise in loan books of 1.9% was generated in 2014 (expectations in 2013: +2.6% growth in loan books). This figure is distorted slightly up by extraordinary circumstances.[1] Given the maturity structures (and early redemptions), very high growth in new business was required in order to keep loan books at a steady level. The pressure to transact new business remains high—which fits well with the abovementioned dynamics of competition.

Figure 4: Growth scenario (loan book and new business) in 2015 and 2016 *(Changes compared to the previous year)*

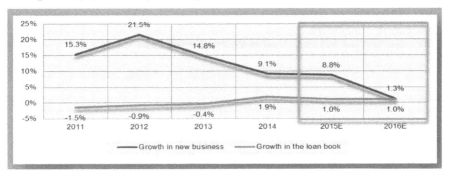

Source: IRE I BS

---

[1]   A large wind-down portfolio formed part of the analysis in the first year. In 2014, the portfolio figure was extrapolated further on the basis of the annual report. This was not done in 2015. A further extrapolation would have brought growth close to the zero line.

According to the expectations for new business surveyed in 2014, the dynamic continued in 2015. The survey has revealed that growth fluctuated in and around 2014 levels during 2015, i.e. around 9%, once again for new business, manifesting itself in a slight growth in loan books of almost 1% according to figures from the financial institutions. Interviews with banks in 2016 suggest that actual growth of new business in 2016 should come in well above the banks' statements in 2014's interviews (i.e. above the 2016 estimates in Figure 4).

18.2.2.2.2   Outstanding CRE loans

There was only slight growth in legacy loan books, despite the high growth in new business. The portfolio analysed in 2014, reveals growth of 1.9% in loan books following on from the virtual flat levels in 2013 and the negative growth of the years prior to that. In other words, the financial institutions used the high growth dynamic in new business, described above, in the previous years to prevent any further dwindling on their legacy loan books, which are the key drivers for the profit and loss accounts of banks. The ratio here is more favourable in 2014 with a slight growth in legacy loan books generated, despite there only having been single-digit growth in new business.

Table 1: Development of the loan book in terms of CRE and institutionally held residential property, Extrapolation of the analysed portfolios to the market as a whole
(in €billions)

	2010	2011	2012	2013	2014
Loan book: Commercial real estate	**241.1**	**240.1**	**241.7**	**242.0**	**252.8**
Relative change (y-o-y)		-0.4%	0.7%	0.1%	4.4%
Absolute change (y-o-y) - in € bn		-1.0	1.6	0.3	10.8
Share of total	55.0%	55.6%	56.5%	56.8%	58.2%
Loan book: Residential (institutionally-held)	**197.1**	**191.8**	**186.3**	**184.3**	**181.7**
Relative change (y-o-y)		-2.7%	-2.8%	-1.1%	-1.4%
Absolute change (y-o-y) - in € bn		-5.4	-5.5	-2.0	-2.6
Share of total	45.0%	44.4%	43.5%	43.2%	41.8%
Total loan book	**438.2**	**431.9**	**428.0**	**426.3**	**434.4**
Relative change (y-o-y)		-1.5%	-0.9%	-0.4%	1.9%
Absolute change (y-o-y) - in € bn		-6.4	-3.9	-1.7	8.1

Source: IRE I BS

A glance at the composition of CRE loan book development reveals much more positive developments in the area of CRE financing than in the institutionally held residential property sector. This is due to the level of maturities in residential.

Figure 5: Distribution by CRE and institutionally held residential property
(Existing: shares in the portfolio as percentages)

Figure 6: Growth in CRE and institutionally held residential property
(Existing: rate of change compared to PY)

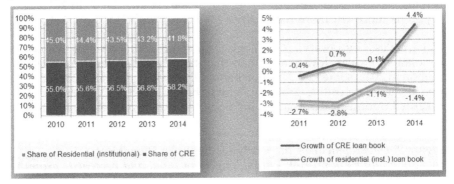

Source: IRE | BS

Source: IRE | BS

18.2.2.2.3 German CRE loan maturities

The share of maturities for 2016 and 2017 has been mostly at similar levels. Therefore, the curve (Figure 7) has seen not much change since 2013. For the year 2013, 21% of the loan book was due to reach maturity the following year, with 13% doing so the year after. For 2015 and 2016, 19% and 13% respectively were due to reach maturity over the next two years, i.e. a very similar maturity pattern.

Figure 7: Maturity profiles
(Maturity profiles of the 2014 loan book, shares as percentages)

Figure 8: Cumulative maturity profiles
(Cumulative maturity profiles of the 2014 loan book, shares as percentages)

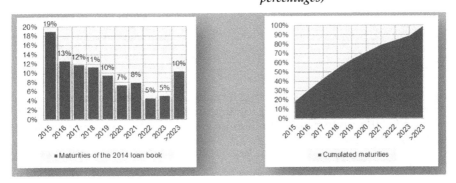

Source: IRE | BS

Source: IRE | BS

421

18.2.2.2.4   Pfandbrief market

The mortgage banks are still proving to be a central essential part of the total German Pfandbrief market. The growth of total shares, of both circulation and new-business divisions of the Hypothekenpfandbriefe, is confirming the extensive upward trend which started after 2007. In 2016, both divisions represent more than half of the shares of the total market.

Nevertheless, by observing the long term trend of the absolute values in circulation, a clear downward trend may be detected in levels of €197,726 million in 2015, some €58.3 million behind the starting levels of 2003. On the positive side, a positive growth rate may be observed in 2015 that may be regarded optimistically as a turning point in the observed excessive decline seen since 2010.

Figure 9: Development of the mortgage banks in Pfandbrief
(absolute values in million Euros, long-term trend and percentile growth
during 2003-2015)

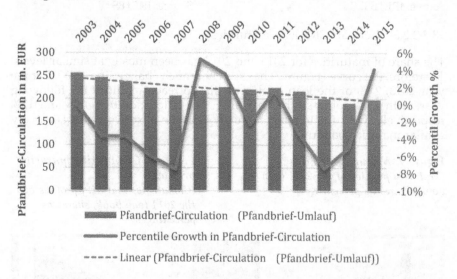

Source: IRE I BS, vdp

In respect of new business, the long term trend does confirm the downward trend. However, the extensive growth in the absolute values from €29,145 million in 2014 up to €40,369 million in 2015 is a high level of new business not observed since 2011.

Figure 10: Development of the mortgage banks (New-business) in Pfandbrief
(absolute values in million Euros, long-term trend and percentile growth during 2003–2015)

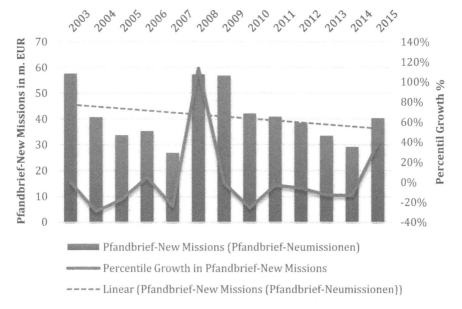

▬▬ Pfandbrief-New Missions (Pfandbrief-Neumissionen)

▬▬ Percentile Growth in Pfandbrief-New Missions

----- Linear (Pfandbrief-New Missions (Pfandbrief-Neumissionen))

Source: IRE I BS

18.2.3 Market segmentation

18.2.3.1 Market Segmentation by locations

18.2.3.1.1 Is there are market for larger players beyond the seven A-cities?

As Germany is a very decentralised market, it is of major importance to dissect the regional sub-markets and a larger number of top A-cities comprising a group of seven cities (Berlin, Düsseldorf, Frankfurt, Hamburg, Köln, Munich, Stuttgart). This is very different from the UK and the French market, which to a large degree are dominated via lending in London and Paris.

The shift away from A-cities did not continue in 2014. On the contrary, the share of the new businesses observed accounted for by A-cities rose significantly from around 55% to 66%. This seems surprising following developments in the previous year. This figure may be slightly distorted upwards by outliers,[2] but it begs the general question: to what extent is regional expansion within Germany practicable for the larger players—

---

[2]   In weighted terms, this question was answered by 51% of the portfolios analysed, representing some €60 billion.

423

which is the cornerstone of our analysis—as a differentiation strategy (to bypass those areas where competition is most intense)? At a second glance, the outlier year in Figure 11 is 2013; the share for 2014 is once again fairly in line with the broad trend of previous years.

Figure 11: Market Segmentation by locations
(The seven A-cities' share of the overall new business, CRE plus institutionally-held residential property)

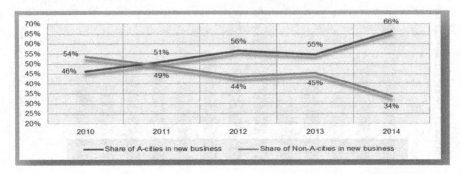

Source: IRE I BS

In Figure 11 Berlin and Munich have the lion's share, although the numbers for the A-cities' shares to the overall market has also been extrapolated. However, the size of the sample combined with a certain home bias may have distorted the figures somewhat. In Berlin, the city's share of the total portfolio analysed in 2014 rose to 21.7% of overall new business (compared to 2013 of 17.4%). Munich is also continuing to boom, with its share rising from 12% to 14%. There are striking rises in the figures in Frankfurt and Cologne, while Hamburg, Düsseldorf and Stuttgart remain stagnated.

The lot sizes soon become smaller in the provinces (i.e. beyond the seven A-cities). Regional expansion outside the A-cities may be a genuine option as a differentiation strategy for the strong competition in the seven A-cities, or at least while rival banks do not follow suit. However, the disadvantage to an expansion of this nature into the provinces is that the lot sizes soon become very small outside the well-known key urban centres. This approach may lead to transaction volumes which fail to deliver adequate economies of scale for the larger institutions, and furthermore, they might end-up in the hard-fought domain of the larger savings banks and cooperative banks (i.e. moving from one hard-fought market to another). This strategy of regional expansion (well outside the A-cities) is generally the preserve of those providers which can operate very intensively within a network strategy (i.e. larger players like Landesbanken teaming up with Sparkassen or coop-erative banks, Volksbanken, teaming up e.g. with DG Hyp.

There would appear to be no need to be concerned about the provision of financing in the regions for two reasons: Firstly, the savings banks and cooperative banks remain very willing to provide finance, on a scale that they had not been doing in 2013-2016.[3] Furthermore, there has been a sharp rise in readiness to provide financing for portfolio deals that frequently contain a mix of properties outside the A-cities, which has generated a surge of interest in portfolio financing. This has also whet the appetite for financing outside the A-cities through the back door, and with adequate lot sizes for financial institutions.

Somewhere between "Out of the frying pan and into the fire" and/or "Hare and Tortoise"? In the case of commitments in the higher seven figure range, a new, equally hard-fought, level of competition, i.e. the sphere occupied by larger savings banks and cooperative banks, as well as their network partners, is encountered. The only suitable strategy for regional expansion would be to target those B- and C-cities with an adequately stable economic profile coupled with adequately large lot sizes for financing transactions. However, many banks also have these types of cities in their sights, and it frequently ends up like a game of "Hare and Tortoise". Outside those obvious cities, it most often only makes sense for supra-regional banks which are structured within a network organisation.

As investors mostly fail to find sufficient transaction volumes in prime locations of A-cities, many investors turned to secondary locations in those cities. Still, as it becomes also more difficult to find sufficient volume in these areas, it is too early to say that the strong focus of large lenders will remain on A-cities. The picture for 2016 is already less evident; it shows some indication of a shift beyond the top seven cities.

18.2.3.1.2   Increasing the share of international lending instead of moving towards smaller cities

One option, which the banks generally regarded as being of less relevance in our first study roughly four years ago, is now clearly coming to the fore: the pronounced willingness to increase their share of lending abroad. Consequently, the alternative is not necessarily to "continue a strategy of provincial sales"; some banks are pursuing the option of increasing their activities abroad instead (many German lenders reduced their international exposure substantially after the GFC). However, the alternatives are frequently in non-Euro countries where potential financing benefits and sought-after diversification advantages may be quickly eroded by foreign currency hedging, and the erosion of margins also unfolds in foreign markets.

---

[3]   Only the change in the volume of new business undertaken by savings banks and cooperative banks on the basis of interviews conducted with a few very large savings banks and cooperative banks may be gauged. None of the savings banks or cooperative banks completed a data questionnaire as part of the data collection project over the past three years. That is due to their being structured as all-purpose banks and to the real estate sector's capacity to set itself apart.

Clear growth in foreign business: Our study focuses on the German market.[4] According to vdp research, foreign loan pledges were already up 16% in 2014. The growth trend has continued in 2015 and 2016.

Is the renewed growth in interest abroad indicative that the international market has normalised or is there increasing scepticism about the potential of the domestic market (or both)? While many financial institutions have primarily focused their attention on domestic markets in recent years following the GFC, those financial institutions who never fully withdrew their interest from the market, have now opted to focus more on foreign markets as an alternative to nationwide expansion.[5] This is further borne out in the figures for 2015 and 2016. It also goes some way towards explaining the lower growth expectations for new business in Germany in 2016.

18.2.3.1.3   New business in project developments

In the area of residential-property development financing, it is true to say that while the cake may have become appreciably bigger, the appetite of suppliers has increased as well. Even though all financial institutions are not involved in the area of residential-property development financing—far from it—there has also been a sharp increase in the competitive pressure in that sub-market. The LTVs have also risen substantially there, which is also reflected in part in significant rises in construction costs.

Table 3: New business in project developments
Extrapolation of the analysed portfolios to the market as a whole
(in €billions)

	2013	2014
New business: Investments	**81.7**	**89.3**
Growth (y-o-y)	20.2%	9.2%
Absolute change (y-o-y) in € bn	13.8	7.5
Share of total	77.5%	77.0%
New business: Project developments	**23.7**	**26.7**
Growth (y-o-y)	8.6%	12.9%
Absolute change (y-o-y) in € bn	1.9	3.1
Share of total	22.5%	23.0%
New business: Commercial developer financing	**13.7**	**12.0**
Growth (y-o-y)		-12.5%
Absolute change (y-o-y) in € bn		-1.7
Share relative to new business	13.0%	10.3%
Share relative to project developmtents	58.0%	44.9%
New business: Residential-property development financing	**9.9**	**14.7**
Growth (y-o-y)		48.0%
Absolute change (y-o-y) in € bn		4.8
Share relative to new business	9.4%	12.7%
Share relative to project developmtents	42.0%	55.1%

Source: IRE I BS

---

[4]   The German market indicates that the relevant finance properties in Germany are localised.
[5]   Given the fact that they are embedded in regional markets, or due to other organisational obstacles or external requirements, this door does of course remain closed to some financial institutions.

Different levels of exposure of the banks in the area of project developments: Furthermore, not all the banks interviewed are involved in the area of project development. Property-development financing requires specialist expertise, and the business can be very cyclical, as discussed in Chapter 8. None of the banks interviewed are new arrivals in this sector; i.e. the banks represented in this area have already accumulated years of experience in this particular field. It became clear during the interviews that the competitive pressure in residential-property development financing has risen significantly and is reflected in higher LTVs. The marked rise in construction costs (i.e. the increased LTC, loan-to-cost) may further have something to do with this. Many developers wish to minimise the impact of their activities on their equity, and the competition that exists between the banks is giving them increasing scope to do so. In addition, covenants in this area gradually seem to have become less restrictive. However, the banks interviewed have an eye on the risks involved and can draw upon the experience that they have built up from many years of relations with customers when weighing up their options. As long as the demand for new housing remains sustainable and is not disrupted by exogenous effects, the risks at least appear manageable in the average assessment.

Insufficient "fodder" for commercial developer financing in 2014: The slowdown in new business in the area of commercial development financing is not attributable to any reluctance on the part of the banks. Quite the opposite, in fact; the financiers involved in this area would happily do more business in this higher-margin sub-market; there is simply a shortage of fundable assets. Figures 14 and 15 illustrate the situation based on figures from the investment market in the A-cities. While the monetarised project volume in the area of residential property has clearly risen in recent years, there has been a continuous slowdown in commercial developer projects in the area of CRE. With a modest rise of 1.3%, 2014 does not mark a sustainable change in trend. Banks seeking to expand their share of project developments either have to secure large market shares in commercial development projects or have to focus more on residential property development financing. The question of risk assessment arises here. Furthermore, with the expansion of shares within the portfolios, there will be increased pressure to have to replace this fast-turning business with further business or to endure reductions in loan books. The appetite in residential property development financing as well as in commercial development financing has increased further in 2015 and 2016—and there are more projects being realised by developers.

In 2014, project financing rose to 23% of all new business (compared to the previous year of 22.5%). Consequently, the growth rate last year of 12.9% was well above the rise in overall new business growth (+9.2%). What drives the growth dynamic in the area of project financing? It is not commercial development financing in CRE (growth there is actually negative at 12.5%); the growth results from the clear expansion in the area of residential-property development financing. The growth figures are characterised by large-volume expansion of financing for new residential units; the rise in this sub-area has been extrapolated to almost €5 billion.

18.2.3.1.4 Market segmentation by property types

Office and retail properties have kept a stable share of the total market. These two segments are still considered by both the investment market and analysed financial institutions to hold the majority share of the whole market. While office spaces have reserved in 2014 a slightly lower share of the overall market than in 2013, it owned a share above the 40% limit (with respect to the investment market), meanwhile the financial institutions showed a constant share levels since 2012. Retail spaces have showed an overall declining trend since 2010, but still have been keeping its share above the 30% limit (with respect to investment market).

Figure 14: Office space—shares of the overall volume
(Shares of new business, shares in the investment volume)

Figure 15: Retail space—shares of the overall volume
(Shares of new business, shares in the investment volume)

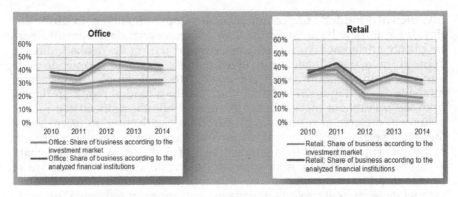

Source: IRE I BS, bulwiengesa   Source: IRE I BS, bulwiengesa

2014 was a year for "other" CRE finance. New business in CRE rose by about 6% in 2014. How is the volume of new business distributed throughout the CRE sector now? Following a boom year in 2013 in retail property, with a volume of financing which is extrapolated at just under €22 billion, this type of property was down slightly in 2014 (−7%; −€1.7 billion). New business in the sub-market of residential property, which is of relevance here, rose markedly in 2014 (+17%; + €6.3 billion). However, the biggest drivers for growth were other commercial financing, which rose by around 39% (+ €5.3 billion).

Around €12 billion in logistics and hotel financing: Based on the figures extrapolated from the portfolio analysed, new business in logistics real estate amounted to €6.3 billion in 2014, closely followed by hotels at €5.5

billion. This is the first year in which the banks interviewed provided an adequate split for the "Other CRE financing" section; consequently, adequately robust figures are not available from 2013 for comparison purposes. The high rise in Others (+39%)—leads to expectation that there will be very dynamic growth, both for logistics, as well as for hotels. There has been a clear rise, both in demand from investors, as well as in the willingness on the part of the banks to finance operator real estate. This is a development which had already taken place in 2013, but which is only now becoming apparent in these financing figures following something of a delay.

18.2.3.1.5 Typical lot sizes over time

The new business of the financial institutions can be divided into different size classes. The average lot size for all the financial institutions analysed in the study lies between €10 million and €50 million. However, the survey reveals two statements about size classes:

(1)   There has been a further significant rise in the share of large-volume financing arrangements.
(2)   There is no indication that lenders have made further strides to leave A-cities (with correspondingly smaller lot sizes).

Both of these observations are consistent with the result of rising shares of new business in A-cities discussed above. Since 2014, it has gradually become increasingly easy to find a source of financing for large nine-digit commitments. The share of smaller lot sizes in the seven-digit range fell markedly from 2010 to 2013, persisting in 2014 at the lower level from the previous year. However, it is important to bear in mind that the data sample does not include any regional cooperative banks and savings banks. Consequently, it cannot be ruled out that these financial institutions may compensate for the downturn.

18.2.3.1.6 Lenders active in the German market (including alternative lenders or funds)

The main active lenders in the German market could be divided into:

• Regional banks
• Branches of foreign banks (Zweigstellen ausländischer Banken)
• Major banks (Großbanken)
• Landesbanken
• Savings banks (Sparkassen)
• Credit Unions/Cooperatives (including the head institutes)
• Mortgage banks (Realkreditinstitute)
• Building societies (Bausparkassen)

The total amount of the commercial lenders' participation amounted to €242.9 billion in 2015 according the reported figures by the German central bank and vdp research GmbH. and the following illustrates that credit unions and savings banks together represent more than half of the contributing shares in commercial lending, while building societies (Bausparkassen) and branches of foreign banks having barely recognised shares not exceeding 1% of the total sum.

Figure 16: Commercial lenders active in the German market-2015 (market shares)

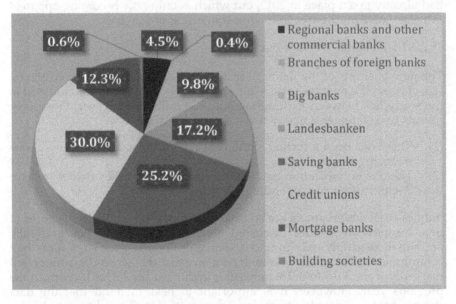

Source: IRE I BS, German Central Bank and vdp Research GmbH

18.2.4   *Typical lending terms*

Both the erosion in margins and the LTV rise in 2014 have proved to be much more modest than the financial institutions had expected in the previous year's study. The margin (net margin after liquidity costs) has dropped to 129 bps instead of 114, i.e. a much more modest development than had been envisaged by the financial institutions in 2014. The same applies to the LTVs. A change in trend, with an average rise to 69.5% was predicted in 2014's interviews for CRE, whereas the current figures show a rise to only 67.2%. The reversal in margin and LTV trends anticipated by the financial institutions also actually materialised in both cases, although not on the scale described in their expectations. Admittedly it is possible that the margins for properties with the same risk may have actually come down more significantly (e.g. there is a mix effect related to higher margin development financing).

Where will the downward spiral end after the down-turn in margins? The perceived pressure on margins is considerably higher than the figures indicated in Figure 17. With regard to the data collected, i.e. the analysis of the data questionnaires, the net margin (net margin active[6]) in 2014, has now dropped by four basis points (to around 129 basis points). The continued slight decline in liquidity costs has made a positive contribution towards this. It should be borne in mind that increasing risks, i.e. rising LTVs and expansion into riskier market segments, as well as more stringent regulations, should normally lead to greater margin demand; instead, the competitive situation brings about a reversal in the trend (downswing of margin). The decline in margin for the market as a whole, indicated in the figures, at least appears lower than the erosion in margins perceived by some of the market operators. The operators anticipated the downturn in margins to continue. According to the 2015 survey, margins will drop a further 20 basis points to 109 basis points through 2016, or at least that is what the interviewees expect to see. Interviews conducted at the time of writing with banks support this expected decline.

This will take margins below the 2010 level, or, in other words, the entire increase in margins achieved in recent years will be more than consumed, despite the more stringent margin requirements. This trend had already become apparent in interviews conducted in previous years. That said, the pressure on margins had been over-compensated for in previous years by portfolio effects ("portfolio streamlining").[7] But this is now largely in the past.

Figure 17: Actual decline in margins with rising LTVs
(Left scale—margins: gross margin and net margin active (after liquidity costs) in basis points; right scale—LTVs in percentage points)

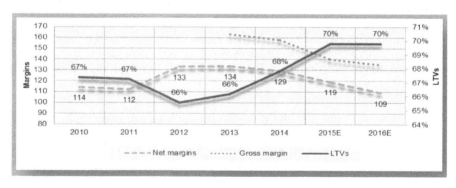

Source: IRE I BS

---

[6] Gross margin less liquidity costs.
[7] These portfolio effects indicate that it is misleading if the margin rises; the financed assets, however, would warrant an even greater rise in margin since the margins would already have gone down in the past adjusted to reflect risk.

LTVs and covenants have come under pressure parallel with the margins: rising competitive pressure is not only stopping at margins—it is increasingly also affecting loan-to-value ratios and covenants.[8] There was frequent reference made in the interviews to the fact that the impact of the competitive pressure was initially felt in the margins, and that the structures, i.e. the LTVs and the covenant requirements, come under pressure at a later point. This is not borne out by our figures for the overall portfolio. The pressure is felt on margins and on LTVs at the same time at least. It did however, occur later in the case of covenants. This may be seen more evidently through 2016.

The weighted LTVs for the entire portfolio analysed—CRE and institutionally-held housing—rose in 2014 to 67.8% (compared with the previous year of 66.1%). While that is not a particularly strong rise, two factors need to be taken into consideration:

(a)   The gradual rise in real estate prices, i.e. the "V" in LTV, has obviously slowed down the rise in LTV.
(b)   The composition of the LTVs in each of the loan books analysed is not known. Cluster risks are possible with high LTVs, which are compensated for in the average assessment by particularly low LTVs (discussed below).

What does that mean specifically? A rising percentage of customers are seeking low LTVs and, based on that, as attractive a margin as possible; they are only looking for low leverage because they wish to identify market investments for their high liquidity and are finding it challenging in any event to gain adequately investable core assets. With slight rises in LTVs on average, there must by necessity be an increase in the percentage of the distribution with clearly expanded LTVs, at the expense of the mean. If this theory of an expansion in high LTVs is correct, the risk profile in respect of LTVs has risen more sharply than the modest average expansion might suggest at first glance.[9]

Nonetheless, it is felt that the financial institutions are keeping a close eye on LTVs and on the capacity to repay the financing, as well as on the financial ability to meet repayments, and this is certainly the case to a very different degree than prior to the GFC. Developments become more challenging but still appear justifiable.

---

[8]   The opinions of the financial institutions on the detail of how to structure their products differ. Some are in favour of fewer covenants, albeit very clearly formulated, and, thus, covenants which can be monitored with a measure of focus. Other financial institutions prefer 50 pages with very detailed documentation about the covenant. In addition to the pressure on margins and LTVs, the pressure of too little margin was much more pronounced in a buyer's market in 2014 than in either of the two previous years.
[9]   This is particularly the case where the increased share of financing with high LTVs has taken place in rather more risky investments.

18.2.4.1   Margin performance over time

Reversal in margin trends is becoming visible in the figures, seen in Figures 18 and 19: net margins (after liquidity costs) are among the banks' central controlling factors for the contribution towards net interest income. In 2012 and 2013, the net margins for new business increased by a good 20 bps, a marked rise. Some of the financial institutions managed to widen their margin slightly in 2014 as well; however, the margin level was down a good 4 bps in the weighted average for the analysed portfolio. The net margin in CRE (–5.5 bps) fell more quickly than that in institutionally held residential property (–2.4 bps). The competitive pressure and according pressure on margins were said by the interviewees to be rather higher in the area of residential property; however, this will most likely tend to be reflected in the 2015 figures.

Figure 18: Active net margin in new business (in basis points)

Figure 19: Active net margin in the loan book (in basis points)

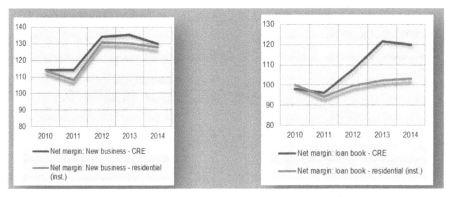

Source: IRE I BS

Source: IRE I BS

18.2.4.2   LTVs over time

LTVs in new business rose by 1.7 percentage points in 2014 (see Figure 20). If one considers the area of CRE separately, the average LTVs were in steady decline from 2010 to 2013 (down 2.1%), but then rose again in 2014 (up 1.9%). 2012 was an outlier in our statistical series for institutionally-held residential property—otherwise, the LTVs for 2013 (67.5%) were virtually at the 2010 level; a further rise was then achieved of 1.2% to 67.8% in 2014 (see Figure 21). In terms of project development (73.9%), the values were virtually at the previous year's level; with the expectation to see the LTVs widen in that case (see Figure 22).

Figure 20: Weighted LTVs in new business from 2010 to 2014 (in percentage points)

Figure 21: Distribution in LTVs in new business in 2014 (in percentage points)[10]

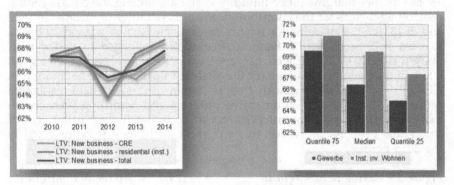

Source: IRE I BS

Source: IRE I BS

Figure 22: LTVs in the loan book—graphical (in percentage points)

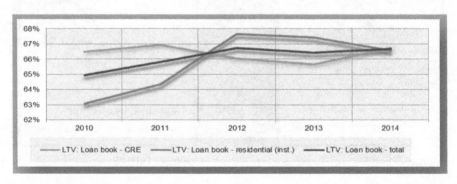

Source: IRE I BS

---

[10] Moreover, deliberately not shown are any maximum and minimum values; otherwise, allocation to specific financial institutions could possibly have been conceivable.

18.2.5 NPL-performance in the German market

Figure 23: Non-performing loans (percentage share relative to the loan book)
      Figure 24: Loan-loss provisions (percentage share relative to the loan book)

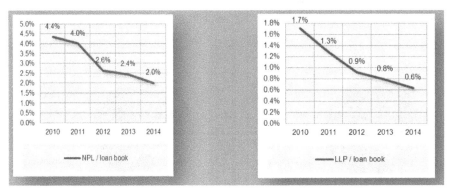

Source: IRE I BS   Source: IRE I BS

The level of NPLs for which there are arrears with debt service payments is also a relevant indicator for the shape of the overall portfolio. The trend in this ratio has been significantly downwards (i.e. improvement) in the few years leading up to 2016. This is no surprise in an upbeat real estate market.

Based upon the portfolios analysed in Figure 23, the ratio of NPL to loan books has more than halved since 2010; the number has dropped from 4.4% to 2.0%. This is an expected development in a booming real estate market. In addition, the portfolio adjustments are reflected in the financial institution's figures. The ratio of specific allowances for bad debts to the loan books seen in Figure 24 has been virtually reduced to a third since 2010 (from 1.7% to 0.6%). This relieves the burden in the financial institutions' income statements.

18.2.6 Brief glance at the German CMBS market[11]

18.2.6.1 Market volume

€9 billion of CMBS analysed by Fitch: At the start of 2015, the European CMBS portfolio analysed by Fitch consisted of 88 loans which were completely or largely secured by real estate in Germany. The portfolio of securitised loans stood at approximately €9.4 billion. This makes Germany the second largest market for CMBS in Europe (after the UK). German loans accounted for 42% of the outstanding European portfolio (by quantity, or 23% by portfolio), see figures 25 and 26.

---

[11] The paper on the topic of CMBS was prepared for the study by Andrew Currie, Christian Ganthaler and Mario Schmidt, Fitch Ratings, London.

Figure 25: Distribution of the German Fitch CMBS portfolio by property type and market value
(Market value: distribution as percentages)

Figure 26: Distribution of the German Fitch CMBS portfolio by property type and quantity of loans
(Quantity of loans: Quantity and percentage distribution as percentages)

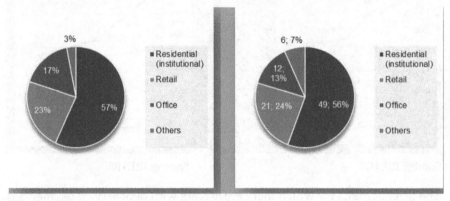

Source: Fitch   Source: Fitch

18.2.6.1.1   LTVs and interest coverage

18.2.6.1.2   Loan-to-values and underlying real estate

The calculated LTV for the loans (as a weighted average) reached a level of 105% at the start of 2015; the figure estimated by Fitch is 110%. This corresponds to a marked rise on 2014 (91% and 104% respectively), whereby the levels reported are moving towards the higher LTVs estimated by Fitch. The rise in the estimate given by Fitch can be explained in part by the aforementioned repayment of large portfolios of multiple-family homes, with relatively lower LTVs. The LTVs throughout the entire European credit portfolio (reported: 93%; Fitch estimate: 96%) are lower than the corresponding German values on average; new issue activity was higher in the likes of the UK or Italy in 2014 than was the case in Germany, and at lower LTVs than prior to the outbreak of the financial crisis. In addition, outstanding German CMBS have a greater exposure to loans from 2006/ 2007 than their European equivalents.

18.2.6.1.3   Interest coverage

The reported interest coverage ratio and debt service coverage ratio of the German portfolio analysed by Fitch were 2.3x and 1.8x better than the European average (2.1x and 1.8x). One reason for a similar level of interest coverage ratio, despite the higher leverage (measured in LTV) is the maturity profile of the German loans: in January 2015, 69 of the 88 German loans were already overdue. A higher ratio than other European countries (the UK has higher shares of long-term CMBS, for instance). Typically, the interest rate swaps expire upon maturity, which means that the interest yield becomes variable. This has a positive influence on interest coverage in the present low-interest climate.

18.2.6.1.4   Maturities and repayments

18.2.6.1.4.1   Maturity extensions

The majority of the loans are either overdue or must be repaid in 2015 or 2016 (83 loans; €5.0 billion). Of the 69 loans which are overdue, 49 had less than four years remaining (15 fewer than two years ago), see figure 27. This makes any further loan maturity extensions less likely and puts pressure on special servicers to work out these loans on schedule. See further Chapters 9, 10 and 11).

Figure 27: CMBS—Distribution of the 88 loans analysed by Fitch by maturity
(Quantity of loans)

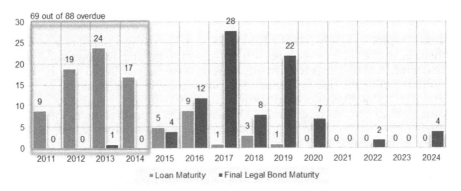

Source: Fitch

18.2.6.1.5   Repayment history

The analysed repayment relates to a portfolio with underlying properties in Germany amounting to (€36.8 billion or 231 loans). In detail:

• 79 loans (€19.7 billion) before scheduled maturity;
• 19 loans (€3.6 billion) at scheduled maturity;
• 49 loans (€6.6 billion) after scheduled maturity;
• 48 loans (€4.7 billion) were bought back by the issuers.
• In addition, there were 36 loss allocations in loans with an original portfolio of €2.2 billion. The weighted loss rate for those loans was 37% (see Figures 28 and 29).

Figure 28: CMBS—Repayment
history of the German portfolio
(Absolute figures in €billion—in
cumulative terms, an analysed portfolio
of €37 billion; percentage figures:
distribution of the values)

Figure 29: CMBS—Repayment
history of the German portfolio—
Quantity of loans
(Quantity of loans in the individual
categories and percentage distribution
of the quantities of loans)

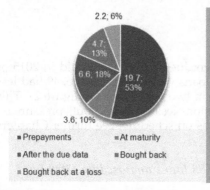

Source: Fitch

Source: Fitch

18.2.7 Conclusion

This Chapter has shown that whilst there is in Germany a rising risk profile, there is, at the time of writing, still no reason to be unduly concerned. The risk profile of the financial institutions is adversely affected by the continued significant rise in competitive pressure, with implications for margins and LTVs. Ever more stringent regulatory requirements and rising real estate prices are creating parallel challenges. On a positive note, the banks are in a position to report high growth in new business which translates into more or less stable loan books.

Despite the increasing challenges, the risk profile for the market as a whole remains manageable, but more and more demanding. In the interviews, in 2015 and 2016, the financial institutions made barely any changes in respect of the basic macro-economic scenario: one of continued solid economic growth in Germany coupled with low interest rates. If this scenario persists, the challenge of getting around further increases in real estate prices will tend to rise further. If expectations are too high for the economy or if interest rates rise higher than expected, the underlying real estate market will cool off significantly. If that period starts, initially being at an average LTV of under 70% would be helpful. It is difficult to predict how long the upswing will last. Furthermore, the individual portfolios should not contain too much exposure simultaneously, which would create inadequately secure cashflow at very high LTVs. Neither the average LTV levels which have been reached, nor the market scenario from an LTV perspective appear to be a particular cause for concern yet, but banks have to remain very selective and the focus on the distribution curve of LTVs per institution and for the market as a whole has become more important to observe.

Are the margins in the scenario for up to 2016 adequate for the risks involved? If the net margins up to 2016 drop below the margin level for 2010 and, at the same time, the margin levels are expanded significantly, due to more stringent regulatory requirements, this begs the question as to whether the capital costs can still be earned. This question is beyond the scope of this Chapter but is certainly worthwhile investigating further going forward. As long as the question can be answered in the affirmative, the financial institutions' growth strategy for preserving the loan books would make sense.

However, if it can—in particular when also taking into account looming impacts from Basel IV—potentially be answered for the German CRE lending market with a "no", this means that it is time to be markedly more selective in the management of new business and, if there is any doubt, to apply the brakes to growth. As things currently stand, other areas of the banks appear to be in a significantly weaker position in the opportunity/ risk profile; otherwise, the financial institutions would not allocate resources to real estate financing to the extent that they currently do. As long as the German macro story holds and interest rate levels remain low, lenders will remain very active in this market with no major relief in terms of competitive pressure. While some German lenders have an increasing appetite to do business abroad, additional international players have entered the German market. However, the German lending market remains largely dominated by domestic players. Insurance companies and pensions funds are becoming more relevant, but have not yet accumulated large market shares; even less so for debt funds.

In terms of market structure, financing conditions and refinancing, the German CRE lending market is substantially different from other key European markets, like France and the UK. In terms of refinancing, the Pfandbrief has been a strong success story while CMBS in Germany has not yet revived after the GFC. But the key differentiator is the highly fragmented market by lenders, as well as the focus on the regions in Germany. Therefore, having in-depth regional analysis capabilities and at the same time being able to offer highly competitive margins is a challenging mix.

18.3 Italian NPL Market

Andrea Pinto,
Partner, K&L Gates LLP

Marco Mazzola,
Trainee, K&L Gates LLP

18.3.1 Introduction

This Chapter, through a legal analysis of the new legislation changes that recently occurred in Italy and the main enforcement procedures and best practices seen in the Italian Market as utilised by international lenders, aims at providing a high level overview of the Italian NPL Market.

Since the occurrence of the GFC, resulting in the worsening of the creditworthiness of the borrowers (in particular the small and medium-sized enterprises), the Italian NPL global change initial case market after NPL has grown to more than €350 billion in 2016 (tripling since 2007).

In the economic context witnessed in mid-July 2016 following the Brexit referendum, the Italian banks—active on the market—have been forced to successfully manage the majority of their non-performing real estate loan portfolios through rescheduling or restructuring transactions. As a result of falling share values, increasing capital requirements and new legislation, Italian banks have also started to consider selling their NPL portfolios to specialised investors (potentially real estate investment funds).

In light of the above, this Chapter presents a high level overview of the Italian NPL Market, with a particular focus on the new legislation changes which might ensure an active market for the NPLs in Italy, together with the possibility to play a more active role for Italian banks in supporting new lending transactions.

18.3.2 Overview of the Italian NPL Market

One of the main reasons behind the accumulation of NPLs in Italy is essentially connected with the increase in the companies' defaults resulting from the GFC, together with the slowness of the recovery and repossessing procedures that made it even more difficult to dispose of NPLs, especially the category of the worst of the NPLs, the so-called *"sofferenze"* or "bad debt" (see Figure 1).

Figure 1. Nonperforming Loans

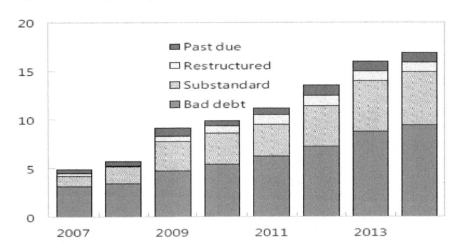

Source: IMF Financial Soundness Indicators: European Central Bank (ECB)

In particular, the Bank of Italy defines *"sofferenze"* as those receivables, the collection of which is not certain by the lenders, because the borrowers are in a state of insolvency (even if a declaration of insolvency has not been issued by a court) or in similar situations.

The basis for such a designation is principally to ensure that the relevant borrower can carry out a restructuring or rescheduling transaction, rather than immediately sell their NPL portfolios to specialised investors. In such a context, the primary pre-condition—requested by the Italian banks—for a debt restructuring, is a cooperative behaviour of the management and of the sponsor of the borrower, so that the Italian banks can also take into consideration the business model and the quality of the asset as criteria necessary to potentially obtain a credit committee's approval of the proposed restructuring transaction. In addition, the Italian bank credit committees may request the availability of additional equity together with the opportunity to increase the bank's margins.

Although the deterioration rates are, at the time of writing, gradually stabilising, the overall amount of the NPLs' exposure in Italy is very significant, such that the process of selling NPLs is a crucial strategy of deleveraging which must occur in Italy. In fact, faced with the falling value of Italian bank shares post Brexit, the Italian banks have been requested to adjust their regulatory capital, so that the disposals of non-core assets are becoming more strategic to limit the use of capital increases.

In this respect, it should be recalled that one of the most important factors that has prevented the NPL sales market not taking off during or post the

441

GFC, is because of the so called "spread bid/ask" which is driven by the wide difference between the price at which banks would sell NPLs and the price at which the trade operators are willing to buy NPLs (see Figure 2).

Figure 2: Who buys and sells Italian NPLs?

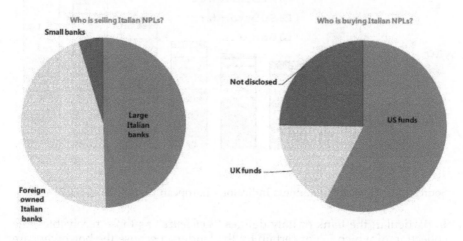

Source: PwC (2013)

In light of the above, in certain instances, some banks are independently creating models for in-house management of the assets which has been granted as security for CRE problematic loans, providing for—for example—the setting up of ad hoc vehicles in which real estate non-core assets and NPLs may be transferred. The purpose is to manage, enhance and then divest the shareholdings in real estate companies lightening the total amount of impaired loans and thus freeing capital available for new investments.

In other instances, certain management companies are promoting the creation of a real estate reserved alternative investment fund, investing, indirectly, in NPLs secured by real estate collateral through the subscription of notes issued by SPVs, such investment may also include a direct investment in such loans and real estate properties.

Furthermore, as occurs in other countries, it may be useful for the Italian banks, in order to reduce their NPL stock, to work more closely with foreign investors, in order to directly purchase NPLs portfolios, or work with banks for the purpose of the restructuring of distressed borrowers. In fact, at the time of writing, the interest in the NPL market is growing in Italy, so much so, that two of the largest Italian banks, UniCredit S.p.A. and Intesa Sanpaolo S.p.A., are considering a partnership with outside investors in order to setting up SPVs to manage a portion of their NPLs.

In order to encourage the purchase of NPLs, the Italian government has introduced, in the context of wider reform that is intended to be implemented, Law no. 49 dated 8 April 2016, which is a new guarantee scheme for the securitisation of NPLs (*Garanzia sulla Cartolarizzazione delle Sofferenze* or GACS) which seeks to increase the liquidity in the NPL market, by facilitating leverage on portfolio sales.

The abovementioned scheme will be effective until 16 August 2017. The Ministry of Economic and Finance may extend such term for another 18-months period, subject to the prior approval of the European Commission. In particular, the Italian government's intervention is limited to the coverage of the timely interests payment and the principal payment obligation on the senior tranches of asset-backed notes issued by Italian SPVs, which are backed by NPLs assets serviced by external servicers, independent from the originating bank.

The GACS is granted pursuant to a decree issued by the Ministry of Economic and Finance, upon request of the originating bank, which shall annually pay a guarantee fee applied out of the securitisation waterfall. In case the GACS is called, it shall refer to the outstanding amount on the senior notes at the respective final maturity date. So, the GACS is payable at first demand, in respect of amounts which are past due for at least 60 days, and the relevant payment shall be made between four and nine months, starting from the date on which a payment request notice has been sent by the representative of noteholders to the securitisation SPV. Once the payment has been made by the Italian State, the latter is subrogated in the rights of the senior holders of the notes.

18.3.3 New legislation changes: how the Banking Monopoly Rules and alternative sources of lending can co-exist

The coming into force of Law no. 49 dated 8 April 2016 (Law 49), has introduced in Italy a new "level one" set of regulatory provisions concerning, inter alia, the direct lending in Italy by EU alternative investment funds (EU AIFs) and Italian alternative investment funds (Italian AIFs), with an aim to try to cut down the scope of the banking monopoly rules.

Indeed, Law 49 supplements a series of legislative acts that have been enacted in Italy since 2012, in response to the GFC and the tightening of regulatory capital requirements for the European banks, with a view to minimising the regulatory and tax hurdles that prevented alternative finance providers from lending to Italian companies, with the intent to diversify firms' debt funding sources and compensate for the drop in bank lending, as has occurred in the UK as witnessed by the opening few Chapters of this book.

Pursuant to the banking monopoly rules, lending to the Italian public on a professional basis has been traditionally reserved in Italy to the licensed banks and financial institutions, such as Italian banks, European banks licensed and/or passported by the Bank of Italy, non-EU banks acting through an Italian facility office and Italian financial intermediaries enrolled in a specific register held by the Bank of Italy pursuant to art.106 (the 106 Register) of the Legislative Decree no. 385, dated 1 September 1993 (Italian Banking Act), and subject to regulatory and prudential provisions broadly mirroring those applicable to banks. In this context, Law no. 116 dated 11 August 2014, (Law 116) and Law 49 have together amended the regulatory framework applicable to direct lending, granting to other entities (subject to a number of conditions), such as insurance companies, securitisation vehicles and alternative investment funds, the opportunity to enter the Italian lending market.

In fact, the possibility for the Italian insurance companies to directly advance loans to Italian borrowers, has been granted by Law 116—which has amended the Italian Banking Act and the Legislative Decree no. 206, dated 6 September 2005—upon satisfaction of the following conditions: (i) the borrowers shall be selected by a bank or by financial intermediary enrolled in the 106 Register; (ii) the bank or the financial intermediary referred to in (i) above shall retain a *"substantial economic interest"* in the transaction (so-called *skin in the game*); and (iii) the insurance company shall have an adequate system of internal controls and credit risk management and an adequate level of capitalisation.

As required by Law 116, on 22 October 2014 the Italian insurance supervisory authority (IVASS) enacted secondary legislation, detailing the conditions and limitations governing the direct lending by Italian insurance companies. Such secondary legislation requires insurance companies to submit to IVASS a detailed plan of their proposed lending activity, describing the process governing the selection and monitoring of the lending operations. In addition, if a bank does not assist them, they must also demonstrate their ability to manage credit risk in accordance with banking standards. The legislation makes a distinction between different categories of credit, to which specific quantitative limits apply. Finally, the new rules state that the capitalisation of insurance companies engaging in lending activity shall be evaluated taking account, at the time of writing, the future prudential regulations governing the insurance sector (Solvency II— see further Chapters 16 and 17), which differ from the existing rules that envisage a risk-based assessment of capital requirements.

As part of the efforts to enhance the role of alternative debt capital providers in the Italian market, Law 116 has amended Law no. 130, dated 30 April 1999 (Italian Securitisation Law), allowing companies established and operating under such law (the Law130 Companies) to directly advance loans to Italian borrowers by issuing notes to finance the disbursement, upon satisfaction of the following conditions: (i) the borrowers are selected by a bank or by financial intermediary enrolled in the 106 Register; (ii) the bank or the financial intermediary referred to in (i) above retains a "skin in the game" in accordance with the criteria set forth in the implementing regulations to be enacted by the Bank of Italy; and (iii) the notes issued by the Law130 Company to finance the disbursement of the loan(s) are held (*detenuti*) by qualified investors (*investitori qualificati*) only.

The securitisation of loans originated by Law130 Companies is governed by the provisions of the Securitisation Law. Therefore, the receivables arising from the disbursement of the loan(s) by the Law130 Company and the relevant collections are segregated from the issuer's own assets and from the assets pertaining to other securitisation transactions (if any) carried out by the same company.

On 8 March 2016, after a public consultation process, the Bank of Italy published the regulatory implementing measures governing the granting of loans by Italian securitisation vehicles incorporated under the Italian Securitisation Law, that implements, among others, the discipline related to the retention requirements provided for under article 1*ter*, letter c) of Italian Securitisation Law.

Prior to the enactment of Law 49, it was unclear whether: (a) EU AIFs were allowed to lend into Italy; (b) AIFs could lend to consumers; and (c) lending by AIFs was subject to the same transparency requirements applying to banks and financial intermediaries. Consequently, Law 49 states that: (i) EU AIFs may, subject to certain conditions, lend directly to Italian borrowers; (ii) Italian and EU AIFs are not permitted to lend to consumers; and (iii) Italian and EU AIFs are subject to the same transparency obligations applicable to banks and financial intermediaries.

According to Law 49, EU AIFs may lend to Italian borrowers (other than Italian consumers) if the following conditions are met: (a) the EU AIF is authorised to carry out lending activities by the competent authority in its home Member State; (b) the EU AIF is set-up as a closed-end undertaking and its operational rules (including those relating to its investors) are comparable to those applicable to Italian AIFs; and (c) the rules on risk diversification and limitation (including limitations on leverage) applicable to the EU AIF under the regulations of its home Member State are equivalent to those applicable to Italian AIFs.

In addition, Law 49 also clarifies that lending by Italian and EU AIFs is subject to the transparency requirements set out under the Bank of Italy's Guidelines. This means that Italian and EU AIFs shall comply with the same pre-contractual, contractual and organisational requirements that normally apply to banks and financial intermediaries when performing lending activities in Italy. In addition, it is worth noting that the Bank of Italy may require EU AIFs to join the Italian Central Credit Register (*Centrale dei Rischi*), either directly or through third party banks or financial intermediaries.

18.3.4 Enforcement procedures and best practices seen in the Italian market as utilised by international lenders

In Italy, in the event the debtor fails to pay its debts, the bilateral relationship between creditor and debtor becomes a trilateral relationship (creditor, debtor, judicial authorities). This is due to the fact that the creditor must seek a judicial order/follow a judicial procedure to enforce his rights. In fact, any action of a creditor to collect his secured or unsecured credit must be filed before the court, which will then issue a title empowering levy execution in favour of the creditor. If such title is already in possession of the creditor (for instance cheques, bills of exchange, authenticated accounting entries, judgments), the judicial system would nevertheless be involved to regulate the repayment of the debt to the creditor by means of the sale of the debtor's goods.

An exception to the above principle can be found in the so called "personal securities", such as sureties and comfort letters. In such cases, if the debtor fails to pay, the creditor can require that the third party guarantor fulfil the debtor's obligations. However, the debtors can stop payment/fulfilment of the obligations by the guarantor by filing a claim to that effect before the court. In this case, the creditor will be required to go through a legal process to enforce his rights.

The assignment by way of security of receivables is one of the most common securities which borrowers grant in favour of a lender in Italy. In order to perfect a valid assignment of receivables, pursuant to art.1264, para.1, of the Italian Civil Code, the assignor shall alternatively notify to the assigned debtor or receive an acceptance of the assignment by the same assigned debtor.

In case the same receivable has been assigned, through following assignments, to a different assignee, then—pursuant to art.1265 of the Italian Civil Code—the first assignment in respect of which the assigned debtor has been notified, or which the assigned debtor has accepted and having a date certain in law (*data certa*), shall prevail in respect of the other assignments.

Upon the occurrence of an enforcement event, and at any time thereafter, the proceeds of the receivables shall become for the benefit of the secured creditors (i.e. the lenders) and may be applied by the same towards discharge of the relevant secured obligations, in the manner and order of application set out in the relevant finance documents of the transaction.

Under Italian law, a so called "pledge in possession" provides the secured creditor with the right to take possession of the goods secured in his favour. The pledge is enforceable with priority against third parties when: (i) the creditor has maintained the possession of the pledged asset; and (ii) the pledge has been created by means of a written instrument bearing a date certain at law (*data certa*), giving a detailed description of the secured obligation, as well as of the relevant pledged asset. Due to the requirement of the transfer of the possession, this security cannot be utilised with reference to plants, machinery and assets that are utilised by the borrower in its ordinary course of business. Pursuant to art.2798 of the Italian civil code, the creditor can always bring an action before the court requiring that the property of the goods be awarded to the creditor, in payment of his credit, up to the full amount of the debt. The value of the goods shall be confirmed by way of appraisal conducted by independent experts or, alternatively, according to the current market price if such price exists. A similar provision also exists in cases where a credit is the object of the pledge (art.2804 of the Italian Civil Code).

Another security granted to the creditors in Italy is the mortgage over real estate assets, which is perfected and enforceable against third parties once it is executed in writing before a Notary public and registered in the Land Registry Office (*Conservatoria dei Registri Immobiliari*) of the place where the property is located. According to art.2891 of the Italian Civil Code, within 40 days of the notice (previously served), any inscribed creditor, or his surety, has a right to demand the expropriation of the property by bringing an enforcement proceeding before the President of the competent court, which has jurisdiction according to the Italian Code of Civil Procedure, provided that certain conditions are met, and notices given to interested parties.

Notwithstanding the above, as part of a wider reform process, the Italian government enacted the Decree no. 59, dated 3 May 2016, which has been converted into law on 30 June 2016 (the Decree 59), which has introduced measures aimed at, inter alia, (i) creating a floating charge called "non-possessory pledge" and (ii) introducing the so called *"patto marciano"* agreement, which allow the creditor to give rise to an out-of-court appropriation of real estate assets securing financings.

In particular the "non-possessory pledge" is a pledge that may be constituted by the borrowers over movable assets used for business purposes, machineries, inventory stocks or raw goods for the business of the borrowers (except for registered movable assets). Just as in the case of a possessory pledge, such non-possessory pledge must be created by means of a written instrument bearing a date certain at law (*data certa*), giving a detailed description of the secured obligation as well as of the maximum secured amount and the relevant pledged asset. Should the pledgor dispose of the object of the pledge, for example selling the relevant assets, the "non-possessory pledge" shall be automatically extended to the replacing goods or assets.

In order to ensure the enforceability, vis-à-vis third parties, the "non-possessory pledge" must be registered—being the registration valid for a 10-year period, that can be extended before the relevant maturity—with an electronic register to be held by the Italian Tax Authorities, ensuring the possibility to have different ranking pledges over the same asset or good.

Upon the occurrence of an enforcement event, the secured creditors may alternatively: (i) dispose of the pledged asset, through a bid procedure, being the value of the pledged asset, evaluated by a third party valuer which has been appointed by the pledgor together with the secured creditor and then the proceeds of the receivables shall be for the benefit of the secured creditors (i.e. the lenders) and may be applied by the same towards discharge of the relevant secured obligations, in the manner and order of application set out in the relevant finance documents of the transaction; (ii) enforce the pledge up to the secured amount; (iii) if provided for under the relevant deed of pledge and registered with the Companies' Register, lease the asset by applying the lease receivable towards discharge of the relevant secured obligations, provided that the relevant agreement outlines the valuation criteria and mechanism, together with a detailed explanation of the secured obligations; and (iv) appropriate the pledged asset up to the secured amount, provided that the relevant agreement outlines the valuation criteria and mechanism, together with a detailed explanation of the secured obligations.

Finally, the Decree 59 introduces a new provision in the Italian Banking Act, a new article 48*bis*, entitled *"Finanziamento alle imprese garantito da trasferimento di bene immobile sospensivamente condizionato"*, pursuant to which the repayment of the loan granted by a bank or a financial institution, authorised to grant loans to the public, can be guaranteed by the transfer to the creditor, or to an affiliate of the creditor authorised to purchase, hold and transfer property rights, the ownership of a property or other right in rem on real estate assets.

In this respect, the relevant agreement must be entered into in a notarial form and, therefore, in order to ensure the enforceability vis-à-vis third parties, *"patto marciano"* shall be registered with the competent Land Registry Office (*Conservatoria dei Registri Immobiliari*).

Therefore, the transfer of the ownership over the property in favour of the creditor (*sospensivamente condisionato*) is subject to the default of the debtor, which may occur if (a) non-payment continues for more than nine months after at least three—not necessarily following—instalments become due and payable, or (b) the non-payment continues for more than nine months after one instalment became due and payable, if the debtor has to reimburse the loan on a monthly basis, or (c) non-payment continues for more than nine months after the final maturity date if the reimbursement is a bullet repayment.

Upon the occurrence of an enforcement event, once the creditor has notified the borrower declaring its intention to benefit from the transfer agreement, within 60 days from such notification, the creditor shall have the right to request the President of the Competent Court of the place where the property is located, to appoint an independent valuer in order to estimate the real estate asset, and the latter shall inform the debtor and the secured creditor of its valuation.

Finally, the abovementioned condition precedent shall be considered fulfilled if (i) the value of the property is communicated to the creditor by the independent valuer or (ii) any exceeding amount has been returned by the creditor to the debtor, in case the estimated value of the property exceeds the amount of the unpaid debt. Once the condition has been fulfilled the parties must enter into a notarial deed of confirmation.

18.3.5 Conclusion

In light of the considerations expressed above and the new legislation changes, an active market for NPLs in Italy may result in a more active role for Italian banks in supporting new lending transactions. In order to have a better organised and functioning market for the NPLs, it is necessary to create a secondary market for NPLs, which can reduce the collection burden on banks, and provide the same banks with a more cost-effective instrument, instead of the lengthy court procedures.

Finally, a well-structured Italian NPL CRE market can also support a secondary market liquidity for CRE loans, attracting the necessary investment to be made by pension funds, private equity funds and insurance companies, which may increase the extra-bank financial resources by providing the corporate sector with the required capital. Such aims are to be applauded and should be closely monitored to ensure they are collectively succeeding.

18.4 Spanish Commercial Real Estate Finance and CMBS in Spain

Borja Oria,
Partner and Head of Retail and Real Estate in the Arcano Investment Banking team

Iñigo de Luisa and Jaime de la Torre,
Partners in the Finance team of Cuatrecasas, Gonçalves Pereira

18.4.1 Introduction

There is no doubt that there is a new real estate sector and a new banking industry in Spain after the deep crisis in the Spanish real estate market which dragged market values to record lows and had a severe impact on Spanish financial institutions, in particular, savings banks and Spanish developers. After several years of inexpensive financing and high property value appreciation, the financial institutions crisis brought illiquidity and the bursting of the bubble in the real estate market, which combined to create a perfect storm in 2007 and subsequent years.

The new regulatory framework both at EU and at Spanish level on supervision and resolution of financial institutions and the creation of the Spanish bad bank SAREB (*Sociedad de Gestión de Activos Procedentes de la Reestructuración Bancaria*) in 2012 set up a new, more stable and solid economic framework. In addition, the transfer of €51 billion of impaired assets (which included almost all types of real estate properties and loans backed by real estate collateral) by troubled financial entities was construed by the market as a floor for real estate prices and the slow starting point of a cyclical change and an economic recovery. Since 2012, the Spanish commercial real estate sector has taken steps to emerge from that crisis and figures now show that the Spanish economic environment is at pre-crisis investment levels (€12 billion investments in 2015).

After a wide process of consolidation between Spanish financial institutions, including nationalisation in some cases, the banking sector was downsized from more than 60 entities to around 12 active financial entities. During this process, surviving banks have significantly cleansed their balance sheets (at least in connection with real estate property holdings) and have bolstered their capital requirements position. However, in general, Spanish banks had very low lending activity in the real estate market until 2014. This situation opened a window of opportunity for institutional investors and debt fund providers which in the past could not compete in pricing terms with local financiers in Spain. Nevertheless, currently low interest rates also discourage both traditional banks and alternative debt funds from entering into plain vanilla lending transactions in real estate.

Traditionally in Spain there was little debt structuring when dealing with real estate projects. In the past, lenders were focused on analysing the balance sheet of Spanish developers and investors rather than their business plans and the viability of the actual real estate investment itself. This means that in this new credit cycle, asset location, its quality and features, cashflow generation and tenant standing are critical drivers in determining whether a transaction will be approved by the relevant financiers' committees. Higher sponsor equity contributions are required and loan to value ratios remain relatively low, normally within the range of 50–60%, while in the past it was not uncommon to obtain 90% or even 100% leverage plus capex. As a result, in order to increase leverage and equity returns, more debt structuring and financial creativity is now required. Thus, in addition to senior debt and first liens, mezzanine debt, junior liens and preferred equity and warrants, together with obtaining funding from debt capital markets, are becoming more popular and a necessity in Spanish real estate transactions. Bond issues as a financing alternative is becoming attractive for deals exceeding €50 million.

During the recovery period, the Spanish real estate market has been very focused on prime assets in both Madrid and Barcelona. Investors now complain about the scarcity of first class assets and increasing yield compression across all asset classes as a result of competitive bidding processes and unreasonable asking prices. The average investors' demanded yield in Spain would now be around 5–7%, but for prime assets we have seen investors accepting 4% or less. Yield compression is compensated by interest rates at records lows. Due to these circumstances, investors' interests have moved on into add value and opportunistic strategies.

Most transactions with international investors involve joint ventures with local partners in order to set up strategic co-investment platforms. Preferred targeted assets are hotels, offices, shopping centres and logistics properties. Investors rely on market expectations regarding the recovery due to a potential strong increase in rents and capital value upside. Non-expensive financing or even increasing leverage at current financial costs allow investors to achieve targeted IRRs. However, we see that property prices are rising faster than rents.

Running in parallel to the real estate market recovery, bank lending activity has been improving as well, but mainly for plain vanilla transactions. In addition, there is wide and improved access to real estate financing in Spain. At present, investors in Spain have access to banks (local and overseas), institutional investors (pension funds, insurance companies), direct lending providers and other alternative debt funds, and debt capital markets (bonds issued at MARF (Alternative Fixed-Income Market), high yield bonds, securitisation). However, many traditional lenders are not ready to participate in new real estate developments. This has opened a potential niche for alternative debt providers, at least for bridge and short term financing. Finally, every debt provider may have a role in the debt structuring process, at different remuneration levels in accordance with the risk taken.

Spain has witnessed the surfacing of new dominant professional partici-
pants in the real estate market on the buy side, the Spanish equivalent of the REITs, SOCIMIs (*Sociedades Anónimas Cotizadas de Inversión Inmobiliaria*). For international investors, efficient tax structuring is critical, both on entry and also on exit. New regulations on SOCIMIs have proved a great success. For instance, in 2014 only four new SOCIMIs (Hispania, Merlin, Axiare and Lar) jointly raised €2.5 billion which was more than 80% deployed in six months and in 2015 these SOCIMIs invested €3.8 billion. On the sale side, Spanish financial entities who acquired foreclosed properties or entered into debt for asset swaps and Sareb, which acquired billions in impaired assets, have become key players. This new market required professional asset managers which have flourished in past years in Spain.

Investors and financiers rely on the Spanish legal framework. Enforcement proceedings are reliable but may take more than one year before the asset is sold in a public auction process. Insolvency proceedings may also delay the process due to the legal moratorium or stay over enforcement which can run up to one year. Restructuring tools are now available and debt for asset swap is a true alternative. However, investors still demand the need for greater transparency and speedier sale processes, especially when dealing with the public administration at different levels (local, regional and state).

18.4.2 *Overview of the Spanish lending market*

After eight years of lender inactivity in the Spanish financial industry (commencing on the advent of the 2008 economic crisis), and now that the Spanish economy has shown clear signs of recovery, activity in the Spanish lending market has begun to rebound.

The Spanish financing market, key in understanding the evolution of the economy, cemented its recovery over the last year. In 2015 banks provided an additional 12% of new credit to the private sector than the previous year. In addition, the amount of mortgages, a key driver for the real estate industry, rose by 33%.

Commercial real estate financing (CRE) is following the general market trend in Spain, as lenders are starting once again to offer competitive financing for CRE projects. Spanish CRE lending activity has historically registered lower levels in comparison to other main European markets such as the UK, Germany or France. The reason is quite simple, as the Spanish real estate market size is far smaller.

According to the Cushman and Wakefield (C&W) January 2016 report "European Lending Trends", the Spanish lending market represents 11% of total lending activity in the main European countries. The UK is the region that accounts for the largest portion, accounting for 24% of total lending activity. On the other hand, Italy (see further the section on the Italian NPL Market above), France, the Nordics and the Baltics are the markets with the lowest levels of lending activity, each of them representing less than 10% of the total.

Figure 1: Geographic focus of lending activity

(Percentages represent lending activity market share by region)

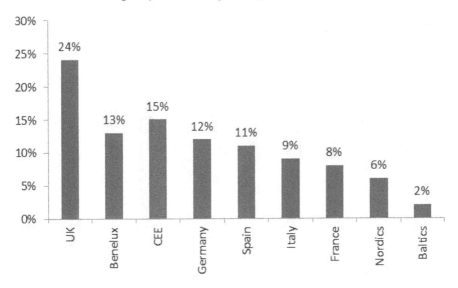

Source: C&W January 2016 report. European Lending Trends

18.4.3 Spanish CRE gearing v other European markets

The Spanish commercial real estate market registered a historical peak in investment volume in 2015, amounting to c. €12 billion.

Intense investment activity, together with the positive trend brought on by key real estate market drivers during the latest quarters (rents, take-up, occupancy rates, etc.), has captured the attention of lenders, leading them to reengage with the market. The upward trend in the Spanish real estate market has led several foreign Tier I financial institutions to relaunch their commercial real estate financing departments, which had slowed down during the years of recession.

Despite intense investment activity in the market, lending needs vary depending on each investor's profile. Even though the market shows liquidity surplus for core investments *(minimizing funding needs in these transactions),* value-added projects demand considerable leverage ratios in order to reach expected returns

The chart below shows a brief comparison of the lending market between different European capital cities.

Figure 2: European Lending Trends

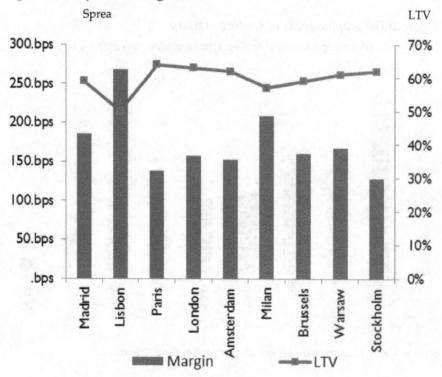

Source: C&W January 2016 report. European Lending Trends

18.4.4 *Spanish CRE loan maturities vs other European markets*

Loan term to maturity for commercial real estate financing in Spain has historically closely followed European lending practice.

Loan maturities have traditionally been strongly conditioned by the type of lender, meaning mid amortising periods for international lenders (between five and seven years) and longer amortisation periods for national/local lenders (between 10 and 15 years).

Despite this tradition and practice, the current tendency is towards establishing a more standardised and shorter loan term for commercial real estate investments of between five and seven years. The reduction of loan maturity length has mainly been caused by higher risk uncertainty (regarding the real estate and financial market) assumed under longer term amortising profiles. Nevertheless, despite the reduction in loan term, those lenders are usually willing to offer refinancing options on maturity.

Although loan length is a key consideration at the time of origination for any project, it must be highlighted that amortisation tranches and balloons are critical issues that will determine the feasibility of the investment and the returns obtained.

In this sense, amortising tranches are gradually being reduced in CRE investments. Due to increasing market confidence in the Spanish real estate market and the moderate returns offered by CRE investments, lenders are assuming significantly low amortising targets during loan term, and consequently, higher balloon amounts payable on maturity.

18.4.5 Alternative lenders operating in Spain

Unlike the North American and European markets, the Spanish lending market has historically been dominated by the local retail banking financing industry.

Competition generated by national retail banks such as Banco Santander or BBVA (two of the main worldwide players in the financial industry) makes Spain a difficult market for alternative lenders to penetrate.

Bank competition is not the only reason that alternative financing has had lower level of success in the Spanish market; the inopportune timing of certain decisions made by alternative lenders should also be considered as part of this equation.

During the recessionary years (2008–2014) main European debt funds focused their activity in the UK, France and Germany (both of these counties are dealt with in lender market sections in this Chapter) even though in Spain at that time traditional CRE lending activity was almost non-existent and alternative lenders did not consider Spain as a target country. This strategic decision did not allow them to position themselves in the Spanish lending market.

Now that the Spanish economy has definitively recovered, retail banks have returned to offering financing to CRE income generating projects under very competitive conditions. Alternative lenders are not expected to be able to compete in this niche market due to their higher equity requirements.

Despite the difficulties experienced by alternative lenders in financing income generating projects, they have been able to conduct their core business in Spain by way of "special situations financing", often related to new developments/refurbishment projects.

These types of projects are hardly ever levered by retail banks due to the higher risk implied in these transactions.

Bridge financing transactions (where alternative lenders provide initial financing at a higher cost, until the project's risk profile decreases sufficiently to access retail banking financing) and special situations financing (projects where high financing structural flexibility is needed) represent an important share of the total activity of alternative lenders.

Subordinated debt (mezzanine debt/participative loans/bonds) has almost no share yet in the Spanish CRE lending market, as the constrained returns offered by these kind of investments (net operating income yields between 3–7%) make it difficult to fit within the expected returns usually required by subordinated lenders, usually above net operating income yields.

No conclusion of this topic is complete without mentioning an emerging alternative funding source: "Real Estate Crowdfunding". Although this alternative funding source has not yet been properly implemented in the Spanish CRE market, other markets like the US/UK have dipped their toes in this nascent industry with apparently positive outcomes (first transaction closed in July 2014, when a group of investors acquired 15% ownership of Hard Rock hotel in Palm Spring, California). According to Crowdnetic, in Q1 of 2015, more than €100m were crowdfunded in the US market. Even though these platforms can be expected to be initially available in the US and the UK financial markets reasonably it can be expected that sooner or later it will spread to other markets. "Housers" is currently one of the main crowdfunding platforms operating in the Spanish real estate market. Currently, the platform has limited its activity to residential projects, thus far avoiding CRE transactions.

18.4.6 Sponsors' expected yields

In the most recent financial quarters the Spanish financial market has changed radically. From a scenario of complete inactivity, the market has seen intense lending activity, with very constrained margins.

Euribor has hit a historical rock-bottom, entering into negative figures during Q1 of 2016. At this point and given tighter spreads being applied by retail banks lenders (due to high competition in the market and the necessity of allocating resources to profitable investments) the cost of debt is at a historical low.

The spreads applied depend on the project's internal characteristics. In commercial real estate lending, key drivers that will determine the terms of financing will include consideration of the type of borrower/sponsor, tenants' credit risk, leasing contract terms, location, lay-out and the asset's technical characteristics.

CRE low risk transactions are being levered under significantly low spread schemes, reaching "all in costs" between 150–250 bps. In terms of risk perception, office and retail (both high street and shopping centres) projects are considered to represent less risk than logistics or hotels investments.

18.4.7 Market Segmentation

18.4.7.1 Market segmentation by borrower and project/asset type (Spanish lenders only)

Borrowers in the Spanish lending market can be segmented into two different categories being institutional and private entities.

Institutional borrowers are mainly comprised of real estate funds, property management companies, SOCIMIs and corporates. These entities, especially when they are considering value added investments, usually try to lever their acquisitions as much as possible in order to maximise their internal returns.

Institutional borrower activity is gaining traction in the market. The Spanish real estate market is experiencing a period of extraordinary investment appetite, which is why achieving optimal financing terms is crucial in allowing potential investors to bid for different investment opportunities that surface in this highly competitive market in order to maximise their probability of success.

On the other hand, private borrowers (usually family offices) are also quite active in the financing market. Despite this type of investor usually conducting acquisitions mainly with equity, the minimum cost of debt prevailing in the market is causing these investors to increase their leverage ratios in these transactions.

18.4.7.2 Market segmentation by lender type

The Spanish CRE lending market is covered by banking entities (retail banks) and alternative lenders. As highlighted previously, the CRE lending market in Spain is dominated by retail banks, leaving a reduced market share available to alternative lenders.

Retail banks can be categorised into Tier I banks and mid-size entities. Tier I banks, are currently particularly active in the market (highlighting national entities such as Santander and BBVA), competing aggressively to cover large deals (with a minimum ticket of €50 million). Currently, retail banks are limiting their financing activity to providing senior debt, usually secured by mortgages on the assets owned the by the borrower/sponsor, or by pledging shares in the case of corporates or share deals.

Mid-size entities are also competing actively in the market. Nevertheless, due to their lower financing capacity, these entities have focused their activity on smaller or syndicated deals, where financing needs do not exceed €30 million.

Alternative lenders can be subdivided into four different categories: investment banks, insurance companies, pension funds and debt funds. Insurance companies and pension funds are competing aggressively with retail banks. Their more efficient internal structure, the inapplicability of Basel III requirements, their large fund capacity and their moderated internal returns are all combining to increase their advantage vis-a-vis retail banks in the lending market.

Investment banks and debt funds cover higher risk transactions. Global players such as Goldman Sachs, JP Morgan, BAML, Chenavari, Deutsche Bank, Bain, Oaktree, Incus, HIG, HayFin, Blackstone, Ben Oldman, etc., are gradually increasing their exposure to the Spanish CRE lending market.

18.4.7.3   Lenders active in the Spanish market (including alternative lenders or funds)

18.4.8   Typical lending terms

18.4.8.1   Prime lending terms

For Spanish standards, in general, prime or core assets in CRE would be those located in prime areas in Madrid or Barcelona with high quality specification and solvent single-tenants.

Local traditional banks are the first choice for transactions with no complexities (including legal issues). Yields for these prime assets have been falling significantly in the past two or three years meaning current levels around 4% or less. LTV ratios are approximately around 60% and only exceptionally would reach 70%. Life term would oscillate between five and seven years and exceptionally 10–15 years for Spanish investors with a long-term business plan. In addition, banks are now accepting bullet payments and balloon amortisations (40% on maturity) in some cases. Traditional security packages would consist of first ranking mortgages and pledges over credit rights. Normally, there is no recourse to sponsors or shareholders.

Most loans are bilateral agreements granted by a single lender as average size would be between €20–40 million. In addition, principal amounts have decreased along with the minimum investment requirements and transactional amounts due to the lack of availability of prime product. Investors have also reduced their capital return expectations. Financing capex for repositioning, refurbishments and new developments is also available since there is significant interest from investors in value add projects. Due to the GFC, owners did not deploy any investment in capex over the past seven years. Capex investment would allow for the potential to witness a significant rental rates for new occupiers and this is becoming an increasing trend.

The average loan size for Spanish deals is now between €30 million and €80 million. Interest rates range at the lower level between 175–225 bps though normally this they start at 400 bps onwards depending on the risk profile. Interest rates remain in most cases variable, meaning Euribor plus margin. Variable interest rates would be expected to be hedged as a result. Such hedge providers would share an interest in the first ranking security with senior lenders. However, we are starting to see fixed interest rates being offered by Spanish banks at 2.25–3.00% over loan term.

It is also usual for international investors, having independent asset managers dealing with the property, to provide periodical asset and financial reporting to the lender (in particular, rental cashflows and appraisal values), complying with financial ratios and taking insurance policies over the asset and loss rentals insurance, and appointing the lenders as beneficiaries under the insurance policies.

According to the 2015 JLL report on CRE finance in Spain, the typical investment transaction would be around €40–50 million, with 50–60% LTV debt financing, five to seven year term, IRR 8–14%, 5–7% annual yield and strong tenants.

18.4.8.2   *Less-Prime/Regional lending terms*

Investing outside Madrid and Barcelona is an increasing trend in CRE in the search for higher returns, focusing, in particular, on asset types such as shopping centres and hotels in certain locations. Except for these or other exceptional assets, the gap in yield between Barcelona and Madrid, and the rest of Spain is increasing. However, it is also expected that the value proposition of properties in secondary locations will be higher than in prime locations as non-prime locations have not recovered at the same speed.

Given strong competition for prime assets, investors are leaving core markets and moving into other areas. Asking prices and bidding process are sometimes not based on fundamentals due to scarcity of prime quality product. This lack of stock has a direct impact on recovery in pricing levels. Value add and opportunistic investments are increasingly on investors' radars. The game now is about potential value uplift and improving asset management.

Consequently, both investors and lenders are looking for riskier projects not involving core assets. Land and development opportunities are back on track. Alternative lenders are more active in this niche. They are more flexible, faster in approval of these deals and execution and have demonstrated that they are willing to take the risk. Local banks would not even venture to start diligence on some of these deals. Evidently, interest rates would be higher and LTV would be lower, requiring more creativity. In general, financing in non-prime areas would require more debt structuring since senior debt LTV requirements fall below 50%.

Dual financing (lending either by banks, institutional investors or debt funds accompanied by a bond issue) is also an increasing trend in order to optimise financial costs. An equity based exit fee can be structured into the transaction as equity is willing to share profits, either through warrants or additional interest payments. Traditional lenders remain conservative on these types of enticements and are leaving an attractive space for debt funds to step in to provide short term financing during the construction phase. However, this type of transaction may require some ultimate recourse to sponsors (at least during a predetermined period) in addition to standard security and higher financial costs during construction or refurbishment periods.

Other challenges faced outside Barcelona and Madrid are, for instance, transactional costs (which, in general, are not very large outside large cities), poor quality of available information for legal due diligence purposes and uncertainties derived from licensing and urban planning requirements which are set by regional local regulation on a region by region basis. Naturally, investors and financiers demand a stable regulatory framework and transparent processes when dealing with the public administration, in particular, municipalities, which is not always available.

18.4.9 Specificities of the Spanish lending market

18.4.9.1 Special reference to SOCIMIs (Spanish equivalent to REITs)

SOCIMIs are incorporated as vehicles aimed at fostering investment in real estate. Inspired by REITs, the SOCIMI was regulated for the first time in Spanish law under Act 11/2009. The Spanish legislator planned to adopt regulations similar to those governing REITs, which on a taxation level hinges on the absence of effective taxation at the corporate level whilst placing the burden on its shareholders instead. However, the regime initially provided for in Act 11/2009 was a failure because the Act provided for direct taxation of SOCIMIs, and because of the number and stringency of the legal requirements that would need to be complied with in setting up these vehicles.

(i) **Corporate requirements**: Under the current legal regime in Act 11/2009, these vehicles must comply with several corporate requirements to qualify as SOCIMIs.

A SOCIMI must be incorporated as a public limited company (*sociedad anónima*). Its corporate name must evidence its status as a *Sociedad Cotizada de Inversión en el Mercado Inmobiliario, Sociedad Anónima* (listed real estate investment company) or include the abbreviation "*SOCIMI, S.A.*". The SOCIMI's main corporate purposes must be: (a) acquisition and developing urban real estate for rental purposes; (b) holding stakes in the share capital of other SOCIMIs; (c) holding stakes in the share capital of other entities (when (i) they have the same corporate purpose as the SOCIMI, and (ii) they are subject, by law or under the company's by-laws, to a similar regime to that applicable to SOCIMIs regarding the obligatory distribution of profits); and (d) holding shares or units of collective real estate investment institutions regulated under Act 35/2003, of 4 November, the Collective Investment Institutions Act. In addition to its main corporate purpose, a SOCIMI can pursue different supplementary business activities. The combined revenues from other supplementary business activities must not exceed 20% of the company's total revenues for each tax period.

Furthermore, to meet the requirement concerning the SOCIMIs' corporate purpose, the SOCIMI must acquire the properties as owner. If properties are located abroad, they must have a similar nature to those located in Spain. Properties with special characteristics for cadastral purposes and real estate assigned to third parties under financial lease agreements (as so defined in the Corporate Income Tax Act) do not qualify as suitable for application of the special regime for SOCIMIs. Properties assigned under operating lease agreements qualify as suitable.

A SOCIMI's share capital must be at least €5 million, represented by one class of registered shares. Contribution of real estate assets to the SOCIMI, at incorporation or through a capital increase, must be accompanied by a report from an independent expert appointed by the commercial registry.

Regarding the distribution of profits, SOCIMIs must distribute their annual profit to their shareholders. They must comply firstly with the corporate requirements necessary to approve the distribution, such as setting-off any losses from preceding years or allocating reserves required by law. A SOCIMI's legal reserve must not exceed 20% of its share capital and its by-laws cannot provide for any other non-disposable reserve. Additionally, profit distribution must include the allocation of: (i) 100% of profit from dividends or any other profit sharing distributed by the companies owned by the SOCIMI; (ii) at least 50% of profits from the transfer of real estate and shares or equity holdings in vehicles dedicated to the development of SOCIMI's main corporate purpose; and (iii) at least 80% of all other profits obtained.

Moreover, under art.3 of Act 11/2009, at least 80% of the value of a SOCIMI's assets must be allocated towards: (a) acquiring and developing urban real estate for rental purposes; (b) acquiring land for real estate development purposes that will be used for rental, as long as the development begins within three years from the date of such property's acquisition; or (c) acquiring equity holdings in qualifying entities for the development of the SOCIMI's main corporate purpose.

The value of the SOCIMI's assets is determined as the average of the individual balance sheet of the companies included in that ad hoc group or based on the group consolidated quarterly balance sheet for the year.

Compliance with the 80% SOCIMI asset value allocation requirement as detailed above is determined in accordance with the group's consolidated balance sheet, where the SOCIMI is the parent company of a group of companies under art.42 of the Commercial Code. In this case, the group will comprise the SOCIMI and the entities in which the SOCIMI holds stakes in the pursuit of its main corporate purpose. It will be calculated based on the consolidated balance sheet regardless of (i) the jurisdiction of the corporate domicile of the different entities and (ii) whether they are obliged or not to draft consolidated annual accounts.

In addition, at least 80% of the SOCIMI's revenues for the tax period must be obtained from one or both of the following: (i) leasing of real estate assets under the SOCIMI's main corporate purpose to non-related persons or entities; and/or (ii) dividends or profit sharing from equity holdings in entities that can be considered suitable to develop the SOCIMI's main corporate purpose. Real estate and equity holdings in entities qualifying to pursue the SOCIMI's main corporate purpose are subject to a minimum holding term: (i) real estate comprising the SOCIMI's assets must be leased for at least three years (this term includes the time during which the properties have been offered for rental but have not yet been leased of up to one year); and (ii) shares or equity holdings in the share capital of companies pursuing the SOCIMI's main corporate purpose must be held as part of the companies' assets for at least three years from their acquisition or from the starting date of the first tax period in which this special tax regime was applied.

For the special tax regime in Act 11/2009 to apply, the SOCIMI's shares must be admitted to trading on:

(a)   a regulated market in Spain, or in a Member State of the EU or the European Economic Area, or in a state that has an effective exchange of information with Spain; or

(b)   a multilateral trading facility in Spain, or in a Member State of the EU or the European Economic Area.

(ii) **Special tax regime applicable to SOCIMIs**: SOCIMIs which fulfil the above described corporate requirements under Act 11/2009, can apply a special tax regime (if specific requirements are fulfilled, the special tax regime can be applicable to entities in which the SOCIMI holds a stake in development of its main corporate purpose), which provides for the SOCIMI's pass-through tax position and for the effective taxation of its shareholders in lieu. A SOCIMI can access the special tax regime even if at the time of that election, not all the legal corporate requirements are fulfilled. Those requirements must be fulfilled within two years from the date the election of this special tax regime was approved. Its main features are:

- the corporate income tax rate for SOCIMIs is 0%. As a consequence, SOCIMIs cannot set off negative tax bases or claim deductions or subsidies on tax payable as an incentive to accomplish specific activities;
- SOCIMIs are obliged to make withholdings on account of dividends and income distributed to its shareholders, unless the shareholders are entities that meet the legal requirements for the application of Act 11/2009. In some circumstances, SOCIMIs must also make partial payments. However, they are exempt from the obligation to make the minimum partial payment of 12% of the income for the year entered on the profit and loss account;
- SOCIMIs are subject to a special corporate additional tax rate of 19% of the gross amount of the dividends or profit sharing distributed to shareholders (i) whose stake in the company's share capital is 5% or more and (ii) whose personal income is exempt from tax or taxed at a rate lower than 10%. Note that the SOCIMI's direct payment of the special corporate additional tax is a financial disadvantage for shareholders whose equity and tax situation is unrelated to circumstances resulting in the generation of that tax. The SOCIMI will account for the special corporate additional tax as an expense for the year, with a negative impact on income for the following year, thus reducing profits available for distribution. Nevertheless, corporate mechanisms can be devised to limit the impact of the SOCIMI's liability for the special corporate additional tax on shareholders whose personal circumstances are unrelated to the accrual of that tax;
- dividends paid out of income or reserves from years in respect of which the special tax regime is applied (dividends taxed for the SOCIMI at 0%) will be taxed at the rate applicable to the shareholders whether for corporate income tax or non-resident income tax, when the dividends are paid (i) to a taxable person for corporate income tax, or (ii) to a taxpayer of non-resident income tax with a permanent

establishment in Spain. In both cases, the exemption for double taxation of dividends in art.21 of the Corporate Income Tax Act cannot be claimed; and

• if the dividend or profit sharing is paid to a personal income taxpayer, it will be taxed in the taxable savings base under the tax category for capital gains from equity holdings, as established in art.25.1 a) of the Personal Income Tax Act. On the other hand, if the dividend or profit sharing is paid to a non-resident income taxpayer without a permanent establishment in Spain, it will be subject to taxation as established in art.24.1 of the Personal Income Tax Act.

Please see below a summary of the main existing SOCIMIs in Spain as of 2016:

Company	Company Profile
Autonomy Spain Real Estate Socimi, S.A.	Autonomy Spain Real Estate Socimi, S.A. was established in 2012 to explore opportunities in the Spanish real estate market. The company is focused on acquiring and managing the highest-quality properties in prime locations.
Axiare Patrimonio Socimi, S.A.	Axiare Patrimonio Socimi, S.A. is a real estate investment company (SOCIMI) focusing on rental properties, created in order to invest in the Spanish property market. Its primary activity is the identification of investment opportunities and the acquisition and management of high-quality properties, in order to add value to the properties and generate sustainable value for its shareholders.
Corpfin Capital Prime Retail II Socimi, S.A.	Corpfin Capital Prime Retail II Socimi, S.A. operates in the Spanish Real Estate market since August 2013 and its main activity is the acquisition and promotion of prime retail assets in the main cities of Spain for its future development, lease and divestment through its subsidiary Corpfin Capital Prime Retail Assets Socimi, S.L. (Ccpr Assets).
Corpfin Capital Prime Retail III Socimi, S.A.	Corpfin Capital Prime Retail III Socimi, S.A. operates in the Spanish Real Estate market since May 2014 and its main activity is the acquisition and promotion of prime retail assets in the main cities of Spain for its future development, lease and divestment through its subsidiary Corpfin Capital prime Retail Assets Socimi, S.L. (Ccpr Assets).

Company	Company Profile
Entrecampos Cuatro Socimi, S.A.	Entrecampos Cuatro Socimi, S.A. is a company which results from a large process of evolution of various real estate companies, originated in the late 50s. All of its assets are currently dedicated to leasing.
Fidere Patrimonio Socimi, S.A.	Fidere Patrimonio Socimi business is focused on the acquisition, leasing and management of residential properties in Spain. Its strategy is based on providing the best service to tenants and increasing shareholder's value through the origination and improvement of recurrent income. The company aims to create value through active asset management of current and future portfolio.
Heref Habaneras, Socimi, S.A.	The main activity of Heref Habaneras Socimi, S.A. is the real estate investment in Europe, pursuing generating attractive returns with minimal risk to their investors. Its business strategy is focused on maximising income from its asset leasing activity that has in its portfolio, which is the Habaneras Shopping Centre, located in Torrevieja, Alicante.
Inversiones Doalca Socimi, S.A.	Inversiones Doalca Socimi, S.A. is a listed company investing in the real estate market, whose main activity is the lease of their real estate assets. It is registered in Madrid. It was established under the name Inversiones Doalca, S.L. on 31 December 1998 after the merger of other companies.
Jaba I Inv. Inmobiliarias Socimi, S.A.	Jaba I Inversiones Inmobiliarias Socimi, S.A. was incorporated in 2014 as a result of the consolidation of various companies and with the goal of analysing unique investment opportunities in the Spanish Real Estate Market. The company is mainly focused on the acquisition and management of properties of the maximum quality and best locations.
Lar España Real Estate, Socimi, S.A.	Lar España's aim is to generate high returns for its shareholders via its business strategy of owning, operating and renting its Real Estate portfolio, which is mainly focused on Commercial Property Assets in Spain. It is investing following a value added approach based on an active management strategy and it is externally managed by Grupo Lar, a family owned, Spanish private Real Estate developer, Investor and Asset Manager with a 40-year track record of international experience.

Company	Company Profile
Mercal Inmuebles, Socimi S.A.	Mercal Inmuebles Socimi, S.A. (hereafter MERCAL) whose purpose is the acquisition and promotion of urban real estate properties for lease. It has a portfolio of first class assets located in the best locations, leased to large companies with long and medium term lease contracts. This maintains high occupancy levels and stable income.
Merlin Properties Socimi, S.A.	Merlin Properties Socimi, S.A. is one of the major Spanish real estate companies trading on the Spanish Stock Exchange and included on the quotation System (Sistema de Interconexión Bursátil—SIBE or Continuous Market) since 30 June 2014. The company is specialised in the acquisition and management of commercial property in the Core and Core Plus segments in the Iberian region. Merlin announced in June 2016 its merger with Metrovacesa, S.A. creating the leading company in the sector.
Obsido Socimi, S.A.	Obsido Socimi, is a patrimonial society, Spanish and Norwegian capital, which aims at investment in hotels in the main Spanish tourist areas to be rented either to hotel chains or to highly specialised managers in this type of asset. The company offers its shareholders and investors the opportunity to obtain a minimum return guaranteed by leasing contracts and, furthermore, also be participants on a percentage of the income earned in the various hotels included in the portfolio.
Promociones Renta y Manten Socimi, S.A.	Promociones Renta y Manten Socimi, S.A. is a listed company whose activity is to manage real estate assets in order to obtain advantages such as, among others, the lease management by a highly experienced, skilled and professional team in the field; the spread out of the individual risk of between the assets of the company; or obtaining high tax benefits.
RREF II Al Breck Socimi, **S.A.**	RREF II Al Breck Socimi, S.A. was incorporated in April 2016 and its main activity is to manage real estate assets and enter into lease agreements for their properties in urban areas.

Company	Company Profile
Testa Inmuebles en Renta Socimi, S.A.	Testa Inmuebles en Renta Socimi, S.A. is a listed company pertaining to Merlin Properties, Socimi, S.A., which holds more than 77% of its share capital. It has an outstanding capacity for generating recurrent revenues, due to the extended lifetime of its managed assets and its customer portfolio. This means that it is an excellent consistent creator of value. Moreover, the potential for appreciation of its real estate assets means that capital gains may be added to the income generated from rent.
Trajano Iberia Socimi S.A.	Trajano Iberia Socimi, SA, is a newly incorporated company, aimed at investing in a mixed portfolio of properties of different types, located in Spain and Portugal, mainly for rental. It is promoted and managed by the Real Estate division of Deutsche Bank in Spain, which has a team of professionals with extensive experience in real estate.
Uro Property Holdings Socimi, S.A.	Uro Property Holdings Socimi, S.A. is a real estate investment trust (REIT) listed on Mercado Alternativo Bursátil (MAB). Its corporate purpose is (i) the asset management of 755 properties rented to Banco Santander; (ii) the acquisition, development and investment management of commercial real estate; (iii) the holding of shares in other REITs or other corporate entities whose principal purpose is the acquisition and management of commercial real estate; and (iv) the holding of shares in commingled funds investing in real estate.
Zambal Spain Socimi, S.A.	Zambal Spain Socimi, S.A., is an investment vehicle created in 2013 whose activity is to invest and subsequently manage prime real estate assets in well-consolidated markets both at a geographical level (Madrid and Barcelona) and at a sectorial level (offices and high-street retail).
Zaragoza Properties Socimi, S.A.U.	Through its Puerto Venecia subsidiary, the company partly owns the "Puerto de Venecia Shopping Resort" commercial complex, located in Zaragoza, whose surface area exceeds 200,000 m2. The strategy of the Board of Zaragoza Properties Socimi is to continue to attract high quality international and national retailers, to grow footfall as a destination centre and ultimately to increase net rental income.

18.4.9.2 Factors that impact Spanish CRE lending and how loans are structured—Security package and costs

As in many other jurisdictions, in CRE transactions in Spain there is usually a vehicle (normally a *sociedad limitada* or SL company) holding the asset in order to have its activities and risks ring-fenced. In most cases, CRE lending is provided through bilateral agreements, meaning one lender for that specific property or project. More recently, "staple financing" (simultaneous financing to purchase offered in a bidding process) is a preferred choice for investors to optimise financing but makes closing more challenging. When dealing with large transactions, it may well be a "club deal" but it may be usual to have a three-month period for syndication. If this is the case, mortgages will be granted through irrevocable powers of attorney at a later stage when the debt piece has been assigned to the new lenders in order to avoid duplicating stamp duty costs.

Other situations involve a bridge facility provided by alternative lenders during licence works and during the construction period at a double digit interest rate and then refinanced by a local bank on non-expensive financial terms once the works on the building have completed and almost fully let. In addition, sale and lease transactions have been quite popular for Spanish companies and highly profitable for international investors, particularly when local banks were not willing to provide any credit facilities. Spanish financial institutions also raised funds through the sale and leaseback transactions. The same type of transaction applies to supermarkets and hypermarkets which used these structures widely in past years. Under Spanish law, sale and lease back transactions are treated as a true sale and are not considered a security interest.

There are also investors who are refinancing their capital structures and replacing equity by debt or refinancing debt by means of bond issues in order to extend maturity terms to match their investment strategies. In some other cases, SOCIMIs purchase assets quickly only with equity to take advantage of this opportunity and afterwards when the distressed situation is cleaned up, they leverage on non-expensive terms.

The typical Spanish security package in CRE finance would comprise the following: (i) first ranking mortgage over the acquired property asset, which comprises not only the plot of land and the building (if any) but also movable assets on the plot, insurance proceeds and other rights; (ii) pledge over shares or quotas of the Spanish vehicle; (iii) pledge over bank accounts; (iv) pledge over receivables and credit rights over any material contracts (construction, leases, PPLs, intercompany loans, insurance, management, etc.); and, (v) if applicable, pledge over VAT refunds (normally VAT would apply to the acquisition of real estate property but this amount would be reimbursed to the buyer within a maximum period of 18 months and for these purposes a specific VAT facility is usually put in place).

Security may be granted over future assets as well, but among other conditions, such proceeds or rights should derive from sufficiently determinable agreements. Promissory mortgages or an undertaking to mortgage upon a trigger event by means of an irrevocable power of attorney could sometimes be an alternative to avoid stamp duty costs. However, note that these structural options are not equivalent to an in rem security per se. In addition, having them granted at a later stage could be impaired and avoided in case of the debtor's insolvency during the two-year clawback period on insolvency.

Adequate security structuring will always cater for cost-efficient solutions. Mortgages and pledges in Spain are granted before a Spanish notary. In addition to notarisation, certain security (such as mortgages) also require, to ensure its validity and enforceability, its filing and registration before the applicable land registry. Therefore, notarial and register fees will arise. In addition, stamp duty would also apply and it is calculated at the ordinary tax rate of 0.75% to 1.50% (depending on the region where the asset is located) over the secured mortgage amount which is usually around 125–140% the principal nominal amount of the underlying debt. Foreign secured lenders are required to apply for a Spanish tax identification number to have the security interest duly registered in their name. Having this Spanish tax id is purely for identification purposes and does not alter the tax regime applicable to such creditor.

Springing mortgages were widely used in the past to avoid part of the stamp duty but it is not an efficient option anymore. Floating mortgages (*hipotecas flotantes* under art.153*bis* of the Spanish Mortgage Law) would be an efficient alternative since a single mortgage could now secure several obligations (existing and future obligations) with no need to amend the mortgage and, as a consequence, stamp duty is not duplicated every time. However, floating mortgages are only available for credit institutions and public bodies of the Spanish administration and not for other ordinary financial entities or debt funds.

A differentiating factor from other jurisdictions is that in Spain, the security interest is granted in favour of all the secured parties. As a result, lenders should duly accept the security interest and be direct beneficiaries at the applicable registers. In Spain it is not possible to appoint a security agent or a trustee as beneficiary of such security on behalf of the secured lenders at the applicable public register. As a result, any subsequent assignment by a lender should be notarised in Spain to become a lender of record. Otherwise assignees or sub participants should rely on contractual arrangements to receive their proceeds in case of mortgage enforcement.

It is also critical to understand that Spanish security may be subject to mandatory legal limitations which may apply to Spanish obligors. For instance, security and guarantees cannot be granted by Spanish entities if it qualifies as financial assistance in a share-purchase deal. No corporate benefit principles apply per se in Spain since it is within the directors' duties towards the company. However, it is increasingly evidenced and documented that there is some consideration for the Spanish entity in exchange for the security granted, particularly within insolvency proceedings. In any case, it is advisable to obtain shareholders' approval before executing the transaction.

Royal Decree-Law 5/2005, of 11 March, on security financial collateral, provides a ring-fenced protection against any effect derived from the debtor's insolvency (mainly, claw-back actions and enforcement stays in insolvency scenarios), and expeditious enforcement proceeding which allows appropriation of collateral in case of default. This would be allowed for certain parties only, such as credit institutions which benefit from this regime, and would apply primarily to pledges over shares and pledges over credit rights. Introducing this enforcement route in the security agreement (if available) is a must to enjoy its application and benefits. Similar enforcement advantages can be obtained when pledge agreements (mainly, pledges over shares or quotas of companies domiciled in Catalunya or pledged over bank accounts located in Catalunya) are governed by Catalonian law.

Imposing limitations to distribution of dividends in the facility agreements is not always possible under Spanish law. For instance, SOCIMIs are forced to distribute 80% EBITDA to shareholders, which makes it incompatible with the usual restrictions contained in a loan agreement. Normally, financial costs including third parties financing and shareholder loans take a large portion of yearly profits. Another issue to be taken into account in CRE financing is that Spanish entities are required to approve the transaction at shareholder level when selling, contributing or charging their "essential assets", meaning a value of more than 25% of its balance sheet (art.160(f) of Spanish Companies Law).

Sometimes, lenders in CRE finance are also tempted to attempt to control the sponsor's decision-making in connection with the running of the SPV or its property asset, even taking direct control and management over the property, bank accounts and other business decisions (i.e. payments, appointing auditors or asset managers, etc.). However, in doing so, the result may be that the creditor can be considered under Spanish insolvency law a de facto director. As a result, its credit claim may be qualified as subordinated within insolvency proceedings and the security it obtained being declared null and void.

18.4.9.3 Banking monopoly rules, alternative sources of lending, NPLs and SAREB

Lending in Spain is not a reserved banking activity requiring an authorisation or licence. Therefore, the same regime applies to domestic and foreign creditors who can freely originate and provide loans and credits (and consequently become beneficiary of security interests and guarantees) in Spain. However, any individual or entity entering into financial transactions or providing financial services in Spain could be required by the Ministry of Economy to disclose periodic information about its activities or be subject to inspections by the Bank of Spain to confirm whether the activity performed is subject to supervision.

A main goal for a lender is avoiding withholding tax over interest which, in summary, requires the lender to either be a Spanish or an EU entity, normally a SL entity or Lux company. There are no exchange control restrictions on loan payments to foreign lenders but complying with money laundering regulation is a must in order avoid payments being blocked. Note that providing loans and credits to consumers in Spain is subject to a special protective regime but this is out of the scope of CRE finance and of this Chapter.

As detailed above, this flexible regime for lending in Spain has allowed for the entry of new players providing alternative financing. "Shadow banking" is an increasing significant phenomenon in Spain and debt funds and other institutional investors are providing tailor-made funding structures and offering greater flexibility and leverage though at higher financial costs. The consolidation process of the Spanish banking sector and the inability of several financial institutions to be exposed to real estate have facilitated this entry to the Spanish market.

Assignment and debt trading is also a major topic in CRE finance. The existing lender may agree to assign and transfer its interests under the loan agreement to a new lender. This could be formalised through English law LMA templates or Spanish law transfer documentation or a mix of them. However, the assignment requirements included in the loan agreement should be complied with in order to become a lender of record. Normally, notarisation is required and no additional costs should arise for the borrower. If there is a mortgage loan, it would also be necessary to enter into a mortgage transfer public deed before a Spanish notary and normally stamp duty tax, notarial and register fees will arise.

The governing law of the finance documentation in CRE transactions in Spain is chosen by the parties. It is usually subject to Spanish law, but although Spanish law offers a reliable enforcement judicial procedure, English law is often an alternative governing law in Spanish lending transactions with foreign creditors. However, in any case Spanish security shall be subject to Spanish law. Notarisation in Spain of the finance documentation, even subject to English law, would also be advisable for eventual enforcement purposes. Among other advantages, English law would allow access to restructuring tools such as the English scheme of arrangement. However, Spanish insolvency law provides several similar tools. As a result, English law choice is (when chosen) typically required by the foreign lender for commercial reasons in almost all cases. At the time of writing, the UK's vote to leave the EU has raised opposition from Spanish borrowers against English law choice in the finance documentation.

Bank portfolios and Sareb sales are expected to remain at the same levels in 2016. Banks need to develerage and release capital. However, this would very much depend on existing capital requirements levels. On the other hand, Sareb has a mandate to sell all its assets (both real estate properties and mortgage secured loans) within 15 years since it was created (i.e. ending in 2027). Sareb has changed its sale strategy from portfolios dispositions to individual sales based on market value. In 2015, Sareb outsourced the asset management to four servicers (Altamira, Solvia, Haya and Servihabitat) which are now leading the sale processes. Notwithstanding, at the end of each year it is usual to see NPLs and real estate portfolios on sale by Sareb.

Together with international investors purchasing secured NPLs and REOs, specialised asset management companies have emerged in Spain to provide the management and servicing of these assets.

18.4.10 *Creditor friendliness, enforcement and insolvency procedures*

Under Spanish Law there are two main types of guarantees, depending on how the obligation is secured:

(a) in rem security, such as mortgages, whereby a specific asset secures the obligation; and

(b) personal guarantees, whereby an individual or entity is personally liable and guarantees performance of such obligations with its own assets.

In the case of insolvency, these guarantees and security rank differently and there are material differences in their enforcement. Mortgage agreements must be drafted in Spanish, executed before a notary public and filed with the applicable land registry, making this type of security more costly since stamp duty tax would also apply.

Broadly speaking, an in rem security interest can only secure one main obligation and its ancillary obligations. If two different main obligations need to be secured, in general, two different in rem securities must be created. Spanish law does not provide for a so-called "universal security" or "all assets security" over all the debtor's assets although there are exceptions, for instance floating mortgages. Nor does it generally provide for the creation of a "floating" or "adjustable" lien or encumbrance.

From the creditors' perspective, it is critical that the in rem security granted will allow enforcement through expeditious executive summary judicial proceedings (*"procedimiento ejecutivo"*), albeit notarial enforcement would also be available. Depending on the type of security, it would also be advisable to cater for enforcement through the mechanisms provided under Royal Decree Law 5/2005 which implements in Spain the EU Directive on financial collaterals, provided all requirements are fulfilled. Finally, under Spanish law, not all breaches and defaults under a facility agreement would lead to an event of default in respect of which Spanish courts would permit enforcement. According to Spanish case law, only essential, continuous and severe breaches would allow lenders to early terminate and to enforce the security. Therefore, it is worth highlighting that certain breaches of less material covenants will not be enough to trigger enforcement, particularly when the borrower is current with its payment obligations. Breaches of financial ratios may be considered of essential nature but borrowers should have the chance to cure such ratio or provide additional security before declaring the early termination of the facility.

Insolvency proceedings are only triggered in the case of a debtor's insolvency. The debtor is considered insolvent when it is regularly unable to meet its obligations as they become due. In this situation, insolvency law aims to protect creditors' interests and to reorganise and preserve the viability of companies that become insolvent. In Spain, there is only one insolvency procedure for all debtors, be they companies or individuals. Insolvency procedures have a common stage (to determine assets and liabilities), which may be followed by a:

- composition stage, the aim of which is to reach an agreement between borrowers and creditors on the payment of debts (so called "*convenio*"); and/or
- liquidation stage, during which the debtor's assets are realised and such proceeds distributed among creditors, following their ranking and preferential treatment as creditors (as the case may be).

18.4.10.1 What are the effects of the declaration of the insolvency ("concurso")?

Effects on debtors: The effects of the declaration of insolvency on the debtor mainly depend on whether insolvency is voluntary or mandatory. In the first case, the debtor usually retains its powers to manage and operate its business supervised by the insolvency administrator that the insolvency judge has appointed. If insolvency is mandatory, debtors lose all rights over their assets, which are then managed directly by the insolvency administrator.

Effects on creditors: One of the keystones and principles of the Spanish Insolvency Act is that all creditors must receive equal treatment (*par conditio creditorum*). However, there are few exceptions to this rule and those permitted by law abide by the rule that "ordinary credits" are considered equal.

On this basis, a distinction is made between privileged, ordinary and subordinated credits. Privileged credits are given preferential treatment over ordinary credits, which in turn have preference over subordinated credits. In addition, there is another special and prioritised category, known as "credits against the insolvency estate" (superprivileged category), which generally arise after the declaration of insolvency and, consequently, will be paid first. These credits are not subject to ranking or acknowledgement and, in principle, must be paid by the insolvency administrator when they fall due. Privileged credits may have a special or general privilege, depending on whether the security is created over a specific asset (special privilege) or over all of the debtor's assets (general privilege).

Credits with special privilege generally include those in which the collateral is specific property or rights (mortgage or pledge) or equivalent rights (financial lease agreement for the leased property). The privilege will only cover the part of the claim not exceeding the value of the respective guarantee. The value of the in rem security will be that resulting from deducting (i) any outstanding debts enjoying a preferential security over the asset or right over which the guarantee lies (ii) from nine-tenths of its fair value as determined by an independent expert.

Ordinary creditors are those who do not meet the requirements to be a privileged or a subordinated creditor. Subordinated creditors are those that the Spanish Insolvency Act considers subordinated to all other creditors. Subordinated claims include those not filed in due time or that are contractually subordinated and interests and penalties and claims owned by a party considered to be "closely related to the debtor", including significant shareholders of the debtor.

18.4.10.2   Enforcement of securities (including mortgages)

With regard to credits secured by assets required for the continuity of the debtor's professional or business activity, the possibilities of enforcing the collateral (mortgage) will be limited, in accordance with the provisions of the Spanish Insolvency Act. Generally, in such cases, enforcement or realisation of the security is subject to automatic stays and may not commence until a composition is approved (which does not affect that entitlement) or one year elapses from the insolvency declaration without liquidation having taken place unless the public auction announcement for the asset or right in question has been published at the time of the insolvency declaration.

18.4.10.3   Clawback period

Clawback in Spain applies to any act or transaction, performed within the two years preceding the debtor's declaration of insolvency and which is deemed to be detrimental to the debtor's estate (even in the absence of fraudulent intent). Actions carried out in the debtor's ordinary course of business and under market terms cannot be challenged.

The following actions are deemed to be detrimental to the debtor's estate (absent evidence to the contrary): (i) acts performed with no consideration, and (ii) payments or other acts cancelling obligations due after the declaration of insolvency (except those with an in rem guarantee). Further, unless proved otherwise the actions will also be detrimental to the estate: (i) acts of disposal for valuable consideration performed in favour of a party closely related to the insolvent party; (ii) granting security interests covering pre-existing debts or new debts incurred to cancel pre-existing debts; and (iii) payments or other actions cancelling obligations secured by an in rem security interest due after the declaration of insolvency.

18.4.11 Case Studies

18.4.11.1 Structured finance/lending

As highlighted throughout this chapter, real estate developers and investors in Spain have traditionally used bank financing to support their activity. It is important to bear in mind that the European economy has been heavily reliant on bank funding, especially compared to the US. According to data provided by Mckinsey in its 2013 report "Financial Globalization: Retreat or Reseat", bank financing represented 93% of all corporate financing whilst corporate bonds only 7%. On the other hand, in the US, the split was 1% bank financing and 99% corporate bonds. Such figures show the importance of bank financing for supporting business growth in Europe and Spain and the real estate industry is not an exception.

Due to the current historically low rate environment, institutional investors have started looking for alternative investments to obtain higher yields. They are adding lending into their business plans, either through debt acquisitions in secondary markets or through direct lending transactions and this has been one of their main options in seeking to obtain higher returns. Investors have revisualised their role and now seek to act as business partners to corporates, offering long-term and tailor made financing solutions in order to help them achieve their business strategies.

A good example of how lenders are supporting the CRE sector is the recent financing of the headquarters of an international tier I corporation in Madrid carried out by Arcano. For this transaction, the landlord of the asset mandated Arcano to carry out a competitive process in which national and international banks, insurance companies and specialised debt funds were contacted and invited to participate.

Due to strong competition among potential lenders, very attractive terms and conditions were achieved:

- Facility: €55 million
- All-in cost: c. 185 bp. Fully hedged with a fixed interest rate swap
- Balloon: c. 40%
- Maturity: 10 years

This kind of transaction has not been an exception in the market. Another example of CRE lending transactions is the €133.6 million loan facility provided by Allianz Real Estate to Merlin Properties, the largest Spanish SOCIMI, to finance Marineda Shopping Center in La Coruña, Spain. The entire complex has a built area of more than 500,000 sqm, a gross leasable area of approximately 196,000 sqm and 6,000 parking spaces. The facility was closed in February 2015, has a fixed interest rate of 2.66%, a tenure of 10 years and the asset secures the facility. Loan-to-cost stood at 51.4%. This transaction marked the company's debut in the Spanish CRE lending market.

18.4.11.2   Bonds/CMBS

Due to the credit crunch during the GFC and the consequential consolidation of the banking industry, European and Spanish companies have realised the importance of diversifying sources of funding and have started looking for new financing alternatives. The emergence of alternative financing follows the tendency in US capital markets and has been supported by the efforts of European public entities.

The bond market, CMBS and direct lending have proved to be the most important alternatives to straight bank financing. CMBS has traditionally been an important source of funding for real estate property owners in Europe. CMBS issuance is far from its historical peak despite several issuances since 2015 suggesting that investor confidence is returning. Note that under Law 5/2015, of 27 April, on promoting corporate financing, securitisation funds are now allowed to grant security interests securing third party obligations.

Spanish corporates have increasingly tapped the bond market in the past few years, highlighting the issuing activity of SOCIMIs. Capital markets have become one of the funding sources available for the acquisition or refinancing of real estate properties in Spain. A few examples are illustrated below:

(i) **LAR ESPAÑA SOCIMI, SA**: Lar España, a real estate company focused on commercial property assets in Spain, completed the first bond issue by a SOCIMI in February 2015 by issuing seven-year senior secured notes for a total amount of €140 million and a fixed coupon of 2.90% per annum. The bonds were unrated.

The transaction was privately placed with institutional non-domestic investors and was listed on the Irish Stock Exchange; the first Euro secured bond transaction to be listed in the Main Securities Market of the Irish Stock Exchange by a REIT.

The purpose for the use of proceeds was to continue deploying the company's investment strategy. The security package included a first ranking mortgage real estate assets for up to c. 60% LTV at bond level and among the first ranking pledges over the shares of the subsidiaries within the bond security net. Such an innovative security package enabled the issuer to minimise its borrowing costs and maintain strategic flexibility while satisfying investors' protection requirements.

(ii) **SAINT CROIX HOLDING IMMOBILIER SOCIMI, SA**: This Socimi has registered a €80,000,000 notes programme under an information memorandum (*documento de base informativo de incorporación*) of medium- and long-term securities on the Alternative Fixed-Income Market (MARF). MARF is a multilateral trading facility and is not a regulated market in accordance with the provisions of Directive 2004/39/EC.

MARF adopts the legal structure of the Multilateral Trading Facility (MTF), making it an alternative unofficial market, similar to those in some neighbouring European countries and within Bolsas y Mercados Españoles (BME), as is the case of the Alternative Stock Market (MAB).

Therefore, access requirements to this market are more flexible than those for the official regulated markets and provide greater speed in processing issues. In this way, companies that use MARF will be able to benefit from processing simplification and lower costs.

As established in its regulation, approved by the Spanish Securities Market Regulator (CNMV), MARF is operated by AIAF Mercado de Renta Fija, S.A.U.

(iii) **URO PROPERTY HOLDINGS SOCIMI, S.A.**: Uro Property Holdings, SOCIMI, S.A. is the owner of 754 properties (consisting mainly of retail bank branches) located in Spain. Those bank branches where acquired and leased to Banco Santander, S.A. on 2007 and their acquisition was partially financed by way of a syndicated facility.

The main purpose of the CMBS transaction that closed in June, 2015 was the repayment in full (approximately €1,259,000,000) of its existing finance facilities entered into in 2007 and originally used to finance part of the original purchase price of the property portfolio.

The tenant of each of the properties within the property portfolio was Banco Santander who is the lessee pursuant to the lease agreements. The tenant will occupy each property within the property portfolio in accordance with the terms of the lease agreements for condominium properties or the lease agreement for non-condominium properties.

The issuer of the bonds was Silverback Finance Limited, incorporated with limited liability in Ireland, and was also the lender pursuant to the loan agreement granted to Uro Property Holdings SOCIMI, S.A. Uro Property Holdings SOCIMI, S.A. was the legal owner of the property portfolio and the borrower pursuant to the loan agreement mentioned above. On the closing date, the proceeds of the issue of the bonds were applied by the issuer, inter alia, in making an advance to Uro Property Holdings SOCIMI, S.A of two euro-denominated term loan facilities totalling in aggregate €1,345 million.

The notes worth €1,345 million, issued in April 2015, which have maturities of 22 years (€868 million) and 24 years (€477 million), were listed on the Irish Stock Exchange and have a rating of BBB+ by S&P. The notes pay a fixed coupon of 3.13% and 3.75% respectively.

The borrower's primary source of funds will be rental payments made by the tenant (Banco Santander) to the borrower (as landlord) pursuant to the lease in respect of the portfolio.

For this purpose, Silverback Finance Limited issued the bonds described below:

	Initial principal amount	Issue price (per cent)	Interest rate (per cent per annum)	Bond Maturity Date	Ratings—S&P
Class A1 Bonds	€867,900,000	100	3.1261	25 February 2037	BBB+
Class A2 Bonds	€476,900,000	100	3.7529	25 May 2039	BBB+

The diagram of the transaction is the following:

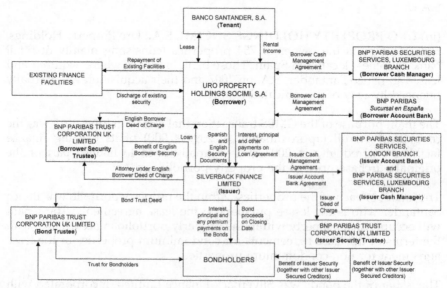

With regard the securities of the issuance, the borrower Uro Property Holdings Socimi, S.A. granted a mortgage over, inter alia, its interests over the property portfolio (other than the non-mortgaged properties) in favour of the issuer as security for the borrower secured obligations.

The Borrower granted English law securities and Spanish law securities. Among the Spanish securities the following is summarised: (i) Spanish law mortgages over each of the initial properties (excluding the non-mortgaged properties) and any incoming properties; (ii) pledge over the borrower accounts; (iii) pledge over the Spanish documents; (iv) any other document governed by Spanish law evidencing or creating security over any asset to secure any obligation of the borrower to the issuer; and (v) each other document governed by Spanish law designed as such in writing by the borrower and the issuer. The creation of the Spanish law mortgages over each of the properties triggered stamp duty tax.

18.4.12   Conclusion

Since 2012, there has been a radical change in the Spanish debt landscape. On one hand, most Spanish developers and local real estate investors, on the borrower side, and all saving entities and some Spanish and international financial institutions, on the lending side, have disappeared from the real estate loan market. On the other hand, there are new players such as the alternative debt funds and other institutional investors willing to originate or trade loans. Moreover, a Spanish equivalent to REITs (SOCIMIs) has become a dominant vehicle acquiring all types of real estate assets. Spanish banks, Sareb and its asset management companies have been active as well on the sale side.

The Spanish real estate market is recovering. Due to the lack of prime assets, investors have moved away from core assets to value add and opportunistic strategies. Currently, there is no room for further yield compression on prime assets. Low interest rates and expectations with regard to rent increases are enabling investors to meet business plan objectives and to improve their returns on equity. There is increasing competition at all levels, investors and lenders/debt providers. Banks may still be adequate for plain vanilla transactions at 50–60% LTV, though for more complex transactions, including land development and capex investment, and an LTV above 60%, alternative lenders are now usually more suitable debt providers.

Debt structuring is now more common and is, in fact, required in order to increase return on capital. Debt structuring will continue to play a significant role in complex and leveraged real estate investments. Combining different layers of debt with different credit providers has proved a good strategy to optimise financial costs. In addition, there are also opportunities in the secondary market. Firstly, banks are still selling secured loan portfolios to free capital (mainly, non-performing mortgage loan portfolios which are purchased at a significant discount by specialist debt funds). Secondly, bilateral mortgage loan agreements are being traded or being syndicated to other lenders.

The Spanish legal system provides a reasonable protective framework for lenders. Enforcement on commercial real estate through judicial executive proceedings is formalistic and reliable but it may take several months until the asset is sold in public auction. Double Luxco structures are also used to facilitate enforcement of over equity in the borrower group. With regard to insolvency procedures, several new tools allow for ring-fenced debt restructuring and debt for asset swaps. However, it is not unusual to see English law governing relevant financial documentation and which follow LMA templates. In any case, security documentation shall always have to be subject to Spanish law.

The efficient structuring of the Spanish security package is also critical in order to minimise costs and stamp duty tax. A usual security package comprises mortgages and pledges, with generally no recourse to the sponsor. A peculiarity under Spanish law is that under a mortgage each secured lender is a directly a holder and beneficiary of that security interest in the applicable register. Under Spanish law, there is no security agent or trustee concept to replace lenders as beneficiaries at public registers.

Since 2014, the SOCIMI is the vehicle which is most widely used in Spain for real estate investments due to the absence of effective taxation at the company level (taxation is applied over dividends distributed to its shareholders). Now SOCIMIs face other challenges such as consolidation, specialisation and leveraging.

Due to the GFC and consequential consolidation of the banking industry, European and Spanish companies have evidenced the importance of diversifying funding sources and have started looking for new financing alternatives. Debt fund providers are increasingly active in CRE lending in Spain. The Spanish bond market is also emerging as an alternative to traditional banking financing albeit the volume of CMBS transactions in Spain remains low (among other reasons, due to the costs related to the granting of real estate mortgages, mainly the payment of stamp duty). An increasing trend for bonds and alternative financial structures for CRE in Spain is expected.

Chapter 19

Islamic-Compliant Financing of Commercial Real Estate

Jonathan Lawrence,
Partner, K&L Gates LLP

19.1 Introduction

CRE has been an increasingly important asset class for Islamic-compliant transactions and banks since the publication of the first edition of this book in 2006. During this period, Islamic-compliant finance has proved to be an alternative source of funds for investors entering the European CRE market, as highlighted by high-profile London CRE deals, such as development finance for The Shard, the Olympic Village, the Battersea Power Station regeneration and the redevelopment of Chelsea Barracks.

In the wake of Brexit, some parameters have changed in relation to Islamic-compliant investment in UK CRE:

- The immediate fall in the pound/US dollar exchange rate made the UK more attractive for those investors in US dollar pegged economies;
- Potential UK tax cuts and incentives were mooted to draw investment;
- A predicted short to mid-term decline in UK real estate values;
- Uncertain impact on the remaining EU economies.

However, most fundamentals of such investment have not changed:

- Islamic finance has never been governed by EU law in the UK or elsewhere;
- The UK has one of the most Islamic friendly legal environments with the most legislation of any of the EU countries to assist Islamic finance from a political and tax perspective;
- The English language, English law and the English courts remain attractions for overseas investors;
- The need to draw overseas investment to the UK became more important than ever.

In 2016, Islamic-compliant financing is on a growth trajectory, based on demographic trends, rising investible income levels and investment in European CRE by Middle Eastern investors led by relatively stable political and legal environments. Brexit may be a spur to further such investment rather than an impediment. In addition, non-Islamic CRE market participants are increasingly looking to Islamic financing structures to supplement conventional equity and debt funding.

It is estimated that 29.7% of the global population will likely be Muslim by 2050, against 23.2% in 2010. The proportion of Muslims in Europe is, at the time of writing, around 6% of the population and projected to be 8% by 2030. This creates a large market and consumer base to consider.

The level of harmonisation is increasing between conventional and Islamic banking regulation, thus eroding barriers to entry. There are further significant growth opportunities, given that the global penetration of Islamic banking is currently below 2% in CRE finance and *sukuk* (*Shari'ah-compliant* capital markets instruments) account for only approximately 1% of global bond issuance. Global assets of Islamic finance were estimated to be $2 trillion at the end of 2014, and have tripled since the start of the economic slowdown in 2007.

The UK has enjoyed an in-built advantage in its attempt to become the hub of Islamic finance in Europe, due to English law often being the governing law of international Islamic finance transactions. An Islamic finance transaction might involve a Swiss bank and a Middle Eastern counterparty, but they may well choose English law to structure their documentation, in order to give flexibility and certainty to both sides.

Successive UK governments have ensured that there is a level legislative and regulatory playing field for both Islamic and conventional financial products. In the UK, more than 20 banks offer Islamic financial services, of which five are fully Islamic-compliant, substantially more than any other European country. In June 2014, the UK government issued a sovereign *sukuk*, the first by a country outside the Islamic world. Rental payments on real estate provide the income for investors in the *sukuk* and it is underpinned by three central government properties.

The acceleration of international real estate investment by Middle East sovereign wealth funds, high net worth individuals, developers and real estate companies outside their own region is most clearly seen in the growth from a recent low of $2 billion in 2009 to $13 billion in 2013, itself a 86% increase over 2012. The biggest growth by investor type is amongst the sovereign wealth funds.

In 2014 and 2015, 44% of the investment went into London. The top four locations of London, Paris, Milan and Lyon were all European and accounted for two-thirds of the total, with US destinations further down the list.

Talk about rivalry over the location of an Islamic finance hub in Europe can be overstated. The UK, Luxembourg, Ireland, the Netherlands and other European locations are complementary to the Islamic finance industry by offering different advantages. The distinctiveness of London has arguably been enhanced by Brexit and investment opportunities increased. Luxembourg is already the leading non-Islamic domicile for Islamic-compliant investment funds and third largest globally behind Saudi Arabia and Malaysia. It is also a popular location for listing *sukuk* on the primary market. However Luxembourg does not have the direct investment targets of CRE and corporate opportunities that the UK possesses. Other popular EU real estate markets such as France, Germany and Italy may have interesting opportunities, but those jurisdictions suffer from tax and legislative hurdles to the use of Islamic finance techniques.

However, other EU countries continue to seek to attract Islamic finance and investment. For example, in 2010, Ireland introduced a tax neutrality regime for Islamic finance. Ireland has signed over 60 double tax treaties ensuring there is no double taxation for such structures (for example, treaties with Malaysia, Saudi Arabia and the United Arab Emirates). The Irish government has called an Irish government *sukuk* "an option" and Dublin is already well developed as a financial centre, with the Irish Stock Exchange having listed its first corporate *sukuk* in 2005. Nevertheless, Ireland has a Muslim population of only approximately 54,000, and this may hamper the development of the industry.

In October 2014, the Luxembourg government issued its own sovereign *sukuk*. Luxembourg, alongside Jersey and Ireland, is a key player in the European Islamic funds sector. However, Islamic-compliant real estate funds account for only 4% of the global market.

Turkey is a country to watch. Straddling Europe and Asia, its nearly 80 million population is over 99% Muslim. Companies are allowed to issue Islamic-compliant debt and Kuveyt Turk issued the first corporate *sukuk* by a European bank. It was listed on the London Stock Exchange.

19.2 CRE as an asset class

Real estate has been a primary focus of the Islamic finance industry since the 1990s. Islamic property investments began in the residential housing sector, but quickly moved to CRE, which now plays a large role in this sector throughout the world. Initial investments were, and continue to be, effected through investment fund structures. However, the emergence of the *sukuk* in 2003 saw significant changes in Islamic-compliant CRE finance.

To date, Islamic finance has viewed CRE as an investible, tangible asset class on which to base its financial structures. The focus has tended to be on prime or trophy assets: for example, hotels or large office headquarter buildings. There is increasing evidence that Chinese investors are aiming for the same type of properties, therefore Middle Eastern investors have been more willing to looking at real estate outside London in the UK.

At the time of writing, a low oil price is leading to mixed predictions about its effect on Middle Eastern CRE investors outside their home regions. Middle East investment was traditionally seen to rise in line with oil prices, as more surplus funds become available. However, it is also likely that the knock-on effect on GDP will be an important reminder of the need to diversify a country's revenue sources away from non-renewable energy. This could lead to an increase in overseas investment into real estate in the medium-to-long term in order to provide stability in an uncertain political and economic climate.

In addition, since 2010, Islamic funds and Islamic banks providing mezzanine finance have multiplied. In such structures, a conventional senior bank lends the majority of the debt on an interest payment basis, the investors inject their equity and the mezzanine finance tranche is put into the structure in an Islamic-compliant way. This is a feasible way of ensuring that deals get done. The senior conventional bank and the Islamic-compliant mezzanine lender enter into an intercreditor agreement which governs the way each loan is treated and takes account of the Islamic sensibilities of the mezzanine lender.

Student accommodation has been a major target for Islamic funds, given the existence of rental guarantees, steady demand and upward only rental payments. Further developments may be seen in this sector due to a broadening view of social infrastructure to include health care, education and social housing sectors. Prime residential properties are still a focus, including the 2011 launch of an Islamic-compliant fund in the UK to offer Islamic investors exposure to this market.

It is worth considering what qualifies as Islamic-compliant finance, as Islamic or *Shari'ah*-compliant finance is a different animal than conventional finance. For example, the payment and receipt of interest are prohibited by the *Shari'ah*, making it impossible to lend against CRE in a conventional manner.

19.3 What is Islamic-compliant finance?

In summary, Islamic finance is the conduct of commercial and financial activities in accordance with the *Shari'ah*. The *Shari'ah* is Islamic religious law, as applied to commercial and financial activities. It is a combination of theology, religion and law. The *Shari'ah* is a guide to how a Muslim leads his or her life (it means, literally, "the way" or "the right path") and is the divine law to Muslims as revealed in the *Qur'an* and the *Sunna*.

Fiqh, literally, is the human understanding of that divine law; the practical rules of *Shari'ah* as determined by the *Shari'ah* scholars. The primary methodology used in this interpretation is *ijtihad* (literally, "effort"), or legal reasoning, using the "roots of the law" (*usul al-fiqh*). The roots (*usul*) upon which Islamic jurisprudence are based, are the:

- *Qur'an*, being the holy book of Islam and the word of Allah (a word for God used in the context of Islam);
- *Sunna* of the Prophet Mohammed, which are the binding authority of his sayings and decisions;
- *Ijma*, or "consensus" of the community of scholars; and
- *Qiyas*, or deductions and reasoning by analogy.

The *Shari'ah* is comprised of principles and rules and, historically, its explanation and application has been largely oral. There are also a number of schools of Islamic jurisprudence (the four main schools of the largest branch of Islam (*Sunni*) are Hanafi, Hanbali, Maliki and Shafi). Historically, the different schools are frequently in conflict with respect to the application of the *Shari'ah* to different factual or structural situations. Even within a school there are variable interpretations, and there is considerable divergence between South East Asia (particularly Malaysia, Indonesia and Brunei) and the Middle East and Western Asia (particularly Pakistan).

As expounded by *Shari'ah* scholars over the last 1,400 years, and as applied to Islamic finance, the *Shari'ah* is a full body of law. It covers virtually every aspect of commerce and finance that is addressed by a mature body of secular law. Thus, for example, it addresses contracts, concepts of consideration, legal capacity, mutuality, sales, leasing, construction activities, partnerships and joint ventures of various types, guarantees, estates, equity and trust, litigation and many other activities and legal structures. As such, it will influence all aspects of an Islamic-compliant CRE finance transaction or the formation of an Islamic investment fund, as well as every aspect of the operation and conduct of a CRE business. However, Islamic finance transactions involving non-Islamic parties are governed by secular law, such as English or New York law.

19.4   *Shari'ah* supervisory boards and Islamic finance regulators

In many CRE finance transactions, only one party may care if the deal is Islamic-compliant. In that case, it is important that each party represents to the other that it is satisfied with the Islamic-compliance from its viewpoint and will not seek to use a later finding of non-compliance as a reason to renege on the transaction.

However, the question remains as to how an investor that wants to make *Shari'ah*-compliant investments ensures that its investment is, in fact, in compliance. Most individuals do not have the expertise to make that determination for themselves. Over the last few decades, the mechanism that has evolved to provide comfort with respect to *Shari'ah*-compliance is the *Shari'ah* supervisory board (a "*Shari'ah* board" or a "board").

Most Islamic banks, financial institutions and CRE companies and many of the higher-net-worth families and individuals in the Islamic world have retained one or more *Shari'ah* scholars that comprise a *Shari'ah* board. Each board oversees the complete range of investment practices, and the principles, methodology and activities of operation of all aspects of the business, of the entity or individual that has retained that particular board. Each board is comprised of a different group of individual scholars. Each board renders determinations with respect to structures and undertakings that are confidential to the entity that retains that board, with the result that explanation of the *Shari'ah*, as applied in competitive financial markets, has occurred in isolated pockets rather than a manner that is coordinated across markets or even schools of Islamic jurisprudence.

Shari'ah boards may be comprised of one scholar or a group of scholars. Frequently, a board is comprised of one or more of the leading "internationalist" scholars, some regional scholars, and some local scholars. Frequently, the internationalist scholars (who most often populate the boards of the major banks and investment funds) have expertise and experience in sophisticated financial transactions in a wide range of jurisdictions throughout the world, including various secular tax and finance laws and other legal and regulatory regimes and the interplay between those regimes and the *Shari'ah* as applied and considered by specific investors.

The Bahrain-based Accounting and Auditing Organisation of Islamic Financial Institutions (AAOIFI) and the Kuala Lumpur-based Islamic Financial Services Board (IFSB) are strong forces in promoting greater uniformity across the schools and across the divide between South East Asian jurisdictions and Middle Eastern and Western Asian jurisdictions. AAOIFI standards prescribe additional international financial reporting standards to reflect the specifics of Islamic finance. The IFSB advises domestic regulators on how Islamic financial institutions should be managed and has published standards on stress testing, liquidity, management, capital adequacy and corporate governance. However, application of these standards is not uniform across countries.

In April 2012, AAOIFI introduced seven new standards for Islamic financial institutions addressing issues including financial rights, bankruptcy, capital protection and contract termination. As a greater number and variety of multinational conventional banks and investment banks enter, and expand their range within, the Islamic finance field, there will be increased pressure toward uniformity, if only to facilitate the implementation of internal policies and procedures of these institutions.

The board will perform a number of different roles including, typically, the following:

• participation in product development activities;
• review and approval of the fund or entity structure and its objectives, criteria and guidelines and issuance of a *fatwa* in respect thereof;
• review and approval of disclosure and offering documents and issuance of a *fatwa* in respect thereof;
• review, approval and oversight of investment and business operational structures and methodology, and issuance of a *fatwa* in respect thereof;
• ongoing review, oversight and approval of transactional or operational variances or applications to unique or changing circumstances; and
• annual audit of the operations of the fund or entity and issuance of an annual certification of *Shari'ah*-compliance.

A *fatwa* (singular; *fatawa* is the plural) is a written certification of a *Shari'ah* scholar or board. It has no binding legal effect under secular law in Europe. Over recent years, *fatawa* have been structured more like Anglo-American legal opinions, with discussion of the underlying *Shari'ah* precepts. It is common to see a copy of a more general *fatwa* reproduced in the offering circular of a *sukuk* issue.

19.5 *Shari'ah* principles

The outlook of the *Shari'ah* on finance is as a type of "ethical investing". It prohibits investment in, or the conduct of, businesses whose core activities:

• include the manufacture or distribution of alcoholic or pork products or, in the case of certain *Shari'ah* boards, firearms;
• have a significant involvement in gaming (gambling, including casinos), brokerage, interest-based banking or impermissible insurance;
• include certain types of entertainment elements (particularly pornography); or
• have impermissible amounts of interest-based indebtedness or interest income.

The activities referred to above are categorised as prohibited business activities. Some *Shari'ah* boards also include the growing, manufacture and distribution of tobacco within prohibited business activities. Some boards interpret the entertainment exclusion more broadly and include cinema and music generally because of the pornography elements of these industries. Hotels are often included because of the presence of alcohol in bars and mini-bars or in-room entertainment. Entities that have prohibited business activities may not be tenants in properties owned and leased by a *Shari'ah*-

compliant investor. These prohibitions fundamentally influence the nature and operations of funds and businesses.

Many large office buildings and complexes have tenants that engage in prohibited business activities, such as retail branches of conventional banks, restaurants that serve alcohol, or supermarkets or convenience stores that sell pork, wine and beer. In the purest case, the entire building or complex would be an impermissible investment. However, the *Shari'ah* scholars have taken a pragmatic view. Rules have been developed that allow investment in these properties for certain impermissible uses, such as those just mentioned. For example, if the branch bank serves a retail market, there are insufficient other banking opportunities in the defined area, and the branch bank occupies a small percentage of the property (say, 1% or less), some *Shari'ah* boards will permit the property acquisition and allow renewal of the lease to that branch bank. The development of these rules as to de minimis impermissible tenancies greatly expanded the universe of properties available for investment.

A fundamental *Shari'ah* principle is the prohibition of *riba*, best known by its prohibition on the payment or receipt of interest. This rule affects every aspect of the manner in which a *Shari'ah*-compliant transaction is structured and implemented. In the securitisation field, it (and other principles) precludes pooling of conventional mortgages, credit card receivables, and all interest-bearing debt instruments.

In the area of joint ventures (including partnerships), numerous principles address allocation of work, profit and loss allocations and distributions and virtually all other operational matters. For example, as a general statement, all distributions of profits and losses must be pro rata. Preferred shares are not permissible. In certain types of partnerships (*mudaraba*), one person contributes services and another person contributes capital. If the arrangement suffers a loss, only the capital provider may be penalised in cash. In other types of partnerships (*Sharikat* and *musharaka*), work and capital contribution may be allocated over all partners with corresponding loss sharing. These rules affect CRE business and fund structures and many operational activities and, directly, *sukuk*.

Shari'ah principles in relation to leasing are of particular importance, because leasing is the primary tool used in the implementation of *Shari'ah*-compliant transactions. Examples include the requirement that a property lessor must maintain the leased property. The lessor may not pass structural maintenance obligations or corresponding obligations, such as the maintenance of buildings insurance, to a lessee. In short, the pervasive fully repairing and insuring lease is prohibited. The end-user tenant may not have prohibited business activities and the lease to the end-user tenant must itself be *Shari'ah*-compliant. These principles have a critical impact on Islamic securitisations.

As one would expect in light of the development of the *Shari'ah* in Middle Eastern societies that were so heavily focused on trading activities, the *Shari'ah* precepts applicable to sales are especially well refined. Leasing, in fact, is treated as a type of sale—sale of the temporary possession (or usufruct) of property. With only limited exceptions, one can sell only tangible assets. Debt cannot be sold, nor can other financial instruments that do not represent an ownership interest in tangible assets. Further, one cannot sell property that one does not own and possess. These principles have a major influence on the structure of Islamic bonds and securitisations. In addition, there are very particular rules addressing delivery, receipt, ownership, allocation of risk, downpayments and virtually all other aspects of sales transactions. These rules affect both the ability to create secondary markets and the tradability of securitisation instruments.

Shari'ah precepts that prohibit gambling and uncertainty also preclude most types of conventional insurance and investments in conventional insurance companies, although the unavailability of *takaful* (*Shari'ah*-compliant insurance) has led to some practical accommodations to the prohibition on the use of insurance.

19.6   Islamic CRE finance structures

To help understand Islamic CRE financing, this Chapter will outline certain of the component structures of Islamic-compliant finance. These are primarily the lease (*ijara*) and sale (particularly *murabaha*) structures. Two structures, the *mudaraba* and *musharaka*, are joint venture structures. Each structure is briefly summarised in this section, and each of these structures is also the basis or a component of Islamic bond and securitisation structures.

19.6.1.   Ijara (lease) structures

The predominant acquisition and operating financing structure in Islamic CRE finance in Europe is the *ijara* (lease). Figure 1 below, shows a basic leasing structure. This example assumes 60% conventional interest-based financing and 40% contribution by the *Shari'ah-compliant* investors; these percentages will vary with each transaction.

The investors make their investment into the "project company". For tax reasons, this investment is usually made through a fund and at least one entity is usually inserted in the structure between that fund and the project company. A special purpose vehicle (SPV), the "funding company", is established to acquire and hold title to the property in which the *Shari'ah-compliant* investment is to be made (the property). The project company contributes its investment (40% of the acquisition price) to the funding company. A conventional interest-bearing loan is made by the "bank" to

Figure 1: Ijara Structure

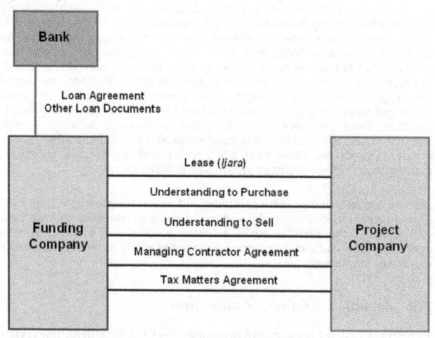

the funding company (equal to 60% of the acquisition price). The funding company then acquires the property from the seller.

Then, the funding company enters into an *ijara* (lease) with the project company, as lessee. The rent payable under the *ijara* is identical to the debt service on the conventional loan from the bank and provides the funds to pay that debt service.

The lease must be *Shari'ah*-compliant, including:

• the lessor must have ownership of the CRE prior to leasing it;
• the lease period must be specified;
• the CRE asset must continue to exist throughout the lease term;
• the lessor must be responsible for maintaining and insuring the property.

Future rents cannot be accelerated under a *Shari'ah*-compliant lease. Given that the outstanding principal is paid through the *ijara*, an acceleration mechanism is necessary outside the *ijara* itself. The understanding to purchase performs that function (it also mirrors all mandatory prepayment provisions of the bank loan). The bank, through the funding company, "puts" the property to the project company at a strike price equal to the outstanding principal (and other outstanding amounts).

The project company may also want to sell the property during the period that the loan is outstanding. The understanding to sell provides the mechanism (and also mirrors the voluntary prepayment provisions of the bank loan).

Under the *Shari'ah* rules noted above, and others, a lessor cannot pass structural maintenance and insurance obligations to a lessee. However, a lessor can hire another entity to perform those functions. In this case, the funding company hires the project company to perform those activities pursuant to the managing contractor agreement.

Finally, the tax matters agreement provides that the project company is the tax owner of the property and for income tax (and other) purposes, this is a loan from the bank to the project company. The tax matters agreement outlines the components as between the conventional loan documentation and the *Shari'ah*-compliant leasing documentation.

This structure is used in essentially all *Shari'ah*-compliant CRE transactions in Europe (with some relatively minor country variations, as appropriate, under relevant tax and CRE laws) and, as noted below, it is easily modified to effect a *Shari'ah*-compliant securitisation.

19.6.2 *Murabaha (sale at a mark-up) structures*

The *murabaha* structure results in OpCo obtaining a cash amount that it can then spend towards purchasing a CRE asset. In Europe, a number of property investors have used this structure as a banking tool, to finance investor purchases of CRE.

As a result, a *murabaha* is a widely used sales structure, and one that is used in some *sukuk* and in many working capital financings. Most simply defined, the *murabaha* is a sale at a mark-up. Figure 2 below, shows a simple *murabaha* transaction.

In the simple *murabaha*, "OpCo", a client of "MBank", wants to purchase a commodity, piece of equipment or other asset. OpCo negotiates the terms of the purchase, including payment terms and precise specifications, with the commodity seller. OpCo then asks MBank to finance the purchase of that asset.

OpCo and MBank enter into a *murabaha* agreement pursuant to which MBank agrees to supply to OpCo a commodity or asset meeting the precise specifications that were negotiated with the commodity seller. The *murabaha* agreement will require OpCo to make payment to MBank for that commodity on a deferred purchase basis.

Figure 2: Basic Murabaha Structure

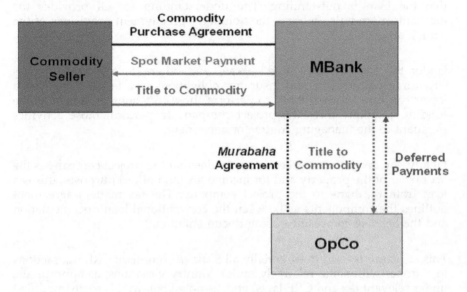

MBank, in turn, will enter into a commodity purchase agreement with the commodity seller and will purchase the commodity from the commodity seller for immediate payment in full.

Upon accepting delivery of the commodity, MBank will fulfil its obligations under the *murabaha* agreement by re-selling the commodity to OpCo. While there are numerous other applicable rules, two are of particular note:

- MBank must have ownership risk with respect to the asset; and
- OpCo can, under most schools of Islamic jurisprudence at the present time, act as the agent for MBank in completing the arrangements between MBank and the commodity seller.

A working capital *murabaha* is shown in Figure 3. This structure is used, in variant forms, in *sukuk* structures.

The transaction, shown in Figure 3, is substantially identical to the *murabaha* transaction shown in Figure 2. The additional element is that OpCo, upon taking title to the commodity (here a permissible metal), immediately sells that metal to the metal purchaser for a cash payment at the same spot market price as obtained in MBank's purchase of that metal from the metal seller (fees ignored). The metal purchaser and metal seller are frequently affiliates. The net result is that OpCo ends up with cash equal to the spot market price of the metal and a deferred *murabaha* payment obligation to MBank in respect of that amount plus a profit factor.

Figure 3: Working Capital Murabaha

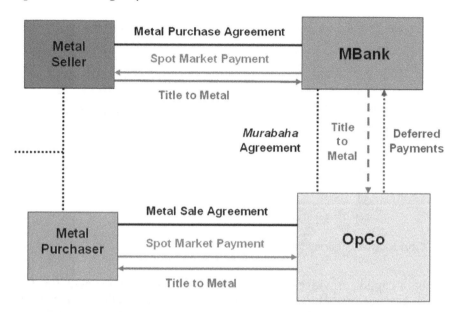

In the CRE context, UK and Irish banks have offered *murabaha* by taking notional possession of a property's title at closing and then selling the property to the investor at a higher price.

If the bank does not want to or cannot acquire title for regulatory reasons, then the bank appoints a transacting party to act as its acquiring agent. The agent then executes the sale in favour of the ultimate investor.

19.6.3 *Mudaraba (service provider—capital provider) structures*

A *mudaraba* is a type of joint venture and is a key method for organising and acquiring CRE investments. It is most frequently formulated as a limited partnership, a limited liability company or a fund. The base structure involves one partner providing services and management (the *mudarib*). One can equate a *mudarib* to a fund manager. In that case, the *mudarib* may subcontract its duties to an experienced CRE management professional. Usually, the *mudarib* does not provide cash or other in-kind capital. Some *Shari'ah* boards prohibit *mudarib* capital; all prohibit it without the consent of the other partner(s). The other partner(s) (the *rabb ul-maal*) provides capital, in cash or in kind, and generally may not interfere in the management or service component. A simple *mudaraba* arrangement with multiple capital providers is shown in Figure 4.

As a general matter, and with a few modifications, a conventional limited partnership agreement works well to structure a *mudaraba*. For example,

Figure 4: Murabaha Structure

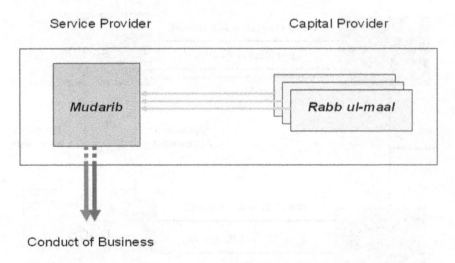

while a capital provider may not interfere in the management function, most *Shari'ah* boards permit "minority rights" protections such as are afforded to limited partners, and other rights are permissible in *mudarib* default, breach and infringement scenarios.

The partnership or fund then acquires CRE assets, most commonly through *ijara* or *murabaha* structures. Profit in a *mudaraba* is that amount that exceeds the capital after deduction of all allowable *mudaraba* expenses. Conversely, loss is the decrease in the *mudaraba* capital. The critical *Shari'ah* rule pertaining to losses is that all losses are borne by the capital provider (the service provider has lost its services and is not seen as having incurred pecuniary losses). Profit allocations must be specified, and must be pro rata (although formulas specifying different allocations upon satisfaction of hurdles have been accepted). Importantly, there can be no predetermined or conclusive profit allocation to any of the parties and arrangements allocating all profit to a single party are impermissible. More difficult issues arise with respect to scenarios in which a clawback of distributions may be necessary, as with losses subsequent to distributions.

19.6.4 *Muisharaka (capital provider) structures*

Al-sharika is a partnership for profit, *Sharikat ul-amwaal* is a property partnership, and *al-musharaka* is a finance method derived from a partnership contract in which a bank participates with one or more clients. The term *musharaka* refers to a wide range of partnership or joint venture arrangements. In a *musharaka*, each of the partners contributes capital, and there is significantly greater flexibility in allocating management responsibilities among partners; joint rights of management are frequent and usual.

Limited partnership agreements are also useful models for structuring *musharaka* arrangements. Profit and loss definitions are mainly the same as with *mudaraba*, with some fundamental differences. Profits may be allocated in accordance with a points system, and that points system may be structured to take account of the amount of capital contributed and the period of participation. Profit from a specific period or operation may not be allocated to a specified partner, nor may a lump sum be allocated to a specific partner. In the majority view, losses, up to the amount of a partner's capital contribution, must be distributed in accordance with the relative capital contributions of the partners. A partner may not assume liability for the capital of another partner, including by way of guarantee.

Shari'ah rules applicable to purchases and sales of interests (*hissas*) from one partner to another (as well as *murabaha* rules) form the basis for securitisation transactions involving *musharaka*.

19.7 The application of CRE finance structures in *sukuk*

Having reviewed some of the typical Islamic finance structures used in CRE acquisition and investment, the next section of this Chapter will consider how such structures have been adapted to develop the market for *sukuk* based on CRE assets. Although a number of significant *sukuk* transactions defaulted (or faced near default) with the advent of the GFC, with issuances of new instruments being very limited during this period, one of the most active areas of Islamic CRE finance, both before and after the GFC, has been *sukuk* issuance. Global annual *sukuk* sales peaked in 2012, and have since declined slightly.

19.8 Asset-based versus asset-backed

Structurally, *sukuk* can be broken into two types of transactions—asset-based or asset-backed. Asset-based issuances are sometimes referred to as "Islamic bonds", whilst asset-backed issuances are generally referred to as "securitisations". There have only been a limited number of *Shari'ah*-compliant securitisations, with the vast majority of *sukuk* issuances being asset-based transactions.

In both types of *sukuk*, the issuing entity (which will usually be an orphan SPV company, as used in CMBS transactions[1]) will issue certificates into the capital markets. The proceeds from the issuance will, depending upon the structure being utilised, either be used to purchase an asset (such as in an *ijara* structure), be invested (as in a *musharaka* or *wakala* structure) or purchase a portfolio of loans (as in a CMBS). It should be noted that in all these structures, the certificates issued are an indivisible ownership interest in the

---

[1] See further Ch.1.

assets of the issuing vehicle. This can cause some tax issues, which will be discussed below.

The difference between the asset-backed structures and asset-based structures lies in the type of credit risk which the investors are taking under each structure.

A *Shari'ah*-compliant securitisation is structurally similar to a conventional securitisation. The issuing vehicle issues certificates and uses the proceeds of the issuance to purchase a portfolio of assets (such as *Shari'ah*-compliant mortgages). The issuing vehicle declares security over this portfolio of assets, and in the event of a default, the security trustee enforces this security and may liquidate the assets. As with conventional securitisations, the investors will not have recourse to the seller of the assets on a default; their recourse will be limited to the assets of the issuing vehicle.

As such, the only structural difference between a *Shari'ah*-compliant securitisation and a conventional securitisation is the fact that the instruments are certificates evidencing an ownership right in the assets in relation to the former, rather than a debt instrument in relation to the latter. As discussed above, there have been a very limited number of *Shari'ah*-compliant securitisations issued (although a larger number have been structured), the most well known of which was the RMBS deal issued by Tamweel in 2008, under which a portfolio of *Shari'ah*-compliant mortgages originated by Tamweel was securitised.

Conversely and from a credit perspective, asset-based *sukuk* structures are most similar to a corporate bond. Islamic bonds are based upon the credit of an entity that is participating in the transaction (which may be the seller, guarantor or other credit support provider and will be referred to as the originator). On execution of the transaction, an asset will be sold to the issuing entity by the corporate, or, funds will be invested with the originator. This asset will generate an income for the issuing vehicle. This income will be generated from payments made by the originator under the contractual arrangements with the issuing entity. However, often there will not be any security over the assets of the issuing entity to secure the certificates (and even where transactions do include security over the assets, it may be that the value of this security is difficult to ascertain). Only a minority of *sukuk* are structured to give *sukuk* holders direct recourse to the underlying asset. The majority are structured so that, following a default, the only recourse is to require the originator to repurchase the income-generating asset (either at a fixed price where fixed-price undertakings are permitted by AAOIFI or at some other price as set out in the documents).

It should be noted that a large number of *sukuk* issued have essentially been capital raising exercises for the underlying corporate, albeit using CRE assets as a way to access this market. However, there have also been a number of *sukuk* transactions that have been used to raise capital for certain CRE and other projects.

Further, a *sukuk* issuance may be one element of a CRE financing. For example, a CMBS transaction could be executed which included both conventional bond financing as well as a tranche structured as a *sukuk*. There is increased market interest in the establishment of multi-funding platforms that incorporate tranches of conventional and Islamic finance and there is no reason why these structures cannot continue to be applied to the CRE market.

19.9   AAOIFI *sukuk* standard

Under the AAOIFI *sukuk* standard, *sukuk* are defined as certificates of equal value put to use as common shares and rights in tangible assets, usufructs and services or as equity in a project or investment activity. The AAOIFI standard carefully distinguishes *sukuk* from equity, notes and bonds. It emphasises that *sukuk* are not debts of the issuer; they are fractional or proportional interests in underlying assets, usufructs, services, projects or investment activities. *Sukuk* may not be issued on a pool of receivables. Further, the underlying business or activity, and the underlying transactional structures (such as the underlying CRE leases) must be *Shari'ah-compliant* (the business or activity cannot engage in prohibited business activities, for example).

AAOIFI has specified 14 categories of permissible *sukuk*. In broad summary, they are securitisations:

- of an existing or to-be-acquired tangible asset (*ijara*);
- of an existing or to-be-acquired leasehold estate (*ijara*);
- of presales of services (*ijara*);
- of presales of the production of goods or commodities at a future date (*salam* (forward sale));
- to fund the cost of construction (*istisna'a* (construction contract));
- to fund the acquisition of goods for future sale (*murabaha*);
- to fund capital participation in a business or investment activity (*mudaraba* or *musharaka*); and
- to fund various asset acquisition and agency management (*wakala* (agency)), agricultural land cultivation, land management and orchard management activities.

A factor that had impinged upon the structuring and issuance of *sukuk* and *Shari'ah*-compliant CMBS transactions was the lack of *Shari'ah*-compliant hedging mechanisms and liquidity structures (which may both be required by rating agencies for a rated transaction). The issue of *Shari'ah*-compliant hedging mechanisms was rectified in March 2010, by the publication of the *Ta'Hawwut* Master Agreement by the International Swaps and Derivatives

Association and the International Islamic Financial Market. However, this development is still in its early stages compared to the conventional hedging market, and is taking time to consolidate. With regard to liquidity structures and other forms of credit enhancement (which in conventional transactions will be provided by facilities), various structures have been considered on a transaction by transaction basis.

Prohibitions on *riba* (interest), and on the sale of instruments that do not represent fractional undivided ownership interest in tangible assets, present a seemingly insurmountable problem for Islamic-compliant securitisation of conventional receivables, such as conventional mortgages, patent and other royalty payments, credit card receivables and the full range of other conventional receivables. Many of these receivables will never be made *Shari'ah*-compliant in and of themselves, but it seems likely that bifurcated structures will be developed to securitise these assets (just as conventional interest-based financing is used in most international *Shari'ah*-compliant CRE and private equity financings).

19.10 Tax and regulatory issues

One issue which needs careful consideration as part of the structuring of any *sukuk* transaction is whether the nature of a *sukuk* can raise any tax or regulatory concerns. These issues, by their very nature, differ across *sukuk* issuances, depending on the jurisdiction(s) of the issuing entity, of the assets and of the investors.

As discussed above, the certificates issued in a *sukuk* are ownership interests in the assets of the issuing vehicle rather than debt instruments. This can raise a number of unexpected tax issues. In a conventional securitisation, it is fundamental that the issuing vehicle be tax neutral. However, the nature of a *sukuk* may mean that this is not the case. The issuing vehicle may not receive the benefit of tax deductions for interest, as no interest is paid on the certificates.

Further, if the instrument is deemed to be an equity-like instrument rather than a debt instrument, transfers of the certificate may incur a transfer tax charge. Additionally, various stamp duty and land taxes may also be triggered in a CRE-based *sukuk* structure.

In a number of jurisdictions (such as the UK and Ireland), regulations have been introduced in order to ensure that *sukuk* structures are not taxed in a manner inconsistent with securitisations and other structured debt transactions. These regulations can take the form of deeming the cashflows under a *sukuk* to be equivalent to cashflows under a securitisation (for example, deeming periodic distribution payments to be payments of interest) and deeming the instruments to be debt rather than equity (and as such, removing the risk of transfer taxes being imposed).

Regarding the collective investment scheme issue, this needs to be considered on a case-by-case basis, as the market has yet to come to a position as to whether or not this is triggered.

19.11   Negotiability of instruments

When structuring a *sukuk*, it is important to understand the nature of the asset underlying the structure. Trading in debt above or below par would breach *riba* principles (being interest) and be impermissible. As such, where the assets underlying the *sukuk* are receivables, either the instruments could only be traded at par, or their transfer must be prohibited. These limitations are generally problematic in capital markets transactions, where the ability to trade freely is critical for the creation of liquidity. Many capital markets instruments are held through central clearing systems (such as Euroclear or Clearstream) which require the instruments to be negotiable and tradeable.

The resolution of the apparent *riba* issue lies in the fact that in a number of *sukuk* structures (such as an *ijara sukuk*) the underlying assets are tangible assets rather than debts and through the trust certificate structure (under which the assets are subject to a trust declared by the issuing vehicle in favour of a trustee to be held on trust for the holders of the certificates) the *sukuk* holders have an interest in a tangible asset. This structure means that these *sukuk* can be traded above or below par, and if required by investors, held in central clearing systems.

19.12   The *sukuk al-ijara*

The *ijara* structure that is so widely used in Islamic finance (see Figure 1) is readily adaptable to *sukuk* in a number of different ways. The simplest *sukuk* issuance utilising the *ijara* structure is shown in Figure 5. In Figure 5, the structure demonstrates the issuing entity issues *sukuk* into the capital markets and uses the proceeds to purchase an asset from the originator. It then leases the asset back to the originator. Often, the *sukuk* holders will not have a security interest in the asset (or, where they do have a security interest in the asset, it may be difficult to enforce). Each *sukuk* holder is entitled to receive the rental income generated under the lease pro rata to its ownership interest in the underlying CRE asset based on the *sukuk* held by it.

The above *sukuk al-ijara* structure in Figure 5 has been utilised in a large number of *sukuk* issuances across the globe, and is seen by some as the "classic *sukuk*".

Figure 5: Ijara Sukuk

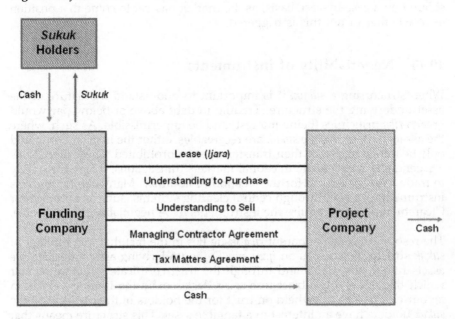

In these structures, the rental stream from the *ijara* can be structured to produce a precise cash flow on the *sukuk* akin to conventional debt capital markets instruments. As such, the rate of return can be set as a fixed rate or a floating rate, and the capital return profile can be structured such that it is either through an amortisation schedule, a bullet repayment or a combination of partial amortisation with partial bullet repayment.

Where the structure involves a bullet repayment or partial bullet repayment at maturity, on the maturity of the certificates (or the occurrence of certain other events, such as an event of default), the originator will repurchase the asset at a price fixed at closing. This price will be equal to all amounts owing to the *sukuk* holders. Unlike some other structures, the scholars are comfortable with a fixed price purchase undertaking being used in *ijara* structures. This may be part of the reason why these structures are so popular in the *sukuk* market.

There are some limitations to the use of the *ijara sukuk*. For example, many originators do not own appropriate underlying assets that are subject to *Shari'ah*-compliant leases or can be made available for such leases during the *sukuk* term, and, as discussed above, in many jurisdictions, there are significant adverse tax consequences associated with the introduction of the assets into a *sukuk* structure. However, a number of authorities such as those in Ireland, France and the UK are keen to encourage the growth of Islamic finance within their jurisdictions and have worked with participants in the Islamic finance market to implement regulations to minimise tax issues in *sukuk* and other Islamic finance structures. In fact, London, Dublin and Paris are all keen to try and be the centres of Islamic finance in Europe and have petitioned their relevant tax authorities accordingly.

19.13   The *sukuk al-musharaka*

In the *sukuk al-musharaka*, the issuing entity enters into a joint venture or partnership arrangement, pursuant to a *"musharaka* management agreement", with the party seeking financing (the *"musharaka* partner"). As noted above, each party may contribute capital to the *musharaka*. Each of the partners receives "units" or *"hissas"* in the *musharaka* in accordance with their respective capital contributions. The issuer's capital contribution is in cash, and equals the proceeds of the *sukuk* issuance. The contribution of the *musharaka* partner is usually an in-kind contribution of a tangible asset (such as a piece of CRE). A *musharaka* structure is depicted in Figure 6.

Figure 6: Sukuk al-Musharaka

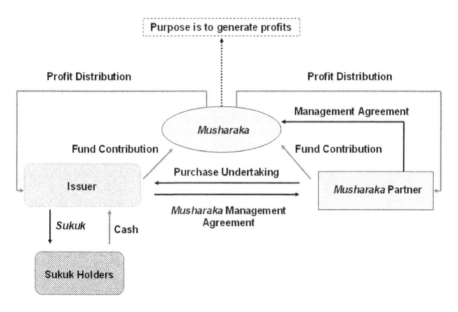

The issuer and the *musharaka* partner enter into a purchase undertaking pursuant to which the issuer can require the *musharaka* partner to purchase designated units or *hissas* on specified dates either during the term of the *sukuk* or at maturity. Where units are purchased throughout the life of the transaction, the structure is referred to as a "diminishing *musharaka*". Economically, this is akin to an amortising bond. However, alternatively, the units may only be repurchased on maturity (or other certain events), in which case the *sukuk* is economically akin to a bond with a bullet repayment.

Under the *musharaka* structure, the issuing entity will receive profit distributions from the *musharaka* and the proceeds from sales of the *hissas*, which are then distributed to the *sukuk* holders in accordance with agreed formulae. Although profits and losses are required to be shared between the partners in accordance with their share of total units in the partnership, a number of *sukuk* transactions have been structured such that all profit has been paid to the issuing entity in priority to the *musharaka* partner, until such time as the issuing entities' contribution has been reduced to zero (and the *sukuk* holders have been repaid in full).

In 2008, AAOIFI issued guidelines (the *AAOIFI Guidelines*) which set out the parameters of how an exercise price under the purchase undertaking could be calculated. Prior to the issuance of the *AAOIFI Guidelines*, the exercise price would have been stipulated under the purchase undertaking as an amount equal to all amounts owing at the time of exercise to the *sukuk* holders. However, following the issuance of the *AAOIFI Guidelines*, where the purchaser under the purchase undertaking is the *musharaka* partner, the exercise price cannot be set at closing, but rather is required to be calculated on the basis of the market value of the assets on the date on which the purchase undertaking is exercised. As such, there is the risk that the exercise price may be less than the amounts owing to *sukuk* holders. Although structural mitigates can be built into a *sukuk* transaction utilising a *musharaka* structure (such as reserve funds and *Shari'ah*-compliant liquidity features) these may not entirely remove the risk of payment default under the certificates on the exercise of the purchase undertaking.

As such, the use of the *sukuk al musharaka* structure has declined in popularity following the issue of the *AAOIFI Guidelines*.

19.14 The *sukuk al-wakala*

One structure which has been utilised on *sukuk* transactions in the Middle East is the *sukuk al-wakala*. This financing structure has been used on a number of funding structures, incorporating both conventional and Islamic finance tranches.

In a *sukuk al-wakala*, the issuing entity as investor appoints the *wakeel* as agent to invest the proceeds of the issuance of certificates in accordance with the terms of a *wakala*. The *wakeel* will invest the funds in a portfolio of *Shari'ah*-compliant assets, which may be a portfolio of assets or parts of an asset already owned by the *wakeel*. At the outset, the parties to the *wakala* will agree the profit return to the issuing vehicle as investor. This profit return will be paid to the issuing vehicle periodically.

A *sukuk al-wakala* structure is shown in Figure 7.

Figure 7: Sukuk al-Wakala

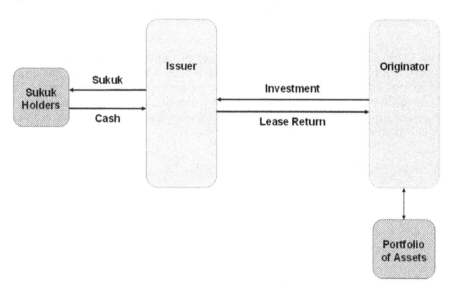

Under a *wakala* structure, any profit is used to pay the profit return to the investor, with the remainder being retained by the *wakeel* as an incentive fee. However, there is a risk that the return generated on the assets may not be sufficient to pay the agreed profit return to the issuing entity, and as such, the *sukuk* holders may suffer a loss. Prior to the *AAOIFI Guidelines*, a guaranteed profit return structure was utilised in the market. However, following the issue of the *AAOIFI Guidelines*, the majority of scholars appear to be of the view that a fixed rate of profit return is not acceptable in a *sukuk al-wakala* structure.

Wakala structures have been considered in capital raisings by CRE companies, where the companies want to access conventional and *Shari'ah*-compliant financing. For example, in the case of a financing of a shopping mall, certain *Shari'ah*-compliant parts of the mall could be used as a base for a *wakala*, with the remainder funded by conventional financing.

19.15 The *sukuk al-istisna*

The *sukuk al-istisna* structure has been discussed as an option for project financing, where general bank debt or other forms of Islamic financing are not available. These structures are often referred to as "Islamic project bonds". However, the structure also has a number of characteristics which have limited its use by originators.

An *istisna* is essentially an order to a manufacturer to manufacture a specific asset for the purchaser. Under a *sukuk al-istisna*, the originator will agree to

503

manufacture or construct certain assets and deliver those assets to the issuing entity in return for an amount equal to the proceeds of the issuance of certificates.

The issuing entity will then agree to lease the assets back to the originator under a forward lease agreement, under which it agrees to make rental payments to the issuing entity. On the maturity of the certificates or the occurrence of other events, such as an event of default, the originator will be required to purchase the assets from the issuing vehicle for an amount equal to amounts owed to the *sukuk* holders.

A *sukuk al-istisna* structure is shown in Figure 8.

Figure 8: Sukuk al-Istisna

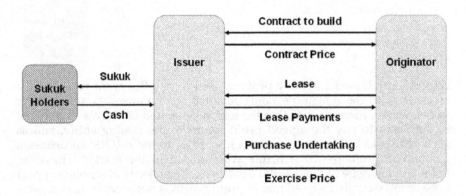

However, as discussed above, there are a number of characteristics relating to these structures. In an *istisna*, there is a construction phase, and then a rental phase. During both phases, the originator will pay periodic rental payments to the issuing entity. There are concerns that during the construction phase, the *sukuk* is only backed by receivables, and as such is not tradable, unless traded at par. Further, some scholars have shown concern about forward leasing, and there is the risk that if the assets are not constructed, any advance rental payments would need to be repaid to the originator.

In light of increased interest in project bonds, it will be interesting to see if these structures become more common, in particular in large multi-funding project finance transactions.

19.16   The *sukuk al-mudaraba*

The *mudaraba* structure may also be incorporated into a *sukuk* offering in a number of different variants of the *sukuk al-mudaraba*. A generalised generic form of a *sukuk al-mudaraba* is set forth in Figure 9.

Figure 9: Sukuk al-Mudaraba

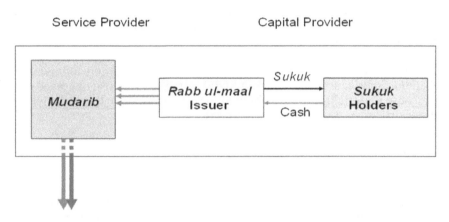

Conduct of Business

The *sukuk al-mudaraba* is quite similar to the standard *mudaraba* structure presented in Figure 4. The *rabb ul-maal* issuer sells the *sukuk* to the *sukuk* holders and the proceeds of that issuance provide the capital for the *mudaraba*. The *mudarib* will conduct the business of the *mudaraba* as the provider of services. As noted above, this is similar to a limited partnership or limited liability company.

This *mudaraba* may constitute the only entity necessary for the conduct of the relevant business. Or, as is more likely in a complex project or undertaking, this *mudaraba* may enter into joint venture and/or other contractual arrangements with other parties. For example, in a complex project financing this *mudaraba* may enter into a further joint venture with a project sponsor in connection with the financing, construction and operation of the project.

Some of the primary structural considerations will focus, at each level of the transaction, on principles pertaining to allocation and distribution of profits and losses, and the permissibility of capital contributions by the *mudarib*.

A separate set of issues arise in any financing in which capital is needed periodically (these issues also affect other structures, such as the *musharaka*). Consider, for example, the construction of a large-scale project where the construction cycle extends over a period of years and there is no project

505

income during that period. All involved parties will desire that there be certainty of capital availability throughout the construction period. Periodic *sukuk* issuances do not provide that certainty. An initial *sukuk* issuance for the full amount of the construction costs will provide that certainty, but is economically inefficient. The issuance proceeds in excess of immediate needs will be invested in short-term investments (such as *murabaha*) that have low rates of return. Further, the *sukuk* holders will probably expect periodic returns from the inception of the transaction. The project itself will be generating no income (it is in the construction phase) and the reinvestment income will be low. Payments on the *sukuk* during the construction and ramp-up phase are essentially self-funded by the *sukuk* holders.

There have been very few *sukuk al-mudaraba* issuances, and following the *AAOIFI Guidelines*, under which AAOIFI stated that the use of a fixed-price purchase undertaking was prohibited in *sukuk* structures, it is expected that these structures will remain rarely used.

19.17 The *sukuk al-murabaha*

One *sukuk* structure which probably has limited utility for CRE transactions, yet merits a short discussion, is the *sukuk al-murabaha*. There have been a limited number of *sukuk al-murabaha* when compared to other forms of *sukuk*; however, under certain circumstances, they may be attractive to parties in a capital raising transaction. These forms of *sukuk* generally raise capital for general purposes and are not linked to a specific CRE asset of the originator. However, the capital raised could be used by the originator for CRE purposes.

Figure 10 below shows a bond-type *sukuk*.

The *sukuk al-murabaha* is issued to the *sukuk* holders by the issuer. The *sukuk* represents a "participation interest" in the underlying *murabaha* transaction. The issuance proceeds are used to purchase a metal on the spot market, the metal is then sold to the originator on a deferred payment basis, and the originator sells the metal to the metal purchaser on the spot market. The net result is that the originator holds cash equal to the spot market price of the metal which it can use in its CRE operations and the originator has a deferred payment obligation on the *murabaha agreement* that is used to service the *sukuk*.

Figure 11 below, illustrates a *murabaha sukuk* in which the deferred *murabaha* payment obligations under a pool of *murabaha* transactions are pooled, and the issuer sells a *sukuk* based on that pool.

Under these *murabaha sukuk* structures, the party needing financing (the originator) obtains cash only by selling the tangible asset (the metal or other asset). Thus, on an ongoing basis, this *sukuk* does not represent an owner-

Figure 10: Sukuk al-Murabaha

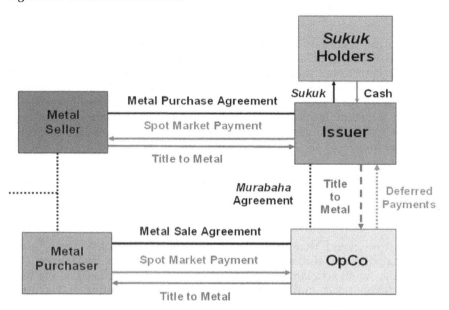

Figure 11: Sukuk al-Murabaha

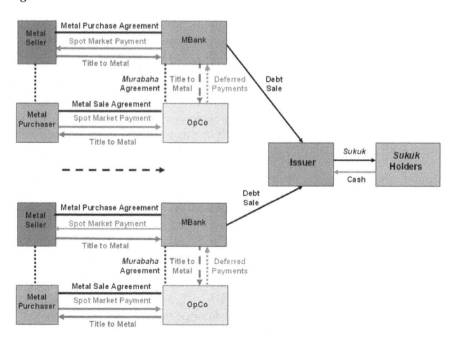

ship interest in a tangible asset—it has been sold—and only the deferred debt obligation (a receivable) remains after sale of the asset.

As such, the assets underlying the *sukuk* are debts. One of the general principles of the *Shari'ah* is that debt cannot be traded except at par. As such, the certificates issued in a *sukuk al-musharaka* cannot be negotiable instruments and traded on the secondary market. This limits the possible investor base for these types of instruments. However, there have been a number of recent transactions which have utilised a *sukuk al-musharaka* structure where the investors have agreed to hold the assets for the term of the transaction.

Further, it is possible for a *sukuk* to have a number of underlying structures, including a *murabaha* structure, where the receivables derived from the *murabaha* are a small proportion of the overall structure.

It should be noted that the position of scholars in South East Asia is somewhat different to the position of scholars outside of that region. The South East Asian scholars accept that a *murabaha* may be used as the basis for a tradeable *sukuk*, making this structure a common feature of the capital markets in that region.

19.18   Conclusion

In 2016, the future for the Islamic finance market is difficult to predict, although the hope is that it will continue to grow and develop globally as a true alternative form of funding. Regulators have shown themselves willing to consider Islamic finance structures and equalise the tax position of Islamic finance structures with their equivalent conventional finance structures.

Regarding Islamic CRE finance, based on recent history, it is hoped that the markets continue to see strong growth in this market. Liquidity needs will focus CRE market players on Islamic finance as an alternative financing channel. Progress in product development, coupled with strong demand, should sharply accelerate growth in Islamic finance due to pent-up demand. For example, there is a forecast need for £1.3 trillion of project finance in GCC countries and £60 billion of mortgage finance in Saudi Arabia.

Conventional banks will, as set out in numerous Chapters throughout this book, increasingly focus on refinancing, de-risking, improving capital ratios and deleveraging. They will continue to vacate a significant part of the CRE finance field and Islamic finance can help to partly meet the remaining demand, with the result that Islamic finance and investment is poised to enter the mainstream of the global CRE market.

Regarding the *sukuk* market, recent *sukuk* defaults and lower issuance rates have led to a focus on the position of *sukuk* holders and, in particular, the rights they have to the underlying assets. This has, as discussed above, highlighted the distinction between asset-backed and asset-based structures, comparable to the rights of bondholders under secured and unsecured bonds. In asset-based *sukuk*, the holders can only require the originator to purchase the underlying *sukuk* assets and would have an unsecured debt claim against the originator from the payment of the purchase price after exercising their rights under the relevant purchase undertaking. This credit risk profile may not be what some investors expected. These are very encouraging signs for the continued growth of the Islamic finance capital markets and Islamic finance market as a whole.

Chapter 20

US Cross-border Investments in European Commercial Mortgage Markets

Anthony R. G. Nolan,
Partner, K&L Gates LLP

Diego Shin,
Special Counsel, K&L Gates LLP

20.1 Introduction[1]

In late 2011 and early 2012, the fragile green shoots of recovery began to peek out from the barren blasted heath of the crisis-blown financial markets. Market activity was spurred by a rare confluence of secular trends, which included the strategic imperative of European financial institutions to deleverage and divest assets in order to improve their regulatory capital, leverage and liquidity ratios, a phenomenon that has been described elsewhere in this book. Markets were also impacted by the liquidity provided by pension and investment funds throughout the world, which have been particularly interested in prime commercial real estate (CRE) assets in major European cities.[2] Whilst investment in European CRE has long been regarded as a relative value play for many global investors, North American interest in European CRE has, in particular, proven to be an effective counterweight to the traditional interest of European investors in US CRE opportunities.

As set out in Chapter 3, as the European CRE sector and related debt markets have emerged from the massive repricing of credit risk and property fundamentals that occurred during the GFC, a significant part of the resurgence in demand for European CRE assets has come from the US. Indeed, it has been estimated that US investors represented almost a quarter of all of investments in European CRE between 2010 and 2015, with US investors deploying €19 billion in 2014 and €16.4 billion in 2015.[3]

---

[1] The authors are grateful for the comments of their tax colleague Tom Lyden to this Chapter.
[2] This Chapter should be read in conjunction with the opportunity for such investors identified in detail in Ch.22.
[3] Cushman & Wakefield, "Investment Market Update: Record investment set to continue—Europe Q4 2015", at *http://www.cushmanwakefield.co.uk/en-gb/research-and-insight/2016/investment-market-update-europe-q4-2015* [Accessed 11 August 2016].

There are many reasons why US investors looked to the Old Continent in the wake of the GFC in the New World. One reason is that European CRE, which had long been valued as a source of diversification, became more attractive as US mortgage markets were broadly affected by the fall in the residential sector and CRE properties were affected by the steep fall off in tenant demand in US markets. Another is the weakening trend of the US dollar in relation to major European currencies, which affected the demand of US investors for future cash flows denominated in those currencies, no more so than what has occurred since the UK's Referendum vote on its continuing membership of the EU that took place on 23 June 2016, where following the positive vote to leave the EU (Brexit), Sterling fell precipitately over 10%. Lastly, European CRE capital markets were relatively active at a time that CRE deal volumes in the US were moribund. While it remains to be seen how the investment story will play out in light of Brexit and the long-running efforts of the EU to avert hard devaluations by Eurozone member states, it appears that continuing uncertainty over European fiscal and monetary policy will provide additional attractive occasions for opportunistic private equity investors to obtain interests in fundamentally strong CRE at favourable prices, as discussed in Chapter 22, albeit caveated and subject to regional and political uncertainty arising from the economic climate in the Southern European jurisdictions and the fallout from Brexit as well as the ramifications of terrorism.

This Chapter will touch on some of the strategic and tactical issues that potential investors should be prepared to address when investing in European CRE. These include country-specific features; differences and similarities between investments through interests in mortgages, mezzanine notes and B-pieces; CMBS in Europe and the US; the CRE debt secondary markets; and problems associated with the economic pressures in the Eurozone.

20.2   Asset-level investment considerations

The confection of a winning bid to acquire CRE assets requires a sound strategy coupled with compelling financing and engaged and competent service providers and asset managers on the ground. Moreover, it requires a proper appreciation of the legal technicalities associated with investments in European CRE by international investors. In some respects, this last ingredient can be particularly challenging for investors whose investment experience has been limited to their own jurisdictions, for CRE is uniquely influenced by the law of the place where the property is located. In law, as in commercial life, it truly can be said that the secret of CRE investment is "location, location, location".

Cross-border considerations in Europe are more complex than in the US not merely because of language and cultural differences, but also because of the fundamentally different evolution of real estate law in Europe and the US despite converging conceptions of a federal system. In the US, whilst real estate law and law governing enforcement or foreclosure is specific to each US State, the laws of each US State—particularly with respect to CRE as opposed to residential real estate—can be viewed as relatively homogenous in a very general way, at least if compared to the hotchpotch of various legal systems and concepts evident across national borders in Europe.

As an example, it is fairly typical in the UK to see borrowing structures with varying degrees of complexity where the borrowers may be located in certain jurisdictions with favourable offshore tax regimes (such as, by way of illustration, Ireland, Netherlands, Luxembourg, Jersey or Gibraltar), or which provide greater tax efficiency, or are required to be used to comply with applicable national law on the basis of the underlying assets collateralising a given loan (the Netherlands or France, among others). Added complexity is introduced to the extent that the underlying CRE securing such financings may be located in one or more European jurisdictions and to the extent that the documentation governing such loan and associated hedging relationships may be subject to the national laws of another EU Member State. Accordingly, European CRE loans involve an appreciation of various legal regimes (each with its own lending and security requirements) that are distinct from each other. This is a fundamental difference from the US legal framework for equivalent transactions to the extent that standards are essentially sui generis or incompatible with other regimes.

The enforcement of rights in a CRE mortgage depends heavily on the local law governing interests in the subject CRE, the enforceability of subordination and intercreditor arrangements, and the local power of eminent domain. In addition to the basic impact of cross-border legal systems on the structure and documentation of a CRE loan, the appraisal of value of a CRE project is often a function of planning (zoning in the US) and land use restrictions, which in the experience of investors with a point of reference in the US, are resolved at the most local level of government. This may depend as much on local conceptions of what is the highest and best use for a loan as on conventional legal doctrine. This consideration should also extend to the political climate in the location of any proposed investment assets where populist governments and/or local authorities have been attempting to curb lender enforcement rights over certain types of properties and limiting development opportunities. Therefore, an important consideration for US investors in European CRE is to strategically map the legal concepts and enforcement rights that are relevant to determinations of value to the corresponding concepts to which they are accustomed in their home jurisdictions.

20.2.1 Strategy

In order to realise the strategic vision, it is also necessary to have in place a robust platform or service provider network that permits realisation of those expectations, bearing in mind that the ultimate strategy will determine the manner in which a CRE portfolio is managed. In the case of a classic long-term equity management play, it will be particularly important to have a strong servicing and property and/or asset management capability on an asset-by-asset basis with disposition or favourable refinancing as an ultimate exit strategy.[4] On the other hand, in the case of a distressed lending "loan to own" strategy the most important elements of investment success will be the ability to obtain value by enforcement and ultimate disposition, refinancing or repositioning of the property after enforcement. The application of these considerations to an individual case will depend on the nature of the parties to a transaction and the character of the acquisition of the interest in CRE, as discussed above. However, in order to have a meaningfully realistic exit strategy, the investor should consider having a captive servicer platform (either in-house or appointed via a non-exclusive third party arrangement) to provide the expertise in resolution strategy.

20.2.2 Financing

The specific implementation of a portfolio acquisition strategy may be affected by the conditions in which the acquiring party will expect to finance its acquisition. Some basic considerations have been discussed above. Financing terms may be affected by a variety of factors, including whether the CRE acquisition is being conducted on an asset-by-asset basis, or as part of a broader portfolio transaction, whether the financing is structured using securitisation techniques. The objectives and timelines of the bidder that may impact the use of leverage may also affect investment decisions. In the case of investment funds these generally relate to the fund guidelines and in the case of joint ventures they may require negotiation between the bidders on a common set of parameters.

A key consideration will be the difficulty of obtaining third party debt or equity financing to support the acquisition. Financial institutions now view with greater interest opportunities to finance portfolio sales on non-performing CRE assets due to the margins and fees payable and relatively quick repayment. CMBS has also been the source of vendor financing in certain occasions. Whilst we have witnessed the opening of sources of third party finance, it remains for evident reasons both portfolio and buyer specific. The availability of third-party financing sources provides greater options for an ultimate exit. Taken together with a steady ream of investment opportunities to finance portfolio acquisitions in Europe, a sustainable level of activity in the short term appears likely. In that sense, there is opportunity for investors to take an equity stake in a transaction or provide straight financing (either alone or in syndicate) to third party purchasers or by investing in related CMBS to allow such parties to gain exposure to transactions they may have not otherwise been able to access, in so-called "loan on loan" financing. Whether such institutions will prefer an equity, financing or capital markets investment role will ultimately depend on the

---

[4]   See further Chs 9, 10 and 11.

risk/return profile of the transaction that may ultimately cater more to certain types of institutions rather than others.

20.2.3 Getting the necessary parties onboard

As discussed above, a crucial element of any strategy that involves a financing option is to determine the optimal source of financing, whether provided by a third party lender or through CMBS, and the terms of the financing. This will involve very different considerations depending on the nature of the financing party and the way in which the financing is structured. It may be necessary to structure a financing in such a way to satisfy rating agency criteria,[5] if the objective is to create highly rated CMBS securities that satisfy investment guidelines of capital market investors, or alternatively to facilitate the issuance of asset-backed commercial paper by permitting the conduit to satisfy its own rating requirements.

The identity of parties to a financing transaction will be dictated to a great extent by the nature of the transaction. A trustee or security trustee, an administrator, a servicer and a special servicer are all potential parties to a financing transaction. Their roles in the European market are dealt with throughout this book.

20.2.4 Certain legal considerations affecting marketing

20.2.4.1 Type of asset or transaction

The amount of due diligence required in respect of a CRE transaction is heavily dependent on the nature of the asset and of the transaction itself. In the case of a whole loan acquisition, the purchaser will have full power to exercise control over the loan and negotiate any work-outs or other resolution strategies with the related borrowers, subject only to restrictions imposed by local law. As described above, a purchaser must appreciate the local laws affecting its proposed exit strategy in relation to each asset it is acquiring. European loan structures can be complex when compared with their US equivalents and can involve a number of very distinct legal regimes. A transaction may involve non-CRE assets such as synthetic swaps and there may also be exposures to third parties that may introduce counterparty credit risk to a transaction where that counterparty may also have rights to administer or influence the decision-making in respect of the reference obligation.

Apart from the predictable impact that the governing laws of the place of incorporation of each member of a given borrower group may have on a structure as well as the location of the underlying income producing properties, it is also important to consider the various tax considerations that can have an impact on such strategies. These tax considerations may

---

[5] See further Ch.14.

not necessarily be limited to the applicable tax regime affecting the location of where the CRE is situated, but may extend to the relevant entity's place of incorporation and/or where it effectively manages and operates its business, among other considerations.

On the other hand, if the asset is a tranche of a loan, or a CMBS security, the ability of the holder to take actions with respect to it may be materially limited if other parties (whether lenders or bondholders) have contractual rights permitting them to exercise control rights over the asset, such as rights to consult on servicing decisions, special servicing transfers or appraisal reductions, each of which have been discussed in previous Chapters. Furthermore, the extent to which the CRE asset may be out of the money may affect the identity of the party entitled to exercise such control rights, as the controlling party is often defined as a majority of the most subordinate class with at least 25% of its principal amount outstanding. It is worth noting that it is not always easy in Europe to identify such controlling party at any given time because publicly placed European securitisations do not maintain a central register of noteholders and because CMBS securities are often held in book-entry form through Euroclear. This problem of identification is similar to that affecting US CMBS in book-entry form that is held through DTEC. Accordingly, purchasers of non-controlling classes of bonds may wish to take additional steps to identify which institutions are represented within the controlling class where the identity of such institutions can have an impact on how the purchaser's realisation strategy is or can be implemented and whether such strategy is ultimately realistic taking into account such third parties' own interests.

20.2.4.2 *Control*

In the case of CMBS securities, the control determinations can be complicated by many factors, including intercreditor issues between the securitisation and subordinate loans that are secured by the same mortgaged property but are held outside the securitisation structure. These types of intercreditor issues are often apparent in tranched A/B loan structures, where the senior (or A) tranche of the loan is placed in a securitisation and the subordinate (or B) tranche is either held, assigned or is itself securitised in a mezzanine CMBS or CRE CDO.[6] The subordination and intercreditor arrangements are of great importance because the party with control over enforcement rights and other functions such as appraisal reductions will have great influence over determinants of value.

The nature of the asset and the nature and existence of other creditors (such as swap counterparties, junior lenders, senior lenders or mezzanine lenders) may affect the extent to which the purchaser may exercise control rights in respect of the asset. For example, swap counterparties to financing structures often have contractually determined rights to share in cashflow from

---

[6] See Chs 5, 6 and 7.

the charged property, with remedies upon certain events that can include changes to payment entitlements and step-up of rights to direct certain determinations. To the extent that there are other lenders in the structure, or that rights are held by CMBS bondholders, other parties (such as third party lenders, swap providers or loan servicers) will be involved in the transaction or the administration of the underlying asset in either an ownership, secured party or agency capacity. Any of such parties may present an obstacle to a purchaser that seeks to implement its own resolution strategy by acquiring a direct interest in the loan CMBS bonds backed by the loan.

A fairly typical example of how such parties to a transaction can directly impact the management of a loan relationship is seen in the rights such parties may have to require the termination and appointment of their nominated special servicer (if any has been appointed). In distressed loans, such special servicers will have primary responsibility in managing the lender/borrower relationship, interfacing with the borrower as to proposed work-out or restructuring plans and ultimately when and whether to take any enforcement action in respect of that loan and its security. It is also possible that such third parties may have certain consent or consultation rights before such prescribed actions are implemented in respect of the related loan or its security. These types of consideration will affect the nature of a CRE investor's interactions with the borrower, as well as the opportunities for realisation of value or liquidity.

20.2.4.3 *Facility agent/security agent transfers*

In order to maximise the opportunities of realisation on a particular loan asset, the purchaser (or its delegates) normally must be able to interface directly with the borrowers on the underlying loans. Effective channels of communication can be crucial to the ability to engage in modifications of the loan and to understand issues involving the borrower that can affect value. To the extent that any of the existing agents in a loan structure are intending to exit the transaction after the purchaser completes its acquisition of the asset by the purchaser, it is important to ensure that such transfers are permitted and to control the costs and liabilities involved in the same, including, such items as transfers of any related security held in any particular agent's own name. Similarly to what has been described above, local law requirements may have an impact on the selection of any replacements, as certain European jurisdictions regulate the types of entities that may perform certain functions in respect of CRE assets. As discussed in other Chapters, securitisations will usually involve other intermediaries as well, such as a loan agent or servicer or a special servicer who will be a point of contact with the underlying obligors. Following its acquisition of the CRE interest, it will be important for the purchaser to assess the extent of its control over the selection and replacement of this intermediary and to ensure that the preferred intermediary is in the role. The considerations discussed above under "control" will be germane to that assessment.

20.2.4.4   Restrictions on assignability

The assignability of a CRE loan that has been acquired is an important element to determining the lender's exit, in the case of a direct loan and of the lender's ability to take necessary actions and make needed determinations, in the case of a loan that is financed through a CMBS structure. In cases where a CRE loan or other asset is not capable of being assigned, it is necessary to consider alternative structures such as loan participations or total return swaps. However, these arrangements pose their own challenges, including the continuing interposition of the lender of record as counterparty, facing the party with the actual credit exposure to the underlying borrower. In order to be viable, any transaction must be structured and implemented in such a way that the purchaser or servicer may effectively take lender decisions in respect of a CRE loan.

20.3   Special considerations for US investors

As discussed in Chapter 1, CMBS has historically represented a source of liquidity for investments in commercial mortgages. The combination of bankruptcy-remote structuring and structured credit enhancement to provide a basis for issuance of highly-rated mortgage-backed securities has long been a potent structuring tool, one that has facilitated capital formation in the CRE markets worldwide.

Although the previous sections of this Chapter have focused on asset-level issues, a crucial set of considerations for transactions sold to US investors relates to the regulatory impact of the structure on US investors, and conversely on the impact that US investors can have on the legal position of a non-US issuer or sponsor.

Commercial mortgage investments that are packaged into securities for sale to investors in the US raise several sets of legal issues. In respect of European issued ABS, these may involve an interplay between US and European legislation, which may impose additional requirements to those which would apply on a purely domestic issuance.[7] From a US perspective, the principal issues involve the registration requirements of and substantive liability under the securities laws, the need to obtain an exemption from registration of the issuer as an investment company, the need to structure the transaction to be eligible for investment by pension plans without causing a prohibited transaction under US pension law and the need to structure the transaction in such a way as to qualify for favourable treatment under US tax law governing real estate mortgage investment conduits.

---

[7]   Recent legislative requirements in respect of European CRE and CMBS are discussed in Chs 16 and 17, whilst this Chapter solely explores US considerations.

In the earlier edition of this Chapter, we omitted discussion of potential regulatory reforms that had not yet affected securitisation or private equity transactions but would possibly have an impact on them depending on how certain rule making activity to implement the Dodd-Frank Wall Street Reform, Consumer Protection and Transparency Act (Dodd-Frank Act) was carried out. At the time, those issues were too uncertain to assess author-itatively. At the time of writing, the passage of Regulation AB II and the Risk Retention provisions of the Dodd-Frank Act are keystone pieces in the regulatory framework affecting CMBS and should play a key role in any investment analysis.

20.3.1 Securities laws

Any offering of securities in the US or to US persons (including European issuances marketed to US investors) must be registered with the US Secu-rities and Exchange Commission (SEC) unless an exemption from regis-tration is available. The typical exemptions used for CMBS offerings are Regulation D and r.144A under the Securities Act of 1933, as amended (Securities Act). Regulation D applies to private placements of securities to "accredited investors", both on initial sale and on resale, but is not intended for broadly distributed offerings, although the US JOBS Act has relaxed the restrictions on general solicitations of such offerings in certain circum-stances. Rule 144A is a resale exemption that applies to offerings to "qua-lified institutional investors", which are institutional investors that own at least $100 million of securities issued by unaffiliated investors.[8]

Registered offerings of CMBS must comply with the registration and dis-closure requirements of the SEC's Regulation AB. This rule sets forth spe-cific requirements for disclosure of information about sponsors, originators, servicers, trustees of a securitisation transaction and also requires sig-nificant information about the pool assets, including detailed information about significant obligors as well as static pool information about the cur-rent pool and prior securitised pools. In addition, registered offerings must comply with the requirements of SEC Rule 193 to provide disclosure about the underwriting of the securitised assets. Regulation AB requires that service providers certify annually as to compliance with servicing stan-

---

[8]   Registered offerings are subject to liability under ss.11 and 12 of the Securities Act of and s.10(b) and 17 of the Securities Exchange Act of 1934 as amended. Section 11 imposes joint and several strict liability to the issuer, its officers and directors, the underwriters and any experts who have consented to be named as such in the prospectus for losses arising from any material misstatement or omissions in the prospectus, although the underwriters can defend against a claim under s.11 by showing that they had conducted "due diligence". Section 12 imposes strict liability against any person who offers or sells a security by means of a prospectus or oral communication which includes a material misstatement or omission. Section 10(b) and s.17(a) require, as a condition to liability, that the defendant knew or was reckless in not discovering that the disclosure contained a material misstatement or omis-sion. As a practical matter, registered offerings expose the sponsor to greater risk of liability than unregistered offerings because under current law only s.10(b) and s.17(a) provides a basis of securities law liability in those transactions.

dards. Regulation AB has been in place since 2004 and CMBS offerings in the US have been structured in reliance on it, with reporting, certification and indemnification provisions that have become quite standard over the years.

In mid-2011 the SEC proposed amendments to Regulation AB that significantly altered how transactions must be handled in the CMBS market. The final rule passed in 2014, with the SEC having adopted many of the proposed changes in Regulation AB in its most current iteration Regulation AB II. Regulation AB effected significant revisions to Regulation AB with respect to the shelf registration eligibility requirements, disclosure requirements and credit risk retention requirements for CMBS offerings. Regulation AB II asset-level disclosures will apply to both CMBS and re-securitisations of CMBS. Regulation AB changed the original standards by enacting new asset-level data disclosure and reporting requirements; new shelf registration eligibility requirements to reduce the undue reliance on credit ratings (CMBS are no longer required to be rated as "investment grade" to be eligible for shelf registration); mechanisms to enforce representation and warranty statements made about underlying assets; filing restrictions requiring that a complete preliminary prospectus be filed at least three days before the first sale in the offering; and the creation of new standardised forms for the registration of CMBS as well as a provision for paying registration fees on a "pay-as-you-go" basis.

Regulation AB does not change the basic substantive definition of an asset backed security, but it does invalidate certain exceptions that impinge on the instruments flexibility. For example, securities backed by assets that arise in non-revolving accounts are no longer considered to be asset-backed securities because they are excluded from the master trust exception to the discrete pool requirement; the revolving period for securities backed by non-revolving assets is now one year instead of three years; for securities backed by a pool with a prefunding period, the prefunding account cannot exceed 25% of the offering proceeds (or the principal balance of the total asset pool in the case of master trusts).

Regulation AB II does not enact public disclosure requirements on private securitisations under Rule 144A, which originally was a key component of the proposed rules in 2011. European or smaller players that find the additional regulatory requirements too onerous for practical, financial or language-related reasons may resort to conducting only 144A transactions instead of coping with the additional burden. The proposed amendments to Regulation AB would have changed this by requiring that the investors in unregistered offerings of CMBS be contractually entitled to require the full suite of Regulation AB disclosure that they would have been entitled to receive in a registered offering. This would have eroded the distinction between registered and unregistered offerings and would have bifurcated the CMBS market into fully SEC-registered deals and truly private deals. Sponsors of CMBS transactions sold into the US would thus be forced to navigate between the Scylla of heightened liability and the Charybdis of reduced liquidity.

Compliance with Regulation AB II requires filing the new Form SF-3 for shelf registrations of all CMBS offerings. Form SF-3 revises the eligibility criteria for shelf offering in four critical ways. First, the CEO of the depositor must certify for each offering, in writing, that (s)he has reviewed the transaction prospectus, acknowledges the content and accuracy of the loan documents, and claims that (s)he believes that the issuance is structured to produce the requisite cash flows. CEO certification about the disclosure contained in the prospectus and the structure of the securitisation must take place at the time of each offering. Secondly, there must be an independent review of the asset pool documents. This "asset reviewer" is tasked with reviewing the representations and warranties of the disclosure and to investigate potential "trigger events" outlined in the loan documents. The review must be carrier out by a CMBS Regulation AB II "certified person". Thirdly, SF-3 requires a dispute resolution clause guaranteeing mediation for repurchase demands that have not been resolved after 180 days.[9] Finally, the party responsible for filing Form 10-D must disclose requests from an investor to communicate with other investors.

One cannot authoritatively discuss the impact of regulatory reforms to the securitisation market without discussing the effect of the Dodd-Frank risk retention rules. Risk retention is now the cornerstone of the US regulatory reform efforts in the securitisation area. Mandated under Section 941 of the Dodd-Frank Act (which also added s.15G to the Securities and Exchange Act of 1934, 15 USC sec. 78o-11), Dodd-Frank was designed to align the interests of securitisers with those of investors in the ABS market. Section 941 mandates that securitisers retain at least 5% of the credit risk of any securitised asset pool for at least five years, or designate a B-piece buyer (third-party risk retention). However Dodd-Frank leaves room for the SEC to determine the scope of any exemptions from these rules for securitisation involving high-quality assets and the form and composition of such risk retention.[10]

US regulators recognise that employing third-party purchasers specifically negotiating for the purchase of a first-loss position is a common feature of

---

9   Buyback demands tend not to occur very often in the CMBS market, therefore the effectiveness of this provision is unknown and untested.
10   Compare the Dodd-Frank Risk Regulation Rules to recent EU proposals to alter risk alignment rules for the ABS market. Current rules in Europe mirror the US' 5% retention requirement. However, EU lawmaker Paul Tang proposes "simple, transparent and standardized rules" that not only increase risk retention rates to upwards of 20% but also establishes a public registry detailing investor positions and loan information. A copy of the draft report can be found at *http://www.europarl.europa.eu/* [Accessed 11 August 2016]. Other proposals involve authorising the European Banking Authority to vary retention rates by type of security or investor risk portfolio.

CMBS transactions typically absent from other asset classes. Section 15G(c)(1)(E)(ii) of the Exchange Act expressly permits the SEC to create rules permitting third-party retention for CMBS transactions. Two, but no more than two, third-party purchasers are permitted to satisfy the risk retention requirement through the purchase of an "eligible residential interest". Third-party purchasers often are, or are affiliated with, special servicers in CMBS transactions. Due to this strong connection and the special servicing rights in CMBS transactions, Dodd-Frank requires the appointment of an Operating Advisor (OA) in all CMBS transactions that rely on the third-party risk retention option. This rule is intended to limit the ability of third-party purchasers to manipulate cash flows through special servicing. Whether the B-piece is initially sold to a third-party purchaser or sold to a third-party purchaser after the initial five year holding period expires, the transaction must have an OA in place at all times that a third-party purchaser holds any portion of the required risk retention.

Credit risk may only be passed onto another qualified B-piece buyer or servicer. The risk retention rules provide an exception to restrictions on transfers of the retained credit risk in CMBS transactions, permitting the transfer of the retained interest by any initial third-party purchaser to another third-party purchaser at any time after five years after the date of the closing of the transaction, provided that the transferee satisfied each of the conditions applicable to the initial third-party purchaser under the CMBS option, in connection with such a purchase. The secondary third-party purchaser can then subsequently transfer the interest to another qualifying third-party purchaser.

While there has been considerable experience with the operation of Regulation AB in US CMBS transactions, many look with trepidation on the potential impact of the proposed amendments to Regulation AB on the wider CRE finance market. In particular, there is a concern that the enhanced disclosure requirements may pose compliance difficulties, particularly where the underlying assets may themselves consist of structured finance securities with respect to which the issuer cannot provide adequate disclosure with respect to underlying assets.

20.3.2 *Investment Company Act*

Securitisation entities are "investment companies" as defined in the Investment Company Act of 1940, as amended (Investment Company Act), and therefore are required to register as such unless an exclusion from the definition applies. As a practical matter it is imperative for CRE structured finance transactions to operate under an exclusion from registration, because the substantive requirements of the Investment Company Act that apply to registered investment companies are antithetical the requirements of securitisations. These requirements include stringent limitations on leverage that would severely curtail the ability to use financing in a manner that is customary for CRE investments, as well as restrictions on transactions with affiliates and certain other business activities that could hinder the relationships among many parties to the CRE transaction. The consequences of failure to register an investment company for which an exclusion does not apply include administrative sanctions and automatic unenforceability under US law of all contracts that the investment company has entered into.

The most common exclusion for CMBS transactions and other CRE transactions is s.3(c)(5)(C) of the Investment Company Act. That section excludes from the definition of investment company "[a]ny person who is not engaged in the business of issuing redeemable securities, face-amount certificates of the installment type or periodic payment plan certificates, and who is primarily engaged ... [in the business of] purchasing or otherwise acquiring mortgages and other liens on and interests in real estate." Many different types of companies in a variety of businesses rely on this exclusion. Such companies include: those that originate and hold CRE interests (such as mortgage participations, mezzanine loans and mortgage-backed securities) and companies that invest in CRE, mortgages and mortgage-related instruments. The SEC staff, in providing guidance on this exclusion, generally has indicated in several No-Action Letters that a company will be considered to be "primarily engaged" in the business of purchasing or otherwise acquiring mortgages and other liens on and interests in CRE if at least 55% of the issuer's assets will consist of mortgages and other liens on and interests in CRE (called "qualifying interests") and the remaining 45% of the issuer's assets will consist primarily of CRE-type interests, such as Tier 1 CRE mezzanine loan.

The SEC is, at the time of writing, engaged in a review of interpretive issues relating to the status of mortgage-related pools under the Investment Company Act in light of the evolution of mortgage-related pools and the development of new and complex mortgage-related instruments. The review was occasioned by concerns that s.3(c)(5)(C) exclusion has been expanded beyond its originally intended scope by CRE-related investors that have sought to rely on it for exclusions of investments in CRE securities, or other interests that are far afield from classic mortgages and CRE equity interests. This review is unlikely to change the applicability of s.3(c)(5)(C) to traditional CMBS transactions (unless by changing the interpretation of what it means to be "primarily engaged"), but it may result in a narrow interpretation of its applicability to non-traditional securitisations or to other CRE-related transactions. If s.3(c)(5)(C) were not available, a CMBS transaction with US investors would have to be structured to rely on Investment Company Act r.3a–7 or s.3(c)(7). Rule 3a–7 is an exemption from the registration requirements for securitisations of eligible assets that meet certain requirements relating to ratings, security interests and the like and do not provide for active management of assets for the purpose of realising gains or avoiding losses, while s.3(c)(7) is available for companies that are not contemplating a public offering and whose securities (or in the case of a foreign issuer, whose securities held by US residents) are held only by "qualified purchasers" that have not been formed for the purpose of the transaction in which they are investing and that generally have $5 million or more in investable assets.

20.3.3 ERISA

Most privately sponsored US pension arrangements are subject to the fiduciary responsibility requirements of the Employee Retirement Income Security Act of 1974, as amended (ERISA). These requirements apply to investment advisers and similar persons who manage assets of certain US pension plans, regardless of where that manager is located. The requirements include a fiduciary standard of conduct as well as strict "prohibited transaction" restrictions, which bar ERISA investors from dealing with certain specified parties ("parties in interest") in the absence of a statutory or administrative exemption.[11] ERISA fiduciaries are prohibited from engaging in certain types of transactions involving self-dealing and conflicts of interest with parties in interest. As an example of the breadth of the prohibited transactions prohibitions, an ERISA fiduciary would be prohibited from investing in securities of the plan sponsor in the absence of an exemption. Actions to recover damages for breach of fiduciary duty may be brought in US courts on behalf of an ERISA investor by another fiduciary for that investor or directly by the US Department of Labor.

The managers of certain private funds in which ERISA plans invest may be considered to be fiduciaries of the ERISA plan, and subject to the standard of care and other restrictions described above. As a result, the servicers of asset pools supporting some CMBS instruments could be considered ERISA fiduciaries. For this reason most CMBS issues that are marketed to ERISA plans comply with the requirements of an ERISA exemption, regardless of whether the sponsor or the assets are outside the US. Also, because of the complexity and severity of the ERISA fiduciary requirements, it is often desirable to structure CRE investment funds to avoid their application. In the case of equity real estate funds, this can be accomplished by structuring the fund as a "real estate operating company" (or REOC).[12] Under the US Department of Labor's new conflict of interest regulation issued in 2016, seeing or promoting investment services to ERISA investors could constitute fiduciary advice. If this were to occur, an exclusion or exemption will be needed to avoid ERISA "Prohibited Transactions". This regulation is

---

[11] ERISA's fiduciary standard is one of the highest standards of care available under US law. A retirement plan fiduciary must act with prudence and undivided loyalty to the participants in that plan.

[12] A REOC is a company that invests in real estate and issues shares that are traded a public exchange. A REOC is in many respects similar to a real estate investment trust, but there are some differences between the two. For example a REOC must reinvest its profits whereas a real estate investment trust is required to distribute profits to its shareholders. REOCs have a greater degree of flexibility than real estate investment trusts with respect to the types of real estate investments in which they can invest.

likely to have an effect on a much broader scope of professionals who make investment-related recommendations. Investment professionals now need to take into consideration whether their dealings may make them a fiduciary, for the purposes of the regulation.

20.3.4 Tax

Tax efficiency is a key consideration for real estate investors, particularly in international transactions. US investors acquiring interests in European CRE would need to consider the effects on a proposed transaction of applicable tax regimes in Europe and the US.

20.3.4.1 EU tax considerations

US investors in European CRE must be familiar with the applicable tax laws in relevant European jurisdictions affecting investments in real estate transactions, including such matters as whether the underlying asset is eligible for depreciation, and if so the depreciation rate that applies, the treatment of depreciation, whether rental income will be taxed as investment income through withholding or on a net income basis and taxation of capital gains. Relevant considerations for this analysis include whether and under what circumstances rental income from CRE located in the relevant EU Member State and any gain from its sale would be considered source income that is subject to tax in that jurisdiction, whether the US investor's personal tax status has a bearing on the conclusion, and whether that member state has an income treaty with the US (or other countries through which investments may be routed) and whether the tax treaty has a bearing on the US investor's tax treatment. Such considerations may only be resolved by analysing applicable local tax law in the relevant EU jurisdictions together with tax specialists so as to structure an optimum tax structure for the investor. These questions may also be affected by the US tax considerations discussed below.

20.3.4.2 US tax considerations

US investors in foreign real estate must also be concerned about US taxation because US income tax is assessed on net income earned throughout the world, subject to credits for taxes paid in other jurisdictions. The timing of US taxation is subject to complex rules.

20.3.4.2.1 Shareholders in controlled foreign corporations and passive foreign investment companies

Even if a US investor structures its holdings of interests in European CRE or its servicing functions through a local corporation or other entity treated as a corporation for US tax purposes, each US shareholder would need to be concerned about current taxation of its pro rata portion of the entity's "subpart F income" related to the entity's ownership or servicing of CRE interests under the rules governing controlled foreign corporations (CFCs) if the entity is majority owned or controlled by US persons, each of which owns at least 10% of the entity's voting stock.[13] The CFC rules represent an exception from the general rule that US shareholders of a foreign corporation can defer US income tax on the corporation's non-US earnings until the corporation repatriates its earnings to the US shareholders through distribution of a dividend. The taxation of the US shareholders' pro rata share of the income of a CFC is subject to mitigating rules designed to avoid double taxation.

However, if 75% or more of the foreign corporation's gross income is passive income or 50% or more of its assets by value generate or could generate passive income or no income at all, the foreign corporation will be subject to the rules governing "passive foreign investment companies" (PFICs). The PFIC rules encourage US shareholders to pay tax on current income (regardless of whether or not it is Subpart F income and treating capital gains as ordinary income for this purpose) by imposing an interest charge on all distributions in excess of 125% of the average distributions for the prior three years and on gain from the sale of PFIC shares, pro rated for each day of the US shareholder's holding period.

A US shareholder may elect out of the punitive PFIC regime by making an election to treat the PFIC as a qualifying electing fund (QEF). By making a QEF election a US shareholder in a PFIC must include in current taxable income its share of the ordinary income and net capital gains of the PFIC, similarly to shareholders of a registered investment company (i.e. a mutual fund), but regardless of whether the PFIC makes an actual distribution. Such election is effective for the year in which it is made and all subsequent years. To the extent such election applies, the PFIC regime is avoided. However, US shareholders making a QEF election may be subject to tax on phantom income to the extent that the PFIC realises taxable income or gain that is not distributed to the electing shareholder. The QEF election can only be made if the PFIC provides information on its earnings to its shareholders each year. A mark-to-market election may also be made to avoid the PFIC regime described above—again at the cost of current inclusion even in the absence of distributions—if shares in the PFIC are regularly traded.

---

[13] Subpart F income generally consists of income that is in principle relatively mobile in the sense of being easily moved between taxing jurisdictions in order to benefit from differences in tax rates between jurisdiction. Subpart F income consists of various types of income, including such things as insurance income and foreign-based company income. This latter is a particularly important income category applicable to most foreign corporations. It includes income from passive investments such as dividends, interest, royalties, capital gains and certain types of rents on real property). It also includes income derived in connection with the performance of technical, managerial, engineering, architectural, scientific, skilled, industrial, commercial or "like services" for or on behalf of any related person outside the country under the laws of which the CFC is created or organised. It also includes services performed by a CFC in a case where substantial assistance contributing to the performance of such services has been furnished by a related person.

20.3.4.2.2   Real estate mortgage investment conduits

US investors financing CRE investments can obtain significant tax efficiencies under the provisions of US tax law relating to entities that properly
elect to be taxed as real estate mortgage investment conduits (REMICs). A
REMIC is a SPV that pools qualifying mortgage loans and certain other
qualifying assets and issues securities that normally represent beneficial
ownership of the pooled assets. By electing to be treated as a REMIC, a
mortgage pool ensures that its "regular interests" will be treated as
indebtedness for US tax purposes and avoids taxation as a taxable mortgage
pool (TMP), which is treated as a corporation for US tax purposes.

In order to qualify for inclusion in a REMIC, a CRE interest would have to
satisfy certain criteria, including that it consist of a mortgage or other lien
on real property, that the holder of the loan have enforcement and foreclosure rights, and that the loan-to-value ratio at the startup of the REMIC
be no greater than 80%. The REMIC rules do not distinguish between US
and non-US mortgage loans in terms of eligibility for inclusion in a REMIC.
However, REMICs have very limited ability to own assets other than
qualifying mortgages and assets closely related to them such as mortgage
insurance and servicing rights, which may make it difficult for REMICs to
use hedging instruments such as swaps.

A REMIC election confers significant advantages, including freedom from
corporate taxation at the entity level and treatment of all regular interests in
the REMIC (including B-pieces) as debt rather than equity for federal
income tax purpose regardless of whether they would qualify as debt under
a traditional debt/equity analysis.

However, a REMIC also brings some disadvantages. One of these is that
notwithstanding the REMIC's treatment as a flow-through entity that does
not pay entity-level taxes, the investors in a REMIC must pay taxes on
earnings on their securities issued by the REMIC, and that tax may be
assessed at both the state and federal level. Thus investors have little ability
to reduce taxes on capital gains. Another disadvantage of a REMIC is that it
is required to issue residual interests to entities that are fully taxable in the
US as corporations. The REMIC residual interest holders are responsible for
paying tax on the income that the REMIC would have paid but for the
entity-level exclusion. These residual interests are distinct from B-pieces
that represent the economic residual interest but that are treated as regular
interests of a REMIC. Because the residual interests in a REMIC are non-
economic interests and not entitled to a share of income or gains, they
involve the payment of significant amounts of tax on phantom income. In
order to sell REMIC residual interests the issuer must pay prospective
investors an amount to cover the expected tax liability, with the pricing
being based on a prospective residual holder's present valuation of the tax
liability over the expected life of the transaction.

Another noteworthy disadvantage of a REMIC is that it is a static pool. Additionally, a REMIC is not permitted to acquire additional assets after the first 90 days from its "start-up date." After that date the mortgage pool is set and the servicer has very little ability to trade or dispose of mortgages. The static pool nature of a REMIC reduces the ability to use pre-funded REMICs to acquire CRE assets opportunistically without a warehouse arrangement. It also makes it difficult to modify or restructure loans, as the REMIC rules generally consider a loan modification to result in a new loan unless the modification is made after default or when default is imminent. A modification that is deemed to be a new loan added to the pool, after the 90-day start up period, will cause the pool to lose its favoured status as a REMIC and to be treated as a TMP. Consequently REMIC structures pose challenges for investors that seek to enhance value from CRE loans by aggressive renegotiation. However, these challenges are not insuperable and can often be managed with knowledgeable advice about US taxation of real estate investments.

20.3.4.2.3 Foreign Account Tax Compliance Act

From 1 January 2013 US investors in European CRE have to be concerned about compliance with the Foreign Account Tax Compliance Act (FATCA), a US law that is designed to clamp down on under-reporting of foreign income by US persons. The implementation will be phased in, and the US Treasury Department has proposed rules and guidance that have raised as many questions as they have suggested solutions.[14]

Under FATCA foreign financial institutions (FFIs) must agree to provide information to the US Internal Revenue Service (IRS) or to their withholding agents for transmission to the IRS about US account holders or substantial US owners. Some countries, where it would be a violation of data protection law to provide such information to the IRS directly, are attempting to negotiate intergovernmental agreements with the US Treasury, pursuant to which FFIs in those countries would provide such information to their own governments, which would provide information in appropriate format to the IRS.

An FFI is broadly defined to include any foreign bank, custodian, broker-dealer, or pooled investment vehicle. The term can also include certain insurance companies. Although direct holdings in real estate would not cause a foreign investment entity to be treated as an FFI, any real estate-related holding that is structured as a security or derivative would cause such an entity to be an FFI.

---

[14] The discussion below of the Foreign Account Tax Compliance Act is general and preliminary because the detailed rules implementing this legislation are only in proposed form and are subject to change.

In the absence of an agreement with the IRS, an FFI would be subject to withholding at a rate of 30% on certain US-source payments that it receives. These include US-source payments of passive income, such as dividends, interest and rents, received on or after 1 January 2014, and gross proceeds from the sale or other disposition of US stocks or bonds received on or after 1 January 2015. Under rules that have not yet been issued and that will not apply any earlier than 1 January 2019, a compliant FFI would itself need to withhold on certain distributions—referred to as "passthru payments"—that it makes to any payee or beneficial owner who does not provide the FFI with a certification that the foreign entity does not have a substantial US owner, or does not provide the name, address and taxpayer identification number (TIN) of each substantial US owner. Although the FATCA regulations have been finalised, the US authorities have postponed publishing an official definition of a passthru payment, making it difficult to discern how foreign passthru payment withholding will actually apply. The IRS has considered a "US assets based approach" to withholding, whereby the Service would designate a non-withholdable portion of the passthru payment as a source of taxable income. But it is unclear whether this will be the final rendition of the passthru rule.

FATCA's regulations create two broad categories of certain regulated FFIs consisting of certain qualified investment vehicles and restricted funds that would be "deemed-compliant" with FATCA and therefore would have a more streamlined means of complying with FATCA in order to avoid the 30% withholding tax. "Compliant" FFIs are not subject to the same requirements as other FFIs. However, note that the scope of such entities is limited and they are still subject to due diligence requirements and registration with the IRS, either directly or through a withholding agent. US investors participating in an investment in European CRE interests now have the additional burden of determining whether the investment vehicle would be deemed compliant under FATCA.

FATCA regulations state that a qualified collective investment vehicle (QIV) may qualify as a deemed-compliant entity if it is an FFI solely because it is an investment vehicle (and not a bank, custodian, or broker-dealer). Under the proposed rules the QIV would have to be regulated in its country of incorporation or organisation as an investment fund and each record holder of debt interests in excess of $50,000 or equity interests in any amount would have to be a participating FFI, a registered deemed-compliant FFI, an exempt beneficial owner, or certain categories of US person (such as a publicly traded company, a regulated investment company, a real estate investment trust). All FFIs in the expanded affiliated group must be participating FFIs or registered deemed-compliant FFIs.

When attempting to allocate risk, US-based CMBS investors should also be wary of the different ways that loan agreements may trigger FATCA's withholding requirements. For example, if the borrower and its guarantor are both a US entity, so that interest payments are US-sourced, the borrower may be subject to FATCA withholding if interest is paid to a noncompliant lender. Similarly, if the borrower is an FFI that earns some US-source income, and rules are issued during the term of the loan requiring withholding on foreign passthru payments, this may also trigger the withholding requirement. However, an existing agreement with an appropriate gross-up provision may not apply to FATCA withholding on passthru payments if this withholding is imposed pursuant to an agreement with the IRS.

20.4 Emerging trends in fintech and P2P lending

Fintech ("financial technology") represents a new trend in the banking industry. Marketplace lending describes how fintech companies use innovative technology and advanced online marketing strategies to match borrowers with lenders without an intermediary. Fintech starts are using technology and new business models to upend a market that was believed to be linked solely to traditional banking institutions. The fintech and marketplace lending space comprises, at the time of writing, of clusters of tech-focused financial companies created during the GFC.[15] Since the beginning of 2015, investors have poured over $20 billion dollars into the fintech sector, providing smaller market players with more access to niche markets as well as alternative financing methods in challenging market conditions.[16] Fintech companies are increasingly playing a key role in the CMBS market at home and in Europe as traditional lending models stagnate.

20.4.1 Peer-to-peer lending

2015 saw the completion of the first US securitisation of peer-to-peer (P2P) consumer loans to obtain an investment grade rating. Such activity in the CMBS market is likely a sign of future growth in the P2P space. Peer-to-peer lending is the practice of lending money to individuals or businesses through online services that match lenders directly with borrowers. P2P began after the GFC in 2008, when banks started tightening their consumer lending policies due to the passage of Dodd-Frank. This led to the emergence of P2P online lending sites such as Prosper and Lending Club. P2P originators tend to target high-yield borrowers, with typical loan amounts ranging from $20,000–$30,000. The European markets could be a huge

---

[15] Oscar Williams-Grut and Ben Moshinsky, Mark Carney's biggest speech of the year is going to be about fintech and the technology behind bitcoin, Business Insider, May 24, 2016, Fintech has been described as the "Uber moment" for banks in Oscar Williams-Grut, *Ex-Barclay's exec: Fintech is a 'fundamental shift' to make finance appeal to millennials*, Business Insider, (26 May 2015), *http://www.businessinsider.com/barclays-rich-ricci-says-fintech-is-fundamental-shift-2016-5?r=UK&IR=T* [Accessed 11 August 2016].

[16] Jennifer Van Grove, *PeerStreet brings real estate investing to Main Street*, The San Diego Union-Tribune (26 October 2015), *http://www.sandiegouniontribune.com/news/2015/oct/26/peerstreet-launches-marketplace-for-real-estate/* [Accessed 11 August 2016].

opportunity for P2P lenders, but most sites are focused on the domestic market in the US (with the exception of Funding Circle).

The European P2P lending market is still nascent compared to the US, but has grown significantly overall. According to the UK P2P Finance Association, its members lent £411 million in 2015 up to 30 October, compared with £279 million in 2014. 2016 may evolve into a strong year for the sector. Funding Circle is the first European P2P lender to have loans from its platform securitised, setting a precedent that could attract additional funding to the fast-growing industry. The deal is a securitisation of at least two billion loans to SMEs since 2010 backed by £130 million of loans. Funding Circle's deal highlights the growing role of hedge funds and banks in a P2P market which has the reputation of being populated by retail investors, not sophisticated ones.

It is unclear how Brexit will affect players in the cross-border P2P lending market. Individual investors and small and medium-sized enterprises (SMEs), which are more likely to participate in the market lending or P2P markets, will likely invest less due to a lack of confidence to hedge risk. Brexit could also have an effect on fintech firms and P2P lending companies that rely on EU "passporting", as losing the ability to cross-sell across members states without having a physical presence within those member-states may render technology-based cross-border lending models difficult to use.

20.4.2 *Crowdfunding*

Crowdfunding has become quite popular in real estate circles, providing a new way to raise capital for a miniscule investment. In the pre-crowd-funding era, investing in private real estate required leveraging personal or professional networks or considerable institutional financing. With better access to pre-vetted deals, crowdfunding platforms also make it possible to begin investing with as little as $1,000. Up until recently, only accredited investors who had a net worth of $1 million or more or earned $200,000 a year were able to invest through crowdfunding platforms. In October 2015, the SEC finalised proposed rules for Title III of the JOBS Act, allowing non-accredited investors entry into the real estate crowdfunding arena on a widespread scale.

One of the benefits of crowdfunding platforms is increased transparency; they operate with a goal of offering investors as much detail about an investment as possible. Additionally, crowdfunding has increased the accessibility of the market, because it provides a platform to market deals to a wider segment of the public. The downside of crowdfunding platforms is risk and the potential for loss. By limiting large-scale real estate investments to accredited investors, the SEC was effectively trying to protect smaller investors. Specifically, there's an increased possibility for non-accredited investors to get hurt because they may have less disposable income to put at risk or may lack the necessary knowledge to make informed investment decisions.

Crowdfunding loans are increasingly appearing in CMBS but remains a largely "untested ownership structure".[17] For example, data analytics company CrediFi is creating a CMBS platform called "CMBS Suite" to enable its customers to more easily parse through opaque loan structures. The CMBS Suite aims to connect lenders with CMBS and non-securitised loan opportunities. Also in 2015, there were three loans (worth $71 million total) made to Colony Hills Capital secured against a portfolio of five properties. These properties received $12 million dollars of crowdfunding through a small site. The consequence of bundling crowdfunded potentially high-risk ABS into CMBS is unknown, however, and will likely depend on the specific lending platform. Incorporating crowdfunding models into CMBS instruments will also depend on the definition of "crowdfunding" being used. For the Colony Hills Capital securitisation, Colony Hills Capital did a series of Regulation D offerings. Only accredited investors can do such offerings, which does not lend itself to attracting the prototype crowdfunding participant.[18]

Examples of Real Estate Fintech companies:

- PeerStreet—a marketplace lending platform for real estate debt.[19]
- LendInvest—an online platform for financing short-term mortgages.[20]
- Patch of Land—originates, underwrites, and services loans in the real estate space.[21]
- LendingHome—issues one-year, first-lien mortgages on one-to-four family homes and passes them on to institutional investors.[22]
- FundingCircle—a peer-to-peer lending platform active across Europe, the UK, and the US.[23]
- SoFi—an online student lender.
- Fundrise—an online crowdfunding platform that offers individual investors a chance to buy shares in commercial real estate projects.[24]

---

[17] *https://www.bisnow.com/national/news/other/morgan-stanley-real-estate-is-the-final-crowdfunding-frontier-50579* [Accessed 11 August 2016].
[18] *http://www.businessalabama.com/Business-Alabama/November-2015/Crowdfunded-Development-or-Investment-Bank-Snipe/* [Accessed 11 August 2016].
[19] *http://www.digitaljournal.com/pr/2918067* [Accessed 11 August 2016].
[20] *http://www.businessinsider.com/macquarie-deal-with-lendinvest-2016-4?r=UK&IR=T* [Accessed 11 August 2016].
[21] *https://www.equities.com/news/patch-of-land-s-new-ceo-on-the-opportunities-in-real-estate-crowdfunding* [Accessed 11 August 2016].
[22] *http://therealdeal.com/2016/04/13/lendinghome-launches-crowdfunding-platform/* [Accessed 11 August 2016].
[23] *http://www.cityam.com/240051/peer-to-peer-securitisation-has-arrived-with-landmark-crowdfunding-deal* [Accessed 11 August 2016].
[24] *http://www.cnbc.com* [Accessed 11 August 2016].

20.5   Conclusion

In recent years global economic forces affecting world financial markets have been consistently drawing capital inexorably towards European CRE. The commercial issues and strategic dynamics posed by the movement of money are similar in many respects to those in any relation of buyers and sellers, although the particular strategic positions of particular players may be influenced by geography. However, a unique confluence of legal issues affects structures for European CRE that are offered for sale to US investors. Cross-border investments also raise unique needs for cross-cultural perception and the ability to translate common concepts of real estate finance into the vernacular, not only of different languages but of different legal systems, in order that US investors can usefully compare their rights in European CRE investments with corresponding rights in US CRE investments with which they are most familiar. The comparison does not stop there, because US investors also need to assess how both emerging and inchoate bodies of regulation in the US and Europe as well as the developing current political climate affect, or may affect, in the near future their position and affect the relative merits of an investment in any particular jurisdiction. The uncertain nature of developments in the law, in the economy, in the political landscape and in commercial practice makes cross-border CRE investments complex undertakings and requires great care in their implementation. However, European CRE investments can continue to represent extraordinary opportunities to achieve high yields for those investors who understand the intricacies and can accurately price risk and reward.

Chapter 21

Improving the effectiveness of CRE debt risk management and regulation

Peter Cosmetatos,

CEO CREFC Europe

21.1   Introduction

The aim of this Chapter is to outline the origins and relevance of, and the prospects for, two proposals for improving financial system resilience in the face of the CRE cycle. One of the proposals—for a comprehensive CRE loan database—seeks to improve the quality of information available to regulators and market participants. The other proposal seeks to introduce a structurally counter-cyclical element in CRE finance markets, by promoting the use of long-term value-based LTV ratios in risk assessment by lenders and regulators.

The proposals were put forward by an independent industry group which was formed in 2012, during an unusually reflective and introspective period for the CRE industry.[1] The group's focus was the UK market, but much of the analysis and many of the recommendations contained in its 2014 report, *A Vision for Real Estate Finance in the UK*,[2] are relevant to the broader European context as well.

21.2   Background to the Vision Project

A significant part of the trauma suffered by the European banking system (and many EU member state economies) in recent years was the result of poor residential or commercial real estate lending decisions before the crisis. Leaving to one side whether regulators correctly diagnosed why that happened and how to stop it happening again, an obvious policy conclusion might be that the concentration of (particularly higher risk) real estate lending in the banking system is a bad thing.

---

[1]   The author was a member of that group, the Real Estate Finance Group, and remains involved in industry efforts to move aspects of its vision towards implementation.

[2]   A *Vision for Real Estate Finance in the UK* was published with the support of the Investment Property Forum and is available on its website at *http://www.ipf.org.uk* [Accessed 11 August 2016].

Regulators seem to have received a slightly different, simpler, message to the effect that CRE debt is generally a bad thing and should be reduced wherever it is found. Increasing capital requirements for banks' safest CRE loans (such as by shifting IRB banks onto slotting, as occurred in the UK— see Chapter 16) might make sense if viewed in that way. Regulatory hostility to CRE debt securitisation in Europe is another, problematic, consequence of that approach.

- In its December 2015 report on CRE and financial stability,[3] the European Systemic Risk Board argued that "there is a growing need to address CRE-related risks in the non-banking sector, given that non-bank financing is becoming more important". It would undoubtedly be right to monitor CRE-related risks across the financial system, as contemplated, indeed, by *Vision* Recommendation 1; it is less obvious that such risks (which have yet to be adequately described, measured or assessed) already need to be addressed in the European context.

  i) No evidence has been presented that securitisation is linked to especially bad CRE lending, or that loans that were (or were intended to be) securitised, performed worse than loans of similar vintage that were (and were intended to be) retained by banks on their balance sheets. What evidence there is (including the travails of many European banks grappling with problematic pre-crisis loan books) suggests that the contrary is true.

  ii) CMBS is, however, the most visible part of the CRE debt market—and thus the messenger bearing bad tidings about the quality of CRE lending more generally at the peak of the last cycle. That was not a good reason for shooting it, particularly since the experience of the crisis offered both a reason and the knowledge to improve the product.[4]

  iii) Indeed, a declining CMBS market since the crisis has resulted in less transparency as a reduced amount of comparable loan-level information is now available, from a less representative sample, to provide insight into (generally much more opaque) broader CRE lending markets. This lack of information does not make the regulator's task easier.

  iv) Since the crisis, there has been a huge increase in the appetite of non-bank, non-originating capital for the risk and return offered by CRE debt. Regulation (most egregiously, the approach to Type 2 Securitisation under Solvency II, as discussed in Chapter 16, but also more recent initiatives) has ensured that different investment channels have generally been favoured over CMBS.

---

[3] The report is available here: *https://www.esrb.europa.eu/pub/pdf/other/2015-12-28_ESRB_ report_on_commercial_real_estate_and_financial_stability.pdf* [Accessed 11 August 2016].

[4] The industry sought to collate learning points from the crisis under the auspices of CREFC Europe. See *http://www.crefceurope.org/wp-content/uploads/2015/02/Market-Principles-for-Issuing-European-CMBS-2-Final.pdf* [Accessed 11 August 2016].

It is encouraging to see the diversification of the CRE debt landscape through a thriving CRE loan syndication market and a multitude of CRE debt funds, as well as new origination platforms set up by insurance companies. But none of those channels provides the comparable information or secondary liquidity available in the bond market, and they have not been road-tested through a boom and bust cycle as CMBS has been.[5] Investors may be genuinely content with the choices they are making; it is less clear whether regulators appreciate how their decisions are driving distribution and investment choices, or how little visibility they now have regarding the size and structure of CRE debt markets and who is exposed to them.

Having said that, CMBS had never become as large and important a part of the CRE debt market as it is on the other side of the Atlantic. Bigger drivers for market change were some of the other regulatory changes discussed in Chapters 16 and 17: changes to banking regulation (in particular through the effective imposition of minimum capital floors via slotting) and the changing regulatory environment for non-bank lenders, whose appetite for CRE debt has grown as fixed income returns from more traditional assets remain depressed.

21.3 The *Vision* project

It was clear in 2012 that multiple regulatory initiatives were affecting CRE markets, and especially CRE finance markets, which remained fragile. It was far less clear whether regulators were thinking strategically and holistically about how those markets would be affected by their interventions, especially on a cumulative basis. Even more fundamentally, in the absence of considered and clearly articulated sector-specific regulatory objectives, it was doubtful whether regulatory interventions were taking the market in the right direction.

It is against that backdrop that the Real Estate Finance Group was formed, on the periphery of the Bank of England's Commercial Property Forum, and with encouragement from the Bank of England. The group's members participated in an individual capacity so that they might bring their expertise and experience to bear without being constrained by the interests of their respective organisations. The group's goal was to take a step back from the current market uncertainty and regulatory frenzy, and consider what should be done to ensure that CRE finance markets could provide a sustainable flow of credit to the CRE market across the cycle without posing unacceptable risks to financial stability. In essence, how can we best max-

---

[5] Besides CMBS, a well-regulated mortgage REIT regime could also have a valuable role to play, offering similar transparency, comparability, diversification and liquidity benefits. Neither in the UK nor in other European jurisdictions have there been meaningful moves to promote such public CRE debt investment channels.

imise the benefits that CRE debt helps deliver to the economy, while minimising the risks it can present to the financial system and the taxpayer?

After an industry consultation in late 2013, the group published a report in May 2014 setting out seven high level recommendations. While the recommendations were conceived as a coherent package, two of them have consistently been singled out as most likely to have a potentially transformational impact (while also being fundamental pre-requisites for progress on other recommendations):

- Recommendation 1 proposed the creation of a mandatory, comprehensive database of UK CRE loans. The database should provide market information not only to the regulator but also (subject to the degree of aggregation required to protect the confidentiality of individual parties, assets and transactions) to the market. Only with relevant, robust and timely information, it was argued, can regulators understand the market they seek to regulate and assess the need for, and effects of, regulatory action. At the same time, improved transparency should support a more competitive and efficient market environment and attract more, better-informed capital to the sector.
- Recommendation 4 proposed that regulatory capital and risk management should use loan-to-value metrics based not on volatile market values, but rather on a long-term measure of collateral value that is insensitive to the CRE cycle. Risk managers and regulators need reliable risk metrics to do their job. The strongest single indicator of systemically significant risk in CRE lending is vintage—the point in the CRE cycle at which a loan is made.[6] It follows that effective risk metrics should reveal where in the cycle the market is at any given moment. Market value viewed in isolation (and LTV ratios based on it) cannot do that, but LTV ratios based on an appropriate long-term measure of collateral value would.

21.3.1 *Official endorsement in the UK and abroad*

The Bank of England consulted[7] on the loan database proposal almost as soon as the *Vision* report was published, and concluded[8] that it should be explored further. More recently, a number of speeches by Bank officials

---

[6] Owing to the generally private and opaque nature of the CRE debt market, there is relatively little reliable data to substantiate this statement, but it is intuitive, and supported by research in this area that the author has seen. A good example is analysis of the historical drivers of CRE loan performance conducted by Bank of America Merrill Lynch in 2015 and 2016 based on securitised UK and European CRE loans.

[7] See *http://www.bankofengland.co.uk/publications/Documents/news/2014/dp300514.pdf* [Accessed 11 August 2016]. The main focus of this consultation was on addressing credit information challenges in the SME lending market.

[8] See *http://www.bankofengland.co.uk/financialstability/Documents/securitisation/responses281114.pdf* [Accessed 11 August 2016].

have reiterated the Bank's desire to work with the industry to take forward both Recommendation 1 and Recommendation 4.[9]

The *Vision* report and these particular recommendations have also attracted broader interest, including from the European Systemic Risk Board,[10] the financial regulation initiative[11] of the Centre for Economic Policy Research, and at the World Economic Forum.[12] With heightened awareness generally of the risks CRE debt can pose (albeit rather lower awareness of the economic value it supports), there is every reason to expect that others may follow successful UK implementation of *Vision* recommendations (Brexit notwithstanding).

21.3.2 Progress and prospects

Following publication of *A Vision for Real Estate Finance in the UK*, custody of the *Vision* project has moved from the Real Estate Finance Group to the Debt Group of the Property Industry Alliance (PIA). The PIA is a forum for a number of industry and professional bodies concerned with UK CRE to work together where it makes sense for them to do so. Among its initiatives and committees is the Debt Group, which was originally established during the crisis years to collect and share CRE industry views and data about the implications of the financial crisis for property. The PIA Debt Group has been re-launched with the primary mission of providing a forum for discussion about, and taking forward implementation of, *Vision* recommendations.

Both the database and long-term value proposals are ambitious and far-reaching, and would likely entail meaningful changes in how individual market participants and the market as a whole operate. Both proposals are complex, and could be approached in different ways—and neither the *Vision* report nor the regulator has sought to mandate any specific path towards implementation. The following paragraphs summarise the progress made as at the time of writing, and set out the author's views about next steps.

---

[9] See *http://www.bankofengland.co.uk/publications/Documents/speeches/2013/speech701.pdf* [Accessed 11 August 2016] for an endorsement by Andy Haldane and *http://www.bankofengland.co.uk/publications/Documents/speeches/2015/speech850.pdf* [Accessed 11 August 2016] for an endorsement by Alex Brazier (each, at the time of the speech, was executive director for financial stability strategy and risk at the Bank).

[10] See *https://www.esrb.europa.eu/pub/pdf/other/2015-12-28_ESRB_report_on_commercial_real_estate_and_financial_stability.pdf* [Accessed 11 August 2016].

[11] See *http://cepr.org/5640* [Accessed 11 August 2016].

[12] See for example *http://www3.weforum.org/docs/WEF_Emerging_Horizons_Real_Estate_Profile_Prescriptions_Proposals_report15.pdf* [Accessed 11 August 2016].

21.3.2.1   Loan database

A working group has been formed under the auspices of the PIA Debt Group to focus on how to take forward this recommendation so as to ensure (in the words of the Bank of England's own consultation response) "that the benefits of developing a CRE loan-level database outweigh the costs". No clear consensus has emerged so far as to precisely what should be done, with the perspectives of different types of market participant diverging sharply at times, often reflecting market and regulatory status. Arguably, it was inevitable (and appropriate) that a reasonable period of discussion would be required as a broader range of industry participants have become involved in a proposal with such significant implications. It is likely that progress towards implementation of the *Vision* recommendation will be achieved in phases, with pragmatism (as well as the ability to test and improve) initially prioritised over ambition.

The *Vision* report proposed a comprehensive database that would provide a view of the entire UK CRE market, and it argued that some form of compulsion would be required to ensure data provision by overseas and unregulated lenders as well as by regulated UK firms. At this stage, however, no legal requirement is being considered; so it is perhaps unsurprising that it has so far proven difficult to build a consensus around the best way forward.

In the author's view, the working group needs to make progress on the following points.

- What questions is it essential, important or desirable that the database should be able to answer? Industry and regulatory stakeholders probably need to make a list. It will then be possible to assess the range of possible information collection requirements, and how the balance should be struck between the burden imposed on those contributing data to the database, and the potential utility of the database (to regulators, data contributors and others).
- What is the appropriate scope for the database—eventually, and initially, assuming phased implementation—in terms of the lenders, loans, borrowers and assets covered? Should particular phases of implementation be subject to any divergences from the comprehensive scope contemplated by the *Vision* report? To the extent that the comprehensive approach is confirmed, how can compliance be delivered?
- What is the appropriate governance structure for the management and oversight of the database and the database operator? What roles should industry and regulatory representatives have? How should access to the database be regulated in the interests of optimising market transparency while protecting the confidentiality of individual transactions and transaction parties? Who should bear the cost of the database, its management and oversight?

- Finally, how should differences in the way different market partici- pants currently define and monitor particular data points be addres- sed so as to optimise data consistency at tolerable cost to data contributing market participants? This most directly affects lenders, but could also affect borrowers and, potentially, tenants, in particular cases.

Throughout, it will also be necessary to consider the technical and tech- nological choices, challenges and opportunities available, as the financial sector gradually moves towards a more digital future. It remains to be seen whether the industry is able to resolve these questions in the absence of regulatory compulsion. In the author's view, the vision remains highly compelling, with enormous potential benefits in financial regulatory and economic policy terms, and for the CRE and CRE debt market, principally in three areas:

- Being able to see where CRE debt is going in the economy: by geo- graphy, borrower type, asset type, ticket size, sub-sector, and so on. It would be possible to gain a far more accurate and granular picture of whether particular market segments were over- or under-served in terms of credit supply.
- Being able to see how CRE market risk is distributed around the financial system: for example, domestic, EU or international; bank balance sheets, institutional or household money; bilateral or shared, retained, intermediated or distributed (syndicated, securitised or in fund structures).
- Being able to assess (including by reference to the segmentation out- lined in the previous two bullets) where we are in the cycle: by lending volumes, LTV (including by reference to long-term values) ratios, interest cover ratios, margins and other financial criteria.

Raising the base level of objective market information would obviously change the competitive environment—and undoubtedly a balance needs to be struck between cost-consciousness, simplicity and pragmatism, on the one hand, and idealistic data-hunger on the other. While different busi- nesses would be affected by that change in different ways, it is difficult to see how the change could be anything other than positive for the market as a whole. In particular, if distribution of CRE debt and non-bank and non- originating investment capital are to have a greater role in the future (as the evolving bank regulatory environment might suggest), upgrading the cur- rent informational environment is surely essential.

21.3.2.2 *Long-term value metrics*

The long-term value recommendation specifically seeks to address the difficulties faced both by lenders and their regulators in identifying and recognising the risk inherent in the CRE cycle. Typically, in the exuberant phase of the cycle, lending volumes increase (often quite dramatically), lending criteria weaken and margins fall—yet confidence remains high. The perception of risk does not reflect the rising likelihood that a whole, large, generation of loans will mature after a CRE market correction, when borrowers will find it harder to repay principal outstanding on loans that typically require no more than modest amortisation during their term.

Market value-based LTV ratios are a widely used measure of borrowing capacity—but a dangerously pro-cyclical one. Not only is "V" inherently volatile; it is driven upwards in a boom by the availability of plentiful, affordable debt, and its fall in a bust is exaggerated by the withdrawal of credit—a dangerous feedback loop for lenders. The *Vision* report argued that this weakness can be addressed by replacing market value with a long-term value metric that, not being a function of prevailing market sentiment, gives a truer impression of the worth of collateral and borrowing capacity.

So the first task for the PIA Debt Group's working group on this recommendation was to identify an appropriate long-term value metric. While there are a number of options, there is surprisingly little comparative data and research in this area. Key assessment criteria are:

- How reliably the relevant approach identifies booms, allowing incremental steps to be taken to moderate over-exuberant lending. It is important to remember, in this context, that booms can have quite different origins, fuelled for example by excess liquidity in investment capital flows or by surging occupier demand. An effective metric would spot the exuberance regardless of its cause.
- How reliably the relevant approach avoids false (or premature) positives. The CRE industry needs to have (and the wider economy needs it to have) a sustainable flow of credit—including for projects that are inherently risky, or risky because of limited equity or debt investor interest. A long-term value metric that severely constrains credit supply to the sector would not be attractive, even if, like a stopped clock, it occasionally tells the right time. This is important not only for CRE businesses, but also for the many other, ordinary businesses whose access to finance is linked to their ability to provide CRE collateral.

The working group short-listed three alternative methodologies:

- An approach based on investment value, a concept drawn from the RICS Red Book;
- An approach based on applying an adjustment factor to long-term market value trends (derived from existing property market indices); and
- An approach based on mortgage lending value as used for the purposes of Germany's Pfandbrief covered bond market.

At the time of writing, these three methodologies were being fine-tuned and tested against a consistent historical dataset covering a number of CRE market cycles, with a view to the publication of a research paper setting out the results of this work.

The working group needs to conduct two further, related, tasks. One is to assess the practical implications for the lending market of any long-term value metric that passes muster. How difficult or costly would it be to integrate into existing lending practices and risk management systems? Is there flexibility as regards whether it is used at the individual loan/property level, at portfolio level, or at market or sub-market levels that would inevitably not be a perfect match for a firm's actual exposures? There has been an ongoing dialogue with lenders to ensure they have an opportunity to consider such questions and provide feedback.

The second task is to consider how any viable metric might be integrated into the regulatory framework.[13] The *Vision* report argued that, while there would be value in developing a reliable methodology for long-term value-based LTV calculation, the full benefits would only be captured if regulatory capital were also linked to it. Here are four possible approaches.

- Perhaps most obviously, one might link the risk weighting (and thus the capital requirements) for every CRE loan written by a bank (and possibly any other lender subject to risk-based capital requirements) to a risk assessment referable to long-term value-based LTV. This approach might be especially effective at encouraging good risk practices at the level of individual lending decisions, and has the virtue of being perfectly sensitive to a lender's actual loan book profile. However, it is unclear how easily such an approach could be accommodated (whether on a permissive or mandated basis) under existing and evolving regulatory capital rules applicable to potentially affected lenders in the UK.[14] This approach also implies asset-by-asset long-term valuation, which may be disproportionately costly and disruptive.
- An alternative approach would be for the regulator to run a periodic stress test, probably at portfolio level, to assess the overall long-term value-based LTV profile of each regulated lender's CRE book. Capital consequences could follow, based on the regulator's use of its powers

---

[13] In his October 2015 speech on nurturing resilience to the financial cycle, Alex Brazier, the Bank of England's executive director for financial stability strategy and risk stated that "in a matter of months, the Bank of England will start reporting market-wide indicators of valuations and gearing based on cashflows capitalised at cycle-neutral rates". The Bank of England's December 2015 financial stability report included a chart showing where "all property" and "prime West End office" indices stood by reference to investment value.
[14] The Capital Requirements Directive allows the use of alternative prudent valuation approaches, but it may not be possible to calibrate rules appropriately to deal with both banks using market value and banks using a long-term value. Of course, it is possible that the UK's exit from the EU will open up more flexibility in this area.

to impose counter-cyclical capital buffers or sectoral capital require-ments (the latter probably being the more useful in this context, as the former apply at firm level and are generally understood to relate primarily to residential mortgages). If there is sufficient clarity and certainty around the regulatory approach, lenders could track their portfolio against the relevant measure to avoid the risk of a stress test surprise.

- Another approach, that would allow lenders a reasonable degree of flexibility over how to structure their overall portfolio and risk profile, would be for the regulator to lay down long-term value-based LTV-related conditions that lenders must comply with to contain risk build-up. For example, the regulator might impose a cap on the pro-portion of each UK-regulated lender's CRE lending exposure with a long-term value-based LTV higher than, say, 100%.[15]
- Finally, regulators could lay down guidelines for underwriting stan-dards that include a clear expectation that lenders will use an approved long-term value methodology.

As in the case of the loan database recommendation, it may be appropriate for implementation to be phased. That would allow any preferred long-term value methodology to find its feet in the market, and lenders and other industry stakeholders to become familiar with it and identify and address any initially unanticipated issues. The regulatory approach could also evolve over time, and should aim to strike a balance between providing certainty and flexing calibrations to take account of improving data about lending risk (including as a result of an evolving CRE loan database).

21.3.3 Continuing relevance

It should be clear that, even if practical results may not yet have made a mark in the real world, the *Vision* report is not gathering dust on the shelf. So is the slow-burning momentum behind at least two of the report's recommendations justified, and is it enough?

The report was conceived in the depths of the crisis, and amid a storm of regulatory reactions to it. Its recommendations were developed during a period of limited market activity, when many in the industry, as well as in the policy world, were feeling chastened, troubled, and more than usually inclined to reflect on the bigger picture and the longer term. However, by the time the report was published in May 2014, the market was recovering, people were busy again, and a degree of regulatory fatigue was beginning

---

[15] The figure of 100% is purely indicative, but seeks to remind readers that the usual frame of reference for LTV percentages would be different if ratios are based on long-term rather than market value. More generally, this approach is comparable to that announced by the Bank of England in June 2014 for the introduction of loan-to-income ratio restrictions for residential mortgage lending (i.e. operating on a proportion-of-loans basis rather than as a hard cap for all loans); see *http://www.bankofengland.co.uk/publications/Pages/news/2014/094.aspx* [Accessed 11 August 2016].

to set in. At the time of writing, the market looks diverse, and lenders and regulators alike are plainly far more attentive to market data and risk than they were before the crisis (at the European level as well as in the UK). Some have been tempted to ask: do we really need more regulation?

It is worth responding to that question.

- The *Vision* report was never about "more" regulation—its stated intention was "to improve the quality and effectiveness of regulation, not to increase or decrease the overall amount of regulation".[16]
- While there have certainly been many and various regulatory responses to the crisis, no doubt making many banks safer in the process, those responses have not been coherent and coordinated. The European Commission effectively recognised as much with its call for evidence on the EU's regulatory framework for financial services.[17] Viewed specifically from the perspective of the CRE sector (which was mostly ignored by that European Commission initiative), regulatory interventions seem rather hit and miss, and unlikely to result in a fundamentally safer and more sustainable market in the longer term, especially if one views regulators as themselves susceptible to the cycle. The role of credit in supporting the CRE industry, and the importance of the CRE industry to the real economy, appear to lie beyond the field of vision of most financial regulators.[18]
- The fundamental, underlying data deficit persists—and while it persists, effective, evidence-based regulation is not possible. As the European Systemic Risk Board noted in its December 2014 report on CRE and financial stability, "data on CRE are in general scarce, incomplete or inconsistent [...] making it difficult to describe accurately and compare risks in and across national markets".[19] Good luck effectively regulating something you cannot describe.

Chapter 16 outlined some of the current regulatory developments—at an EU or global, rather than UK, level—that are relevant to the shape, structure, effectiveness and risk profile of CRE debt markets. Two persistent and fundamental failures can be discerned. The first is the way a deeply-ingrained perception of income-producing CRE as intrinsically and generically risky gets in the way of both focusing on the CRE cycle as a critical

---

[16] See paragraph 1.3 of *A Vision for Real Estate Finance in the UK* (*http://www.ipf.org.uk* [Accessed 11 August 2016]).

[17] See *http://ec.europa.eu/finance/consultations/2015/financial-regulatory-framework-review/index%5Fen.htm* [Accessed 11 August 2016].

[18] Given how slow the industry itself has been to articulate these points, financial regulators can perhaps be forgiven. Only in 2016 was a first major report published that explores the contribution of CRE debt to the European economy (see *http://www.crefceurope.org*) [Accessed 11 August 2016].

[19] See *https://www.esrb.europa.eu/pub/pdf/other/2015-12-28_ESRB_report_on_commercial_real_estate_and_financial_stability.pdf* [Accessed 11 August 2016].

risk factor, and recognising that this is an asset class that spans a very broad risk spectrum (from the very safe to the very risky). The second is the failure to understand how CRE lending risk can be distributed around the financial system, and how regulatory interventions affect that distribution. Regulation cannot succeed while these blind spots persist, and the sector as a whole will remain vulnerable to misallocation of capital, mispriced risk and systemic risk build-up.

The *Vision* report seeks to provide a sounder, more sustainable foundation for a successful CRE finance market, supported by better regulation. Time and experience may enable its recommendations to be improved upon, but the essential first step is for all interested parties to engage with it constructively and support the informed, holistic and strategic approach at its heart.

21.4   Conclusion

So how might a sustainable, diversified and efficient CRE finance market look?

- Banks should dominate lower risk lending, most importantly (from an economic point of view) in the smaller ticket and regional lending markets, which their branch networks and local knowledge positions them well to serve. In appropriate cases, and supported by better market and cycle data, they should be able to lend to those markets at low rates (where the risk is low), with correspondingly low regulatory capital requirements. Private capital—such as unleveraged or modestly geared specialist CRE debt funds—should be free to provide more expensive loans at higher risk levels, such as mezzanine tranches.
- Shorter-term, floating rate bank loans should be complemented by wide availability of longer-term and fixed rate loans funded (directly or through the securitisation market) by life companies seeking to match assets and liabilities.
- Robust, historical performance data should allow evidence-backed kite-marking of low risk loans—something that could in turn facilitate easier volume production and distribution of smaller ticket, quality-assured loans. Better data would also help lenders, non-originating investors and regulators (among others) understand the cycle and identify both risk build-up and areas of opportunity, where the market is failing to meet the needs of the economy.
- The use of long-term value metrics would reduce the amplitude of the cycle. Reducing the damaging consequences of excessive exuberant lending at the peak would undoubtedly soften the extent and impact of credit drought after a crash.

Most of the ingredients are to be found in the *Vision* report. The UK can show the way, albeit some of the controls for building an effective informational and regulatory environment are in the hands of global and (for now, at least) EU regulators.

Chapter 22

Challenges and Opportunities for Commercial Mortgage Loan Markets

Craig B Prosser,

Landesbank Baden-Württemberg

22.1 Introduction

As the concluding Chapter of the book is finalised in mid-2016 and the news-flows around the world are considered, many market participants would agree that it is a challenge to be optimistic, given the backdrop of macro-economic uncertainty, geo-political stress and political uncertainty present in the world. Commentators argue that bond prices seem too high, equity indexes are overpriced and certain sectors of CRE are overvalued. Against this backdrop, investors and lenders alike need to be underwriting with an exit strategy in mind and to be confident on the assets and their fundamental investment qualities over time. In June 2016, the game-changing vote in favour of Brexit for the UK was witnessed, possibly the biggest disruptive shock to UK politics during the last 40 or 50 years and, at the time of writing, a controversial US election campaign is reaching a conclusion. It is not difficult to say that there are many challenges in allocating capital in existing financial markets, where many asset classes are trading at or close to all-time highs and it is often difficult to calculate an asset's intrinsic value. In short, asset markets, including the CRE lending market, are experiencing an Age of Great Uncertainty, as a result of extraordinary central bank monetary stimulus, and with uncertainty comes both challenge and opportunity. Global stock and real estate markets, fuelled by central bank intervention on both a co-ordinated basis and at unprecedented levels, have been in a bull market since 2009. In fact, most asset prices during this period have surpassed the peak of their previous highs in 2007, as the following selection of charts demonstrate.

Figure 1: Annual US Housing Existing Sales Median Prices: US housing Indexes now at higher levels than in 2007

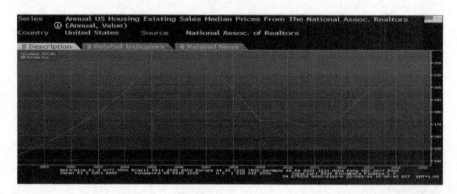

Source Bloomberg

Furthermore, the S&P 500 index traded in mid-2016 at a c. 26 times price earning multiple and has now recovered in excess of 3 times the value of its nadir in 2009, and some c. 50% higher than in 2007, as Figure 2 illustrates.

Figure 2: S&P 500 Index Historical Chart

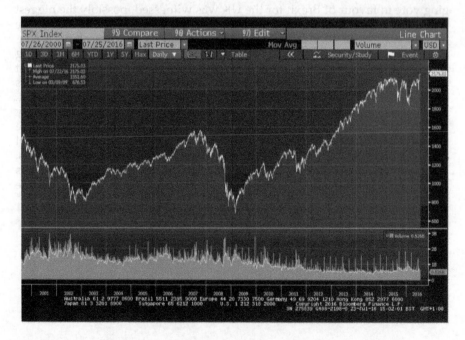

One of the challenges in allocating equity or debt in the existing markets is to have an awareness of the past and how this can predict the future, and this is reflected in a phrase borrowed from Winston Churchill, that if we want to predict the future, then: "The farther back you can look, the farther forward you are likely to see." So, as discussed in Chapter 2 at the start of this book, over the last 100 years or so, economic setbacks have occurred every five to eight years and therefore it may well be that the markets are getting nearer to a correction in asset values. The last two bubbles were the dotcom bubble of 2000 and the GFC which led to the correction of asset prices globally.

In mid-2016, fixed income investors are faced with the dilemma of paying to hold debt, at the time of writing some $13 trillion of global debt now yields a negative interest rate, according to Bank of America Merrill Lynch. For example, the 10 year German Bund has a negative yield and Swiss Government Bond yields are negative out to 50 years. A combination of central bank buying, concern about the future prospects for economic growth and inflation means that investors are effectively paying sovereign governments for the privilege of lending to them. Never before in hundreds of years of recorded economic history have interest rates been at zero or negative (see further Chapter 12). The implications of this for the pension fund and annuity industry are tremendous. Many pension schemes face the dual challenges of increasing longevity of their members and decreasing yield on assets. Most research indicates that in order to fund such liabilities, an 8% return is required on investments. With UK gilt yields at historic lows, the spread between gilts on UK CRE is at historic highs and on a relative and historical basis, the asset class both for debt and equity investors alike is certainly compelling. This means that increased activity for UK and Overseas Pension funds in the UK CRE sector is likely.

This Chapter will highlight some of the opportunities and challenges for participants in the CRE loan markets, against a background of deflation, as evidenced by low and negative yielding sovereign debt, combined with asset values that have seen dramatic inflation post GFC. However, such opportunities come with a health warning: investors must focus on prudent underwriting, must understand their exit strategies and lender's underwriting and lending criteria should, in an Age of Uncertainty be robust.

The aim of this Chapter is not to offer a prediction on current or future prices of debt, or yields on CRE, as these will surely fluctuate over time, but rather to take a panoramic view as to where the main opportunities and challenges lie, based on thematic trends highlighted by various commentators in real estate journals and conference discussions. This Chapter will look at some of the basic insights gained by examining the context of where European CRE loan markets are at the time of writing as reported in various market surveys, including the De Montford Report, and to highlight opportunities and challenges these markets present to the financier and investor, with consideration to the market structure and participants.

22.2   Dynamics in the CRE debt and investment markets

Post the GFC, CRE markets across Europe have, since 2013–2014, enjoyed a healthy growth in volumes particularly in prime investment properties in core markets across Europe, in fact records were broken in 2015. This has been particularly evident in the UK real estate investment market. According to the *De Montford Report* (2015), the net aggregate value of CRE loan books in the UK stood at £168.4 billion at the end of 2015, an annual increase on 2014 of 1.9% and is the first annual increase recorded since 2008 (see further Chapter 15).

Prime investment markets across the UK and Europe experienced strong rental growth and yield compression throughout 2015. The picture on loan margins is more nuanced; according to the 2015 *De Montfort University Report*, margins had compressed during 2012-mid 2015 though had begun to widen across most UK sectors from mid 2015 to end 2015, although remained lower than those reached at year-end 2014. This is despite increase in volumes of activity being recorded during the second half of the year. The survey reports that the only exceptions to this were loans secured by prime offices and loans secured by secondary industrial projects. Also, according to the survey, loan to value ratios having increased during 2014 had begun to fall across all sectors from mid 2015 to end of 2015. According to the published data, it is too early to say whether this is the beginning of a general widening trend, though this it is interesting to observe from published data that at a time of record real estate transactional volume activity as witnessed in 2015 increases in margins and decreases in LTVs were observed.

During 2015 CMBS activity once again remained subdued, and largely comprised of European Real Estate. In the UK CRE market financings via sole underwrites or club deals have remained the predominant form debt source for real estate transactions. Higher risk, secondary properties, transitional and development projects both on residential and commercial have tended to be funded by debt funds.

Additionally, lenders are looking to identify new up and coming markets and seek to deploy capital there, early and prudently. Such markets in the UK previously included the South Bank for CRE and Shoreditch which has become a hub for the fintech and more broadly the IT and technology sectors. Since 2014 these markets, which were once the poor cousins of the City of London, have developed into markets of their own and are able to command rents equalling, if not exceeding, traditional markets for occupiers. Aldgate and Whitechapel in London potentially exhibit many of the characteristics which typified the South Bank and Shoreditch in 2011. Investment into these sub-markets has been evidenced through press reports during 2016 of Brookfield and China Life's purchase of Aldgate Tower and Derwent London's Aldgate Union (renamed the Whitechapel

Building). Lenders who do not normally engage in development financing, discussed further in Chapter 8, should consider this very carefully. It is one area where the risk-reward ratio is still strongly in favour of the reward for both investor and financier. Supporting the best in class, well capitalised sponsors in a fully pre-let development financing in many instances, may offer lenders a superior risk position on a capital per-square foot basis than a 60% LTV loan on a fully let prime office in mid-2016. Set against a back-drop of uncertainty due to the UK's vote to leave the EU following the June 2016 referendum, it will be interesting to see how future transactional volume, LTVs and loan margins develop in the UK and indeed how this will influence European CRE and lending markets. There exists little con-crete public data, at the time of writing, to offer a definitive view on the direction of travel of these parameters, although according to JLL, European transactional volumes are down some 15% compared to Q1 2015, with the central London real estate market showing a particularly large fall in volume compared to Q1 2015. As uncertainty increases risk perceptions will change and CRE markets are likely to see increased risk awareness. This has already been evidenced by valuation tables published by the major sur-veying firms showing that prime investment yields widening by some 25bps for City of London offices. As markets change rapidly those who are able to be nimble and opportunistic may benefit from the current changing macro-economic environment in the UK. Opportunistic debt and equity funds are likely to see an increase in activity during 2016 and indeed during any periods of market dislocation that global asset markets may face over the next 12 months.

In the UK market looking at the published five-year Libor rates shown in Figure 3 below, Libor rates have decreased steadily since 2011, in particular one can observe that on this metric alone since 2014 to today five year Libor has fallen by some 150bps which when combined with the margin data published by De Montfort indicates that all in financing costs have shown a steady decrease during the last 18 months or so. As long as the all in rate of such financings remains below the yield of real estate assets investors are able to benefit from positive leverage and increased returns, set against the backdrop of the returns of other assets mentioned above. This perhaps goes some way to explain increased transaction volumes in UK and European CRE markets during 2015.

Figure 3: Chart Showing five Year Swap Rates

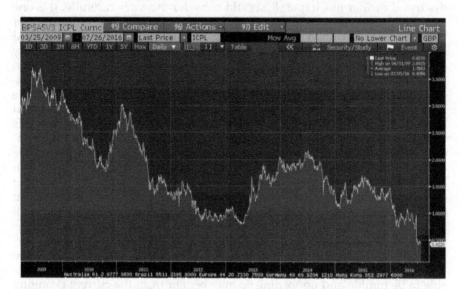

Source: Bloomberg

22.3 Alternative Lenders—The Debt Funds

As the 2015 *De Montford Report* highlights, with the supply of senior debt increasing in the UK real estate markets and the corresponding compression in investment margins, it has been evident that the Debt Funds have chosen to allocate capital to core-plus, value add regional assets and development assets that they have successfully built up post GFC. Interestingly, according to the 2015 *De Montfort Report*, as at the end of 2015, some 51% of non-bank lender's development exposure was to residential development. Traditionally a more volatile sector than CRE this may be a cause of concern. During periods of market uncertainty and temporary dislocations as mentioned above Debt Funds can not only take advantage to increase allocations but also to bring diversity to their real estate loan books.

At the time of writing, numerous institutions have entered or increased their presence in the market with either a mandate to raise a fund for senior CRE debt, or are already lending directly into the market on CRE debt. In the main, these institutions are insurance companies or asset managers seeking to benefit from the relatively high margins available on CRE debt compared to corporate debt and sovereign bonds. Estimates for the firepower that these funds have, or will have, are said to be in excess of some €40 billion.

As discussed above, with global pension funds seeking 8% to meet their liabilities and dividend yields on the S&P 500 and FTSE 100 Indexes standing at 2.11% and 4% respectively, at the time of writing, both senior debt all in yields of c. 2.5%–3.5% and mezzanine yields of c. 6–12% (as reported in the 2015 *De Montford Report*), these funds should continue to see solid inflows of capital seeking stable yield. Senior debt funds should seize the opportunities that will come from the increased tail-risk that is present in global markets and take advantage of pricing dislocations.

22.3.1   *Secondary property versus prime property*

Prime office yields in the City of London are, at the time of writing, around the 4%–4.5% yield range and generally speaking, not too far off where they were in 2006 (c. 4.25%). Secondary properties around the UK are less well bid and yields have not compressed as much and show both a healthy pick up versus both prime real estate and yield levels seen in 2006. It is worth noting, that at the height of the CRE markets in 2007, secondary asset pricing and prime pricing had very small yield differentials. Price discrimination in the CRE loan and CMBS markets between primary and secondary properties was also largely absent. In mid-2016, with European commercial banks, in the main, focusing on well-let core real estate, there remains a window of opportunity to deploy both equity and debt capital to regional secondary properties which present a modest pick up in returns to long-run average pricing in both cases. Through backing the right property, prudent underwriting and importantly the right sponsor, capital allocation in the form of senior debt to this sector, at this stage in the cycle, is likely to prove a good opportunity for the senior debt funds. Similarly, focusing on light infrastructure, transitional assets in superior locations and operating assets are also areas where senior debt fund managers may be able to offer above average returns in the debt space. Notwithstanding the earlier comments on residential development financing, the advent of the PRS sector in the UK would be a sensible asset class for many debt funds when they consider their capital allocations.

22.4   The mezzanine debt market opportunity

Prior to the GFC, according to market commentary, the LTV ratios that banks and CMBS markets were willing to offer were often up to the 80%–95% range at reported margins of c1-1.5%. At the time of writing, the LTV ratio most banks are willing to offer is rarely higher than 60–65% and is much more sensitive to asset type than before the GFC. Many German lenders often cut off their LTV's towards the lower end of a 55–65% range and a percentage of this loan, known as the *"Beleihungswert"*, an independently assessed value that means a loan is able to be refinanced through the Pfandbrief (covered bond) markets to those institutions that have programmes in place (see further the German lending market chapter contained in Chapter 18). Many borrowers, especially those seeking financing for core-plus assets, seek to achieve a 70–75% LTV advance rate. Due to increased capital requirements on traditional lenders, discussed in Chapters 16 and 17, it is the non-bank lending sector which is and will continue to provide capital in this space.

The LTV gap that is present at the time of writing, has presented non-traditional lenders with an opportunity to enter into the CRE mortgage markets. Some have long been present and were seasoned buyers of B notes from investment banks prior to the GFC, though there have been many new entrants seeking to achieve private equity type returns of 5–10% IRR from CRE debt. Whilst this funding may be dilutive to prime core real estate and hence not appealing to most property investors, for those investing in the secondary and transitional sector this is an attractive proposition. Although the main challenge for most real estate investors is often not in achieving the last 10% or 15% of funding, but rather the first 50–60% via the senior banking market, hence once again, there is an opportunity for senior debt funds. The challenge for the mezzanine and junior debt funds to deploy their capital relies upon senior lenders (whether traditional providers or debt funds as referred to above) being active in financing to facilitate the offering of their product. Given the continued resilience of the Pfandbrief market and the lower range LTV cut off mentioned above, a key opportunity, and one which is likely to increase as the real estate cycle matures, will be the increased use of stretch senior by borrowers that will offer the ability for mezzanine funds to deploy capital in this space.

22.5 Insurance companies

As discussed above, due to the requirements of pension funds attempting to achieve returns to match their liabilities; the insurance sector will continue to increase its presence as a permanent source of debt capital for real estate going forward; often targeting the opportunity to provide long-term financing where is it favourable, both from a regulatory perspective and from an asset-liability matching perspective. Alongside insurance companies investing in this space will be large institutional investors (pension funds, insurance companies, sovereign wealth funds, etc.), which look to increase their exposure to CRE, either directly or indirectly. In particular, the attractiveness of lending to CRE has increased for insurance companies, compared to directly investing into CRE, as a result of Solvency II regulation (see further Chapter 16). This is because, upon implementation of Solvency II regulations, insurance companies will be required to put aside an increased amount of capital for direct CRE investments, thereby making indirect CRE investments, such as CRE debt, relatively more attractive. Some of these investors have historically low allocations to CRE, in particularly CRE debt. These allocations are likely to increase over time, once the attractive risk/return profiles offered by the CRE debt markets become more widely advertised.

22.6 Private Equity

Due to its existing infrastructure to invest in CRE, its wide relationship networks and its flexible investment approach, the private equity industry is another source of debt capital that will take on the opportunity and help address the funding gap in Europe. Private equity funds generally have the ability to invest opportunistically across the capital structure. The combination of a sustained supply/demand imbalance in the availability of debt and the consequent increase in the cost of debt described above, are gradually leading to a closing of the often observed "pricing gap", i.e. the gap between the cost expectations of the borrower and the return expectations of private equity funds. The market environment, at the time of writing, therefore represents a very attractive investment opportunity for the private equity industry and other institutional investors. In essence, the uncertain global environment that exists in mid-2016, creates opportunities for CRE private equity that will allow it to invest in CRE in the alternative form of debt, at compelling risk-adjusted returns. Of course, given the cash constraint nature of many refinancing situations in the NPL sector, equity capital can also provide attractive returns to private equity investors.

22.7 Conclusion

This Chapter has presented a market participant's view of some of the main opportunities and challenges facing the European CRE loan markets that exist in mid 2016. Many market participants are, to a certain extent, struggling to forecast in the face of the global uncertainty that is faced. The outcome of the Brexit referendum in the UK demonstrates the uncertainty and fragility of global markets. Volatilities in currencies and interest rates globally contribute to an uncertain back-drop for making investment and lending decisions. Concerns abound about debt to GDP ratios across all advanced economies, which have without exception increased since 2007, indeed China's debt to GDP ratio has quadrupled since 2007, standing at 240%, outmatched only by Japan, whose debt to GDP ratio stands at 245%. Eventually, such monetary easing measures will become exhaustive and policy makers will be faced with the fact that the world has borrowed more from the future than in any time in recorded economic history, and will have to focus on reducing this debt. Unless such borrowing has been allocated to investment and increasing productivity, and it appears that this has not been the case, then this only serves to increase economic tail-risk in the global financial system. Whether economies, already flooded with credit, will be driven further by central bank stimulus is a key question investors and lenders have to answer, to tailor their capital allocation strategies accordingly. Key signs that investors should watch closely are NPL rates in jurisdictions which have a high debt to GDP ratio, as a small percentage of these loans going into default and subsequent losses would have an outsized effect on these countries GDPs (e.g. 2.4x for China and

2.45x for Japan) which would have the propensity to develop a truly significant global financial shock. Once again global housing markets are flashing warning signs of bubble territory.

It is set against such a backdrop that this Chapter has summarised some of the main challenges facing the CRE loan markets where capital is scarce. On a more positive note, the Chapter highlights the opportunities this presents for senior debt and mezzanine debt funds. The most striking and greatest challenge discussed in the Chapter is for banks to find low risk real estate upon which to lend. In conclusion, banks will remain the predominant source of debt capital to investment loans in core markets backed by strong sponsors. One challenge, perhaps better described as a threat to the market, is that of a shift in the focus of the central banks when the market becomes faced with the prospect of rising interest rates, or worse still—suddenly rising interest rates. However, this seems remote at the time of writing and as discussed in Chapter 12, banks in 2016 are the recipients of cheap funding via various central bank programmes across the world. It should be reflected upon that in 2017 and the coming years, central banks may shift their focus from one of easing and therefore increase interest rates. Such a move is perhaps some time away in the UK, and has already had a false start in the US at the end of 2015, although signs are, once again, pointing towards a more hawkish attitude from the Federal Reserve on interest rates. Lenders and investors should not grow complacent to rising borrowing costs, even though since 2008, the markets have witnessed an era of low interest rates. It is worth noting that if five year LIBOR rates in the UK were to increase to 2014 levels, this would be a 300% increase from five year LIBOR levels. This potential move, however remote commentators may view it, is one that financiers and investors alike should consider in their underwriting and capital allocation decisions. Are the expectations of circa 50bps for five year Libor correct? Or could rates rapidly return to the expectations of five year Libor of 2%, as was the case two years ago, in 2014. The former may seem certainly too low, however one only has to look to Europe to see that rates can go lower still. Much of the existing real estate pricing can be explained along the lines of relative value to other global real estate markets, the weight of money investing into the sector and strong rental growth prospects. As mentioned above, the requirement to fund pension liabilities, requiring returns of some c. 8%, combined with central bank activities, is distorting pricing in many asset markets including real estate. However, whilst any sudden and material corrections in real estate markets for the next 12–24 months are unlikely, market participants must be mindful of the fundamentals, both as lenders and investors in such markets. It is during such a time of uncertainty that investors, be they debt or equity should not be distracted by noise and lose sight of the fundamentals. Whilst it is often discussed that the current yields of real estate are attractive relative to sovereign bonds it is the fundamentals that count.

The key to real estate investing, as with all asset classes, is to find Quality at the right Price; be this in the debt or equity space. This means focusing on real estate assets that are well-located and are in markets which are showing strong and innovative potential and allocate capital when these assets are cheap.

If investors can allocate capital to real estate assets when these three factors align: Growth, Quality and Price, then history has shown that over time the patient investor be it in debt or equity will be rewarded with such a strategy.

Moreover, investors following such an approach may also be able to benefit from the current low levels of interest rates across the globe and combine this strategy with positive leverage. It is interesting to note that that some 10 years ago the five year UK Libor rate stood more than 400bps higher than it is at the time of writing. Whilst interest rates look favourable today, and the pick up on real estate versus gilts at historic highs all may point to the fact that the UK CRE sector is in good health for both investors and lenders alike. On the cautionary side, if rates revert towards their mean and the degree of positive leverage maybe diminished or even turn negative. The hope is that for central banks to raise interest rates significantly is that rents and therefore values will have increased proportionately. Most mainstream press reports do not expect significant tightening of central bank interest rates, however the fact that this is not expected or anticipated could exacerbate the eventual effect of a modest and sustained tightening in central bank interest rate policy. Global markets seem very comfortable that this is unlikely to happen any time soon. However, such tail risk is increasing and has caused volatility and corrections in asset markets previously e.g. "The Taper Tantrum in 2013". Sudden shifts in expectations on central bank activity are likely to be painful for many participants and this tail risk is something that investors should not discount.

In light of the challenges and opportunities discussed, there is a further challenge facing the markets which is worth mentioning, although there is not the scope to discuss its implications in full in this Chapter. In the face of such an unprecedented downturn that the financial services experienced with the GFC and increased regulatory changes, combined with the profitability and return challenges that lie within the sector, perhaps the greatest issue of all faced by the market will be the ability to attract and retain the human capital necessary to face the challenges of restructuring, origination and servicing of CRE loans discussed throughout this book. Without doubt, the upheaval that has taken place in CRE markets over the last decade has affected both assets and talent in the sector. As the banks have withdrawn and re-entered CRE lending, the expertise and transactional knowledge has become more dispersed. For platforms with the appropriate expertise and creativity the CRE lending market, despite all its challenges, presents one of the best opportunities in a generation.

As discussed throughout this book, CRE is a capital intensive business and as the balance of economic power shifts from West to East, to overcome the challenges in the CRE markets, participants will need to adapt to seek out the changing pockets of capital. Innovation in adapting to the challenges faced by the sector will continue, as is already seen in the arrival of specialist debt funds and fixed rate products of short and long durations on offer. In addition to traditional sources of capital, debt market participants in Europe will need a more global perspective in seeking out capital to allocate to CRE debt. South-East Asia, the Americas, the Middle East, Russia, Japan and importantly China, will all have an increased role to play in the European CRE debt markets post 2016 and for the next decade and beyond. Those individuals and organisations that can embrace this by realising that we are in an Age of Great Uncertainty on a global scale, and be the quickest to adapt to this shifting landscape and rise and adapt to these challenges, will succeed and prosper. After all it was the teachings of Charles Darwin that taught us: it is not the most intellectual of the species that survives; it is not the strongest that survives; but the species that survives is the one that is able best to adapt and adjust to the changing environment in which it finds itself.

Glossary

A

ABCP conduits
Asset backed commercial paper conduits.

A-cities
The dominant cities in the German CRE market, comprising Berlin, Düsseldorf, Frankfurt, Hamburg, Köln, Munich, Stuttgart.

A Lender or A Loan Holder or A Note Holder
The Lender which holds the A Loan in an AB Structure.

A-IRB approach
An advanced variant of the IRB approach proposed under Basel II, allowing banking institutions to develop their own risk weighting models.

A Loan or A Note
The senior tranche in an AB Structure typically securitised or placed within a CMBS.

A Loan Holder
See A Lender.

A Note
See A Loan.

A Note Holder
See A Lender.

AAOIFI
Accounting and Auditing Organisation of Islamic Financial Institutions.

ABCDS
Credit Derivatives referencing CMBS, MBS, ABS or CDO Securities. ABCDS are typically drafted using the CPS Template or the PAUG Template.

ABCP
Asset Backed Commercial Paper.

AB Structure
A senior-subordinate debt structure whereby the ownership of a single mortgage loan is tranched into one or more senior tranches and one or more subordinate tranches.

ABS
See Asset Backed Securitisation/Securities.

Abandonment
The voluntary relinquishment of a property or an interest in a property where there is no intention of resuming possession of the property or of keeping rights therein.

Acceleration
The process whereby a Loan is declared due and payable prior to its scheduled repayment date, usually following the occurrence of an Event of Default.

Accounting Records
The manual or computerised records of assets and liabilities, monetary transactions, various journals, ledgers, and supporting documents (such as agreements, cheques, invoices and vouchers), which certain organisations are required to keep for a certain number of years.

Accrued Interest
Interest charged or due on a loan which is unpaid. This is often added to the outstanding principal balance and must be paid before any reduction in the principal balance is allowed.

Accrued Rate
The rate at which interest is charged or is due on a loan.

Adjustable Rate Mortgage
A mortgage loan whereby the interest rate changes on specific dates.

Administration
The procedure under the Insolvency Act 1986 where a company may be reorganised or its assets realised under the protection of a statutory moratorium. At the end of the administration, the company will usually have been restructured or the business and/or assets will have been sold by the Administrator. Administration can be commenced by obtaining a court order or the company, its directors or the holder of a Qualifying Floating Charge may use the out-of-court appointment route.

Administration Rate
The annual servicing fee as a percentage of the outstanding principal balance of each loan.

Administrative Receivership
The remedy by which a secured Creditor may realise assets subject to its Security. Creditors with a Floating Charge (created prior to 15 September 2003) over the whole (or substantially the whole) of the assets of the company can appoint an administrative receiver. For Floating Charges created on or after 15 September 2003, Administrative Receivership is only available in a limited number of exceptional circumstances. The holder of a Qualifying Floating Charge created on or after 15 September 2003 can appoint an Administrator.

Administrator
An insolvency practitioner appointed by the court or by a company, its directors or the holder of a Qualifying Floating Charge using the out-of-court appointment route, to carry out the Administration. An Administrator is given wide powers to manage the company's affairs, business and property and at the end of the Administration the company is usually either returned to the directors or liquidated.

ADR
See American Depository Receipts.

Advance
In the context of a Mortgage Loan, an advance made by a Lender to a Borrower. In the context of a CMBS transaction, a payment by the Special Servicer (in respect of Non-Performing Loans) or the Master Servicer (in respect of Performing Loans) so that payments due on the CMBS can continue as scheduled.

Advances
Payments by the Special Servicer (in respect of delinquent loans) or the Master Servicer (in respect of performing loans) so that note payments can continue as scheduled. These can be required for a variety of payments alongside principal and interest payments (for example taxes and insurance) but do not include fees which the trustee or an officer of the trustee deems non-recoverable.

Adverse Selection
The process by which the risk profile of an asset pool is assumed to worsen over time due to a presumption that more creditworthy borrowers are more likely to prepay their loans resulting over time in less creditworthy borrowers predominating.

Advisory Committee
A committee consisting of representatives of a private equity fund's larger investors established to review and approve conflict items and certain major decisions relating to the fund.

AFFO
Adjusted funds from operations, recurring income delivered by properties owned by REITs adjusted for non-real estate depreciation and amortisation and a straight line rent adjustment.

Agent
See Facility Agent.

Aggregation Risk
The risk assumed while mortgages are being warehoused during the process of pooling them for ultimate securitisation. The mortgage holder faces the risk that the value of the mortgages will decline before the securitisation can be executed due to factors such as adverse interest rate movements or credit losses.

AIF
See Authorised Investment Funds.

AIFM

Alternative Investment Fund Manager.

AIM
The Alternate Investment Market of the London Stock Exchange.

ALA
Allocated Loan Amount.

All in Cost
The total cost of a securitisation to the issuer or sponsor (including the interest rate paid to investors' underwriting expenses and various other expenses such as legal and documentation fees) amortised over the expected average life of the issue. This is often quoted in basis points to indicate what would have been added to the yield had these expenses not been incurred in the creation of the security.

Allocated Percentage
The proportion of the principal amount of a mortgage loan secured by multiple properties which is associated with each individual property. The proportion is usually calculated by dividing the net operating income or net cash flow produced by the one property by the cumulative net operating income or net cash flow produced by all of the properties that secure the loan. Consequently the sum of all of the allocated percentages should be 100%.

Allocation of Realised CMBS Losses
A CMBS provision that defines how realised losses will be allocated to each class of certificate holders.

A Loan
The senior tranche in an AB Structure.

Al-Musharaka
An Islamic financing method derived from a partnership contract in which a bank participates with one or more clients.

Alpha
The return delivered when the manager uses skill to out-perform the market competition at the relevant risk level.

Al-Sharika
An Islamic finance term meaning a partnership for profit.

Alternative A Loan
A first ranking residential mortgage loan that generally conforms to traditional prime credit guidelines, although the LTV ratio, loan documentation, occupancy status, property type, or other factors cause the loan not to qualify under standard underwriting programs. Less than full documentation is typically the reason for classifying a loan as Alternative A.

Alternative Investment Funds (AIFs)
Defined under the Alternative Investment Fund Managers Directive (2011/61/EU) (AIFMD) as an entity which raises capital from a number of investors with a view to investing it in accordance with a defined investment policy and does not require authorisation.

American Depository Receipts
A mechanism designed to facilitate trading in shares of non-US companies in the US stock markets. The main purpose is to create an instrument which can easily be settled through US stock market clearing systems.

Amortisation
The scheduled repayment of debt in regular instalments over a period of time until repaid in full. For non-scheduled repayment, see Prepayment.

Amortisation Polled
A period during which the outstanding balance of any related securities of a transaction are partially repaid. This may follow the revolving period of a transaction.

Ancillary Rights
Contractual and security rights attaching to underlying loans which are transferred by the originator as part of the sale process.

Anchor Tenant(s)
One or more large shops or supermarkets introduced to a shopping centre in key positions to attract shoppers into the centre in order to encourage other retailers to Lease units.

Annual Payment Cap
In relation to an adjustable rate mortgage loan, the maximum percentage in any one year by which the due payments of principal and interest can be increased.

Annualised Net Rents
In any year, the sum of all gross rent proceeds received by a Landlord plus, where any rent reviews are outstanding, the estimated increase in gross rents (as determined by external valuers) for that year, less any ground rents payable under the head Leases.

A Notes
The most senior tranche of an ABS or MBS issue. These rank senior to other tranches both in priority of repayment of principal and credit terms. A Notes are rated as Investment Grade and are thus appropriate for regulated institutional investors.

Appraisal
The assessment of the likely future performance of an investment, which can be used to determine value or to assess risk. In the context of a US real estate financing, a term used to mean a Valuation.

Appraisal Reduction
Following certain events based on loan delinquency, an appraisal will be performed to determine if the property value justifies any further advances by the Servicer. If the value is reduced below the loan balance plus authorised advances, the Servicer will stop or reduce principal and interest payments on the loan to the Trustee. The Trustee will then reduce principal and interest payments to the certificate holders in order of their priority, beginning with the first-loss security.

Arbitrage
The simultaneous purchase and sale of an asset in order to profit from a difference in its price, usually on different exchanges or marketplaces. An example of this is where a domestic stock also trades on a foreign exchange in another country, where its price has not adjusted in line with the exchange rate. A trader purchases the stock where it is undervalued and short sells the stock where it is overvalued, thus profiting from the difference.

Arbitrage CDO
A CDO transaction which is based on assets the aggregate yield of which is less than the aggregate yield for which the securities issued in connection with the transaction can be sold or funded.

AREA
The Asian Real Estate Association.

Arrangement Fee
The fee payable by a Borrower to the Arranger of a Loan.

Arranger
The bank which arranges a Loan involving more than one Lender.

Asking Rent
A prospective rent offered by the landlord to a prospective tenant. The actual rent paid will often be less than this following negotiations and concessions.

Asset-Backed Securities (ABS)
Bonds or notes collateralised (or ''backed'') by a specific pool of financial assets. Such financial assets will generally have predictable income flows (for example credit card receivables or vehicle loans) and are originated by banks and other credit providers.

Asset-Backed Commercial Paper
A short-term investment vehicle with a maturity that is typically between 90 and 180 days issued by a bank or other financial institution. The notes are backed by physical assets and used for short-term financing needs.

Asset-Independent Approach
An approach to rating synthetic securities which is not based on a credit evaluation of the SPE's assets. Instead the credit rating is in accordance with the creditworthiness of the swap counterparty or its guarantor.

Asset Liquidity
The quality of a real estate asset assessed in terms of the ease with which ownership and/or the financial structure of the asset can be changed.

Asset Manager
An entity appointed by a real property holding vehicle to provide investment advisory services and/or discretionary investment management services in respect of real property or a beneficial interest in real property held by such vehicle. The services of the asset manager will be particularly necessary where the holding vehicle is a SPV with independent directors unfamiliar with the management of real property. The regulatory status of the manager can differ depending on whether the manager makes investment decisions on behalf of the vehicle, and therefore provides discre-

tionary investment management services, or the manager does not make investment decisions on behalf of the vehicle, and therefore provides only investment advisory services. See also Investment Manager and Property Manager.

Asset Originator
The party that has originated an asset or group of assets by extending credit to one or more creditors.

Asset Protection Scheme
A UK Government scheme announced in June 2009 to enable the UK Government to provide participating institutions with protection against future credit losses on defined portfolios of assets in exchange for a fee.

Asset Reliability
The quality of a real estate asset assessed in terms of criteria relating to ownership and/or use.

Assignment
The transfer of an interest, right, claim or property from one party to another.

Attachment
The point in time at which a Lender's Security is deemed to attach to the asset in question. Attachment occurs, in the case of a legal Mortgage, when legal title is conveyed to the Mortgagee and, in the case of a charge or equitable Mortgage, when the Security interest is created.

Attribution Analysis
The method for explaining returns on the basis of stock selection, sector allocation, active management and target style, such as core real estate investment, core plus real estate investment or opportunistic.

Ausbietungsgarantie
A German term for a guarantee from a secured lender to a bidder to release its security if a reserve price is met.

Authorised Investment Funds (AIF)
Tax-exempt unlisted UK funds.

Authorised Unit Trust
A UK based unit trust that has been authorised by the FSA to market its units to the general public (often referred to as retail investors). See also Unauthorised Unit Trust.

Automated Valuation Models or AVMs
Computer based valuation packages, designed to provide a basic valuation of assets based on standard information inputted into the program. They

are used mainly for large scale valuations, such as residential apartment blocks.

Available Funds
All funds available or collected from the borrower or borrowers (for example principal and interest payments, prepayments) to make payment obligations under a loan.

Available Funds Cap
A ceiling applied to the amount of interest payable to noteholders being the extent of interest accrued on a pool of loans.

Average Life
A measure of the anticipated life span of an investment based on the average length of time required before all principal invested in repaid.

AVM
See Automated Valuation Models.

B

B Lender or *B Loan Holder* or *B Note Holder*
The Lender which holds the B Loan in an AB Structure.

B Loan or *B Note*
The subordinate tranche in an AB Structure, held outside a CMBS, but can be held in a CRE CDO.

B Loan Holder
See B Lender.

B Note
See B Loan.

B Note Holder
See B Lender.

B Piece
The most subordinated tranche in a CMBS issuance and represents the First Loss Piece. These are often confused with B Loan.

B Piece Holder
The holder of a B Piece. The term is often confused with B Lender.

Backstop Facility
A facility provided by a highly rated entity which can be drawn on should the entity with the primary obligation to make the payment be unable to do so.

Balance Sheet
A condensed statement that shows the financial position of an entity on a specified date (usually the last day of an accounting period) and will, amongst other things, contain details as to the assets and liabilities of the entity. It is often part of the Accounting Records.

Balance-Sheet CDO
A CDO transaction in which the sponsor securitises assets which it already owns.

Balance Sheet Lender
A bank or other financial institution that originates Loans for the purpose of holding those Loans on its balance sheet until such time as they are repaid. By comparison, a bank may originate Loans for the purpose of selling those Loans into a CMBS transaction via the OTD model and therefore removing such Loans from its balance sheet.

Balloon Loan
A Loan that requires the Borrower to make relatively small principal and/ or interest repayments during the life of the Loan and a much larger principal repayment at maturity. The final payment is often referred to as the balloon repayment.

Bank for International Settlements (BIS)
An international bank based in Basel, Switzerland, which monitors and collects data on international banking activity and circulates rules concerning international bank regulation.

Bankruptcy-Remote
A description of an entity which is protected from or is unlikely to be the subject of insolvency, bankruptcy or similar proceedings from third party Creditors. A Bankruptcy Remote entity is typically used in Securitisation and many commercial Mortgage Loan transactions to provide comfort to the transaction parties that the credit risk of the Bankruptcy Remote entity is isolated.

Basel I, II, III
Basel Accords are recommendations on banking laws and regulations issued by the Basel Committee on Banking Supervision. Basel guidelines aim to provide the national regulators with a set of requirements to ensure that banks have adequate capital for the risk they expose themselves to through their lending and investment practices. The number (I, II, III) refers to revised version of the Basel Accords.

Basel I or *Basel Accord*
A set of international banking regulations introduced in 1988 by the Basel Committee, which set out the minimum capital requirements of financial institutions with the goal of minimising credit risk.

Basel II
A revision of Basel I designed to make the framework more risk sensitive and representative of modern banks' risk management practices. Basel II was implemented in the European Union via the Capital Requirements Directive (Directive 2006/48/EC and Directive 2006/49/EC).

Basel III
A revision of Basel II which is designed to strengthen both capital requirements and introduce new regulatory requirements on both liquidity and bank leverage.

Basel Committee (BCBS)
The Basel Committee for Banking Supervision. The organisation which carries out consultation and aims to develop capital requirements which reflect the risks faced by the banking industry.

Basis Point (bp)
One-hundredth of one percentage point. One basis point is the smallest measure used to quote yields on bills, notes and bonds.

Basis Risk
The risk that payments received from the underlying mortgage loans do not match the necessary payments out to bondholders. This arises from discrepancy between the indices to which the mortgage and the bonds are linked. For example, if mortgages are at fixed rates but bonds are at floating rates the bonds could accrue interest at a higher rate than the underlying mortgage loans. The resulting shortfall is known as the basis risk shortfall.

BBA
See British Banking Association.

BCO
British Council for Offices. An organisation which researches, develops and communicates best practice in all aspects of the office sector.

Behavioural finance
The study of the influence of psychology on the behaviour of financial practitioners and the subsequent effect on markets.

Beleihungswert
Beleihungswert or mortgage lending value is the German independently assessed valuation metric that shows the extent to which a loan is able to be refinanced through the Pfandbrief market.

Beta
The return delivered when the manager exposes the client's capital to the market taking a particular amount of market risk.

Bifurcation
The process of splitting a loan into a senior and a junior tranche.

BIPRU
The FSA's Prudential Sourcebook for Banks, Building Societies and Investment Firms.

BIS
See Bank for International Settlements.

Blind-Pool Funds
The assets of Private Equity Real Estate Funds or other investment vehicles which are not determined and/or communicated to investors at the time of investment.

Blockers
Entities used to block a certain action (such as certain tax effects) from flowing from a fund through to particular investors (often special types of feeders) or another fund as a whole (often special subsidiary entities).

Boilerplate
The collective name given to provisions, often of a standard nature, which are typically included in most agreements and which do not relate to the substantive provisions of an agreement. Governing law, assignment, notices and amendment provisions are examples of boilerplate clauses.

Bond
A certificate of debt issued by a government or corporate entity promising payment of the original investment plus interest by a specified future date. Bonds typically have a longer maturity than Notes. See also Notes and Securities.

Borrower
The entity borrowing money from a Lender.

BPF
British Property Federation. This is a membership organisation which represents the interests of those involved in property ownership and investment.

B Loan
The subordinate tranche in an AB Structure.

B Notes
A subordinated tranche in a CMBS structure.

B Pieces
Tranches of a CMBS issuance which are rated BB or lower and are therefore below investment grade.

Bracket
Categorising loans according to a sole shared attribute. For example in a term bracket all loans will have the same average life.

Break Clause
See Break Option.

Break Option or *Break Clause*
An option incorporated in a Lease, which allows the Landlord, Tenant, or in some cases, both, to terminate the Lease before its contractual expiry date. It is usually subject to a notice period and is sometimes subject to a premium payment in the case of a Tenant. In some Leases, there is a provision for a rolling break option, whereby it can be exercised at any point after a certain date, subject to notice.

Break Cost
The cost to the lender whenever a loan is repaid or cancelled on or before the last day of an interest period or the expiry of the term.

Brexit
The departure of the United Kingdom from the European Union.

Bridge Finance
Short-term interim funding made available to a Borrower until funding of a more permanent nature is put in place.

British Banking Association or *BBA*
An association for the United Kingdom banking and financial services sector that speaks for over 200 banking members from 60 countries on a full range of UK and international banking issues, which is responsible for, amongst other things, publishing the daily LIBOR rate.

Broker's Opinion of Vaule (BOV)
An assessment of what an asset will trade for in the market.

Brownfield Site
A site that has previously been developed and is available for redevelopment. Such sites may be contaminated.

Building Society
A financial institution, owned by its members, that offers banking and other financial services. Building Societies are authorised under the Building Societies Act 1986.

Bull Run
A sustained period of strong performance. This term may be applied to a market, a sector, or a single Security.

Bullet Loan
A loan whereby principal is repaid in its entirety through a single payment at maturity.

Buy To Let
Real estate that is purchased with the intention of letting to Tenants for profit.

C

Callable
A loan or securities over which the borrower has the option to require repayment ahead of schedule.

Call Protection
Protection against the risk that loans will be prepaid early, or protection against prepayment risk.

Cap
A maximum price or an upper limit on the total amount of a party's obligation.

Capex
In the CRE context, capital expenditure or capex means the average annual expenses that should be invested into the property by a prudent property owner to maintain the property's condition and to retain its tenants or attract new tenants.

Capital Adequacy
The obligation on a regulated entity (such as a bank or building society) to maintain a certain minimum level of capital in proportion to the risk profile of its assets. Such regulated entities may be able to meet the capital adequacy requirement by securitising their assets and removing them from their balance sheet without recourse, thereby negating the obligation to maintain capital with respect to the securitised assets.

Capital Allowances
One of several kinds of benefit available to an owner against income tax or Corporation Tax for capital expenditure on certain qualifying buildings.

Capital Calls
Notifications by a private equity fund to its investors made at any time during the investment period (and often on a limited basis for certain specific items after the investment period) requiring the investors to make payments to the fund in lieu of their Capital Commitments.

Capital Commitments
Contractual commitments to make a capital contribution to a private equity fund by the fund investors, which are drawn down through a series of Capital Calls, primarily during the investment period.

Capital Gain
A gain that arises when an investment is sold at a higher price than originally paid.

Capital Gains Tax or CGT
Tax payable on a Capital Gain.

Capital Markets
A financial market in which long-term debt and equity Securities are bought and sold.

Capital Markets Union (CMU)
A European Commission proposal intended to create a single, integrated European market for capital.

Capital Requirements Directive (CRD)
The CRD aligns European legislation with international standards on capital by implementing the Basel Accords in the European Union. CRD 2 and CRD 3 update and refine the CRD and strengthens the EU regulatory framework. CRD 4 is a set of further reforms to prudential requirements for credit institutions and investment firms, introduced alongside Basel III.

Capital Requirements Regulation (CRR)
Capital Requirements Regulation (Regulation 575/2013) forms part of CRD 4, aiming to further reform and replace CRD, alongside the Basel III legislative framework.

Capitalisation
In a Loan context, the process of adding interest to the principal amount of the Loan rather than the interest being paid periodically during the term of the Loan. In a corporate context, see Market Capitalisation.

Capitalisation Rate or Cap Rate
A measure of a property's value based on current performance and also a measure of investor's expectations. Calculated by dividing the net operating income for the year by the value of the property.

Capped Floating-Rate Note
A floating rate note with an upper limit or cap on the coupon rate. This prevents the investor from benefiting from interest rate movements which would take the coupon above the cap.

Carried Interest
An allocation of a private equity fund's profits made from the capital accounts of the fund's limited partners to the capital account of the fund's general partner or manager. Carried interest is often equal to 20% of the realised gains actually distributed to the investors. Carried interest may be calculated on a Portfolio-wide basis or on a modified deal-by-deal level.

Cash Collateral
A reserve fund that can be accessed in the event of credit losses and subsequent claims by investors. A type of credit enhancement. The account in which the funds are held is the Cash Collateral Account (CCA) and lent to the issuer by a third party under a loan agreement.

Cash Collateral Account
A bank account that serves to secure and service a loan. It is essentially a zero-balance account and no sums may be withdrawn.

Cash Flow Note
A note which is not based on an interest rate but repaid periodically based on a portion of cash flow derived by the secured property.

Cash Flow Waterfall
The order in which the cash flow available to an Issuer, after covering all expenses, is allocated to the debt service owed to holders of the various classes of issued securities.

Cash-on-Cash return
A measure of the short term return on property investment calculated by dividing cash flow received from the property by the equity invested in the property.

Cash-Out Refinance Mortgage Loan
A mortgage loan taken in order to refinance an existing mortgage loan in a situation where the amount of the new loan exceeds (by more than 1%) the amount required to cover repayment of the existing loan, closing costs and repayment of any outstanding subordinate mortgage loans. The borrower can put the additional cash to whatever use it pleases.

Cash Trap
A provision often seen in intercreditor agreements whereby all amounts that would be distributable to a junior lender commencing immediately on a payment default or borrower insolvency are held in escrow (trapped) pending the senior lender's decision to enforce or the junior leader's decision to cure the borrower default.

Cash Sweep
Where cash is taken or swept from the borrower's bank accounts and applied to pay down the outstanding balance of the loan.

Casualty
Unexpected damage or destruction to a property.

Catch-Up
Form of promoted interest designed to achieve a certain split of return between the General Partner and the Limited Partners after a preferred interest has been provided.

CBO
See Collateralised Bond Obligation.

CDO
See Collateralised Debt Obligation.

CDO^2
See Collateralised Debt Obligation Squared.

CDS
See Credit Default Swap.

Cédulas
Cédula hipotecaria (Spanish covered bonds) are notes issued by financial institutions which pay a fixed interest rate and which are guaranteed by mortgage loans granted by the issuing entity. Such cédula hipotecaria can only be issued by Spanish credit institutions (*entidades de crédito oficial*), Spanish savings banks (*cajas de ahorro*) or specialised companies formed with the sole object of, among other things, granting loans or mortgage guarantees (*sociedades de crédio hipotecario*).

Cession Dailly
Mechanism under French law for the security assignment of lease receivables.

CEE
Central and Eastern Europe.

577

CGT
See Capital Gains Tax.

Centre of Main Interest (COMI)
The term relevant with respect to insolvency. An entity's centre of main interests is generally (in an EU context) where the main insolvency proceedings against that entity will be taken.

Certificate
A formal certificate evidencing beneficial ownership in a trust fund. Owned by a certificate holder.

Charge
Security over a particular asset or class of assets that gives the chargee the right to have the particular asset or class of assets (and all proceeds from the sale of such asset or class of assets) appropriated to the discharge of the debt in question. A charge does not transfer legal ownership. It is merely an encumbrance on the asset.

Cherry-Picking
The practice of applying specific criteria to select assets from a portfolio; the opposite of a sample selected at random.

Civil Law
Legal systems (codified and uncodified) based mainly on concepts and principles of Roman law.

CIL
Community Infrastructure Levy.

Clawback
A repayment by a private equity fund's general partner or manager of all or a portion of Carried Interest previously received from the fund to the extent required by the fund's investors to ensure that the Carried Interest is not paid on previous successful deals to protect investors against any losses sustained on any subsequent failed deals. A mechanism for investors to protect their capital and preferred return.

Clean-Up Call
An optional redemption of securities at a point when there is 15% or less of the original principal balance of the underlying collateral pool outstanding and the cost of servicing the remaining pool of assets has become uneconomic. The issuing SPE will sell the remaining assets (usually at par) to the senior or the originator/sponsor of the assets and use the proceeds to effect the redemption. The benefit to investors of such a redemption is that it provides assurance that they will not be left with a tiny, illiquid fraction of their original investment.

Clearstream International
A subsidiary of Deutsche Borse AG that provides clearing, settlement and custody services for stocks and bonds traded in European domestic and cross-border markets.

Clearing House
A financial institution that provides clearing, settlement and custody services for stocks and Bonds traded in domestic and cross-border markets. Clearstream International, Euroclear and the Depository Trust Company (DTC) are examples of clearing houses.

Clearing System
The trading system used for trading publicly traded Securities designed to promote world trade and market efficiency. Most international clearing transactions are administered by an international clearing house.

CLO
See Collateralised Loan Obligations.

CLN
See Credit-Linked Note.

Close Company
A company in which the directors control more than half the voting shares, or where such control is exercised by five or fewer people and their associates.

Closed-Ended Fund
A Real Estate Fund from which investors cannot demand to have their capital redeemed or paid back, and which are not normally open to new investors to subscribe for new units for cash other than when the fund is formally raising additional capital. Closed-ended funds are normally limited life structures, but the term 'closed-ended' means that a finite number of units will be in issue for long periods of time. Compare with Open-Ended Fund.

Club Deal
Term for CRE transactions involving several lenders.

Comisión Nacional del Mercado de Valores (CNMV)
The Spanish securities market regulator.

CMBS
See Commercial Mortgage Backed Securities/Securitisation.

Co-Insurance
The sharing of risk by insurer and insured or by two or more insurers each taking liability for an agreed proportion of the whole amount at risk either immediately or in sequential layers.

Collar
The lowest rate acceptable to a note purchaser or the lowest price acceptable to the issuer.

Collateral
Those assets belonging to a Borrower or Issuer which are secured in favour of the Lender or Noteholders, respectively. Should the Borrower or Issuer default on its obligations under the Loan Agreement or conditions of the Notes, the Lender or the Noteholders can apply the secured or pledged assets to make good any amounts owed to them (in the case of Securitisation, subject to any priority of payments).

Collateralised Bond Obligation (CBO)
A security backed by a pool of corporate bonds.

Collateralised Debt Obligation (CDO)
A security backed by a pool of various types of debt, which may include corporate bonds sold in the capital markets, loans made to corporations by institutional lenders and tranches of securitisations.

Collateralised Debt Obligation Squared (CDO^2)
A CDO backed by a Portfolio of Securities issued by other CDOs.

Collateral Debt Security
The underlying debt obligations (or Collateral) that comprise the Portfolio of a CDO or a CLO.

Collateralised Loan Obligation (CLO)
CLO can be used in two contexts. First, it can refer to the Debt Securities backed by a Portfolio of Loans made to corporations by institutional Lenders, usually commercial banks. Second, to the overall transaction by which the Securities are issued and sold in the Capital Markets.

Collateralised Mortgage Obligation (CMO)
A security backed by a pool of mortgage loans or some combination of residential mortgage loans and agency securities. CMO issuances usually involves multiple classes of securities with varying maturities and coupons.

Collection Account
The account into which (generally) all payments and collectables received on mortgages are deposited.

Combined LTV Ratio
An LTV ratio calculated in situations where a property secures more than one mortgage loan.

Comfort Letter
Either: (a) a letter from one party to an agreement to the other that certain actions which are not contemplated by the agreement will not taken; or (b) an independent auditor's letter providing assurance that information in the registration statement and prospectus is correct and that no material changes have occurred since its preparation. This does not positively state the information is correct, only that the accountants are not aware of any-thing to indicate it is not correct. This is therefore sometimes called a cold comfort letter.

COMI
See Centre of Main Interest.

Commercial Mortgage Backed Securities or Commercial Mortgage Backed Secur-itisations (CMBS)
The CMBS abbreviation is used in two contexts. The former refers to securities that are backed by one or more pools of mortgages secured by commercial real estate, such as shopping centres, industrial parks, office buildings and hotels. All principal and interest from the mortgages flow to the noteholders in a pre-determined sequence. The latter refers to the overall transaction by which the securities are issued and sold in the capital markets.

CMBS 2.0
A term used to describe the new self-imposed industry standards, and regulatory and legislative changes to the CMBS market.

CMBS Noteholder Forum
A method used by CMBS noteholders to identify and communication with each other, managed by a forum co-ordinatior

Commercial Real Estate Collateralised Debt Obligations (CRE CDOs)
CRE CDO can be used in two contexts. First, it can refer to Debt Securities that are backed by a Portfolio of Mortgage Loans, Securities, B Loans or other debt interests related to commercial real estate. Second, it can refer to the overall transaction by which the Securities are issued and sold in the Capital Markets.

Commonhold
A form of land ownership in England and Wales, established by the Commonhold and Leasehold Reform Act 2002. It combines Freehold ownership of a single property within a larger development, with mem-bership of a limited company that will own and manage the common parts of the development. Although most likely to be used in relation to resi-

581

dential flats, Commonhold is also suitable for houses, mixed use and commercial developments.

Commercial Paper (CP)
Short-term promissory Notes with a maturity of generally less than 270 days and most commonly between 30 and 50 days or less.

Commercial Real Estate Finance Council - Europe
A trade association which promotes the strength and liquidity of commercial real estate finance. Formerly the Commercial Mortgage Securities Association - Europe.

Commingling Risk
The risk that cash belonging to an issuing SPE is mixed with cash belonging to a third party (for example, the originator or Servicer) with the result that, should the third party become insolvent/bankrupt, such cash cannot be separately identified or such cash is frozen in the accounts of the third party.

Common Security
Where the Senior and Mezzanine Lenders have a common security package over the assets of the Borrower entity.

Company Voluntary Arrangement (CVA)
A compromise or other arrangement with Creditors under the Insolvency Act 1986, which is implemented under the supervision of an insolvency practitioner (known as the nominee before the proposals are implemented, who then becomes known as the supervisor). The arrangement will be binding on Creditors if the relevant majorities vote in favour of the proposals at properly convened meetings of Creditors and Shareholders of the company. The arrangement does not affect the rights of secured or preferential Creditors unless they agree to the proposals. Small companies have an optional *moratorium* before any CVA is put into place.

Compliance Certificate
A certificate typically signed by a director of a Borrower confirming that the Borrower is in compliance with the financial covenants and certain other obligations set out in the Loan Agreement.

Compulsory Purchase Order
An order issued by the government, or local authority, which enables the local authority to compulsorily purchase land in order to enable development, whether it be for highways purposes, or for building construction.

Concentration Risk
A risk that a pool which is not particularly diverse will suffer disproportionately from certain economic or market developments or changes. Having a diverse pool of loans mitigates this risk.

582

Concessions
An incentive offered to attract and retain tenants whereby payments under a lease are reduced, most often through a rent free period. These make the calculation of net cash flow (and correspondingly debt service coverage ratios) difficult to calculate.

Conciliateur
French term for an insolvency administrator.

Conditions Precedent
Those conditions which must be satisfied before a Lender is prepared to advance funds to a Borrower. The conditions precedent required by a Lender will be listed in the Loan Agreement and include, amongst other things, board resolutions of the Obligors, valuations of the property and a legal report on title. Sometimes referred to as "closing conditions".

Conduit
The legal entity which provides the link between the lender(s) originating loans and the ultimate investor(s). The conduit purchases loans from third parties and once sufficient volume has been accumulated, pools these loans to sell in the CMBS market. In the European CMBS market the pool is generally of less than twenty loans with a wide or narrow range of properties. On the other hand, in the US market the pool may consist of anything between 50 to 100 loans secured on a wide range of properties.

Confirmation
A document that evidences the economics of a Derivative trade and governs the performance of the dealer and end user upon the occurrence of certain contemplated events that may occur during the term of the trade. A Confirmation may be either a short-form or long-form. The short form version is executed in connection with an existing ISDA Master Agreement and a long-form Confirmation is typically executed in anticipation of the dealer and counterparty entering into an ISDA Master Agreement, which is the best practice.

Contrat de Reservation
A reservation contract between the buyer and the developer in French development transactions, which deals with the guaranteed price of the property when built, payment stages and technical specifications.

Control Valuation Event or CVE
A term relevant to AB Structure as being the point in time when the value of the property serving as Collateral for the whole Loan has decreased to such an extent that the B Lender is not likely to get a meaningful economic recovery on their investment (i.e. repayment of the B Loan). Following the occurrence of a Control Valuation Event the relevant B Lender can no longer exercise its Cure Rights.

Controlling Class

The class of Noteholders in a Securitisation that has the contractual right to control the occurrence of certain events, such as forced redemptions, following an Event of Default or certain tax related events. In CMBS transactions the Controlling Class is normally the most subordinate class of Notes, while in CDO transactions the Controlling Class is normally the most Senior Class of Notes. In order to address conflicts of interest among different parts of the capital structure, other classes or parties (including the Controlling Party) may have a right to vote on or to veto certain actions of or with respect to the issuing entity.

Controlling Class Representative (CCR)

Appointed by the Controlling Class, the Controlling Class Representative has contractual consent or consultation rights in connection with the proposed actions of the Servicer/Special Servicer in connection with a serviced loan.

Controlling Party

The party with the contractual right to approve and direct certain acts of the Servicer or Special Servicer. In the context of AB Structures, the Controlling Party is typically the holder of the B Loan pending the occurrence of a Control Valuation Event and thereafter the Controlling Class in a CMBS. See also Operating Advisor.

Constant Prepayment Rate

The percentage of the outstanding principal which will theoretically be prepaid in one year, estimated based on a constant (rather than variable) rate of prepayment.

Controlled Amortisation

A period that may follow the revolving period of a transaction, during which the outstanding balance of the related securities is partially repaid. A controlled amortisation period is usually 12 months in length.

Core Real Estate Investments

Property investments that have the following defining characteristics: they are substantially rented, they have an orderly Lease expiration schedule, they are of high quality and are from the four basic property types—offices, industrial, retail and multi-family. Core Real Estate Investments must also be well maintained in a major city, carry no more than 50% debt, have an internal rate of return of approximately 6-8%, have low roll-over and an investment structure with significant control.

Core-Plus Real Estate Investments

Property investments that are relatively safe but are riskier than Core Real Estate investments. Core-Plus Real Estate Investments generally have an internal rate of return from 8% to 11% and involve debt at 50% to 60% of the property's value.

Corporate Guarantee
A form of credit enhancement whereby the issuer or a third party provides a guarantee in respect of certain losses up to a specified sum. The guarantor will be subject to minimum rating requirements.

Corporation Tax
Tax payable by a company on its profits.

Corrected Loan
A loan which, after being transferred to the Special Servicer for handling has been corrected and is now reperforming.

Cost of Funds
The cost of borrowing money. For a Borrower, it is the effective rate it pays on its current debt, namely interest and fee charges. Cost of funds can be measured before and after tax however, because interest expense is deductible, the after-tax cost is seen most often.

Counterparty
A party to a Derivatives or Hedging contract that may be, in the case of a Derivatives trade, either the dealer or the end user and, in the case of Hedging transaction, the Hedge Counterparty.

Covenant
In a legal context, a promise to do or not to do something. In a financial context, the term used to describe the financial worth of a company and is normally ascertained by reference to trading figures or other financial assessments. In a contractual context, the term refers to the contractual obligations contained in a Lease or Loan Agreement. Contractual covenants can be positive (requiring the covenantor to take action) or negative (requiring the covenantor to refrain from taking action).

Core Capital
Core Capital or Tier 1 Capital is a term used to describe the capital adequacy of a bank and includes equity capital and disclosed reserves.

Cost of Equity
The return a company theoretically pays to its shareholders.

Coupon
The rate of interest payable on a bond or other debt security.

Covered Bonds
Debt Securities backed by a Portfolio of Mortgages or other public sector Loans. Covered Bonds are issued by banks and remain on the issuing bank's balance sheet and provide the holders of the Covered Bonds will full recourse to the assets of the originator. Covered Bonds can be contrasted to

CMBS, which are off-balance sheet debt obligations entitling the holders of the CMBS recourse only to the assets securitised.

CP
See Commercial Paper.

CPS Template
The template for Credit Derivative Transaction on Asset Backed Security With Cash or Physical Settlement published by ISDA in 2005, as amended. This template adopts the Credit Derivatives Definitions to address trading of ABCDS in European markets.

CRA Regulation
See European Communities Regulation on Credit Rating Agencies.

CRD
See Capital Requirements Directive.

CRD 2
A 2007 European directive which makes changes to CRD by improving the quality of firms' capital by establishing a clear EU-wide criteria for assessing the eligibility of hybrid capital to be considered as part of a firm's overall capital, risk management of securities, supervision of cross-border banking groups and amending certain technical provisions of CRD to correct unintentional errors.

CRD 3
A 2009 European directive which makes further changes to CRD to complement CRD 2 which includes higher capitalisation requirements for re-securitisations, updating disclosure standards for securitisation exposures to increase market confidence and strengthening trading book capital requirements.

CRD 4
A 2014 European directive which makes further changes to CRD by reforming the EU's prudential requirements for credit institutions and investment firms, as well as EU legislation relating more generally to credit institutions.

Crédit-Bail Immobilier
The French property leasing market.

Credit Committee
The committee within a bank, building society or other financial institution that assesses the credit risk to the bank of it making a Loan to a Borrower. The credit committee ultimately approves the terms on which a Loan is made to that Borrower and the Security it requires from the Borrower.

Credit Default Swap
A credit default swap is a contract whereby the protection seller agrees to pay to the protection buyer the settlement amount should certain credit events occur. This gives protection to the protection buyer, in return for which the protection buyer will pay the protection seller a premium.

Credit Derivatives
Instruments used in the capital markets to re-allocate credit risk from one party to another, such as credit default swaps, total return swaps and credit-linked notes.

Credit Derivatives Definitions
The ISDA 2003 Credit Derivatives Definitions. These were published by ISDA in order to facilitate the trading of credit risk of operating companies with a large public float of Debt Securities.

Credit Enhancement
An instrument or mechanism which operates alongside the mortgage collateral to enhance the credit quality of the mortgage backed securities and thereby support the desired credit rating of the securities. Basically these are elements within the structure of a securitisation which are designed to ensure that investors do not suffer from decreases in the value of the underlying assets.

Credit Enhancer
A party that agrees to provide credit enhancement for a pool of assets by making payments, usually up to a specified amount, should the cash flow produced by the underlying pool of assets be less than the amounts contractually required due to defaults by the underlying obligors.

Credit Guarantee Scheme
A UK Government scheme launched in October 2008 and closed to new issuance in February 2010 that was intended to provide sufficient liquidity in the short term, make available new capital to UK banks and building societies to strengthen their resources, and ensure that the banking system has the funds necessary to maintain lending in the medium term.

Credit-Linked Note
A note, payment of which is dependant on a credit event occurring or credit measure existing with respect to a reference entity or pool of assets.

Credit Rating Agency (CRA)
See Rating Agency.

Credit Risk
The risk that the lender will be either (1) repaid less than the amount owed to it, (2) repaid over a longer period than originally agreed or, in the worst case, (3) not be repaid at all.

587

Credit Support Annex (CSA)
A document often entered into in connection with a Credit Derivative transaction that states the parties' duties to deliver and return Collateral as a method of credit protection for the parties to the Credit Derivative transaction.

Credit Tenant
A tenant which is rated as investment grade.

Credit Tenant Lease
A lease of part or all of a commercial property to a credit tenant.

Credit Tenant Lease Loans (CTL)
Mortgage loan secured by commercial properties occupied by investment-grade credit tenants. The loans are underwritten and structured based on the anticipated cash flow from the leases rather than on the value of the underlying real estate.

Creditor
An entity to whom money is owed.

Creditors' Voluntary Liquidation (CVL)
A CVL commences when the members of a company pass a special resolution to the effect that the company should be wound up.

CRE Finance Council Investor Reporting Package (CREFC IRP)
Package of bond, loan and property level information provided for CMBS securitisations.

Cross-Collateralisation
A provision by which collateral for one mortgage also serves as collateral for other mortgage(s) in the structure. This is a technique for enhancing the protection provided to a lender which adds value to the structure and therefore is a form of credit enhancement. Generally seen in connection with commercial mortgage loans.

Cross-Default
Where a borrower automatically defaults under one loan in the event that it has defaulted under another loan, effectively giving the lender the benefit of the default provisions under both loans.

Crystallisation
The point in time following a default or similar event when a Floating Charge is converted into a Fixed Charge over the assets to which it attaches.

CSA
See Credit Support Annex.

Cure Payments
Payments made by a B Lender when exercising its Cure Rights. Cure Payments can comprise: (a) Prepayment of the A Loan in an amount necessary to ensure compliance with the underlying remediable default, together with all other related payments in respect of the A Loan which the Borrower would have had to make as a result of such Prepayment had the Borrower made the Prepayment itself; (b) placing on deposit or posting of Collateral or a Letter of Credit in an amount equal to any shortfall that triggered a remediable default; and (c) placing on deposit on behalf of the A Lenders in an amount equal to the Prepayment of the A Loan which would have been required to have been received from the Borrower to ensure that the Borrower could have remedied the remediable default.

Cure Loan
A loan deemed to be made by a Mezzanine Lender to a Mezzanine Borrower in an amount equal to any cure payment made by a Mezzanine Lender to a Senior Lender to remedy, typically, a non-payment default or a financial covenant default by a Senior Borrower, in accordance with the terms of the relevant intercreditor agreement.

Cure Rights
Rights given to a subordinated lender which enables it to cure certain remediable Loan level defaults within a certain time period and include, amongst others, the right to make Cure Payments.

Current Delinquency Status
The delinquency status of a loan as of the current date.

Custodian
A bank or other financial institution that holds Securities and other financial assets for safe custody and record keeping on behalf of investors. A Custodian will usually be required to hold Securities on behalf of those entities which are not participants in the clearing systems.

Customary Laws
Traditional common rule or practice that has become an intrinsic part of the accepted and expected conduct in a community, profession or trade and is treated as a legal requirement.

Cut off date
The date the underlying pool of assets which secures a CMBS issuance is identified, calculations are based on this before issuing the securities.

CVA
See Company Voluntary Arrangement.

CVE
See Control Valuation Event.

CVL
See Creditors' Voluntary Liquidation.

D

Dach und Fach
German leases which require the tenant to pay all expenses, with the exception of expenses associated with the roof and structure of the building.

Dark Space
Empty space in a property for which the tenant continues to pay rent. Tenants in large properties may exercise break rights in leases should any other tenant go dark.

DCF
See Discounted Cash Flow.

Dealer
An entity, usually a bank or broker, whose economic function is to make a market so that buyers and sellers can readily transact in that market.

Debenture
A document evidencing the indebtedness of one party to another and the terms and conditions governing the relationship between the creditor who lends funds to the debtor who in turn repays the principal amount lent to it with or without interest.

Debenture (UK)
An instrument executed by a Borrower as a deed in favour of a Lender, providing the Lender with Security over the whole or substantially the whole of the Borrower's assets and undertaking. A Debenture typically creates a Fixed Charge over the assets of the Borrower which are not disposed of in the ordinary course of business of the company and a Floating Charge over the rest of the company's undertaking and reserving to the Lender the power to appoint an Administrator or a Receiver with extensive authority to get in the assets, run the Borrower's business and dispose of the assets either piecemeal or as part of a sale of the business as a going concern.

Debenture (US)
A document evidencing the indebtedness of one party to another and the terms and conditions governing the relationship between the Creditor who lends funds to the Debtor who in turn repays the principal amount lent to it with or without interest.

Debt Service Payments
Payments which the borrower is required to make under the relevant credit agreement.

Debt Securities
Debt obligations issued in the form of a Bond or Note representing a promise from the Issuer to repay at some future date. In Securitisation transactions, Issuers will issue various classes of Debt Securities with varying risk and return profiles.

Debtor
An entity who owes money.

Deed of Trust
A US real estate Security instrument pursuant to which a grantor (the Borrower) grants a Lien on real property to the Trustee for the benefit of the beneficiary (the Lender) to secure a debt. A deed of trust usually also includes an assignment of Leases and rents and a Security interest in fixtures and personal property.

Debt Service
The scheduled payments on a loan, including principal, interest and other fees stipulated in the credit agreement.

Debt Service Coverage Ratio (DSCR)
The net cash flow generated by an income-generating property on an annual basis divided by the annual debt service payments required under the terms of the mortgage loan or loans entered into for the purpose of financing the property. This is generally expressed as a multiple and gives a measure of a property's ability to cover debt service payments. Should this ratio drop below 1.0, there will be insufficient cash flow from the property to cover debt payments.

Debt Yield
A financial metric considered in the underwriting process of a CRE loan. The Debt Yield is calculated as the ratio of total annual cashflows generated by the property (and available for debt servicing) to the principal balance of the CRE loan.

Default
A violation of the terms and conditions set out in the relevant credit agreement.

Default
An event which with the passing of time or the giving of notice would constitute an Event of Default. Default is often used loosely to refer to an Event of Default.

Defeasance
The setting aside of cash or a portfolio of high-quality assets to cover the remaining interest and principal payments due with respect to a debt.

Defective Title
A title to land affected by a matter which leaves the ownership or use of the land open to challenge or otherwise unmarketable.

Deferred Consideration
A term used by practitioners to refer to consideration that will or may be payable sometime in the future rather than at completion. Deferred Consideration may be payable in a number of different ways including cash, loan notes and shares.

Deferred Interest
The amount of interest that is added to the principal balance of a debt obligation (whether a Loan or Bond) when the contractual terms of that debt obligation allow for a payment of interest to be made in an amount that is less than the scheduled amount of interest due.

Deferred Maintenance Account
An account set up by a borrower to cover the cost of any repairs or future maintenance of a property.

Deleveraging
The reduction of the ratio of debt to equity.

Delinquency
Failure to comply with a debt obligation by the specified due date.

Demand Notes
Short-term loans or notes which include a provision that repayment can be demanded or the note called should the lender choose. Such notes often require all cash flows net of debt service to be applied to amortise a loan should the borrower fail to demonstrate progress towards refinancing. These can be fast pay whereby if the balloon payment of a balloon mortgage is not met, the borrower must apply excess cash flows to pay down the loan balance.

Depreciation
The decline in value of an asset as it ages.

Derivative
A financial instrument whose value depends on the characteristics and value of an underlying asset, typically a commodity, Bond, Interest Rate, equity or currency.

592

Determination Date
The date of the month used as a set off date for calculations of the payments due on securities.

Development
The making of any material change in the use of any buildings or other land, not including internal alterations that do not materially affect its appearance.

Development Construction Cost
The total cost of construction of a project to completion, excluding site values and finance costs.

Development Finance
A Loan made to a Borrower to fund the Development Construction Costs in respect of a Development.

Development Pipeline
Typically the combination of a development programme, together with proposed schemes that are not yet included in the Development programme but are more likely to proceed than not.

Direct Property Fund
A fund that invests 100% in Direct Property Investment and holds no property shares, REITs, other equities or other indirect holdings.

Direct Property Investment
The acquisition of legal and/or beneficial title to real estate.

Discounted Cash Flow or DCF
A financial appraisal based on analysis of future income flow on an asset, allowing for a discount back to present day values.

Discounted Purchase Option/Pay-Off (DPO)
The settlement of debt for less than the entire outstanding balance under the loan.

Discount Margin
The difference between the price and the face value of a security.

Discount to NAV
The percentage difference between the Net Asset Value of the assets of the company (subject to certain adjustments for debt etc) and the market capitalisation of the company.

Distressed Mortgage Loan
Another term for a non performing loan.

Distribution Date
The date of the month when payments on securities are made to investors. Necessarily this falls a few days after the Determination Date.

Dodd–Frank Wall Street Reform and Consumer Protection Act
The Dodd-Frank Act is a US Act which changes the regulatory structure through creating new agencies and merging or removing others in an effort to streamline the regulatory process, increasing oversight of specific institutions regarded as a systemic risk, amending the Federal Reserve Act and promoting transparency.

Dominant Tenement
See Easement.

Double Lux-co
CRE loan structuring solution used by foreign lenders and in larger transactions, allowing the Security Agent to enforce its enforce its share pledge in Luxembourg.

Double Net Lease
See Net Net Lease.

Double Taxation Avoidance Agreements
The Double Tax Avoidance Agreements (DTAA) is a bilateral agreement entered into between two countries. The basic objective is to avoid taxation of income in both the countries (i.e. Double taxation of same income) and to promote and foster economic trade and investment between the two countries.

Dow Jones US Real Estate Index
An index that is designed to provide measures of real estate Securities and is composed primarily of REITs.

downREIT
A REIT structure similar to that of an UPREIT, except that the downREIT may own property directly as well as property being held by one or more Limited Partnerships of which the REIT is general partner and a limited partner.

DSCR
See Debt Service Coverage Ratio.

DTAA
See Double Taxation Avoidance Agreements.

Due Diligence
In practical terms this is the investigation and fact finding exercise carried out by a potential purchaser to allow him to make a more well-informed

decision about whether to purchase or invest. In legal terms this is a measure of prudence as can be expected from a reasonable and prudent person in the circumstances of the particular deal. The degree of prudence depends on the facts of the case and is judged on industry standards. In a CMBS transaction, investors rely on the expertise of the professionals involved as it is impossible for them to inspect properties, financial records and the due diligence such professionals have carried out.

E

Earn Out Loans
A credit agreement under which the original principal balance can be resized for further advances should the operating performance of a property be able to service the additional debt.

Easement
A right benefiting a piece of land (known as the dominant tenement) that is enjoyed over land owned by someone else (known as the servient tenement).

EBA
European Banking Authority. Established in January 2011 by the European Parliament; it has taken over all existing and ongoing tasks and responsibilities from the Committee of European Banking Supervisors (CEBS). It is responsible for EU-wide stress testing and recapitalisation needs.

EBITA
Accounting term to mean the earnings of a company (or group of companies) before the deduction of interest, tax and amortisation.

EC
European Community (often used interchangeably with EU).

ECON
European Parliament's Committee on Economic and Monetary Affairs, responsible for the regulation of financial services and the free movement of capital within the EU.

EEA
The European Economic Area, a common market (established in 1994) among members of the EU and EFTA.

EFTA
The European Free Trade Association.

EMEA
Regional designation for Europe, the Middle East and Africa.

EMIR
European Markets and Infrastructure Regulation.

Encumbrance
A claim or a right to property by a party that is not the property owner. Typical encumbrances include issues such as Leases, Mortgages and restrictive covenants.

End User
An entity that enters a Derivatives contract in order to hold the position whether for Hedging, speculative or arbitrage purposes and not for the purpose of market making.

Enforceability Opinion
A legal opinion stating that the obligations imposed on a party by an agreement will be legal, valid and binding on that party in accordance with its terms, subject to certain standard assumptions and qualifications.

Enforcement
The process whereby the lender takes control of the collateral including the cash flow from the mortgaged property.

Environmental Risk
The risk of the value of a property being decreased by the presence of hazardous materials (for example asbestos). Rating agencies may include the possibility of non-compliance with future environmental standards in their analysis even if a property complies with current environmental standards.

EPF
The European Property Federation.

EPRA
European Public Real Estate Association; an industry body for quoted property companies and investors in quoted property stocks.

Equitable Mortgage
See Mortgage.

Equitable Transfer
The transfer of the beneficial ownership, as opposed to legal ownership, of property. This is often seen in European RMBS.

Equitable Transfer
The transfer of the beneficial ownership, as opposed to legal ownership, of property. This is often seen in European securitisation transactions as it is often significantly cheaper to arrange than a legal transfer.

Equity
A provision allowing a lender or an investor to receive an equity based return in addition to normal rates upon the occurrence of certain events.

Equity Finance
Money in the form of share capital made available to a company, generally for a specific venture such as a development where the subscriber, as part of the bargain, becomes entitled to a share of any profit, whether or not in receipt of dividends.

Equity Release
Retail financial product, usually in the form of a lifetime Mortgage or home reversion plan, that allows residential property owners to realise some or all of the equity and remain living in their house.

Equivalent Yield
The return on an investment calculated by dividing the mean income by the value/purchase price and expressed in terms of a percentage.

ERISA (or Employee Retirement Income Security Act of 1974)
US legislation which stipulates the standard of risk suitable and acceptable for private pension plan investments.

ERV
See Estimated Rental Value.

Escrow Account
An account jointly held by the Borrower and Lender containing funds for capital expenses, such as improvement or insurance.

ESMA
The European Securities and Markets Association.

Establishment
In the context of cross-border insolvencies any place of operations where the Debtor carries out a non-transitory economic activity.

Estate
A term used in common law to signify all the property belonging to a person.

Estimated Rental Value
The rent that a property might reasonably be able to command in the open market at a given time, subject to the terms of the relevant Lease.

ETF
See Exchange Traded Fund.

EU
The European Union (established in 1993), a political and economic union of sovereign states aimed at maintaining freedom of trade and developing community of legal and economic structures.

EU Insolvency Regulation
The EU Insolvency Regulation (1346/2000) came into effect on May 31 2002. The primary function of the regulation is to codify the manner in which a member state determines whether it has jurisdiction to open insolvency proceedings.

EU Securitisation Regulation
Legislative proposal published in September 2015 by the European Commission to create a European framework for simple, transparent and standardised (STS) securitisations.

European Communities Regulation on CRAs
This came into force in 2009 and introduced a harmonised approach to the regulation of credit rating activities in the European Union and established a registration system for CRAs.

Eurobond
Bond denominated in a currency other that the home currency of the country or market in which it is issued.

Euro Interbank Offered Rate (EURIBOR)
The interest rate at which interbank term deposits denominated in Euros are offered by one prime bank in the euro zone to another prime bank in the euro zone. EURIBOR is established by a panel of about 60 European banks. As with LIBOR, there are EURIBOR rates for deposits of various maturities.

Euroclear
One of two principal clearing systems in the Eurobond Market, functioning much like the Depository Trust Company in the US market. Euroclear began operations in 1968, is located in Brussels and is managed by Morgan Guaranty Bank.

European Central Bank (ECB)
The European Central Bank is the central bank for the euro and administers monetary policy of the Eurozone.

European Insurance and Occupational Pension Authority (EIOPA)
An independent advisory body to the European Parliament, European Council and European Commission which monitors and identifies trends as well as potential risks and vulnerabilities stemming from the micro-prudential level across borders and sectors.

European Investor Reporting Package (E-IRP)
A product designed by CREFC-Europe which provides relevant data that loan and securities investors can use to compare loans and bonds across multiple European transactions.

European Systemic Risk Board
The European Systemic Risk Board (ESRB) was established in 2010 to oversee the financial system of the European Union (EU) and prevent and mitigate systemic risk.

Event of Default
An event specified in a commercial agreement where a non-defaulting party can terminate the agreement. In the context of debt finance and Securitisation transactions, an Event of Default will entitle the Lender or Noteholders (respectively) to declare all amounts owing by the Borrower or Issuer (as applicable) to accelerate the debt obligations as being immediately due and payable thereby enabling Enforcement. Typical events of default include non-payment of interest or principal, breach of representation, breach of covenant, cross-default, material adverse change and insolvency. See also Default.

Event Risk
Certain events (for example natural disaster, industrial accident and takeover) cannot be predicted via a standard method of credit analysis. The risk that such events pose to an issuer's ability to make its debt service payments is the Event Risk.

Excess Interest/Excess Spread
Interest or other income received by a Securitisation Issuer which exceeds the stated amount of interest required to be paid on the various classes of Securities.

Excess Servicing Fee
The portion of the interest charged to underlying obligors in a securitisation structure that is in excess of the interest portion of debt service payments or the regular servicing fee.

Excess Spread
Interest or other income received by a Securitisation Issuer which exceeds the stated amount of interest required to be paid on the various classes of Securities.

Exchange
The exchange of contracts in a real estate acquisition.

Exchange Controls
Restrictions on conversion of a country's currency for another imposed by its government in an attempt to improve its balance of payments position.

Exchange Traded Fund (ETF)
Funds traded like normal shares which allow investors to spread investments by tracking the performance of an entire index.

Exit Value
The value of a property on a particular date, either at the end of an agreed Loan term, or applied to a date an investor has targeted to sell an investment in the future.

Exit Debt Yield
A measure of the recoverable proceeds of a loan based on current cash flow and the balance of the loan at maturity.

Expected Maturity
The date as of which securities are expected to be repaid in full based on a specified assumption regarding the rate of repayment of the underlying assets.

Expense Ratio
The ratio of operating expenses and operating revenues.

Expense Stops
Lease clauses which limit the amount of a landlords obligation for expense on a property, with expenses in excess of this amount being met by the tenant.

Exposure at Default
A lender's exposure at the time of default and is equal to the outstanding amount of loan principal and interest accruing at that time.

Extend and Amend
This is an extension to the loan maturity date usually in exchange for an uplift in margin or a more punitive amortisation profile.

Extend and Pretend
See Extend and Amend.

Extension Adviser
A third party with the right or obligation to approve loan extensions or notifications recommended by the Master or Special Servicer.

Extension/Extension Option
A grace period following the contractual termination date given to a borrower to repay a loan (through refinancing or sale). Used to prevent foreclosing on the property and the additional cost this incurs.

600

Extension Risk
The potential inability to refinance balloon mortgages in a timely manner, with the result that the life of the security may be extended beyond the expected life.

External Credit Enhancement
Credit support provided by a highly rated third-party to enhance the rating of the securitisation structure.

Extraordinary General Meeting ("EGM")
An unscheduled meeting of shareholders called to approve non-routine matters. Under the Companies Act 2006, the term "extraordinary general meeting" is no longer applicable and instead the term "general meeting" is used to describe a meeting of company members.

F

Face Rent
Rental payments without adjustments for any lease concessions (for example rent-free periods).

Facility Agent
The entity that deals with the day-to-day administration of a Loan on behalf of the Lenders.

Facility Office
The office or branch of a Lender through which it performs its obligations under a Loan Agreement.

Fair Value
A valuation system that requires banks to mark the value of their assets to market price. The fair value concept focuses on the price that would be received upon the sale of an asset or paid to transfer a liability.

Fast Pay
A descriptive term applied to a security or a transaction structure aimed at ensuring repayment of principal on an accelerated schedule.

Fannie Mae (or Federal National Mortgage Association or FNMA)
A quasi private US corporation which purchases and pools conventional mortgages then issues securities using these as collateral. Holders of Fannie Mae certificates are guaranteed full and timely payment of principal and interest.

Fatwa/Fatawah
A written confirmation of a Sharia'a scholar or board. This has no binding effect under secular law. Historically this was a short summary of the

decision, and more recently these have been structured like Anglo–American legal opinions.

FCA
See Financial Conduct Authority.

FDI
See Foreign Direct Investment.

FDIC
See Federal Deposit Insurance Corporation.

Federal Deposit Insurance Corporation (FDIC)
A US government agency that insures deposits of depository institutions.

Feeders
Entities created above the fund to accommodate the special (often tax-related) requirements of one or more investors.

Feuhold
The Scottish equivalent of Freehold.

FFO
FFO or funds from operations is a term for the recurring income delivered by properties owned by REITs.

FHCMC
See Freddie Mac.

Fiduciary
A person to whom power or property is entrusted for the benefit of another (e.g. a director owes fiduciary duties to the company of which he is a director).

Final Maturity
See Legal Maturity.

Finance Documents
A collective term used to refer to those documents entered into between the Lender, the Borrower and any Obligors. A Lender will require all Finance Documents to be entered into before the Lender will advance funds to the Borrower. Typically, the Finance Documents will include the Loan Agreement, Security Documents, Hedging Documents, Intercreditor Agreement and fee letters. A breach of any Finance Document will typically constitute an Event of Default under the Loan Agreement.

Finance Lease
A Lease that transfers the risks and rewards of a fixed asset without transferring legal ownership. The Lender (often a finance house) buys the asset and then Leases it to the Borrower (lessee). The lessee is required to make Lease payments over the life of the Lease equivalent to the full value of the fixed asset and will also pay a return on capital to the Lender. At the end of the Lease, provided the lessee has paid the Lender all amounts due to it, the asset is transferred to the lessee.

Finance Parties
A collective term used in syndicated or securitised Loans to refer to those entities within the Lender group and includes the current Lenders, the Facility Agent, the Arranger, the Security Trustee and any Hedge Counterparty. Obligors owe obligations to all the Finance Parties and so the Security is held on trust by the Security Trustee for the benefit of all Finance Parties. Also referred to as the Secured Parties.

Financial Conduct Authority (FCA)
A body that oversees the regulation of all providers of financial services in the UK.

Financial Covenants
Positive or negative obligations on the borrower relating purely to financial matters, for example to maintain LTV to a certain percentage.

Financial Institutions and Reform, Recovery and Enforcement Act 1989 (FIRREA)
A US federal act that revamped the regulation and insurance of depositary financial institutions. The Act created several new institutions including the Resolution Trust Corporation.

Financial Stability Board (FSB)
Established in 2009 at the London G-20 summit, the FSB is an international body that monitors and makes recommendations about the global financial system.

Financial Stability Forum (FSF)
Established in 1999 at the behest of G7 finance ministers and central bank governors, the purpose of the FSF was to identify and over see action to remove threats and vulnerabilities to the international financial system. The FSF was succeeded by the FSB in 2009.

Fintech
A term for the emerging financial services sector composed of companies seeking to use technology to bring innovation and efficiency to traditional financial services.

603

First Loss Piece
The most junior class of a CMBS which suffers losses from a mortgage pool before any other classes suffer.

Fixed Charge
A form of Security by which an asset or group of assets owned by a company are charged as Security for borrowings or other indebtedness. The chargor remains the legal owner of the asset subject to the Fixed Charge but is prohibited from dealing with such assets without the Lender's consent. A Fixed Charge will rank ahead of any Floating Charge in the order of repayment on insolvency. See also Floating Charge.

Fixed Charge Receiver
A Receiver appointed to deal with assets which are the subject of a Fixed Charge. See also Receiver.

Fixed Income Investor
An investor seeking a fixed (and therefore certain) rate of return on their investments.

Fixed Rate Interest
An Interest Rate that will not change during the term of a Loan.

Floating Charge
A form of Security by which an asset or group of assets owned by a company are charged as Security for borrowings or other indebtedness. The Lender's interest attaches to a changing Pool of assets until Crystallisation. The advantage of a Floating Charge is that, before insolvency, it allows the chargor to deal with charged assets during the course of a company's business without the consent of the Lender (e.g. by transferring or selling the assets). See also Fixed Charge, Crystallisation and Qualifying Floating Charge.

Floating Rate Interest
An Interest Rate which may vary during the term of the Loan. Typical Floating Rate Interest include LIBOR and EURIBOR.

Floating-Rate Notes
A class of securities having a variable (or floating), rather than fixed interest rate, but typically a margin above a market index.

Floor
A minimum price or a bottom limit on price.

FNMA
See Fannie Mae.

Fonds Commun de Créance (FCC)
A type of closed-end mutual debt fund used as a funding vehicle in French securitisations.

Forbearance
Relief from repayments under a loan, granted by the Lender in lieu of enforcing its security.

Foreclosure
A proceeding, in or out of court, brought a lender holding a mortgage on real property seeking to enable the lender to sell the property and apply the sale proceeds to satisfy amounts owned by the owner under the related loan.

Foreign Account Tax Compliant Act (FACTA)
FACTA is a US act that aims to improve tax compliance involving foreign financial assets and offshore accounts. Under FATCA, US taxpayers with specified foreign financial assets that exceed certain thresholds must report those assets to the IRS. FATCA will require foreign financial institutions to report directly to the IRS information about financial accounts held by US taxpayers, or held by foreign entities in which US taxpayers hold a substantial ownership interest.

Foreign Court
A judicial or other authority competent to control or supervise a Foreign Proceeding.

Foreign Direct Investment or *FDI*
A company from one country making a physical investment into real estate in another country.

Foreign Main Proceeding
A Foreign Proceeding pending in the country where the Debtor has its COMI.

Foreign Nonmain Proceeding
A Foreign Proceeding, other than a Foreign Main Proceeding, pending in a country where the Debtor has an establishment.

Foreign Proceeding
A judicial or administrative proceeding in a foreign country, including an interim proceeding, under a law relating to insolvency or adjustment of debt in which proceeding the assets and affairs of the Debtor are subject to control or supervision by a foreign court, for the purpose of reorganisation or liquidation.

Foreign Representative
A person or body, including a person or body appointed on an interim basis, authorised in a foreign proceeding to administer the reorganisation of the liquidation of the Debtor's assets or affairs or to act as a representative of such foreign proceeding.

Forwards
A contract that calls for the sale, in the future, of an asset. The price and quantity (as well as other terms) are agreed upon by the parties to a forward at the outset.

Forward Curve
The forward variable rate, often referred to generically as "the LIBOR forward rate" or simply a "forward" and, in aggregate, the "forward curve", which approximates what the relevant variable index will be at the beginning of each future interest period being considered.

Freddie Mac (or Federal Home Loan Mortgage Corporation or FHCMC)
A quasi private US corporation. This entity is charged with providing liquidity to the secondary market for single family mortgages and issues securities using these mortgages as the underlying collateral. Holders of Freddie Mac certificates are assured of timely payment of interest and eventual payment of principal.

Freehold
An estate in land which provides the holder of the estate with rights of ownership. There are several different types of Freehold estate. The most common are 'Fee simple' that is effectively absolute ownership of the land and 'Life estate' which effectively means ownership for the duration of the holder's life.

Freeholder
The owner of a Freehold.

FTSE 100
The benchmark index of the London Stock Exchange. It is a market value weighted index of the 100 largest UK stocks by market capitalisation.

FTSE NAREIT All REITs Index
A stock market index containing all qualified REITs with common stock traded on the New York Stock Exchange of NASDAQ National Market, without regard to any minimum size, liquidity criteria or free float adjustments. The index is maintained by FTSE Group, an independent company that began as a joint venture between the Financial Times and the London Stock Exchange.

Full Service Lease
A Lease which provides that the Landlord pays all building expenses. Also called a Gross Full Service Lease or a Gross Rent Lease.

Fully repairing and insuring (FRI) leases
Leases that are fully repairing and insuring (FRI or in US "triple-net"), such that while a property or part of a property is let, the tenant is assumed to pay the rent and all outgoings.

Funds of Funds
An investment fund that invests in other investment funds rather than investing directly in shares, Bonds or other Securities.

Fusion Deals
A CMBS which features a combination of conduit loans, small loans and large loans.

Futures
Highly standardised Forwards that are traded on an exchange.

G

G-7
Abbreviation for the Group of Seven, a forum of the world's leading industrial nations to meet and discuss global economic matters. G-7 members are: Canada, France, Germany, Italy, Japan, the UK and the US.

G-8
The G-7 plus Russia.

G-20
Established in 1999, the group of 20 finance ministers and central bank governors is a forum for discussion between industrial and emerging market countries on issues of global economic stability. The G-20 is comprised of 19 countries and the European Union. The 19 countries are: Argentina, Australia, Brazil, Canada, China, France, Germany, India, Indonesia, Italy, Japan, Mexico, Russia, Saudi Arabia, South Africa, South Korea, Turkey, the UK and the US.

GAAP
Acronym for generally accepted accounting principals. A standardised framework of guidelines for the preparation of financial statements. There are various sets of generally accepted accounting principals worldwide, such as US, UK and German.

Garantie Financière d'Achèvement (GFA)
A French completion guarantee or construction bond provided by the bank in French development finance transactions.

Garanzia sulla Cartolarizzazione delle Sofferenze (GACS)
An Italian guarantee scheme for the securitisation of non-performing loans which seeks to increase the liquidity in the Italian non-performing loan market by facilitating leverage on portfolio sales.

Gearing
An accounting term used to define the debt-to-equity ratio of a company. SPEs will typically be more highly geared than operating companies.

General/Multiline Insurer
An insurer which transacts business over a range of classes of insurance. Contrast with Monoline Insurer.

Generally Accepted Accounting Principals
See GAAP.

General Meeting
Formerly known as an extraordinary general meeting. A general meeting can be either a non-routine meeting of a company called for a specific purpose or an annual general meeting.

Global Financial Crisis (GFC)
The 2007-2009 global financial crisis.

GIC
See Guaranteed Investment Contract.

Ginnie Mae or *Governmental National Mortgage Association* or *GNMA*
A wholly-owned government corporation within the US Department of Housing and Urban Development. This entity is charged with providing liquidity to the secondary market for single family Mortgages by guaranteeing that investors will receive the timely payment of principal of and interest on Mortgage-backed Securities that are backed by federally insured or guaranteed Loans.

Globally Systematically Important Financial Institutions (GSIFIs)
A list of financial institutions produced by the Financial Stability Board whose failure in the Financial Stability Board's view could trigger a global financial crisis.

GNMA
See Ginnie Mae.

GOEF
German Open-Ended Funds; indirect real estate investment vehicles that are of particular importance in Germany. Shares are directly backed by properties and liquid assets held by the fund; as an open-ended vehicle, a fund can create new shares on demand, and investors buy shares at net asset value.

"Golden Share" Structure
A loan structure used in French transactions allowing the Agent to dismiss managers of the French entity and to appoint new managers of its choice without having to enforce its security interest over the shares of the French or Luxembourg entity.

Government National Mortgage Association (Ginnie Mae or GNMA)
This is a US government related agency which guarantees securities which use mortgages initially issued by approved lenders as their underlying collateral.

Government Sponsored Enterprise (GSE)
The collective description for the US government agencies formed to provide a secondary market for residential real estate loans. Includes Fannie Mae, Freddie Mac and Ginnie Mae.

Grace Period
The period of time during which a party, typically a Debtor, has to pay overdue amounts or remedy any other defaults before it incurs further interest and/or the relevant Creditor initiates enforcement proceedings.

Graduated Payment Mortgage
A mortgage where the individual loan payments are graduated on the basis of pre-defined schedules.

Granularity
This is achieved where an underlying pool of loans is made up of smaller loans. Pools which contain a small number of higher value loans are said to be less granular, or more lumpy.

Green Property Funds
Socially responsible property funds which invest in sustainable and/or carbon-neutral property investments and developments.

Greenfield Site
Previously undeveloped land which is, or is potentially, available for development, e.g. agricultural land.

Gross Asset Value
The appraised value of the properties in a REIT or Real Estate Fund.

Gross Development Value
The value of a development based on the assumption that such development has been completed and the building is fully let.

Gross Full Service Lease
A lease which provides that the landlord pays all building expenses. Also called a full service lease or a gross rent lease.

Gross Rent Lease
See Full Service Lease.

Ground Lease
A long Lease granted at a ground rent, i.e. a rent disregarding the value of any buildings or other improvements of the land but reflecting any right to develop the land.

Ground Rent
Rent paid for vacant land which is suitable for development.

GSE
See Government Sponsored Enterprise.

G-SIFIs
Globally systemically important financial institutions.

Guarantee
A promise from a third party to repay a debt if the original Borrower fails to do so. The Guarantee may extend beyond the payment obligations.

Guaranteed Investment Contract (GIC)
A deposit account provided by a financial institution that guarantees a minimum rate of return, thereby mitigating interest rate risk.

Guarantor
An entity which provides a Guarantee.

H

Haircut
The expression given to the reduction in the value attributed to an asset or the income or cash flow anticipated to be received from a property, usually by applying a percentage to this value.

Hard Costs
The element of the building cost or purchase cost of real estate which includes the land, building material, plant, machinery and inventory.

Head Lease
A Lease of property between the Freeholder and a Tenant which grants overall contractual responsibility of the property to one particular Tenant. The head lessee will usually sublet the property or part of the property to occupational Tenants pursuant to an Occupational Lease.

Head Rent
The rent paid by a head lessee to the Freeholder under a Head Lease.

Heads of Terms (HoTs)
A document which sets out the main commercial terms of a transaction. In a real estate Loan transaction the Heads of Terms would typically include the Interest Rate, the term of the Loan, the repayment schedule, fees, Events of Default, Financial Covenants and Conditions Precedent. Sometimes called a Term Sheet.

Hedge Counterparty
The entity which enters into Hedging transaction with a Borrower.

Hedge Fund
An investment fund that buys and sells assets on a speculative basis in order to out perform the market or index in which it is invested.

Hedging
A general term used to refer to strategies adopted to offset investment risks. Examples of hedging include the use of derivative instruments to protect against fluctuations in interest rates or currency exchange rates, or investment in assets whose value is expected to rise faster than inflation to protect against inflation (interest rate hedging, currency hedging and inflation rate hedging respectively).

Hedging Documents
The documents that document the Hedging arrangements entered into between the Borrower and the Hedge Counterparty and will usually include and ISDA Master Agreement and Schedule, a Confirmation and possibly a CSA.

Hipotecas Flotantes
A Spanish term for floating rate mortgages.

Hissas
An Islamic finance term referring to the sale and purchase of partnership interests from one partner to another.

HMRC (UK)
HM Revenue & Customs. A UK Government department formed on 18 April 2005 from a merger between the Inland Revenue and HM Customs &

Excise. The Government department responsible for the collection of taxes and the payment of some forms of state support.

HoldCo
An abbreviation for holding company. A holding company is established in order to exercise control over one or more other companies.

Horizontal Slice Option
The risk retention requirement introduced pursuant to the Dodd–Frank Wall Street Reform and Consumer Protection Act and the Alternative Investment Fund Managers Directive (AIFMD) for the sponsor to retain a first-loss position in an amount equal to at least 5% of the par value of all CMBS interests in the issuing entity issued as part of the securitisation transaction.

Housing Associations
Independent not-for-profit UK bodies that principally provide low-cost social housing.

Hurdle Rate
A break-even debt service calculation which establishes the maximum interest rate a mortgaged property can handle at maturity if the property must be refinanced. Also called break even debt service analysis.

Hybrid
A term used to refer to a whole-business securitisation. Such a transaction entails risks that are a hybrid of pure corporate risk and the risks associated with traditional securitisations backed by financial assets or diversified pools of corporate credits.

Hybrid Debt
Investments that have equity and debt features such as participating Mortgages, convertible Mortgages and convertible participating Mortgages.

Hyper-Amortisation
The accelerated paydown of a CMBS class achieved through the allocation of all principal and interest to that class.

Hypothekenpfandbriefe
See Pfandbriefe.

I

IBOR

IBOR or "Inter-Bank Offered Rate" is used generically as the variable-rate index in a CRE financing. The specific rate will have a prefix such as with

USD LIBOR, GBP LIBOR, EURIBOR, and others representing the variable rates most commonly used in any given currency.

ICE Benchmark Administration Limited (ICE)
Established in July 2013 following an announcement by the Hogg Tendering Advisory Committee, the ICE is an independent committee set up by the UK government to select the new administrator for LIBOR, replacing the British Banking Association.

ICE LIBOR
The ICE Benchmark Administration Limited's fixing of the London Inter-Bank Offered Rate. ICE LIBOR is often used as a benchmark or reference rate for short term interest rates. It is compiled by ICE and released to the market at about 11.00 each day. It replaced BBA LIBOR on 1 February 2014.

ICR
See Interest Cover Ratio.

IDB
Islamic Development Bank.

IFRS
International Financial Reporting Standards

IFRS Accounting Standards
A single set of accounting standards, developed and maintained by the International Accounting Standards Board.

IFSB
The Islamic Financial Services Board.

Ijara
An Islamic finance term meaning a lease. A predominant structure in Islamic real estate finance. Securitisations which use this structure are termed Ijara al Sukuk.

Illiquid
An asset which is not easily tradable, the opposite of liquid.

Impound or Escrow Account
An account jointly held by the borrower and lender containing funds for capital expenses, such as improvement or insurance.

In the Money
An option is described as being in the money when the price of the underlying instrument is above the strike or exercise price for a call option and below the strike price for a put option. The more an option is in the

money the more expensive it becomes. Options are described as being deep in the money when they are likely to expire in the money.

Income
The excess of revenue over expenses for an accounting period.

Income-to-interest cover
See Interest Cover Ratio.

Income-Producing Real Estate Exposure (IPRE)
Term to describe exposure to real estate assets such as office, retail space and multi-family, for the purposes of the IRB Approach.

Indenture
An agreement between the Issuer and the Trustee that specifies the terms and conditions of the securities.

Indemnity
An obligation undertaken by one party (rather than one imposed by force of law) to pay another party in the event that the second party suffers a specified loss.

Independent Commission on Banking
A commission established by the UK Government in June 2010 to consider structural and non related structural reforms to the UK banking sector to promote stability and competition.

Independent Director
A key component of SPEs. This is a member of the board of directors of the borrowing or issuing entity where a vote is required for certain important acts of the entity such as declaration of bankruptcy. This removes control of the entity from the hands of affiliated principals.

Indirect Property Fund
A fund that invests 100% in Indirect Property Investment.

Indirect Property Investment
Ownership of shares or units in a company or Partnership which holds legal and/or beneficial title to real estate, such as REITs and PUTs.

Initial Yield
The return on an investment calculated by dividing the current income by the purchase price of the investment.

INREV
Investors in Non-listed Real Estate Vehicles; the European industry association for investors in non-listed real estate funds.

Insolvency
The inability to pay debts when they fall due. Although not specifically defined in the Insolvency Act 1986, a company is deemed unable to pay its debts if: (i) a statutory demand as been served on it and not paid on time, (ii) it has failed to pay a judgement debt, (iii) the court is satisfied that it is unable to pay their debts as they fall due (the cash-flow test) or (iv) the court is satisfied that the value of its assets is less than the amount of its liabilities taking into account contingent and prospective liabilities (the balance sheet test). If a company is unable to pay its debts a Creditor may petition the court for it to be placed into compulsory liquidation.

Insuring Capacity
The financial amount which an insurer wishes and/or is able within its capital structure to commit to a particular risk or class of risks.

Intercreditor Agreement
An agreement which governs the relationship between the holders of senior and junior loans. Whilst this is expressed as an agreement, this document will usually be executed as a deed.

Interest Cover Ratio (ICR)
A ratio used to determine how easily a Borrower or Securitisation Issuer can pay interest due on a Loan or class of Securities. Generally calculated by dividing the amount of income a Borrower or Issuer receives by the amount of interest the Borrower or Issuer is required to pay in any given period.

Interest in Arrears
A rating designation where the full monthly payment on an underlying loan is not being advanced.

Interest Only Strip (IO Strip)
Should the interest rate on the underlying loans exceed the interest paid on the issued securities backed by the same, the surplus is removed and added as a further class, the IO strip. Usually sold for a small percentage of the price of the whole security, these can be very volatile, for example if there is a large amount of pre-payment this could remove the interest stream to pay the IO strip, usually curtailing the life span of the IO strip.

Interest Paid versus Interest Impacted
This clause in the CMBS structure determines how and when losses are allocated, for example before or after principal is paid. This has a major impact on the yield of the most junior noteholders.

Interest Payment Date
The date on which interest on the Loan is paid. Often shortened to IPD.

Interest Period
The period between two successive Interest Payment Dates. Interest on a Loan accrues during an Interest Period and is paid on the Interest Payment Date falling at the end of Interest Period.

Interest Proceeds
Collections received from underlying debt instruments that consist of interest payments and other non-principal receipts, such as finance charges.

Interest Rate
The rate at which interest is charged or is due on a debt obligation and typically consists of a Margin, an interest basis (such as LIBOR) and, in Loans, mandatory costs. See also Fixed Rate Interest and Floating Rate Interest.

Interest Rate Cap
Limits the rate to a maximum or cap thereby protecting the borrower from rising rates. Often purchased by the borrower.

Interest rate collar
Where an interest rate cap and an interest rate floor are sold simultaneously. If the interest rates move outside the range between the interest rate cap and the interest rate floor, the buyer will receive payment from the seller.

Interest Rate Hedge
A Derivative instruments that protects the Protection Buyer against Interest Rate Risk. Typically, the Protection Buyer will pay interest at a fixed rate to the Protection Seller and in return receive interest at a variable rate from the Protection Seller.

Interest Rate Risk
A change in interest rates may mean that interest earned on assets in a low interest rate environment will not be sufficient to service payments required in respect of liabilities incurred in a higher interest rate environment, thereby leading to shortfall. The risk of such shortfall (and the corresponding change in a security's value), is the interest rate risk.

Interest Rate Swap
A binding agreement between two counterparties to exchange periodic interest payments on a predetermined principal amount, which is referred to as the notional amount. Typically, one counterparty will pay interest at a fixed rate and in return receive interest at a variable rate, with the opposite applying to the other counterparty.

Interest Shortfall
The difference between the aggregate amount of interest payments received from the borrowers and the accrued interest on the certificates.

Internal Approach
A method of calculating credit risk under Basel II which allows banks to use their internal methods and procedures to model, assess and regulate risk, rather than relying on external assessments. See also Standardised Approach.

Internal Credit Enhancement
Mechanisms inherent within the securitisation structure designed to improve the credit quality of the senior classes of securities, most commonly involving the channelling of asset cash flow in ways that protect those senior classes from experiencing shortfalls.

Internal Rate of Return (IRR)
A compounded rate of return on an investment, calculated to show the rate at which the present values of future cash flows from an investment is equal to the cost of the investment.

Internal Rating Based (IRB) Approach
Established by the Basel Accords, this provides a single framework by which a given set of risk components or inputs are translated into minimum capital requirements. The framework allows for a foundation method and more advanced methodologies. In the foundation method, banks estimate the probability of default associated with each borrower and the bank supervisors supply other inputs. In the advanced methodology, a bank with a sufficiently developed internal capital allocation process is permitted to supply other necessary inputs as well.

In The Pool
A tranche of a loan which is included in the pool of loans which is to be securitised.

Investment Grade
A term used to describe Securities rated in one of the top four rating categories (AAA, AA, A and BBB or equivalent) by one or more Rating Agencies.

Investment Manager
The party responsible for managing a Portfolio of assets on behalf of the owner of that Portfolio. An Investment Manager will typically be responsible for actively managing the Portfolio and making investment related decisions. In the context of a Portfolio of real property this may also include carrying out the function of Property Manager. See also Asset Manager.

Investment Period
The period that commences on a private equity fund's initial closing date (when capital contributions are first accepted) and runs for the period (typically two to three years) negotiated with the fund's investors (often with some provisions for transactions in process at the end of the period).

Investment Property
Any property purchased with the primary intention of retaining it and enjoying the total return (rental income and appreciation in capital value) over the life of the interest acquired.

Investment Property Databank
A provider of performance data and analysis for owners, investors and manager of real estate.

Involuntary Repayment
Pre-payment on a mortgage loan due to default.

IO Strip
See Interest Only Strip.

IPD
The Investment Property Databank. The term IPD is also used to refer to an Interest Payment Date.

IPF
The Investment Property Forum.

IRR
Internal Rate of Return; a rate of return used in capital budgeting to measure or compare profitability. It is the discount rate that makes the net present value of all cashflows from a particular project equal to zero.

Irrational Exuberance
A term coined by former Federal Reserve chairman, Alan Greenspan to describe unsustainable investor enthusiasm that drives asset prices up to levels that are not supported by the fundamentals.

Irritancy
The right of the landlord to end a lease prematurely, extinguishing the lease and any rights under it, such as any subleases.

IRS
The US Internal Revenue Service.

ISCR
Interest service coverage ratio.

ISDA
International Swaps and Derivatives Association, a global trade association for privately negotiated derivates and the leading organisation that promulgates industry-standard Swaps and Derivatives documentation.

618

ISDA Master Agreement
An umbrella agreement that documents Derivative transactions which is amended and supplemented by a Schedule.

Issue Credit Rating
A rating agency opinion of the creditworthiness of an obligor with respect to a specific financial obligation, a specific class of financial obligations, or a specific financial program (including MTN programs and CP programs). Relevant factors in determining the issue credit rating are the creditworthiness of guarantors, insurers, the currency of the obligation as well as other forms of credit enhancement.

Issuer
A party that has authorised the creation and sale of securities to investors. In a securitisation structure, the issuer is usually established as an SPE in a jurisdiction that offers a favourable legal regime in terms of the ability to achieve bankruptcy-remote status for the issuer and the security arrangements provided for the investors and which affords favourable the tax treatment. Common jurisdictions used for establishing SPEs are England, Italy, Ireland, The Netherlands, Luxemburg and Jersey.

Issuer Collection Account
An account opened in the name of the Issuer at the Issuer's cash management bank into which the Servicer deposits payments from the borrower.

Issuing Bank
A bank that issues a Letter of Credit.

Issuer Credit Rating (ICR)
A rating agency opinion of an obligor's overall financial capacity to pay its financial obligations. This is basically an opinion of creditworthiness. An ICR focuses on the obligor's general capacity and willingness to meet its financial commitments as they fall due. Unlike the issue credit rating, this does not apply to any specific financial obligations.

Istisna'a
An Islamic finance term meaning construction contract. Sukuk Al-Istisna'a is one of the 14 categories of permissible sukuk specified by the AAOIFI.

Istisna' –Ijara Structure
An Islamic finance term meaning a construction-lease financing structure.

IVASS
Italian insurance supervisory authority.

J

J-curve
The time-variant profile of the performance of an unlisted fund which expends fees and taxes as it acquires assets.

JPUT
A JPUT is a unit trust governed by Jersey law and used to hold real estate. Under a unit trust, legal ownership of the trust assets is vested in one or more trustees, who holds them on trust for the benefit of holders of units in the trust (unit holders) in accordance with the terms of the trust instrument. JPUTs have been used to acquire and hold property in the United Kingdom in recent years, since they can be attractive property investment vehicles for single investors, joint venture arrangements and investment funds.

Junior Class or Junior Notes
See Subordinated Class or Subordinated Notes.

Junior Debt
See Subordinated Debt.

Junior Notes
See Junior Class.

Junior Tranche
See Tranche.

Junk Bonds
A colloquial term applied to below investment grade securities.

K

Kalte Zwangsverwaltung
German term for cold forced administration.

Key Persons
One or more persons designated by a private equity fund or a Lender as key to the expected success of the fund or a Borrower. Key persons must often devote a certain amount of time to the business, and a violation of the key person provisions usually allows the investors to either stop funding new transactions or to remove the general partner or manager or call an Event of Default of the Loan (as appropriate).

Kick off
The point at which the process of creating and issuing the CMBS commences.

L

Landlord
The owner of an interest in land who, in consideration of rents, grants the right to exclusive possession of that land to another person for a specific period by way of a Lease.

Land Registration
The process by which a state body records transfers of ownership of interests in real estate for the purpose of making the transfer conclusively effective and/or a matter of public knowledge.

Large Loan Sizing Model
CMBS loan rating model to determine the appropriate debt capacity at each rating category, sizing each loan separately.

"Last Look"
Provisions in an intercreditor allowing a lender to step in if another lender is looking to transfer its interest.

LC
See Letter of Credit.

Lead Manager
An investment bank or securities dealer that manages a syndicate of dealer banks and agrees to place a securities issuance. It is usually allocated a larger share of the issuance and therefore has more at stake in terms of the success of the effort to market and place the securities. As a result, the lead manager often takes on the role of chief advisor to the issuer or, in a securitisation structure, to the seller of the assets that are being securitised and is responsible for structuring the securities to be issued and liaising with other parties such as rating agencies, lawyers and credit enhancers. The lead manager is also closely involved in the preparation of the offering circular and advises its client on the pricing of the related securities. The lead manager may have legal liability as to the compliance of the issuance with relevant securities laws and regulations.

Leakage
Cash which escapes or is lost during its movement through a securitisation structure from underlying tenants to the issuer which has not been built into the structure and is unexpected.

Lease
The grant of a right to the exclusive possession of land for a definite period (which is less than that held by the grantor), or the document granting the right.

Lease Assignment
A form of credit enhancement whereby lease payments are made directly to
the Servicer.

Leasehold
An estate in land which provides the holder of the estate with rights of
possession and use of the land but not ownership. The Freehold is retained
by the Freeholder who grants the Lease (also referred to as a tenancy) as the
Landlord (also referred to as the lessor) to the holder of the estate, who is
referred to as the Tenant or lessee.

Legacy CMBS
Term for pre-2010 (before the introduction of CMBS 2.0) CMBS transactions.

Legal Final Maturity
The date by which the principal balance of securities must be repaid.

Legal Mortgage
See Mortgage.

Lender
An individual, bank, building society or other financial institution who/
that lends money to a Borrower.

Letter of Credit (LOC or LC)
A form of credit enhancement whereby a third party agrees to make funds
available. The third party rating is generally required to be at least equal to
the highest rating of the securities. to or upon the order of a third party
Creditor of a Borrower upon receiving a demand for payment.

Leverage
The use of debt in addition to the investment of equity as a means to finance
an acquisition. The greater (lesser) the level of debt in proportion to equity
the greater (lesser) the Leverage.

LIBOR or London Interbank Offered Rate
The rate of interest at which interbank term deposits are offered by one
prime bank in the London interbank market to another prime bank in the
London Interbank Market. There are LIBOR rates for deposits of various
maturities.

Licence
The lawful grant of a permission to do something that would otherwise not
be legal or allowed, for example, to occupy a property, or to assign a Lease
where the Landlord's consent is required.

Lien

An encumbrance against a property which may be voluntary (as in the case of a mortgage) or involuntary (as in the case of a lien for unpaid property taxes), and acts as security for amounts owed to the holder of the lien.

Limited Partnership (LP)

A Partnership structure which enables a pool of investors to invest together in one or more assets. The general partner (GP) must have unlimited liability while the other partners have limited liability. The investment vehicle is tax transparent.

Limited Purpose Entity (LPE)

A corporate vehicle (whether in the form of a limited company, partnership, trust, limited partnership or other form) which complies with rating agency LPE criteria. An LPE is usually the property owner. Due to inherent risks which stem from property ownership, LPEs are not fully insolvency remote but instead are structured so that insolvency risks are mitigated to the fullest possible extent. Characteristics which mitigate insolvency risk include: use of newly formed entities, contractual restrictions on activities and powers, non-petition covenants, separateness covenants and no employees.

Line-of-Credit Mortgage Loan

A mortgage loan that is linked to a revolving line of credit upon which the borrower can draw at any time during the life of the loan. The interest rate charged on the loan is usually variable and accrues on the basis of the outstanding balance only, while the undrawn principal limit grows at an annual rate.

Liquidation

Either a voluntary liquidation or a compulsory liquidation. Voluntary liquidation is a non-court based procedure to wind up a company commenced by the company's Shareholders. There are two types of voluntary liquidation: (i) members' voluntary liquidation which can be commenced if the directors of the company are able to swear a declaration that the company is solvent and 75% of the company's members have agreed to place the company into liquidation and (ii) creditors' voluntary liquidation where the directors cannot swear that the company is solvent. A compulsory liquidation is commenced by a petition to the court, usually presented by a Creditor who is owed money by the company.

Liquidation Fee

The fee ordinarily payable to a Special Servicer in respect of a specially serviced loan as percentage of the proceeds of sale (net of costs and expenses of sale) arising form the sale of a loan, any obligor of such loan or any part of any property or properties securing such loan.

Liquidator
Insolvency practitioner appointed by a company's Shareholders or unsecured Creditors, or on a court order, to manage the winding up of an entity.

Liquidity
A measure of the ease and frequency with which assets can be traded. It is a function of both the time it takes to close a particular action and the ability to trade the asset at market prices. Those traded more readily are said to be more liquid.

Liquidity Facility (LF)
A facility, such as an LOC, used to enhance the liquidity (but not the creditworthiness) of securitised assets. This facility provides cash to make the necessary payments of principal and interest on securities in the event of a shortfall in the cash available to the Issuer to make these payments. Amounts drawn on this facility become a senior obligation of the Issuer and will rank at least pari passu with the related securities.

Liquidity Provider
The provider of a liquidity facility.

Liquidity Risk
The risk that there will only be a limited number of buyers interested in buying an asset if and when the current owner of the asset wishes to sell it. Basically the risk that an owner of an asset will not be able to dispose of that asset.

Listed
Listed (quoted) on a stock exchange for public trading.

Listed Building
A building of special architectural or historical interest which the owner may not alter, extend or demolish without listed building consent.

Listed Real Estate Investments
Property investments that are traded on exchanges and priced on the basis of supply and demand for shares in the companies.

Listing Agent
The agent responsible for carrying out the procedures required to have securities listed on the appropriate stock exchange.

Loan
The advance of monies from one party (the Lender) to another party (the Borrower) which must be repaid on some future date.

Loan Agreement
The document which sets out the terms and conditions on which the Lender is prepared to lend monies to the Borrower. The Loan Agreement will contain the commercial terms of the Loan as well as, amongst other things, representations, covenants, undertakings and Events of Default.

Loan to Cost Ratio
This is the proportion of the cost of a development project that a lending institution will be prepared to lend.

Loan Files
A record maintained by the Servicer of, amongst other things, debt service payments, property protection advances, property inspection reports, financial statements, property level intelligence, modifications to any loan documents and records of special servicing transfer events.

Loan Market Association (LMA)
A market-led organisation established in December 1996 whose key objective is improving
liquidity, efficiency and transparency in the primary and secondary syndicated loan markets.

Loan Loss Provisions
An expense set-aside as an allowance for bad loans (when a customer defaults or terms of a loan have to be renegotiated, for example).

Loan on Loan
A loan (typically a senior whole loan but may also be mezzanine) made by a Senior Lender to a Borrower (typically a newly created acquisition vehicle) used to purchase (or refinance the purchase of) a pool of CRE loans. The underlying loans (and their security) will typically be for the benefit of the Borrower and not the Senior Lender and the Borrower (which will be the lender of record under the underlying loans) grants security over its interests in such loans to the Senior Lender.

Loan to Value Covenant
A covenant by the Borrower that the Loan will not exceed a certain LTV threshold.

Loan-to-Value (LTV) Ratio
The balance of a mortgage loan over either the value of the property financed by the loan or the price paid by the borrower to acquire the property and provides a measure of the equity the borrower has in the asset that secures the loan. The greater the LTV ratio, the less equity the borrower has at stake and the less protection is available to the lender by virtue of the security arrangement.

Loan Warranties
An assurance or promise in relation to a loan, the breach of which may give rise to a claim for damages.

LOC
See Letter of Credit.

Lock Box Provision
A provision giving trustees the control of the underlying properties in a CMBS so that property owners only have a claim to cash flows net of expenses.

Lock-Out Period
The time period following origination during which the borrower cannot prepay the mortgage loan.

London Interbank Offered Rate (LIBOR)
The rate of interest that major international banks in London charge each other for borrowings. There are LIBOR rates for deposits of various maturities.

Loss Curve
A graphical representation of the pattern of losses experienced over time regarding a sample of loans or receivables, based on plotting the defaults or losses that occur over the life of all loans or receivables in the sample.

Loss Given Default (LGD)
This represents the loss as a percentage of Exposure at Default.

Loss Ratio
The proportion of an insurer's premium income in any one year expended on paying and/or adjusting claims expressed as a percentage of the premium revenue.

Loss Security
The ratio of the outstanding principal paid on the loans minus the realised loss to the outstanding principal on the mortgage loans. Gives a rate of loss on a liquidated mortgage.

Loss to Lease
The difference between the rent being paid for property and the market rental rate for such a property.

Long Term Refinancing Operation (LTRO)
The ECB controls liquidity in the banking system via Refinancing Operations, which are basically repurchase agreements. Banks put up acceptable collateral with the ECB and receive a cash loan in return. In December 2011,

the ECB extended the time frame to borrow to allow banks access to relatively inexpensive funding for up to 3 years.

LP
See Limited Partnership.

LPA Receiver
A person (not necessarily an insolvency practitioner) appointed under the Law of Property Act 1925 by a Lender holding a Fixed Charge over property in order to enforce the Lender's Security. A LPA Receiver has the powers and duties specified in the Law of Property Act 1925 but these can be modified by express provisions in the Security Document. An LPA Receiver is usually appointed with a view to selling the charged property or collecting the rental income from it for the Lender.

LPE
See Limited Purpose Entity.

LSA
Liquidity Subordinated Amounts.

LTV
See Loan to Value.

LTV Covenant
See Loan to Value Covenant.

M

MAD
See Market Abuse Directive.

Main Proceedings
Insolvency proceedings which are brought in the member state in which the Debtor has its COMI. Once these proceedings are commenced all the assets of the Debtor are subject to the main proceedings, regardless of the member state where they are situated, unless Secondary/Territorial Proceedings are opened or already in place.

Majority Lenders
A term used in a syndicated or securitisable Loan Agreement to refer to that percentage (typically set at 66 2/3%) of Lenders (by size of commitment) that are required to approve certain decisions in respect of the Loan and related documentation.

Management Fee
In a private equity context, a fee paid by investors in a Private Equity Real Estate Fund to the general partner or an Investment Manager of the fund. The management fee is typically calculated as a percentage of the total capital commitments to the fund during the investment period, and as a percentage of the invested capital thereafter.

Mandatory Cost
The cost to a Lender incurred by complying with its regulatory funding requirements. This is not to be confused with Capital Adequacy requirements. The cost is paid by way of deposit to the Bank of England and the interest earned on that deposit helps fund the Bank of England's supervisory role. This cost is typically passed on to the Borrower and calculated as a percentage of that Lender's commitment in the Loan.

Mandatory Prepayment
A Prepayment following the occurrence of certain events, for example, on disposal of an asset, a change in control of the Borrower, or on receipt of insurance proceeds.

Marchlands de Biens
Interest-only loans to French developers or estate agents with high LTVs and maturities shorter than 3 years.

Margin
(i) In a Loan context, the percentage rate above a Lender's Cost of Funds that a Borrower has to pay on a Loan. The Margin reflects both the Lender's profit element for making the Loan as well as its pricing of the risk in advancing funds to a Borrower. (ii) In a Securitisation context, the percentage rate paid on each class of Securities above a particular interest basis (such as EURIBOR). The Margin paid on the Senior Class will be less than the Margin paid on the more Subordinated Classes.

Mark to Market
To re-state the value of an asset based on its current market price.

Market Abuse Directive (MAD)
EU Directive 2003/6/EC. The Market Abuse Directive sets a common framework for tackling insider dealing and market manipulation in the EU and the proper disclosure of information to the market.

Market Abuse Regulation (MAR)
Regulation (EU) No 596/2014. The Market Abuse Regulation repealed and replaced the Market Abuse Directive and its implementing legislation with effect from 3 July 2016. MAR establishes a new, common regulatory framework on market abuse.

Market Capitalisation
The value of a company determined by reference to the market price of its shares and the total number of shares in issue.

Market to Market
The act of recording the value of a position or portfolio based on the day's closing price. Instead of being valued at the original purchase price, the portfolio is valued at its current worth, reflecting any profit or loss which is not yet realised but which would be if the position was sold immediately.

Market Value
The estimated amount which a property should be exchanged on the date of valuation between a willing buyer and willing seller in an arm's length transaction.

Master Servicer
The party responsible for servicing mortgage loans.

Master Servicing Fee
The main fee paid to the Master Servicer for the servicing services it provides. Generally payable monthly from interest on the loan.

Master Trust
An SPE that issues multiple series of securities backed by a single pool of assets, with the cash flow generated by the assets being allocated between the series according to a predetermined formula.

Maturity Date
The date on which a bond or other security becomes due and payable in full.

MBS
See Mortgage Backed Securities.

Medium-Term Note (MTN)
A corporate debt instrument that is continuously offered over a period of time by an agent of the Issuer. Investors can select from maturity bands of nine months to one year, more than one year to 18 months, more than 18 months to two years, etc., up to 30 years.

Mezzanine Debt
Debt (often more expensive, highly leveraged) which is subordinated to the Senior Debt.

Mezzanine Pieces
Classes or tranches rated in the middle range of a multi-class security. These are more secure than the first loss piece but less secure than senior classes.

Mezzanine Investor
A party who actively invests in mezzanine debt.

Modelling/Cash Flow Modelling
When converted into securities, all payments are chronologically collated to the class created in the issuance. Cash flows are estimated in a variety of circumstances using multiple variables (or models).

Money Laundering
Legitimisation of illegally obtained money to hide its true nature or source.

Moratorium
A period of time during which a certain activity is not allowed or required. In the context of a workout, an agreed period during which the Creditors cannot enforce their rights to enable a restructuring plan to be agreed. In the context of an Administration, the period during which a Creditor may not commence or continue any legal action against the company or enforce its Security without the consent of the court or the Administrator.

Monoline Insurer
An insurance company which may only write insurance policies relating to a single type of risk. In a financial context, the monoline insurer unconditionally guarantees the repayment of certain securities issued in connection with specified types of transactions (usually a securitisation) in return for the payment of a fee or premium.
The financial guarantee provided by a monoline insurer will generally allow the insured class or classes of a securitisation to be rated based on the financial guarantee rating of the insurer, with the result that the classes are rated higher than they would be were the financial guarantee not in place.

Monte Carlo Approach or Method
Monte Carlo methods are used in finance and mathematical finance to value and analyze instruments, portfolios and investments by simulating the various sources of uncertainty affecting their value, and then determining their average value over the range of resultant outcomes

MoRE Analysis
Moody's ratings approach to real estate analysis in EMEA.

Mortgage
A security interest in real property given as security for the repayment of a loan.

Mortgage (UK)
The transfer of the ownership in real property by way of Security for repayment of a Loan on the express or implied condition that it will be re-transferred on the discharge of the secured obligations. A Legal Mortgage transfers legal title to the Mortgagee and prevents the Mortgagor from

dealing with the mortgaged asset while it is subject to the Mortgage. An Equitable Mortgage arises where the formalities to create a Legal Mortgage have not been completed or where the asset subject to the Mortgage is only an equitable interest. An Equitable Mortgage only transfers a beneficial interest in the asset to the Mortgagee with legal title remaining with the Mortgagor.

Mortgage (US)

A two party real property Security instrument in which the Mortgagor grants a Lien on real property to the Mortgagee to secure a debt. The Mortgage usually also includes an assignment of Leases and rents as well as a Security interest in personal property.

Mortgage-Backed Securities (MBS)

MBS include all securities whose security for repayment consists of a mortgage loan (or a pool of mortgage loans) secured on real property. Payments of interest and principal to investors are derived from payments received on the underlying mortgage loans.

Mortgage Loan

A Loan for the financing or refinancing of real estate whereby the Loan is secured by way of Mortgage over the real estate.

Mortgagee

The party taking the benefit of the Mortgage, usually a Lender.

Mortgagee in Possession

Where the Mortgagee takes possession of the property either by taking physical possession of the property or by bringing an action for possession.

Mortgagor

The borrower with respect to a Mortgage Loan.

MTN

See Medium Term Note.

Mudaraba

An Islamic finance term meaning a partnership whereby one party contributes services and another party capital. Securitisations which use this structure are termed Sukuk al-Mudaraba.

Mudarib

An Islamic finance term meaning the partner in a mudaraba structure which provides services and capital and usually no cash.

Multi-family Property
A building with at least five residential units, often classed as high rise, low rise or garden apartments. The quality of such properties is distinguished as:
Class A—command the highest rental rates in the market due to design/ construction/location. Usually managed by large management companies.
Class B—command average rental rates in the market due to outdated design and finish but still which are of adequate construction quality and are well maintained. Again usually managed by large management companies. This class compiles the majority of properties collateralising up RMBS.
Class C—command below average rental rates due to poor maintenance/ build in less desirable areas/occupied by tenants in less stable income streams. Generally managed by smaller, local property management companies.

Murabaha
Islamic finance term meaning sale at a mark-up. A prevalent structure in Islamic financing. Securitisations which use this structure are termed Sukuk al-Murabaha.

Murubaha
Islamic finance term meaning a partnership. Securitisations which use this structure are termed Sukuk al-Murubaha.

Musharaka
An Islamic finance term meaning a capital provider structure. Here each partner contributes capital and there is a much greater flexibility in allocating management responsibilities among partners, with joint rights of management being frequent and usual. Securitisations which use this structure are termed Sukuk al-Musharaka.

Mutual Fund
A professionally managed collective investment fund that distributes its shares to both retail and professional investors and that invests in stocks, Bonds, short-term money market instruments, and/or other Securities. The term is used as a generic descriptive identifier for various types of collection investment vehicles, such as unit trusts, open-ended investment companies, unitized insurance funds and UCITs.

N

NAREIT
The National Association of Real Estate Investment Trusts, a US organisation.

National Asset Management Agency (NAMA)
A body created by the Irish Government in 2009, to function as a 'bad bank', acquiring property developments loans from Irish banks in response to the Irish financial crisis.

NAV
See Net Asset Value.

NCREIF
The National Council of Real Estate Investment Fiduciaries, a US member-supported non-profit association that publishes various real estate returns including total return, income and capital appreciation returns varying by property type and region.

Negative Amortisation
This occurs when the principal balance of a loan based on the amount paid periodically by the borrower is less than the amount required to cover the amount of interest due. The unpaid interest is generally added to the outstanding principal balance.

Negative Amortisation Limit
The maximum amount by which the balance of a negatively amortising loan can increase before the LTV ratio exceeds a pre-defined limit. When this limit is reached, the repayment schedule for the loan is revised to ensure that the full balance will be repaid by maturity.

Negative Equity
Where the outstanding value of an asset falls below the amount of the loan taken out to purchase it.

Negative Pledge
An undertaking by a Borrower or other Obligor not to create, or permit to subsist, Security over its assets without the prior consent of the Lender.

Net Asset Value (NAV)
The appraised value of an entity's assets less the value of its liabilities.

Net Effective Rent
The gross rent less all operating expenses, rental concessions, tenant improvements etc. This can be a negative figure.

Net Net Lease (or double net lease)
A lease which requires the tenant to pay for property taxes and insurance in addition to the rent.

Net Net Net Lease (or triple net lease)
A lease which requires the tenant to pay for property taxes, insurance and maintenance in addition to the rent.

Net Operating Cash Flow (NOCF)
Total income less operating expenses and adjustments but before mortgage payments, tenant improvements, replacement revenues and leasing commissions. This is used as the basis for many financial calculations (for example debt service coverage ratios).

Net Operating Income (NOI)
Total income less operating expenses and adjustments and after mortgage payments, tenant improvements, replacement revenues and leasing commissions.

Net Present Value (NPV)
The sum of the present values of all future incomes less the sum of the present values of all costs, including purchase price, discounted at the required return.

Net Receivables
The principal balance of receivables minus any portion of the interest due with respect to those receivables.

Net Rent
The income from a property after deduction of all outgoings, including repairs, insurance and management costs, but excluding taxes payable by the recipient.

Net Stable Funding Ratio (NSFR)
A measurement of the amount of long-term, stable sources of funding employed by an institution relative to the liquidity profiles of the assets it has funded and the potential for contingent calls on funding liquidity arising from off-balance sheet commitments and obligations, which has been proposed within the Basel III Accord.

Netting
The process of terminating or cancelling reciprocal obligations enjoyed by two parties to an agreement or contract, where those terminated or cancelled obligations are replacement by a single payment obligation from one party to the other.

NICE
A term used to describe a period of non inflationary consistent expansion that followed the UK Government's move to give the Bank of England the freedom to set interest rates soon after the 1997 General Election.

NOCF
See Net Operating Cash Flow.

Non-Consolidation Opinion
A key feature of an SPE or bankruptcy remote entity. This is a legal opinion which confirms that the assets of an entity would not be substantially consolidated with those of its affiliates.

Non-Performing Loan (NPL)
A Mortgage Loan or other debt instrument with respect to which the Borrower or Obligor has failed to make at least three scheduled payments.

Non-Recourse
Whereby a Borrower does not have any liability for a Loan beyond the assets it has granted as Security to a Lender. The Lender will have no right of recourse to a Borrower if those secured assets are insufficient to satisfy its liability to the Lender.

Note
A certificate of debt issued by a government or corporate entity promising payment of the original investment plus interest by a specified future date. Notes typically have a shorter maturity than Bonds. See also Bonds and Securities.

Noteholder
The holder of a Note or other Security.

Notice Rights
Rights often given to subordinated lenders allowing them notice that the loan is non-performing, or that a special servicing transfer event has occurred. Twinned with Cure Rights.

Notional Amount
The figure used as the basis for calculating the interest due with respect to an obligation that either has no principal balance or has a principal balance that is not the balance used for calculating interest.

Novation
The transfer of contractual obligations from one party to another and which requires the consent of the counterparty.

O

Obligor
The party that has taken on the responsibility for taking certain actions under the terms of a contractual agreement. These actions often include making payments to parties. In a securitisation structure, the term generally refers to the parties making payments on the assets being securitised; these payments are the source of cash flows from which investors are repaid.

OECD
The Organisation for Economic Co-operation and Development.

OEIC
See Open-Ended Investment Company.

OER
The operating expense ratio, given by operating expenses/gross effective income.

Off-Balance Sheet Pass Through Securitisation
Where assets are transferred to a trustee for the sole purpose of issuing asset-back securities.

Off-Balance Sheet Pay Through Securitisation
A development of Off-Balance Sheet Pass Through Securitisation due to the diversity of the European market in terms of types of underlying assets, types of security and applicable taxes, regulations and laws.

Offentliche Pfandbriefe
See Pfandbriefe.

Offering Circular
A document used to promote a new securities issuance to prospective investors. This describes the transaction, including the features of each class of securities to be issued (such as the basis for interest payments, credit rating, expected average life and priority with respect to other classes). In a securitisation structure, the offering circular also gives details of the underlying assets, for example the type of assets and their credit quality. The offering circular is usually prepared by the lead manager of the securities issuance and its legal advisors.

Official List
The FSA's list of securities that have been admitted to listing. As the competent authority, the FSA must maintain the official list in accordance with Part VI of the Financial Services and Markets Act 2000.

Official Receiver
An officer of the court and civil servant who deals with bankruptcies and compulsory company liquidations. Such person has various functions which include becoming the first liquidator when the court makes a winding up order against the company, being appointed by the court as interim Receiver or provisional liquidator once the winding-up order has been presented and investigating the conduct of the company and directors.

OIC
The Organisation of the Islamic Conference.

On-Balance Sheet securitisation
Examples include covered mortgage bonds and Pfandbriefe style products.

One-Tier Transaction
A securitisation in which the transferor sells or pledges assets directly to the issuing SPE and/or the bond trustee or custodian and in doing so does not involve multiple transfers of the assets and one or more intermediate SPEs (thereby reducing transaction costs).

OpCo/PropCo Structure
This arises where an operating borrower with significant property assets (such as pubs and care homes) is acquired and restructured into two separate companies. OpCo is the operating company and operates the business, PropCo holds all the property assets. OpCo then takes a lease from PropCo on all of the operating properties.

Open-Ended Commingled Investment Funds
Investment funds where the number of shares outstanding changes when new shares are sold or old shares are redeemed and pricing is Net Asset Value.

Open-Ended Fund
A Real Estate Fund from which investors can demand to have their capital redeemed or paid back. These are usually also open to new investors who can subscribe for new units for cash. Compare with Closed-Ended Fund.

Open-Ended Investment Company (OEIC)
UK open-ended collective investment scheme of variable size that is structured as a company (rather than a trust) which invests in a broad range of assets.

Open Pre-Payment
A clause permitting prepayment of all or a portion of a loan without incurring a fee or penalty often restricted to a specified period.

Open Standards Consortium for Real Estate (OSCRE)
A Non-profit organization dedicated to the development of industry standards for data exchange.

Operating Advisor (OA)
A party appointed by the Controlling Class whom the Servicer or Special Servicer must consult with before making certain decisions with respect to the loans.

Opportunistic Real Estate Investments
Investments that are the most risky, are in non-traditional property types, including speculative development, seek internal rates of return of 15+% or more and have debt levels at more than 70% of the property value. They are

characterised by property assets that have low economic occupancy, high tenant roll-over, are in secondary or tertiary markets and have investment structures with minimal control.

Option
Contracts that entitle the holder to the right to purchase or sell an asset for a specific price at a specific time in the future.

Option Adjusted Spreads
A representation of incremental return incorporating interest rate volatility and variations in cash flow due to changes in rates. Used in RMBS to price the prepayment risk to an investor. Less relevant to CMBS given the prevalence of prepayment penalties.

Option Pledge
The right but not the obligation to deliver goods or personal property as Security for a debt or obligation.

Optional Termination
A right granted to certain classes of Noteholders in a Securitisation defining when and under what circumstances a Securitisation can be redeemed ahead of its Expected Maturity or Final Maturity.

Original Issue Discount
A bond which is sold below, or at a discount to, par.

Original Lender
See Lender.

Original LTV Ratio
The original amount owed with respect to a mortgage loan divided by the value of the property on which the loan is secured. In the case of commercial mortgage loans, value is generally taken to mean the current appraised value of the property.

Original Valuation
The initial amount the asset was considered to be worth.

Originate-to-Distribute (OTD)
The process of originating Loans for the purpose of securitising or syndicating where the Originator intends to retain no, or only a small, interest in that Loan. By using the OTD model, an Originator is able to remove an asset from its balance sheet relatively quickly which allows it to originate more assets.

Origination
The process of making loans.

Originator
An entity that underwrites and makes loans; the obligations arising with respect to such loans are originally owed to this entity before the transfer to the SPE. See also Origination.

Orphan Company
Where the SPV issuer is owned by a trust for quasi-charitable purposes resulting in the underlying entity being removed from the originator group's ownership.

OTC
See Over the Counter.

OTD
See Originate-to-Distribute

Out of the Money
An option is described as being out of the money when the price of the underlying instrument is below the strike or exercise price for a call option (an option to buy) and above the strike price for a put option (an option to sell). The more an option is out of the money the cheaper it becomes as the likelihood that it will be exercised becomes smaller. Options can also be described as being deeply out of the money when they are likely to expire out of the money.

Out of The Pool
A tranche of a loan which is not included in the pool of loans which are to be securitised.

Outstanding Principal Amount
The primary amount left unpaid.

Over Collateralisation
A capital structure in which the value of assets exceed liabilities and thereafter a form of credit enhancement (used most regularly in certain asset-backed transactions). For example, an issuance of £100 million of senior securities might be secured by a pool of assets valued at £150 million, in which case the overcollateralisation for the senior securities would be 33%.

Over-Hedged
A hedged position in which the offsetting position is for a greater amount than the underlying position held by the firm entering into the hedge.

Over-Rented
A property is over-rented when it is subject to a Lease, or Leases, where the current rent passing is greater than could be achieved in the open market at the current time.

Over-the-Counter (OTC)
A description for Derivatives that are not traded over an organised exchange. Derivative contracts are entered into directly between the parties, enabling them to tailor the contract to match the terms of a particular transaction.

P

PAIF
See Property Authorised Investment Fund.

Partnership
A type of business organisation in which persons pool money, skills and other resources, and share profit and loss in accordance with the terms of a Partnership Agreement.

Partnership Agreement
A written agreement between partners to a Partnership who join as partners to form and carry on a business.

Passing Rent
The rent which is currently payable under the terms of a Lease or tenancy agreement.

"Patto Marciano" Agreement
Italian law agreement which allows the creditor to give rise to an out-of-court appropriation of secured real estate assets.

PAUG Template
The template for Credit Derivative Transaction on Mortgage-Backed Securities with Pay-As-You-Go or Physical Settlement published by ISDA in 2005, as amended. The PAUG Template adopts the Credit Derivatives Definitions to address trading of ABCDS in North American markets. This template addresses the settlement and credit issues associated with CDS referencing MBS and certain types of ABS more specifically than does the CPS Template through the innovation of so-called pay-as-you-go settlement of floating amount events.

Pay Rate
The periodic rate at which interest is paid on a mortgage. May differ from the accrual rate.

Paying Agent
A bank of international standing and reputation that is responsible for making payments on commercial mortgage loans. In general, payment is made via a clearing system (in Europe usually through Euroclear or Clearstream International). In Europe, this role is often assumed by an

entity affiliated with the trustee or the administrator; by contrast, in the US, the trustee itself is generally responsible for making payments to investors.

Payment History
A record of a borrower's payments.

Payment in Kind
See PIK or PIK able.

Payout Event
An early amortisation event.

PC
Practical Completion.

Peer-to-Peer (P2P) Lending
A method of debt financing that enables individuals and companies to borrow and lend money without the use of an official financial institution as an intermediary.

Percentage Lease
Rent payments which include overage as a percentage of gross expenses which exceed a certain amount as well as minimum of base rent. Common in large rental stores.

Perfection
A generic term used to describe the process that must be taken in order that a charge holder's Security has the intended priority over the chargor's other Creditors.

Performing
Term used to describe a loan or other receivable with respect to which the borrower has made all scheduled interest and principal payments under the terms of the loan.

Performing Loan
A Mortgage Loan or other receivable in respect of which the Borrower has made all scheduled interest and principal payments on the due date for payment.

Pfandbrief (plural Pfandbriefe)
A debt instrument issued by German mortgage banks and certain German financial institutions. There are two types of Pfandbriefe: "Hypothekenpfandbriefe" that banks use to finance their lending activities and "Offentliche Pfandbriefe" that they use to finance their lending to public sector entities.

Phase Rent
Rental payments without adjustments for any lease concessions (for example rent free periods).

PIA
See Property Industry Alliance.

PIC
See Property Investment Certificate.

PID
See Property Income Distribution.

PIK or PIK-able
Payment in Kind. CDO Bonds (typically Mezzanine Pieces) that provide for the deferral of interest if funds available to the Issuer from the underlying Portfolio of assets are insufficient to pay interest in full and on time on those CDO Bonds.

Pledge (US)
A Security interest in property of the Debtor or third party which includes the right of the Creditor to enforce it in case of the Debtor's default by way of public sale. The Creditor's right to levy on pledged property is senior to the rights of subsequent pledge Creditors and unsecured Creditors. Whilst a pledge is a type of possessory Security where the Creditor takes possession of the pledged property, title to the pledged property does not pass to the Creditor.

PLN
See Property Linked Note.

Plumbing
To remedy or cure any leakage from a securitisation structure.

Pool
See Portfolio.

Pool Factor
The percentage of the original aggregate principal balance of a pool of assets which is still outstanding as of a particular date.

Pooling and Servicing Agreement
A contract that documents a transaction in which a defined group of financial assets are aggregated and details how the future cash flows to be generated by those assets will be divided between the parties to the contract. This also details the responsibilities of the Master Servicer and the Special Servicer for managing a CMBS.

Portfolio
The combination or spread of investments or assets held by an investor, fund or Issuer.

Portfolio Lender
A company that not only originates mortgage loans, but also holds a portfolio of their loans instead of selling them off in a secondary market.

Portfolio Manager
An individual or institution that manages a portfolio of investments.

Preferred Equity
Financing that is similar to mezzanine loan but structured to a senior equity position rather than as a loan. A preferred equity interest will typically have a stated preferred return and control rights similar to or greater than those of a mezzanine lender.

Preferred Returns
The second form of cash flow distribution in a fund, payable after the initial capital investment has been returned. A preferred return resembles a dividend payment on a preferred stock, and is paid prior to other claims on the underlying property cash flows.

Pre-Let
A legally enforceable agreement for letting to take effect at a future date, upon completion of a development that is proposed or under construction at the time of the agreement.

Preliminary Prospectus
A prospectus which includes all or nearly all the information which will be included in the final version, identified by red printing on the front cover. This is essentially a marketing tool allowing investors to assess the utility of the security for meeting their investment objectors and allows the issuer to gauge interest in the proposed issues. Also known as the Red Herring or The Red.

Premium
An amount in excess of the regular price paid for an asset (or the par value of a security), usually as an inducement or incentive.

Prepayment
A payment by the borrower which is greater than and/or earlier than the scheduled repayments.

Prepayment Interest Shortfall
The shortfall between the interest accrued on the corresponding mortgages and that accrued from a prepayment, generally when interest received from the prepayment is less than the interest on notes. Such shortfall may be

allocated to certain classes of notes and, if so, that class will be adversely affected.

Prepayment Penalty or Prepayment Premium
A levy imposed on prepayments made on a mortgaged loan to discourage prepayment.

Prepayment Rate
The rate at which the mortgage loans (or other receivables in discrete pools) are reported to have been prepaid, expressed as a percentage of the remaining principal balance of the pool. Prepayment rates are often sensitive to market rates of interest.

Prepayment Risk
The risk that the yield on an investment will be adversely affected if some or all of the principal amount invested is repaid ahead of schedule. Commercial mortgages often reduce this risk through lockout periods, prepayment premiums and/or yield maintenance. Prepayment risk can also be taken to include extension risk, which is related to the repayment of principal more slowly than expected.

Prescribed Part
The fund required under section 176A of the Insolvency Act 1986 to be set aside out of the net realisations of property subject to a Floating Charge and made available to unsecured Creditors. The prescribed part was introduced by the Enterprise Act 2002.

Pricing
The process of determining the coupon and the price for securities prior to their issuance. The price of any financial instrument should be equal to the present value of the cost flow that it is expected to produce. In a securitisation structure, due to the effect of prepayment on the timing of the cash flows, the pricing process generates expected-case cash flows using a prepayment scenario.

Primary Servicer
The Primary Servicer collects payments from the underlying borrower and applies them to the relevant creditors and is responsible for the general administration of the loan, dealing with communications received from the borrower, monitoring compliance and reporting on loan performance to the finance and securitisation parties.

Primary Servicing Fee
Low basis point per annum fee payable to the Primary Servicer calculated against the outstanding balance of all loans and payable on each note payment date.

Prime Property
A property investment regarded as the best in its class and location.

Principal Only Notes
Classes of Notes that are only entitled to principal distribution but not distribution of interest. See also Interest Only Strips.

Principal Proceeds
Collections received from underlying debt instruments that consist of principal payments, whether scheduled or unscheduled.

Priority
The right of a secured creditor to take enforcement action and to receive payment in priority to other competing interests.

Priority of Distributions
Provisions which dictate how, when and to whom available funds will be distributed.

Priority of Payments
The provisions in a Securitisation (or any other transaction involving structural subordination) which dictate how, when and to whom available funds will be distributed. Generally, available funds will be distributed to each class of Securities in accordance with their respective seniority. Once interest and principal due on the most Senior Class of Securities has been paid, interest and principal due on the next most Senior Class of Securities will be paid and so on. Also known as the Waterfall.

Private Equity
Money invested in entities which are not listed on any stock exchange.

Private Equity Real Estate Funds
Pooled investment vehicles formed to allow multiple investors to collectively invest in a series of real estate projects to achieve certain economic goals within certain risk tolerances.

Private Label Securitisation
Privately sponsored MBS and CMBS Securitisations using investment bank and commercial bank lending conduits.

Private Placement
The sale of securities to investors who meet certain criteria who are deemed to be sophisticated investors (for example insurance companies, pension funds).

Private Real Estate Investments
Direct real estate investments and indirect real estate investments, such as open-ended and closed-ended funds, that directly invest in real estate that are not traded on the exchanges.

Probability of Default (PD)
A borrower's likelihood of defaulting under a set of economic conditions.

Procédure de Sauvegarde
French safeguarding procedure akin to Administration.

Professional Indemnity Insurance
Insurance purchased by a provider of professional services to protect the provider against claims made by the person to whom the services are provided alleging loss caused by the provider's negligence.

Profit Share
A loan or investment provision that allows the lender/investor to receive an equity-based return in addition to normal rates upon some event. Typically this involves a lender/investor receiving a disproportionate percentage share of the proceeds in refinancing or sale.

Profit Stripping
The process whereby a company that has sold its assets in a securitisation continues to extract value from those assets by siphoning off the profits earned by the securitisation vehicle. The company therefore retains the economic benefits of ownership of the securitised assets.

Prohibited Business Activities
In an Islamic finance context, the conduct of business whose core activities (a) include manufacture or distribution of alcohol beverages or pork products for human consumption (or in some cases firearms); (b) have a significant involvement in gaming, brokerage, interest based banking or impermissible insurance; (c) accrue certain types of entertainment elements (especially pornography); or (d) have impermissible amounts of interest based indebtedness or interest income. Activities (a) through (c) are prohibited under the Sharia'a.

Property Authorised Investment Fund
An AIF that invests in real estate.

Property Derivative
A Derivative which has a price and value derived from a published commercial or residential property index. A Property Derivative presents the opportunity to hedge or speculate with respect to property values for a period of time.

Property Income Distribution (PID)
Dividends paid by UK REITs from the profits of its Property Investment Business.

Property Industry Alliance (PIA)
Alliance of four UK property trade bodies—the British Property Federation (BPF), British Council for Offices (BCO), Investment Property Forum (IPF) and the Royal Institution of Chartered surveyors (RICS)—that work together on issues of mutual concern.

Property Investment Certificate (PIC)
A British, publicly-traded Debt Security representing a holding in a special purpose vehicle that owns real estate. PIC coupons and redemption value depend on the performance of a real estate index such as an index published by the IPD.

Property Linked Notes (PLN)
A Debt Security with a return that is based on the performance of property. A PLN may be structured to give its holder control rights with respect to the underlying property. PLNs have been issued by owners of real property in order to divest themselves of the income stream, expenses and responsibilities relating to the ownership of property. The holder of the PLN in essence steps into the shoes of the real property owner for the term of the PLN.

Property Manager
The party responsible for the management of a property.

Property Protection Advance
A mechanism by which the Servicer or Special Servicer can provide amounts required to protect the property serving as collateral for the loan, for example payment of insurance premiums. In the event that a property protection payment is not made by the borrower, the Servicer or Special Servicer can require a property protection advance to be made either by the borrower drawing on a liquidity facility or the Servicer or Special Servicer making the payment out of its own funds then being reimbursed by the Issuer.

Property Protection Payment
A payment required to be made by the borrower in respect of the property serving as collateral such as insurance, real estate taxes or rent due under a headlease.

Property Unit Trust
An unincorporated fund established under a trust structure for the purpose of investing in real estate. The investors in PUTs are the beneficiaries under the trust. See also Authorised Unit Trust and Unauthorised Unit Trust.

Prospectus
The document which contains all the material information about a security. Termed the black as opposed to the red. In a CMBS this includes details of the properties, the payment sequence amongst classes and the treatment of defaults and prepayments. All relevant information about a security must be included in the prospectus. In connection with European deals, an Offering Circular ("OC") issued in accordance with the Prospectus Directive. See also Offering Circular.

Prospectus Directive
EC Directive 2003/71/EC. The Prospectus Directive sets out the disclosure obligations for Issuers of Securities that are to be offered to the public or admitting to trading on any regulated market within the EU. The European Commission issued a further amending directive designed to simplify and improve the application of the Prospectus Directive which came into force on 1 July 2012 across the EU.

Protection Buyer
The party transferring the credit risk associated with certain assets to another party in return for payment often seen in transactions such as credit default swaps. Payment is typically an up-front premium.

Protection Seller
The party that accepts the credit risk associated with certain assets (often seen in transactions such as credit default swaps, as mentioned above). Should losses on the assets exceed a specified amount, the protection seller makes credit protection payments to the protection buyer.

PRS
Private rental sector.

100% PSA
The benchmark mortgage prepayment scenario. Under this scenario, the monthly prepayment rate is assumed to be 0.2% per annum in the first month after issuance and to increase by 20 bps per year each month for the next 28 months. Beginning in the 30th month after issuance, the monthly prepayment rate is assumed to level off at 6% per annum and to remain at that level for the life of the mortgage pool to which the scenario is being applied.

200% PSA
A prepayment scenario in which prepayments are assumed to be made twice as fast as under the benchmark mortgage prepayment scenario. Under the 200% PSA scenario, the monthly prepayment rate is assumed to be 0.4% per year in the first month after issuance and to increase by 40 bps per year each month for the next 28 months. Beginning in the 30th month after issuance, the monthly prepayment rate is assumed to level off at 12%

per year and to remain at that level for the life of the mortgage pool to which the scenario is being applied.

Public Real Estate Investments
Indirect Property Investments in exchange traded companies that invest in real estate.

Purchase Event of Default
A right given to subordinated lenders to purchase the senior portion of a loan which has gone into default.

PUT
See Property Unit Trust.

Q

QFC
See Qualifying Floating Charge.

QIS
See Qualified Investor Scheme.

QRS
See Qualified REIT Subsidiary.

Qualified Investor Scheme (QIS)
A type of Authorised Investment Fund (AIF) which has wider investment powers and is subject to lighter regulation than other types of AIF. Investment in a QIS is open only to 'qualified investors', who will either be corporates or sophisticated individual investors who are expected to understand the risks involved in a wide range of investments.

Qualified Mortgage
A mortgage which can appropriately be included in a CMBS.

Qualified REIT Subsidiary (QRS)
A wholly-owned subsidiary of a REIT that is disregarded for tax purposes. A QRS may only own REIT qualified assets and generate REIT qualified income.

Qualifying Floating Charge (QFC)
A Floating Charge over the whole or substantially the whole of the company's property created by an instrument which (i) states that paragraph 14 of Schedule B1 to the Insolvency Act 1986 applies to it, (ii) purports to empower the holder of the Floating Charge to appoint an Administrator of the company or (iii) purports to empower the holder of the Floating Charge

to make an appointment of an administrative receiver within the meaning given by section 29(2) of the Insolvency Act 1986.

Qualifying Lender
A party to whom a Lender can assign all or part of its interest in a Loan. Generally, a Qualifying Lender must be a bank or other financial institution which, were it to acquire an interest in the Loan, would not cause an increase in tax liability to the Borrower.

R

Rabb ul-Maal
An Islamic finance term meaning partners in a mudaraba structure which provide capital in cash or in kind and generally do not interfere with the management or service component.

Rack Rent
Rent that represents the full open market annual value of a holding.

Rake Bonds
Loan specific securities backed by a B Note, or the junior component of a single commercial mortgage loan.

Ramp Up
The period of time following closing of a Securitisation (typically found in CDOs) during which the Issuer may acquire additional Collateral in order to "Ramp Up" a Portfolio at least equal in principal value to the amount of Securities issued by the Issuer.

Ramp Up Period
The period in a CDO during which the Issuer can "Ramp Up" the Portfolio. During the Ramp Up Period certain collateral tests are disapplied.

Rate Creep
This arises where the principal amount allocated sequentially (to the senior loan in priority to the junior) causes the weighted average rate on the senior and junior loans set out in the intercreditor agreement to creep above the weighted coverage whole loan rate that the tenant pays, with the result that there is an available funds shortfall with an increasing portion of junior loan interest becoming non-recoverable.

Rate Step-Ups
Agreed increases in interest rates. These can occur at certain specified times or upon the occurrence of certain events, for example if the borrower is unable to obtain a signed sales contract on the underlying property.

Rated Obligations
The obligation on an issuer to pay principal and interest which has been assigned a rating by a rating agency according to the likelihood they would be able to comply with those obligations.

Rated Securities
Securities of an Issuer which have been assigned a credit rating by a Rating Agency.

Rating Agency
Organisations which examine the likelihood of timely receipt of interest and ultimate repayment of principal on Securities issued by, amongst others, Securitisation Issuers. The process involves examining the credit strength of the underlying Portfolio, the cashflows of the transaction and the levels of subordination at each level of the capital structure. Ratings range from AAA (highest) to CCC (lowest).

Rating Agency Confirmation
A written statement issued by a rating agency that confirms, post-closing, that a proposed action in respect of the relevant transaction will not result in a downgrade or the withdrawal of current ratings of notes.

RBC
See Risk Based Capital.

RCF
Revolving Credit Facility.

Real Estate Derivatives Special Interest Group or *RED-SIG*
A US industry alliance established to offer insight and perspective on the use and implementation of US commercial property Derivative products and to facilitate the exchange of information on the use and implementation of commercial property directives.

Real Estate Fund
A legal entity which acts as a wrapper or vehicle into which investors place capital and which then invests in property.

Real Estate Investment Trust (REIT)
A tax election option which allows a specially formed vehicle to invest in real estate and/or securities backed by real estate. Such entities receive favourable tax breaks.

Real Estate Mortgage Investment Conduit (REMIC)
A legislation financial vehicle which allows for the issuance of multi-class securities with no adverse tax consequences. A REMIC is a pass-through entity that can hold loans secured by real property without the regulatory, accounting and economic obstacles inherent in other forms of mortgage-

backed securities. A REMIC is a bankruptcy-remote legal entity which distributes the cash flow to bondholders of various classes or tranches of securities without being taxed at the entity level.

Realised Loss
The amount unrecovered when a foreclosed loan is sold, equal to (i) the unpaid balance of the loan; plus (ii) all unpaid scheduled interest; plus (iii) all fees applied to the sale of the property; minus (iv) the amount received from the sale.

Receivables
General term referring to principal and interest related cash flows generated by an asset and are payable to (or receivable by) the owner of the asset.

Receiver
A person appointed by the holder of a charge to enforce its Security. The appointment of a Receiver by a secured Creditor is a contractual remedy without recourse to the courts. A Receiver can be a Fixed Charge Receiver, LPA Receiver or administrative receiver. The Receiver's primary duty is to the appointing secured Creditor.

Recognised Investment Exchange
A Securities market which has been recognised as meeting the requirements stipulated by the UK Financial Services Authority.

Red Book
Otherwise known as the 'Royal Institution of Chartered Surveyors Valuation—Professional Standards'. The current edition of the Red Book became effective on 6 January 2014 and sets out procedural rules and guidance within a best practice framework covering the preparation of valuations for many purposes, including loan security and capital taxation.

Red Book Valuation
A new independent valuation commissioned by a loan servicer.

Red Herring or The Red
See Preliminary Prospectus.

RED-SIG
See Real Estate Derivatives Special Interest Group.

Redemption
The process of repaying all amounts due on Securities in a Securitisation. Redemption can occur on final maturity, following the occurrence of an Event of Default, on prepayment of the underlying assets, at the option of certain classes of Noteholders following the occurrence of certain events, and following the occurrence of certain tax events.

Redevelopment
Development of land which entails or follows the removal of all or most of the already existing buildings or structures.

Refinancing Risk
The risk that a borrower will not be able to refinance the mortgage on maturity thus extending the life of a security which uses this mortgage as collateral. See also Balloon Risk.

Reinsurance
Where an insurer relieves itself of all or part of an insurance risk by passing that risk on to another insurance company.

Reinvestment Period
The period in a CDO during which the Issuer may acquire new assets and substitute existing assets.

Reinvestment Risk
The risk that income from an investment can not be reinvested at the same rate of return as the investment that generated such income.

REIT
See Real Estate Investment Trust.

REIT debt securities
Securities issued by a real estate investment trust which are generally unsecured and may be subordinated to other obligations of the issuer.

Release provision
Either (a) a provision to release collateral under a mortgage for a pre-agreed amount or (b) a provision which requires the borrower, if it prepays the loan associated with one property in the pool which is consolidated and cross collaterised, to prepay a portion of all other loans in the pool (thereby stopping the borrower cherry picking properties in a pool).

Release Price
The price as part of the release provisions in loan agreements secured by portfolios of properties, sometimes set at a predetermined factor above the ALA or incorporating the sale price.

Relevant Information Summary or RIS
RIS refers to a summary of any information relating to a loan or any property that the Servicer or the Special Servicer reasonably determines is likely to have a material impact on the value of the loan (or whole loan as applicable).

REMIC
See Real Estate Mortgage Investment Conduit.

Remittance Report
A report sent to noteholders on each distribution date by the Servicer containing information about the current distribution.

Rent Free Period
A defined period of time commencing from the start of the Lease during which the Tenant does not pay any rent.

Rent Step-Up
A lease whereby the rent increases at set intervals for a certain pre-agreed period or for the life of the lease.

Rental Growth
The rate of growth over a specified period of the Estimated Rental Value of a property.

Rental Income Yield
Rental income expressed as a percentage of the value of a real estate investment.

REOC
A real estate operating company.

Repatriation
Return of a financial asset (such as earnings) from a foreign country to an entity's home country.

Representations and Warranties
Clauses in an agreement in which various parties to the agreement confirm certain factual matters and agree that, should those statements of fact be untrue or incorrect, they will take steps to ensure that the statements are corrected or otherwise compensate the other parties to the agreement because the statements are not correct. In the context of a securitisation, the representations and warranties usually cover the condition and quality of the assets at the time of their transfer from the originator to the SPE or an intermediate transferor. They generally also specify the remedies available to the SPE or the intermediate transferor in the event that any of the representations are subsequently found to have been untrue. These may still be enforceable once the asset has been included in a securitised pool of assets.

Reserve Account
A funded account available for use by an SPE for certain specified purposes and often used as a form of credit enhancement. Virtually all reserve accounts are at least partially funded at the start of the related transactions, but many are structured to be built up over time using the excess cash flow that is available after making payments to investors.

Reserving
An amount maintained by an insurer in liquid form from its premium revenue against future claims, whether imposed by an insurance regulator or which the insurer itself chooses to maintain.

Residential Mortgage-Backed Securities (RMBS)
The RMBS abbreviation is used in two contexts. Residential Mortgage Backed Securities refers to Debt Securities that are backed by one or more Pools of Mortgages secured by residential real estate. All principal and interest from the Mortgages flow to the Noteholders in a pre-determined sequence. Residential Mortgage Backed Securitisation also refers to the overall transaction by which the Securities are issued and sold in the Capital Markets.

Residual
The term applied to any cash flow remaining after the liquidation of all security classes in a CMBS.

Resolution Trust Corporation (US)
A US Government owned asset management company that was responsible for liquidating assets (primarily real estate assets) that had been assets of saving and loan associations declared insolvent.

Retail Sector
A sector of commercial property types that includes high street shops, shopping centres and retail warehouses.

Retention of Title
A contractual provision by which the passing of title in goods supplied under the contract is made conditional on payment of the full purchase price by the buyer.

Return on Equity
The ratio of a company's profits to its shareholder equity expressed as a percentage.

Reverse Earn-Out Loans
Loans in respect of which provisions concerning resizing are made at origination on the basis of criteria not yet met, or not yet achieved consistently. Criteria will be specified and, if these are not met by specified dates, the loan will be resized downwards. The difference between the original balance of the loan and the resized balance must be paid down by the borrower.

Reversion
The ultimate sale of a property after a holding period (can be a theoretical sale).

Reversionary Cap Rate
The capitalisation rate applied to the expected sale price of a property after a holding period. This will be higher than the going-in cap rate.

Reversionary Estate
Where a property owner makes an effective transfer of a property to another but retains some future right to the property.

Reversionary Rent/Income
A change in income that will arise following a rent review or renewal of a Lease or re-letting of a property.

Reversionary Value
The expected value of a property upon reversion.

Reversionary Yield (RY)
The return on an investment calculated by dividing the reversionary income by the value/purchase price and expressed in terms of a percentage.

Revolving Period
The period during which newly originated loans or other receivables may be added to the asset pool of a revolving transaction.

Riba
An Islamic finance term meaning interest. The payment or receipt of riba is prohibited under Sharia'a law.

RICS
The UK Royal Institution of Chartered Surveyors.

RIE
See Recognised Investment Exchange.

Right in Personam
A right which is only enforceable against the person originally bound. Personal or contractual Security is a promise by the Borrower to pay the underlying debt and is usually augmented by a Right in Rem and real Security.

Right in Rem
A right available against the world at large (i.e. a right of property) save for a purchaser without notice, in contrast to a Right in Personam. Real Security gives the Lender a right in rem enforceable against a specific asset of the Borrower.

Right to Cure
The right for a specified interested third party to assume the responsibilities of a party who has breached a contractual obligation with a view to remedying the breach and preserving their interests.

Right of Substitution
The right to replace collateral, parties or other components in a contractual obligation.

Risk Based Capital (RBC)
An amount of capital or net worth an investor must identify and allocate to absorb a potential loss on an instrument. The amount of RBC varies amongst asset classes and is usually expressed as a percentage of the amount at risk.

Risk Diversity
The pooling of diverse loans to avoid and reduce concentration risk.

Risk-Weighting
The practice of classifying assets on the basis of the degree of risk that they entail.

Risk-weighted assets (RWA) approach
The risk weighted assets (RWA) approach used by banks to price loans. The (simplified) principles involve determining the risk profile of the loan; assigning a rating based on a determination of what proportion of the loan balance counts for RWAs by applying a percentage; multiplying the loan balance by the RWA percentage to determine the total RWA and then multiplying the total RWA by the bank's capital ratio target to determine the amount of equity that is to be allocated against that loan. The anticipated returns net of costs are then compared against the equity allocated in order to determine whether the return on equity over the life of the loan is of a sufficient high level.

Risk-Weighting Bucket
A risk-weighting category that is defined as including assets that involve a similar degree of risk.

RMBS
See Residential Mortgage Backed Securitisation.

ROE
See Return on Equity.

ROY Table
In order to understand default risk and value break points in a variety of stress scenarios, a sensitivity analysis for three of the key determinants of property value and consequently loan repayment: rent, occupancy and

Commercial Mortgage Loans and CMBS: Developments in the European Market

yield can be undertaken and the results shown in a ROY (rent, occupancy, yield) table.

Russell NCREIF Index
Numerous indexes complied by the Frank Russell Company and the National Council and Real Estate Investment Fiduciaries on commercial real estate performance. Often used in the US as a benchmark for real estate investment performance.

Russell 2000 Index
A stock market index compiled by the Tacoma, Washington-based Russell Investment Group. Using a rules-based and transparent process, Russell forms its indexes by listing all companies in descending order by market capitalisation adjusted for float, which is the actual number of shares available for trading. In the US, the top 3,000 stocks (those of the 3,000 largest companies) make up the broad-cap Russell 1000 Index, and the bottom 2,000 (the smallest companies) make up the small-cap Russell 2000 Index.

S

S&P 500
An index of the 500 largest publically traded companies in the United States. It is a market value weighted index which is also float adjusted.

Sakk
An Islamic finance term which is the singular of Sukuk.

Salam
An Islamic finance term meaning forward sale. One of the 14 categories of permissible Sukuk specified by the AAOIFI.

Sale and Lease Back
A transaction where the seller sells real property to the purchaser and the purchaser Leases the real property back to the seller.

Sanierungsgutachten
German term for a restructuring opinion.

Santiago Principles
A set of generally accepted principles and practices for sovereign wealth funds, established by The International Working Group of Sovereign Wealth Funds (IWG).

Sarbanes-Oxley
A US statute which became law in July 2002, which brought about significant corporate governance and disclosure reforms and made substantial

changes to the regulation of the accounting profession. The legislation extends to certain non-US companies, mainly those that are US reporting companies, and to the non-US auditors of these companies.

SAREB
The Spanish Management Company for Assets arising from the Banking Sector Reorganisation created in November 2012 to clean up institutions that had excessive exposure to the real estate sector, also known as the Spanish bad bank.

Schedule
An agreement that supplements, amends and customises an executed ISDA Master Agreement to fit the particular contractual needs of the counterparties.

Scheduled Interest
The amount of interest owed at the end of the current period.

Scheduled Principal
The amount of principal scheduled to be repaid at the end of the current period.

Scheme of Arrangement
An arrangement between a company and creditors under Part 26 of the Companies Act 2006 to effect insolvent restructurings.

Schuldschein or Schuldscheindarlehen
Loans made in the domestic German market that are evidenced by a promissory note.

Schützschreiben
Preventative declaration made by creditors under German law.

SDLT
See Stamp Duty Land Tax.

Seasoning
Descriptive term used to refer to the age of an asset being securitised. This gives an indication of how long the obligor has been making payments and satisfying its other obligations with respect to the asset prior to its securitisation. An asset becomes more seasoned as the period it has been performing to its terms increases. It is presumed that more seasoned assets have a lower likelihood of default.

SEC
See Securities and Exchange Commission.

Second-Lien Mortgage Loan
A loan secured by a mortgage or trust deed, the security of which is junior to the security of another mortgage or trust deed.

Secondary Market
A market in which existing securities are re-traded (as opposed to a primary market in which assets are originally sold by the entity that made those assets).

Secondary Mortgage Market
The market for the buying, selling and trading of individual mortgage loans and MBS.

Secondary/Territorial Proceedings
In the context of the EC Regulation, insolvency proceedings which are brought in any place where the debtor carries out a non-transitory economic activity with human means and goods but which is not the member state where the Debtor has its Centre of Main Interests or COMI.

Section 106 Agreement
Section 106 agreements (Town and Country Planning Act 1990) are signed subsequent to a planning consent being granted, that impose upon the developer obligations financially, or otherwise, that are conditions precedent to the implementation of any planning consent.

Secured Debt
Borrowing that is made, in part, on the basis of security pledged by the borrower to the lender.

Secured Parties
See Finance Parties.

Securities
See Debt Securities.

Securities and Exchange Commission (SEC)
A US government agency which issues regulations and enforces provisions of federal securities laws and its own regulations, including regulations governing the disclosure of information provided in connection with offering securities for sale to the public. The SEC is also responsible for regulating the trading of these securities.

Securitisation
A means of raising finance secured on the back of identifiable and predictable cash flows derived from a particular class of assets (such as rents, receivables, mortgages or operating properties).

Securitisation Liquidity Facility
See Liquidity Facility.

Security
Assets that one party pledges to another party to safeguard amounts lent to that party. Following the occurrence of certain events, the party benefiting from the grant of Security can use the secured assets towards recovering the amounts owed to it. See also Legal Mortgage, Fixed Charge, Floating Charge, Perfection and Enforcement.

Security Documents
The collective name for those Finance Documents granting Security in favour of the Secured Parties/Finance Parties.

Security Interest
An interest that makes the enforcement of a Lender's rights more secure or certain, for example, by granting the Lender recourse to particular property in Priority to other Creditors.

Security Package
The name given to the overall Security granted by the Obligors and documented in the Security Documents.

Security Trustee
The entity which holds the Security Package on trust for all Secured Parties.

Self-Amortising Loans
A loan whereby the full amount of principal will be paid off at termination.

Senior/Junior
A common structure of securitisations that provides credit enhancement to one or more classes of securities by ranking them ahead of (or senior to) other classes of securities (junior classes). In a basic two-class senior/junior relationship, the senior classes are often called the class A notes and the junior (or subordinated) classes are called the class B notes. The class A notes will receive all cash flow up to the required scheduled interest and principal payments. The class B notes provide credit enhancement to the class A notes and experience 100% of losses on the security until the amount of the class B notes is exceeded, when class A will experience all future losses.

Senior Class or *Senior Notes*
A class of Investment Grade Securities issued in a Securitisation that rank senior in priority to the Subordinated Classes issued in the same transaction.

Senior Debt
A debt obligation that is paid in priority to all other debts pursuant to the terms of an Intercreditor Agreement. The Senior Debt is typically repaid in full before the Subordinated Debt is repaid.

Senior Notes
See Senior Class.

Senior Pieces
Classes or tranches rated above BBB (or an investment grade) which are appropriate for regulated institutional investors.

Senior Tranche
See Tranche.

Serviced Offices
A general term used to describe offices which are let on an inclusive basis. They are normally subject to relatively short term licences. The rent is usually calculated on a per desk/room basis and is inclusive of all rates and service charges, as well as power and communication costs.

Servicer
The organisation that is responsible for collecting loan payments from individual borrowers and for remitting the aggregate amounts received to the owner or owners of the loans.

Servicer Event of Defaults
An event allowing the issuer to terminate the appointment of the Servicer or Special Servicer.

Servicer Modification Fee

Fee payable to the Primary Servicer for work involved in deciding whether or not to agree to consents, waivers and modifications where the loans are heading towards a distressed position but have not yet been transferred to Special Servicing.

Servicers Watch List
A list of Loans maintained and published by a Servicer which indicates those Loans that should be elevated to a higher level of monitoring because, for example, the Borrower may have breached covenants or the Sponsor faces financial trouble.

Servicing Advances
The customary, necessary and reasonable out-of-pocket expenses incurred by the Master Servicer or Special Servicer in performing their duties. These are generally paid directly and then reimbursed from future payments.

Servicing Agreement
The contract that governs the responsibilities of the Master Servicer and the Special Servicer for managing and collecting payments on a Portfolio of Mortgage Loans that are held in a CMBS.

Servicing Override
The rights of the Controlling Class (in particular in any concert rights they may have) can be overridden by the servicer if it determines that following the course of action proposed by the Operating Advisor or the Controlling Class would violate the Servicing Standard.

Servicing Standard
The standard that the Servicer and Special Servicer must adhere to when performing their respective functions. The wording of the standard will be set out in the Servicing Agreement.

Servicing Standard Override
A right given to the Servicer and Special Servicer to override a course of action proposed by the Controlling Class or Operating Advisor in the exercise of their rights if the Servicer or Special Servicer determines that the proposed course of action would violate the Servicing Standard.

Servicing Tape
A record maintained by the Servicer of the current and historical loan payment profile of a loan.

Servicing Transfer Event
An event that triggers the transfer of the management of a mortgage loan from the Servicer to Special Servicer. A Servicing Transfer Event occurs when a borrower has defaulted or, in the reasonable adjustment of the Servicer, is likely to default and not be cured/corrected within a reasonable time. In this event the Servicer can transfer the day-today handling of the account to the Special Servicer until such time as the Special Servicer determines that the default has been cured/corrected.

Servicing Power of Attorney
A power of attorney (usually in a prescribed form in the Servicing Agreement) in favour of the Servicer and Special Servicer enabling the Special Servicer and Servicer to act on behalf of the relevant Finance Parties under the Finance Documents.

Servient Tenement
See Easement.

Set-Off
Where a Debtor has a cross-claim against a Creditor to the reduction or extinguishment of the Creditor's claim by the amount of his cross-claim.

Shadow banking
The term used to describe financial intermediaries that perform the services of financial institutions but that are not regulated as financial institutions.

Share Capital
Invested money that is not repaid to the investors in the normal course of business.

Shareholder
An individual, group or organisation that holds one or more shares in a company and in whose name a share certificate is issued.

Shareholders Agreement
A contract entered into between the Shareholders of a company which defines the Shareholders mutual obligations, privileges, protections and rights.

Sharia'a Board or Sharia'a Supervisory Board
The panel of Islamic scholars who determine whether an Islamic financial structure is sharia'a compliant.

Sharikat
An Islamic finance term meaning a partnership whereby work and capital may be allocated over all persons with correlative loss sharing.

Sharkat ul-amwaal
An Islamic finance term meaning a musharaka which is a property partnership.

Sharpe Ratio
An investment ratio used to measure the risk-adjusted performance in respect of a financial asset. The Sharpe Ratio provides an indication as to whether an asset's return is due to a smart investment choice or excessive risk.

Shell Rent
A portion of rental rates intended to amortise the cost of extraordinary tenant improvements.

SIV
See Structured Investment Vehicle.

"Skin in the game"
Term for the risk retention regulatory requirements introduced after the GFC to ensure that the issuers of securitised assets retain risk in the underlying assets.

664

Slotting
The methods set out in BIPRU Regulation 4.5.8 R for assigning risk weights for specialised commercial real estate lending exposures.

Small and Medium Sized Enterprises (or SME)
A company which by virtue of its number of employees, turnover or balance sheet total is classed as a small or medium enterprise.

SOCIMIs (Sociedades Anónimas Cotizadas de Inversión Inmobiliaria)
Spanish law vehicles aimed at fostering investment in real estate, which are equivalent to REITs.

Soft Costs
The element of the building cost or purchase cost of real estate which includes the due diligence fees, legal fees, accounting fees, surveyor fees and architect fees.

Solvency II
A review of the capital adequacy regime for the European insurance industry. It aims to establish a revised set of EU-wide capital requirements and risk management standards that will replace the current solvency requirements.

Sospensivamente Condisionato
Term for the transfer of the ownership over a property in favour of the Lender in Italian law.

Sovereign Wealth Fund (SWF)
A state-owned investment fund composed of financial assets derived from a country's reserves that have accumulated from budget and trade surpluses, often from revenue from generated from the export of natural resources.

Special Liquidity Scheme
A Bank of England scheme introduced in April 2008 which closed in January 2012 that was designed to improve the liquidity position of the banking system by allowing banks and building societies to swap their high quality mortgage backed and other securities for UK Treasury Bills for up to 3 years.

Special-Purpose Entity (SPE)
A Bankruptcy Remote corporate vehicle (whether in the form of a limited company, Partnership, trust, Limited Partnership or other form) often used in debt finance and Securitisation transactions. The Bankruptcy Remoteness protects Lenders or Noteholders from having the underlying assets involved in insolvency proceedings against the Borrower or Issuer.

Special Purpose Vehicle (SPV)
See Special Purpose Entity.

Special Servicer
This can be the same or a different party to the Master Servicer, but is responsible for managing loans which have defaulted and carrying out the work of process.

Special Servicing
A term used to describe when a Mortgage Loan is being serviced by a Special Servicer following the occurrence of a Special Servicing Transfer Event.

Special Servicing Fee
The portion of the Special Servicer's fee which accrues with each specially serviced mortgaged loan.

Special Servicing Transfer Event
An event triggering the transfer of the servicing responsibilities from the Master Servicer to the Special Servicer. The trigger event is generally when the borrower has defaulted or, in the Master Servicer's reasonable opinion, is likely to default and be unable to cure the same within a reasonable time.

Specially Serviced Loan
A Mortgage Loan serviced by a Special Servicer.

Specialised Lending Exposures (SLEs)
Exposure categories under the Basel II framework to which the IRB Approach is difficult to apply, including secured real estate lending.

Sponsor
Either (i) the entity that sponsors a Securitisation; or (ii) the entity that provides equity to a Borrower in a real estate finance transaction.

Spread Accounts
A revenue account into which is paid any collateral interest which is in excess of note interest which is not directed at any particular class. This provides credit enhancement in that it absorbs mortgage losses up to a structured cap.

S&P 500 Index
A stock market index containing the stocks of 500 large capitalisation corporations, most of which are American. The index is float weighted; that is, movements in price of companies that have higher float-based market values (share price multiplied by the number of shares which Standard & Poors determines are available for public trading) have a greater effect on the index than companies with smaller market values. The index is owned and maintained by Standard & Poors, a division of McGraw-Hill. S&P 500 is used in reference not only to the index but also to the 500 companies that have their common stock included in the index.

SPV
See Special Purpose Vehicle.

Stamp Duty Land Tax
Tax on transactions involving the acquisition of interests in UK land.

Stand Alone Securitisation
A securitisation based on a single loan. This has a very high concentration risk.

Standard Prepayment Assumption
This is a measure of prepayment rates on loans based on a variable rate of prepayments each month relative to the outstanding principal balance of the loans. Contrast with the Constant Prepayment Rate which assumes a constant rate of prepayment each month.

Standardised Approach
A method of calculating credit risk under Basel II involving the categorisation of banking book exposures.

Standstill Period
The period during which a standstill agreement is in effect, postponing enforcement action for a sufficient period of time to allow a formal restructuring to take place.

Static Pool
A pool of assets made up solely of assets originated during a finite period of time, such as a month or a quarter.

Statutory Declaration of Solvency
A written statement by the directors of a UK company that they have made a full inquiry into the company's affairs and that, having done so, they believe that the company will be able to pay its debts in full within 12 months from the start of the winding up. The declaration is signed by the directors and declared to be true before a solicitor or person authorised to take oaths. The declaration will include a statement of the company's assets and liabilities as at the latest practicable date before making the declaration.

Strategic Land
A general reference to land holdings which are purchased or held with a view to add value by development at some future stage. Typically this only includes land which does not yet have consent for alternative and more valuable uses, and is principally applied to residential land, such as land banks, held by house buildings.

Stress Testing
The process used to evaluate whether the assets that will form the collateral for a securitisation are likely to produce sufficient cash flows in a variety of

economic scenarios to be able to continue to make the principal and interest payments due on the related securities. The scenarios generally include a worst case and provide an indication of whether the proposed structure and level of credit enhancement is sufficient to achieve a particular credit rating for some or all of the various tranches issued in connection with the transaction. (See also WAFF and VIALS.)

Stretched senior loans
Financing provided by a senior lender at a higher LTV ratio than a senior lender would normally be willing to lend and which would ordinarily be provided by additional Mezzanine Debt.

Strike Rate
The purchaser of a cap or floor receives the difference between the variable-rate index and a chosen rate for a defined term. The chosen rate is called the strike rate.

Stripped Interest Notes
Note classes entitled to interest distributions but no (or a nominal) distribution of principal.

Stripped Principal Notes
Note classes entitled to principal distribution but no (or a nominal) distribution of interest.

Structural Subordination
The concept that the lender will not have access to the assets of the company's subsidiary until after all of the subsidiary's creditors have been paid and the remaining assets have been distributed up to the company as an equity holder.

Structured Finance
A type of financing in which the credit quality of the debt is assumed to be based not on the financial strength of the debtor itself, but on a direct guarantee from a creditworthy entity or on the credit quality of the debtor's assets, with or without credit enhancement.

Structured Investment Vehicle (SIV)
A type of SPE that funds the purchase of its assets, which consist primarily of highly rated securities, through the issuance of both CP and MTNs. Should an SIV default, its pool of assets may need to be liquidated; therefore, the rating on an SIV reflects the risks associated with potential credit deterioration in the portfolio and market value risks associated with selling the assets.

Structuring
The process by which combinations of mortgages and security classes are put together to achieve the highest price for a CMBS based on the current market position.

Structuring Bank
The investment bank responsible for co-ordinating the execution of a securitisation with respect to the originator/client, law firms, rating agencies, and other third parties. Typically, the structuring bank performs a due diligence exercise with respect to the assets to be securitised and the capacity of the Servicer including an identification of historical information and often an asset audit. The structuring bank is also responsible for developing and documenting the legal structure of the transaction and for identifying and resolving accounting and tax issues. In the case of a public issue, the structuring bank oversees the preparation of an information memorandum or offering circular to be used for the offering and listing of the related securities. The structuring bank ensures that the transaction complies with local regulatory requirements.

STS Securitisation
Proposed category of simple, transparent and standardised (STS) securitisations for favourable capital treatment under the proposed EU Securitisation Regulation.

Subordinated Class
A class of securities with rights that are subordinate to the rights of other classes of securities issued in connection with the same transaction. Subordination usually relates to the rights of holders of the securities to receive promised debt service payments, particularly where there is a shortfall in cash flow to pay promised amounts to the holders of all classes of securities, although this could be related to the voting rights of noteholders.

Subordinated Debt
Debt which ranks junior to other debt. Such debt is usually paid after amounts currently due (or previously due) to holders of senior debt before paying amounts currently due (or previously due) to holders of the subordinated debt.

Subordinated Notes
See Subordinated Class.

Subordination
Where one Creditor (or group of Creditors) agrees not to be paid by a Borrower or other common Debtor (such as an Issuer) until another Creditor (or group of Creditors) have been paid. A form of Credit Enhancement where the risk of credit losses is disproportionately allocated amongst the Creditors. See also Senior Debt, Subordinated Debt, Senior Class and Subordinated Class.

Subordination Agreement
Formal document acknowledging that one party's claim or interest is inferior (junior) to that of the other party of parties. See also Intercreditor Agreement.

Sub-Performing Loan
A loan which is producing payments (even the full principal and interest payments required) but with an unacceptable debt coverage ratio. Some investors also apply this term to loans making all necessary payments but the LTV ratio (or other indicatory value) suggest it is unlikely to be fully paid off at maturity.

Sub-Prime
Residential Mortgage Borrowers with a tarnished or limited credit history. Loans made to sub-prime Borrowers carry a greater credit risk than Loans made to non sub-prime Borrowers.

Subrogation
The succession by one party, often an insurer, to another party's legal right to collect a debt from or enforce a claim against a third partly.

Subscription Facility
A Loan advanced to a Private Equity Real Estate Fund secured by unfunded commitments of the fund's investors that allow the fund to minimise the number of capital calls on its investors by serving as working capital and for bridge financing and giving the fund a way to quickly finance the day to day needs of its operations.

Sub-Servicing
This is when the Servicer and/or the Special Servicer sub-contracts some or all of their obligations. This is generally prohibited if it would result in the downgrade in the rating of the notes. The Servicer and Special Servicer would remain liable for any breach by the sub-servicer of their obligations under the servicing agreement.

Sukuk
An Islamic finance term which refers to both Islamic bonds and Islamic securitisations.

Survivability
A term applied to contractual terms which are still enforceable once the loan has been included in a security. Often the case with representations and warranties.

Swap
An agreement pursuant to which two counterparties agree to exchange one cash flow stream for another, for example fixed-to-floating interest-rate

swaps, currency swaps, or swaps to change the maturities or yields of a bond portfolio.

Swap Provider
The party that writes a swap contract.

Syndicate
A group of Lenders that together make a Loan available to a Borrower.

Syndicated Loan
A large loan arranged by a group of international banks that form a syndicate, headed by a lead manager. The borrower pays the lead manager a fee whose size depends of the complexity of the loan and the risk involved.

Synthetic CDO
A CDO transaction in which the transfer of risk is effected through the use of a Credit Derivative as opposed to a True Sale of the assets. See also Synthetic Securitisation.

Synthetic CMBS
A CMBS transaction in which the transfer of risk is effected through the use of a Credit Derivative as opposed to a True Sale of the assets. See also Synthetic Securitisation.

Synthetic Securities
Securities designed to modify the cash flows generated by underlying asset securities that are rated primarily on the creditworthiness of the asset securities and currency or interest rate swaps or other similar agreements.

Synthetic Securitisation
A Synthetic Securitisation or synthetic risk transfer achieves the same economic result as in a True Sale Securitisation of physical assets, but relies on the transfer of credit risk through Derivative contracts in respect of the Portfolio. The Issuer (as Protection Seller) agrees to pay the legal owner of those assets (the Protection Buyer) an amount equal to the losses it suffers as a result of certain credit events occurring on the underlying Portfolio (such as an underlying obligor payment default). These payments are funded from the proceeds of issuing CLNs to Capital Market investors. Until such time as a credit event occurs, the proceeds from the issuance of the CLNs are invested by the Issuer in risk-free investments such as government Securities. The principal amount of each class of CLNs is written down in line with a principal reduction in the market value of the reference Portfolio resulting from a credit event.

T

Ta'Hawwut Master Agreement
Sharia'a compliant hedging agreement published by the International
Swaps and Derivatives Association and the International Islamic Financial
Market.

Takaful
Sharia'a compliant insurance.

Taxable REIT Subsidiary
A wholly-owned subsidiary of a REIT that is taxed as a corporation. Dividends from a Taxable REIT Subsidiary are good REIT income which means
a REIT can conduct operations through a Taxable REIT Subsidiary that
benefit the REIT even though those operations generate non-qualifying
REIT income.

Tenant
An individual or corporate body holding a tenancy.

Tenant Improvements
The expense, generally met by the tenant, of physically improving the
leased property or space.

Term
The lifespan of a Loan being the period of time from the borrowing of the
Loan to the repayment of the Loan.

Term Asset-Backed Securities Loan Facility (TALF)
A program created by the United States Federal Reserve to help market
participants meet the credit needs of households and small businesses by
supporting the issuance of ABS. Closed for loan extensions against newly
issued CMBS on June 30, 2010 and for new loan extensions against all other
types of collateral on March 31, 2010.

Term Sheet
See Heads of Terms.

Third Party Pool Insurance
A form of credit enhancement whereby the issuer pays a bond issuer an
annual premium, in return for which the issuer will absorb the loss on
mortgaged loans. This therefore protects investors from any losses on the
mortgage loans. The CMBS is usually never rated higher than the credit
rating of the third party insurer. See also monoline insurer.

Tier 1 Capital
See Core Capital.

Time-weighted rate of return (TWRR)
The single rate of compound interest which will produce the same accumulated value over more than one period as would be produced by a series of single period returns or interest rates. Some commentators refer to this as the geometric mean rate of return, although this is not strictly accurate.

Title Insurance
The application of insurance to the ownership and/or use of interests in real estate.

TOGC
A term indicating the transfer of a business as a going concern.

Top-Down Approach to Investing
A strategy adopted by an investor whereby large scale trends in the general economy are examined and industries and companies to invest in selected which are likely to benefit from those trends, contrast with a bottom-up approach to investing.

Torrens Systems
An approach to transfers of interests in real estate which creates a real right through the act of registration carried out by a state body and which typically provides both a plan-based record and an indemnity from the state.

Total Return Swap (TRS)
A Derivative trade between a dealer and end user whereby one of the two parties exchanges the total return of an asset (including, for example, appreciation and dividends or other distributions relating to that asset) for a fixed or floating amount plus a spread that reflects the credit profile of a counterparty and other factors, plus any depreciation with respect to the underlying asset. A TRS may be structured as a Property Derivative, a Credit Derivative or as other Derivatives.

Tranche
A term used to refer to a class of Securities and the collective description of the discreetly rated classes of CMBS securities. Each class is paid a predetermined coupon and principal based on a payment sequence. The lower rated tranches generally have higher coupons (to compensate for increased risk) and longer life spans as they do not receive principal payments until higher rated tranches have been paid off.. See also Subordination, Senior Class, Mezzanine Piece and Subordinated Class.

Tranching Account
An account opened by the security trustee pursuant to the terms of the intercreditor agreement pursuant to which it agrees to hold all amounts received on the whole mortgage loan in its entirety on trust for the holders

of each tranche and to disburse such amounts pursuant to the terms of the intercreditor agreement.

Treasuries
Negotiable debt obligations of the US government issued with varying maturities and backed by the credit of the US government.

Trigger Event
In a securitisation structure, the occurrence of an event which indicates that the financial condition of the issuer or some other party associated with the transaction is deteriorating. Such events will often be defined in the transaction documents, as are the changes to the transaction structure and/or priority of payments that are to be made following the occurrence of such an event.

Triple Net Lease
See Net Net Net Lease.

Trophy Asset
A large commercial property that enjoys a high profile as a result of some combination of prestigious location, highly visible owners, prominent tenants and often striking design.

Troubled Asset Relief Program (TARP)
A United States Government program to purchase assets and equity from financial institutions to strengthen the financial sector.

TRS
See Total Return Swap.

True Sale
A sale transaction which is recognised by the courts as a sale, not a grant of Security interest by the seller. Recognition as a True Sale is necessary to ensure that the title to the underlying real property, and not merely a Security interest on the real property, is effectively transferred to the purchaser. Although there is no court precedent defining the requirements of a True Sale, it is generally understood that various factors, including the parties' intention, need to be taken into consideration when determining whether the sale transaction is recognised as a True Sale.

True Sale Opinion
With respect to a securitisation, a legal opinion to the effect that the assets that are being securitised have been transferred from the originator to the issuing SPE that these assets will not form part of the bankruptcy estate of the originator or be subject to any applicable automatic stay or moratorium provisions.

Trustee
A third party, often a specialist trust corporation or part of a bank, appointed to act on behalf of investors. In the case of a securitisation, the trustee is given responsibility for making certain key decisions that may arise during the life of the transaction. The role of the trustee may also include holding security over the securitised assets and control over cash flows. It is often a requirement of listing ABS that an independent trustee be appointed. The trustee receives regular reports on the performance of the underlying assets in order to check whether, for instance, cash flow procedures are being followed. Subject to appropriate indemnity and other protections, the trustee is also typically responsible for finding a replacement servicer when necessary, taking up legal proceedings on behalf of the investors, and, as the case may be, selling the assets in order to repay investors. To enable the trustee to perform its duties and to provide adequate remuneration, it receives a fee paid senior to all other expenses and a senior ranking indemnity to cover all unexpected costs and expenses.

Turner Review
A review carried out by Lord Turner, the chairman of the FSA, of the UK's approach to bank regulation with recommendations for reforming the ways banks are regulated. This review was commissioned by the British Chancellor of the Exchequer.

U

UBTI
Unrelated Business Taxable Income. A tax placed on the income of otherwise non-taxable entities with respect to certain specified types of income.

UCC
The US Uniform Commercial Code, the uniform law adopted in all 50 US States and the District of Columbia (with minor local variations), which, amongst other things, governs the creation, perfection, priority and enforcement of Security interest in most types of US personal property.

UCIT
See Undertakings for Collective Investment in Transferable Securities.

UK Asset Resolution Limited (UKAR)
UKAR was established on 1 October 2010 to facilitate the orderly management of the closed mortgage books of both Bradford & Bingley and NRAM (formerly Northern Rock Building Society).

Umbrella Partnership REIT or UPREIT
A REIT structured to be the general partner and a limited partner of an operating Limited Partnership that holds all of the real estate assets. The UPREIT structure allows owners of property to exchange their property for

interest in the Limited Partnership in a tax-free exchange while diversifying their holdings. The Limited Partnership interests can be exchanged for REIT shares at a later time giving the holder of Limited Partnership interests liquidity, but such conversion will result in a realisation of the deferred tax on the gain of the contributed property.

Unauthorised Unit Trust
An unregulated unit trust which may only be offered to institutional investors. See also Authorised Unit Trust.

Undertakings for Collective Investment in Transferable Securities or *UCIT*
Retail collective investment funds established in accordance with European Union directives that are permitted to operate freely throughout the EU on the basis of a single authorisation from one member state. In practice many EU member nations have imposed additional regulatory requirements that have impeded free operation with the effect of protecting local asset managers. These are similar in many respects to Mutual Funds.

Underwriter
Any party that takes on risk. In the context of the capital markets, a securities dealer will act as underwriter to an issuance and commit to purchasing all or part of the securities at a specified price thereby giving the issuer certainty that the securities will be placed and at what price and eliminating the market risk. In return for assuming this risk, the underwriter will charge a fee.

Unlisted Real Estate Investments
Property investments that are not traded on exchanges.

UPREIT
See Umbrella Partnership REIT.

Upward Only Rent Review
A clause in a Lease that specifically states that the rent can only be reviewed to the greater of the previous rent or the current market rent. The rent can never go down but can stay the same. This is a standard clause in most UK Leases.

V

Vacant Possession
A term used to describe a property which is not subject to an occupational Lease or licence that may produce income. It does not, however, refer to a property that is occupied by the owner.

Vacant possession value (VPV)
Valuer's opinion of the price that could be achieved if a property was sold on the valuation date fully vacant.

Valuation
An appraisal of a property carried out by independent valuers in order to establish the approximate value of the property.

Valuation Report
A report prepared by valuation surveyors attributing a value to a property usually for financing purposes.

Valuation Shopping
A process whereby borrowers select and present their choice of valuer from the outset of a transaction based on who they know will give them the highest potential value.

Value
Unless specified to the contrary the fair market value of a property determined in an appraisal made by the originator when the loan is first made.

Value-Added Real Estate Investments
Property investments that are slightly more risky than Core-Plus and generally seek internal rates of 11% to 15%. Value-Added Real Estate Investments carry debt of between 50% to 75% of the property's value, and rely more on local knowledge than Core or Core-Plus Investment.

VAT
Value Added Tax.

VATA 1994
Value Added Tax Act 1994.

Vertical Slice Option
The risk retention requirement pursuant to the Dodd–Frank Wall Street Reform and Consumer Protection Act and the Alternative Investment Fund Managers Directive (AIFMD) for the sponsor to retain at least 5% of each class of securities issued in the securitisation.

VEFA ("Vente en État Futur d'Achèvement") contracts
VEFA or "sale in future state of completion" contracts are French law regulated development contracts, which represent the largest portion of the CRE development financing market.

Vickers Report
This is the final report of the Independent Commission on Banking, chaired by Sir John Vickers. The Commission was asked to consider structural and

related non-structural reforms to the UK banking sector to promote financial stability and competition.

Vision Project
"A Vision for Real Estate Finance in the UK" report published in 2014 with the support of the Investment Property Forum, which put forward proposals to improve the resilience of the CRE market.

Void Periods
A period of time during which a property, or part of a property, does not generate any income, either where there is no Lease in place, or where there is a Lease in place but there is a Rent Free Period that has not yet expired.

Volcker Rule
This refers to Section 619 of the Dodd-Frank Wall Street Reform and Consumer Protection Act, which adds section 13 to the Bank Holding Company Act of 1956. Section 13 contains certain restrictions on the ability of a banking entity and nonbank financial company supervised by the Board of Governors of the Federal Reserve System to engage in proprietary trading and have certain interests in a hedge fund or private equity fund.

Voluntary Prepayments
Prepayments by the borrower so to reduce or pay off the outstanding principal, often due to the borrower refinancing at lower interest rates.

Voting Rights Enforcement
A type of Enforcement action whereby the rights attaching to pledged shares are exercised by the Secured Parties/Finance Parties. A Voting Rights Enforcement is often used to replace the board of directors of the Borrower vehicle.

W

Wakala
An Islamic finance term meaning agency. One of the 14 categories of permissible Sukuk specified by the AAOIFI. Securitisations which use a *wakeel* as agent under the terms of a *wakala* are known as Sukuk al-Wakala.

Wakeel
The agent to the issuing entity, appointed to invest the proceeds of the issuance certificates in accordance with the terms of the *Wakala*.

Waterfall
The term applied to the cash flow pay-out priority in a CMBS. Generally, cash flow pays principal and interest to the highest rated tranche but interest only to lower rated tranches. Once the notes from the highest rated tranche are paid down, cash flow then pays principal and interest on next

highest rated tranche and so on. The sequence will be stipulated in the prospectus at the time of issue. See Priority of Payments.

Weighted-Average Cost of Funds
The weighted-average rate of return that an issuer must offer to investors in the event of a combination of borrowed funds and equity investments. Also referred to as the weighted-average cost of capital.

Weighted-Average Coupon (WAC)
The average interest rate for a group of loans or securities, calculated by multiplying the coupon applicable to each loan or security in the group by the proportion of the outstanding principal balance of the entire pool made up by the loan or security to which the coupon relates.

Weighted-Average Foreclosure Frequency (WAFF)
The estimated percentage of assets in the securitisation pool that will go into default under an economic scenario designed to test whether the cash flow that is expected to be generated by the pool plus available credit enhancement will be sufficient to repay all securities rated at a certain rating category or higher. The WAFF is used in conjunction with the WALS to determine the expected level of losses at different rating categories.

Weighted Average Life
The average time until all scheduled principal payments are expected to have been made, weighted by the size of each mortgage in the pool.

Weighted-Average Loss Severity (WALS)
The average loss that is expected to be incurred in the event that any one asset in a securitisation pool goes into default, expressed as a percentage of outstanding principal balance of such asset as of the date of the default. The expected loss is predicted by making various assumptions about the potential decline in the market value of collateral that may secure the asset. The WALS is used in conjunction with the WAFF to determine the expected level of losses at different rating categories.

Weighted–Average Maturity (WAM)
A measure of the remaining term to maturity of a group of loans, calculated by multiplying the remaining months to maturity of each loan in the group by the proportion of the outstanding principal balance of the entire pool made up by the loan or security to which the coupon relates.

Weighted Average Unexpired Lease Term (WAULT)
The average lease term remaining to expiry or lease break across the investment portfolio, weighted by rental income. Excludes short-term lettings such as car parks and advertising hoardings, residential leases and long ground leases.

Whole Business Securitisation
A whole-business or corporate securitisation refers to the issuance of bonds backed by a company's cash flow generating assets and/or its inventory. The security may have been legally isolated in favour of the holders of the notes and might be managed by a backup operator, thereby prolonging the security's cash flow generating capacity in favour of the noteholders should bankruptcy proceedings be brought against the company or the company become insolvent. With appropriate enhancements to the securitised debt structure in place, securitisation can achieve a higher rating on (and longer term of) the securitised debt than a company's secured or unsecured corporate debt.

Whole Loan
A whole Mortgage Loan and the term used in AB Structures to refer to a Mortgage Loan before it is bifurcated into an A Loan and B Loan.

Withholding Tax
A tax levied on income (interest and dividends) from debt obligations owned by foreign investors. This can be claimed back if there is a double tax treaty in place between the relevant countries.

Workout
Term for out-of-court debt restructuring.

Workout Fee
The fee the Special Servicer is entitled to for any specialist serviced loan which becomes corrected. It provides an incentive for the Special Servicer to correct a non-performing loan as soon as possible. This fee is paid only whilst the loan remains a corrected mortgaged loan.

X

X-Class Coupon
This is a deal's profit taken by the issuing bank.

X-Notes
The term usually given to the notes which form the IO strip in a CMBS.

Y

Yield
The return on an investment, calculated by dividing the income at any particular moment, divided by the value/purchase price and expressed in terms of a percentage.

Yield Maintenance
A prepayment provision to ensure investors attain the same yield as if the borrower had made all scheduled payments until maturity, therefore removing the prepayment risk.

Yield Shift
The movement in the yield of an investment, whether upwards of downwards.

Yield Spread
The difference in yield between a security and a separate benchmark (for example UK treasuries of the same maturity).

Yield to Average Life
A calculation based on the expected term of the class rather than its final stated maturity. Used in lieu of yield to maturity.

Yield to Maturity
The calculation of the return an investor will receive if a note is held to its maturity date. This takes into account purchase price, redemption value, time to maturity, coupon and the time between interest payments.

Z

Zero Coupon Note
A note that does not pay interest and therefore does not have a coupon but is traded at a deep discount, rendering profit at maturity when the bond is redeemed for its full face value. Another name for a stripped interest note.

Zscore
A score used by Lenders indicating their assessment of the financial strength of the Borrower, taking into account factors such as experiences of the Sponsor/Borrower, reliability and payment history.

Zwangsverwaltung

German term for a forced administration where the court appoints a receiver to take over management of a property from its owners.

Zwangsversteigerung
German term for where a court forces an auction process over a property.

Index

All indexing is to heading number.